Third Edition

Modern Drama
for Analysis

PAUL M. CUBETA
Middlebury College

HOLT, RINEHART AND WINSTON, INC.

New York - Chicago - San Francisco - Toronto

To the Instructor

This book provides an approach to modern drama that demands close textual analysis. Because plays are written for the theater, their full dimensions cannot be appreciated through reading alone. Yet studying drama is a satisfying and rewarding experience if a play is not viewed simply as a story nor read as one would read a novel.

I believe that the student should become acquainted first with the drama of his own time so that when he attends the theater he will better understand the significance of a modern dramatic production. I have, consequently, limited this collection to relatively modern plays. If Greek, Elizabethan, or Restoration drama were included, an understanding of their conventions, styles of acting, and theaters would be necessary.

Most drama anthologies of this size are based on principles different from those followed here. One possible basis of selection is dramatic type; another is national representation; still others exemplify major modern theatrical developments or mirror cultural changes. Excellent as these approaches may be for specialized study, I have found that they teach the student little about either the play-going or the play-reading experience.

Although I have included plays of various national origins and dramatic types, my primary concern has been to select readable plays of intrinsic merit that demonstrate the techniques of the playwright and the resources of the modern theater. I have avoided theatrical novelty for its own sake, for only the best plays successfully use the assets of the stage.

Each play is preceded by a brief biographical sketch of the dramatist, a list of his important works, a selected descriptive bibliography, a headnote when necessary, and ground plans for each set. A partial analysis of the play and questions that raise problems not discussed in the critical apparatus follow each play. Also included are a brief introduction on how to read drama, a general descriptive bibliography, and a glossary of terms as they are used in this text. The descriptive bibliographies are not exhaustive; they are meant to introduce the student to the best criticism (readily available in most college libraries) of each playwright and especially of the play included in this anthology. Extensive footnotes are provided for *The Devil's Disciple* to alert the student to the possibility that he may be hastily passing over words that he should look up in his dictionary. For subsequent plays only foreign words and expressions and proper nouns, probably unfamiliar to the student and relevant for an understanding of the play, have been footnoted.

The plays in this book are arranged in a sequence designed to introduce a variety of the themes, techniques, and problems found in modern drama. The first play, *The Devil's Disciple,* is relatively simple to analyze; it presents a broad range of theatrical devices as well as problems of character, language, structure, and theme. The commentaries on the following plays deal in greater detail and on more difficult levels with one or more topics central to the drama. The commentary on *Rosmersholm* studies the relationship of exposition to character and theme; that on *Desire under the Elms* further explores the nature of character and the tragic situation. *The Glass Menagerie* and *The Cherry Orchard* provide an opportunity for a comparative study of two worlds created by a rich variety of symbols and tonal effects. The critical apparatus for *A View from the Bridge* examines Miller's views of the modern tragic hero and his world and includes the original version of the ending so that the student may gain an insight into the playwright's creative process. *Murder in the Cathedral* and *Becket* dramatize the sharp differences in content and technique that can occur when two dramatists treat the same historical character. *The Skin of Our Teeth* presents traditional themes in a highly novel and experimental manner. The text concludes with *The Sandbox* as an example of a recent Off-Broadway play that parodies many of the themes, characters, and techniques studied earlier. The book suggests, but does not insist upon, this organization of the plays. Many of the questions explore other relationships that are valid and useful in designing a course in modern drama.

The commentaries are not exhaustive. Discussion in detail of a wide range of dramatic issues is left open to the instructor. Some major problems are not raised at all; others are deliberately considered only briefly. The purpose of the commentary is to point a way into the plays, to sharpen the student's critical responses, and to suggest topics that can be fully discussed in class. It is hoped that the explications will provide ample scope for disagreement. When possible, an author's own comments on his play are included, and for two plays excerpts from the comments of professional reviewers and academic critics, chosen for their contradictory points of view, are incorporated into the critical material. Technical and critical terminology is kept to a minimum.

If the commentary helps an instructor to save class time, it will serve a purpose. By turning the student's attention to crucial issues, the analyses should free class time for a more exciting and intensive investigation of the rich complexity of dramatic literature. A frequent frustration is that the instructor often needs to spend so much time helping the student with fundamental critical questions that the limited time of the course is exhausted in preliminaries, to the inevitable impoverishment of the student's view of the play. The apparatus should enable the instructor to move more readily to the consideration of problems beyond those of primary meaning and technique, or perhaps to find time for the reading of more plays.

The questions appended to each play go beyond the mere testing of a student's thoroughness in preparation. The commentary and questions draw the plays together by comparisons and by exploration of recurrent themes, attitudes, characterizations, and techniques. The questions suggest the kind of insights attained when two or more plays are studied in relation to one another. Occasionally a question has been imprecisely phrased so that the student may challenge its validity and thus see an issue by having to rephrase the problem more accurately. Others suggest larger dramatic problems, often insoluble, rather than "right" answers. Questions are sometimes deliberately deceptive, appearing to call for only a ready-made and stereotyped response. Because many of the questions recall earlier plays in the volume, they should provide a good, continual review. The questions should also lead the student to consider the dimensions of modern dramatic literature not confined by the boundaries of nationalities, periods, or types.

I am grateful to the staff of the Egbert Starr Library at Middlebury College for their kind and generous assistance and to my able colleagues John F. Butler, who offered many useful insights and suggestions for viewing Eliot's and Anouilh's Becket, and David J. Littlefield, whose painstaking reading and intelligent criticism of the commentaries put me much in his debt. To my friend and former student Peter G. Thompson go my thanks for his help in drawing the ground plans. But most of all I have a debt to my wife, Beth, who has endured all three editions and yet remains indefatigable typist, patient listener, perceptive critic, and perennial morale-booster.

P. M. C.

Middlebury, Vermont
October, 1962

To the Student

This is a book on how to read drama. The assumption upon which it is based may at first seem insulting and fallacious: any educated person knows how to read, and furthermore, one should see drama, not read it. This book has been prepared in the belief that most people read only superficially, and that, although reading drama is different from seeing a theatrical production and cannot be substituted for it, studying a play as dramatic literature is both entertaining and intellectually stimulating.

In the theater much of the hard work of interpreting a play is done for an audience by the actors, the director, the designer, the electricians, the stagehands, the wardrobe mistress, and all the others involved in mounting a production. There dramatic literature is transformed into something alive through the complex resources of the modern theater. Communication of character, meaning, and mood is established by dialogue, movement, and gesture or even by complete silence. Costumes and make-up play a significant role, as do sets, lighting, properties, and sound and musical effects.

Reading drama presents a greater challenge than seeing a play for the very reason that the reader must create in imagination his own theatrical production. In reading, one can only approximate the staging of a play; but if something is lost, something more is gained, for there are depths and dimensions to dramatic art lost on the stage. The opportunity for a deliberate and thoughtful evaluation of a play is not permitted an audience. A line lost in laughter, a subtle gesture or verbal implication missed, cannot be retrieved. In watching a play we do not exhaust its artistic riches; in reading a play, on the other hand, we shift the area of inspection, to some extent, from the technical and theatrical to the literary. The thematic, tonal, structural, and symbolic elements of drama receive increased attention, even though plot, action, scene, character, and dialogue must not be overlooked. But simply to reduce drama to a story in dialogue is to lose its literary significance.

Story, however, is where one begins. Thus, it is essential first to read a play quickly for the sheer enjoyment of discovering the outcome. If possible, one should read a play through at a single sitting, re-creating as far as possible the actual experience of an evening in the theater and responding to the pace of the drama, the different tones of voice, and the variety of speech rhythms. The thoughtful, detailed analysis which must then follow ought not to be a painful bore. Deeper understanding and a refined imagination enhance one's enjoyment of dramatic literature.

Drama, like all modes of art, gives structure and form to experience, allowing us to see our lives in more meaningful terms than everyday existence permits. The aim of this book is to explore these patterns of meaning and to develop an awareness of the artistic processes and techniques by which the playwright transforms experience into dramatic art. The way to obtain this insight is not by reading dramatic criticism or, worse, critics' criticisms of the criticism, but by turning to the plays themselves. Long, involved introductions dealing with drama and literary history and extended definitions of critical terminology often get badly in the way of the play and have therefore been omitted. The most valuable part of this anthology is, of course, the ten plays. The additional material, at most, will help to intensify and increase understanding and enjoyment. The criticism can be ignored; the plays cannot. The commentaries following the plays are not intended to be *the* reading of the play, but only *a* reading, and an incomplete one at that. It is hoped that they will be useful and meaningful elucidations and that the questions will stimulate further thinking about these plays in particular and drama in general; but the primary purpose of the critical apparatus is to focus attention upon the plays as works of art and thus gradually to cultivate and enhance the reader's critical ability so that it will serve him long after he has left the classroom.

P. M. C.

Contents

GEORGE BERNARD SHAW

The Devil's Disciple

a melodrama

Biography

GEORGE BERNARD SHAW (1856-1950) belongs to a distinguished line of Irish writers of English comedy—Congreve, Goldsmith, Sheridan, Wilde. He was born in Dublin, the "upstart son of a downstart," as he put it. His family claimed descent from Macduff; "it was as good as being descended from Shakespeare," said Shaw. But his father was a poor and unsuccessful member of a Protestant family that was once a part of the landed gentry of Ireland; the elder Shaw was an alcoholic whose only bequest to his son was a delightfully rich sense of humor and a hearty, mocking skepticism. From his mother, a remarkable woman and a gifted singer, Shaw inherited his interest in music.

Shaw's early career hardly gave promise that he would become one of the great writers of comedy in English. Up to the age of forty he seems to have tried everything but playwriting. As one commentator characterizes his kaleidoscopic career:

> We may describe Shaw as a socialist and propagandist for the socialist cause; a journalist-critic of music, fine arts, and drama; a novelist, a dramatist, and a director of plays; an astute manager of his own financial interests; an enormously successful lecturer; a reformer concerned with social problems (such as housing, women's rights, prison reform, and prostitution); a propounder of scientific theories and a critic of science, a philosopher, a preacher of a peculiar evolutionary religion and of socialist Christianity; an anti-vivisectionist, a vegetarian, and an advocate of spelling reform (the cause for which he left the bulk of his estate).[1]

After joining his mother in London when he was twenty, he did an assortment of odd jobs and wrote five novels, about which the kindest thing that could be said is that they were unsuccessful. His last novel, and the only one published, *An Unsocial Socialist,* was probably the first Marxist novel in English literature. In 1884 Shaw became an eloquent partisan of the newly organized Fabian Society, which broke from the revolutionary Marxian theories of economics and of political violence and advocated instead a process of social evolution; from these roots grew England's Labor Party.

---

[1] Reuben A. Brower, "George Bernard Shaw," in *Major British Writers* (New York, 1954), II, 521.

At twenty-nine, Shaw became a music critic in London, startling Victorians with the brash, impudent, and witty criticisms which continued to be a Shavian trademark when he became a drama critic in 1895. His first play, *Widowers' Houses* (1892), attacking landlords in slum areas, was as unsuccessful as his novels. Not until *Arms and the Man* (1894) did Shaw achieve an artistic blend of comedy with a philosophical and social purpose. Even then his popularity as a dramatist was by no means established; for example, *Candida* (1894) had to wait a decade before it became an international box-office triumph. Shaw first received substantial recognition as a dramatist in the United States with the highly successful New York run of *The Devil's Disciple* in 1897. The handsome royalties from this play enabled Shaw to marry Charlotte Payne-Townshend, like himself a person of liberal views, whom he had met while a member of the Fabians.

For nearly half a century Shaw continued to write not only plays, which he frequently directed, but also critical essays as long prefaces to his plays and political and social tracts. Thus he built his reputation as the greatest dramatic genius in English letters since the eighteenth century. When Shaw was offered the Nobel Prize for literature in 1925, he first refused it, saying, "The money is a lifebelt thrown to a swimmer who has already reached the shore in safety." Prevailed upon to accept the award, he donated the prize-money to the Anglo-Swedish Literary Alliance.

In November, 1950, at the age of ninety-four, his extraordinary career came to an end. His will provided that the residue of his large estate should be used to encourage a reform of the English alphabet, but the courts ruled that this was not in the public interest, and the estate was divided among the British Museum, the National Gallery of Ireland, and the Royal Academy of Dramatic Art.

To understand Shaw's historical contribution to the modern theater one must be aware that in 1879 Matthew Arnold, Victorian England's greatest critic-poet, could write: "In England we have no modern drama at all." Not only was England—and America too—without distinguished dramatists, but the theater itself was in disrepute as a mode of artistic expression. The Victorian middle class had inherited from their Puritan ancestors the firmly held belief that the theater was an instrument of the devil. No really respectable lady would ever have considered a theatrical career. And the plays that were produced were largely dramatic clap-trap—romantic and sentimental melodrama. Shaw's historical achievement lies in his returning along with Oscar Wilde, his most famous contemporary in the English theater, to an older tradition of English drama—the comedy of manners which flourished in the Restoration and the eighteenth century. Shaw was also inspired by eighteenth-century comic opera, particularly those operas in the style of Mozart. Like his dramatic and operatic predecessors, Shaw placed great emphasis upon characters who have their genesis in simplified and traditional comic types and upon sparkling, witty dialogue which often sounds more like the counterpointing of the rhythms and tones of individualized operatic voices than the utterance of full-bodied characters. It is little wonder that *Arms and the Man* should perhaps be even better known in its musical reincarnation, Oscar Straus's *The Chocolate Soldier,* or that *Pygmalion* should be transformed into the most highly successful musical of our day, *My Fair Lady.*

But Shaw was not content with writing simply a comedy of manners in many of his plays. Deeply influenced by his Norwegian contemporary Henrik Ibsen, Shaw demanded that the English theater become a vehicle for the realistic dramatic presentation of serious moral and social ideas.

Principal Works

PLAYS

Mrs. Warren's Profession (1893)

Arms and the Man (1894)

Candida (1894)

The Devil's Disciple (1897)

Caesar and Cleopatra (1898)

Captain Brassbound's Conversion (1899)

Man and Superman (1903)

Major Barbara (1905)

The Doctor's Dilemma (1906)

Misalliance (1910)

The Dark Lady of the Sonnets (1910)

Fanny's First Play (1911)

Androcles and the Lion (1912)

Pygmalion (1912)

Great Catherine (1913)

Heartbreak House (1919)

Back to Methuselah (1920)

Saint Joan (1923)

The Millionairess (1935)

ESSAYS AND NOVELS

An Unsocial Socialist (1883)

Fabian Essays in Socialism (1889)

The Quintessence of Ibsenism (1891)

The Perfect Wagnerite (1898)

Dramatic Opinions and Essays (1906)

The Intelligent Woman's Guide to Socialism and Capitalism (1928)

Everybody's Political What's What (1944)

Sixteen Self Sketches (1949)

Selected Descriptive Bibliography

Bentley, Eric, *Bernard Shaw,* amended edition, Norfolk, Conn., 1947.
One of the best criticisms of Shaw as dramatist and philosopher, pene-trating and judicious. Good selected Bibliography.

Brower, Reuben, "George Bernard Shaw" in *Major British Writers,* Vol. II, New York, 1954.
An excellent, brief introductory essay, incisive and illuminating.

Chesterton, G. K., *George Bernard Shaw,* New York, 1909.
The best early biographical study of Shaw, but limited as literary criticism.

Ervine, St. John, *Bernard Shaw: His Life, Work and Friends,* New York, 1956.
A judicious, modern biography with emphasis on the people in Shaw's life.

Farley, Earl and Marvin Carlson, "George Bernard Shaw: A Selected Bibliography (1945-1955)," *Modern Drama,* II (1959), 188-202, 295-325.
A detailed Bibliography of recent books and articles on Shaw.

Fuller, Edmund, *George Bernard Shaw: Critic of Western Morale,* New York, 1950.
A cursory review of Shaw's plays from a didactic point of view. Shaw is frequently used as a vehicle for Fuller's own moral pronouncements about the nature of the world.

Harris, Frank, *Bernard Shaw,* New York, 1931.
A colorful, but unreliable view of Shaw.

Henderson, Archibald, *Bernard Shaw, Playboy and Prophet,* New York, 1932.
A detailed and fully documented biography of a friend and admirer, largely superseded by Henderson's later volume.

————, *George Bernard Shaw: Man of the Century,* New York, 1956.
The richest Shavian biography. A monumental study of almost one thousand pages.

Kronenberger, Louis, ed., *George Bernard Shaw: A Critical Survey,* Cleveland and New York, 1953.
A collection of some of the best articles on Shaw written over the last sixty years.

Mander, Raymond and Joe Mitchenson, *Theatrical Companion to Shaw,* London, 1954.
A pictorial record of productions of Shaw's plays with synopses and production notes.

Nethercot, Arthur H., *Men and Supermen,* Cambridge, Mass., 1954.
A fine critical study of the Shavian portrait gallery. The characters are grouped by types and categories so that the discussion of the plays is scattered and sometimes repetitious.

Pearson, Hesketh, *G.B.S., A Full Length Portrait* and *A Portrait,* New York, 1952.
A gossipy and informal, but informative series of impressions covering the

full span of Shaw's career. Of value also because it contains many of Shaw's delightful conversations.

Purdom, C. B., ed., *Bernard Shaw's Letters to Granville-Barker,* New York, 1957.
Shaw's letters to his friend Harley Granville-Barker, actor and director, cover a period from 1900 to 1943 and afford interesting commentary on the practical problems of the theater that Shaw faced daily as well as on Shaw's views of himself as playwright.

Ward, A. C., *Bernard Shaw,* London, 1951.
A slight study containing a brief biography and a survey of the plays and other writings.

Wilson, Edmund, "Bernard Shaw at Eighty," *The Triple Thinkers,* New York, 1938.
A vigorous discussion of Shaw as a political thinker.

The Devil's Disciple GEORGE BERNARD SHAW

CHARACTERS

RICHARD DUDGEON, *the Devil's Disciple*

CHRISTOPHER DUDGEON, *Richard's brother*

REV. ANTHONY ANDERSON, *the Presbyterian minister in Websterbridge*

GENERAL BURGOYNE, *a British general*

MAJOR SWINDON, *the commander of British troops in Websterbridge*

THE SERGEANT, *one of Burgoyne's army*

LAWYER HAWKINS

WILLIAM DUDGEON, *Richard's uncle*

TITUS DUDGEON, *Richard's uncle*

MR. BRUDENELL, *the British chaplain*

THE EXECUTIONER

MRS. DUDGEON, *Richard's mother*

JUDITH ANDERSON, *Rev. Anderson's wife*

MRS. WILLIAM DUDGEON, *Richard's aunt*

MRS. TITUS DUDGEON, *Richard's aunt*

ESSIE, *illegitimate daughter of Peter Dudgeon*

The Devil's Disciple was first presented at the Harmanus Bleecker Hall, Albany, New York, on October 1, 1897, and on October 4 began a successful run at the Fifth Avenue Theatre in New York City.

Acknowledgment is made to the Public Trustee and The Society of Authors for The Devil's Disciple *by Bernard Shaw.*

9

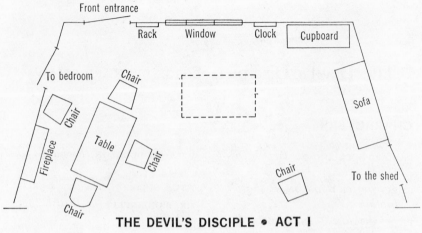

THE DEVIL'S DISCIPLE • ACT I

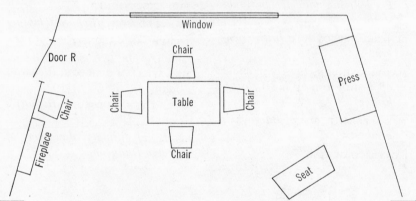

THE DEVIL'S DISCIPLE • ACT II

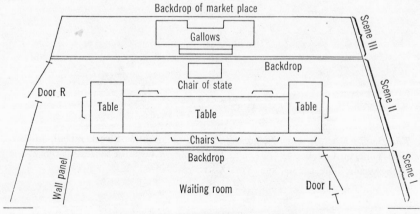

THE DEVIL'S DISCIPLE • ACT III

Act One

At the most wretched hour between a black night and a wintry morning in the year 1777, MRS. DUDGEON, *of New Hampshire, is sitting up in the kitchen and general dwelling room of her farm house on the outskirts of the town of Websterbridge. She is not a prepossessing woman. No woman looks her best after sitting up all night; and* MRS. DUDGEON'S *face, even at its best, is grimly trenched by the channels into which the barren forms and observances of a dead Puritanism can pen a bitter temper and a fierce pride. She is an elderly matron who has worked hard and got nothing by it except dominion and detestation in her sordid home, and an unquestioned reputation for piety and respectability among her neighbors, to whom drink and debauchery are still so much more tempting than religion and rectitude, that they conceive goodness simply as self-denial. This conception is easily extended to others-denial, and finally generalized as covering anything disagreeable. So* MRS. DUDGEON, *being exceedingly disagreeable, is held to be exceedingly good. Short of flat felony, she enjoys complete license except for amiable weaknesses of any sort, and is consequently, without knowing it, the most licentious woman in the parish on the strength of never having broken the seventh commandment or missed a Sunday at the Presbyterian church.*

The year 1777 is the one in which the passions roused by the breaking-off of the American colonies from England, more by their own weight than by their own will, boiled up to shooting point, the shooting being idealized to the English mind as suppression of rebellion and maintenance of British dominion, and to the American as defense of liberty, resistance to tyranny, and self-sacrifice on the altar of the Rights of Man. Into the merits of these idealizations it is not here necessary to inquire: suffice it to say, without prejudice, that they have convinced both Americans and English that the most high-minded course for them to pursue is to kill as many of one another as possible, and that military operations to that end are in full swing, morally supported by confident requests from the clergy of both sides for the blessing of God on their arms.

Under such circumstances many other women besides this disagreeable MRS. DUDGEON *find themselves sitting up all night waiting for news. Like her, too, they fall asleep towards morning at the risk of nodding themselves into the kitchen fire.* MRS. DUDGEON *sleeps with a shawl over her head, and her feet on a broad fender of iron laths, the step of the domestic altar of the fireplace, with its huge hobs[2] and boiler, and its hinged arm above the smoky mantelshelf for roasting. The plain kitchen table is opposite the fire, at her elbow, with a candle on it in a tin sconce.[3] Her chair, like all the others in the room, is uncushioned and unpainted; but as it has a round railed back and a seat conventionally moulded to the sitter's curves, it is comparatively a chair of state. The room has three doors, one on the same side as the fireplace, near the corner, leading to the best bedroom; one, at the opposite end of the opposite wall, leading to the scullery[4] and washhouse; and the housedoor, with its latch, heavy lock, and clumsy wooden bar, in the front wall, between the window in its middle and the corner next the bedroom door. Between the door and the window a rack of pegs suggests to the deductive observer that the men of the house are all away, as there are no hats or coats on them. On the other side of the window the clock hangs on a nail, with its white wooden dial, black iron weights, and brass pendulum. Between the clock and the corner, a big cupboard, locked, stands on a dwarf dresser full of common crockery.*

On the side opposite the fireplace, between the door and the corner, a shamelessly ugly black horsehair sofa stands against the wall. An inspection of its stridulous surface shows that MRS. DUDGEON *is not alone. A girl of sixteen or seventeen has fallen asleep on it. She is a wild, timid-looking creature with black hair and tanned skin. Her frock, a scanty garment, is rent, weather-stained, berry-stained, and by no means scrupulously clean. It hangs on her with a freedom which, taken with her brown legs and bare feet, suggests no great stock of underclothing.*

Suddenly there comes a tapping at the door, not loud enough to wake the sleepers. Then knocking, which disturbs MRS. DUDGEON *a little. Finally the latch is tried, whereupon she springs up at once.*

MRS. DUDGEON (*threateningly*) : Well, why don't you open the door? (*She sees that the girl is asleep, and immediately raises a clamor of heartfelt vexation*) Well, dear, dear me! Now this is— (*shaking her*) wake up, wake up; do you hear?

THE GIRL (*sitting up*) : What is it?

MRS. DUDGEON : Wake up; and be ashamed of yourself, you unfeeling, sinful girl, falling asleep like that, and your father hardly cold in his grave.

THE GIRL (*half asleep still*) : I didn't mean to. I dropped off—

---

[2] Projections at the back or side of a fireplace on which something may be kept warm.

[3] A candlestick.

[4] A small room off the kitchen where the kitchen utensils are cleaned and kept.

MRS. DUDGEON (*cutting her short*): Oh yes, you've plenty of excuses, I daresay. Dropped off! (*Fiercely, as the knocking recommences*) Why don't you get up and let your uncle in? After me waiting up all night for him! (*She pushes her rudely off the sofa*) There; I'll open the door; much good you are to wait up. Go and mend that fire a bit. (*The girl, cowed and wretched, goes to the fire and puts a log on.* MRS. DUDGEON *unbars the door and opens it, letting into the stuffy kitchen a little of the freshness and a great deal of the chill of the dawn, also her second son* CHRISTY, *a fattish, stupid, fair-haired, roundfaced man of about 22, muffled in a plaid shawl and grey overcoat. He hurries, shivering, to the fire, leaving* MRS. DUDGEON *to shut the door.*)

CHRISTY (*at the fire*): F—f—f! but it is cold. (*Seeing the girl and staring lumpishly at her*) Why, who are you?

THE GIRL (*shyly*): Essie.

MRS. DUDGEON: Oh, you may well ask. (*To* ESSIE) Go to your room, child, and lie down, since you haven't feeling enough to keep you awake. Your history isn't fit for your own ears to hear.

ESSIE: I—

MRS. DUDGEON (*peremptorily*): Don't answer me, Miss; but show your obedience by doing what I tell you. (ESSIE, *almost in tears, crosses the room to the door near the sofa*) And don't forget your prayers. (ESSIE *goes out*) She'd have gone to bed last night just as if nothing had happened if I'd let her.

CHRISTY (*phlegmatically*): Well, she can't be expected to feel Uncle Peter's death like one of the family.

MRS. DUDGEON: What are you talking about, child? Isn't she his daughter— the punishment of his wickedness and shame? (*She assaults her chair by sitting down.*)

CHRISTY (*staring*): Uncle Peter's daughter!

MRS. DUDGEON: Why else should she be here? D'ye think I've not had enough trouble and care put upon me bringing up my own girls, let alone you and your good-for-nothing brother, without having your uncle's bastards—

CHRISTY (*interrupting her with an apprehensive glance at the door by which* ESSIE *went out*): Sh! She may hear you.

MRS. DUDGEON (*raising her voice*): Let her hear me. People who fear God don't fear to give the devil's work its right name. (CHRISTY, *soullessly indifferent to the strife of Good and Evil, stares at the fire, warming himself*) Well, how long are you going to stare there like a stuck pig? What news have you for me?

CHRISTY (*taking off his hat and shawl and going to the rack to hang them up*): The minister is to break the news to you. He'll be here presently.

MRS. DUDGEON: Break what news?

CHRISTY (*standing on tiptoe, from boyish habit, to hang his hat up, though he is quite tall enough to reach the peg, and speaking with callous placidity, considering the nature of the announcement*): Father's dead too.

MRS. DUDGEON (*stupent*) : Your father!

CHRISTY (*sulkily, coming back to the fire and warming himself again, attending much more to the fire than to his mother*) : Well, it's not my fault. When we got to Nevinstown, we found him ill in bed. He didn't know us at first. The minister sat up with him and sent me away. He died in the night.

MRS. DUDGEON (*bursting into dry, angry tears*) : Well, I do think this is hard on me—very hard on me. His brother, that was a disgrace to us all his life, gets hanged on the public gallows as a rebel; and your father, instead of staying at home where his duty was, with his own family, goes after him and dies, leaving everything on my shoulders. After sending this girl to me to take care of, too! (*She plucks her shawl vexedly over her ears*) It's sinful, so it is; downright sinful.

CHRISTY (*with a slow, bovine cheerfulness, after a pause*) : I think it's going to be a fine morning, after all.

MRS. DUDGEON (*railing at him*) : A fine morning! And your father newly dead! Where's your feelings, child?

CHRISTY (*obstinately*) : Well, I didn't mean any harm. I suppose a man may make a remark about the weather even if his father's dead.

MRS. DUDGEON (*bitterly*) : A nice comfort my children are to me! One son a fool, and the other a lost sinner that's left his home to live with smugglers and gypsies and villains, the scum of the earth!
(*Someone knocks.*)

CHRISTY (*without moving*) : That's the minister.

MRS. DUDGEON (*sharply*) : Well, aren't you going to let Mr. Anderson in? (CHRISTY *goes sheepishly to the door.* MRS. DUDGEON *buries her face in her hands, as it is her duty as a widow to be overcome with grief.* CHRISTY *opens the door and admits the minister,* ANTHONY ANDERSON, *a shrewd, genial, ready Presbyterian divine of about 50, with something of the authority of his profession in his bearing. But it is an altogether secular authority, sweetened by a conciliatory, sensible manner not at all suggestive of a quite thorough-going other-worldliness. He is a strong, healthy man too, with a thick sanguine neck; and his keen, cheerful mouth cuts into somewhat fleshy corners. No doubt an excellent parson, but still a man capable of making the most of this world, and perhaps a little apologetically conscious of getting on better with it than a sound Presbyterian ought.*)

ANDERSON (*to* CHRISTY, *at the door, looking at* MRS. DUDGEON *whilst he takes off his cloak*) : Have you told her?

CHRISTY: She made me. (*He shuts the door; yawns; and loafs across to the sofa, where he sits down and presently drops off to sleep.*)
(ANDERSON *looks compassionately at* MRS. DUDGEON. *Then he hangs his cloak and hat on the rack.* MRS. DUDGEON *dries her eyes and looks up at him.*)

ANDERSON: Sister, the Lord has laid His hand very heavily upon you.

MRS. DUDGEON (*with intensely recalcitrant resignation*) : It's His will, I suppose; and I must bow to it. But I do think it hard. What call had Timothy to go to Springtown and remind everybody that he belonged to a man that was being hanged?—and (*spitefully*) that deserved it, if ever a man did.

ANDERSON (*gently*): They were brothers, Mrs. Dudgeon.

MRS. DUDGEON: Timothy never acknowledged him as his brother after we were married; he had too much respect for me to insult me with such a brother. Would such a selfish wretch as Peter have come thirty miles to see Timothy hanged, do you think? Not thirty yards, not he. However, I must bear my cross as best I may; least said is soonest mended.

ANDERSON (*very grave, coming down to the fire to stand with his back to it*): Your eldest son was present at the execution, Mrs. Dudgeon.

MRS. DUDGEON (*disagreeably surprised*): Richard?

ANDERSON (*nodding*): Yes.

MRS. DUDGEON (*vindictively*): Let it be a warning to him. He may end that way himself, the wicked, dissolute, godless—(*She suddenly stops; her voice fails; and she asks, with evident dread*) Did Timothy see him?

ANDERSON: Yes.

MRS. DUDGEON (*holding her breath*): Well?

ANDERSON: He only saw him in the crowd; they did not speak. (MRS. DUDGEON, *greatly relieved, exhales the pent up breath and sits at her ease again*) Your husband was greatly touched and impressed by his brother's awful death. (MRS. DUDGEON *sneers.* ANDERSON *breaks off to demand with some indignation*) Well, wasn't it only natural, Mrs. Dudgeon? He softened towards his prodigal son in that moment. He sent for him to come to see him.

MRS. DUDGEON (*her alarm renewed*): Sent for Richard!

ANDERSON: Yes; but Richard would not come. He sent his· father a message; but I'm sorry to say it was a wicked message—an awful message.

MRS. DUDGEON: What was it?

ANDERSON: That he would stand by his wicked uncle and stand against his good parents, in this world and the next.

MRS. DUDGEON (*implacably*): He will be punished for it. He will be punished for it—in both worlds.

ANDERSON: That is not in our hands, Mrs. Dudgeon.

MRS. DUDGEON: Did I say it was, Mr. Anderson? We are told that the wicked shall be punished. Why should we do our duty and keep God's law if there is to be no difference made between us and those who follow their own likings and dislikings, and make a jest of us and of their Maker's word?

ANDERSON: Well, Richard's earthly father has been merciful to him; and his heavenly judge is the father of us all.

MRS. DUDGEON (*forgetting herself*): Richard's earthly father was a soft-headed—

ANDERSON (*shocked*): Oh!

MRS. DUDGEON (*with a touch of shame*): Well, I am Richard's mother. If I am against him who has any right to be for him? (*Trying to conciliate him*) Won't you sit down, Mr. Anderson? I should have asked you before; but I'm so troubled.

ANDERSON: Thank you. (*He takes a chair from beside the fireplace, and turns it so that he can sit comfortably at the fire. When he is seated he adds, in the tone of a man who knows that he is opening a difficult subject)* Has Christy told you about the new will?

MRS. DUDGEON *(all her fears returning)* : The new will! Did Timothy—? *(She breaks off, gasping, unable to complete the question.)*

ANDERSON: Yes. In his last hours he changed his mind.

MRS. DUDGEON *(white with intense rage)* : And you let him rob me?

ANDERSON: I had no power to prevent him giving what was his to his own son.

MRS. DUDGEON: He had nothing of his own. His money was the money I brought him as my marriage portion. It was for me to deal with my own money and my own son. He dare not have done it if I had been with him; and well he knew it. That was why he stole away like a thief to take advantage of the law to rob me by making a new will behind my back. The more shame on you, Mr. Anderson,—you, a minister of the gospel—to act as his accomplice in such a crime.

ANDERSON *(rising)* : I will take no offense at what you say in the first bitterness of your grief.

MRS. DUDGEON *(contemptuously)* : Grief!

ANDERSON: Well, of your disappointment, if you can find it in your heart to think that the better word.

MRS. DUDGEON: My heart! My heart! And since when, pray, have you begun to hold up our hearts as trustworthy guides for us?

ANDERSON *(rather guiltily)* : I—er—

MRS. DUDGEON *(vehemently)* : Don't lie, Mr. Anderson. We are told that the heart of man is deceitful above all things and desperately wicked. My heart belonged, not to Timothy, but to that poor, wretched brother of his that has just ended his days with a rope round his neck—aye, to Peter Dudgeon. You know it; old Eli Hawkins, the man to whose pulpit you succeeded, though you are not worthy to loose his shoe latchet,[5] told it you when he gave over our souls into your charge. He warned me and strengthened me against my heart, and made me marry a God-fearing man—as he thought. What else but that discipline has made me the woman I am? And you, you, who followed your heart in your marriage, you talk to me of what I find in my heart. Go home to your pretty wife, man; and leave me to my prayers. *(She turns from him and leans with her elbows on the table, brooding over her wrongs and taking no further notice of him.)*

ANDERSON *(willing enough to escape)* : The Lord forbid that I should come between you and the source of all comfort! *(He goes to the rack for his coat and hat.)*

MRS. DUDGEON *(without looking at him)* : The Lord will know what to forbid and what to allow without your help.

ANDERSON: And whom to forgive, I hope—Eli Hawkins and myself, if we have ever set up our preaching against His law. *(He fastens his cloak, and is now ready to go)* Just one word—on necessary business, Mrs. Dudgeon. There is the reading of the will to be gone through; and

---

[5] Shoelace.

Richard has a right to be present. He is in the town; but he has the grace to say that he does not want to force himself in here.

MRS. DUDGEON: He shall come here. Does he expect us to leave his father's house for his convenience? Let them all come, and come quickly, and go quickly. They shall not make the will an excuse to shirk half their day's work. I shall be ready, never fear.

ANDERSON (*coming back a step or two*): Mrs. Dudgeon, I used to have some little influence with you. When did I lose it?

MRS. DUDGEON (*still without turning to him*): When you married for love. Now you're answered.

ANDERSON: Yes, I am answered. (*He goes out, musing.*)

MRS. DUDGEON (*to herself, thinking of her husband*): Thief! Thief! (*She shakes herself angrily out of her chair; throws back the shawl from her head; and sets to work to prepare the room for the reading of the will, beginning by replacing* ANDERSON'S *chair against the wall and pushing back her own to the window. Then she calls, in her hard, driving, wrathful way*) Christy. (*No answer: he is fast asleep*) Christy. (*She shakes him roughly*) Get up out of that; and be ashamed of yourself—sleeping, and your father dead! (*She returns to the table; puts the candle on the mantelshelf; and takes from the table drawer a red table cloth which she spreads.*)

CHRISTY (*rising reluctantly*): Well, do you suppose we are never going to sleep until we are out of mourning?

MRS. DUDGEON: I want none of your sulks. Here: help me to set this table. (*They place the table in the middle of the room, with* CHRISTY'S *end towards the fireplace and* MRS. DUDGEON'S *towards the sofa.* CHRISTY *drops the table as soon as possible, and goes to the fire, leaving his mother to make the final adjustment of its position*) We shall have the minister back here with the lawyer and all the family to read the will before you have done toasting yourself. Go and wake that girl; and then light the stove in the shed: you can't have your breakfast here. And mind you wash yourself and make yourself fit to receive the company. (*She punctuates these orders by going to the cupboard; unlocking it; and producing a decanter of wine, which has no doubt stood there untouched since the last state occasion in the family, and some glasses, which she sets on the table. Also two green ware[6] plates, on one of which she puts a barn-brack[7] with a knife beside it. On the other she shakes some biscuits out of a tin, putting back one or two, and counting the rest*) Now mind: there are ten biscuits there; let there be ten there when I come back after dressing myself. And keep your fingers off the raisins in that cake. And tell Essie the same. I suppose I can trust you to bring in the case of stuffed birds without breaking the glass? (*She replaces the tin in the cupboard, which she locks, pocketing the key carefully.*)

CHRISTY (*lingering at the fire*): You'd better put the inkstand instead, for the lawyer.

MRS. DUDGEON: That's no answer to make to me, sir. Go and do as you're

---

[6] Pottery.
[7] A currant bun, also spelled "barm brack."

told. (CHRISTY *turns sullenly to obey*) Stop; take down that shutter before you go, and let the daylight in; you can't expect me to do all the heavy work of the house with a great lout like you idling about.

(CHRISTY *takes the window bar out of its clamps and puts it aside; then opens the shutter, showing the grey morning.* MRS. DUDGEON *takes the sconce from the mantelshelf; blows out the candle; extinguishes the snuff[8] by pinching it with her fingers, first licking them for the purpose; and replaces the sconce on the shelf.*)

CHRISTY (*looking through the window*) : Here's the minister's wife.

MRS. DUDGEON (*displeased*) : What! Is she coming here?

CHRISTY: Yes.

MRS. DUDGEON: What does she want troubling me at this hour, before I am properly dressed to receive people?

CHRISTY: You'd better ask her.

MRS. DUDGEON (*threateningly*) : You'd better keep a civil tongue in your head. (*He goes sulkily towards the door. She comes after him, plying him with instructions*) Tell that girl to come to me as soon as she's had her breakfast. And tell her to make herself fit to be seen before the people. (CHRISTY *goes out and slams the door in her face*) Nice manners, that! (*Someone knocks at the house door; she turns and cries inhospitably*) Come in. (JUDITH ANDERSON, *the minister's wife, comes in.* JUDITH *is more than twenty years younger than her husband, though she will never be as young as he in vitality. She is pretty and proper and ladylike, and has been admired and petted into an opinion of herself sufficiently favorable to give her a self-assurance which serves her instead of strength. She has a pretty taste in dress, and in her face the pretty lines of a sentimental character formed by dreams. Even her little self-complacency is pretty, like a child's vanity. Rather a pathetic creature to any sympathetic observer who knows how rough a place the world is. One feels, on the whole, that* ANDERSON *might have chosen worse, and that she, needing protection, could not have chosen better*) Oh, it's you, is it, Mrs. Anderson?

JUDITH (*very politely—almost patronizingly*) : Yes. Can I do anything for you, Mrs. Dudgeon? Can I help to get the place ready before they come to read the will?

MRS. DUDGEON (*stiffly*) : Thank you, Mrs. Anderson; my house is always ready for anyone to come into.

MRS. ANDERSON (*with complacent amiability*) : Yes, indeed it is. Perhaps you had rather I did not intrude on you just now.

MRS. DUDGEON: Oh, one more or less will make no difference this morning, Mrs. Anderson. Now that you're here you'd better stay. If you wouldn't mind shutting the door! (JUDITH *smiles, implying "How stupid of me!" and shuts it with an exasperating air of doing something pretty and becoming*) That's better. I must go and tidy myself a bit. I suppose you don't mind stopping here to receive anyone that comes until I'm ready.

JUDITH (*graciously giving her leave*) : Oh yes, certainly. Leave that to me,

---

[8] The charred portion of a candlewick.

Mrs. Dudgeon; and take your time. (*She hangs her cloak and bonnet on the rack.*)

MRS. DUDGEON (*half sneering*): I thought that would be more in your way than getting the house ready. (ESSIE *comes back*) Oh, here you are! (*Severely*) Come here; let me see you. (ESSIE *timidly goes to her*. MRS. DUDGEON *takes her roughly by the arm and pulls her round to inspect the results of her attempt to clean and tidy herself—results which show little practice and less conviction*) Mm! That's what you call doing your hair properly, I suppose. It's easy to see what you are and how you were brought up. (*She throws her arm away and goes on, peremptorily*) Now you listen to me and do as you're told. You sit down there in the corner by the fire; and when the company comes, don't dare to speak until you're spoken to. (ESSIE *creeps away to the fireplace*) Your father's people had better see you and know you're there; they're as much bound to keep you from starvation as I am. At any rate they might help. But let me have no chattering and making free with them, as if you were their equal. Do you hear?

ESSIE: Yes.

MRS. DUDGEON: Well, then go and do as you're told. (ESSIE *sits down miserably on the corner of the fender*[9] *furthest from the door*) Never mind her, Mrs. Anderson; you know who she is and what she is. If she gives you any trouble, just tell me; and I'll settle accounts with her. (MRS. DUDGEON *goes into the bedroom, shutting the door sharply behind her as if even it had to be made do its duty with a ruthless hand.*)

JUDITH (*patronizing* ESSIE *and arranging the cake and wine on the table more becomingly*): You must not mind if your aunt is strict with you. She is a very good woman and desires your good too.

ESSIE (*in listless misery*): Yes.

JUDITH (*annoyed with* ESSIE *for her failure to be consoled and edified, and to appreciate the kindly condescension of the remark*): You are not going to be sullen, I hope, Essie.

ESSIE: No.

JUDITH: That's a good girl! (*She places a couple of chairs at the table with their backs to the window, with a pleasant sense of being a more thoughtful housekeeper than* MRS. DUDGEON) Do you know any of your father's relatives?

ESSIE: No. They wouldn't have anything to do with him; they were too religious. Father used to talk about Dick Dudgeon; but I never saw him.

JUDITH (*ostentatiously shocked*): Dick Dudgeon! Essie, do you wish to be a really respectable and grateful girl, and to make a place for yourself here by steady good conduct?

ESSIE (*very half-heartedly*): Yes.

JUDITH: Then you must never mention the name of Richard Dudgeon— never even think about him. He is a bad man.

ESSIE: What has he done?

JUDITH: You must not ask questions about him, Essie. You are too young

---

[9] A low metal guard before an open fireplace, to keep back falling coals.

to know what it is to be a bad man. But he is a smuggler; and he lives with gypsies; and he has no love for his mother and his family; and he wrestles and plays games on Sunday instead of going to church. Never let him into your presence, if you can help it, Essie; and try to keep yourself and all womanhood unspotted by contact with such men.

ESSIE: Yes.

JUDITH (*again displeased*): I am afraid you say Yes and No without thinking very deeply.

ESSIE: Yes. At least I mean—

JUDITH (*severely*): What do you mean?

ESSIE (*almost crying*): Only—my father was a smuggler; and— (*Someone knocks.*)

JUDITH: They are beginning to come. Now remember your aunt's directions, Essie; and be a good girl. (CHRISTY *comes back with the stand of stuffed birds under a glass case, and an inkstand, which he places on the table*) Good morning, Mr. Dudgeon. Will you open the door, please; the people have come.

CHRISTY: Good morning. (*He opens the house door.*)

(*The morning is now fairly bright and warm; and* ANDERSON, *who is the first to enter, has left his cloak at home. He is accompanied by* LAWYER HAWKINS, *a brisk, middleaged man in brown riding gaiters and yellow breeches, looking as much squire as solicitor. He and* ANDERSON *are allowed precedence as representing the learned professions. After them comes the family, headed by the senior uncle,* WILLIAM DUDGEON, *a large, shapeless man, bottle-nosed and evidently no ascetic at table. His clothes are not the clothes, nor his anxious wife the wife, of a prosperous man. The junior uncle,* TITUS DUDGEON, *is a wiry little terrier of a man, with an immense and visibly purse-proud wife, both free from the cares of the William household.*

HAWKINS *at once goes briskly to the table and takes the chair nearest the sofa,* CHRISTY *having left the inkstand there. He puts his hat on the floor beside him and produces the will.* UNCLE WILLIAM *comes to the fire and stands on the hearth warming his coat tails, leaving* MRS. WILLIAM *derelict near the door.* UNCLE TITUS, *who is the lady's man of the family, rescues her by giving her his disengaged arm and bringing her to the sofa, where he sits down warmly between his own lady and his brother's.* ANDERSON *hangs up his hat and waits for a word with* JUDITH.)

JUDITH: She will be here in a moment. Ask them to wait. (*She taps at the bedroom door. Receiving an answer from within, she opens it and passes through.*)

ANDERSON (*taking his place at the table at the opposite end to* HAWKINS): Our poor afflicted sister will be with us in a moment. Are we all here?

CHRISTY (*at the house door, which he has just shut*): All except Dick.

(*The callousness with which* CHRISTY *names the reprobate jars on the moral sense of the family.* UNCLE WILLIAM *shakes his head slowly and repeatedly.* MRS. TITUS *catches her breath convulsively through her nose. Her husband speaks.*)

UNCLE TITUS: Well, I hope he will have the grace not to come. I hope so.

(*The* DUDGEONS *all murmur assent, except* CHRISTY, *who goes to the window and posts himself there, looking out.* HAWKINS *smiles secretively as if he knew something that would change their tune if they knew it.* ANDERSON *is uneasy; the love of solemn family councils, especially funeral ones, is not in his nature.* JUDITH *appears at the bedroom door.*)

JUDITH (*with gentle impressiveness*): Friends, Mrs. Dudgeon. (*She takes the chair from beside the fireplace, and places it for* MRS. DUDGEON, *who comes from the bedroom in black, with a clean handkerchief to her eyes. All rise, except* ESSIE. MRS. TITUS *and* MRS. WILLIAM *produce equally clean handkerchiefs and weep. It is an affecting moment.*)

UNCLE WILLIAM: Would it comfort you, sister, if we were to offer up a prayer?

UNCLE TITUS: Or sing a hymn?

ANDERSON (*rather hastily*): I have been with our sister this morning already, friends. In our hearts we ask a blessing.

ALL (*except* ESSIE): Amen.

(*They all sit down, except* JUDITH, *who stands behind* MRS. DUDGEON'S *chair.*)

JUDITH (*to* ESSIE): Essie, did you say Amen?

ESSIE (*scaredly*): No.

JUDITH: Then say it, like a good girl.

ESSIE: Amen.

UNCLE WILLIAM (*encouragingly*): That's right; that's right. We know who you are; but we are willing to be kind to you if you are a good girl and deserve it. We are all equal before the Throne.

(*This republican sentiment does not please the women, who are convinced that the Throne is precisely the place where their superiority, often questioned in this world, will be recognized and rewarded.*)

CHRISTY (*at the window*): Here's Dick.

(ANDERSON *and* HAWKINS *look round sociably.* ESSIE, *with a gleam of interest breaking through her misery, looks up.* CHRISTY *grins and gapes expectantly at the door. The rest are petrified with the intensity of their sense of Virtue menaced with outrage by the approach of flaunting Vice. The reprobate appears in the doorway, graced beyond his alleged merits by the morning sunlight. He is certainly the best looking member of the family; but his expression is reckless and sardonic, his manner defiant and satirical, his dress picturesquely careless. Only, his forehead and mouth betray an extraordinary steadfastness; and his eyes are the eyes of a fanatic.*)

RICHARD (*on the threshold, taking off his hat*): Ladies and gentlemen: your servant, your very humble servant. (*With this comprehensive insult, he throws his hat to* CHRISTY *with a suddenness that makes him jump like a negligent wicket keeper,[10] and comes into the middle of the room, where he turns and deliberately surveys the company*) How happy you all look! how glad to see me! (*He turns towards* MRS. DUDGEON'S *chair;*

---

[10] In cricket the player on the fielding side who stands behind the wicket to stop balls that pass it.

and his lip rolls up horribly from his dog tooth as he meets her look of undisguised hatred) Well, mother: keeping up appearances as usual? that's right, that's right. (JUDITH *pointedly moves away from his neighborhood to the other side of the kitchen, holding her skirt instinctively as if to save it from contamination.* UNCLE TITUS *promptly marks his approval of her action by rising from the sofa and placing a chair for her to sit down upon)* What! Uncle William! I haven't seen you since you gave up drinking. (*Poor* UNCLE WILLIAM, *shamed, would protest; but* RICHARD *claps him heartily on his shoulder, adding)* You have given it up, haven't you? (*Releasing him with a playful push)* Of course you have; quite right too; you overdid it. (*He turns away from* UNCLE WILLIAM *and makes for the sofa)* And now, where is that upright horse-dealer Uncle Titus? Uncle Titus, come forth. (*He comes upon him holding the chair as* JUDITH *sits down)* As usual, looking after the ladies!

UNCLE TITUS (*indignantly)* : Be ashamed of yourself, sir—

RICHARD (*interrupting him and shaking his hand in spite of him)* : I am, I am; but I am proud of my uncle—proud of all my relatives—(*Again surveying them)* Who could look at them and not be proud and joyful? (UNCLE TITUS, *overborne, resumes his seat on the sofa.* RICHARD *turns to the table)* Ah, Mr. Anderson, still at the good work, still shepherding them. Keep them up to the mark, minister, keep them up to the mark. Come! (*With a spring he seats himself on the table and takes up the decanter)* Clink a glass with me, Pastor, for the sake of old times.

ANDERSON: You know, I think, Mr. Dudgeon, that I do not drink before dinner.

RICHARD: You will, some day, Pastor; Uncle William used to drink before breakfast. Come, it will give your sermons unction. (*He smells the wine and makes a wry face)* But do not begin on my mother's company sherry. I stole some when I was six years old; and I have been a temperate man ever since. (*He puts the decanter down and changes the subject)* So I hear you are married, Pastor, and that your wife has a most ungodly allowance of good looks.

ANDERSON (*quietly indicating* JUDITH) : Sir, you are in the presence of my wife. (JUDITH *rises and stands with stony propriety.)*

RICHARD (*quickly slipping down from the table with instinctive good manners)* : Your servant, madam; no offense. (*He looks at her earnestly)* You deserve your reputation; but I'm sorry to see by your expression that you're a good woman. (*She looks shocked and sits down amid a murmur of indignant sympathy from his relatives.* ANDERSON, *sensible enough to know that these demonstrations can only gratify and encourage a man who is deliberately trying to provoke them, remains perfectly good-humored)* All the same, Pastor, I respect you more than I did before. By the way, did I hear, or did I not, that our late lamented Uncle Peter, though unmarried, was a father?

UNCLE TITUS: He had only one irregular child, sir.

RICHARD: Only one! He thinks one a mere trifle! I blush for you, Uncle Titus.

ANDERSON: Mr. Dudgeon, you are in the presence of your mother and her grief.

RICHARD: It touches me profoundly, Pastor. By the way, what has become of the irregular child?

ANDERSON (*pointing to* ESSIE): There, sir, listening to you.

RICHARD (*shocked into sincerity*): What! Why the devil didn't you tell me that before? Children suffer enough in this house without—(*He hurries remorsefully to* ESSIE) Come, little cousin! never mind me; it was not meant to hurt you. (*She looks up gratefully at him. Her tear-stained face affects him violently; and he bursts out, in a transport of wrath*) Who has been making her cry? Who has been ill-treating her? By God—

MRS. DUDGEON (*rising and confronting him*): Silence your blasphemous tongue. I will bear no more of this. Leave my house.

RICHARD: How do you know it's your house until the will is read? (*They look at one another for a moment with intense hatred; and then she sinks, checkmated, into her chair.* RICHARD *goes boldly up past* ANDERSON *to the window, where he takes the railed chair in his hand*) Ladies and gentlemen, as the eldest son of my late father and the unworthy head of this household, I bid you welcome. By your leave, Minister Anderson: by your leave, Lawyer Hawkins. The head of the table for the head of the family. (*He places the chair at the table between the minister and the attorney; sits down between them; and addresses the assembly with a presidential air*) We meet on a melancholy occasion: a father dead! an uncle actually hanged, and probably damned. (*He shakes his head deploringly. The relatives freeze with horror*) That's right: pull your longest faces (*His voice suddenly sweetens gravely as his glance lights on* ESSIE) provided only there is hope in the eyes of the child. (*Briskly*) Now then, Lawyer Hawkins: business, business. Get on with the will, man.

TITUS: Do not let yourself be ordered or hurried, Mr. Hawkins.

HAWKINS (*very politely and willingly*): Mr. Dudgeon means no offense, I feel sure. I will not keep you one second, Mr. Dudgeon. Just while I get my glasses—(*He fumbles for them. The* DUDGEONS *look at one another with misgiving.*)

RICHARD: Aha! They notice your civility, Mr. Hawkins. They are prepared for the worst. A glass of wine to clear your voice before you begin. (*He pours out one for him and hands it; then pours one for himself.*)

HAWKINS: Thank you, Mr. Dudgeon. Your good health, sir.

RICHARD: Yours, sir. (*With the glass half way to his lips, he checks himself, giving a dubious glance at the wine, and adds, with quaint intensity*) Will anyone oblige me with a glass of water?

(ESSIE, *who has been hanging on his every word and movement, rises stealthily and slips out behind* MRS. DUDGEON *through the bedroom door, returning presently with a jug and going out of the house as quietly as possible.*)

HAWKINS: The will is not exactly in proper legal phraseology.

RICHARD: No, my father died without the consolations of the law.

HAWKINS: Good again, Mr. Dudgeon, good again. (*Preparing to read*) Are you ready, sir?

RICHARD: Ready, aye ready. For what we are about to receive, may the Lord make us truly thankful. Go ahead.

HAWKINS (*reading*): "This is the last will and testament of me Timothy

Dudgeon on my deathbed at Nevinstown on the road from Springtown to Websterbridge on this twenty-fourth day of September, one thousand seven hundred and seventy seven. I hereby revoke all former wills made by me and declare that I am of sound mind and know well what I am doing and that this is my real will according to my own wish and affections."

RICHARD (*glancing at his mother*): Aha!

HAWKINS (*shaking his head*): Bad phraseology, sir, wrong phraseology. "I give and bequeath a hundred pounds[11] to my younger son Christopher Dudgeon, fifty pounds to be paid to him on the day of his marriage to Sarah Wilkins if she will have him, and ten pounds on the birth of each of his children up to the number of five."

RICHARD: How if she won't have him?

CHRISTY: She will if I have fifty pounds.

RICHARD: Good, my brother. Proceed.

HAWKINS: "I give and bequeath to my wife Annie Dudgeon, born Annie Primrose"—you see he did not know the law, Mr. Dudgeon: your mother was not born Annie: she was christened so—"an annuity of fifty-two pounds a year for life (MRS. DUDGEON, *with all eyes on her, holds herself convulsively rigid*) to be paid out of the interest on her own money"—there's a way to put it, Mr. Dudgeon! Her own money!

MRS. DUDGEON: A very good way to put God's truth. It was every penny my own. Fifty-two pounds a year!

HAWKINS: "And I recommend her for her goodness and piety to the forgiving care of her children, having stood between them and her as far as I could to the best of my ability."

MRS. DUDGEON: And this is my reward! (*Raging inwardly*) You know what I think, Mr. Anderson; you know the word I gave to it.

ANDERSON: It cannot be helped, Mrs. Dudgeon. We must take what comes to us. (*To* HAWKINS) Go on, sir.

HAWKINS: "I give and bequeath my house at Websterbridge with the land belonging to it and all the rest of my property soever to my eldest son and heir, Richard Dudgeon."

RICHARD: Oho! The fatted calf, Minister, the fatted calf.

HAWKINS: "On these conditions—"

RICHARD: The devil! Are there conditions?

HAWKINS: "To wit: first, that he shall not let my brother Peter's natural child starve or be driven by want to an evil life."

RICHARD (*emphatically, striking his fist on the table*): Agreed.

(MRS. DUDGEON, *turning to look malignantly at* ESSIE, *misses her and looks quickly round to see where she has moved to; then, seeing that she has left the room without leave, closes her lips vengefully.*)

HAWKINS: "Second, that he shall be a good friend to my old horse Jim"— (*again shaking his head*) he should have written James, sir.

RICHARD: James shall live in clover. Go on.

---

[11] A pound was worth about four dollars at the time Shaw wrote the play, but the purchasing power of a pound was considerably more in Revolutionary times than it is today.

HAWKINS: —"and keep my deaf farm labourer Prodger Feston in his service."

RICHARD: Prodger Feston shall get drunk every Saturday.

HAWKINS: "Third, that he make Christy a present on his marriage out of the ornaments in the best room."

RICHARD (*holding up the stuffed birds*): Here you are, Christy.

CHRISTY (*disappointed*): I'd rather have the china peacocks.

RICHARD: You shall have both. (CHRISTY *is greatly pleased*) Go on.

HAWKINS: "Fourthly and lastly, that he try to live at peace with his mother as far as she will consent to it."

RICHARD (*dubiously*): Hm! Anything more, Mr. Hawkins?

HAWKINS (*solemnly*): "Finally I give and bequeath my soul into my Maker's hands, humbly asking forgiveness for all my sins and mistakes, and hoping that He will so guide my son that it may not be said that I have done wrong in trusting to him rather than to others in the perplexity of my last hour in this strange place."

ANDERSON: Amen.

THE UNCLES AND AUNTS: Amen.

RICHARD: My mother does not say Amen.

MRS. DUDGEON (*rising, unable to give up her property without a struggle*): Mr. Hawkins, is that a proper will? Remember, I have his rightful, legal will, drawn up by yourself, leaving all to me.

HAWKINS: This is a very wrongly and irregularly worded will, Mrs. Dudgeon: though (*turning politely to* RICHARD) it contains in my judgment an excellent disposal of his property.

ANDERSON (*interposing before* MRS. DUDGEON *can retort*): That is not what you are asked, Mr. Hawkins. Is it a legal will?

HAWKINS: The courts will sustain it against the other.

ANDERSON: But why, if the other is more lawfully worded?

HAWKINS: Because, sir, the courts sustain the claim of a man—and that man the eldest son—against any woman, if they can. I warned you, Mrs. Dudgeon, when you got me to draw that other will, that it was not a wise will, and that though you might make him sign it, he would never be easy until he revoked it. But you wouldn't take advice; and now Mr. Richard is cock of the walk. (*He takes his hat from the floor; rises; and begins pocketing his papers and spectacles.*)

(*This is the signal for the breaking-up of the party.* ANDERSON *takes his hat from the rack and joins* UNCLE WILLIAM *at the fire.* TITUS *fetches* JUDITH *her things from the rack. The three on the sofa rise and chat with* HAWKINS. MRS. DUDGEON, *now an intruder in her own house, stands inert, crushed by the weight of the law on women, accepting it, as she has been trained to accept all monstrous calamities, as proofs of the greatness of the power that inflicts them, and of her own wormlike insignificance. For at this time, remember, Mary Wollstonecraft[12] is as yet only a girl of eighteen, and her Vindication of the Rights of Women*

---

[12] The wife of William Godwin, English political philosopher. Her *Vindication of the Rights of Women* (1792) was a courageous attack on eighteenth-century attitudes toward women.

is still fourteen years off. MRS. DUDGEON *is rescued from her apathy by* ESSIE, *who comes back with the jug full of water. She is taking it to* RICHARD *when* MRS. DUDGEON *stops her.*)

MRS. DUDGEON (*threatening her*): Where have you been? (ESSIE, *appalled, tries to answer, but cannot*) How dare you go out by yourself after the orders I gave you?

ESSIE: He asked for a drink—(*She stops, her tongue cleaving to her palate with terror.*)

JUDITH (*with gentler severity*): Who asked for a drink? (ESSIE, *speechless, points to* RICHARD.)

RICHARD: What! I!

JUDITH (*shocked*): Oh Essie, Essie!

RICHARD: I believe I did. (*He takes a glass and holds it to* ESSIE *to be filled. Her hand shakes*) What! afraid of me?

ESSIE (*quickly*): No. I—(*She pours out the water.*)

RICHARD (*tasting it*): Ah, you've been up the street to the market gate spring to get that. (*He takes a draught*) Delicious! Thank you. (*Unfortunately, at this moment he chances to catch sight of* JUDITH'S *face, which expresses the most prudish disapproval of his evident attraction for* ESSIE, *who is devouring him with her grateful eyes. His mocking expression returns instantly. He puts down the glass; deliberately winds his arm round* ESSIE'S *shoulders; and brings her into the middle of the company.* MRS. DUDGEON *being in* ESSIE'S *way as they come past the table, he says*) By your leave, mother (*and compels her to make way for them*). What do they call you? Bessie?

ESSIE: Essie.

RICHARD: Essie, to be sure. Are you a good girl, Essie?

ESSIE (*greatly disappointed that he, of all people, should begin at her in this way*): Yes. (*She looks doubtfully at* JUDITH) I think so. I mean I— I hope so.

RICHARD: Essie, did you ever hear of a person called the devil?

ANDERSON (*revolted*): Shame on you, sir, with a mere child—

RICHARD: By your leave, Minister; I do not interfere with your sermons; do not you interrupt mine. (*To* ESSIE) Do you know what they call me, Essie?

ESSIE: Dick.

RICHARD (*amused; patting her on the shoulder*): Yes, Dick; but something else too. They call me the Devil's Disciple.

ESSIE: Why do you let them?

RICHARD (*seriously*): Because it's true. I was brought up in the other service; but I knew from the first that the Devil was my natural master and captain and friend. I saw that he was in the right and that the world cringed to his conqueror only through fear. I prayed secretly to him; and he comforted me, and saved me from having my spirit broken in this house of children's tears. I promised him my soul and swore an oath that I would stand up for him in this world and stand by him in the next. (*Solemnly*) That promise and that oath made a man of me. From this day this house is his home; and no child shall cry in it: this hearth is his altar; and no soul shall ever cower over it in the dark evenings and be afraid. Now (*turning forcibly on the rest*) which of you good men will take this child and rescue her from the house of the devil?

JUDITH (*coming to* ESSIE *and throwing a protecting arm about her*): I will. You should be burnt alive.

ESSIE: But I don't want to. (*She shrinks back, leaving* RICHARD *and* JUDITH *face to face.*)

RICHARD (*to* JUDITH): Actually doesn't want to, most virtuous lady!

UNCLE TITUS: Have a care, Richard Dudgeon. The law—

RICHARD (*turning threateningly on him*): Have a care, you. In an hour from this there will be no law here but martial law. I passed the soldiers within six miles on my way here; before noon Major Swindon's gallows for rebels will be up in the market place.

ANDERSON (*calmly*): What have we to fear from that, sir?

RICHARD: More than you think. He hanged the wrong man at Springtown: he thought Uncle Peter was respectable, because the Dudgeons had a good name. But his next example will be the best man in the town to whom he can bring home a rebellious word. Well, we're all rebels; and you know it.

ALL THE MEN (*except* ANDERSON): No, no, no!

RICHARD: Yes, you are. You haven't damned King George up hill and down dale as I have; but you've prayed for his defeat; and you, Anthony Anderson, have conducted the service and sold your family bible to buy a pair of pistols. They mayn't hang me, perhaps; because the moral effect of the Devil's Disciple dancing on nothing wouldn't help them. But a minister! (JUDITH, *dismayed, clings to* ANDERSON) or a lawyer! (HAWKINS *smiles like a man able to take care of himself*) or an upright horsedealer! (UNCLE TITUS *snarls at him in rage and terror*) or a reformed drunkard! (UNCLE WILLIAM, *utterly unnerved, moans and wobbles with fear*) eh? Would that show that King George meant business—ha?

ANDERSON (*perfectly self-possessed*): Come, my dear; he is only trying to frighten you. There is no danger. (*He takes her out of the house. The rest crowd to the door to follow him, except* ESSIE, *who remains near* RICHARD.)

RICHARD (*boisterously derisive*): Now then: how many of you will stay with me; run up the American flag on the devil's house; and make a fight for freedom? (*They scramble out,* CHRISTY *among them, hustling one another in their haste*) Ha ha! Long live the devil! (*To* MRS. DUDGEON, *who is following them*) What, mother! Are you off too?

MRS. DUDGEON (*deadly pale, with her hand on her heart as if she had received a deathblow*): My curse on you! My dying curse! (*She goes out.*)

RICHARD (*calling after her*): It will bring me luck. Ha ha ha!

ESSIE (*anxiously*): Mayn't I stay?

RICHARD (*turning to her*): What! Have they forgotten to save your soul in their anxiety about their own bodies? Oh yes, you may stay. (*He turns excitedly away again and shakes his fist after them. His left fist, also clenched, hangs down.* ESSIE *seizes it and kisses it, her tears falling on it.*)

He starts and looks at it) Tears! The devil's baptism! (*She falls on her knees, sobbing. He stoops good-naturedly to raise her, saying*) Oh yes, you may cry that way, Essie, if you like.

(*The Curtain Falls.*)

Act Two

MINISTER ANDERSON'S *house is in the main street of Websterbridge, not far from the town hall. To the eye of the eighteenth-century New Englander, it is much grander than the plain farmhouse of the* DUDGEONS; *but it is so plain itself that a modern house agent would let both at about the same rent. The chief dwelling room has the same sort of kitchen fireplace, with boiler, toaster hanging on the bars, movable iron griddle socketed to the hob, hook above for roasting, and broad fender, on which stand a kettle and a plate of buttered toast. The door, between the fireplace and the corner, has neither panels, fingerplates nor handles: it is made of plain boards, and fastens with a latch. The table is a kitchen table, with a treacle-colored cover of American cloth,*[13] *chapped*[14] *at the corners by draping. The tea service on it consists of two thick cups and saucers of the plainest ware, with milk jug and bowl to match, each large enough to contain nearly a quart, on a black japanned*[15] *tray, and, in the middle of the table, a wooden trencher*[16] *with a big loaf upon it, and a square half-pound block of butter in a crock. The big oak press*[17] *facing the fire from the opposite side of the room, is for use and storage, not for ornament; and the minister's house coat hangs on a peg from its door, showing that he is out; for when he is in, it is his best coat that hangs there. His big riding boots stand beside the press, evidently in their usual place, and rather proud of themselves. In fact, the evolution of the minister's kitchen, dining room and drawing room into three separate apartments has not yet taken place; and so, from the point of view of our pampered period, he is no better off than the* DUDGEONS.

---

[13] A molasses-colored oilcloth.
[14] Split or cracked.
[15] Varnished in the Japanese manner.
[16] A flat wooden platter on which meat or bread was cut and served.
[17] An upright cupboard or closet with full-length doors for storing clothes.

But there is a difference, for all that. To begin with, MRS. ANDERSON *is a pleasanter person to live with than* MRS. DUDGEON. *To which* MRS. DUDGEON *would at once reply, with reason, that* MRS. ANDERSON *has no children to look after; no poultry, pigs nor cattle; a steady and sufficient income not directly dependent on harvests and prices at fairs; an affectionate husband who is a tower of strength to her: in short, that life is as easy at the minister's house as it is hard at the farm. This is true; but to explain a fact is not to alter it; and however little credit* MRS. ANDERSON *may deserve for making her home happier, she has certainly succeeded in doing it. The outward and visible signs of her superior social pretensions are a drugget*[18] *on the floor, a plaster ceiling between the timbers, and chairs which, though not upholstered, are stained and polished. The fine arts are represented by a mezzotint*[19] *portrait of some Presbyterian divine, a copperplate*[20] *of Raphael's*[21] *St. Paul preaching at Athens, a rococo*[22] *presentation clock on the mantelshelf, flanked by a couple of miniatures, a pair of crockery dogs with baskets in their mouths, and, at the corners, two large cowrie shells.*[23] *A pretty feature of the room is the low wide latticed window, nearly its whole width, with little red curtains running on a rod half way up it to serve as a blind. There is no sofa; but one of the seats, standing near the press, has a railed back and is long enough to accommodate two people easily. On the whole, it is rather the sort of room that the nineteenth century has ended in struggling to get back to under the leadership of Mr. Philip Webb*[24] *and his disciples in domestic architecture, though no genteel clergyman would have tolerated it fifty years ago.*

The evening has closed in; and the room is dark except for the cosy firelight and the dim oil lamps seen through the window in the wet street, where there is a quiet, steady, warm, windless downpour of rain. As the town clock strikes the quarter, JUDITH *comes in with a couple of candles in earthenware candlesticks, and sets them on the table. Her self-conscious airs of the morning are gone: she is anxious and frightened. She goes to the window and peers into the street. The first thing she sees there is her husband, hurrying home through the rain. She gives a little gasp of relief, not very far removed from a sob, and turns to the door.* ANDERSON *comes in, wrapped in a very wet cloak.*

---

[18] A coarse rug made of cotton and wool.
[19] A copper or steel engraving.
[20] A plate of polished copper on which a picture is engraved.
[21] Famous Renaissance Italian painter (1483-1520).
[22] A florid, often tasteless, style of ornamentation, characterized by curved lines and decoration of pierced shellwork, popular in the eighteenth century.
[23] Large, oval, mottled shells from clam-like mollusks.
[24] Philip Webb (1831-1915) was an English architect associated with the manufacturing and decorating firm that was established by the poet William Morris to revolutionize the taste of the Victorian public.

JUDITH (*running to him*): Oh, here you are at last, at last! (*She attempts to embrace him.*)

ANDERSON (*keeping her off*): Take care, my love; I'm wet. Wait till I get my cloak off. (*He places a chair with its back to the fire; hangs his cloak on it to dry; shakes the rain from his hat and puts it on the fender; and at last turns with his hands outstretched to* JUDITH) Now! (*She flies into his arms*) I am not late, am I? The town clock struck the quarter as I came in at the front door. And the town clock is always fast.

JUDITH: I'm sure it's slow this evening. I'm so glad you're back.

ANDERSON (*taking her more closely in his arms*): Anxious, my dear?

JUDITH: A little.

ANDERSON: Why, you've been crying.

JUDITH: Only a little. Never mind; it's all over now. (*A bugle call is heard in the distance. She starts in terror and retreats to the long seat, listening*) What's that?

ANDERSON (*following her tenderly to the seat and making her sit down with him*): Only King George, my dear. He's returning to barracks, or having his roll called, or getting ready for tea, or booting or saddling or something. Soldiers don't ring the bell or call over the banisters when they want anything: they send a boy out with a bugle to disturb the whole town.

JUDITH: Do you think there is really any danger?

ANDERSON: Not the least in the world.

JUDITH: You say that to comfort me, not because you believe it.

ANDERSON: My dear, in this world there is always danger for those who are afraid of it. There's a danger that the house will catch fire in the night; but we shan't sleep any the less soundly for that.

JUDITH: Yes, I know what you always say; and you're quite right. Oh, quite right: I know it. But—I suppose I'm not brave: that's all. My heart shrinks every time I think of the soldiers.

ANDERSON: Never mind that, dear; bravery is none the worse for costing a little pain.

JUDITH: Yes, I suppose so. (*Embracing him again*) Oh how brave you are, my dear! (*With tears in her eyes*) Well, I'll be brave too: you shan't be ashamed of your wife.

ANDERSON: That's right. Now you make me happy. Well, well! (*He rises and goes cheerily to the fire to dry his shoes*) I called on Richard Dudgeon on my way back; but he wasn't in.

JUDITH (*rising in consternation*): You called on that man!

ANDERSON (*reassuring her*): Oh, nothing happened, dearie. He was out.

JUDITH (*almost in tears, as if the visit were a personal humiliation to her*): But why did you go there?

ANDERSON (*gravely*): Well, it is all the talk that Major Swindon is going to do what he did in Springtown—make an example of some notorious rebel, as he calls us. He pounced on Peter Dudgeon as the worst character there; and it is the general belief that he will pounce on Richard as the worst here.

JUDITH: But Richard said—

ANDERSON (*goodhumoredly cutting her short*): Pooh! Richard said! He said what he thought would frighten you and frighten me, my dear. He said what perhaps (God forgive him!) he would like to believe. It's a terrible thing to think of what death must mean for a man like that. I felt that I must warn him. I left a message for him.

JUDITH (*querulously*): What message?

ANDERSON: Only that I should be glad to see him for a moment on a matter of importance to himself, and that if he would look in here when he was passing he would be welcome.

JUDITH (*aghast*): You asked that man to come here!

ANDERSON: I did.

JUDITH (*sinking on the seat and clasping her hands*): I hope he won't come! Oh, I pray that he may not come!

ANDERSON: Why? Don't you want him to be warned?

JUDITH: He must know his danger. Oh, Tony, is it wrong to hate a blasphemer and a villain? I do hate him. I can't get him out of my mind; I know he will bring harm with him. He insulted you; he insulted me; he insulted his mother.

ANDERSON (*quaintly*): Well, dear, let's forgive him; and then it won't matter.

JUDITH: Oh, I know it's wrong to hate anybody; but—

ANDERSON (*going over to her with humorous tenderness*): Come, dear, you're not so wicked as you think. The worst sin towards our fellow creatures is not to hate them, but to be indifferent to them; that's the essence of inhumanity. After all, my dear, if you watch people carefully, you'll be surprised to find how like hate is to love. (*She starts, strangely touched—even appalled. He is amused at her*) Yes, I'm quite in earnest. Think of how some of our married friends worry one another, tax one another, are jealous of one another, can't bear to let one another out of sight for a day, are more like jailers and slave-owners than lovers. Think of those very same people with their enemies, scrupulous, lofty, self-respecting, determined to be independent of one another, careful of how they speak of one another—pooh! haven't you often thought that if they only knew it, they were better friends to their enemies than to their own husbands and wives? Come: depend on it, my dear, you are really fonder of Richard than you are of me, if you only knew it. Eh!

JUDITH: Oh, don't say that; don't say that, Tony, even in jest. You don't know what a horrible feeling it gives me.

ANDERSON (*laughing*): Well, well: never mind, pet. He's a bad man, and you hate him as he deserves. And you're going to make the tea, aren't you?

JUDITH (*remorsefully*): Oh yes, I forgot. I've been keeping you waiting all this time. (*She goes to the fire and puts on the kettle.*)

ANDERSON (*going to the press and taking his coat off*): Have you stitched up the shoulder of my old coat?

JUDITH: Yes, dear. (*She goes to the table and sets about putting the tea into the teapot from the caddy.*[25])

ANDERSON (*as he changes his coat for the older one hanging on the press*

---

[25] A small can or chest for tea leaves.

and replaces it by the one he has just taken off) : Did anyone call when I was out?

JUDITH: No, only— (*Someone knocks at the door. With a start which betrays her intense nervousness, she retreats to the further end of the table with the tea caddy and spoon in her hands, exclaiming*) Who's that?

ANDERSON (*going to her and patting her encouragingly on the shoulder*) : All right, pet, all right. He won't eat you, whoever he is. (*She tries to smile and nearly makes herself cry. He goes to the door and opens it.* RICHARD *is there, without overcoat or cloak*) You might have raised the latch and come in, Mr. Dudgeon. Nobody stands on much ceremony with us. (*Hospitably*) Come in. (RICHARD *comes in carelessly and stands at the table, looking round the room with a slight pucker of his nose at the mezzotinted divine on the wall.* JUDITH *keeps her eyes on the tea caddy*) Is it still raining? (*He shuts the door.*)

RICHARD: Raining like the very (*his eye catches* JUDITH'S *as she looks quickly and haughtily up*)—I beg your pardon; but (*showing that his coat is wet*) you see—!

ANDERSON: Take it off, sir; and let it hang before the fire a while; my wife will excuse your shirtsleeves. Judith, put in another spoonful of tea for Mr. Dudgeon.

RICHARD (*eyeing him cynically*) : The magic of property, Pastor! Are even you civil to me now that I have succeeded to my father's estate?

(JUDITH *throws down the spoon indignantly.*)

ANDERSON (*quite unruffled and helping* RICHARD *off with his coat*) : I think, sir, that since you accept my hospitality, you cannot have so bad an opinion of it. Sit down. (*With the coat in his hand, he points to the railed seat.* RICHARD, *in his shirtsleeves, looks at him half quarrelsomely for a moment; then, with a nod, acknowledges that the minister has got the better of him, and sits down on the seat.* ANDERSON *pushes his cloak into a heap on the seat of the chair at the fire and hangs* RICHARD'S *coat on the back in its place.*)

RICHARD: I come, sir, on your own invitation. You left word you had something important to tell me.

ANDERSON: I have a warning which it is my duty to give you.

RICHARD (*quickly rising*) : You want to preach to me. Excuse me; I prefer a walk in the rain. (*He makes for his coat.*)

ANDERSON (*stopping him*) : Don't be alarmed, sir; I am no great preacher. You are quite safe. (RICHARD *smiles in spite of himself. His glance softens; he even makes a gesture of excuse.* ANDERSON, *seeing that he has tamed him, now addresses him earnestly*) Mr. Dudgeon, you are in danger in this town.

RICHARD: What danger?

ANDERSON: Your uncle's danger. Major Swindon's gallows.

RICHARD: It is you who are in danger. I warned you—

ANDERSON (*interrupting him good-humoredly but authoritatively*) : Yes, yes, Mr. Dudgeon, but they do not think so in the town. And even if I were in danger, I have duties here which I must not forsake. But you are a free man. Why should you run any risk?

RICHARD: Do you think I should be any great loss, Minister?

ANDERSON: I think that a man's life is worth saving, whoever it belongs to. (RICHARD *makes him an ironical bow.* ANDERSON *returns the bow humorously*) Come, you'll have a cup of tea, to prevent you catching cold?

RICHARD: I observe that Mrs. Anderson is not quite so pressing as you are, Pastor.

JUDITH (*almost stifled with resentment, which she has been expecting her husband to share and express for her at every insult of* RICHARD'S) : You are welcome for my husband's sake. (*She brings the teapot to the fireplace and sets it on the hob.*)

RICHARD: I know I am not welcome for my own, madam. (*He rises*) But I think I will not break bread here, Minister.

ANDERSON (*cheerily*) : Give me a good reason for that.

RICHARD: Because there is something in you that I respect, and that makes me desire to have you for my enemy.

ANDERSON: That's well said. On those terms, sir, I will accept your enmity or any man's. Judith, Mr. Dudgeon will stay to tea. Sit down; it will take a few minutes to draw[26] by the fire. (RICHARD *glances at him with a troubled face, then sits down with his head bent, to hide a convulsive swelling of his throat*) I was just saying to my wife, Mr. Dudgeon, that enmity— (*She grasps his hand and looks imploringly at him, doing both with an intensity that checks him at once*) Well, well, I mustn't tell you, I see; but it was nothing that need leave us worse friend—enemies, I mean. Judith is a great enemy of yours.

RICHARD: If all my enemies were like Mrs. Anderson, I should be the best Christian in America.

ANDERSON (*gratified, patting her hand*) : You hear that, Judith? Mr. Dudgeon knows how to turn a compliment.

(*The latch is lifted from without.*)

JUDITH (*starting*) : Who is that?

(CHRISTY *comes in.*)

CHRISTY (*stopping and staring at* RICHARD) : Oh, are you here?

RICHARD: Yes. Begone, you fool; Mrs. Anderson doesn't want the whole family to tea at once.

CHRISTY (*coming further in*) : Mother's very ill.

RICHARD: Well, does she want to see me?

CHRISTY: No.

RICHARD: I thought not.

CHRISTY: She wants to see the minister—at once.

JUDITH (*to* ANDERSON) : Oh, not before you've had some tea.

ANDERSON: I shall enjoy it more when I come back, dear. (*He is about to take up his cloak.*)

CHRISTY: The rain's over.

ANDERSON (*dropping the cloak and picking up his hat from the fender*) : Where is your mother, Christy?

CHRISTY: At Uncle Titus's.

---

[26] To extract the essence by soaking; to steep.

ANDERSON: Have you fetched the doctor?

CHRISTY: No: she didn't tell me to.

ANDERSON: Go on there at once; I'll overtake you on his doorstep. (CHRISTY *turns to go*) Wait a moment. Your brother must be anxious to know the particulars.

RICHARD: Psha! not I; he doesn't know, and I don't care. (*Violently*) Be off, you oaf. (CHRISTY *runs out.* RICHARD *adds, a little shamefacedly*) We shall know soon enough.

ANDERSON: Well, perhaps you will let me bring you the news myself. Judith, will you give Mr. Dudgeon his tea and keep him here until I return.

JUDITH (*white and trembling*): Must I—

ANDERSON (*taking her hands and interrupting her to cover her agitation*): My dear, I can depend on you?

JUDITH (*with a piteous effort to be worthy of his trust*): Yes.

ANDERSON (*pressing her hand against his cheek*): You will not mind two old people like us, Mr. Dudgeon. (*Going*) I shall not say good evening; you will be here when I come back. (*He goes out.*)

(*They watch him pass the window and then look at each other dumbly, quite disconcerted.* RICHARD, *noting the quiver of her lips, is the first to pull himself together.*)

RICHARD: Mrs. Anderson, I am perfectly aware of the nature of your sentiments towards me. I shall not intrude on you. Good evening. (*Again he starts for the fireplace to get his coat.*)

JUDITH (*getting between him and the coat*): No, no. Don't go; please don't go.

RICHARD (*roughly*): Why? You don't want me here.

JUDITH: Yes, I— (*Wringing her hands in despair*) Oh, if I tell you the truth, you will use it to torment me.

RICHARD (*indignantly*): Torment! What right have you to say that? Do you expect me to stay after that?

JUDITH: I want you to stay; but (*suddenly raging at him like an angry child*) it is not because I like you.

RICHARD: Indeed!

JUDITH: Yes, I had rather you did go than mistake me about that. I hate and dread you; and my husband knows it. If you are not here when he comes back, he will believe that I disobeyed him and drove you away.

RICHARD (*ironically*): Whereas, of course, you have really been so kind and hospitable and charming to me that I only want to go away out of mere contrariness, eh?

(JUDITH, *unable to bear it, sinks on the chair and bursts into tears.*)

RICHARD: Stop, stop, stop, I tell you. Don't do that. (*Putting his hand to his breast as if to a wound*) He wrung my heart by being a man. Need you tear it by being a woman? Has he not raised you above my insults, like himself? (*She stops crying and recovers herself somewhat, looking at him with a scared curiosity*) There, that's right. (*Sympathetically*) You're better now, aren't you? (*He puts his hand encouragingly on her shoulder. She instantly rises haughtily and stares at him defiantly. He at once drops into his usual sardonic tone)* Ah, that's better. You are yourself again; so is Richard. Well, shall we go to tea like a quiet respectable couple and wait for your husband's return?

JUDITH *(rather ashamed of herself)* If you please. I—I am sorry to have been so foolish. *(She stoops to take up the plate of toast from the fender.)*

RICHARD: I am sorry, for your sake, that I am—what I am. Allow me. *(He takes the plate from her and goes with it to the table.)*

JUDITH *(following with the teapot)*: Will you sit down? *(He sits down at the end of the table nearest the press. There is a plate and knife laid there. The other plate is laid near it; but* JUDITH *stays at the opposite end of the table, next the fire, and takes her place there, drawing the tray towards her)* Do you take sugar?

RICHARD: No, but plenty of milk. Let me give you some toast. *(He puts some on the second plate and hands it to her, with the knife. The action shows quickly how well he knows that she has avoided her usual place so as to be as far from him as possible.)*

JUDITH *(consciously)*: Thanks. *(She gives him his tea)* Won't you help yourself?

RICHARD: Thanks. *(He puts a piece of toast on his own plate, and she pours out tea for herself.)*

JUDITH *(observing that he tastes nothing)*: Don't you like it? You are not eating anything.

RICHARD: Neither are you.

JUDITH *(nervously)*: I never care much for my tea. Please don't mind me.

RICHARD *(looking dreamily round)*: I am thinking. It is all so strange to me. I can see the beauty and peace of this home; I think I have never been more at rest in my life than at this moment; and yet I know quite well I could never live here. It's not in my nature, I suppose, to be domesticated. But it's very beautiful; it's almost holy. *(He muses a moment and then laughs softly.)*

JUDITH *(quickly)*: Why do you laugh?

RICHARD: I was thinking that if any stranger came in here now, he would take us for man and wife.

JUDITH *(taking offense)*: You mean, I suppose, that you are more my age than he is.

RICHARD *(staring at this unexpected turn)*: I never thought of such a thing. *(Sardonic again)* I see there is another side to domestic joy.

JUDITH *(angrily)*: I would rather have a husband whom everybody respects than—than—

RICHARD: Than the devil's disciple. You are right; but I daresay your love helps him to be a good man, just as your hate helps me to be a bad one.

JUDITH: My husband has been very good to you. He has forgiven you for insulting him and is trying to save you. Can you not forgive him for being so much better than you are? How dare you belittle him by putting yourself in his place?

RICHARD: Did I?

JUDITH: Yes, you did. You said that if anybody came in they would take us for man and— (*She stops, terror-stricken, as a squad of soldiers tramps past the window*) The English soldiers! Oh, what do they—

RICHARD (*listening*): Sh!

A VOICE (*outside*): Halt! Four outside: two in with me. (JUDITH *half rises, listening and looking with dilated eyes at* RICHARD, *who takes up his cup prosaically and is drinking his tea when the latch goes up with a sharp click, and an English* SERGEANT *walks into the room with two privates, who post themselves at the door. He comes promptly to the table between them.*)

THE SERGEANT: Sorry to disturb you, mum. Duty! Anthony Anderson: I arrest you in King George's name as a rebel.

JUDITH (*pointing at* RICHARD): But that is not— (*He looks up quickly at her, with a face of iron. She stops her mouth hastily with the hand she has raised to indicate him, and stands staring affrightedly.*)

THE SERGEANT: Come, parson; put your coat on and come along.

RICHARD: Yes, I'll come. (*He rises and takes a step towards his own coat; then recollects himself, and, with his back to the* SERGEANT, *moves his gaze slowly round the room without turning his head until he sees* ANDERSON'S *black coat hanging up on the press. He goes composedly to it, takes it down, and puts it on. The idea of himself as a parson tickles him; he looks down at the black sleeve on his arm and then smiles slyly at* JUDITH, *whose white face shows him that what she is painfully struggling to grasp is not the humor of the situation but its horror. He turns to the* SERGEANT, *who is approaching him with a pair of handcuffs hidden behind him, and says lightly*) Did you ever arrest a man of my cloth before, Sergeant?

THE SERGEANT (*instinctively respectful, half to the black coat and to* RICHARD'S *good breeding*): Well, no sir. At least, only an army chaplain. (*Showing the handcuffs*) I'm sorry sir; but duty—

RICHARD: Just so, Sergeant. Well, I'm not ashamed of them; thank you kindly for the apology. (*He holds out his hands.*)

SERGEANT (*not availing himself of the offer*): One gentleman to another, sir. Wouldn't you like to say a word to your missis, sir, before you go?

RICHARD (*smiling*): Oh, we shall meet again before—eh? (*Meaning "before you hang me".*)

SERGEANT (*loudly, with ostentatious cheerfulness*): Oh, of course, of course. No call for the lady to distress herself. Still— (*in a lower voice, intended for* RICHARD *alone*) your last chance, sir.

(*They look at one another significantly for a moment. Then* RICHARD *exhales a deep breath and turns towards* JUDITH.)

RICHARD (*very distinctly*): My love. (*She looks at him, pitiably pale, and tries to answer, but cannot—tries also to come to him, but cannot trust herself to stand without the support of the table*) This gallant gentleman is good enough to allow us a moment of leavetaking. (*The* SERGEANT *retires delicately and joins his men near the door*) He is trying to spare you the truth; but you had better know it. Are you listening to me? (*She signifies assent*) Do you understand that I am going to my death?

(*She signifies that she understands*) Remember, you must find our friend who was with us just now. Do you understand? (*She signifies yes*) See that you get him safely out of harm's way. Don't for your life let him know of my danger; but if he finds it out, tell him that he cannot save me: they would hang him; and they would not spare me. And tell him that I am steadfast in my religion as he is in his and that he may depend on me to the death. (*He turns to go and meets the eyes of the* SERGEANT, *who looks a little suspicious. He considers a moment and then, turning roguishly to* JUDITH *with something of a smile breaking through his earnestness, says*) And now, my dear, I am afraid the sergeant will not believe that you love me like a wife unless you give one kiss before I go. (*He approaches her and holds out his arms. She quits the table and almost falls into them.*)

JUDITH (*the words choking her*): I ought to—it's murder—

RICHARD: No; only a kiss (*softly to her*) for his sake.

JUDITH: I can't. You must—

RICHARD (*folding her in his arms with an impulse of compassion for her distress*): My poor girl!

(JUDITH, *with a sudden effort, throws her arms round him; kisses him; and swoons away, dropping from his arms to the ground as if the kiss had killed her.*)

RICHARD (*going quickly to the* SERGEANT): Now, Sergeant; quick, before she comes to. The handcuffs. (*He puts out his hands.*)

SERGEANT (*pocketing them*): Never mind, sir; I'll trust you. You're a game one. You ought to a bin a soldier, sir. Between them two, please. (*The soldiers place themselves one before* RICHARD *and one behind him. The* SERGEANT *opens the door.*)

RICHARD (*taking a last look round him*): Goodbye, wife; goodbye, home. Muffle the drums and quick march!

(*The* SERGEANT *signs to the leading soldier to march. They file out quickly.*******************When ANDERSON *returns from* MRS. DUDGEON'S, *he is astonished to find the room apparently empty and almost in darkness except for the glow from the fire; for one of the candles has burnt out, and the other is at its last flicker.*)

ANDERSON: Why, what on earth—? (*Calling*) Judith, Judith! (*He listens; there is no answer*) Hm! (*He goes to the cupboard; takes a candle from the drawer; lights it at the flicker of the expiring one on the table; and looks wonderingly at the untasted meal by its light. Then he sticks it in the candlestick; takes off his hat; and scratches his head, much puzzled. This action causes him to look at the floor for the first time, and there he sees* JUDITH *lying motionless with her eyes closed. He runs to her and stoops beside her, lifting her head*) Judith.

JUDITH (*waking; for her swoon has passed into the sleep of exhaustion after suffering*): Yes. Did you call? What's the matter?

ANDERSON: I've just come in and found you lying here with the candles burnt out and the tea poured out and cold. What has happened?

JUDITH (*still astray*): I don't know. Have I been asleep? I suppose— (*She stops blankly*) I don't know.

ANDERSON (*groaning*): Heaven forgive me, I left you alone with that scoundrel. (JUDITH *remembers. With an agonized cry, she clutches his shoulders and drags herself to her feet as he rises with her. He clasps her tenderly in his arms*) My poor pet!

JUDITH (*frantically clinging to him*): What shall I do? Oh my God, what shall I do?

ANDERSON: Never mind, never mind, my dearest dear: it was my fault. Come, you're safe now; and you're not hurt, are you? (*He takes his arms from her to see whether she can stand*) There, that's right, that's right. If only you are not hurt, nothing else matters.

JUDITH: No, no, no, I'm not hurt.

ANDERSON: Thank Heaven for that! Come now: (*leading her to the railed seat and making her sit down beside him*) sit down and rest; you can tell me about it tomorrow. Or (*misunderstanding her distress*) you shall not tell me at all if it worries you. There, there! (*Cheerfully*) I'll make you some fresh tea; that will set you up again. (*He goes to the table and empties the teapot into the slop bowl.*[27])

JUDITH (*in a strained tone*): Tony.

ANDERSON: Yes, dear?

JUDITH: Do you think we are only in a dream now?

ANDERSON (*glancing round at her for a moment with a pang of anxiety, though he goes on steadily and cheerfully putting fresh tea into the pot*): Perhaps so, pet. But you may as well dream a cup of tea when you're about it.

JUDITH: Oh stop, stop. You don't know— (*Distracted, she buries her face in her knotted hands.*)

ANDERSON (*breaking down and coming to her*): My dear, what is it? I can't bear it any longer; you must tell me. It was all my fault; I was mad to trust him.

JUDITH: No, don't say that. You mustn't say that. He—oh no, no: I can't. Tony, don't speak to me. Take my hands—both my hands. (*He takes them, wondering*) Make me think of you, not of him. There's danger, frightful danger; but it is your danger; and I can't keep thinking of it; I can't, I can't; my mind goes back to his danger. He must be saved— no, you must be saved: you, you, you. (*She springs up as if to do something or go somewhere, exclaiming*) Oh, Heaven help me!

ANDERSON (*keeping his seat and holding her hands with resolute composure*): Calmly, calmly, my pet. You're quite distracted.

JUDITH: I may well be. I don't know what to do. I don't know what to do. (*Tearing her hands away*) I must save him. (ANDERSON *rises in alarm as she runs wildly to the door. It is opened in her face by* ESSIE, *who hurries in full of anxiety. The surprise is so disagreeable to* JUDITH *that it brings her to her senses. Her tone is sharp and angry as she demands*) What do you want?

ESSIE: I was to come to you.

---

[27] A bowl for receiving the rinsings of tea cups at the table.

ANDERSON: Who told you to?

ESSIE (*staring at him, as if his presence astonished her*): Are you here?

JUDITH: Of course. Don't be foolish, child.

ANDERSON: Gently, dearest; you'll frighten her. (*Going between them*) Come here, Essie. (*She comes to him*) Who sent you?

ESSIE: Dick. He sent me word by a soldier. I was to come here at once and do whatever Mrs. Anderson told me.

ANDERSON (*enlightened*): A soldier! Ah, I see it all now! They have arrested Richard. (JUDITH *makes a gesture of despair.*)

ESSIE: No. I asked the soldier. Dick's safe. But the soldier said you had been taken.

ANDERSON: I! (*Bewildered, he turns to* JUDITH *for an explanation.*)

JUDITH (*coaxingly*): All right, dear: I understand. (*To* ESSIE) Thank you, Essie, for coming; but I don't need you now. You may go home.

ESSIE (*suspicious*): Are you sure Dick has not been touched? Perhaps he told the soldier to say it was the minister. (*Anxiously*) Mrs. Anderson, do you think it can have been that?

ANDERSON: Tell her the truth if it is so, Judith. She will learn it from the first neighbor she meets in the street. (JUDITH *turns away and covers her eyes with her hands.*)

ESSIE (*wailing*): But what will they do to him? Oh, what will they do to him? Will they hang him? (JUDITH *shudders convulsively and throws herself into the chair in which* RICHARD *sat at the tea table.*)

ANDERSON (*patting* ESSIE'S *shoulder and trying to comfort her*): I hope not. I hope not. Perhaps if you're very quiet and patient, we may be able to help him in some way.

ESSIE: Yes—help him—yes, yes, yes. I'll be good.

ANDERSON: I must go to him at once, Judith.

JUDITH (*springing up*): Oh no. You must go away—far away, to some place of safety.

ANDERSON: Pooh!

JUDITH (*passionately*): Do you want to kill me? Do you think I can bear to live for days and days with every knock at the door—every footstep—giving me a spasm of terror? to lie awake for nights and nights in an agony of dread, listening for them to come and arrest you?

ANDERSON: Do you think it would be better to know that I had run away from my post at the first sign of danger?

JUDITH (*bitterly*): Oh, you won't go. I know it. You'll stay; and I shall go mad.

ANDERSON: My dear, your duty—

JUDITH (*fiercely*): What do I care about my duty?

ANDERSON (*shocked*): Judith!

JUDITH: I am doing my duty. I am clinging to my duty. My duty is to get you away, to save you, to leave him to his fate. (ESSIE *utters a cry of distress and sinks on the chair at the fire, sobbing silently*) My instinct is the same as hers—to save him above all things, though it would be so much better for him to die! so much greater! But I know you will take your own way as he took it. I have no power. (*She sits down sullenly on the railed seat*) I'm only a woman; I can do nothing but sit here and suffer. Only, tell him I tried to save you—that I did my best to save you.

ANDERSON: My dear, I am afraid he will be thinking more of his own danger than of mine.

JUDITH: Stop; or I shall hate you.

ANDERSON (*remonstrating*): Come, come, come! How am I to leave you if you talk like this? You are quite out of your senses. (*He turns to* ESSIE) Essie.

ESSIE (*eagerly rising and drying her eyes*): Yes?

ANDERSON: Just wait outside a moment, like a good girl; Mrs. Anderson is not well. (ESSIE *looks doubtful*) Never fear; I'll come to you presently; and I'll go to Dick.

ESSIE: You are sure you will go to him? (*Whispering*) You won't let her prevent you?

ANDERSON (*smiling*): No, no: it's all right. All right. (*She goes*) That's a good girl. (*He closes the door and returns to* JUDITH.)

JUDITH (*seated—rigid*): You are going to your death.

ANDERSON (*quaintly*): Then I shall go in my best coat, dear. (*He turns to the press, beginning to take off his coat*) Where—? (*He stares at the empty nail for a moment; then looks quickly round to the fire; strides across to it; and lifts* RICHARD'S *coat*) Why, my dear, it seems that he has gone in my best coat.

JUDITH (*still motionless*): Yes.

ANDERSON: Did the soldiers make a mistake?

JUDITH: Yes, they made a mistake.

ANDERSON: He might have told them. Poor fellow, he was too upset, I suppose.

JUDITH: Yes, he might have told them. So might I.

ANDERSON: Well, it's all very puzzling—almost funny. It's curious how these little things strike us even in the most— (*He breaks off and begins putting on* RICHARD'S *coat*) I'd better take him his own coat. I know what he'll say—(*imitating* RICHARD'S *sardonic manner*) "Anxious about my soul, Pastor, and also about your best coat." Eh?

JUDITH: Yes, that is just what he will say to you. (*Vacantly*) It doesn't matter; I shall never see either of you again.

ANDERSON (*rallying her*): Oh pooh, pooh, pooh! (*He sits down beside her*) Is this how to keep your promise that I shan't be ashamed of my brave wife?

JUDITH: No, this is how I break it. I cannot keep my promises to him; why should I keep my promises to you?

ANDERSON: Don't speak so strangely, my love. It sounds insincere to me. (*She looks unutterable reproach at him*) Yes, dear, nonsense is always insincere; and my dearest is talking nonsense. Just nonsense. (*Her face darkens into dumb obstinacy. She stares straight before her and does not look at him again, absorbed in* RICHARD'S *fate. He scans her face; sees that his rallying has produced no effect; and gives it up, making no further effort to conceal his anxiety*) I wish I knew what has frightened you so. Was there a struggle? Did he fight?

JUDITH: No. He smiled.

ANDERSON: Did he realize his danger, do you think?

JUDITH: He realized yours.

ANDERSON: Mine!

JUDITH (*monotonously*): He said "See that you get him safely out of harm's way." I promised: I can't keep my promise. He said, "Don't for your life let him know of my danger." I've told you of it. He said that if you found it out, you could not save him—that they will hang him and not spare you.

ANDERSON (*rising in generous indignation*): And you think that I will let a man with that much good in him die like a dog, when a few words might make him die like a Christian. I'm ashamed of you, Judith.

JUDITH: He will be steadfast in his religion as you are in yours; and you may depend on him to the death. He said so.

ANDERSON: God forgive him! What else did he say?

JUDITH: He said goodbye.

ANDERSON (*fidgeting nervously to and fro in great concern*): Poor fellow, poor fellow! You said goodbye to him in all kindness and charity, Judith, I hope.

JUDITH: I kissed him.

ANDERSON: What! Judith!

JUDITH: Are you angry?

ANDERSON: No, no. You were right; you were right. Poor fellow, poor fellow! (*Greatly distressed*) To be hanged like that at his age! And then did they take him away?

JUDITH (*wearily*): Then you were here; that's the next thing I remember. I suppose I fainted. Now bid me goodbye, Tony. Perhaps I shall faint again. I wish I could die.

ANDERSON: No, no, my dear, you must pull yourself together and be sensible. I am in no danger—not the least in the world.

JUDITH (*solemnly*): You are going to your death, Tony—your sure death, if God will let innocent men be murdered. They will not let you see him; they will arrest you the moment you give your name. It was for you the soldiers came.

ANDERSON (*thunderstruck*): For me!!! (*His fists clinch; his neck thickens; his face reddens; the fleshy purses under his eyes become injected with hot blood; the man of peace vanishes, transfigured into a choleric and formidable man of war. Still, she does not come out of her absorption to look at him; her eyes are steadfast with a mechanical reflection of* RICHARD'S *steadfastness.*)

JUDITH: He took your place; he is dying to save you. That is why he went in your coat. That is why I kissed him.

ANDERSON (*exploding*): Blood an' owns![28] (*His voice is rough and dominant, his gesture full of brute energy*) Here! Essie, Essie!

---

[28] A violent blasphemy, "by God's blood and wounds."

ESSIE (*running in*): Yes.

ANDERSON (*impetuously*): Off with you as hard as you can run, to the inn. Tell them to saddle the fastest and strongest horse they have (JUDITH *rises breathless and stares at him incredulously*)—the chestnut mare, if she's fresh—without a moment's delay. Go into the stable yard and tell the black man there that I'll give him a silver dollar if the horse is waiting for me when I come, and that I am close on your heels. Away with you. (*His energy sends* ESSIE *flying from the room. He pounces on his riding boots; rushes with them to the chair at the fire; and begins pulling them on.*)

JUDITH (*unable to believe such a thing of him*): You are not going to him!

ANDERSON (*busy with the boots*): Going to him! What good would that do? (*Growling to himself as he gets the first boot on with a wrench*) I'll go to them, so I will. (*To* JUDITH *peremptorily*) Get me the pistols; I want them. And money, money: I want money—all the money in the house. (*He stoops over the other boot, grumbling*) A great satisfaction it would be to him to have my company on the gallows. (*He pulls on the boot.*)

JUDITH: You are deserting him, then?

ANDERSON: Hold your tongue, woman; and get me the pistols. (*She goes to the press and takes from it a leather belt with two pistols, a powder horn, and a bag of bullets attached to it. She throws it on the table. Then she unlocks a drawer in the press and takes out a purse.* ANDERSON *grabs the belt and buckles it on, saying*) If they took him for me in my coat, perhaps they'll take me for him in his. (*Hitching the belt into its place*) Do I look like him?

JUDITH (*turning with the purse in her hand*): Horribly unlike him.

ANDERSON (*snatching the purse from her and emptying it on the table*): Hm! We shall see.

JUDITH (*sitting down helplessly*): Is it of any use to pray, do you think, Tony?

ANDERSON (*counting the money*): Pray! Can we pray Swindon's rope off Richard's neck?

JUDITH: God may soften Major Swindon's heart.

ANDERSON (*contemptuously—pocketing a handful of money*): Let him, then. I am not God; and I must go to work another way. (JUDITH *gasps at the blasphemy. He throws the purse on the table*) Keep that. I've taken 25 dollars.

JUDITH: Have you forgotten even that you are a minister?

ANDERSON: Minister be—faugh! My hat: where's my hat? (*He snatches up hat and cloak and puts both on in hot haste*) Now listen, you. If you can get a word with him by pretending you're his wife, tell him to hold his tongue until morning; that will give me all the start I need.

JUDITH (*solemnly*): You may depend on him to the death.

ANDERSON: You're a fool, a fool, Judith. (*For a moment checking the torrent of his haste and speaking with something of his old quiet and impressive conviction*) You don't know the man you're married to. (ESSIE *returns. He swoops at her at once*) Well, is the horse ready?

ESSIE (*breathless*) : It will be ready when you come.

ANDERSON : Good. (*He makes for the door.*)

JUDITH (*rising and stretching out her arms after him involuntarily*) : Won't you say goodbye?

ANDERSON : And waste another half minute! Psha! (*He rushes out like an avalanche.*)

ESSIE (*hurrying to* JUDITH) : He has gone to save Richard, hasn't he?

JUDITH : To save Richard! No: Richard has saved him. He has gone to save himself. Richard must die.

(ESSIE *screams with terror and falls on her knees, hiding her face.* JUDITH, *without heeding her, looks rigidly straight in front of her, at the vision of* RICHARD, *dying.*)

(*The Curtain Falls.*)

Act Three

SCENE ONE

Early next morning the SERGEANT, *at the British headquarters in the Town Hall, unlocks the door of a little empty panelled waiting room and invites* JUDITH *to enter. She has had a bad night, probably a rather delirious one; for even in the reality of the raw morning, her fixed gaze comes back at moments when her attention is not strongly held.*

The SERGEANT *considers that her feelings do her credit and is sympathetic in an encouraging military way. Being a fine figure of a man, vain of his uniform and of his rank, he feels specially qualified, in a respectful way, to console her.*

SERGEANT : You can have a quiet word with him here, mum.

JUDITH : Shall I have long to wait?

SERGEANT : No, mum, not a minute. We kep' him in the Bridewell[29] for the night; and he's just been brought over here for the court martial. Don't fret, mum; he slep' like a child, and has made a rare good breakfast.

JUDITH (*incredulously*) : He is in good spirits!

SERGEANT : Tip top, mum. The chaplain looked in to see him last night; and he won seventeen shillings off him at spoil five.[30] He spent it among

---

[29] A prison. The name comes from a former penitentiary, near St. Bride's Well in London.

[30] A round game of cards which is "spoiled" if no player wins three out of a possible five tricks.

us like the gentleman he is. Duty's duty, mum, of course; but you're among friends here. (*The tramp of a couple of soldiers is heard approaching*) There: I think he's coming. (RICHARD *comes in, without a sign of care or captivity in his bearing. The* SERGEANT *nods to the two soldiers and shows them the key of the room in his hand. They withdraw*) Your good lady, sir.

RICHARD (*going to her*): What! My wife. My adored one. (*He takes her hand and kisses it with a perverse, raffish gallantry*) How long do you allow a brokenhearted husband for leave-taking, Sergeant?

SERGEANT: As long as we can, sir. We shall not disturb you till the court sits.

RICHARD: But it has struck the hour.

SERGEANT: So it has, sir; but there's a delay. General Burgoyne's just arrived—Gentlemanly Johnny we call him, sir—and he won't have done finding fault with everything this side of half past. I know him, sir; I served with him in Portugal. You may count on twenty minutes, sir; and by your leave I won't waste any more of them. (*He goes out, locking the door.* RICHARD *immediately drops his raffish manner and turns to* JUDITH *with considerate sincerity.*)

RICHARD: Mrs. Anderson, this visit is very kind of you. And how are you after last night? I had to leave you before you recovered; but I sent word to Essie to go and look after you. Did she understand the message?

JUDITH (*breathless and urgent*): Oh, don't think of me; I haven't come here to talk about myself. Are they going to—to—(*meaning "to hang you"*)?

RICHARD (*whimsically*): At noon, punctually. At least, that was when they disposed of Uncle Peter. (*She shudders*) Is your husband safe? Is he on the wing?

JUDITH: He is no longer my husband.

RICHARD (*opening his eyes wide*): Eh?

JUDITH: I disobeyed you. I told him everything. I expected him to come here and save you. I wanted him to come here and save you. He ran away instead.

RICHARD: Well, that's what I meant him to do. What good would his staying have done? They'd only have hanged us both.

JUDITH (*with reproachful earnestness*): Richard Dudgeon, on your honor, what would you have done in his place?

RICHARD: Exactly what he has done, of course.

JUDITH: Oh, why will you not be simple with me—honest and straightforward? If you are so selfish as that, why did you let them take you last night?

RICHARD (*gaily*): Upon my life, Mrs. Anderson, I don't know. I've been asking myself that question ever since; and I can find no manner of reason for acting as I did.

JUDITH: You know you did it for his sake, believing he was a more worthy man than yourself.

RICHARD (*laughing*): Oho! No, that's a very pretty reason, I must say; but I'm not so modest as that. No, it wasn't for his sake.

JUDITH (*after a pause, during which she looks shamefacedly at him, blushing painfully*): Was it for my sake?

RICHARD (*gallantly*): Well, you had a hand in it. It must have been a little for your sake. You let them take me, at all events.

JUDITH: Oh, do you think I have not been telling myself that all night? Your death will be at my door. (*Impulsively, she gives him her hand and adds, with intense earnestness*) If I could save you as you saved him, I would do it, no matter how cruel the death was.

RICHARD (*holding her hand and smiling, but keeping her almost at arms length*): I am very sure I shouldn't let you.

JUDITH: Don't you see that I can save you?

RICHARD: How? by changing clothes with me, eh?

JUDITH (*disengaging her hand to touch his lips with it*): Don't (*meaning "Don't jest"*). No, by telling the Court who you really are.

RICHARD (*frowning*): No use: they wouldn't spare me; and it would spoil half his chance of escaping. They are determined to cow us by making an example of somebody on that gallows today. Well, let us cow them by showing that we can stand by one another to the death. That is the only force that can send Burgoyne back across the Atlantic and make America a nation.

JUDITH (*impatiently*): Oh, what does all that matter?

RICHARD (*laughing*): True, what does it matter? What does anything matter? You see, men have these strange notions, Mrs. Anderson; and women see the folly of them.

JUDITH: Women have to lose those they love through them.

RICHARD: They can easily get fresh lovers.

JUDITH (*revolted*): Oh! (*Vehemently*) Do you realize that you are going to kill yourself?

RICHARD: The only man I have any right to kill, Mrs. Anderson. Don't be concerned; no woman will lose her lover through my death. (*Smiling*) Bless you, nobody cares for me. Have you heard that my mother is dead?

JUDITH: Dead!

RICHARD: Of heart disease—in the night. Her last word to me was her curse; I don't think I could have borne her blessing. My other relatives will not grieve much on my account. Essie will cry for a day or two; but I have provided for her; I made my own will last night.

JUDITH (*stonily, after a moment's silence*): And I!

RICHARD (*surprised*): You?

JUDITH: Yes, I. Am I not to care at all?

RICHARD (*gaily and bluntly*): Not a scrap. Oh, you expressed your feelings towards me very frankly yesterday. What happened may have softened you for the moment; but believe me, Mrs. Anderson, you don't like a bone in my skin or a hair on my head. I shall be as good a riddance at 12 today as I should have been at 12 yesterday.

JUDITH (*her voice trembling*): What can I do to show you that you are mistaken?

RICHARD: Don't trouble. I'll give you credit for liking me a little better than you did. All I say is that my death will not break your heart.

JUDITH (*almost in a whisper*): How do you know? (*She puts her hands on his shoulders and looks intently at him.*)

RICHARD (*amazed—divining the truth*): Mrs. Anderson! (*The bell of the town clock strikes the quarter. He collects himself and removes her hands, saying rather coldly)* Excuse me: they will be here for me presently. It is too late.

JUDITH: It is not too late. Call me as witness; they will never kill you when they know how heroically you have acted.

RICHARD *(with some scorn)*: Indeed! But if I don't go through with it, where will the heroism be? I shall simply have tricked them; and they'll hang me for that like a dog. Serve me right too!

JUDITH *(wildly)*: Oh, I believe you want to die.

RICHARD *(obstinately)*: No I don't.

JUDITH: Then why not try to save yourself? I implore you—listen. You said just now that you saved him for my sake—yes *(clutching him as he recoils with a gesture of denial)* a little for my sake. Well, save yourself for my sake. And I will go with you to the end of the world.

RICHARD *(taking her by the wrists and holding her a little way from him, looking steadily at her)*: Judith.

JUDITH *(breathless—delighted at the name)*: Yes.

RICHARD: If I said—to please you—that I did what I did ever so little for your sake, I lied as men always lie to women. You know how much I have lived with worthless men—aye, and worthless women too. Well, they could all rise to some sort of goodness and kindness when they were in love. *(The word "love" comes from him with true Puritan scorn)* That has taught me to set very little store by the goodness that only comes out red hot. What I did last night, I did in cold blood, caring not half so much for your husband, or *(ruthlessly)* for you *(she droops, stricken)* as I do for myself. I had no motive and no interest; all I can tell you is that when it came to the point whether I would take my neck out of the noose and put another man's into it, I could not do it. I don't know why not; I see myself as a fool for my pains; but I could not and I cannot. I have been brought up standing by the law of my own nature; and I may not go against it, gallows or no gallows. *(She has slowly raised her head and is now looking full at him)* I should have done the same for any other man in the town, or any other man's wife. *(Releasing her)* Do you understand that?

JUDITH: Yes, you mean that you do not love me.

RICHARD *(revolted—with fierce contempt)*: Is that all it means to you?

JUDITH: What more—what worse—can it mean to me? *(The SERGEANT knocks. The blow on the door jars on her heart)* Oh, one moment more. *(She throws herself on her knees)* I pray to you—

RICHARD: Hush! *(Calling)* Come in. *(The SERGEANT unlocks the door and opens it. The guard is with him.)*

SERGEANT *(coming in)*: Time's up, sir.

RICHARD: Quite ready, Sergeant. Now, my dear. *(He attempts to raise her.)*

JUDITH *(clinging to him)*: Only one thing more—I entreat, I implore you. Let me be present in the court. I have seen Major Swindon; he said I should be allowed if you asked it. You will ask it. It is my last request; I shall never ask you anything again. *(She clasps his knee)* I beg and pray it of you.

RICHARD: If I do, will you be silent?

JUDITH: Yes.

RICHARD: You will keep faith?

JUDITH: I will keep—(*She breaks down, sobbing.*)

RICHARD (*taking her arm to lift her*): Just—her other arm, Sergeant.

(*They go out, she sobbing convulsively, supported by the two men.*)

SCENE TWO

Meanwhile, the Council Chamber is ready for the court martial. It is a large, lofty room, with a chair of state in the middle under a tall canopy with a gilt crown, and maroon curtains with the royal monogram G.R. In front of the chair is a table, also draped in maroon, with a bell, a heavy inkstand, and writing materials on it. Several chairs are set at the table. The door is at the right hand of the occupant of the chair of state when it has an occupant: at present it is empty. MAJOR SWINDON, *a pale, sandy-haired, very conscientious looking man of about 45, sits at the end of the table with his back to the door, writing. He is alone until the* SERGEANT *announces the* GENERAL *in a subdued manner which suggests that Gentlemanly Johnny has been making his presence felt rather heavily.*

SERGEANT: The General, sir.

(SWINDON *rises hastily. The* GENERAL *comes in; the* SERGEANT *goes out.* GENERAL BURGOYNE *is 55 and very well preserved. He is a man of fashion, gallant enough to have made a distinguished marriage by an elopement, witty enough to write successful comedies, aristocratically-connected enough to have had opportunities of high military distinction. His eyes, large, brilliant, apprehensive, and intelligent, are his most remarkable feature: without them his fine nose and small mouth would suggest rather more fastidiousness and less force than go to the making of a first-rate general. Just now the eyes are angry and tragic, and the mouth and nostrils tense.*)

BURGOYNE: Major Swindon, I presume.

SWINDON: Yes. General Burgoyne, if I mistake not. (*They bow to one another ceremoniously*) I am glad to have the support of your presence this morning. It is not particularly lively business, hanging this poor devil of a minister.

BURGOYNE (*throwing himself into* SWINDON'S *chair*): No, sir, it is not. It is making too much of the fellow to execute him; what more could you have done if he had been a member of the Church of England? Martyrdom, sir, is what these people like: it is the only way in which a man can become famous without ability. However, you have committed us to hanging him; and the sooner he is hanged the better.

SWINDON: We have arranged it for 12 o'clock. Nothing remains to be done except to try him.

BURGOYNE (*looking at him with suppressed anger*): Nothing—except to save your own necks, perhaps. Have you heard the news from Springtown?

SWINDON: Nothing special. The latest reports are satisfactory.

BURGOYNE (*rising in amazement*): Satisfactory, sir! Satisfactory!! (*He stares at him for a moment and then adds, with grim intensity*) I am glad you take that view of them.

SWINDON (*puzzled*): Do I understand that in your opinion—

BURGOYNE: I do not express my opinion. I never stoop to that habit of profane language which unfortunately coarsens our profession. If I did, sir, perhaps I should be able to express my opinion of the news from Springtown—the news which you (*severely*) have apparently not heard. How soon do you get news from your supports here?—in the course of a month, eh?

SWINDON (*turning sulkily*): I suppose the reports have been taken to you, sir, instead of to me. Is there anything serious?

BURGOYNE (*taking a report from his pocket and holding it up*): Springtown's in the hands of the rebels. (*He throws the report on the table.*)

SWINDON (*aghast*): Since yesterday!

BURGOYNE: Since two o'clock this morning. Perhaps we shall be in their hands before two o'clock tomorrow morning. Have you thought of that?

SWINDON (*confidently*): As to that, General, the British soldier will give a good account of himself.

BURGOYNE (*bitterly*): And therefore, I suppose, sir, the British officer need not know his business; the British soldier will get him out of all his blunders with the bayonet. In future, sir, I must ask you to be a little less generous with the blood of your men and a little more generous with your own brains.

SWINDON: I am sorry I cannot pretend to your intellectual eminence, sir. I can only do my best and rely on the devotion of my countrymen.

BURGOYNE (*suddenly becoming suavely sarcastic*): May I ask are you writing a melodrama, Major Swindon?

SWINDON (*flushing*): No, sir.

BURGOYNE: What a pity! What a pity! (*Dropping his sarcastic tone and facing him suddenly and seriously*) Do you at all realize, sir, that we have nothing standing between us and destruction but our own bluff and the sheepishness of these colonists? They are men of the same English stock as ourselves: six to one of us (*repeating it emphatically*) six to one, sir; and nearly half our troops are Hessians, Brunswickers, German dragoons, and Indians with scalping knives. These are the countrymen on whose devotion you rely! Suppose the colonists find a leader! Suppose the news from Springtown should turn out to mean that they have already found a leader! What shall we do then? Eh?

SWINDON (*sullenly*): Our duty, sir, I presume.

BURGOYNE (*again sarcastic—giving him up as a fool*): Quite so, quite so. Thank you, Major Swindon, thank you. Now you've settled the question, sir—thrown a flood of light on the situation. What a comfort to me to feel that I have at my side so devoted and able an officer to support me in this emergency! I think, sir, it will probably relieve both our feelings if we proceed to hang this dissenter without further delay (*he strikes the bell*) especially as I am debarred by my principles from the customary military vent for my feelings. (*The* SERGEANT *appears*) Bring your man in.

SERGEANT: Yes, sir.

BURGOYNE: And mention to any officer you may meet that the court cannot wait any longer for him.

SWINDON (*keeping his temper with difficulty*): The staff is perfectly ready, sir. They have been waiting your convenience for fully half an hour. Perfectly ready, sir.

BURGOYNE (*blandly*): So am I. (*Several officers come in and take their seats. One of them sits at the end of the table furthest from the door and acts throughout as clerk of the court, making notes of the proceedings. The uniforms are those of the 9th, 20th, 21st, 24th, 47th, 53rd, and 62nd British Infantry. One officer is a Major General of the Royal Artillery. There are also German officers of the Hessian Rifles, and of German dragoon and Brunswicker regiments*) Oh, good morning, gentlemen. Sorry to disturb you, I am sure. Very good of you to spare us a few moments.

SWINDON: Will you preside, sir?

BURGOYNE (*becoming additionally polished, lofty, sarcastic, and urbane now that he is in public*): No, sir; I feel my own deficiencies too keenly to presume so far. If you will kindly allow me, I will sit at the feet of Gamaliel.[31] (*He takes the chair at the end of the table next the door and motions* SWINDON *to the chair of state, waiting for him to be seated before sitting down himself.*)

SWINDON (*greatly annoyed*): As you please, sir, I am only trying to do my duty under excessively trying circumstances. (*He takes his place in the chair of state.*)

(BURGOYNE, *relaxing his studied demeanor for the moment, sits down and begins to read the report with knitted brows and careworn looks, reflecting on his desperate situation and* SWINDON'S *uselessness.* RICHARD *is brought in.* JUDITH *walks beside him. Two soldiers precede and two follow him, with the* SERGEANT *in command. They cross the room to the wall opposite the door; but when* RICHARD *has just passed before the chair of state the* SERGEANT *stops him with a touch on the arm and posts himself behind him, at his elbow.* JUDITH *stands timidly at the wall. The four soldiers place themselves in a squad near her.*)

BURGOYNE (*looking up and seeing* JUDITH): Who is that woman?

SERGEANT: Prisoner's wife, sir.

SWINDON (*nervously*): She begged me to allow her to be present; and I thought—

BURGOYNE (*completing the sentence for him ironically*): You thought it would be a pleasure for her. Quite so, quite so. (*Blandly*) Give the lady a chair; and make her thoroughly comfortable.

---

[31] The Pharisee doctor of law and teacher of St. Paul.

(*The* SERGEANT *fetches a chair and places it near* RICHARD.)

JUDITH: Thank you, sir. (*She sits down after an awestricken curtsy to* BURGOYNE, *which he acknowledges by a dignified bend of his head.*)

SWINDON (*to* RICHARD, *sharply*) : Your name, sir?

RICHARD (*affable, but obstinate*) : Come, you don't mean to say that you've brought me here without knowing who I am?

SWINDON: As a matter of form, sir, give your name.

RICHARD: As a matter of form then, my name is Anthony Anderson, Presbyterian minister in this town.

BURGOYNE (*interested*) : Indeed! Pray, Mr. Anderson, what do you gentlemen believe?

RICHARD: I shall be happy to explain if time is allowed me. I cannot undertake to complete your conversion in less than a fortnight.

SWINDON (*snubbing him*) : We are not here to discuss your views.

BURGOYNE (*with an elaborate bow to the unfortunate* SWINDON) : I stand rebuked.

SWINDON (*embarrassed*) : Oh, not you, I as—

BURGOYNE: Don't mention it. (*To* RICHARD, *very politely*) Any political views, Mr. Anderson?

RICHARD: I understand that that is just what we are here to find out.

SWINDON (*severely*) : Do you mean to deny that you are a rebel?

RICHARD: I am an American, sir.

SWINDON: What do you expect me to think of that speech, Mr. Anderson?

RICHARD: I never expect a soldier to think, sir.

(BURGOYNE *is boundlessly delighted by this retort, which almost reconciles him to the loss of America.*)

SWINDON (*whitening with anger*) : I advise you not to be insolent, prisoner.

RICHARD: You can't help yourself, General. When you make up your mind to hang a man, you put yourself at a disadvantage with him. Why should I be civil to you? I may as well be hanged for a sheep as a lamb.

SWINDON: You have no right to assume that the court has made up its mind without a fair trial. And you will please not address me as General. I am Major Swindon.

RICHARD: A thousand pardons. I thought I had the honor of addressing Gentlemanly Johnny.

(*Sensation among the officers. The* SERGEANT *has a narrow escape from a guffaw.*)

BURGOYNE (*with extreme suavity*) : I believe I am Gentlemanly Johnny, sir, at your service. My more intimate friends call me General Burgoyne. (RICHARD *bows with perfect politeness*) You will understand, sir, I hope, since you seem to be a gentleman and a man of some spirit in spite of your calling, that if we should have the misfortune to hang you, we shall do so as a mere matter of political necessity and military duty, without any personal ill-feeling.

RICHARD: Oh, quite so. That makes all the difference in the world, of course.

(*They all smile in spite of themselves, and some of the younger officers burst out laughing.*)

JUDITH (*her dread and horror deepening at every one of these jests and compliments*): How can you?

RICHARD: You promised to be silent.

BURGOYNE (*to* JUDITH, *with studied courtesy*): Believe me, madam, your husband is placing us under the greatest obligation by taking this very disagreeable business so thoroughly in the spirit of a gentleman. Sergeant, give Mr. Anderson a chair. (*The* SERGEANT *does so.* RICHARD *sits down*) Now, Major Swindon, we are waiting for you.

SWINDON: You are aware, I presume, Mr. Anderson, of your obligations as a subject of His Majesty King George the Third.

RICHARD: I am aware, sir, that His Majesty King George the Third is about to hang me because I object to Lord North's[32] robbing me.

SWINDON: That is a treasonable speech, sir.

RICHARD (*briefly*): Yes. I meant it to be.

BURGOYNE (*strongly deprecating this line of defense, but still polite*): Don't you think, Mr. Anderson, that this is rather—if you will excuse the word —a vulgar line to take? Why should you cry out robbery because of a stamp duty and a tea duty and so forth? After all, it is the essence of your position as a gentleman that you pay with a good grace.

RICHARD: It is not the money, General. But to be swindled by a pig-headed lunatic like King George—

SWINDON (*scandalized*): Chut, sir—silence!

SERGEANT (*in stentorian tones, greatly shocked*): Silence!

BURGOYNE (*unruffled*): Ah, that is another point of view. My position does not allow of my going into that, except in private. But (*shrugging his shoulders*) of course, Mr. Anderson, if you are determined to be hanged (JUDITH *flinches*) there's nothing more to be said. An unusual taste! however (*with a final shrug*)— !

SWINDON (*To* BURGOYNE): Shall we call witnesses?

RICHARD: What need is there of witnesses? If the townspeople here had listened to me, you would have found the streets barricaded, the houses loopholed, and the people in arms to hold the town against you to the last man. But you arrived, unfortunately, before we had got out of the talking stage; and then it was too late.

SWINDON (*severely*): Well, sir, we shall teach you and your townspeople a lesson they will not forget. Have you anything more to say?

RICHARD: I think you might have the decency to treat me as a prisoner of war and shoot me like a man instead of hanging me like a dog.

BURGOYNE (*sympathetically*): Now there, Mr. Anderson, you talk like a civilian, if you will excuse my saying so. Have you any idea of the average marksmanship of the army of His Majesty King George the Third? If we make you up a firing party, what will happen? Half of them will miss you; the rest will make a mess of the business and leave you to the provo-marshal's pistol. Whereas we can hang you in a perfectly workmanlike and agreeable way. (*Kindly*) Let me persuade you to be hanged, Mr. Anderson?

---

[32] British prime minister during the Revolutionary War.

JUDITH (*sick with horror*): My God!

RICHARD (*To* JUDITH): Your promise! (*To* BURGOYNE) Thank you, General; that view of the case did not occur to me before. To oblige you, I withdraw my objection to the rope. Hang me, by all means.

BURGOYNE (*smoothly*): Will 12 o'clock suit you, Mr. Anderson?

RICHARD: I shall be at your disposal then, General.

BURGOYNE (*rising*): Nothing more to be said, gentlemen. (*They all rise.*)

JUDITH (*rushing to the table*): Oh, you are not going to murder a man like that, without a proper trial—without thinking of what you are doing—without— (*she cannot find words*).

RICHARD: Is this how you keep your promise?

JUDITH: If I am not to speak, you must. Defend yourself; save yourself; tell them the truth.

RICHARD (*worriedly*): I have told them truth enough to hang me ten times over. If you say another word you will risk other lives; but you will not save mine.

BURGOYNE: My good lady, our only desire is to save unpleasantness. What satisfaction would it give you to have a solemn fuss made, with my friend Swindon in a black cap and so forth? I am sure we are greatly indebted to the admirable tact and gentlemanly feeling shown by your husband.

JUDITH (*throwing the words in his face*): Oh, you are mad. Is it nothing to you what wicked thing you do if only you do it like a gentleman? Is it nothing to you whether you are a murderer or not, if only you murder in a red coat? (*Desperately*) You shall not hang him; that man is not my husband.

(*The officers look at one another, and whisper; some of the Germans asking their neighbors to explain what the woman had said.* BURGOYNE, *who has been visibly shaken by* JUDITH'S *reproach, recovers himself promptly at this new development.* RICHARD *meanwhile raises his voice above the buzz.*)

RICHARD: I appeal to you, gentlemen, to put an end to this. She will not believe that she cannot save me. Break up the court.

BURGOYNE (*in a voice so quiet and firm that it restores silence at once*): One moment, Mr. Anderson. One moment, gentlemen. (*He resumes his seat.* SWINDON *and the officers follow his example*) Let me understand you clearly, madam. Do you mean that this gentleman is not your husband, or merely—I wish to put this with all delicacy—that you are not his wife?

JUDITH: I don't know what you mean. I say that he is not my husband—that my husband has escaped. This man took his place to save him. Ask anyone in the town—send out into the street for the first person you find there, and bring him in as a witness. He will tell you that the prisoner is not Anthony Anderson.

BURGOYNE (*quietly, as before*): Sergeant.

SERGEANT: Yes, sir.

BURGOYNE: Go out into the street and bring in the first townsman you see there.

SERGEANT (*making for the door*): Yes, sir.

BURGOYNE (*as the* SERGEANT *passes*) : The first clean, sober townsman you see.

SERGEANT: Yes, sir. (*He goes out.*)

BURGOYNE: Sit down, Mr. Anderson—if I may call you so for the present. (RICHARD *sits down*) Sit down, madam, whilst we wait. Give the lady a newspaper.

RICHARD (*indignantly*) : Shame!

BURGOYNE (*keenly, with a half smile*) : If you are not her husband, sir, the case is not a serious one—for her. (RICHARD *bites his lip, silenced.*)

JUDITH (*to* RICHARD, *as she returns to her seat*) : I couldn't help it. (*He shakes his head. She sits down.*)

BURGOYNE: You will understand, of course, Mr. Anderson, that you must not build on this little incident. We are bound to make an example of somebody.

RICHARD: I quite understand. I suppose there's no use in my explaining.

BURGOYNE: I think we should prefer independent testimony, if you don't mind.

(*The* SERGEANT, *with a packet of papers in his hand, returns conducting* CHRISTY, *who is much scared.*)

SERGEANT (*giving* BURGOYNE *the packet*) : Dispatches, sir. Delivered by a corporal of the 33rd. Dead beat with hard riding, sir.

(BURGOYNE *opens the dispatches and presently becomes absorbed in them. They are so serious as to take his attention completely from the court martial.*)

SERGEANT (*to* CHRISTY): Now then. Attention; and take your hat off. (*He posts himself in charge of* CHRISTY, *who stands on* BURGOYNE'S *side of the court.*)

RICHARD (*in his usual bullying tone to* CHRISTY) : Don't be frightened, you fool: you're only wanted as a witness. They're not going to hang you.

SWINDON: What's your name?

CHRISTY: Christy.

RICHARD (*impatiently*) : Christopher Dudgeon, you blatant idiot. Give your full name.

SWINDON: Be silent, prisoner. You must not prompt the witness.

RICHARD: Very well. But I warn you you'll get nothing out of him unless you shake it out of him. He has been too well brought up by a pious mother to have any sense or manhood left in him.

BURGOYNE (*springing up and speaking to the* SERGEANT *in a startling voice*) : Where is the man who brought these?

SERGEANT: In the guard-room, sir.

(BURGOYNE *goes out with a haste that sets the officers exchanging looks.*)

SWINDON (*to* CHRISTY) : Do you know Anthony Anderson, the Presbyterian minister?

CHRISTY: Of course I do (*implying that* SWINDON *must be an ass not to know it*).

SWINDON: Is he here?

CHRISTY (*staring round*) : I don't know.

SWINDON: Do you see him?

CHRISTY: No.

SWINDON: You seem to know the prisoner?

CHRISTY: Do you mean Dick?

SWINDON: Which is Dick?

CHRISTY (*pointing to* RICHARD): Him.

SWINDON: What is his name?

CHRISTY: Dick.

RICHARD: Answer properly, you jumping jackass. What do they know about Dick?

CHRISTY: Well, you are Dick, ain't you? What am I to say?

SWINDON: Address me, sir; and do you, prisoner, be silent. Tell us who the prisoner is.

CHRISTY: He's my brother Dick—Richard—Richard Dudgeon.

SWINDON: Your brother!

CHRISTY: Yes.

SWINDON: You are sure he is not Anderson.

CHRISTY: Who?

RICHARD (*exasperatedly*): Me, me, me, you—

SWINDON: Silence, sir.

SERGEANT (*shouting*): Silence.

RICHARD (*impatiently*): Yah! (*To* CHRISTY) He wants to know am I Minister Anderson. Tell him and stop grinning like a zany.

CHRISTY (*grinning more than ever*): *You* Pastor Anderson! (*To* SWINDON) Why, Mr. Anderson's a minister—a very good man, and Dick's a bad character; the respectable people won't speak to him. He's the bad brother; I'm the good one. (*The officers laugh outright. The soldiers grin.*)

SWINDON: Who arrested this man?

SERGEANT: I did, sir. I found him in the minister's house, sitting at tea with the lady with his coat off, quite at home. If he isn't married to her, he ought to be.

SWINDON: Did he answer to the minister's name?

SERGEANT: Yes, sir, but not to a minister's nature. You ask the chaplain, sir.

SWINDON (*to* RICHARD, *threateningly*): So, sir, you have attempted to cheat us. And your name is Richard Dudgeon?

RICHARD: You've found it out at last, have you?

SWINDON: Dudgeon is a name well known to us, eh?

RICHARD: Yes, Peter Dudgeon, whom you murdered, was my uncle.

SWINDON: Hm! (*He compresses his lips and looks at* RICHARD *with vindictive gravity.*)

CHRISTY: Are they going to hang you, Dick?

RICHARD: Yes. Get out; they've done with you.

CHRISTY: And I may keep the china peacocks?

RICHARD (*jumping up*): Get out. Get out, you blithering baboon, you. (CHRISTY *flies, panicstricken.*)

SWINDON (*rising—all rise*): Since you have taken the minister's place, Richard Dudgeon, you shall go through with it. The execution will take place at 12 o'clock as arranged; and unless Anderson surrenders before then, you shall take his place on the gallows. Sergeant, take your man out.

JUDITH (*distracted*): No, no—

SWINDON (*fiercely dreading a renewal of her entreaties*): Take that woman away.

RICHARD (*springing across the table with a tiger-like bound, and seizing* SWINDON *by the throat*): You infernal scoundrel—

(*The* SERGEANT *rushes to the rescue from one side, the soldiers from the other. They seize* RICHARD *and drag him back to his place.* SWINDON, *who has been thrown supine on the table, rises, arranging his stock.[33] He is about to speak, when he is anticipated by* BURGOYNE, *who has just appeared at the door with two papers in his hand: a white letter and a blue dispatch.*)

BURGOYNE (*advancing to the table, elaborately cool*): What is this? What's happening? Mr. Anderson, I'm astonished at you.

RICHARD: I am sorry I disturbed you, General. I merely wanted to strangle your understrapper[34] there. (*Breaking out violently at* SWINDON) Why do you raise the devil in me by bullying the woman like that? You oat-meal faced dog, I'd twist your cursed head off with the greatest satisfaction. (*He puts out his hands to the* SERGEANT) Here: handcuff me, will you; or I'll not undertake to keep my fingers off him.

(*The* SERGEANT *takes out a pair of handcuffs and looks to* BURGOYNE *for instructions.*)

BURGOYNE: Have you addressed profane language to the lady, Major Swindon?

SWINDON (*very angry*): No, sir, certainly not. That question should not have been put to me. I ordered the woman to be removed, as she was disorderly; and the fellow sprang at me. Put away those handcuffs. I am perfectly able to take care of myself.

RICHARD: Now you talk like a man; I have no quarrel with you.

BURGOYNE: Mr. Anderson—

SWINDON: His name is Dudgeon, sir, Richard Dudgeon. He is an impostor.

BURGOYNE (*brusquely*): Nonsense, sir; you hanged Dudgeon at Spring-town.

RICHARD: It was my uncle, General.

BURGOYNE: Oh, your uncle. (*To* SWINDON, *handsomely*) I beg your pardon, Major Swindon. (SWINDON *acknowledges the apology stiffly.* BURGOYNE *turns to* RICHARD) We are somewhat unfortunate in our relations with your family. Well, Mr. Dudgeon, what I wanted to ask you is this. Who is (*reading the name from the letter*) William Maindeck Parshotter?

RICHARD: He is the Mayor of Springtown.

BURGOYNE: Is William—Maindeck and so on—a man of his word?

RICHARD: Is he selling you anything?

BURGOYNE: No.

RICHARD: Then you may depend on him.

---

[33] A close-fitting, wide necktie.
[34] A subordinate or underling.

BURGOYNE: Thank you, Mr.—'m Dudgeon. By the way, since you are not Mr. Anderson, do we still—eh, Major Swindon? (*meaning "do we still hang him?"*)

RICHARD: The arrangements are unaltered, General.

BURGOYNE: Ah, indeed. I am sorry. Good morning, Mr. Dudgeon. Good morning, madam.

RICHARD (*interrupting* JUDITH *almost fiercely as she is about to make some wild appeal, and taking her arm resolutely*) : Not one word more. Come. (*She looks imploringly at him but is overborne by his determination. They are marched out by the four soldiers; the* SERGEANT *very sulky, walking between* SWINDON *and* RICHARD, *whom he watches as if he were a dangerous animal.*)

BURGOYNE: Gentlemen, we need not detain you. Major Swindon, a word with you. (*The officers go out.* BURGOYNE *waits with unruffled serenity until the last of them disappears. Then he becomes very grave and addresses* SWINDON *for the first time without his title*) Swindon, do you know what this is (*showing him the letter*) ?

SWINDON: What?

BURGOYNE: A demand for a safe-conduct for an officer of their militia to come here and arrange terms with us.

SWINDON: Oh, they are giving in.

BURGOYNE: They add that they are sending the man who raised Springtown last night and drove us out; so that we may know that we are dealing with an officer of importance.

SWINDON: Pooh!

BURGOYNE: He will be fully empowered to arrange the terms of—guess what.

SWINDON: Their surrender, I hope.

BURGOYNE: No, our evacuation of the town. They offer us just six hours to clear out.

SWINDON: What monstrous impudence!

BURGOYNE: What shall we do, eh?

SWINDON: March on Springtown and strike a decisive blow at once.

BURGOYNE (*quietly*) : Hm! (*Turning to the door*) Come to the adjutant's office.

SWINDON: What for?

BURGOYNE: To write out that safe-conduct. (*He puts his hand to the door knob to open it.*)

SWINDON (*who has not budged*) : General Burgoyne.

BURGOYNE (*returning*) : Sir?

SWINDON: It is my duty to tell you, sir, that I do not consider the threats of a mob of rebellious tradesmen a sufficient reason for our giving way.

BURGOYNE (*imperturbable*) : Suppose I resign my command to you, what will you do?

SWINDON: I will undertake to do what we have marched south from Quebec to do and what General Howe has marched north from New York to do: effect a junction at Albany and wipe out the rebel army with our united forces.

BURGOYNE (*enigmatically*): And will you wipe out our enemies in London, too?

SWINDON: In London! What enemies?

BURGOYNE (*forcibly*): Jobbery and snobbery, incompetence and Red Tape. (*He holds up the dispatch and adds, with despair in his face and voice*) I have just learnt, sir, that General Howe is still in New York.

SWINDON (*thunderstruck*): Good God! He has disobeyed orders!

BURGOYNE (*with sardonic calm*): He has received no orders, sir. Some gentleman in London forgot to dispatch them; he was leaving town for his holiday, I believe. To avoid upsetting his arrangements, England will lose her American colonies; and in a few days you and I will be at Saratoga with 5,000 men to face 18,000 rebels in an impregnable position.

SWINDON (*appalled*): Impossible!

BURGOYNE (*coldly*): I beg your pardon?

SWINDON: I can't believe it! What will History say?

BURGOYNE: History, sir, will tell lies, as usual. Come, we must send the safe-conduct. (*He goes out.*)

SWINDON (*following distractedly*): My God, my God! We shall be wiped out.

SCENE THREE

As noon approaches, there is excitement in the market place. The gallows which hangs there permanently for the terror of evildoers, with such minor advertisers and examples of crime as the pillory,[35] the whipping post, and the stocks,[36] has a new rope attached, with the noose hitched up to one of the uprights, out of reach of the boys. Its ladder, too, has been brought out and placed in position by the town beadle,[37] who stands by to guard it from unauthorized climbing. The Websterbridge townsfolk are present in force, and in high spirits; for the news has spread that it is the devil's disciple and not the minister that King George and his terrible general are about to hang: consequently the execution can be enjoyed without any misgiving as to its righteousness, or to the cowardice of allowing it to take place without a struggle. There is even some fear of a disappointment as midday approaches and the arrival of the beadle with the ladder remains the only sign of preparation. But at last reassuring shouts of "Here they come: Here they are" are heard; and a company of soldiers with fixed bayonets, half British infantry, half Hessians, tramp quickly into the middle of the market place, driving the crowd to the sides.

---

[35] A wooden framework erected on a post with holes for securing the head and hands and used to expose an offender to public ridicule.

[36] Another instrument of punishment consisting of a framework with holes for the ankles and wrists of the offender.

[37] A parish officer having various subordinate duties.

SERGEANT: Halt. Front. Dress. (*The soldiers change their column into a square enclosing the gallows, their petty officers, energetically led by the* SERGEANT, *hustling the persons who find themselves inside the square out at the corners*) Now then! Out of it with you; out of it. Some o' you'll get strung up yourselves presently. Form that square there, will you, you damned Hoosians. No use talkin' German to them; talk to their toes with the butt ends of your muskets; they'll understand that. Get out of it, will you. (*He comes upon* JUDITH, *standing near the gallows*) Now then, you've no call here.

JUDITH: May I not stay? What harm am I doing?

SERGEANT: I want none of your argufying. You ought to be ashamed of yourself, running to see a man hanged that's not your husband. And he's no better than yourself. I told my major he was a gentleman; and then he goes and tries to strangle him, and calls his blessed Majesty a lunatic. So out of it with you, double quick.

JUDITH: Will you take these two silver dollars and let me stay?

(*The* SERGEANT, *without an instant's hesitation, looks quickly and furtively round as he shoots the money dexterously into his pocket. Then he raises his voice in virtuous indignation.*)

SERGEANT: Me take money in the execution of my duty! Certainly not. Now I'll tell you what I'll do, to teach you to corrupt the King's officer. I'll put you under arrest until the execution's over. You just stand there; and don't let me see you as much as move from that spot until you're let. (*With a swift wink at her he points to the corner of the square behind the gallows on his right and turns noisily away, shouting*) Now then, dress up and keep 'em back, will you.

(*Cries of "Hush" and "Silence" are heard among the townsfolk; and the sound of a military band, playing the Dead March from Saul,*[38] *is heard. The crowd becomes quiet at once; and the* SERGEANT *and petty officers, hurrying to the back of the square, with a few whispered orders and some stealthy hustling cause it to open and admit the funeral procession, which is protected from the crowd by a double file of soldiers. First come* BURGOYNE *and* SWINDON, *who, on entering the square, glance with distaste at the gallows, and avoid passing under it by wheeling a little to the right and stationing themselves on that side. Then* MR. BRUDENELL, *the chaplain, in his surplice, with his prayer book open in his hand, walking beside* RICHARD, *who is moody and disorderly. He walks doggedly through the gallows framework and posts himself a little in front of it. Behind him comes the executioner, a stalwart soldier in his shirtsleeves. Following him, two soldiers haul a light military wagon. Finally comes the band, which posts itself at the back of the square and finishes the Dead March.* JUDITH, *watching* RICHARD *painfully, steals down to the gallows and stands leaning against its right post. During the conversation which follows, the two soldiers place the cart under the gallows and stand by the shafts, which point backwards. The executioner takes a set of*

---

[38] The celebrated Dead March is a part of George Frederick Handel's oratorio *Saul*, produced in London in 1739.

steps from the cart and places it ready for the prisoner to mount. Then he climbs the tall ladder which stands against the gallows, and cuts the string by which the rope is hitched up; so that the noose drops dangling over the cart, into which he steps as he descends.)

RICHARD (*with suppressed impatience, to* BRUDENELL): Look here, sir: this is no place for a man of your profession. Hadn't you better go away?

SWINDON: I appeal to you, prisoner, if you have any sense of decency left, to listen to the ministrations of the chaplain, and pay due heed to the solemnity of the occasion.

CHAPLAIN (*gently reproving* RICHARD): Try to control yourself and submit to the divine will. (*He lifts his book to proceed with the service.*)

RICHARD: Answer for your own will, sir, and those of your accomplices here (*indicating* BURGOYNE *and* SWINDON); I see little divinity about them or you. You talk to me of Christianity when you are in the act of hanging your enemies. Was there ever such blasphemous nonsense! (*To* SWINDON, *more rudely*) You've got up the solemnity of the occasion, as you call it, to impress the people with your own dignity—Handel's music and a clergyman to make murder look like piety! Do you suppose *I* am going to help you? You've asked me to choose the rope because you don't know your own trade well enough to shoot me properly. Well, hang away and have done with it.

SWINDON (*to the* CHAPLAIN): Can you do nothing with him, Mr. Brudenell?

CHAPLAIN: I will try, sir. (*Beginning to read*) Man that is born of woman hath—

RICHARD (*fixing his eyes on him*): "Thou shalt not kill." (*The book drops in* BRUDENELL'S *hands.*)

CHAPLAIN (*confessing his embarrassment*): What am I to say, Mr. Dudgeon?

RICHARD: Let me alone, man, can't you?

BURGOYNE (*with extreme urbanity*): I think, Mr. Brudenell, that as the usual professional observations seem to strike Mr. Dudgeon as incongruous under the circumstances, you had better omit them until—er—until Mr. Dudgeon can no longer be inconvenienced by them. (BRUDENELL, *with a shrug, shuts his book and retires behind the gallows*) You seem in a hurry, Mr. Dudgeon.

RICHARD (*with the horror of death upon him*): Do you think this is a pleasant sort of thing to be kept waiting for? You've made up your mind to commit murder; well, do it and have done with it.

BURGOYNE: Mr. Dudgeon, we are only doing this—

RICHARD: Because you're paid to do it.

SWINDON: You insolent— (*He swallows his rage.*)

BURGOYNE (*with much charm of manner*): Ah, I am really sorry that you should think that, Mr. Dudgeon. If you knew what my commission cost me and what my pay is, you would think better of me. I should be glad to part from you on friendly terms.

RICHARD: Hark ye, General Burgoyne. If you think that I like being hanged, you're mistaken. I don't like it; and I don't mean to pretend that I do.

And if you think I'm obliged to you for hanging me in a gentlemanly way, you're wrong there too. I take the whole business in devilish bad part; and the only satisfaction I have in it is that you'll feel a good deal meaner than I'll look when it's over. (*He turns away and is striding to the cart when* JUDITH *advances and interposes with her arms stretched out to him.* RICHARD, *feeling that a very little will upset his self-possession, shrinks from her, crying*) What are you doing here? This is no place for you. (*She makes a gesture as if to touch him. He recoils impatiently*) No, go away, go away; you'll unnerve me. Take her away, will you.

JUDITH: Won't you bid me goodbye?

RICHARD (*allowing her to take his hand*): Oh goodbye, goodbye. Now go—go—quickly. (*She clings to his hand—will not be put off with so cold a last farewell—at last, as he tries to disengage himself, throws herself on his breast in agony.*)

SWINDON (*angrily to the* SERGEANT, *who, alarmed at* JUDITH'S *movement, has come from the back of the square to pull her back and stopped irresolutely on finding that he is too late*): How is this? Why is she inside the lines?

SERGEANT (*guiltily*): I dunno, sir. She's that artful—can't keep her away.

BURGOYNE: You were bribed.

SERGEANT (*protesting*): No, sir—

SWINDON (*severely*): Fall back. (*He obeys.*)

RICHARD (*imploringly to those around him and finally to* BURGOYNE, *as the least stolid of them*): Take her away. Do you think I want a woman near me now?

BURGOYNE (*going to* JUDITH *and taking her hand*): Here, madam: you had better keep inside the lines; but stand here behind us; and don't look. (RICHARD, *with a great sobbing sigh of relief as she releases him and turns to* BURGOYNE, *flies for refuge to the cart and mounts into it. The executioner takes off his coat and pinions him.*)

JUDITH (*resisting* BURGOYNE *quietly and drawing her hand away*): No, I must stay. I won't look. (*She goes to the right of the gallows. She tries to look at* RICHARD *but turns away with a frightful shudder and falls on her knees in prayer.* BRUDENELL *comes towards her from the back of the square.*)

BURGOYNE (*nodding approvingly as she kneels*): Ah, quite so. Do not disturb her, Mr. Brudenell; that will do very nicely. (BRUDENELL *nods also and withdraws a little, watching her sympathetically.* BURGOYNE *resumes his former position and takes out a handsome gold chronometer*[39]) Now then, are those preparations made? We must not detain Mr. Dudgeon.

(*By this time* RICHARD'S *hands are bound behind him, and the noose is round his neck. The two soldiers take the shafts of the wagon, ready to pull it away. The executioner, standing in the cart behind* RICHARD, *makes a sign to the* SERGEANT.)

SERGEANT (*to* BURGOYNE): Ready, sir.

---

[39] A timepiece of greater accuracy than an ordinary pocket watch.

BURGOYNE: Have you anything more to say, Mr. Dudgeon? It wants two minutes of twelve still.

RICHARD (*in the strong voice of a man who has conquered the bitterness of death*): Your watch is two minutes slow by the town clock, which I can see from here, General. (*The town clock strikes the first stroke of twelve. Involuntarily the people flinch at the sound, and a subdued groan breaks from them*) Amen! my life for the world's future!

ANDERSON (*shouting as he rushes into the market place*): Amen; and stop the execution. (*He bursts through the line of soldiers opposite* BURGOYNE *and rushes, panting, to the gallows*) I am Anthony Anderson, the man you want.

(*The crowd, intensely excited, listens with all its ears.* JUDITH, *half rising, stares at him, then lifts her hands like one whose dearest prayer has been granted.*)

SWINDON: Indeed. Then you are just in time to take your place on the gallows. Arrest him.

(*At a sign from the* SERGEANT, *two soldiers come forward to seize* ANDERSON.)

ANDERSON (*thrusting a paper under* SWINDON'S *nose*): There's my safe-conduct, sir.

SWINDON (*taken aback*): Safe-conduct! Are you— !

ANDERSON (*emphatically*): I am. (*The two soldiers take him by the elbows*) Tell these men to take their hands off me.

SWINDON (*to the men*): Let him go.

SERGEANT: Fall back.

(*The two men return to their places. The townsfolk raise a cheer and begin to exchange exultant looks, with a presentiment of triumph as they see their Pastor speaking with their enemies in the gate.*)

ANDERSON (*exhaling a deep breath of relief and dabbing his perspiring brow with his handkerchief*): Thank God, I was in time!

BURGOYNE (*calm as ever, and still watch in hand*): Ample time, sir. Plenty of time. I should never dream of hanging any gentleman by an American clock. (*He puts up his watch.*)

ANDERSON: Yes, we are some minutes ahead of you already, General. Now tell them to take the rope from the neck of that American citizen.

BURGOYNE (*to the executioner in the cart—very politely*): Kindly undo Mr. Dudgeon.

(*The executioner takes the rope from* RICHARD'S *neck, unties his hands, and helps him on with his coat.*)

JUDITH (*stealing timidly to* ANDERSON): Tony.

ANDERSON (*putting his arm round her shoulders and bantering her affectionately*): Well, what do you think of your husband now, eh?—eh? ?—eh? ? ?

JUDITH: I am ashamed— (*She hides her face against his breast.*)

BURGOYNE (*to* SWINDON): You look disappointed, Major Swindon.

SWINDON: You look defeated, General Burgoyne.

BURGOYNE: I am, sir; and I am humane enough to be glad of it. (RICHARD *jumps down from the cart,* BRUDENELL *offering his hand to help him, and runs to* ANDERSON, *whose left hand he shakes heartily, the right being occupied by* JUDITH) By the way, Mr. Anderson, I do not quite understand. The safe-conduct was for a commander of the militia. I understand you are a—(*He looks as pointedly as his good manners permit at the riding boots, the pistols, and* RICHARD'S *coat, and adds*)—a clergyman.

ANDERSON (*between* JUDITH *and* RICHARD): Sir, it is in the hour of trial that a man finds his true profession. This foolish young man (*placing his hand on* RICHARD'S *shoulder*) boasted himself the Devil's Disciple; but when the hour of trial came to him, he found that it was his destiny to suffer and be faithful to the death. I thought myself a decent minister of the gospel of peace; but when the hour of trial came to me, I found that it was my destiny to be a man of action and that my place was amid the thunder of the captains and the shouting. So I am starting life at fifty as Captain Anthony Anderson of the Springtown militia; and the Devil's Disciple here will start presently as the Reverend Richard Dudgeon, and wag his pow[40] in my old pulpit, and give good advice to this silly sentimental little wife of mine (*putting his other hand on her shoulder. She steals a glance at* RICHARD *to see how the prospect pleases him*). Your mother told me, Richard, that I should never have chosen Judith if I'd been born for the ministry. I am afraid she was right; so, by your leave, you may keep my coat and I'll keep yours.

RICHARD: Minister—I should say Captain. I have behaved like a fool.

JUDITH: Like a hero.

RICHARD: Much the same thing, perhaps. (*With some bitterness towards himself*) But no; if I had been any good, I should have done for you what you did for me, instead of making a vain sacrifice.

ANDERSON: Not vain, my boy. It takes all sorts to make a world—saints as well as soldiers. (*Turning to* BURGOYNE) And now, General, time presses; and America is in a hurry. Have you realized that though you may occupy towns and win battles, you cannot conquer a nation?

BURGOYNE: My good sir, without a Conquest you cannot have an aristocracy. Come and settle the matter at my quarters.

ANDERSON: At your service, sir. (*To* RICHARD) See Judith home for me, will you, my boy. (*He hands her over to him*) Now, General. (*He goes busily up the market place towards the Town Hall, leaving* JUDITH *and* RICHARD *together.* BURGOYNE *follows him a step or two, then checks himself and turns to* RICHARD.)

BURGOYNE: Oh, by the way, Mr. Dudgeon, I shall be glad to see you at lunch at half-past one. (*He pauses a moment and adds, with politely veiled slyness*) Bring Mrs. Anderson, if she will be so good. (*To* SWINDON, *who is fuming*) Take it quietly, Major Swindon; your friend the British soldier can stand up to anything except the British War Office. (*He follows* ANDERSON.)

SERGEANT (*to* SWINDON): What orders, sir?

SWINDON (*savagely*): Orders! What use are orders now! There's no army. Back to quarters; and be d— (*He turns on his heel and goes.*)

---

[40] Shoot off his gunpowder.

SERGEANT (*pugnacious and patriotic, repudiating the idea of defeat*): 'Tention. Now then: cock up your chins, and show 'em you don't care a damn for 'em. Slope arms![41] Fours! Wheel! Quick march!

(*The drums mark time with a tremendous bang; the band strikes up British Grenadiers; and the* SERGEANT, BRUDENELL, *and the English troops march off defiantly to their quarters. The townsfolk press in behind and follow them up the market, jeering at them; and the town band, a very primitive affair, brings up the rear, playing Yankee Doodle.* ESSIE, *who comes in with them, runs to* RICHARD.)

ESSIE: Oh, Dick!

RICHARD (*good-humoredly, but wilfully*): Now, now; come, come! I don't mind being hanged; but I will not be cried over.

ESSIE: No, I promise. I'll be good. (*She tries to restrain her tears, but cannot*) I—I want to see where the soldiers are going to. (*She goes a little way up the market, pretending to look after the crowd.*)

JUDITH: Promise me you will never tell him.

RICHARD: Don't be afraid.

(*They shake hands on it.*)

ESSIE (*calling to them*): They're coming back. They want you.

(*Jubilation in the market. The townsfolk surge back again in wild enthusiasm with their band and hoist* RICHARD *on their shoulders, cheering him.*)

(*The Curtain Falls.*)

Shaw's Notes to *The Devil's Disciple*

BURGOYNE

GENERAL JOHN BURGOYNE, who is presented in this play for the first time (as far as I am aware) on the English stage, is not a conventional stage soldier, but as faithful a portrait as it is in the nature of stage portraits to be. His objection to profane swearing is not borrowed from Mr. Gilbert's H.M.S. Pinafore[42]: it is taken from the Code of Instructions drawn up by himself for his officers when he introduced Light Horse into the English Army. His opinion that English soldiers should be treated as thinking beings was no doubt as unwelcome to the military authorities of his time, when nothing was thought of ordering a soldier a thousand lashes, as it will be to those modern victims of the flaggelation neurosis who are so anxious to revive that discredited sport.

---

[41] Bring weapons into a sloping position.

[42] *H.M.S. Pinafore* (1878) is one of the most popular of the comic operas written by Sir William S. Gilbert and Sir Arthur Sullivan for the D'Oyly Carte opera company.

His military reports are very clever as criticisms, and are humane and enlightened within certain aristocratic limits, best illustrated perhaps by his declaration, which now sounds so curious, that he should blush to ask for promotion on any other ground than that of family influence. As a parliamentary candidate, Burgoyne took our common expression "fighting an election" so very literally that he led his supporters to the poll at Preston in 1768 with a loaded pistol in each hand, and won the seat, though he was fined £1000, and denounced by Junius,[43] for the pistols.

It is only within quite recent years that any general recognition has become possible for the feeling that led Burgoyne, a professed enemy of oppression in India and elsewhere, to accept his American command when so many other officers threw up their commissions rather than serve in a civil war against the Colonies. His biographer De Fonblanque,[44] writing in 1876, evidently regarded his position as indefensible. Nowadays, it is sufficient to say that Burgoyne was an Imperialist. He sympathized with the colonists; but when they proposed as a remedy the disruption of the Empire, he regarded that as a step backward in civilization. As he put it to the House of Commons, "while we remember that we are contending against brothers and fellow subjects, we must also remember that we are contending in this crisis for the fate of the British Empire." Eighty-four years after his defeat, his republican conquerors themselves engaged in a civil war for the integrity of their Union. In 1885 the Whigs, who represented the anti-Burgoyne tradition of American Independence in English politics, abandoned Gladstone[45] and made common cause with their political opponents in defense of the Union between England and Ireland. Only the other day England sent 200,000 men into the field south of the equator to fight out the question whether South Africa should develop as a Federation of British Colonies or as an independent Afrikander United States.[46] In all these cases the Unionists who were detached from their parties were called renegades, as Burgoyne was. That, of course, is only one of the unfortunate consequences of the fact that mankind, being for the most part incapable of politics, accepts vituperation as an easy and congenial substitute. Whether Burgoyne or Washington, Lincoln or Davis,[47] Gladstone or Bright,[48] Mr. Chamber-

---

[43] The pseudonym of the writer of a series of letters (1769-1771) appearing in the *Public Advertiser,* a London paper, which bitterly and satirically attacked George III and Lord North, among others.

[44] Edward Barrington de Fonblanque, *Biography of the Right Honorable General John Burgoyne,* London, 1876.

[45] William Ewart Gladstone (1809-1898), a great Liberal statesman and prime minister four times between 1868 and 1894.

[46] Shaw refers to the Boer War (1899-1902).

[47] Jefferson Davis (1808-1889), president of the Confederate States of America, 1861-1865.

[48] John Bright (1811-1889), English Liberal statesman and orator, who refused to support Gladstone when the prime minister in 1886 urged Irish home rule.

lain[49] or Mr. Leonard Courtney[50] was in the right will never be settled, because it will never be possible to prove that the government of the victor has been better for mankind than the government of the vanquished would have been. It is true that the victors have no doubt on the point; but to the dramatist, that certainty of theirs is only part of the human comedy. The American Unionist is often a Separatist as to Ireland; the English Unionist often sympathizes with the Polish Home Ruler; and both English and American Unionists are apt to be Disruptionists as regards that Imperial Ancient of Days, the Empire of China. Both are Unionists concerning Canada, but with a difference as to the precise application to it of the Monroe doctrine. As for me, the dramatist, I smile, and lead the conversation back to Burgoyne.

Burgoyne's surrender at Saratoga made him that occasionally necessary part of our British system, a scapegoat. The explanation of his defeat given in the play (p. 57) is founded on a passage quoted by De Fonblanque from Fitzmaurice's Life of Lord Shelburne, as follows: "Lord George Germain,[51] having among other peculiarities a particular dislike to be put out of his way on any occasion, had arranged to call at his office on his way to the country to sign the dispatches; but as those addressed to Howe had not been fair-copied, and he was not disposed to be balked of his projected visit to Kent, they were not signed then and were forgotten on his return home." These were the dispatches instructing Sir William Howe, who was in New York, to effect a junction at Albany with Burgoyne, who had marched from Quebec for that purpose. Burgoyne got as far as Saratoga, where, failing the expected reinforcement, he was hopelessly outnumbered, and his officers picked off, Boer fashion, by the American farmer-sharpshooters. His own collar was pierced by a bullet. The publicity of his defeat, however, was more than compensated at home by the fact that Lord George's trip to Kent had not been interfered with, and that nobody knew about the oversight of the dispatch. The policy of the English Government and Court for the next two years was simply concealment of Germain's neglect. Burgoyne's demand for an inquiry was defeated in the House of Commons by the court party; and when he at last obtained a committee, the king got rid of it by a prorogation. When Burgoyne realized what had happened about the instructions to Howe (the scene in which I have represented him as learning it before Saratoga is not historical: the truth did not dawn on him until many months afterwards) the king actually took

---

[49] Joseph Chamberlain (1836-1914), English Liberal statesman and the South Africa colonial secretary during the Boer War.

[50] Leonard Courtney (1832-1918), British statesman and pacifist, who was opposed to England's involvement in the Boer War.

[51] Lord George Germain, his majesty's secretary of state for the colonies during the Revolutionary War.

advantage of his being a prisoner of war in England on parole, and ordered him to return to America into captivity. Burgoyne immediately resigned all his appointments; and this practically closed his military career, though he was afterwards made Commander of the Forces in Ireland for the purpose of banishing him from parliament.

The episode illustrates the curious perversion of the English sense of honor when the privileges and prestige of the aristocracy are at stake. Mr. Frank Harris[52] said, after the disastrous battle of Modder River,[53] that the English, having lost America a century ago because they preferred George III, were quite prepared to lose South Africa today because they preferred aristocratic commanders to successful ones. Horace Walpole,[54] when the parliamentary recess came at a critical period of the War of Independence, said that the Lords could not be expected to lose their pheasant shooting for the sake of America. In the working class, which, like all classes, has its own official aristocracy, there is the same reluctance to discredit an institution or to "do a man out of his job." At bottom, of course, this apparently shameless sacrifice of great public interests to petty personal ones, is simply the preference of the ordinary man for the things he can feel and understand to the things that are beyond his capacity. It is stupidity, not dishonesty.

Burgoyne fell a victim to this stupidity in two ways. Not only was he thrown over, in spite of his high character and distinguished services, to screen a court favorite who had actually been cashiered for cowardice and misconduct in the field fifteen years before; but his peculiar critical temperament and talent, artistic, satirical, rather histrionic, and his fastidious delicacy of sentiment, his fine spirit and humanity, were just the qualities to make him disliked by stupid people because of their dread of ironic criticism. Long after his death, Thackeray,[55] who had an intense sense of human character, but was typically stupid in valuing and interpreting it, instinctively sneered at him and exulted in his defeat. That sneer represents the common English attitude towards the Burgoyne type. Every instance in which the critical genius is defeated and the stupid genius (for both temperaments have their genius) "muddles through all right," is popular in England. But Burgoyne's failure was not the work of his own temperament, but of the stupid temperament. What man could do under the circumstances he did, and did handsomely and loftily. He fell, and his ideal empire was dismembered, not through his own misconduct, but because Lord George Germain overestimated the importance of his Kentish holiday, and underestimated the difficulty of con-

---

[52] Shaw's friend and biographer.
[53] One of the first battles (December, 1899) of the Boer War, in which the British suffered heavy losses.
[54] British writer (1717-1797) who served in Parliament for many years prior to the American Revolution.
[55] William Makepeace Thackeray (1811-1863), Victorian novelist, author of *Vanity Fair*.

quering those remote and inferior creatures, the colonists. And King George and the rest of the nation agreed, on the whole, with Germain. It is a significant point that in America, where Burgoyne was an enemy and an invader, he was admired and praised. The climate there is no doubt more favorable to intellectual vivacity.

I have described Burgoyne's temperament as rather histrionic; and the reader will have observed that the Burgoyne of the Devil's Disciple is a man who plays his part in life, and makes all its points, in the manner of a born high comedian. If he had been killed at Saratoga, with all his comedies[56] unwritten, and his plan for turning As You Like It[57] into a Beggar's Opera[58] unconceived, I should still have painted the same picture of him on the strength of his reply to the articles of capitulation proposed to him by the victorious Gates (an Englishman). Here they are:

PROPOSITION.

ANSWER.

1. General Burgoyne's army being reduced by repeated defeats, by desertion, sickness, etc., their provisions exhausted, their military horses, tents and baggage taken or destroyed, their retreat cut off, and their camp invested, they can only be allowed to surrender as prisoners of war.

Lieut-General Burgoyne's army, however reduced, will never admit that their retreat is cut off while they have arms in their hands.

2. The officers and soldiers may keep the baggage belonging to them. The Generals of the United States never permit individuals to be pillaged.

Noted.

3. The troops under his Excellency General Burgoyne will be conducted by the most convenient route to New England, marching by easy marches, and sufficiently provided for by the way.

Agreed.

4. The officers will be admitted on parole and will be treated with the liberality customary in such cases, so long as they, by proper behaviour, continue to deserve it; but those who are apprehended having broke their parole, as some British officers have done, must expect to be close confined.

There being no officer in this army under, or capable of being under, the description of breaking parole, this article needs no answer.

---

56 Burgoyne was the author of two comedies, *The Maid of the Oaks* (1774) and *The Heiress* (1786).
57 A Shakespearean pastoral comedy (1599) set in the Forest of Arden.
58 A musical play by John Gay (1728). Its hero, Captain Macheath, a romantic highwayman, would surely have appealed to "Gentlemanly Johnny" Burgoyne.

5. All public stores, artillery, arms, ammunition, carriages, horses, etc., etc., must be delivered to commissaries appointed to receive them.

All public stores may be delivered, arms excepted.

6. These terms being agreed to and signed, the troops under his Excellency's, General Burgoyne's command, may be drawn up in their encampments, where they will be ordered to ground their arms, and may thereupon be marched to the river-side on their way to Bennington.

This article is inadmissible in any extremity. Sooner than this army will consent to ground their arms in their encampments, they will rush on the enemy determined to take no quarter.

And, later on, "If General Gates does not mean to recede from the 6th article, the treaty ends at once: the army will to a man proceed to any act of desperation sooner than submit to that article."

Here you have the man at his Burgoynest. Need I add that he had his own way; and that when the actual ceremony of surrender came, he would have played poor General Gates off the stage, had not that commander risen to the occasion by handing him back his sword.

In connection with the reference to Indians with scalping knives, who, with the troops hired from Germany, made up about half Burgoyne's force, I may cite the case of Jane McCrea, betrothed to one of Burgoyne's officers. A Wyandotte chief attached to Burgoyne's force was bringing her to the British camp as a prisoner of war, when another party of Indians, sent by her betrothed, claimed her. The Wyandotte settled the dispute by killing her and bringing her scalp to Burgoyne. Burgoyne let the deed pass. Possibly he feared that a massacre of whites on the Canadian border by the Wyandottes would follow any attempt at punishment. But his own proclamations had threatened just what the savage chief executed.

BRUDENELL

Brudenell is also a real person. At least, an artillery chaplain of that name distinguished himself at Saratoga by reading the burial service over Major Fraser[59] under fire, and by a quite readable adventure, chronicled, with exaggerations, by Burgoyne, concerning Lady Harriet Acland. Others have narrated how Lady Harriet's husband killed himself in a duel, by falling with his head against a pebble; and how Lady Harriet then married the warrior chaplain. All this, however, is a tissue

---

[59] General Simon Fraser was one of Burgoyne's ablest commanders, leading his troops to victory in the battle of Hubbardton, Vermont, during the advance upon Albany. At his burial service the Americans ceased hostilities and fired a cannon salute out of respect for a gallant foe.

of romantic lies, though it has been repeated in print as authentic history from generation to generation, even to the first edition of this book. As a matter of fact, Major Acland died in his bed of a cold shortly after his return to England;[60] and Lady Harriet remained a widow until her death in 1815.

The rest of the Devil's Disciple may have actually occurred, like most stories invented by dramatists; but I cannot produce any documents. Major Swindon's name is invented; but the man, of course, is real. There are dozens of him extant to this day.

A Note on the Battle of Saratoga

Shaw reveals a cavalier disregard for historical and geographical accuracy in The Devil's Disciple. General Burgoyne left Canada in the late spring and proceeded down the west side of Lake Champlain to Saratoga, New York, where he was defeated on October 8, 1777, by an American army under the command of Major General Horatio Gates. At no time was he in New Hampshire. In the first edition of his play Shaw has Burgoyne marching south from Boston through New Hampshire to effect the union with Howe at Albany. Although Shaw later got his geography straightened out, he seems content to allow Burgoyne a diversionary thrust into New Hampshire.

The strategy of the British war office, planned by King George III, his Cabinet, and Lord George Germain, who was the American colonial secretary, was to separate New England from the rest of the states by having Lord William Howe move up the Hudson River from his headquarters in New York City to meet Burgoyne at Albany. This was at best a dubious strategy since Burgoyne's lines from Canada were inevitably overextended and subjected to constant harassment from New England's militia men.

Historians today question the legend which Shaw accepts concerning Lord Germain's Kentish weekend. Although Howe never received definite orders from Germain, he was fully aware that a junction of the two British armies at Albany was contemplated, and he had been politely encouraged to support the operation. Lord Howe, however, was more interested in his favorite project of capturing Philadelphia than in proceeding up the Hudson. He argued that he did not have time or

---

[60] Major John Dyke Acland, whose devoted wife Lady Harriet accompanied him throughout Burgoyne's campaign, engaged in a duel on Bampton Down in Devonshire in November, 1778. He escaped unhurt but died of pneumonia brought on from exposure.

troops enough to launch two attacks and that Burgoyne should not expect assistance. Apparently Lord Howe believed that Burgoyne could himself proceed directly down Lake Champlain, capture Albany, and continue on down the Hudson to New York City without reinforcements. This assumption was a disastrous miscalculation.

On October 16 Burgoyne signed the treaty of surrender—the Convention of Saratoga, to which Shaw refers in his Notes. Under this agreement Burgoyne's whole army would be granted free passage from Boston to England with the condition that they would not serve again in North America. One of the buildings of Harvard College was commandeered for the housing of Burgoyne's officers until their embarkation. But Congress refused to honor the Convention and sent the British troops to a town south of the Potomac, where they remained until the war was over.

On Diabolonian Ethics[61]

[*The Devil's Disciple*] does not contain a single even passably novel incident. Every old patron of the Adelphi pit[62] would, were he not beglamored in a way presently to be explained, recognize the reading of the will, the oppressed orphan finding a protector, the arrest, the heroic sacrifice, the court martial, the scaffold, the reprieve at the last moment, as he recognizes beefsteak pudding on the bill of fare at his restaurant. Yet when the play was produced in 1897 in New York by Mr. Richard Mansfield, with a success that proves either that the melodrama was built on very safe old lines, or that the American public is composed exclusively of men of genius, the critics, though one said one thing and another another as to the play's merits, yet all agreed that it was novel—*original*, as they put it—to the verge of audacious eccentricity.

Now this, if it applies to the incidents, plot construction, and general professional and technical qualities of the play, is nonsense; for the truth is, I am in these matters a very old-fashioned playwright. . . .

[But] The Devil's Disciple has, in truth, a genuine novelty in it. Only, that novelty is not any invention of my own, but simply the novelty of the advanced thought of my day. As such, it will assuredly

[61] George Bernard Shaw, "On Diabolonian Ethics," *Three Plays for Puritans* (New York, 1906), pp. xxiii-xxvii. Reprinted by permission of The Society of Authors and The Public Trustee.
[62] A London theater popular in the nineteenth century for its conventional melodramas.

lose its gloss with the lapse of time, and leave the Devil's Disciple exposed as the threadbare popular melodrama it technically is.

Let me explain (for, as Mr. A. B. Walkley[63] has pointed out in his disquisitions on Frames of Mind, I am nothing if not explanatory). Dick Dudgeon, the devil's disciple, is a Puritan of the Puritans. He is brought up in a household where the Puritan religion has died, and become, in its corruption, an excuse for his mother's master passion of hatred in all its phases of cruelty and envy. This corruption has already been dramatized for us by Charles Dickens in his picture of the Clennam household in Little Dorrit: Mrs. Dudgeon being a replica of Mrs. Clennam with certain circumstantial variations, and perhaps a touch of the same author's Mrs. Gargery in Great Expectations. In such a home the young Puritan finds himself starved of religion, which is the most clamorous need of his nature. With all his mother's indomitable selffulness, but with Pity instead of Hatred as his master passion, he pities the devil; takes his side; and champions him, like a true Covenanter, against the world. He thus becomes, like all genuinely religious men, a reprobate and an outcast. Once this is understood, the play becomes straightforwardly simple. The Diabolonian position is new to the London playgoer of today, but not to lovers of serious literature. From Prometheus[64] to the Wagnerian Siegfried,[65] some enemy of the gods, unterrified champions of those oppressed by them, has always towered among the heroes of the loftiest poetry. Our newest idol, the Overman,[66] celebrating the death of godhead, may be younger than the hills; but he is as old as the shepherds. Two and a half centuries ago our greatest English dramatizer of life, John Bunyan,[67] ended one of his stories with the remark that there

---

[63] Arthur Bingham Walkley, dramatic critic of *The London Times,* to whom Shaw dedicated his play *Man and Superman.*

[64] One of the titans in Greek mythology and the hero of a tragedy by Aeschylus. When Zeus hid fire from man, Prometheus stole it and brought it back to earth. In revenge Zeus chained him to a rock and sent an eagle to eat his liver, which, because Prometheus was immortal, grew at night as fast as the eagle could devour it by day. Hercules finally rescued the god from his agony.

[65] A legendary Germanic prince, the hero of the third of the operas in the tetralogy, *The Ring of Nibelung,* by Richard Wagner (1813-1883). In Act III of *Siegfried* Wagner's fearless hero challenges the god Wotan, who was responsible for the death of Siegfried's father, and with his sword Nothung splinters the shaft of the god's spear. Wotan vanishes in a flash of lightning and a crash of thunder.

[66] The Superman of the German philosopher Friedrich Nietzsche (1844-1900), proclaimed in his best known work, *Thus Spake Zarathustra.* Nietzsche's hero is a pitiless aristocratic leader, contemptuous of the codes of Christian morality, who would unscrupulously trample on the mass of mankind in his will to dominate.

[67] John Bunyan (1628-1688), Baptist preacher who did most of his writing during the twelve years he was imprisoned for his religious beliefs. Shaw is recalling the end of Bunyan's dream allegory *Pilgrim's Progress* (1678): "Then I saw that there was a way to hell, even from the gates of heaven, as well as from the City of Destruction! So I awoke, and behold it was a dream."

is a way to hell even from the gates of heaven, and so led us to the equally true proposition that there is a way to heaven even from the gates of hell. A century ago William Blake[68] was, like Dick Dudgeon, an avowed Diabolonian: he called his angels devils and his devils angels. His devil is a Redeemer. Let those who have praised my originality in conceiving Dick Dudgeon's strange religion read Blake's Marriage of Heaven and Hell; and I shall be fortunate if they do not rail at me for a plagiarist. But they need not go back to Blake and Bunyan. Have they not heard the recent fuss about Nietzsche and his Good and Evil Turned Inside Out? Mr. Robert Buchanan[69] has actually written a long poem of which the Devil is the merciful hero, which poem was in my hands before a word of The Devil's Disciple was written. There never was a play more certain to be written than The Devil's Disciple at the end of the nineteenth century. The age was visibly pregnant with it.

I grieve to have to add that my old friends and colleagues the London critics for the most part showed no sort of connoisseurship either in Puritanism or in Diabolonianism when the play was performed for a few weeks at a suburban theatre (Kennington) in October 1899 by Mr. Murray Carson. They took Mrs. Dudgeon at her own valuation as a religious woman because she was detestably disagreeable. And they took Dick as a blackguard, on her authority, because he was neither detestable nor disagreeable. But they presently found themselves in a dilemma. Why should a blackguard save another man's life, and that man no friend of his, at the risk of his own? Clearly, said the critic, because he is redeemed by love. All wicked heroes are, on the stage: that is the romantic metaphysic. Unfortunately for this explanation (which I do not profess to understand) it turned out in the third act that Dick was a Puritan in this respect also: a man impassioned only for saving grace, and not to be led or turned by wife or mother, Church or State, pride of life or lust of the flesh. In the lovely home of the courageous, affectionate, practical minister who marries a pretty wife twenty years younger than himself, and turns soldier in an instant to save the man who has saved him, Dick

---

[68] William Blake (1757-1827), poet and mystic who engraved the texts and illustrations for many of his works. His principal prose work, The Marriage of Heaven and Hell (1790), declares that "The Messiah fell, and formed a heaven of what he stole from the Abyss."
[69] Robert Buchanan (1841-1901), poet, novelist, playwright, is the butt of Shaw's anticlimactic joke. An incredibly bad poet, Buchanan hardly merits mention in a list of illustrations including Aeschylus, Bunyan, Blake, and Wagner. Shaw apparently refers to Buchanan's "The Vision of the Man Accurst." In Book VIII no sooner has Buchanan's un-Miltonic Devil been cast from Heaven than

". . . The Man arose,
With teeth gnashed beast-like, waved wild feeble hands
At the white Gate (that glimmered far away, . . .)
Cast a shrill curse at the pale judge within
Then groaning, beast-like crouched."

looks round and understands the charm and the peace and the sanctity, but knows that such material comforts are not for him. When the woman nursed in that atmosphere falls in love with him and concludes (like the critics, who somehow always agree with my sentimental heroines) that he risked his life for her sake, he tells her the obvious truth that he would have done as much for any stranger—that the law of his own nature, and no interest nor lust whatsoever, forbad him to cry out that the hangman's noose should be taken off his neck only to be put on another man's.

But then, said the critics, where is the motive? *Why* did Dick save Anderson? On the stage, it appears, people do things for reasons. Off the stage they don't: that is why your penny-in-the-slot heroes, who only work when you drop a motive into them, are so oppressively automatic and uninteresting. The saving of life at the risk of the saver's own is not a common thing: but modern populations are so vast that even the most uncommon things are recorded once a week or oftener. Not one of my critics but has seen a hundred times in his paper how some policeman or fireman or nursemaid has received a medal, or the compliments of a magistrate, or perhaps a public funeral, for risking his or her life to save another's. Has he ever seen it added that the saved was the husband of the woman the saver loved, or was that woman herself, or was even known to the saver as much as by sight? Never. When we want to read of the deeds that are done for love, whither do we turn? To the murder column; and there we are rarely disappointed.

Need I repeat that the theatre critic's professional routine so discourages any association between real life and the stage, that he soon loses the natural habit of referring to the one to explain the other? The critic who discovered a romantic motive for Dick's sacrifice was no mere literary dreamer, but a clever barrister. He pointed out that Dick Dudgeon clearly did adore Mrs. Anderson; that it was for her sake that he offered his life to save her beloved husband; and that his explicit denial of his passion was the splendid mendacity of a gentleman whose respect for a married woman, and duty to her absent husband, sealed his passion-palpitating lips. From the moment that this fatally plausible explanation was launched, my play became my critic's play, not mine. Thenceforth Dick Dudgeon every night confirmed the critic by stealing behind Judith, and mutely attesting his passion by surreptitiously imprinting a heartbroken kiss on a stray lock of her hair whilst he uttered the barren denial. As for me, I was just then wandering about the streets of Constantinople, unaware of all these doings. When I returned all was over. My personal relations with the critic and the actor forbad me to curse them. I had not even a chance of publicly forgiving them. They meant well by me; but if they ever write a play, may I be there to explain!

Commentary

The most difficult problem in reading drama is to realize that a play is a theater piece to be seen and heard; hence it is important to understand the contribution of such basic stage devices as sets, costumes, properties, and sound and lighting effects to the literary and dramatic achievement of the play as a whole. We shall take up these theatrical devices in turn, studying the way in which they help establish Shaw's artistic purposes. Since Shaw intended his plays to be read as well as produced, he incorporated in the text many stage directions which would ordinarily be left to a director's discretion. At other times it is not possible for an actor to convey the nuances of mood Shaw calls for in his witty stage directions; for example, when Uncle William declares, "We are all equal before the Throne," Shaw reports that "This republican sentiment does not please the women, who are convinced that the Throne is precisely the place where their superiority, often questioned in this world, will be recognized and rewarded" (p. 21).

As the curtain rises on the sleeping figures of Mrs. Dudgeon and Essie, and before a word of dialogue is spoken, we gain an immediate impression of the values of Mrs. Dudgeon's Puritan world. The plain kitchen table, the uncushioned and unpainted chairs, and the "shamelessly ugly black horsehair sofa" suggest her bleakly severe Puritanism. The shutters are drawn, and the only light comes from the glow of a dying fire. The dark kitchen with its rigid furniture foreshadows the sense of death running as an undercurrent through the play. Mrs. Dudgeon berates Essie for falling asleep when her father is "hardly cold in his grave"; and Christy soon bursts in to declare, "Father's dead too." Mrs. Dudgeon herself dies before a day has passed, and Dick Dudgeon has a hair's breadth escape from the gallows. But the opening atmosphere also suggests "the barren forms and observances of a dead Puritanism" reflected not only in Mrs. Dudgeon's face but also in the mourners who come to console her.

In a letter to Harley Granville-Barker on August 12, 1907, Shaw writes: "I have purposely put the fireplace on the same side in Acts I and II, so as to make the contrast between Judith's notion of a living room and Mrs. Dudgeon's as marked as possible by giving them similar material to work on." This contrast is pointed up in many details: there are stained and polished chairs, a rug, a tablecloth, prints on the wall, red curtains, and on the mantelpiece a clock flanked by knickknacks. Everything in the room evokes a vitality and an affection missing in the somber, uncomfortable Dudgeon home. Although it is evening, the room is brighter and pleasanter; there is a cozy fire burning on the grate. The glow of the streetlamps can be seen through the window, which is considerably wider than the Dudgeons'; Judith brings in candles. The loving care evident in the Anderson home sets the stage for the embrace of the happy couple which begins Act Two. Contrast Mrs. Dudgeon's angry shaking of Essie, who is called an "unfeeling, sinful girl," at the opening of the drama.

A good playwright will use stage properties for a more significant purpose than merely providing stage business. Shaw's adroit handling of the wine decanter in Act One and the tea service in Act Two is a case in point. In Mrs. Dudgeon's Puritan household wine is not a beverage, but a symbol of a "state occasion." It is kept carefully locked away for weddings and funerals, and even on this occasion no member of the Dudgeon family has a drink. Instead, the decanter becomes the means whereby Shaw can throw light on his characters. When Dick teasingly offers Anderson a glass, the minister responds stuffily that he does not drink before dinner, thus giving Dick the opening he needs to jibe at his Uncle William, a reformed drunkard. Yet Dick, who supposedly leads a life of wild dissipation, does not drink; he wryly proclaims that his temperance was induced at an early age by the wretched quality of his mother's sherry. His request for water allows Essie an opportunity to show her devotion to him. The decanter kept under lock and key suggests the niggardly puritanical attitudes of Mrs. Dudgeon; the tea service standing on the Anderson table enhances the hospitality and friendliness of the Anderson home. And ironically because Dick does make himself at home over a cup of tea, he is suddenly confronted with his "hour of trial." Thus, these two pieces of stage property underscore the same cleavage in attitudes implied in the sets of the first two acts.

Similarly, Shaw uses costume in Act Two as a crucial device for the development of plot, character, and theme. He prepares for the exchange of coats by carefully planting Anderson's wet cloak in full view before the fire and then replacing it there with Richard's. As Anderson changes into his old coat, attention is called to it through dialogue. Twice Richard starts toward the fireplace for his coat, and his decision to stay results in his capture. Note the number of times these coats are involved in dialogue and action. They become an important structural device in dramatizing the climax of The Devil's Disciple, for Dick's spontaneous decision to sacrifice himself so that Anthony may be saved is silently conveyed by his first instinctively going again for his coat and then with deliberate composure putting on the minister's instead. Later Anderson too moves toward an heroic act by donning Richard's coat and then imitating his sardonic tone (p. 40); a few moments later he explodes with a shocking blasphemy one would have thought only a devil's disciple capable of. Thus Shaw also uses costume as symbol: outer garment suggests an inner nature hitherto unrevealed.

Each man seems to exchange his character as he does his coat. Richard at the moment of decision is the man of peace; his usual display of verbal pyrotechnics gives way to dignified silence and an inner composure. Conversely, Anderson is galvanized into an energy such as we had seen earlier only when Dick presided at his family conclave: "His energy sends Essie flying from the room. He pounces on his riding boots; rushes with them to the chair at the fire; and begins pulling them on" (p. 42). As Anderson buckles on his pistols, counts out his money, and contemptuously dismisses the efficacy of prayer at such a moment— actions and thought more appropriate to a supposed smuggler living with gypsies than to a Presbyterian minister—Judith is convinced that her husband is a craven coward fleeing for his life. But the audience, who has witnessed the paradoxical reversal of roles, understands Anderson's meaning when he declares to his wife: "You don't know the man you're married to."

Besides such fundamental stage devices as sets, props, and costumes, Shaw also calls into comic play a wide range of conventional theater tricks long familiar in nineteenth-century opera and melodrama— and indeed still evident in today's television westerns. In fact, Shaw deprecatingly calls attention to *The Devil's Disciple* as "the threadbare popular melodrama it technically is" (p. 71) and catalogues such hackneyed devices as "the reading of the will, the oppressed orphan finding a protector, the arrest, the heroic sacrifice, the court martial, the scaffold, the reprieve at the last moment" (p. 70). And Shaw has not exhausted his list. One could also point out the solemn gathering of the clan (without the black sheep), the posturing entrance of the hero, and the sentimental tableaux on which the curtain falls in Acts One and Two. What others come to mind? What Shaw fails to note, however, is that he is quite ready to upset convention by having a son throw his widowed mother out of the house or by ringing the final curtain down on a hero and a heroine shaking hands. Point out other examples.

Shaw's play never descends to the level of claptrap melodrama because the playwright brilliantly turns his exhilarating wit upon the very techniques he uses and parodies them with masterly skill. The entrance of the widow (p. 21) is an illustration. Mrs. Dudgeon with calculated effect waits in her room until the audience of mourners is seated and quiet; then Judith announces her entrance as though she were a member of the royal family: "Friends, Mrs. Dudgeon." Mrs. Dudgeon sweeps in dressed in widow's weeds, handkerchief at her eyes. The audience rises, the women weep, the men stand ready to pray or sing if it will comfort their "poor afflicted sister." But the somber, brooding tone of the opening is gone. There is no grief for a dead relative, only "the barren forms and observances of a dead Puritanism" (p. 11). Shaw converts the ritual of mourning into a travesty which exposes the empty pieties of the Dudgeons, even as Mrs. Dudgeon's earlier vindictive selfishness now ironically

undercuts her pretense of grief. Dick Dudgeon's melodramatic entrance
a moment later also unmasks this sanctimony, although in its own terms
it is as calculated a bit of posturing as Mrs. Dudgeon's. Again the
announcement, the door swings open, and the "villain" poses cavalierly
in the entrance, his figure carefully silhouetted in the sunlight. With a
sweeping theatrical bow, Richard mockingly announces his presence and
destroys the solemnity of the occasion by tossing his hat to the startled
Christy and then turning with cheerful nonchalance to expose the sham
and cant of his relatives, starting with his mother.

Shaw thus dramatizes the conflict of attitudes here by juxtaposing
two conventionally melodramatic entrances so that the second undercuts
the first. In like manner Shaw develops the central conflict of character
by the use of gestures, facial expressions, and speech rhythms. Mrs.
Dudgeon's strident voice and sharp staccato rhythms are still heard,
although not so frequently: "And this is my reward!/ You know what
I think, Mr. Anderson;/ you know the word I gave to it"/ (p. 24).
"My curse on you!/ My dying curse!"/ (p. 27). But she is over-
whelmed by her older son's witty sophistications—"No, my father died
without the consolations of the law"—stunned by his blasphemous grace—
"For what we are about to receive, may the Lord make us truly thankful" (p. 23)—and finally hounded off stage in humiliated defeat—
"What, mother! Are you off too?" (p. 27). Richard's breezy vitality
sparkles in his idiom as he dominates the scene, seemingly never silent
nor still. In contrast to his flamboyant movements, his family is "petrified
with the intensity of their sense of Virtue menaced with outrage by the
approach of flaunting Vice" (p. 21); "Judith rises and stands with stony
propriety"; Mrs. Dudgeon "sinks, checkmated, into her chair" (pp. 22–
23); "the relatives freeze with horror"; and Mrs. Dudgeon "holds herself
convulsively rigid." Through gesture and posture Dick reflects the force
of life, whereas the stone-like persons he confronts suggest a moral and
spiritual death.

Shaw is not merely playing games with his melodramatic tricks;
they are his means for launching a mockingly ironic attack on a Puritan
ideology which he believes has been perverted. But Shaw never preaches
in The Devil's Disciple, nor are his characters simply spokesmen for his
ideas and attitudes. Dramatic technique, character, and theme are all
brilliantly unified. Mrs. Dudgeon is a good example of Shaw's embodi-
ment of the Puritan point of view which becomes self-destructive. Her
Puritanism is essentially a self-denial. On the advice of her pastor, old
Eli Hawkins, Mrs. Dudgeon did not marry the one man she truly
loved, Peter Dudgeon, but chose instead his "God-fearing" brother
Timothy. With an irony she cannot appreciate, Peter's illegitimate child
Essie is now her charge, and she maliciously takes revenge on the poor
child.

The word "heart" has become for her a term of derision (p. 16), and she cannot forgive Anderson his marrying for love. Mrs. Dudgeon is incapable of affection or compassion. Note the stage directions preceding her speeches and the epithets she flings at every member of her family. The only love she knows is a callous self-love, and the first-person pronoun looms large in her talk. She receives even the news of her husband's death by crying angrily: "Well, I do think this is hard on me—very hard on me" (p. 14). Since love is anathema to Mrs. Dudgeon, she finds her values in the Puritan ideal of "duty"—a word which echoes throughout *The Devil's Disciple.* "Why should we do our duty . . . ?" (p. 15). She shuts the door sharply "as if even it had to be made to do its duty with a ruthless hand" (p. 19). She criticizes her dead husband for not staying at home "where his duty was" (p. 14). In Act Three this verbal motif is picked up by the Sergeant and Major Swindon on several occasions. Why does Shaw transfer to British soldiers a view of life previously associated with New England Puritanism?

One critic has written that Shaw's central comic technique is the dramatization of paradox in his character relationships:

> A received moral opinion or social doctrine is embodied in a character who at first seems to the audience perfectly sensible, honorable, right-minded. To this person is opposed a character who embodies the Shavian contradiction of this conventional attitude. Their conflict—mostly verbal—is the central action of the play.[70]

Such conflicts are also Shaw's means of organizing each act. His hero Dick Dudgeon confronts Mrs. Dudgeon and his Puritan relatives in Act One, Judith in Act Two and Act Three, scene one, and Burgoyne in Act Three, scene two. Shaw playfully dramatizes the paradox that his diabolonian hero is "genuinely religious," whereas the "religious" Puritan mother is devilish. He has, of course, neatly stacked his dramatic cards, for the "sins" charged against Dick are unsubstantiated and far from heinous: "But he is a smuggler; and he lives with gypsies; and he has no love for his mother and his family; and he wrestles and plays games on Sunday instead of going to church" (p. 20). What evidence does Shaw provide that Dick's affirmation of allegiance to the Devil (p. 26) is ethically Christian? What does Shaw imply is un-Christian about the Puritanism he dramatizes? Why is Anderson not a true Puritan?

At the Anderson home Dick more than once drops the extravagant poses and sardonic tone of the reprobate to reveal his true nature. At one point he apologizes to Judith, "I am sorry, for your sake, that I am—what I am" (p. 35), and as he studies a home so unlike his own, he adds, ". . . and yet I know quite well I could never live here. It's not

---

[70] Alan R. Thompson, *The Dry Mock* (Berkeley and Los Angeles, 1948), pp. 112-113.

in my nature, I suppose, to be domesticated." As he leaves for prison, he urges Judith to tell her husband "that I am steadfast in my religion as he is in his and that he may depend on me to the death" (p. 37). But Judith fails to understand him, even as she misunderstood her husband's changed behavior, because she herself is torn by the central dramatic conflict between duty and instinct, a confusion created by her prudish, puritanical attitudes and her romantic blindness. It is Dick's problem to make her realize that he does not act out of either noble or ignoble motives, that his sacrifice is done not for love, friendship, or patriotism. He pronounces the word "love" with a "true Puritan scorn" (p. 46) like Mrs. Dudgeon's. But if he repudiates love as severely as his mother does, he does not assert "duty" as his code of conduct. When he is forced to choose between sacrificing his life or that of another, he acts instinctively and unhesitantly: "I have been brought up standing by the law of my own nature; and I may not go against it, gallows or no gallows." Shaw relishes the irony that a man who repudiates conventional romantic notions of conduct and insists he is a realist should himself "in the hour of trial" make an essentially romantic commitment, acting, not by reason nor by any traditional religious code, but on impulse. Shaw carries the paradox further, for his diabolonian hero in responding to an inner moral compulsion is acting according to the traditional Protestant belief in an "inner light" as a moral guide. The devil's disciple is ready, if necessary, to become a martyr and a saint.

This major theme of a man's revelation of his identity makes *The Devil's Disciple* more than a conventional melodrama with its hackneyed stage business of mistaken identity. This is the theme which underlies the theatrical suspense and brilliant dialogue of Act Three. Shaw makes the point in a letter written on March 13, 1897, to the famous actress Ellen Terry:

> It is not enough, for the instruction of this generation, that Richard should be superior to religion and morality as typified by his mother and his home, or to love as typified by Judith. He must also be superior to gentility: that is, to the whole ideal of modern society. . . . Burgoyne pleads all through for softening and easing the trial by reciprocal politeness and consideration between all the parties, and for ignoring the villainy of his gallows, the unworthiness of his cause, and the murderousness of his profession. The picture is completed by the band playing Handel's music, and the Christian clergyman reading the Bible to give the strangling an air of being an impressive ceremony.

Richard is pitted against Burgoyne in Act Three, not because he is the commanding general of the British army, but because he is Gentlemanly Johnny. For a time it appears that Burgoyne and Dudgeon are counterparts. Burgoyne calls his prisoner "a gentleman and a man of some spirit" (p. 50), and the British general has the urbane elegance and wit we have seen in the devil's disciple. Burgoyne's biting attack on the cant and hypocrisy of Swindon is reminiscent of an earlier conflict in the Dudgeon household. Both Burgoyne and Richard speak with the same rhetorical flair and graceful rhythms. But by keeping us aware of Judith's consternation and desperation, Shaw does not permit his audience to forget—despite the polished surface of Burgoyne's repartee—that a man is unjustly condemned to death and that Burgoyne's main concern is avoiding "unpleasantness" and "solemn fuss" (p. 52). He misjudges Richard's "admirable tact and gentlemanly feeling," and when he continues his urbane game of social banter even at the gallows, Richard will have none of it. Richard's manner becomes sharp and direct as he decisively repudiates the general's superficiality: "Hark ye, General Burgoyne. If you think that I like being hanged, you're mistaken. I don't like it; and I don't mean to pretend that I do. And if you think I'm obliged to you for hanging me in a gentlemanly way, you're wrong there too. I take the whole business in devilish bad part; and the only satisfaction I have in it is that you'll feel a good deal meaner than I'll look when it's over" (pp. 59–60). Burgoyne and Richard here part company as Richard moves toward the heroic. Burgoyne is defeated as a general and as a man, but he at least has the grace and integrity to admit it.

To illuminate further the ideal character of his diabolonian hero, Shaw cleverly introduces Christy as a comic foil. Dick best gets at the playwright's purpose when he says that his younger brother "has been too well brought up by a pious mother to have any sense or manhood left in him" (p. 53). Burgoyne fails as a man because he begs "political necessity and military duty" (p. 50) and is unwilling to accept moral responsibility for his act, but Christy is something less than a man. When we first meet him, he is "standing on tiptoe, from boyish habit, to hang his hat up" (p. 13), and callously announcing his father's death; but he is not just an overgrown boy. His mother likens him to a "stuck pig," and Shaw mentions his "slow, bovine cheerfulness" and notes that he "goes sheepishly to the door." He flees from each of the three acts in cowardice or panic. As he bobs in and out of the play, he is labeled variously a "fool" (p. 14), a "great lout" (p. 18), an "oaf" (p. 34), a "blatant idiot" (p. 53), a grinning "zany" (p. 54), a "jumping jackass" (p. 54), and a "blithering baboon" (p. 54). Christy's happiest moment in the play comes when he is promised both the stuffed birds and the china peacocks as his inheritance. Christy may believe he is the good brother, but Shaw has with mischievous irony denied him his manhood and even his humanity.

Questions and Problems

1. Shaw contradicts himself on the time of his play. Where? How can we ascertain the correct date?

2. Shaw frequently has fun with his characters' names. Why is his hero named Dudgeon? What is Mrs. Dudgeon's full name? Are there other characters with ironic names?

3. What purposes does Essie serve? Why should each act end with Essie in tears?

4. Although Richard's father does not appear in the play, explain how his character and influence are felt.

5. Point out instances where Shaw uses the technique of foreshadowing.

6. Shaw's problem in the second part of Act Two is to delay Anderson's realization of what happened during his absence. How does the dramatist hold Anderson back from this knowledge? How does Anderson gradually learn the truth?

7. Discuss the significance of these properties in Act Three: the blue dispatch, the Bible, Burgoyne's chronometer.

8. Why does Shaw introduce Brudenell in Act Three?

9. Trace the development of Anderson, Shaw's secondary hero, from Puritan to Diabolonian. One critic argues that Anderson "fails when it is incumbent on him to give his life to save Dick." Discuss.

10. On page 62 Anderson declares that he and Richard have now reversed roles, having discovered their "true professions." Do you agree with his assessment? Is Shaw parodying the neat conclusion of the "well-made play"? Or has the play come full circle?

11. In Act One the inhabitants of Websterbridge receive the brunt of Shavian wit. Discuss their role in Act Three and the implications of the triumphal procession which ends the play.

12. Although the trial scene is a travesty of justice, how does Shaw maintain his comic tone?

13. What is Shaw suggesting when he describes Judith on page 18? Does the play bear out the accuracy of his character analysis? Would any modifications be in order by the time Dick and she pledge to keep their secret?

14. Discuss the differences between Mrs. Dudgeon's view of self-sacrifice and Dick's.

HENRIK IBSEN

Rosmersholm

Translated by Ann Jellicoe

Biography

SEVEN YEARS AFTER Henrik Ibsen's birth on March 20, 1828, in Skien, a small Norwegian coastal town, his family lost their money and social position. On the wretched farm to which they moved there were no outlets for the boy's literary and artistic talents. At sixteen he left home to become a druggist's apprentice in the seaport village of Grimstad; during these unhappy, lonely years of adolescence and young manhood he was interested in the revolutionary causes sweeping Europe. In 1850 he entered the university at Christiania (now Oslo) as a medical student, but the publication of his first play, *Catalina*, a blank-verse tragedy, made him decide on a theatrical career.

For the next two years Ibsen wrote plays, and virtually starved doing so, until he was appointed dramatist for the Norwegian Theater at Bergen, where he later became stage manager. After six years of hard work writing, translating, and directing plays there, he was appointed "artistic director" of the Norwegian Theater of Christiania, a post he held until the theater failed in 1862. Several years of hardship and poverty followed before he moved in self-imposed exile to Rome and, later, to Dresden and Munich, where during the next quarter of a century he wrote his most famous plays. In 1891 he returned to Norway, where the earlier hostility and bitterness aroused by his dramas had turned to acclaim. For a decade he enjoyed extravagant but controversial success in Europe and America, but a stroke made his last days ones of lonely suffering. He died in Christiania in 1906 and was given a ceremonial public funeral attended by the king of Norway.

Ibsen is an historic figure in modern dramatic literature, for he was the first to create the modern problem play, set in realistic contemporary surroundings. He introduced into the drama of the late nineteenth century a serious intent where previously there had been only an effort to entertain the middle class or to flatter their respectable Victorian social and economic attitudes. Ibsen repudiated the dramatic assumptions of his day; he violently disturbed his audiences by focusing attention on crises in the moral and social life of their age. Although he was always a painstaking craftsman, he also rejected the conventions of the "well-made" play. Instead of making use of the traditional soliloquies and asides, for example, he erected an imaginary fourth wall for his box-like

85

stage so that a drama could work itself out independently, separated from an audience whose presence is never recognized until the final curtain calls break the illusion.

In the early part of his career Ibsen made no revolutionary innovations in dramatic technique. His first plays were experimental efforts to dignify Norwegian folklore and history, and here his bent was toward poetic and satiric dramas. It is Ibsen's so-called second period that produced the plays for which he is best known. From *Pillars of Society* (1877) to *Hedda Gabler* (1890) Ibsen dealt with many of the social and ethical problems that existed in a complacent world, showing to Shaw and his contemporaries that the theater could not only entertain but enlighten and that it could be the artistic instrumentality for presenting serious, even revolutionary, views about the freedom and dignity of the individual in conflict with the pressures of modern society. His attack on the conventional treatment of women in *A Doll's House* (1879) made the play a milestone in dramatic history, marking the beginning of the modern theater. In Ibsen's last four plays, however, he moved away from the social toward the symbolic, the psychological, and the introspective as experimental modes of creating human beings and human destinies—always the goal of Ibsen's dramatic impulses.

Principal Plays

Catalina (1850)

Love's Comedy (1862)

The Pretenders (1863)

Brand (1866)

Peer Gynt (1867)

The League of Youth (1869)

Emperor and Galilean (1873)

Pillars of Society (1877)

A Doll's House (1879)

Ghosts (1881)

An Enemy of the People (1882)

The Wild Duck (1884)

Rosmersholm (1886)

The Lady from the Sea (1888)

Hedda Gabler (1890)

The Master Builder (1892)

Little Eyolf (1894)

John Gabriel Borkman (1896)

When We Dead Awaken (1899)

Selected Descriptive Bibliography

Bentley, Eric, *In Search of Theater,* New York, 1953.
Bentley's chapter on Ibsen is a provocative dialogue assessing the playwright's strengths and weaknesses.

Bradbrook, M. C., *Ibsen the Norwegian,* London, 1948.
An intelligent revaluation of Ibsen's dramatic career set against his historical background.

Downs, Brian W., *A Study of Six Plays by Ibsen,* Cambridge, England, 1950.
A modern critical revaluation of Love's Comedy, Brand, Peer Gynt, A Doll's House, The Wild Duck, *and* The Master Builder.

Jorgenson, Theodore, *Henrik Ibsen: A Study in Art and Personality,* Northfield, Minnesota, 1945.
A detailed, but pedestrian, account of Ibsen's life and works. The dramatic criticism is limited to plot paraphrases and character sketches.

Koht, Halvdan, *The Life of Ibsen,* 2 vols., New York, 1931.
The most comprehensive and satisfactory biography of Ibsen.

Lavrin, Janko, *Ibsen: An Approach,* London, 1950.
An introductory study with brief commentary on each of the plays.

McFarlane, James Walter, *Ibsen and the Temper of Norwegian Literature,* London, 1960.
A study that views Ibsen in the context of modern Norwegian literature.

Northam, John, *Ibsen's Dramatic Method,* London, 1953.
Northam analyzes the visual implications of the plays as revealed through stage directions. Illuminating study of the earlier drafts of Ibsen's manuscripts.

Reichardt, Konstantin, "Tragedy of Idealism: Henrik Ibsen" in *Tragic Themes in Western Literature,* ed. Cleanth Brooks (New Haven, 1955), pp. 128-149.
This essay, one of the best on Rosmersholm, *focuses mainly upon its ethical and philosophical implications.*

Shaw, George Bernard, *The Quintessence of Ibsenism,* New York, 1912.
A colorful defense of Ibsen's ideas by an articulate admirer, but one which throws more light on Shaw than on Ibsen.

Tennant, P. F. D., *Ibsen's Dramatic Technique,* Cambridge, England, 1948.
Rather than studying each play separately, Tennant analyzes Ibsen's craftsmanship in terms of settings, stage directions, plot, exposition, and ending. He also investigates Ibsen's method of composition and the sources of his inspiration.

Weigand, Hermann J., *The Modern Ibsen: A Reconsideration,* New York, 1925.
The standard critical study of Ibsen's plays from Pillars of Society *to the end of his dramatic career. Weigand's approach is largely psychological.*

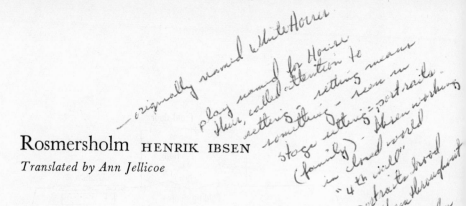

Rosmersholm HENRIK IBSEN

Translated by Ann Jellicoe

CHARACTERS

JOHN ROSMER, *owner of Rosmersholm, formerly the parish clergyman*

REBECCA WEST, *one of Rosmer's household*

MR. KROLL, *Rosmer's brother-in-law, headmaster of the local school*

ULRIC BRENDEL

PETER MORTENSGARD

MRS. HELSETH, *housekeeper at Rosmersholm*

SCENE: *The action takes place at Rosmersholm, an old manor house near a small town on a fjord in Western Norway.*

Rosmersholm was published on November 23, 1886, and first produced in Bergen, Norway, on January 17, 1887.

Acknowledgment is made to Ann Jellicoe for permission to publish her translation of Rosmersholm *by Henrik Ibsen.*

All performing rights are reserved and no professional or amateur performance of this translation of the play may be given without authorization from Miss Jellicoe's agents, Margaret Ramsay, Ltd., 14 Goodwin's Court, London, W. C. 2, England, or Toby Cole, 234 West 44th Street, New York 36, N. Y.

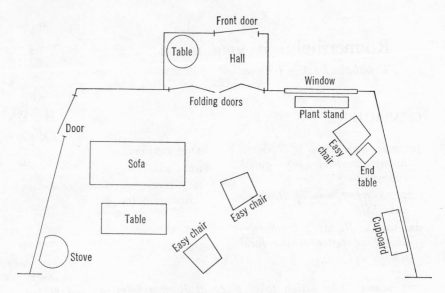

ROSMERSHOLM • ACTS I, III, IV

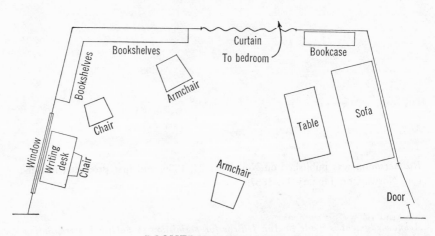

ROSMERSHOLM • ACT II

Act One

The living room at Rosmersholm: spacious, old-fashioned and comfortable. Downstage right stands a tiled stove decorated with fresh birch branches and wild flowers. Further upstage is a door. In the back wall folding doors lead into the hall. On the left wall is a window and, in front of it, a stand with flowers and plants. Near the stove is a table with sofa and easy chairs. Round the walls hang portraits, old and more recent, of priests, officers and government officials in uniform. The window stands open as does the door into the hall and the outer door of the house. Outside can be seen an avenue of tall old trees leading up to the house. A summer evening, the sun is down.

REBECCA WEST sits in an easy chair by the window and crochets a large white shawl which is nearly finished. Every now and then she spies out watchfully between the flowers. After a while enter MRS. HELSETH *right.*

MRS. HELSETH: It might be as well if I began to lay the supper, Miss?

REBECCA: Yes do. Mr. Rosmer will be back soon.

MRS. HELSETH: Isn't it drafty where you're sitting, Miss?

REBECCA: A little. Perhaps you'll close the window?

(MRS. HELSETH *goes and closes the folding doors; then she crosses to the window.*)

MRS. HELSETH (*looking out before she closes it*): Isn't that the Pastor there now?

REBECCA (*quickly*): Where? (*Rising*) Yes, it's him. (*Keeping behind the curtains*) Keep back. Don't let him see us.

MRS. HELSETH (*moving back into the room*): Fancy, he's starting to use the mill path again.

REBECCA: He took the mill path the day before yesterday as well. (*Peeping out between the curtains and the window frame*) But now we shall see—

MRS. HELSETH: Is he going over the footbridge?

REBECCA: That's what I want to see. (*After a moment*) No, he's turned off. Going by the upper road today as well. (*Leaves window*) The long way round.

MRS. HELSETH: Oh dear me yes. It must be hard for the Pastor to cross the footbridge where a thing like that's happened, and—

REBECCA (*putting her crochet together*): They cling to their dead here at Rosmersholm.

MRS. HELSETH: I'd say myself, Miss, it's the dead that cling to Rosmersholm.

REBECCA (*looking at her*): The dead?

MRS. HELSETH: Almost as if they couldn't tear themselves away from them they leave behind.

REBECCA: What makes you think so?

MRS. HELSETH: Oh yes, indeed, otherwise there'd be no white horse,—I know.

REBECCA: Yes, now just what is all this about a white horse, Mrs. Helseth?

MRS. HELSETH: Oh it doesn't do to speak lightly of it. Anyway you don't believe in that sort of thing.

REBECCA: Do you believe in it?

MRS. HELSETH (*crossing to shut window*): Oh I'm not going to have you laugh at me, Miss. (*Looking out*) But—isn't that the Pastor on the mill path again?

REBECCA (*looking out*): That man. There. (*Goes to window*) Why— It's Mr. Kroll!

MRS. HELSETH: Yes that's right, it is Mr. Kroll.

REBECCA: This is splendid; he must be coming to see us.

MRS. HELSETH: He comes straight over the footbridge, he does. Even though she was his own sister. Well, I'll go and lay the supper, Miss. (*Exit* MRS. HELSETH *right.* REBECCA *stands a little while at the window; then she nods and smiles, greeting someone outside. It begins to grow dark.*)

REBECCA (*crossing, she speaks through door right*): Mrs. Helseth dear, could we have a little something extra special for supper? You know what Mr. Kroll likes.

MRS. HELSETH (*off*): Yes of course, Miss. I'll see to it.

REBECCA (*opening the door into the hall*): Well, after all this time—! How nice to see you, my dear Mr. Kroll.

KROLL (*in the hall putting down his stick*): Thank you. I hope I don't disturb you?

REBECCA: You! Nonsense, you're joking!

KROLL (*coming in*): Always so kind. Is Rosmer perhaps up in his room?

REBECCA: No, he's gone out for a walk but he's sure to be back soon. (*Gesturing to sofa*) Won't you sit down and wait?

KROLL (*putting down his hat*): Many thanks. (*Sits down and looks around*) Well, how neat and pretty you've made this old room, flowers everywhere.

REBECCA: Mr. Rosmer likes to have fresh living flowers around him.

KROLL: And you too, I think.

REBECCA: Yes, the scent is so delicious and we've had to deny ourselves until recently.

KROLL: Poor Beate didn't like the smell. *1ˢᵗ time name appears.*

REBECCA: Nor the colors, she was so easily upset.

KROLL: Yes, I remember. (*In lighter tone*) Well now, how is everything out here?

REBECCA: Oh, everything goes on the same quiet way, one day just like another. —And how is it with you? Is your wife—?

flowers represent new things bringing into house. Reb. represents new ideas— Beate old ideas etc.

KROLL: Oh, my dear Miss West, don't let's talk about me; there's always something going wrong in a family, especially in times like these.

REBECCA (*after a pause she sits in an easy chair by the sofa*): Why haven't you been out to see us once during all the school holidays?

KROLL: Well, one didn't want to be a nuisance—

REBECCA: If you knew how we've missed you—

KROLL: —and of course I've been away—

REBECCA: Yes, for a couple of weeks. I hear you've been going in for politics —attending meetings.

KROLL (*nodding*): What do you think of that, eh? You didn't think I'd become a political agitator in my old age, did you?

REBECCA (*smiling*): You've always been something of an agitator, Mr. Kroll.

KROLL: Maybe, just for my own benefit and amusement. But it's going to be serious in future. Do you ever see the radical press?

REBECCA: Yes, Mr. Kroll. I won't deny that—

KROLL: Oh, there's nothing wrong in it, Miss West, not in your case.

REBECCA: No, I think so too. I like to follow what's happening, to be informed—

KROLL: In any case you, a woman, would scarcely take an active part in the civil dispute—I could almost say civil war,—that's raging here. But have you seen how these leaders of the people have seen fit to treat me, the filthy abuse they have allowed themselves?

REBECCA: Yes, but I think you gave quite as good as you got.

KROLL: I did indeed, though I say it myself. I've tasted blood now, and they'll soon see, I'm not a man to give up easily. (*Breaking off*) Well but, come come. Don't let's talk of such painful things this evening.

REBECCA: No, don't let's, dear Mr. Kroll.

KROLL: You tell me instead how you are getting on here at Rosmersholm, now that you're alone, since our poor Beate—

REBECCA: Oh, I manage quite well thank you. There is a great emptiness, even after so many months, and sadness naturally. But apart from that—

KROLL: Are you thinking of staying here? I mean permanently.

REBECCA: I really haven't thought much, one way or the other. I've become so used to it here, I almost feel I belong here too.

KROLL: You! Yes indeed you do.

REBECCA: And so long as Mr. Rosmer feels that I can be of any comfort or use to him, well then, I expect I shall stay.

KROLL (*looking at her, much moved*): You know, there is something fine in this—a woman sacrificing her youth for the sake of others.

REBECCA: Oh, but what else have I had to live for?

KROLL: When you first came here, you had your foster father: crippled, unreasonable.

REBECCA: You mustn't think Dr. West was so unreasonable up there in Finmark. It was those terrible sea journeys he had to make that broke him. But when we came down here—well yes, then there were a couple of difficult years before he found peace.

KROLL: And the years that followed, weren't they even more difficult?

REBECCA: No, how can you say that! I was so fond of Beate—and she was so helpless, poor dear, and so badly needed tenderness and care.

KROLL: Heaven will bless you, that you remember her with such charity.

REBECCA (*sitting a little closer*): My dear Mr. Kroll, you say that so kindly and sincerely that I am sure there is no resentment behind it.

KROLL: Resentment? What do you mean?

REBECCA: Well, it wouldn't have been so very difficult to understand if you *had* found it painful to see me, a stranger, running things here at Rosmersholm.

KROLL: What on earth—!

REBECCA: But you don't. (*Holding out her hand*) Thank you, dear Mr. Kroll. Thank you, thank you for that.

KROLL: But what on earth gave you such an idea?

REBECCA: I began to be a little frightened when you came out to see us so seldom.

KROLL: Then you've been on quite the wrong track, Miss West. And besides—nothing is really changed. You and only you looked after everything here during poor Beate's last unhappy years.

REBECCA: That was just a kind of regency in the wife's name.

KROLL: Well anyway—do you know, Miss West—for my part, I should have nothing against it if you—but I suppose I shouldn't say that.

REBECCA: What do you mean?

KROLL: If it should so happen, that you took the empty place.

REBECCA: I have the place I want, Mr. Kroll.

KROLL: In effect, yes, but not in—

REBECCA (*interrupting him gravely*): You should be ashamed, Mr. Kroll; how can you joke about such things?

KROLL: Ah well, probably our good John Rosmer feels he's had more than enough of marriage. But all the same—

REBECCA: You know I could almost laugh at you.

KROLL: All the same—tell me, Miss West, if it's not a rude question—how old are you?

REBECCA: I'm ashamed to say I'm over twenty-nine, Mr. Kroll; I'm nearly thirty.

KROLL: Yes, and Rosmer—how old is he? Let me see, he is five years younger than I; that makes him forty-three. I think that would do very well.

REBECCA (*rising*): Yes, yes, it would do beautifully. —You'll stay and have some supper?

KROLL: Thank you, yes, I had thought of staying. There's something I want to discuss with our good friend—and so, Miss West—in case you have any more silly ideas, I'm going to come out here just as often as I can—like the old days.

REBECCA: Oh yes, please do. (*Shaking his hand*) Thank you, thank you. You're so kind really.

KROLL (*a little gruff*): That's more than they say at home.

(*Enter* JOHN ROSMER *by door right.*)

REBECCA: Mr. Rosmer—look who's sitting here.

ROSMER: Mrs. Helseth told me.

(KROLL *has risen.*)

ROSMER (*quiet and gentle takes* KROLL'S *hands*): Welcome to this house again, my dear Kroll. (*Lays his hand on* KROLL'S *shoulders and looks into his eyes*) My dear old friend, I knew that one day things would be right again between us.

KROLL: But my dear fellow—have you been imagining that there was something wrong too?

REBECCA (*to* ROSMER): Isn't it wonderful—it was just our imagination.

ROSMER: Was it really that, Kroll? But why didn't you come to see us?

KROLL (*quietly and gravely*): Because I didn't want to come here as a living reminder of those unhappy years—and of her—who ended in the mill race.

ROSMER: That was very thoughtful of you, you're always so considerate. But there was absolutely no need to stay away because of that. —Come, let's sit down on the sofa. (*They sit*) No, it doesn't hurt me any more to think of Beate. We talk of her every day. We almost feel as if she was still part of the house.

KROLL: Do you really?

REBECCA (*lighting the lamp*): Yes, indeed we do.

ROSMER: It's not so strange. We were both so deeply attached to her—and both Rebecc—both Miss West and I, we each know that we did everything we could for the poor invalid. We've no need to reproach ourselves—and so I think there is something sweet and peaceful in thinking of Beate now.

KROLL: You dear good people. From now on, I shall come out and see you every day.

REBECCA (*sitting down in the easy chair*): Yes, and mind you keep your word.

ROSMER (*hesitating a little*): You know, Kroll, I wish our friendship had never been interrupted. I've always relied on you for advice, for as long as we've known each other, ever since I was a student.

KROLL: Well, yes, and it's always meant a great deal to me. Why, is there something specially—?

ROSMER: There are many things I want to talk to you about, so much. Things that are very near my heart.

REBECCA: Oh yes, why not, Mr. Rosmer? I think it would be such a comfort —between old friends—

KROLL: Well, I've even more to tell you. Now I'm an active politician as you know.

ROSMER: Yes, you are indeed. How did it happen?

KROLL: I had to, you know. Had to, whether I liked it or not. You can't stand by any longer. Now that the radicals have become so abominably powerful—it's high time—. And so I made our little band of friends in the town get together—and high time too, I say.

REBECCA (*with a slight smile*): Isn't it even a little late?

KROLL: Doubtless, we should have stopped the rot sooner. But who could have known what was coming? I didn't anyway. (*Rises, and walks about the floor*) But now I've really had my eyes opened for me. There's a spirit of revolt in the school itself.

ROSMER: In the school? Surely not in your school.

KROLL: There certainly is. In my school. What do you think? It has come to my knowledge that the Sixth Form boys—some of them at least—have had a secret society for the past half year, and they've been taking Mortensgard's paper.

REBECCA: Ah, the *Signal*.

KROLL: Yes, nice sound nourishment for future public servants, eh? But the pity of it is, it's all the most gifted boys who've hatched this conspiracy against me. Only the dunces have kept out.

REBECCA: Does this really mean so much to you, Mr. Kroll?

KROLL: Mean much! To see my life work checked and thwarted! (*More quiet*) Still, that must look after itself. There's something even worse. (*Looking round*) There's nobody listening at the door?

REBECCA: No, of course not.

KROLL: Then let me tell you this . . . dissension and rebellion have crept into my own house. Into my own peaceful home. My family life has been utterly destroyed.

ROSMER (*rising*): What do you say? At home, in your house—?

REBECCA (*going to* KROLL): But my dear Mr. Kroll, what has happened?

KROLL: You won't believe it, but my own children—. In short—it's Laurits who is leader in the school plot. And Hilde has embroidered a red folder to keep the *Signal* in.

ROSMER: I would never have dreamed—that your family—in your house—

KROLL: Who could have dreamed such a thing? In my house, where there's always been peace and order—which, until now, has been ruled by a single will.

REBECCA: How does your wife take this?

KROLL: That's the most extraordinary thing of all, she, who all her life— in everything great and small—has shared my views, has thought as I have thought—she is tending to side with the children, and she blames *me* for what has happened. She says I'm too strict with them, as if I didn't have to be—. Well, that's the kind of battle that's going on at home. Of course I talk about it as little as possible. Things like this are best kept quiet. (*Walking about the room*) Oh well, well, well.

(*He stands in front of the window and looks out, his hands behind his back.*)

REBECCA (*crosses to* ROSMER *and speaks quickly, unnoticed by* KROLL): Tell him.

ROSMER (*likewise*): Not tonight.

REBECCA (*as before*): Yes, now.

(*She goes and adjusts the lamp.*)

KROLL (*coming back into the room*): Well, my dear Rosmer, now you see how the spirit of today has cast its shadow over my private and my public life. And shall I not fight this subversive and destructive anarchy with every weapon I can lay my hands on? I most certainly shall, in speech and print.

ROSMER: Do you think you can achieve anything by such methods?

KROLL: I shall be doing my duty as a citizen anyway, and I think it's up to every man with a spark of patriotism to do the same—and this is the main reason I came out to see you this evening.

ROSMER: But my dear fellow, what do you mean—? How can I—?

KROLL: You are going to help your old friends. Do as we do. Join the struggle and give the best you can.

REBECCA: But Mr. Kroll, you know how Mr. Rosmer dislikes that kind of thing.

KROLL: Then he must get over his dislike—you don't keep up with things, Rosmer. You bury yourself here in your historical research—all respect to scholarship and all that. But this is no time for that sort of thing—unfortunately. You've no idea what a state things have reached in the country. There's hardly a single accepted idea that isn't being challenged. It's going to be a huge task to stamp out these wild ideas.

ROSMER: I think so too. But that kind of work is not for me.

REBECCA: And I rather think that Mr. Rosmer has come to take a broader view of life than he used to.

KROLL (surprised): Broader?

REBECCA: Yes, or maybe freer, more open-minded.

KROLL: What does this signify? Rosmer—you're not so weak surely that you let yourself be swayed by the mere chance that these mobleaders have won a temporary advantage?

ROSMER: My dear Kroll, you know how little I know about politics, but really I do think that in the last few years people have begun to think more for themselves—more independently.

KROLL: Well! And you think that's a good thing! You're wrong, my friend. Just make a few inquiries and see what the radicals are thinking—out here and in town. Nothing more or less than the wisdom published in the *Signal*.

REBECCA: Yes, Mortensgard has great influence round here.

KROLL: It's fantastic. A fellow with such a disgraceful past. A schoolmaster dismissed for immoral behavior—! sets himself up as a leader of the people. And he gets away with it, he actually gets away with it! Now I hear he's going to enlarge his paper. I know for certain he's looking for a capable assistant.

REBECCA: I'm surprised you and your friends don't start something in opposition.

KROLL: That's just what we're going to do. Today we bought the *County News*. There was no difficulty about the money, but—(*turning to* ROSMER) and this is the real reason for my visit, it's the leadership, the editorship that's the problem. Now look here, Rosmer, don't you feel, for the good of the cause, that you should undertake it?

ROSMER (*almost in consternation*): I!

REBECCA: Oh, how can you think such a thing!

KROLL: That you shrink from public meetings and don't want to expose yourself to vulgarity, I can quite understand. But an editor can keep in the background, or rather—

ROSMER: No, no, my dear friend, you mustn't ask this of me.

KROLL: I wouldn't mind trying it myself, but I've far too much to do already—but you are no longer tied down in public work. We others will naturally help as much as we can.

ROSMER: I can't, Kroll, I'm not fitted for it.

KROLL: Not fitted? You said the same thing when your father gave you your living.

ROSMER: And I was right; that's why I resigned.

KROLL: If you are as good an editor, as you were a priest, we shall be satisfied.

ROSMER: My dear Kroll—I say now, once and for all, I cannot do it.

KROLL: Well, at least you'll let us use your name.

ROSMER: My name?

KROLL: Yes, the mere name of John Rosmer will help the paper. The rest of us are all looked upon as party politicians. I hear that I'm thought of as a raging fanatic. So we can't use our own names if the paper is going to influence the people—the misguided mass. But you now—you've always kept out of the fight. Everyone round here knows and respects you: your gentle honest nature, your polished mind, your absolute integrity, and then there's the deference and prestige you still have as a former clergyman. And above all, there is the luster of your family name.

ROSMER: Oh, the family name—

KROLL (pointing to the portraits): Rosmers of Rosmersholm, priests, officers and statesmen. True gentlemen, all of them. A family, that for nearly two hundred years has stood first in the district. (Laying his hands on ROSMER's shoulders) Rosmer, you owe it to yourself and to the high traditions of your family to come with us and defend those things which until now have always been held sacred in our society. (Turning) What do you say, Miss West?

REBECCA (with a gentle little laugh): My dear Mr. Kroll, I find all this utterly ludicrous.

KROLL: What! Ludicrous?

REBECCA: Yes, for now I will tell you—

ROSMER (quickly): No, no!—Don't!—Not now.

KROLL (looking from one to the other): Dear friends, what on earth— (Breaking off) Hm!

(Enter MRS. HELSETH right.)

MRS. HELSETH: There's a man at the back door wants to know if Mr. Rosmer is at home.

ROSMER (more lightly): Oh, oh, well ask him to come in.

MRS. HELSETH: Here in the sitting room?

ROSMER: Yes, of course.

MRS. HELSETH: He doesn't look quite the sort of man to have in the sitting room.

REBECCA: How does he look, Mrs. Helseth?

MRS. HELSETH: Well nothing very much, Miss.

ROSMER: Did he say who he is?

MRS. HELSETH: Yes, I think he said his name was Hekman, or something like that.

ROSMER: I don't know that name.

MRS. HELSETH: And he said his other name was Ulric.

ROSMER (*starting*): Ulric Hetman—was that it?

MRS. HELSETH: Yes, Hetman, that's right.

KROLL: I've heard that name before.

REBECCA: Wasn't that the name he used to write under, that extraordinary—

ROSMER (*to* KROLL): It's Ulric Brendel's pseudonym.

KROLL: That rascal, Ulric Brendel. Of course.

REBECCA: So he's still alive.

ROSMER: I thought he was with a troupe of actors.

KROLL: The last I heard, he was in the workhouse.

ROSMER: Ask him to come in, Mrs. Helseth.

MRS. HELSETH: Very well.

(*Exit* MRS. HELSETH.)

KROLL: Are you really going to have that fellow in here?

ROSMER: Oh well, you know, he was once my tutor.

KROLL: Yes, I know, and I know he went and stuffed your head with so many revolutionary ideas that your father showed him to the door with a horsewhip.

ROSMER: Yes, father never forgot he commanded a regiment, even at home.

KROLL: Be grateful to his memory for that, my dear Rosmer. Well!

(MRS. HELSETH *opens door right for* ULRIC BRENDEL *and then exits, closing the door after her. He is a good-looking man, somewhat gaunt, but vigorous and active. His hair and beard are grey. He is dressed like a common tramp: threadbare frock coat, worn out shoes and no shirt to be seen. He wears an old pair of black gloves and carries a dirty soft hat under his arm. He has a walking stick.*)

BRENDEL (*hesitates a moment, then goes quickly up to* KROLL *and holds out his hand*): Good evening, John!

KROLL: I beg your pardon.

BRENDEL: Did you ever think to see me again—and that within these hated walls.

KROLL: I beg your pardon. (*Pointing*) There.

BRENDEL (*turning round*): Of course, there he is. John—my dear boy—my favourite pupil—!

ROSMER (*taking his hand*): My old tutor.

BRENDEL: In spite of certain painful memories, I could not pass Rosmersholm by, without paying a flying visit.

ROSMER: You are very welcome here now.

BRENDEL: And this delightful lady (*bows*), Mrs. Rosmer of course.

ROSMER: Miss West.

BRENDEL: A near relation no doubt. And yonder stranger, a colleague I can see.

ROSMER: Mr. Kroll, the headmaster of our school.

BRENDEL: Kroll? Kroll? Just a minute. Didn't you study philology in your younger days?

KROLL: Yes, of course I did.

BRENDEL: But—*Donnerwetter!*[1]—I must have known you!

KROLL: Excuse me—

BRENDEL: Were you not—

KROLL: Excuse me—

BRENDEL: —one of those pillars of virtue that had me kicked out of the debating society.

KROLL: Quite possibly, but I disclaim any closer acquaintance.

BRENDEL: Well! Well! *Nach Belieben, Herr Doktor.*[2] I dare say I'll get over it. It takes more than that to upset Ulric Brendel.

REBECCA: Are you on your way into town, Mr. Brendel?

BRENDEL: Reverend madame, you have hit it. Now and again, I am obliged to strike a blow for existence. It goes against the grain but—*enfin*[3]—stern necessity—

ROSMER: Oh, but my dear Mr. Brendel, won't you let me help you? In one way or another, I am sure—

BRENDEL: Hah! What a suggestion! Will you sully the bond that unites us? Never, John—never!

ROSMER: But what do you plan to do in town? You know, I don't think you'll find it so easy—

BRENDEL: Leave that to me, my boy, the die is cast. You see before you a man engaged in a vast campaign. Vaster than all my previous campaigns put together. (*To* KROLL) Dare I ask the Herr Professor—*unter uns*[4]—is there a respectable, decent and commodious assembly hall in your excellent town?

KROLL: The largest is the working men's club.

BRENDEL: And has the Herr Professor any official influence with this doubtless highly worthy organization?

KROLL: I have nothing whatever to do with it.

REBECCA (*to* BRENDEL): You should speak to Peter Mortensgard.

BRENDEL: Pardon, madame, what kind of a fool is he?

ROSMER: What makes you think he's a fool?

BRENDEL: The mere name sounds so plebeian.

KROLL: There's an answer I didn't expect.

BRENDEL: But there is no alternative. I shall have to conquer my natural reluctance. When a man stands—as I do—at a turning point in his life—it is done! I shall put myself in touch with this individual. Enter into direct negotiation—

ROSMER: Are you seriously at a turning point in your life?

BRENDEL: Does not my own pupil know, that wherever Ulric Brendel stands, there stands he seriously? I am about to become a new man. Hitherto I have shrouded myself with modest reserve. I shall cast it off.

---

[1] Literally, German for "thunderstorm"; an exclamation like "by Jove."
[2] German for "as you please, doctor."
[3] French for "at last."
[4] German for "between us."

ROSMER: But how—?

BRENDEL: I shall lay hold on life with a firm hand, tread forward, tread upward. We live in a stormy equinoctial age. I want to lay my mite on the altar of freedom.

KROLL: You too—?

BRENDEL (to them all): Has anybody round here any acquaintance with my uncollected works?

KROLL: No. I must confess that—

REBECCA: I have read some of them. My foster father had them.

BRENDEL: Then, beautiful lady of the house, you have wasted your time. For let me tell you, they are so much trash.

REBECCA: Indeed?

BRENDEL: Those you have read, yes! My really important works are known to neither man nor woman. To no one—but myself.

REBECCA: How is this?

BRENDEL: Because they are not written yet.

ROSMER: But dear Mr. Brendel—

BRENDEL: You know, John, I'm a bit of a Sybarite. A *Feinschmecker*.[5] Have been all my days. I like my pleasures in solitude. Thus I enjoy them twice as much, ten times as much. When golden dreams drifted over me, enfolded me, when new thoughts were born in me—shadowy, infinite— wafting me away on their sustaining pinions, I shaped them into visions, poems, pictures: only in rough outline of course.

ROSMER: Yes, yes.

BRENDEL: Oh, I have known joy, rapture, the mysterious ecstasy of creation —in the rough, as I said. Applause, gratitude, fame, the laurel wreath— I have garnered all with joyful, trembling hands. In my innermost thoughts tasted a delight—so intoxicating! So intense—!

KROLL: Hm—

ROSMER: But never written it down.

BRENDEL: Not a word. The drudgery of penpushing nauseates me. And why should I prostitute my visions when I can enjoy their purity all by myself? But now they shall be sacrificed. You know, I really feel like a mother laying her little daughter in the bridegroom's arms. But all the same, I shall sacrifice them. Sacrifice them on the altar of freedom. A series of well-planned lectures—all over the country—

REBECCA: That's fine of you, Mr. Brendel—You're giving your most precious —your most cherished—

ROSMER: The only thing.

REBECCA (looking significantly at ROSMER): How many others would do the same, would dare do it?

ROSMER (returning her look): Who knows?

BRENDEL: My audience is moved. That warms my heart and steels my will. And so I proceed to action. But one moment. (To KROLL) Mr. School-master, can you tell me if there is a Temperance Society in the town? An Association of Total Abstainers. I'm quite sure there is.

---

[5] German for "a gourmet."

KROLL: Yes, we are at your service. I myself am the President.

BRENDEL: I should have known it! Well, it's quite possible that I may come and join for a week.

KROLL: I beg your pardon—we don't take weekly members.

BRENDEL: *A la bonne heure,*[6] Herr President. Ulric Brendel never forced himself into that sort of society. (*Turning*) But I must not tarry longer in this house so rich in memories. I shall to town and there select a suitable lodging. I trust there is a decent hotel.

REBECCA: Won't you have something before you go? A warm drink?

BRENDEL: A warm drink, gracious lady?

REBECCA: A cup of tea, or—

BRENDEL: I thank the gracious chatelaine,[7] but I am loath to trespass on private hospitality. (*Waves his hand*) Farewell, gentles! (*Goes to the door and turns*) Oh, by the way John—Reverend Mr. Rosmer—would you do your erstwhile tutor a service, for old times' sake?

ROSMER: Yes, with all my heart.

BRENDEL: Good. Well, just for a day or two, will you lend me a starched white shirt—with cuffs?

ROSMER: Nothing more?

BRENDEL: You see I'm travelling on foot—this time. My luggage is following.

ROSMER: Quite. But isn't there anything else I can do?

BRENDEL: Well, I tell you what—perhaps you could spare an oldish summer coat—fairly worn.

ROSMER: Yes, yes of course I can.

BRENDEL: And if there should be a presentable pair of boots, to go with the coat—

ROSMER: I'm sure they can be arranged. As soon as we have your address, we'll send them on.

BRENDEL: Not at all. I couldn't put you to so much trouble. I can take the little trifles now.

ROSMER: Good, good. Come upstairs with me then.

REBECCA: Let me go. Mrs. Helseth and I will see to it.

BRENDEL: I could never suffer this distinguished lady—

REBECCA: Oh, nonsense. Just you come along, Mr. Brendel. (*She exits right.*)

ROSMER (*holding* BRENDEL *back*): Tell me, isn't there something else I could do for you?

BRENDEL: I really can't think of anything—why yes, dammit—! John—you haven't got eight crowns[8] on you?

ROSMER: Let me see—(*Opens his purse*) I've got two ten crowns.

BRENDEL: Oh, they'll do. I can take them. They can always be changed in town. Thanks for now. And don't forget, that's two tens I had. Goodnight, my own dear boy. Goodnight, good Sir.

---

[6] French idiom for "good for you."

[7] Lady of the house; hostess.

[8] The Norwegian krone is equivalent to about twenty cents.

(*He goes out right, where* ROSMER *takes leave of him and then shuts the door after him.*)

KROLL: Merciful Heaven! So that's the Ulric Brendel that people once thought would do something big in the world.

ROSMER (*quietly*): At least he's had the courage to live life in his own way. I don't think that's such a small thing after all.

KROLL: What? A life like his! I almost think that man could confuse your mind again.

ROSMER: Oh no, I'm quite clear now on everything.

KROLL: I wish I could think so, my dear Rosmer. You are so easy to influence.

ROSMER: Let's sit down. I want to talk to you.

KROLL: Yes.

(*They sit on the sofa.*)

ROSMER: We've made it pleasant and comfortable here, haven't we?

KROLL: Yes, it's pleasant and comfortable here now—and peaceful. Yes, you've made yourself a home here, Rosmer, and I have lost mine.

ROSMER: Oh, my friend, don't say that. There may be a wound now, but surely it will heal.

KROLL: Never, never. There'll always be a sting. It will never be the same as it was.

ROSMER: Listen, Kroll. You and I have been friends for many and many a year. Do you think our friendship could ever be broken?

KROLL: There's nothing in the world that could come between us. What gives you such an idea?

ROSMER: Well, it is so important to you that people should agree in their ideas and opinions.

KROLL: No doubt, but then we two do agree about important things anyway.

ROSMER (*low*): Not any more.

KROLL (*wanting to jump up*): What's this?

ROSMER (*holding him*): Don't get up, Kroll, I beg you.

KROLL: What is all this? I don't understand you. Tell me right out.

ROSMER: A new summer has come to me. I see through eyes new again, young again. And so I stand now—

KROLL: Where—where—?

ROSMER: Where your children stand.

KROLL: You! You! It isn't possible. You stand where, do you say?

ROSMER: On the same side as Laurits and Hilde.

KROLL (*his head sinking*): Apostate. John Rosmer an apostate.

ROSMER: I should have been so happy, so deeply content about this, apostasy as you call it. But I suffered very much, for I knew it would cause you bitter distress.

KROLL: Rosmer—Rosmer! I shall never get over this. (*Looks at him gloomily*) That you too could go and help the work of ruin and destruction in this unhappy country.

ROSMER: It is the work of emancipation I want to help.

KROLL: Oh yes, I know all about that. That's what the leaders call it, and their dupes. But do you really think you'll get emancipation from the spirit that threatens to poison our whole national life?

ROSMER: I don't like the spirit behind either of the parties. I want to try and bring people together, from all sides; I want to give my life and my life's work to this end—to create a real democracy in this country.

KROLL: So you don't think we've enough democracy! I think myself we're all in a fine way to be dragged down into the mud, among the common people.

ROSMER: That's why I want to awaken democracy to its real task.

KROLL: What task?

ROSMER: To help every man in this country to real nobility.

KROLL: Every man—!

ROSMER: As many as possible, at any rate.

KROLL: How?

ROSMER: I think, by freeing their minds and refining their wills.

KROLL: You're a dreamer, Rosmer. Will *you* free them? Will *you* refine them?

ROSMER: No my dear friend, I will only try and waken them to the idea. They must do the real work themselves.

KROLL: And do you think they can?

ROSMER: Yes.

KROLL: By their own strength?

ROSMER: Yes by their own strength. There is no other.

KROLL (*rising*): Is that a fitting observation for a priest?

ROSMER: I am no longer a priest.

KROLL: Yes, but—the faith you were reared in—?

ROSMER: I have it no longer.

KROLL: Have it no—!

ROSMER (*rising*): I have given it up. I had to give it up, Kroll.

KROLL (*shaken, but controlling himself*): I see, yes, yes, yes. The one led to the other. I suppose this was why you left the service of the Church?

ROSMER: Yes, when I was clear in my own mind—when I was quite sure it wasn't just a passing temptation, but that it was a conviction from which I never could or would be free—then I resigned.

KROLL: So this has been brewing all this time—and we—your friends, you told us nothing. Rosmer, Rosmer, how could you hide it from us?

ROSMER: I thought it concerned only me and I didn't want to give you and the others any unnecessary pain. I thought I could stay here and live as before, quiet and contented and happy. I wanted to read and absorb all the works that have been closed to me. To really become one with the great world of truth and freedom that has opened before me.

KROLL: Apostate. Every word shows it. But why do you confess your apostasy like this? And why just now?

ROSMER: You yourself forced me to it, Kroll.

KROLL: I—I force you—?

ROSMER: When I heard how violent you were at meetings—when I read your vicious speeches, the bitter attacks on those who were on the other side—the sneering denunciations of your opponents—oh Kroll—that you, you could come to that! My duty was plain. People are growing evil in this struggle. They need peace and joy and forbearance. That's why I come forward now and confess what I am. And I too want to try my strength. Kroll, couldn't you—from your side—meet me in this?

KROLL: Never as long as I live, will I compromise with the forces of destruction in the community.

ROSMER: Then let us at least fight with honorable weapons—since it seems we must fight.

KROLL: Whoever is not with me in the vital matters of life, him I no longer know. And to him I owe no consideration.

ROSMER: Does that apply to me too?

KROLL: It is you that have broken with me, Rosmer.

ROSMER: But is this a break?

KROLL: This! This is a break with all who, till now, have stood near to you. Now you must take the consequences.

(REBECCA WEST *enters right and opens the door wide.*)

REBECCA: Well, that's that. He's on his way to his great sacrifice and we can go into supper. Won't you come through, Mr. Kroll?

KROLL (*takes his hat*): Goodnight, Miss West. There is nothing more for me here.

REBECCA (*excited*): What's this? (*Shuts door and comes nearer*) Have you told him?

ROSMER: He knows now.

KROLL: We shan't let you slip through our fingers, Rosmer. We shall force you back to us.

ROSMER: I shall never come back.

KROLL: We shall see. You're not a man to stand alone.

ROSMER: But I am not quite alone.—There are two of us to bear the loneliness here.

KROLL: Ah—! (*A suspicion arising in him*) That too! Beate's words—!

ROSMER: Beate—?

KROLL (*dismissing the thought*): No, no—that was vile—forgive me.

ROSMER: What? What was that?

KROLL: Nothing. Ugh! Forgive me, goodbye. (*Going through hall door.*)

ROSMER (*following him*): Kroll, we mustn't part like this. I'll come and see you tomorrow.

KROLL (*in the hall, turning*): You shall not set foot in my house.

(*He takes his stick and goes.* ROSMER *stands a moment in the open door; then he closes it, and crosses to the table.*)

ROSMER: That doesn't matter, Rebecca. We shall see it through all right, we two faithful friends, you and I, Rebecca.

REBECCA: What do you think he meant when he said "that was vile"?

ROSMER: Don't trouble yourself about that, dear. He didn't know what he meant himself. But tomorrow I'll go in and see him. Goodnight.

REBECCA: You're going up early as usual? After this?

ROSMER: Tonight as always. I feel so relieved now it's over. See how calm I am, Rebecca dear. You take it calmly too. Goodnight.

REBECCA: Goodnight, dear friend, and sleep well.

(*Rosmer goes out through the hall door and his steps are heard going upstairs.* REBECCA *rises and pulls a bell cord by the stove. Soon after,* MRS. HELSETH *enters right.*)

REBECCA: You may as well clear the table, Mrs. Helseth. Mr. Rosmer doesn't want anything and Mr. Kroll has gone home.

MRS. HELSETH: Has Mr. Kroll gone? What was the matter with him then?

REBECCA (*taking her crochet*): He fears it will blow up for a big storm.

MRS. HELSETH: That's funny, there's not a speck of cloud to be seen in the sky.

REBECCA: Let's hope he doesn't meet the White Horse, for I'm afraid we may hear from a ghost of some sort—now.

MRS. HELSETH: Lord forgive you, Miss! Don't talk like that.

REBECCA: Well, well, well—

MRS. HELSETH (*low*): Miss, do you really think that someone here may—pass on?

REBECCA: No, I'm not thinking that. But there are so many kinds of white horses in this world, Mrs. Helseth—well, goodnight, I'm going to my room.

MRS. HELSETH: Goodnight, Miss.

(REBECCA *exits right with her crochet work.*)

MRS. HELSETH (*turns down the lamp, shaking her head and muttering to herself*): Bless us—bless us. That Miss West, the things she says sometimes.

(*The Curtain Falls.*)

Act Two

JOHN ROSMER'S *study. An entrance door in the left hand wall. In the back wall, a doorway with curtains drawn back, which leads to the bedroom. A window to the right, and in front of it a writing desk covered with books and papers. Bookshelves and cupboards against the walls. Plain furniture. An old-fashioned sofa with a table in front of it stands left.* JOHN ROSMER, *dressed in an indoor jacket, sits in a high-backed chair at the writing desk. He is cutting the pages of a pamphlet, turning them over and reading a little here and there.*

There is a knock at the door, left.

ROSMER (*without turning round*): Come in.

(*Enter* REBECCA WEST *dressed in a morning robe.*)

REBECCA: Good morning.

ROSMER: Good morning, dear. Do you want something?

REBECCA: I just wanted to know if you had slept well.

ROSMER: Oh I slept very well, very peacefully. No dreams—(*Turning round*) And you?

REBECCA: Oh yes, thank you. Towards morning—

ROSMER: I don't know when I felt so lighthearted. Oh, I'm glad I said it at last.

REBECCA: Yes, you shouldn't have kept quiet so long.

ROSMER: I don't understand how I could be such a coward.

REBECCA: Well, it wasn't quite cowardice—

ROSMER: Oh yes, yes, dear. Inside myself, I know there was some cowardice.

REBECCA: All the braver then, that you overcame it. (*Sitting down beside him at a chair by the writing desk*) But now I want to tell you about something I've done—and you mustn't be annoyed with me.

ROSMER: Annoyed? My dear, how can you think—?

REBECCA: Perhaps I took too much upon myself, but—

ROSMER: Well then, let me hear it.

REBECCA: Last night, when that Ulric Brendel was going—I gave him a note to take to Mortensgard.

ROSMER (*a little thoughtful*): But my dear Rebecca—well, what did you write?

REBECCA: I said that he would be doing you a service if he would take a little notice of that poor fellow and help him in any way he could.

ROSMER: Dear, you shouldn't have done that. You have only harmed Brendel. And Mortensgard is a man whom I would much rather avoid. You know very well I had some trouble with him once.

REBECCA: But don't you think it might be as well if you made it up with him now?

ROSMER: I? With Mortensgard? What do you mean?

REBECCA: Well, you can't feel absolutely safe now—since this has become between you and your friends.

ROSMER (*looking at her and shaking his head*): Can you really think that Kroll, or any of them, would want to take revenge, that they could bring themselves to—?

REBECCA: In the first heat of anger, my dear—nobody can be quite sure—after the way Mr. Kroll took—

ROSMER: Oh, you should know him better than that. Kroll is an honorable man through and through. I'll go into town this afternoon and talk to him. I'll talk to all of them. And you just see, it will be so easy. (MRS. HELSETH *enters through door left.*)

REBECCA (*rising*): What is it, Mrs. Helseth?

MRS. HELSETH: Mr. Kroll is downstairs in the hall.

ROSMER (*hastily rising*): Kroll!

REBECCA: Mr. Kroll!

MRS. HELSETH: He wants to know if he can come up and speak to the Pastor.

ROSMER (*to* REBECCA): What did I say!—Yes, of course he can. (*He*

goes to the door and shouts down the stairs) Come up, my dear fellow.
I'm so glad to see you!

(ROSMER *stands and holds open the door— Exit* MRS. HELSETH—
REBECCA *pulls the curtains across the doorway center back and then
tidies one or two things. Enter* KROLL, *his hat in his hand.*)

ROSMER (*quietly, moved*): I knew very well that it was not the last
time—

KROLL: Today I see this affair in a quite different light from yesterday.

ROSMER: Really, Kroll? Do you really? Now that you've thought it over—

KROLL: You completely misunderstand me. (*He puts his hat on the table
by the sofa*) I would much prefer to speak to you alone.

ROSMER: Why, cannot Miss West—?

REBECCA: No, no, Mr. Rosmer. I'll go.

KROLL (*looking her up and down*): And I must beg Miss West's pardon
for coming here so early. For catching her unawares before she's had
time to—

REBECCA: What's that? Do you find something wrong in my wearing a
morning coat here at home?

KROLL: Heaven forbid, I have no notion of what may now be the custom
at Rosmersholm.

ROSMER: Why, Kroll!—You're very strange today!

REBECCA: If you will excuse me, Mr. Kroll.

(*She goes out left.*)

KROLL: With your permission—

(*He sits on the sofa.*)

ROSMER: Yes, my dear fellow, let's sit down and talk.

(*He sits in a chair opposite* KROLL.)

KROLL: I haven't so much as closed my eyes since yesterday. I have been
lying the whole night, thinking, thinking.

ROSMER: And what have you to say today?

KROLL: It will take some time, Rosmer. Let me begin with a kind of
introduction. I can tell you something of Ulric Brendel.

ROSMER: Has he been to see you?

KROLL: No. He landed up in a squalid tavern in the lowest company.
Drank and stood drinks as long as he could pay. Then he turned on the
lot of them and called them filthy rabble. An accurate description.
Then he was beaten up and thrown into the gutter.

ROSMER: So he is really incorrigible.

KROLL: The coat he had pawned. But that will be redeemed for him. Can
you guess by whom?

ROSMER: Perhaps by you yourself?

KROLL: No. By the noble Mr. Mortensgard.

ROSMER: Ah hah.

KROLL: I understand that Mr. Brendel's first visit was to the fool and
plebeian.

ROSMER: It was very lucky for him—

KROLL: It was indeed. (*He leans across the table a little nearer to* ROSMER)
But this brings me to something which for our old—our former friendship's sake it is my duty to warn you.

ROSMER: My dear fellow, what is it?

KROLL: It's this: there is some sort of a little game going on in this house behind your back.

ROSMER: How can you think—is it Reb—is it Miss West, you mean?

KROLL: Just so. I can see her point of view, of course; she's been used to being in control here for so long. But all the same—

ROSMER: My dear Kroll. You're quite wrong about this. She and I—we don't hide anything from each other.

KROLL: Has she also confessed to you that she has entered into correspondence with the editor of the *Signal*?

ROSMER: Oh, you mean the couple of lines she gave Ulric Brendel.

KROLL: So you have found out. And do you approve that she should so enter into an association with that scandal writer, who tries week after week to make me a laughing stock in both my school work and my public life?

ROSMER: My dear Kroll, I'm sure she never thought of it like that. And besides she is free to behave exactly as she wishes, naturally. Just as I am free.

KROLL: Indeed? Yes, that fits in very well with your new way of thinking. For what you think, presumably Miss West thinks as well?

ROSMER: Yes, she does. We two have worked our way forward faithfully together.

KROLL (*looking at him, slowly shakes his head*): Oh, you are blind, bewitched.

ROSMER: Why do you say that?

KROLL: Because I dare not—will not think worse. No, no, let me finish. Do you really value my friendship, Rosmer? And my respect? Do you?

ROSMER: Surely I need not answer that question.

KROLL: Well then, there are other matters that demand answers—full explanations by you—will you agree if I hold a sort of enquiry—?

ROSMER: Enquiry?

KROLL: Yes. If I ask you one or two questions about things that it may distress you to recall? You see—this apostasy of yours—this emancipation as you call it—is tied up with so much that for your own sake you must explain to me.

ROSMER: My dear friend, ask whatever you like. I have nothing to hide.

KROLL: Well then, tell me this—what do you really think was the fundamental reason that made Beate put an end to her life?

ROSMER: Can you have any doubt? Or rather, can one rationalize the actions of someone who was ill, unhappy and deranged?

KROLL: Are you sure that Beate really was insane? The doctors seemed to think it was not so certain.

ROSMER: If the doctors could have seen her as I have seen her so often, night and day, they would have had no doubts.

KROLL: I didn't doubt it either then.

ROSMER: Oh no, unhappily there could be no doubt, at all. Of course I've told you of her wild uncontrolled passion—that she longed for me to return—oh it was horrible. And then, in the last years, her consuming tortures of self-reproach, which were utterly without foundation.

KROLL: Yes. When she was told she could never have a child.

ROSMER: Consider for yourself—such haunted agonized brooding over something not her fault at all. How could she be considered sane?

KROLL: Hm. Can you remember if there were any books in the house at that time about the purpose of marriage—according to today's advanced ideas?

ROSMER: I remember Miss West once lent me a book of that kind. The doctor left her his library as you know. But my dear Kroll, you can't think we were so careless as to let that poor invalid see such things? I can solemnly swear that we were not to blame. It was her own disordered brain.

KROLL: I can tell you one thing anyway, and that is poor Beate, miserable and obsessed, put an end to her own life so that you should be able to live happily—freely—as you desired.

ROSMER (half starting from his chair): What do you mean?

KROLL: Now you're to listen to me quietly, Rosmer. I can speak about it now. In the last years of her life, she came to me twice to pour out her dread and her despair.

ROSMER: About this same thing?

KROLL: No. The first time she declared that you were on your way to apostasy. That you would break with your religious faith.

ROSMER (eagerly): It's impossible, Kroll! Quite impossible! You must have made a mistake.

KROLL: Why?

ROSMER: Because as long as Beate was alive I was still in doubt, wrestling with myself. And I fought that battle out alone and in silence. I don't think even Rebecca—

KROLL: Rebecca?

ROSMER: Oh—Miss West. I call her Rebecca for convenience.

KROLL: I have noticed it.

ROSMER: So I cannot understand how Beate got the idea. And why didn't she speak to me about it herself? She never did. Not a word.

KROLL: Poor thing—she begged and implored me to speak to you.

ROSMER: Why didn't you?

KROLL: I never doubted that she was out of her mind. Such an accusation against a man like you!—Well, about a month later she came again. She seemed calmer. But as she was going she said: "They can soon expect the white horse at Rosmersholm."

ROSMER: Oh yes, the white horse—she was always talking of it.

KROLL: And when I tried to take her mind off such morbid thoughts she just said: "I have not much time left. For John must marry Rebecca at once."

ROSMER (almost speechless): What's that you say—! I marry—!

KROLL: That was Thursday afternoon—Saturday evening she threw herself from the bridge down into the mill race.

ROSMER: And you never warned us—!

KROLL: You know yourself she was always saying that her end was near.

ROSMER: Yes—but all the same—you should have warned us!

KROLL: I did think of it. But by then it was too late.

ROSMER: But afterwards—why didn't you—why have you kept quiet about all this?

KROLL: What was the point of my coming here to torture and harass you further? I thought it was just some of her wild fantasies—until yesterday evening.

ROSMER: But now no longer?

KROLL: Didn't Beate see rather clearly when she said you would lapse from your faith?

ROSMER (*staring straight ahead*): Yes, I don't understand that; it's quite incomprehensible.

KROLL: Incomprehensible or not—there it is. And now I ask you, Rosmer—how much truth is there in her other accusation?

ROSMER: Accusation? *Was* it an accusation?

KROLL: Perhaps you didn't notice how it was put? She was to go, she said—why? Well?

ROSMER: Well, so that I could marry Rebecca—

KROLL: That wasn't quite how it was put. Beate expressed herself differently. She said: "I haven't much time left. For now John *must* marry Rebecca *at once*."

ROSMER (*looks at him a while, then rises*): Now I understand you, Kroll.

KROLL: Well? What is your answer?

ROSMER (*still quiet and restrained*): To something so unheard of—the only proper answer would be to ask you to go.

KROLL (*rising*): Well and good.

ROSMER (*standing in front of him*): Now listen, for over a year—ever since Beate died—Rebecca West and I have lived alone here at Rosmersholm. All this time you have known Beate's accusation against us. But never for one instant have I noticed that you disapproved of Rebecca and I living here together.

KROLL: I did not know before yesterday evening that it was a free thinking man and an emancipated woman living together.

ROSMER: Ah!—So you think that purity cannot be found in the free thinking and the emancipated. You don't believe that morality can be part of their natures.

KROLL: I have no great trust in any morality that is not rooted in religion.

ROSMER: And you apply that to Rebecca and me as well? To Rebecca's and my relationship?

KROLL: I can't make an exception for you two from my opinion that there is no great gulf between free thought and—hm.

ROSMER: And what—?

KROLL: —And free love, if you want to know.

ROSMER (*low*): Are you not ashamed to say that to me? You, who have known me ever since I was a boy.

KROLL: It's just because of that that I know how easily you let yourself be led by people around you. And as for your Rebecca—oh well, your Miss West—we don't really know very much about her. In short Rosmer, I am not going to give you up—and you—you must try to save yourself in time.

ROSMER: Save myself? How—?

(MRS. HELSETH *peeps in at the door left.*)

ROSMER: What do you want?

MRS. HELSETH: I wanted to ask Miss West to come down.

ROSMER: Miss West isn't up here.

MRS. HELSETH: Oh? Isn't she? (*Looks round*) That's funny.

(*Exit* MRS. HELSETH.)

ROSMER: You were saying—?

KROLL: Listen to me. What went on in secret here while Beate was alive—and may still be going on—I will not seek to enquire. Of course you were very unhappy in your marriage and I suppose that could in a way excuse you.

ROSMER: Oh how little you really know me—

KROLL: Don't interrupt me. This is what I want to say. If this living with Miss West is to continue, you simply must keep quiet about this change—this miserable apostasy—that she has led you into. Let me speak! Let me speak! I say, think and believe and hold any opinion you like, however bad it may be, but for God's sake keep it to yourself. It's an entirely personal matter. There's absolutely no need to go shouting it all over the countryside.

ROSMER: There is a need for me to get out of a false and equivocal position.

KROLL: But Rosmer! You have a duty towards the tradition of your line. Remember that! Rosmersholm has always stood like a stronghold of law and order—for respect and esteem for all that is reverenced and preserved by the best people in our community. The whole district has taken its tone from Rosmersholm. It will create disorder and irreparable confusion if it gets known that you yourself have broken with what I will call the Rosmer family tradition.

ROSMER: My dear Kroll, I can't see it that way. I feel it my imperative duty to bring some light and happiness here where the race of Rosmer has spread gloom and oppression all this long long time.

KROLL (*looking sternly at him*): Yes indeed. That will be a worthy task for the man with whom the race dies out. Let it alone. It's not your work. You were made to be a peaceful scholar.

ROSMER: Yes, that may be so. But now I want to join in the struggle of life for once. I too.

KROLL: The struggle of life!—Do you know what that will be for you? It will be a fight to the death with all your friends.

ROSMER (*quietly*): They can't all be as fanatical as you.

KROLL: You are so simple, Rosmer! So inexperienced. You just don't realize what violence will break over you.

(MRS. HELSETH *looks in at the door left.*)

MRS. HELSETH: Miss West sent to say—

ROSMER: What is it?

MRS. HELSETH: There's a man downstairs wants a word with the Pastor.

ROSMER: Is it the man who was here last night?

MRS. HELSETH: No, it's that Mr. Mortensgard.

ROSMER: Mortensgard!

KROLL: Aha! So we've got that far! That far already.

ROSMER: What does he want with me? Why didn't you send him away?

MRS. HELSETH: Miss West said I was to ask if he could come up.

ROSMER: Tell him I have someone—

KROLL (*to* MRS. HELSETH): Let him come up please, Mrs. Helseth.

(*Exit* MRS. HELSETH.)

KROLL (*taking his hat*): I retire from the field—for the moment. But the real battle is yet to come.

ROSMER: On my word of honor, Kroll, I have nothing whatever to do with Mortensgard.

KROLL: I don't believe you any more. Not in anything. And in nothing hereafter will I believe you. It is war to the knife now. We'll try and see if we can't make you harmless.

ROSMER: Oh Kroll—how low—how very low you have sunk!

KROLL: I! And that from a man like you! Remember Beate.

ROSMER: That again!

KROLL: No, you must solve the secret of the mill race after your own conscience—if you still have such a thing.

(PETER MORTENSGARD *enters quietly and unobtrusively left. He is a small, spare man with sparse reddish hair and beard.*)

KROLL (*with a look of hatred*): Well, here is the *Signal*-lighter at Rosmersholm. (*Buttoning his coat*) Well! Now I can be in no doubt as to what course I should take.

MORTENSGARD: The *Signal* will always be ready to show Mr. Kroll the way home.

KROLL: Yes, you've always shown your goodwill. Of course there is a commandment which says we shouldn't bear false witness against our neighbor—

MORTENSGARD: Mr. Kroll need not instruct me in the commandments.

KROLL: Not even in the seventh?

ROSMER: Kroll!

MORTENSGARD: If that were needed, the Pastor is the proper man.

KROLL (*with heavy sarcasm*): The Pastor? Oh yes, the Reverend Mr. Rosmer is without question the proper man in this case. Enjoy yourselves, gentlemen.

(*Exit* KROLL, *slamming the door after him.*)

ROSMER (*stands looking at the door and speaks to himself*): Well, well— there it is. (*Turns*) Will you tell me, Mr. Mortensgard, what brings you out here to see me?

MORTENSGARD: I really came to see Miss West. I wanted to thank her for the kind letter I had yesterday.

ROSMER: I know she wrote to you. Have you spoken to her?

MORTENSGARD: For a moment. (*With a slight smile*) I hear that in one way and another there has been a change of ideas out here at Rosmersholm.

ROSMER: My ideas have changed in many ways, indeed in almost—every way.

MORTENSGARD: So Miss West said. She thought I ought to come up and have a little talk to the Pastor about it.

ROSMER: About what, Mr. Mortensgard?

MORTENSGARD: May I be allowed to announce in the *Signal* that you have changed your ideas?—That you now support the liberal and progressive party?

ROSMER: You may certainly do so; indeed I request you to announce it.

MORTENSGARD: It shall appear first thing tomorrow. It's sensational news that Pastor Rosmer of Rosmersholm means to strive for the light in *this* way as well.

ROSMER: I don't quite understand you.

MORTENSGARD: I mean that our party gets a strong moral backing every time we gain serious Christian support.

ROSMER (*somewhat surprised*): So you don't know—? Hasn't Miss West told you?

MORTENSGARD: Mr. Rosmer? Miss West seemed in rather a hurry. She said I must go upstairs and hear the rest from you yourself.

ROSMER: Well then, I must tell you that I have freed myself entirely. From everything. I now have no connection with the Church. Such things will not concern me in the future.

MORTENSGARD (*looking at him amazed*): Well!—If the moon fell out of the sky, I couldn't be more—Pastor Rosmer says himself—

ROSMER: Yes, I stand now where you have long stood. You can print this in tomorrow's *Signal* as well.

MORTENSGARD: This as well?—No, dear Mr. Rosmer—pardon me, but it would be wiser not to mention this aspect.

ROSMER: Not to mention it?

MORTENSGARD: I mean, not at first.

ROSMER: But I don't understand.

MORTENSGARD: Yes, well you see, Mr. Rosmer—. I expect you're probably not quite so familiar with the ins and outs as I am. But if you have now come over to the Liberals—and if you—as Miss West says—want to take part in the movement—you obviously want to be as much use to the party and to the movement as you possibly can.

ROSMER: Yes, I do indeed, most sincerely.

MORTENSGARD: Quite. Well, I will only point out to you, Mr. Rosmer, that if you come forward openly with all this about your leaving the Church, you immediately tie your own hands.

ROSMER: Do you think so?

MORTENSGARD: Yes. You wouldn't be much use in this part of the country, and besides—we've plenty of freethinkers already, Mr. Rosmer. I nearly said, almost too many of that sort. What the party needs now is a Christian element—something that everybody must respect. So I think it would be best if you kept quiet about these things that don't really concern the public.

ROSMER: I see. You don't want to risk getting mixed up with me if I openly declare that I have left the Church?

MORTENSGARD (*shaking his head*): I wouldn't like to, Mr. Rosmer. I've made it a rule recently not to support anyone or anything that is anti-Church.

ROSMER: You yourself have returned to the Church?

MORTENSGARD: That is my business.

ROSMER: Ah. Now I understand you.

MORTENSGARD: Mr. Rosmer, you should remember that I—I especially—am not free to behave just as I choose.

ROSMER: What prevents you?

MORTENSGARD: I'm a marked man; that's what prevents me.

ROSMER: Ah—yes.

MORTENSGARD: A marked man, Mr. Rosmer. You surely should remember. It was mostly due to you.

ROSMER: If I had thought then as I think now, I should have looked upon your offense with more sympathy.

MORTENSGARD: I think so too, Mr. Rosmer. But it's too late now. You have marked me, once and for always. Branded me for my whole life. I don't suppose you can really know what that means. But now, perhaps, you may experience it yourself.

ROSMER: I?

MORTENSGARD: Yes. You don't imagine Mr. Kroll and his circle will have much loving-kindness for such a break as yours? I hear the *County News* will be pretty bloodthirsty. It could be that you will be a marked man now. You too.

ROSMER: I think my private life is safe, Mr. Mortensgard. There is nothing in my personal conduct to justify an attack.

MORTENSGARD (*with a slight smile*): That is saying a good deal, Mr. Rosmer.

ROSMER: Perhaps. But I have a right to claim a good deal.

MORTENSGARD: Even if you ransack your life as thoroughly as you once ransacked mine?

ROSMER: You say that very oddly. What are you hinting? Is it anything definite?

MORTENSGARD: Yes. There is one thing. Only one. But it could be quite enough if a malicious enemy got hold of it.

ROSMER: Will you be so good as to tell me what it may be?

MORTENSGARD: Can't you guess, Mr. Rosmer?

ROSMER: No, certainly not. I have no idea.

MORTENSGARD: Oh well. You drag it out of me.—I have in my possession a curious letter written here at Rosemersholm.

ROSMER: Miss West's letter? Is that so curious?

MORTENSGARD: No, that letter isn't curious. But I once had another letter from this house.

ROSMER: Also from Miss West?

MORTENSGARD: No, Mr. Rosmer.

ROSMER: Well then, who sent it? Who?

MORTENSGARD: The late Mrs. Rosmer.

ROSMER: My wife! *You* had a letter from my wife?

MORTENSGARD: Yes, I had.

ROSMER: Well?

MORTENSGARD: It was just before Mrs. Rosmer's death. About a year and a half ago. And that is the curious letter.

ROSMER: Of course you knew my wife was mentally ill at that time.

MORTENSGARD: Yes. I know that there were many who thought so. But I doubt if there is anything to show it in the letter. When I say this letter is curious, I mean in another way.

ROSMER: And what in the world did my poor wife find to write to you about?

MORTENSGARD: I have the letter at home. She begins more or less by saying that she lives in great fear and dread. There are so many wicked people round here, she says. And these people only want to do you harm.

ROSMER: Me?

MORTENSGARD: Yes, so she says. Then comes the strange part. Shall I go on, Mr. Rosmer?

ROSMER: Yes, of course. Tell me everything.

MORTENSGARD: The late Mrs. Rosmer begs and implores me to be magnanimous. She knows, she says, that it was Mr. Rosmer who had me dismissed from my job as a teacher. And she earnestly begs me not to take revenge.

ROSMER: How did she think that you could take revenge?

MORTENSGARD: It says in the letter that if I should hear rumors of sinful goings on at Rosmersholm, I mustn't take them seriously because it would only be bad people trying to harm you.

ROSMER: Is this in the letter?

MORTENSGARD: You can read it yourself, sir, whenever you like.

ROSMER: But I don't understand!—What did she think they would spread rumors about?

MORTENSGARD: First, that you should have broken with your religion. This the lady absolutely denied—at that time. And next—hm—

ROSMER: Next?

MORTENSGARD: Well, she writes next—and this is rather confused—that she knows of no sinful behavior at Rosmersholm. That no wrong has been done her. And if rumors of this kind should get about, she implores me not to refer to them in the *Signal*.

ROSMER: She gives no names?

MORTENSGARD: No.

ROSMER: Who brought you this letter?

MORTENSGARD: I have promised not to say. It was handed to me one evening after dark.

ROSMER: If you had enquired at the time, you would have found that my poor unhappy wife could not be held fully responsible for her actions.

MORTENSGARD: I did enquire, Mr. Rosmer, but I must say, I didn't get quite *that* impression.

ROSMER: You didn't?—but then why do you choose to tell me now about this old, confused letter?

MORTENSGARD: To advise you to be extremely careful, Mr. Rosmer.

ROSMER: You mean, in my way of life?

MORTENSGARD: Yes. Remember you won't be quite so protected after this.

ROSMER: So you persist in thinking I have something to hide?

MORTENSGARD: I don't see why a freethinking man should not be allowed to live his life as fully as he can, but as I said, just be careful after this.

If some rumor or other gets around that's against popular prejudice, you can be sure that it will harm the whole Liberal movement—Goodbye, Pastor Rosmer.

ROSMER: Goodbye.

MORTENSGARD: Well, I'm going straight to the printers to put this great news in the *Signal*.

ROSMER: Put it all in.

MORTENSGARD: I'll put in everything that the good public needs to know.

(*He bows and exits.* ROSMER *remains standing in the doorway as he goes downstairs. The front door is heard to shut.*)

ROSMER (*in the doorway, calls softly*): Rebecca! Re—hm. (*Loud*) Mrs. Helseth, is Miss West downstairs?

MRS. HELSETH (*down in the hall*): No, sir, she's not here.

(*The curtain in the back wall is pulled aside.* REBECCA *appears in the doorway.*)

REBECCA: John!

ROSMER (*turning*): What! Were you in my bedroom? My dear, what were you doing there?

REBECCA (*goes up to him*): I have been listening.

ROSMER: Oh but Rebecca. How could you?

REBECCA: Oh, indeed I could. He was so hateful—about my morning coat.

ROSMER: So you were in there when Kroll—?

REBECCA: Yes, I wanted to know what was behind it all.

ROSMER: But I would have told you.

REBECCA: You wouldn't have told me everything. And certainly not in his own words.

ROSMER: Then you heard everything?

REBECCA: Most of it. I had to go down for a moment when Mortensgard came.

ROSMER: And then you came up again—

REBECCA: Don't think ill of me, dear friend.

ROSMER: Do whatever you yourself think right and proper. You are completely free.—But what do you say to all this, Rebecca? Oh I don't think I've ever needed you so much as now.

REBECCA: Surely we were both prepared for what had to come sometime.

ROSMER: No, no, not for this.

REBECCA: Not for this?

ROSMER: I certainly thought that sooner or later our pure beautiful friendship would be misrepresented. Not by Kroll. I could never have believed it of him. But by all those many others with their coarse and sordid minds. Oh yes, I was right to conceal our relationship so jealously. It was a dangerous secret.

REBECCA: Oh why worry yourself what all these others think? We know ourselves that we're free of guilt.

ROSMER: I? Free of guilt? Yes, I really thought so—until today. But now—now, Rebecca—

REBECCA: Well, what now?

ROSMER: How can I explain to myself Beate's terrible accusation?

REBECCA (*impetuously*): Oh don't talk about Beate! Don't think about Beate any more! You've just got free of her. She's dead.

ROSMER: Since I've heard all this, it's somehow as if, in some disturbing way, she'd come alive again.

REBECCA: Oh no—you mustn't, John! You mustn't!

ROSMER: Yes, I tell you. We must try to get to the bottom of this. How can she have strayed into such a terrible error?

REBECCA: You're not beginning to doubt yourself that she was very nearly mad?

ROSMER: Oh, my dear—that's just what I can't be certain of any longer. And besides—if it was so—

REBECCA: If it was so? Yes, what then?

ROSMER: I mean—what was the thing that finally drove her sick mind over into madness?

REBECCA: Oh what's the use of wearing yourself out with this brooding?

ROSMER: I can't help it, this gnawing doubt, Rebecca. I can't shake it off however much I want to.

REBECCA: But it can be dangerous to go on thinking in circles around this one dreary thing.

ROSMER (*walks round restlessly, thinking*): I must have given myself away somehow. She must have noticed how happy I began to feel after *you* came to us.

REBECCA: Yes, but dear, even if she did—!

ROSMER: Yes, you see—she would see that we read the same books. That we sought each other out and talked about all the new ideas. But I don't understand! I was so careful to protect her. When I think back, I did everything I could to keep her from knowing anything about it; I did, didn't I, Rebecca?

REBECCA: Yes, yes, of course you did.

ROSMER: And so did you. And yet in spite of that—oh, it's terrible to think of. She must have gone about—watching us—full of her morbid love— never saying a word—noticing everything and mistaking everything.

REBECCA (*kneading her hands*): Oh, I should never have come to Rosmersholm.

ROSMER: Just think what she must have suffered in silence. All the evil that her sick mind conjured up and built around us—didn't she ever say anything to you to make you suspect?

REBECCA (*as if startled*): To me? Do you think I should have stayed here a day longer?

ROSMER: No, no, that's obvious—oh, what a battle she must have fought. And fought alone, Rebecca. In despair and quite alone—and then finally —the poignant, accusing victory—in the mill race. (*Throws himself down into a chair by the desk, puts his elbows on the desk and covers his face with his hands.*)

REBECCA (*approaches him cautiously from behind*): Listen, John, if you could call Beate back—to you—to Rosmersholm—would you do it?

ROSMER: Oh I don't know what I would do or not do. I can only think of this thing—that can't be undone.

REBECCA: You should begin to live now, John; you *had* begun. You'd freed yourself of everything. You were feeling so happy and lighthearted—

ROSMER: Yes, dear. I really was—and then came this terrible shock—

REBECCA (*behind him, with her arms on the back of the chair*) : How beautiful it was, when we used to sit down there in the sitting room in the dusk. How we helped each other to plan a new life. You wanted to get out into real life—into the real life of today, you called it. You wanted to go from home to home bringing freedom. To win over the souls of men. To make them noble. More and more of them. Noble men!

ROSMER: Happy and noble.

REBECCA: Yes—happy.

ROSMER: For it's happiness that ennobles, Rebecca.

REBECCA: Don't you think—suffering as well? Deep suffering?

ROSMER: Yes—if you can get through it, over it, overcome it.

REBECCA: That is what you must do.

ROSMER (*shakes his head gloomily*) : I shall never get over this—altogether. There'll always be doubts and questions. Never again can I rejoice in what makes life so blissful and sweet.

REBECCA (*speaking softly over the back of the chair*) : What is it you mean, John?

ROSMER (*looking up at her*) : Peaceful, happy freedom from guilt.

REBECCA (*takes a step backwards*) : Yes, freedom from guilt. (*A short pause.*)

ROSMER (*with his elbows on the table, holds his head in his hands and stares ahead*) : And she pieced it together so systematically. First she begins to suspect my belief.—How did she get *that* idea? But she did get it. And then she became certain. And then—then of course it was so easy for her to believe all the rest. (*Sits upright in his chair and runs his hand through his hair*) Oh, these wild visions. I shall never be rid of them. I feel it. I know it. All of a sudden they'll come surging back to call up the dead.

REBECCA: Like the white horse of Rosmersholm.

ROSMER: Yes. Rushing onwards in the dark. And no sound.

REBECCA: Because of this pointless fantasy, are you going to let slip the real life you had started to make for yourself?

ROSMER: Yes, it's hard, hard, Rebecca. But I have no choice. How can I overcome this?

REBECCA (*back of the chair*) : Work to make a new life.

ROSMER (*starting, looks up*) : A new life!

REBECCA: Yes, a new life in the world outside. Live! Work! Act! Don't sit here, grubbing and brooding over insoluble riddles.

ROSMER (*rising*) : A new life! (*Walks to the door and then comes back*) There is a question in my mind. Haven't you asked yourself this question, Rebecca?

REBECCA (*breathing with difficulty*) : Tell me—what it is.

ROSMER: What do you think *our* life will be after this?

REBECCA: I think our friendship can endure—whatever may come.

ROSMER: Yes. But I didn't mean just that. I was thinking of what brought us together—that binds us so closely to each other—our common belief that a man and woman can live together in purity—

REBECCA: Yes, yes,—and so?

ROSMER: I mean that such a relationship—as ours has been—surely works best in a life that's serene and happy—

REBECCA: And so?

ROSMER: But now I see before me a life of strife and unrest and violent emotion. For I will live my life, Rebecca! I won't let myself be dragged down by misgivings. I won't have my way of life dictated by the living or—anyone else.

REBECCA: No, no! Don't let them. Be free, John!

ROSMER: But don't you see what I'm thinking? Don't you know? Don't you see how I can free myself from nagging memories—from all the unhappy past?

REBECCA: Well!

ROSMER: By creating a new living reality.

REBECCA (*fumbling for the back of the chair*): A living—? What do you—mean?

ROSMER (*nearer*): Rebecca—if I asked you now—will you be my second wife?

REBECCA (*speechless a moment, cries out in joy*): Your wife!—yours—! I! I!

ROSMER: Come. Let us try. We two will be one. Then there will be no place left empty by the dead.

REBECCA: I—in Beate's place—!

ROSMER: Then there is an end of her. Forever and ever.

REBECCA (*low and trembling*): Do you think so, John?

ROSMER: It must be so! It must! I can't—I won't go through life with a corpse on my back. Help me to throw it off, Rebecca. And let us stifle all memories in freedom and joy and passion. You shall be to me the only wife I ever had.

REBECCA (*controlled*): Never talk of this again; I shall never be your wife.

ROSMER: What! Never! Oh, then don't you think you could come to love me? Isn't there already a hint of love in our friendship?

REBECCA (*stopping her ears as if in terror*): Don't say that, John, don't talk like that!

ROSMER (*seizes her by the arm*): Yes, yes—our relationship could develop and grow. Oh I can see you feel the same, don't you, Rebecca?

REBECCA (*once more firm and calm*): Listen to me. I tell you—if you persist in this, I shall leave Rosmersholm.

ROSMER: Leave! You! You can't. It's impossible.

REBECCA: It's even more impossible that I can be your wife. Never in this world can I be that.

ROSMER (*looking at her surprised*): You say "can" and you say it so strangely. Why can you not?

REBECCA (*seizing both his hands*): Dear friend—for your sake and for mine—don't ask me why. (*Lets him go*) So there it is, John.
(*She goes to the door, left.*)

ROSMER: But after this, there can only be one question—why?

REBECCA (*turns and looks at him*) : Then it is finished.

ROSMER : Between you and me?

REBECCA : Yes.

ROSMER : It will never be finished between us two. You will never leave Rosmersholm.

REBECCA (*with her hand on the door handle*) : No, perhaps not. But if you question me any more—then it is finished.

ROSMER : Finished? How—?

REBECCA : Yes, because then I will go the way Beate went. Now you know, John.

ROSMER : Rebecca—!

REBECCA (*in the doorway, nodding slowly*) : Now you know.
    (*Exit* REBECCA.)

ROSMER (*staring at the door, as if fainting, says to himself*) : What—is—this?

(*The Curtain Falls.*)

Act Three

The sitting-room at Rosmersholm. The window and the door into the hall are open. The morning sun is shining outside.

> REBECCA WEST *dressed as in Act One stands by the window watering and arranging the flowers. Her crochet work lies on the easy chair.* MRS. HELSETH *goes round with a feather duster dusting the furniture.*

REBECCA (*after a pause*) : It's strange Mr. Rosmer is down so late today.

MRS. HELSETH : Oh, he's often late. But I expect he'll be down soon.

REBECCA : Have you seen him?

MRS. HELSETH : Just for a moment, when I was up with the coffee. He was in his bedroom, dressing.

REBECCA : I ask because he wasn't really very well yesterday.

MRS. HELSETH : No, he didn't look at all well. I wondered if there wasn't something wrong between him and his brother-in-law.

REBECCA : What do you think it could be?

MRS. HELSETH : I wouldn't know. Perhaps it's that Mortensgard set them against each other.

REBECCA : That's very possible.—Do you know anything about this Peter Mortensgard?

MRS. HELSETH : No indeed. How can you ask, Miss, a man like that?

REBECCA : You mean because he edits that deplorable paper?

MRS. HELSETH: Oh, not just that, Miss—you must have heard that he had a child by a married woman? Her husband had deserted her.

REBECCA: I have heard some talk of it. But it was such a long time before I came.

MRS. HELSETH: Bless me, yes—he was young enough then. And she should have had more sense. He would have married her, too, but of course he couldn't. Well, he's certainly had to suffer for it.—But since then, my goodness, Mr. Mortensgard has pulled himself together. There are lots of people run after him now.

REBECCA: Most of the poor people go to him when they're in trouble.

MRS. HELSETH: Oh, there could be others as well—

REBECCA (*looks at her covertly*): Really?

MRS. HELSETH (*by the sofa, dusting and rubbing vigorously*):—It could be people you'd least expect, Miss.

REBECCA (*arranging the flowers*): Surely that's just your idea, Mrs. Helseth. *You* couldn't be certain about a thing like that.

MRS. HELSETH: So I couldn't be sure eh, Miss? Well I could, for—if I let it out after all this time—I myself once took a letter to Mortensgard.

REBECCA (*turning*): No—*you* did!

MRS. HELSETH: Yes, I certainly did. And that letter was written here at Rosmersholm.

REBECCA: Really, Mrs. Helseth?

MRS. HELSETH: Yes, believe me, it was. And fine paper it was written on. And a fine red seal on the outside too.

REBECCA: And you were entrusted to go with it? Well, dear Mrs. Helseth, it's not difficult to guess who it was from.

MRS. HELSETH: Well?

REBECCA: Of course it was something poor Mrs. Rosmer wrote when she was ill—

MRS. HELSETH: You say so, Miss. I'm not saying whether it was or not.

REBECCA: What was in the letter? No, but of course—you couldn't know that.

MRS. HELSETH: Hm. But perhaps I could all the same.

REBECCA: Did she say what she was writing about?

MRS. HELSETH: No, she didn't quite do that. But when he—Mortensgard—had read it, he started asking me questions about this and that and the other and I soon guessed what was in it all right.

REBECCA: What was in it, then? Oh dear Mrs. Helseth, do tell me. Be a dear.

MRS. HELSETH: Oh no, Miss. Not for anything.

REBECCA: Oh you can tell me, we two are such friends.

MRS. HELSETH: Heaven forbid that I should tell you anything about *that*, Miss. I'll only say this: it was something horrible they had gone and got that poor sick lady to believe—

REBECCA: Who made her believe it?

MRS. HELSETH: Wicked people, Miss West, wicked people.

REBECCA: Wicked—?

MRS. HELSETH: Yes, and I'll say it again. Downright wicked they must have been.

REBECCA: Who could they be?

MRS. HELSETH: Oh I know very well what I think but please heaven, I'll keep *my* mouth shut. Mind you, there's a certain lady in the town—hm!

REBECCA: I see you mean Mrs. Kroll.

MRS. HELSETH: Oh, she's a fine one, she is. Very high and mighty she's always been with me. And she doesn't like you much either.

REBECCA: Do you think Mrs. Rosmer was quite in her right mind when she wrote that letter to Mortensgard?

MRS. HELSETH: It's a funny thing, the mind, Miss. Clean off her head I don't think she ever was.

REBECCA: But she went quite wild when she heard she could never have a child. That was when the madness started.

MRS. HELSETH: Yes, she took that very badly, poor thing.

REBECCA (*takes her crochet work and sits in chair by window*): After all, don't you think it was just as well for the Pastor, Mrs. Helseth?

MRS. HELSETH: What, Miss?

REBECCA: That there were no children. Hm?

MRS. HELSETH: Hm. I don't really know what to say.

REBECCA: Oh yes, Pastor Rosmer was never made to put up with crying children, in the house.

MRS. HELSETH: Little children don't cry at Rosmersholm, Miss.

REBECCA (*looking at her*): They don't cry?

MRS. HELSETH: Children have never cried here for as long as anyone can remember.

REBECCA: That's very strange.

MRS. HELSETH: Yes, it is strange, isn't it? It runs in the family. And there's another strange thing. When they grow up they don't laugh, never as long as they live.

REBECCA: But that would be very curious—

MRS. HELSETH: Have you ever once heard or seen the Pastor laugh?

REBECCA: No—now I think of it, you may be right. But nobody seems to laugh much round here.

MRS. HELSETH: No they don't. They say it started at Rosmersholm and then I suppose it spread itself round like a sort of infection.

REBECCA: You're a very wise woman, Mrs. Helseth.

MRS. HELSETH: Oh, don't sit there making fun of me, Miss—(*Listens*) Tut, tut—the Pastor's coming down. He doesn't like to see me dusting. (*She exits by door right.* JOHN ROSMER *with stick and hat in hand enters from the hall.*)

ROSMER: Good morning, Rebecca.

REBECCA: Good morning, dear. (*After a moment's pause, during which she crochets*) Are you going out?

ROSMER: Yes.

REBECCA: It's a beautiful day.

ROSMER: You didn't come up to see me this morning.

REBECCA: No—I didn't. Not today.

ROSMER: And will you not come up, from now on?

REBECCA: I don't know yet, dear.

ROSMER: Has anything come for me?

REBECCA: The *County News* has come.

ROSMER: The *County News*—!

REBECCA: It's on the table.

ROSMER (*puts down his hat and stick*): Is there anything—?

REBECCA: Yes.

ROSMER: You didn't send it up—

REBECCA: You'll read it soon enough.

ROSMER: Oh, I see. (*Takes up the paper and reads, standing by the table*) What!—"Cannot warn too strongly against traitors, men of no character"— (*Looks at her*) They call me a traitor, Rebecca.

REBECCA: They name no names.

ROSMER: It makes no difference. (*Reads on*)—"Secret traitors to the good cause"—"Judases who boldly announce their apostasy as soon as they think the moment propitious and—profitable." "Reckless outrage upon the good name of an ancient family"—"In the confident expectation that those temporarily in power will not disappoint them of a suitable reward." (*Lays paper on table*) And they write this about me. They, who have known me so long and so well. This, that they don't even believe themselves. This, that they know hasn't a true word in it—but they write it all the same.

REBECCA: There is more.

ROSMER (*takes up the paper*):—"Some excuse in inexperience and lack of judgement," "pernicious influence"—"Perhaps extending to matters which, for the moment we will forbear to make the subject of public discussion and condemnation"—(*Looks at her*) What's this?

REBECCA: That's aimed at me, clearly.

ROSMER (*puts the paper down*): Rebecca, this is the behavior of dishonorable men.

REBECCA: Yes, they've not much to learn from Mortensgard.

ROSMER (*walking about the floor*): This *must* be put right. Everything that's good in people will be lost if this goes on. But it shan't! It mustn't. Oh, how glad—how happy I'd feel if I could let some light into this filth and nastiness.

REBECCA (*rising*): Yes! This is true. Here's something great and sublime!

ROSMER: If I could bring them to see themselves! Make them angry and ashamed of themselves. Bring them together in forbearance—in love, Rebecca.

REBECCA: Yes. There is something great to live for. Put all your strength into it and you must succeed.

ROSMER: I think it might come. Oh, what joy it would be to live then. No more bitter competition, only emulation. All eyes fixed on the same goal. All thoughts and energies drawn forward—upward, each in its own natural way.—Happiness for all—through all. (*Happens to look outside, starts, and says gloomily*) Ah! Not through me.

REBECCA: Not—? Not through you—?

ROSMER: And not for me.

REBECCA: Oh, don't think like that.

ROSMER: Happiness—Rebecca—happiness above all things is that peaceful sense of freedom from guilt.

REBECCA (*staring in front of her*) : Guilt—

ROSMER: You don't know what guilt means. But I—

REBECCA: You least!

ROSMER (*points out of the window*) : The mill race.

REBECCA: Oh, John—!

(MRS. HELSETH *looks in at the door right.*)

MRS. HELSETH: Miss West!

REBECCA: Later, later. Not now.

MRS. HELSETH: Just a word, Miss.

(REBECCA *goes to the door.* MRS. HELSETH *tells her something. They whisper together for a while.* MRS. HELSETH *nods and goes.*)

ROSMER (*uneasy*) : Something for me?

REBECCA: No, just the housekeeping.—Now John dear, you should go and get some fresh air. Have a good long walk.

ROSMER (*takes his hat*) : Yes, come along, we'll go together.

REBECCA: No, dear, I can't just now. You must go alone. But no more sad thoughts. Promise me.

ROSMER: I can't stop thinking about it—I'm afraid.

REBECCA: Oh that something so without foundation can take such a hold of you—!

ROSMER: But—is it so without foundation, Rebecca? I've lain thinking all night, perhaps Beate was right after all.

REBECCA: What do you mean?

ROSMER: When she thought I loved you, Rebecca.

REBECCA: Right in *that!*

ROSMER (*puts his hat on the table*) : I keep asking myself if we two haven't deceived ourselves all along when we called our feeling for each other friendship?

REBECCA: Do you mean that it might well have been called—

ROSMER: Love. Yes, my dear, I mean that. Even while Beate was alive I only thought of you. It was you I longed for. It was with you I felt that serene passionless joy. Rebecca—wasn't the life we shared like the sweet hidden love between children? Without desire and without dreams. Don't you think so? Tell me.

REBECCA (*fighting with herself*) : Oh, I don't know what I should answer.

ROSMER: And this living with each other, for each other, that we have called friendship—no, my dear—our relationship has been a spiritual marriage— perhaps from the very first. That's why I'm guilty—I had no right to it— no right for Beate's sake.

REBECCA: No right to be happy, John? Do you believe that?

ROSMER: She saw our relationship through the eyes of *her* love. Judged our relationship by *her* kind of love. Of course, Beate could not judge other- wise than she did.

REBECCA: But why blame yourself for Beate's delusion?

ROSMER: Because she loved me—in *her* way—she threw herself into the mill race. That actually happened, Rebecca. I can never forget that.

REBECCA: Oh, don't think of anything but the wonderful task you've set yourself!

ROSMER (*shaking his head*) : Not now. Not by me. Not after what I know.

REBECCA: Not by you?

ROSMER: A cause that has its roots in sin can never succeed.

REBECCA: Oh this is something born in you—family doubts, family anxieties, family scruples. They chatter round here about the dead coming back like a rushing white horse. I think this is the same sort of thing.

ROSMER: What does it matter what it is if I can't be rid of it? What I say is true, Rebecca; the cause that's to win through to lasting victory must be led by a man who's happy and free from guilt.

REBECCA: Is happiness so absolutely necessary for *you*, John?

ROSMER: Happiness. Oh yes, dear—it is indeed.

REBECCA: For you, who can never laugh?

ROSMER: Oh yes, in spite of that, I have a great capacity for happiness.

REBECCA: Now you must go for your walk, dear, a good long one. Yes? Here's your hat and here's your stick.

ROSMER (*takes them*): Thank you. And you're not coming with me?

REBECCA: No, I can't come now.

ROSMER: Ah well, you're always with me all the same.

(*He goes out through the hall door. After a moment* REBECCA *peeps out from behind the open door and then she goes over to the door right.*)

REBECCA (*opens the door and speaks at half-voice*): All right, Mrs. Helseth, you can let him in now.

(*She crosses to window. Shortly afterwards,* KROLL *enters right. He greets her silently and formally and keeps his hat in his hand.*)

KROLL: Has he gone?

REBECCA: Yes.

KROLL: Does he stay out long?

REBECCA: Generally. But he's not himself today. So, if you don't want to meet him—

KROLL: No, no. I want to speak to you. Alone.

REBECCA: Then we'd better not waste time. Sit down, Mr. Kroll.

(*She sits in the easy chair by the window;* KROLL *sits on a chair beside her.*)

KROLL: Miss West, you can hardly appreciate how deeply and painfully I have taken to heart this change in John Rosmer.

REBECCA: We were ready for this—at first.

KROLL: Only at first?

REBECCA: Mr. Rosmer was quite confident that sooner or later you would join him.

KROLL: I!

REBECCA: You and all his other friends.

KROLL: You see! So feeble is his judgement when it comes to people and the real business of living.

REBECCA: However—since he now feels he must free himself from everybody—

KROLL: Yes, but look—that's *precisely* what I don't believe.

REBECCA: What do you believe then?

KROLL: I think it's *you* who are behind it all.

REBECCA: You got that from your wife, Mr. Kroll.

KROLL: It doesn't matter where I got it from. The point is, I have a strong suspicion—I say, an extremely strong suspicion when I look back and consider your behavior since you came here.

REBECCA (*looks at him*): I seem to remember that once upon a time you had an extremely strong *belief* in me, dear Mr. Kroll. I nearly said, a warm belief.

KROLL (*low*): Whom could you not bewitch—if you put your mind to it.

REBECCA: Put my mind to it—!

KROLL: Yes, you did. I'm no longer such a fool as to think there was any feeling in your little game. You simply wanted to get a footing at Rosmersholm. To settle yourself here. And I had to help you, I see that now.

REBECCA: So you have quite forgotten that it was Beate who begged and implored me to move out here.

KROLL: Yes, when you'd bewitched her too. Can it be called friendship what she came to feel for you? It was adoration, idolatry. It turned into—what shall I say?—into a sort of desperate passion. Yes, that's it.

REBECCA: Be so good as to remember the state your sister was in. You certainly can't call me unbalanced.

KROLL: No, certainly not. But that makes it all the more dangerous for those whom you want to get into your power. It's so easy for you to work things out, to control yourself. Just because you're so cold-hearted.

REBECCA: Cold? Are you so sure?

KROLL: I'm absolutely certain now. Otherwise you couldn't have continued here, year after year, pursuing your purpose so relentlessly. Well, well—you've got what you wanted. He and everything else here are in your power. But in order to achieve this, you haven't scrupled to make him unhappy.

REBECCA: That's not true. It's not me. It is you yourself who have made him unhappy.

KROLL: Have I?

REBECCA: Yes. When you led him to believe that he was responsible for Beate's terrible death.

KROLL: Did he feel it so deeply?

REBECCA: You know he did. A sensitive man like him—

KROLL: I thought that a so-called emancipated man was above such scruples.—But there it is! Ah well—it was to be expected. The descendant of the men who gaze down on us here,—he won't be able to free himself so easily from what's been handed down from generation to generation.

REBECCA (*looking down thoughtfully*): John Rosmer's roots are deep in his family. That's very true.

KROLL: Yes, and you should have thought of that if you had any sympathy for him. But I suppose such consideration was beyond you. Your starting point was worlds away from his.

REBECCA: What starting point do you mean?

KROLL: I mean starting point in origin, in parentage—Miss West.

REBECCA: It's quite true,—I come from fairly poor people but all the same—

KROLL: I am not speaking of rank or position. I'm thinking of a moral starting point.

REBECCA: Starting point—? For what?

KROLL: For your birth.

REBECCA: What's this you're saying?

KROLL: I only allude to it because it explains your entire conduct.

REBECCA: I don't understand. Will you please explain!

KROLL: I really thought you knew. Otherwise it seems very odd that you let yourself be adopted by Dr. West.

REBECCA (*rising*): So that's it! Now I understand.

KROLL: —And took his name. Your mother's name was Gamvik.

REBECCA (*crosses the room away from* KROLL): My father's name was Gamvik, Mr. Kroll.

KROLL: Your mother's occupation must of course have often brought her into contact with the local doctor.

REBECCA: You're quite right.

KROLL: And as soon as your mother was dead, he takes you to live with him. He treats you badly. And still you stay with him. You know that he won't leave you a penny. In fact you only get a case full of books. And yet you stay with him. Put up with him. Care for him right to the end.

REBECCA (*by the table, looks at him scornfully*): And since I did all this— it's clear to you that there is something immoral—something criminal in my birth!

KROLL: What you did for him I attribute to unconscious filial instinct. All the rest of your actions are, I consider, the result of your origin.

REBECCA (*vehement*): But there is not one single word of truth in what you're saying. And I can prove it. For Dr. West did not come to Finmark till after I was born.

KROLL: Excuse me—Miss West. He came up the year before. This I have ascertained.

REBECCA: You're wrong! You're absolutely wrong!

KROLL: You said yesterday that you were twenty-nine. Getting on for thirty.

REBECCA: Really? Did I say that?

KROLL: Yes you did. And from that I can calculate—

REBECCA: Stop! That won't help you to calculate. I may as well tell you, I'm a year older than I give myself out to be.

KROLL (*smiling incredulously*): Really? This is something new. How did this happen?

REBECCA: When I reached twenty-five, I felt—unmarried as I was—I was getting altogether too old. And so I began to take a year off my age.

KROLL: You? An emancipated woman. Do you cherish prejudices about a marriageable age?

REBECCA: Yes, it was stupid and silly. But there's always some little thing or other that you can't shake off. That's how we are.

KROLL: That's as may be. But the calculation could be right all the same. Dr. West was up for a flying visit the year before he was appointed.

REBECCA (*impetuously*): That's not true!

KROLL: Is it not true?

REBECCA: No, because my mother never spoke of it.

KROLL: She didn't, eh?

REBECCA: No, never. Nor did Dr. West. Not a word.

KROLL: Could it be because they both had good reason to skip a year? Just like you, Miss West. Perhaps it runs in the family.

REBECCA (*walks about, kneading and wringing her hands*): It's not possible. You just want to trap me. This can never be true. It can't be true. Never, never—!

KROLL (*rising*): But my dear—why in heaven's name do you take on in this way? You quite alarm me. What am I to think—!

REBECCA: Nothing. You mustn't think anything.

KROLL: Then you really must explain to me why this matter—this possibility—so upsets you.

REBECCA (*controlling herself*): It's really quite simple, Mr. Kroll. I've no desire to be known here as an illegitimate child.

KROLL: Quite so. Well yes, let us be content with that explanation—for the moment. But you seem to have retained yet another—prejudice.

REBECCA: Yes, I suppose I have.

KROLL: Well I think it's the same with most of what you call your emancipation. You read yourself into a whole heap of new thoughts and ideas. You've made a sort of acquaintance with researches going on in various fields—researches which seem to upset much of what has hitherto been accepted amongst us without question. But all this has been merely booklearning to you, Miss West. An intellectual acquaintance. It hasn't got into your blood.

REBECCA (*thoughtfully*): You may be right.

KROLL: You think about it and you'll see. And if it's like this with you, it's easy to see how it is with John Rosmer. It's sheer madness—it's plunging straight into disaster for *him* openly to declare himself an apostate! Think—with his sensitivity! Imagine *him* disowned—hounded out of his own circle. Bitterly attacked by all the best people. He'll never be able to stand it.

REBECCA: He *must* stand it! It's too late now to turn back.

KROLL: It's not too late. Not by any means. What's done can be quietly undone—or at least it can be explained away as a temporary though regrettable aberration. But—*one* of the conventions really must be observed.

REBECCA: And what on earth is that?

KROLL: You must get him to legalize the relationship, Miss West.

REBECCA: His relationship with me?

KROLL: Yes, you must see to that.

REBECCA: You simply cannot get rid of the idea that we have a relationship that needs—legalizing?

KROLL: I don't want to mix myself up in the business any more. But I have certainly noticed that the *point* where it becomes easiest to break with so-called convention is in—hm.

REBECCA: In the relations between men and women you mean?

KROLL: Yes, frankly I do.

REBECCA (*crosses room and looks out of the window*): I almost said—if only you were right, Mr. Kroll.

KROLL: What do you mean? You said that very strangely.

REBECCA: Ah, what indeed! Let's not say anything more about it.—Ah—here he comes.

KROLL: Already! I'll go.

REBECCA (*goes to him*): No—stay here. Because now you're going to hear something.

KROLL: Not now. I don't think I could bear to see him.

REBECCA: I beg you to stay. Please do. If you don't, you will regret it later. It's the last time I shall ask you anything.

KROLL (*looks at her surprised and puts down his hat*): Very well, Miss West, so be it.

(*There is a short silence; then* JOHN ROSMER *enters from the hall.*)

ROSMER (*sees* KROLL *and stops in the doorway*): What!—Are you here?

REBECCA: He didn't want to see you, John.

KROLL (*involuntarily*): John!

REBECCA: Yes, Mr. Kroll. John and I—we call each other by our Christian names. That is due to our relationship.

KROLL: Is that what you promised I should hear?

REBECCA: That—and something more.

ROSMER (*coming nearer*): What is the purpose of your visit here today?

KROLL: I wanted to try once more to stop you and to win you back.

ROSMER (*pointing to the paper*): After that?

KROLL: I did not write it.

ROSMER: Did you do anything to stop it?

KROLL: That would have been disloyal to the cause I serve. And besides it was not in my power.

REBECCA (*tears newspaper into pieces, crumples them together and throws them into the back of the stove*): There now! It's out of sight. Let it be out of mind. There's going to be no more of that, John.

KROLL: Oh, if only you could really make sure of that.

REBECCA: Let's sit down, dear. All three. Then I'll tell you everything.

ROSMER (*sits without thinking*): What has happened to you, Rebecca? This unnatural calm—whatever is it?

REBECCA: The calm of resolution. (*She sits*) You sit down too, Mr. Kroll. (KROLL *sits on the sofa.*)

ROSMER: The calm of resolution!

REBECCA: I want to give you back what you need in order to live your life. You shall have your happiness, your freedom from guilt, my dear friend.

ROSMER: But what *is* all this?

REBECCA: I will just tell you what happened. Nothing else is needed.

ROSMER: Well!

REBECCA: When I came down here from Finmark—with Dr. West—I felt as if a great new and wide world opened before me. The Doctor had taught me a few things. The little I knew about life at that time— (*Low and almost impossible to hear*) And then—

KROLL: And then?

ROSMER: But Rebecca—I know all this.

REBECCA (*pulls herself together*): Yes, yes—you're quite right. You know it all really.

KROLL (*looking hard at her*) : Perhaps I had better go.

REBECCA: No, my dear Mr. Kroll, you must stay. (*To* ROSMER) Well, it was like this, you see—I wanted to take part in the new era, that was coming, take part in the new thinking. Then, one day, Mr. Kroll told me that Ulrich Brendel had had a great influence on you when you were a boy, and I thought I might be able to make use of that.

ROSMER: You came here with a hidden design—!

REBECCA: I wanted us both to go forward together in freedom. Further—and further forward. But there was this gloomy insurmountable wall between you and real freedom.

ROSMER: What wall?

REBECCA: I mean this, John. That you could only develop out in the bright sunshine. And here you were languishing and sickening in the gloom of your marriage.

ROSMER: You have never spoken of my marriage in *this* way before.

REBECCA: No, I didn't dare. I would have frightened you.

KROLL (*nods to* ROSMER) : Do you hear that?

REBECCA (*going on*) : —But I saw well enough there was a way out for you. But only one way. And so I took action.

ROSMER: Took action? What do you mean?

KROLL: Do you mean to say—?

REBECCA: Yes, John— (*Rises*) No, sit still. You too, Mr. Kroll. But it must be said now. It was not you, John. You are free of guilt. It was I who lured,—who finally ended by luring, Beate into her delusion.

ROSMER (*jumping up*) : Rebecca!

KROLL (*rises from the sofa*) : —into the delusion!

REBECCA: Into the delusion—that led to the mill race. Now you know. Both of you.

ROSMER (*as if stunned*) : But I don't understand—what's she standing there and saying? I don't understand—!

KROLL: Oh, yes. I'm beginning to understand.

ROSMER: But what did you do? What was there you could say to her? There was nothing. Absolutely nothing!

REBECCA: She came to know that you meant to free yourself from your old beliefs.

ROSMER: Yes, but I didn't know myself then.

REBECCA: I knew that you soon would.

KROLL (*nodding to* ROSMER) : Aha!

ROSMER: And then? What else? I want to know everything now.

REBECCA: Some time afterwards—well, I asked, begged her to let me leave Rosmersholm.

ROSMER: Why did you want to leave?

REBECCA: I didn't want to leave, I wanted to stay here. But I told her it would be best for us all—for me to go away in time. I let her understand that if I stayed here any longer—it could be—that something might happen.

ROSMER: You said and did this?

REBECCA: Yes, John.

ROSMER: *This* is what you call taking action.

REBECCA (*in a broken voice*): I called it that, yes.

ROSMER (*after a pause*): Have you confessed everything, Rebecca?

REBECCA: Yes.

KROLL: Not everything.

REBECCA (*looks at him, frightened*): What else should there be?

KROLL: In the end didn't you give Beate to understand that it was necessary—not just that it was best—but that it was necessary, for your sake and
Rosmer's, that you should leave—as soon as possible—well?

REBECCA (*low and indistinct*): Perhaps I did say something like that.

ROSMER (*sinking into the easy chair by the window*): And she believed it,
this web of lies and deceit—that sick woman believed it, utterly. (*Looks
at* REBECCA) And she never came to me, never spoke a word of it. O
Rebecca—I see it in your face—you persuaded her not to!

REBECCA: She had got it into her head that she—as a childless wife—had no
right to be here. And so she began to imagine that it was her duty to
make way.

ROSMER: And you—didn't you do anything to dissuade her?

REBECCA: No.

KROLL: Perhaps you even encouraged her? Answer! Did you?

REBECCA: I believe she may have thought so.

ROSMER: Yes, yes—and she followed you in everything. And so she made
way. (*Jumping up*) How could—how could you carry through this horrible game?

REBECCA: I felt it was a choice between two lives, John.

KROLL (*strong and authoritative*): *You* had no right to make such a choice!

REBECCA (*impetuous*): Do you think it was done coldly, cunningly? I was
not the same person that I am now, standing here telling you this. Besides, I think there are two sorts of will in everyone. I wanted Beate out
of the way. Somehow or other. But I never thought it would happen all
the same. With every step I took, with every step I ventured forward, I
felt as if something seemed to shriek inside me. No further! Not a step
further!—But I *couldn't* stop. I *had* to venture just a little bit further.
Just one step—and then another—always one more. And so it happened.
That's the way things like that do happen.

(*Short silence.*)

ROSMER (*to* REBECCA): What do you think will become of you? After this?

REBECCA: It doesn't matter much.

KROLL: Not a word that suggests remorse. Perhaps you feel none?

REBECCA (*coldly dismissive*): Excuse me, Mr. Kroll, that is my concern.
I shall have to settle it with myself.

KROLL (*to* ROSMER): And you have lived under the same roof with this
woman. In the closest confidence. (*Looking at the portraits*) Ah—those
that are gone—if they could only see us now!

ROSMER: Are you going into the town?

KROLL (*taking his hat*): Yes. The sooner the better.

ROSMER (*takes his hat as* KROLL *has done*): Then I will go with you.

KROLL: You will! Ah, I was sure we hadn't quite lost you.

ROSMER: Come, Kroll! Come along!

(*They both exit by the hall, without looking at* REBECCA. *Pause.* REBECCA *goes cautiously to the window and glances covertly through the flowers.*)

REBECCA: Not over the footbridge today either. The long way round. Never over the mill race. Never. (*Moves away from window*) Well, well then! (*She crosses and pulls the bell rope. Shortly after, enter* MRS. HELSETH *from the right.*)

MRS. HELSETH: Yes, Miss?

REBECCA: Mrs. Helseth, I wonder if you would be kind enough to have my trunk brought down from the attic?

MRS. HELSETH: Trunk?

REBECCA: Yes, you know, the brown sealskin.

MRS. HELSETH: Yes, of course, but bless me, are you going on a journey, Miss?

REBECCA: Yes—I am going away on a journey, Mrs. Helseth.

MRS. HELSETH: Straight away!

REBECCA: As soon as I've packed.

MRS. HELSETH: Well, I never heard the like! But I'm sure you'll be back soon, Miss.

REBECCA: I'm never coming back.

MRS. HELSETH: Never? But goodness me, what's to become of Rosmersholm if Miss West isn't here any more? Just as everything was getting so nice and comfortable for the Pastor.

REBECCA: Yes, but I had a scare today, Mrs. Helseth.

MRS. HELSETH: A scare. Oh, my good Lord—what was that?

REBECCA: Yes, I think I may have caught a glimpse of the white horse.

MRS. HELSETH: The white horse! In broad daylight.

REBECCA: Oh, they are out early and late—the white horses of Rosmersholm. (*With a change of voice*) Well then—the trunk, Mrs. Helseth.

MRS. HELSETH: Very well, the trunk.

(*They both exit right.*)

(*The Curtain Falls.*)

Act Four

The living room at Rosmersholm. It is late evening. The lamp, with a shade over it, stands burning on the table.

REBECCA WEST *stands by the table packing small articles into a travelling bag. Her cloak, hat and the white crocheted shawl are lying over the back of the sofa. Enter* MRS. HELSETH *right.*

MRS. HELSETH (*speaking low and constrainedly*): All the things have been brought down, Miss. They're in the kitchen passage.

REBECCA: Good. You've told the coachman?

MRS. HELSETH: Yes. He wants to know what time he should bring the carriage.

REBECCA: I think about eleven o'clock. The steamer leaves at midnight.

MRS. HELSETH (*hesitates a little*): But the Pastor? Suppose he's not back by then?

REBECCA: I shall go in any case. If I don't see him, you can say that I'll write. A long letter. Say that.

MRS. HELSETH: I suppose a letter will do. But poor Miss West—I think you ought to try and speak to him again.

REBECCA: Perhaps—and yet, perhaps not.

MRS. HELSETH: Well, I never thought I should live to see this!

REBECCA: Why, what did you think, Mrs. Helseth?

MRS. HELSETH: Well, I really thought Mr. Rosmer was more of a man than that.

REBECCA: More of a man?

MRS. HELSETH: Yes, really I did.

REBECCA: But my dear Mrs. Helseth, what do you mean?

MRS. HELSETH: I mean what's true and right, Miss. He shouldn't get out of it in *this* way.

REBECCA (*looking at her*): Now look here, Mrs. Helseth. Just tell me why you think I'm going away.

MRS. HELSETH: I suppose it can't be helped, Miss, goodness knows. Oh well, well, well. But I still don't think the Pastor's behaved very well. Mortensgard had some excuse. Her husband was still alive. Those two couldn't get married however much they wanted to. But the Pastor, well —hm!

REBECCA (*with a faint smile*): Can you really think such a thing of me and Pastor Rosmer?

MRS. HELSETH: Of course not, I mean—not before today.

REBECCA: But today—?

MRS. HELSETH: Well—after all the dreadful things about the Pastor that people say is in the papers—

REBECCA: Aha!

MRS. HELSETH: Well I mean to say, you can believe anything of a man that'll go over to Mortensgard's religion.

REBECCA: Ah, yes, perhaps. But me then? What about me?

MRS. HELSETH: Heaven help us, Miss—I don't think you're so much to blame. It can't be so easy for a woman to resist that's on her own.— We're all human—after all, Miss West.

REBECCA: Yes, Mrs. Helseth. We are all human.—What are you listening for?

MRS. HELSETH (*low*): Oh gracious—I believe it's him coming back.

REBECCA (*starting*): So after all—! (*Firmly*) Well then. So be it.

(JOHN ROSMER *enters from the hall.*)

ROSMER (*sees travelling things, turns to* REBECCA *and asks*): What is this?

REBECCA: I am leaving.

ROSMER: Now?

REBECCA: Yes. (*To* MRS. HELSETH) Well then, eleven o'clock.

MRS. HELSETH: Very good, Miss.

(*She exits right.*)

ROSMER (*after a short pause*): Where are you going then, Rebecca?

REBECCA: Up north, with the steamer.

ROSMER: North? What will you do in the north?

REBECCA: It's where I came from.

ROSMER: But there is nothing for *you* up there now.

REBECCA: There is nothing for me down here, either.

ROSMER: What do you think you will do?

REBECCA: I don't know. I just want to finish with it all.

ROSMER: Finish with it?

REBECCA: Rosmersholm has broken me.

ROSMER (*his attention roused*): What?

REBECCA: Broken me utterly to pieces. I was so strong. I had the courage of a free will when I came here. Now I have submitted to a law that was quite alien to me. After this, I don't think I'll have the courage for anything ever again.

ROSMER: Why not? What is this law you say that you—?

REBECCA: Don't let's talk of it now, my dear—what happened with you and Mr. Kroll?

ROSMER: We have made peace.

REBECCA: Ah well. So it came to that.

ROSMER: He got all our old friends together at his house. They've made me see that the work of ennobling men's minds—is not for me—and besides you know, it's a hopeless idea anyway—I'm going to let it alone.

REBECCA: Well, well—perhaps it's best like that.

ROSMER: Is *that* what you say now? Do you think so *now?*

REBECCA: I've come to think so. In the last couple of days.

ROSMER: You are lying, Rebecca.

REBECCA: Lying—!

ROSMER: Yes, you're lying. You never believed in me. You've never believed that I was the man to lead the cause through to victory.

REBECCA: I thought that we two could do it together.

ROSMER: That's not true. You thought that you yourself could do something big in the world. That you could use me to help you. That I could serve your purpose. *That's* what you thought.

REBECCA: Listen, John—

ROSMER (*sits drearily on the sofa*): Oh let me be! I see it all now. I've been like a tool in your hand.

REBECCA: Listen now, John. Let's talk a bit more about this. It'll be for the last time. (*Sits in a chair by the sofa*) I was going to write to you about all this—when I got north again. But it's much better for you to hear it now.

ROSMER: Have you still more to confess?

REBECCA: The greatest of all.

ROSMER: The greatest?

REBECCA: The thing you've never guessed. But it gives shape and meaning to everything else.

ROSMER (*shaking his head*): I don't know what you're talking about.

REBECCA: It's quite true that I once played my cards so as to gain an entrance here into Rosmersholm. I thought I might be able to do myself some good here. In one way or another—

ROSMER: Well, you got what you wanted.

REBECCA: I think I could have got anything I wanted, anything—in those days. I still had my courage, my free will. I had nobody to consider. Nothing to turn me from my path. But then came the beginning of what's broken my will and made me a miserable coward for the rest of my life.

ROSMER: What came? Do speak so that I can understand.

REBECCA: It came over me—that fierce, passionate, uncontrollable desire—. Oh John—!

ROSMER: Desire?—You! For what?

REBECCA: For you.

ROSMER (*wanting to jump up*): What is this!

REBECCA (*restraining him*): Don't get up, my dear. I'll tell you more about it.

ROSMER: You mean to say—you have loved me—in that way?

REBECCA: I called it loving—then,—I felt it was love. But it wasn't. It was what I said: a wild uncontrollable desire!

ROSMER (*with difficulty*): Rebecca—is it really you yourself—you—sitting there and telling me all this!

REBECCA: Yes, it's hard to believe, isn't it!

ROSMER: Out of this—because of this—you took action, as you called it.

REBECCA: It swept over me like a storm at sea. It was like one of those storms we get up north in wintertime. It takes you up and carries you with it, you know—as long as it lasts. There's no use resisting.

ROSMER: So it swept the unhappy Beate out into the mill race.

REBECCA: Yes, it was like a fight for life between Beate and me.

ROSMER: You were certainly the strongest at Rosmersholm. Stronger than Beate and me put together.

REBECCA: I knew you well enough to see—that there was no way out for you until you were made free in body—and mind.

ROSMER: But I don't understand you, Rebecca. You—you yourself—everything you do puzzles me. I am free now—in body, in mind, in my actions. You stand right before the goal you first set yourself. And yet—

REBECCA: Never have I stood further from my goal than I do now.

ROSMER: —and yet—when I asked you yesterday—begged you: be my wife—you cried out that it could never be as though you were terrified.

REBECCA: I cried out in despair, my dear.

ROSMER: Why?

REBECCA: Because Rosmersholm has broken my spirit. Sapped my courage, crushed it. Once upon a time I would have dared anything, everything. But now I have lost the power to act.

ROSMER: Tell me how it has happened.

REBECCA: It has happened through living here together with you.

ROSMER: But how? How?

REBECCA: When I was alone with you here—and you had become yourself—

ROSMER: Yes, yes?

REBECCA: —For you were never completely yourself so long as Beate was alive—

ROSMER: Alas, you're right.

REBECCA: But when I was living with you here—in solitude—in peace—when you told me all your thoughts—without reserve—every fine and sensitive feeling—just as it came to you—then began the great change in me. Little by little. Almost unnoticed—but in the end overwhelming. Right to my very depths.

ROSMER: Oh, what is this, Rebecca?

REBECCA: All the other—that ugly desire that drowns the senses, ebbed far, so far away from me. All those violent passions sank down into stillness. And I was wrapped in peace—tranquil like the mountain cliffs at home where the birds nest under the midnight sun.

ROSMER: Tell me more. Tell me everything.

REBECCA: There isn't much more. There is only *this*. That then love came to me. The great selfless love that was content in the life we shared together.

ROSMER: Oh, if only I had had the smallest idea of all this.

REBECCA: It's better like this. Yesterday—when you asked me if I would be your wife—my heart sang—

ROSMER: Yes, you were happy, weren't you, Rebecca! I felt it!

REBECCA: For a moment, yes. I forgot myself. It was my free buoyant will of the old days trying to take hold again. But it's so weak now, there's no strength left.

ROSMER: How do you think this has happened to you?

REBECCA: It's the Rosmer family view of life—or *your* view of life anyway, that has infected my will.

ROSMER: Infected?

REBECCA: Made it sick. Bound me under a law that used to mean nothing to me. You—living together with you—has made me noble—

ROSMER: Oh, if I could believe that!

REBECCA: You can confidently believe it. The Rosmer view of life does make men noble. But—(*Shaking her head*)—but—but—

ROSMER: But? What?

REBECCA: But it kills happiness, my dear.

ROSMER: Do you feel that, Rebecca?

REBECCA: For me, at least.

ROSMER: Yes, but are you so sure? If I asked you again—? Begged you—

REBECCA: Ah, my dear. Let's not talk of that again. It's impossible—! Yes, John, you have to know, something happened in the past.

ROSMER: Something more than you have told me already?

REBECCA: Yes. Something different and something more.

ROSMER (*with a faint smile*): It's odd, isn't it, Rebecca? You know, I've had a sort of feeling that there might have been something like that.

REBECCA: And yet you still—? Even so—?

ROSMER: I never thought of it seriously. I only played with it in my mind.

REBECCA: If you like, I'll tell you about that as well.

ROSMER (*putting it aside*): No, no. Don't tell me anything. Whatever it is, I can forget it.

REBECCA: But I cannot.

ROSMER: Oh Rebecca—!

REBECCA: That's the terrible thing, that now, when you freely offer me every happiness, now I am changed so that my own past stands in my way.

ROSMER: Your past is dead, Rebecca. It's no longer part of you—nothing to do with you—as you are *now*.

REBECCA: Oh my dear, those are only words. And freedom from guilt? Where shall I find that?

ROSMER (*heavily*): Yes, yes—freedom from guilt.

REBECCA: Freedom from guilt means joy and happiness. *That* was the message you were to make a reality for all men.

ROSMER: Oh don't remind me of that. It was only a dream, Rebecca; a half considered impulse. I don't believe in it myself any more—people cannot be taught honor from outside.

REBECCA (*low*): Not even by serene love?

ROSMER (*thoughtfully*): Yes—of course. That would be immense. That would be so beautiful.—If it were so. (*Moves about restlessly*) But how can I ever be sure? Absolutely sure?

REBECCA: Don't you believe me, John?

ROSMER: Oh Rebecca, how can I believe you? In you, who've lived here hiding so much!—Now you bring up something new. Is there a secret behind this? If there is, tell me straight out. Perhaps you want to gain something by it. I would so gladly do anything I can for you.

REBECCA (*wringing her hands*): Oh, this killing doubt—! John—John—!

ROSMER: It's horrible, isn't it? But I can't get away from it. I'll always doubt. I'll never know for certain that I have your love, pure and whole.

REBECCA: But isn't there something in you, that tells you that I am transformed? And that this transformation is due to you—only to you.

ROSMER: Oh my dear, I don't believe any more in my power to transform people. I don't believe in myself any more. I don't believe in myself or in you.

REBECCA (*looks at him gloomily*): Then how will you be able to live?

ROSMER: I don't know. I can't think. I don't believe I *can* go on living—there's nothing worth living for.

REBECCA: Oh life—life renews itself. Let's hold fast to it. We shall be out of it soon enough.

ROSMER (*springing up restlessly*): Then give me my faith again! Faith in you! Faith in your love! Proof! I want proof!

REBECCA: Proof? How can I give you proof—!

ROSMER: You *must*. (*Crosses the room*) I can't bear this emptiness—this awful desolation—this—this—(*Knocking at the hall door.*)

REBECCA (*starts from her chair*): Ah!—Listen!

(*The door opens and* ULRIC BRENDEL *enters. He wears a white shirt, black*

*coat and a good pair of boots outside his trousers. Otherwise he is dressed
as before. He looks excited.*)

REBECCA: Oh it's you, Mr. Brendel!

BRENDEL: John, my boy—hail—farewell!

ROSMER: Where are you going so late?

BRENDEL: Downhill.

ROSMER: How—?

BRENDEL: I'm going home, my cherished little pupil. I am homesick for the
great nothingness.

ROSMER: Something has happened to you, Mr. Brendel. What is it?

BRENDEL: So you observe the transformation? Yes—well you may. When I
last bestrode these halls—I stood before you, a man of substance, slapping
my breast pocket.

ROSMER: What! I don't quite understand—

BRENDEL: But as you see me this night, I am a deposed monarch amid the
ashes of my burnt-out castle.

ROSMER: If there is anything *I* can do to help—

BRENDEL: You have preserved your childlike heart, John. Can you grant
me a loan?

ROSMER: Yes, yes, most gladly.

BRENDEL: Can you spare me an ideal or two?

ROSMER: What do you say?

BRENDEL: A couple of cast-off ideals. For I'm cleaned out, my dear boy.
Empty. Finished.

REBECCA: Weren't you able to give your lectures?

BRENDEL: No, enticing lady. What do you think! Just as I stood ready to
empty my overflowing cornucopia, I made the *penible* discovery that I
am bankrupt.

REBECCA: But what about your unwritten works?

BRENDEL: For five and twenty years I have sat, as a miser sits, on his locked
treasure chest, and then yesterday—when I went to open it to take out
the treasure—there was nothing. The teeth of time have ground it to dust.
There was *nichts*[9] and nothing.

ROSMER: But are you quite sure?

BRENDEL: There was no possibility of doubt, my youngling. The president
has convinced me.

ROSMER: The president?

BRENDEL: Well then—His Excellency *ganz nach Belieben.*[10]

ROSMER: Yes, but who do you mean?

BRENDEL: Peter Mortensgard, of course.

ROSMER: What!

BRENDEL (*with an air of secrecy*): Sh! sh! sh! Peter Mortensgard is lord
and master of the future. Never have I stood in a greater presence. Peter
Mortensgard has almighty power. He can do whatever he wants.

ROSMER: Oh, don't believe that.

---

[9] German for "nothing."

[10] German for "entirely as you wish."

BRENDEL: Oh yes, my boy! For Peter Mortensgard never wants more than he can do. Peter Mortensgard is able to live without ideals. And *that*—look you—*that* is the secret of success. It's the sum of all worldly wisdom. *Basta!*[11]

ROSMER *(low)* : Now I see—you leave here poorer than you came.

BRENDEL: *Bien!*[12] Then take a *Beispel*[13] from your old teacher. Strike out everything he printed in your mind. Build not your house on shifting sands. And look ahead—and consider well—before you build upon the graceful creature that here sweetens your life.

REBECCA: Do you mean me?

BRENDEL: Yes, you bewitching mermaid.

REBECCA: Why am I not to be built upon?

BRENDEL *(coming a step nearer)* : I am told that my former little pupil has a life work to carry to victory.

REBECCA: So—

BRENDEL: Victory is assured. But—mark well—upon one unavoidable condition.

REBECCA: What condition?

BRENDEL *(takes her gently by the wrist)* : That the woman who loves him goes gladly out into the kitchen and chops her rosy little finger off—*here*—just at the middle joint. Item. That the aforesaid loving woman—likewise gladly—snips off her incomparably moulded left ear. *(Lets her go and turns to* ROSMER*)* Farewell, my victorious John.

ROSMER: Are you going now? It's dark night outside.

BRENDEL: Dark night is best. Peace be with you.

(He exits. There is a short silence in the room.)

REBECCA *(breathing heavily)* : Oh how close it is in here.

(She goes to the window, opens it and stands there.)

ROSMER *(sitting in an easy chair by the sofa)* : There's nothing else for it, after all, Rebecca. I see that. You *must* go.

REBECCA: Yes, I see no choice.

ROSMER: Let's make the most of our last hour. Come here and sit by me.

REBECCA *(goes and sits on the sofa)* : What do you want to say, John?

ROSMER: First I want to tell you that you need have no anxiety about your future.

REBECCA *(smiles)* : Hm. *My* future.

ROSMER: I have seen to everything. Long since. Whatever happens you are provided for.

REBECCA: That as well, my dear one.

ROSMER: You might have known I should.

REBECCA: It's many a long day since I thought of anything like that.

ROSMER: Yes, yes of course. You thought that things could never be different between us.

REBECCA: Yes, I thought that.

---

[11] Italian and Spanish idiom for "that will do."
[12] French for "well."
[13] German for "example."

ROSMER: So did I. But if anything happened to me now—

REBECCA: Oh John—you will live longer than I.

ROSMER: My useless life lies in my own hands.

REBECCA: What! You're never thinking of—!

ROSMER: Would it be so strange? After this pitiful defeat? I was going to bear my life's work to victory—and now I run away from it all—even before it had properly begun.

REBECCA: Try again, John, only try!—And you'll win!—you'll ennoble hundreds, thousands of souls. Only try!

ROSMER: Oh Rebecca—I who no longer believe in my own life's work.

REBECCA: But your work has already been proved. One person at least you have made noble. Me, for as long as I live.

ROSMER: Yes, if I dared believe you.

REBECCA (*kneading her hands*): Oh John—don't you know of anything—anything that could make you believe.

ROSMER (*starting, as if in fear*): Don't pursue this, Rebecca. No further. Not another word.

REBECCA: This is just what we must pursue. Do you know of anything that could stifle your doubts? Because I don't know.

ROSMER: Better for you not to know. Better for us both.

REBECCA: No, no, no.—I won't have that! If you know of something that can acquit me in your eyes, then I demand, as my right, that you speak.

ROSMER (*as though powerless, driven against his own will*): Well, let's see then. You say that you are filled with great love. That your soul has been made noble through me. Yes? Is that right? Have you worked it out correctly, my dear? Shall we check it and see? Well?

REBECCA: I am ready.

ROSMER: Whenever it may be.

REBECCA: Whenever you like. The sooner the better.

ROSMER: Then show me, Rebecca—if you—for my sake—this very night— (*Breaking off*) oh, no, no, no!

REBECCA: Yes, John, yes, yes! Say it and you shall see.

ROSMER: Have you the courage to—are you willing to—gladly as Ulric Brendel said—for my sake, now, tonight—gladly—to go the same way—as Beate went?

REBECCA (*getting up slowly from the sofa and speaking nearly inaudibly*): John—!

ROSMER: Yes, my dear. I'll never be able to get away from this—when you are gone. Every hour of the day I will come back to this. Oh I seem to see you before me. You stand on the footbridge, out in the middle. Now you lean forward over the rail, mesmerized down to the mill race below. No. You draw back. You daren't do—what she dared.

REBECCA: But supposing I was brave enough—and glad? What then?

ROSMER: I should have to believe in you. I should have to have faith in my life's work. Believe that I can make men noble. Believe that men can be ennobled.

REBECCA (*slowly takes her shawl and throws it over her head, saying with self-control*): You shall have your faith again.

ROSMER: Are you brave and strong enough—for that, Rebecca?

REBECCA: You must judge in the morning—or later, when they fetch me up.

ROSMER (*puts his hand to his forehead*): There's a horrible fascination about this—!

REBECCA: I don't want to stay lying down there. Any longer than need be. You must see that they find me.

ROSMER (*jumping up*): But this—it's madness of course. Go—or stay! I believe you on your bare word.

REBECCA: Mere words, John. No more evasions or cowardice now, my dear. How can you believe my bare word after today?

ROSMER: But I don't want to see you fail, Rebecca.

REBECCA: I won't fail.

ROSMER: You will. You're not the sort of person to do as Beate did.

REBECCA: You don't think so?

ROSMER: Never. You're not like Beate. Your way of thinking isn't distorted, like hers.

REBECCA: My way of thinking is the Rosmersholm way—now. Where I have sinned, it is right that I should atone.

ROSMER: Do you think like *that?*

REBECCA: Yes.

ROSMER (*resolved*): Very well then. *I* think according to our unfettered view of life. There is no judge over us, so we ourselves must see that justice is done.

REBECCA (*misunderstanding him*): That too. That too. My going will save what is best in you.

ROSMER: Oh there is nothing to save in me any more.

REBECCA: There is. But I—after this I would only be like a sea troll hanging onto the ship that you should sail forward, hampering it. I must go overboard. Or shall I drag out my stunted life up here in the world? Brooding over the happiness I have lost because of my past? I must throw in my hand, John.

ROSMER: If you go, then I will go with you.

REBECCA (*smiling almost imperceptibly, says gently*): Yes, come with me, dear—and be witness—

ROSMER: I go with you, I said.

REBECCA: To the footbridge. You never dare go out onto it.

ROSMER: Have you noticed that?

REBECCA: Yes. (*Sadly and heavily*) That's what made my love hopeless.

ROSMER: Rebecca—now I lay my hand on your head (*He does as he says*) and take you in marriage for my true wife.

REBECCA (*takes both his hands and bows her head to his breast*): Thank you, John. (*Lets him go*) And now I go—gladly.

ROSMER: Man and wife should go together.

REBECCA: Only to the bridge, John.

ROSMER: Out onto it as well. I shall go as far as you go. For now I dare.

REBECCA: Are you absolutely sure—that this way is the best for you?

ROSMER: I know it is the only one.

REBECCA: What if you deceive yourself? If it's only a delusion. One of those white horses of Rosmersholm.

ROSMER: It may well be. We never escape from them, we of this house.

REBECCA: Then stay, John!

ROSMER: The man shall go with his wife, as the wife with her husband.

REBECCA: Yes, but tell me. Is it you who follow me? Or is it I who follow you?

ROSMER: We shall never know, Rebecca.

REBECCA: I should dearly like to know.

ROSMER: We follow each other, Rebecca. I you, and you me.

REBECCA: I almost think that too.

ROSMER: For now we two are one.

REBECCA: Yes, now we are one! So we go gladly.

(*They go out through the hall, hand in hand, and are seen to turn left. The door remains open after them. The room remains empty a little while; then* MRS. HELSETH *enters right.*)

MRS. HELSETH: Miss West—the carriage is—(*Looks round*) Not here? Out together at this time? Well now—that I must say—! Hm! (*Goes into the hall, looks round and comes in again*) Not on the garden seat. Well, well. (*Goes to window and looks out*) Good gracious! That white—!—well upon my soul, both of them on the footbridge! God forgive the sinful creatures! If they're not putting their arms round each other. (*Screams loudly*) Ah! Over—both of them—down into the mill race. Help! Help! (*Her knees shaking, she holds herself up by the back of the chair and can scarcely get the words out*) No, no help here. The dead wife has taken them.

(*The Curtain Falls.*)

Commentary

The striking differences in situation and tone between *The Devil's Disciple* and *Rosmersholm* may at first obscure the fact that both Shaw and Ibsen are concerned with the problem of self-discovery and self-sacrifice, with the conflict between convention and the individual, and with characters who change in an hour of moral crisis. But Shaw's treatment is satirical, whereas Ibsen's is psychological, if not tragic. Shaw gives answers; Ibsen asks questions.

One of the first and most troublesome problems a dramatist faces is that of exposition. The novelist, by comparison, has no such difficulty:

either he can begin his plot at a point early enough to permit the reader to build a necessary body of facts, or he can narrate past events at the juncture most suitable for his purpose. The dramatist does not have this freedom; his situation must develop immediately, and his audience must be efficiently informed of the background while the action is in full swing. The dramatic clichés of the French maid who talks to herself while she dusts the furniture, or of the butler who gives lengthy exposition over the telephone, are just two examples of the pitfalls which may trap the unskilled dramatist.

Ibsen's problem is more complex because he has written a play of exposition in which there are few facts and only attitudes, motives, opinions. *Rosmersholm* is a drama in which nothing happens, but much is discovered. What happens happens not so much on stage as in the minds of Ibsen's characters. The only significant action—the suicide of Rosmer and Rebecca—takes place off stage in the manner of Greek tragedy. Their confrontation of the past destroys them even as they discover it and themselves.

If one were to close his eyes and listen to the dialogue of Act One, he might get the impression that the conflicts in *Rosmersholm* were political (conservatism versus liberalism), or religious (orthodoxy versus apostasy), or social (the community versus the individual). But like much else in the play the dialogue is misleading. The stage setting and apparently irrelevant small talk are Ibsen's means of preparing for ethical and psychological conflicts, deeper than a clash between past and present. Like Shaw in *The Devil's Disciple* Ibsen uses his setting as exposition to hint at a way of life. Whereas Shaw dramatizes a clash of values by juxtaposing Judith Anderson's living room in Act Two and Mrs. Dudgeon's in Act One, Ibsen creates a tension in the set of the Rosmersholm living room. The past seems to hang heavy in the old house. There is no sunlight filtering through the avenue of tall old trees outside and into the heavily curtained windows. The ancestral portraits gaze bleakly down from the walls. The atmosphere is quiet and subdued, and voices are rarely raised. Even when there were children at Rosmersholm, legend has it that they never cried. But Rebecca remarks that neither does anyone laugh—a condition which Mrs. Helseth says has "spread itself round like a sort of infection" (p. 123). The sound of the millrace, soon to be associated with violent death, is heard always in the background. Noting Rosmer's ritualistic avoidance of the footbridge, Rebecca remarks, "They cling to their dead here at Rosmersholm" (p. 91). On the other hand, Rebecca's touch can be felt in the fresh birch branches and wild flowers decorating the tile stove, accentuating the contrast between her vitality and the dead hand of Beate, who did not like either their color or their fragrance. After she found Rosmer "languishing and sickening in the gloom" of his marriage to Beate, Rebecca believed that it was her mission in life to destroy the "gloomy insurmountable wall" between Rosmer and freedom and to bring him into "bright sunshine" (p. 131).

Ibsen employs more than the exposition of set and dialogue to establish the tension between life and death, present and past at Rosmersholm. Almost at once he introduces, tentatively and obliquely, the symbol of the white horse, which rushes soundlessly onward in the darkness. Like Beate, its presence makes itself constantly felt at Rosmersholm, and it is alluded to at the end of each act. Why? What associations build up around this phantom? The original title of *Rosmersholm* was *White Horses*. What reasons may Ibsen have had for changing it?

Closely related to dramatic exposition is the device of foreshadowing. Just as exposition brings time past into time present, foreshadowing hints of time future in time present. Although it is easy to see how the symbol of the white horse serves this function, it is equally easy to overlook an apparently insignificant stage prop, the large white shawl which Rebecca works on in Acts One and Three and which she completes before Act Four. At the beginning and the end of Act One Ibsen pointedly calls attention to Rebecca's crochet when the white horse is mentioned. She takes the shawl to her room and, haunted by rising anxieties, lies awake until nearly morning. Her crocheting in Act Three is not simply Ibsen's way of giving his actress a piece of stage business. Rebecca is rapidly completing her shawl on the morning of the day of her death, and in Act Four it lies completed on the sofa before us until at the end of the drama it is worn for the only time, as Rebecca's shroud. In an earlier draft Mrs. Helseth cries out, upon seeing Rebecca move toward the footbridge, "Good God!—What's that?—the White Horse!" But now her broken cry—"Good gracious! That white——!" leaves the conclusion ambiguously poised between "horse" and "shawl," uniting both implications as the dead wife takes Rebecca and Rosmer.

Set and props are only two of the theatrical devices available to the playwright to establish exposition and foreshadowing. Note how the dialogue in Act One, for example, also serves this purpose. Ibsen is careful not to reveal the background and the personality of his characters in simple, straightforward statements. The excitement and difficulty of *Rosmersholm*, however, is that even when one understands Ibsen's dramatic techniques and their function, the exposition has not really clarified the past. Ibsen's indirection has not created an intelligible, coherent body of facts. The more deeply one moves into the drama the more perplexing the questions raised. Consider Beate, for example. Although she has been dead for a year before the action begins, her character and her control over the lives of those at Rosmersholm are felt from the moment the curtain rises on Rebecca observing Rosmer's careful avoidance of the footbridge until it falls on Mrs. Helseth's anguished scream, "The dead wife has taken them." Yet Beate never appears on stage. She exists only through memory, opinions, and attitudes. We know her only through others, but the characters all view Beate differently. Furthermore, the attitudes of even her husband are reassessed and changed during the drama. Our knowledge deepens as we are forced to modify and revaluate the first impressions we gained from the exposition. Was she insane? Why did she write Mortensgard? Did she really have a "wild uncontrolled passion"? How did Beate learn more than Rosmer knew himself about his religious skepticism and his relationship with Rebecca? How are we to judge what Beate was like when the testimony of her relatives and friends is often contradictory, prejudiced, or distorted? It soon becomes apparent that Ibsen's exposition reveals, not only Beate, but those who knew her, for they often betray themselves reminiscing about her.

Ibsen's exposition, therefore, does not present facts about the past, but only possibilities. Ambiguities, evasions, equivocations, deceptions, and self-deceptions—*how* is exposition possible in the world of *Rosmersholm*? Rebecca's first action foreshadows this question and offers a clue to conduct which in *Rosmersholm* is not hers alone: "Every now and then she spies out watchfully between the flowers"; "Keeping behind the curtains"; "Peeping out between the curtains and the window frame." In Act Two she openly admits to eavesdropping. In what way are both acts characteristic of Rebecca? Who else in a figurative sense spies but is not so frank to confess it?

In the world of *The Devil's Disciple* truth is not equivocal, hypocrisy stands exposed, and Shaw's values are clearly affirmed. Not so with Ibsen. No character is his disciple and his final judgments are reserved. Rosmer is a man of great integrity and high ideals, but he is weak and naïve when, as Kroll observes, "it comes to people and the real business of living" (p. 126). Rebecca uses morally dubious means as she ruthlessly pursues noble ends. Brendel is a sensitive and drunken idealist nauseated by the thought of the intellectual discipline required to articulate his liberal ideas. His admiration for Mortensgard's worldly success does not hide the fact that the editor is an opportunist ready to sacrifice principle for expediency. And Kroll, intolerant, overbearing bigot though he is, has the strength of character not to press the advantage that on more than one occasion is his. How does Ibsen present both the traditions of Rosmersholm and Rosmer's ideals of emancipation so that an audience must view them with critical reservations?

By adhering closely to the traditional dramatic unities of time, place, and action, Ibsen focuses only upon the climactic moments of confrontation with moral issues which Rosmer and Rebecca have for some time evaded. The past is included in the present, not for reasons of dramatic exposition, but because of its moral implications which hero and heroine are now forced to recognize. In what sense are both bound by their pasts? What does the past include? The problem for Rosmer is that as he is enlightened about the past, he must come to terms with himself. "We each know that we did everything we could for the poor invalid. We've no need to reproach ourselves—and so I think there is something sweet and peaceful in thinking of Beate now," says Rosmer with smug satisfaction early the first evening (p. 95). Ibsen ironically underscores Rosmer's moral blindness by having Rebecca light the lamp as he speaks. But by page 110 he will insist for the last time: "I can solemnly swear that we were not to blame. It was her own disordered brain." How do Kroll and Mortensgard undermine Rosmer's simple confidence in himself and his world? Rosmer's growing uncertainty and bewilderment are accentuated by his numerous questions and by his repeated remarks: "Yes, I don't understand that; it's quite incomprehensible" (p. 111); "I don't quite understand you" (p. 114); "But I don't understand" (p. 114).

On the surface the structure of Act Two would seem to be three scenes in each of which Rosmer's education is painfully furthered. The conservative headmaster is followed by the liberal journalist, and the act concludes with a deeply personal moment with his enlightened friend. But the struggle is not just political or religious, Kroll opposed to Mortensgard, ideals. Ibsen's larger concern is with Rosmer's moral crisis, his increasing for both men reveal a common pragmatic willingness to sacrifice their awareness of his deep involvement in guilt. The shattering question which concludes Act Two—"What—is—this?"—is not directed alone at Rebecca's enigmatic refusal of marriage and sinister threat of suicide but at the incomprehensible events of the whole day of Act Two, a day which started with Rosmer's declaration that after a peaceful, dreamless sleep he could not recall when he felt more lighthearted. By the end of the act Rosmer is less able than ever to face his world because he is now less able to face himself.

Act Three is Rebecca's act. Like Rosmer, she has less knowledge of herself and of the forces working upon her at Rosmersholm than she believed she had. Except for brief introductory and concluding scenes between Mrs. Helseth and Rebecca, which repeat the design of Act One, Act Three has the same threefold division as Act Two. Why does Ibsen repeat this structural arrangement in this act? What is revealed about Rebecca's past, and what does she discover? With the knowledge that there is no escape from or breaking with one's guilty involvement in the past, Rosmer and Rebecca renounce the thing which is to them most meaningful—Rosmer, his career of "bringing freedom" to ennoble men; Rebecca, the powerful control she has exercised over Rosmer. Both for the first time are confronted with their moral responsibility and their failure. Rosmer tries desperately to find a solution which will obliterate the knowledge—marriage with Rebecca: "I won't go through life with a corpse on my back. Help me to throw it off, Rebecca. And let us stifle all memories in freedom and joy and passion. You shall be to me the only wife I ever had" (p. 120). Why does Rebecca refuse him? When she declares that if Rosmer again asks her to marry him, she "will go the way Beate went" (p. 121), her words are more than a dark foreshadowing of suicide. Beate's way, although at times it approached madness, moved through a guilty sense of personal failure and renunciation to a sacrifice of her life so that her husband might be free. Was it courage and devotion, or insanity? Unlike Rosmer's efforts at evasion and escape, Rebecca's confession at the end of Act Three is motivated by an integrity not always so strong a part of her character: "I was not the same person that I am now, standing here telling you this" (p. 132). In an heroic effort to save Rosmer's innocence she exonerates him from the guilt of Beate's death and accepts full moral responsibility for it. But the gesture miscarries, and Rosmer goes off to effect a reconciliation with Kroll.

In Act Four Rebecca has only to complete her confession by declaring her motive for engaging in her fierce struggle with Beate as well as for making the idealistic sacrifice in Rosmer's behalf—"that fierce, passionate, uncontrollable desire" (p. 136), a passion which Beate could surely have understood. But Rosmersholm has brought Rebecca ironic retribution and now bears out the truth of Rosmer's first naïve mention of Beate: "We almost feel as if she was still part of the house" (p. 95). At first Rebecca speaks only of Rosmer's involvement in the traditions of Rosmersholm—"Oh this is something born in you—family doubts, family anxieties, family scruples. They chatter around here about the dead coming back like a rushing white horse" (p. 126)—but by Act Four she confesses that the Rosmer family view of life has infected and broken her will (p. 137). Rebecca, too, has become a "part of the house."

If Rosmer has ennobled Rebecca's passions, his way of life has also killed her happiness, as it had Beate's, by creating in her a sense of guilt. If Rebecca has refined his intellect and given him purpose and direction, she herself has lost courage and the power to act—until Brendel, now a nightmarish vision of Rosmer's bankrupt idealism, symbolically suggests the victorious way out: "That the woman who loves him goes gladly out into the kitchen and chops her rosy little finger off—here—just at the middle joint. Item. That the aforesaid loving woman—likewise gladly—snips off her incomparably moulded left ear" (p. 140). Here, as Beate also knew, would be a sacrificial act of utter selflessness, the destruction of the self. As Rebecca had tempted Beate, so now Rosmer toys, fascinated, with the idea in his testing of Rebecca. In suicide Rebecca not only would attain redemption through atonement for Beate's death but also would redeem Rosmer's faith in himself by proving that "one person at least you have made noble. Me, for as long as I live" (p. 141). So speaks Rebecca in the last ten minutes of her life. The marriage which she had once rejected as leading to the way Beate went, Rebecca now accepts. Hand in hand, hesitantly, neither of the lovers quite believing that the other has the courage of a final commitment, Rosmer and Rebecca enter a marriage which is death. Rosmer dies to prove his emancipation, as one would have earlier expected of Rebecca; Rebecca dies in a curiously un-Christian way, more according to the ancient Norse code of justice or doom, "the Rosmersholm way," to expiate her sin, as one would have earlier expected of Rosmer. The irony has completed itself. What has it proved? "Is it you who follow me? Or is it I who follow you?" asks Rebecca, and Rosmer replies, in a manner suggesting the final truth of *Rosmersholm,* "We shall never know, Rebecca." Each has been profoundly changed by the other's love; each becomes much like the other's old self, and ironically, the place where their lives finally join is the footbridge over the millpond at the moment of death.

Questions and Problems

1. What is Mrs. Helseth's role? How does Ibsen turn the stereotyped action of her dusting in Act Three to good dramatic use? Why does she appear at the beginning and end of each act except the second?

2. Ibsen uses letters on more than one occasion as a means of exposition. What do they reveal? What are the motives of the sender in each case?

3. At first Ibsen intended to include two young daughters of Rosmer and Beate in his drama. Why may he finally have decided to omit them?

4. In an earlier draft Rebecca says that when she came down from Finmark with Dr. West, she was "no longer what people call an—innocent woman." Why has Ibsen made her relationship with Dr. West ambiguous in the final version?

5. Brendel is a standard dramatic device of Ibsen's: a character returning from the past to fill in background. How is he used for the purpose of foreshadowing? What other functions does he serve? Why should Ibsen have him break in as he does in Acts One and Four?

6. In an earlier version of Act Four Ibsen made no mention of Brendel's borrowed clothes. Why does he in the final revision? Contrast the dramatic purposes achieved by the device of borrowed clothes with Shaw's use of the same technique in *The Devil's Disciple.*

7. Rebecca's home is in Finmark, in northern Norway, the land of the midnight sun and the legendary home of the trolls. Brendel calls Rebecca a "bewitching mermaid," and Kroll says that she could bewitch anyone. At the end of the drama she compares herself to a sea-troll which clung to a ship to prevent its sailing. Note also the descriptions of Finmark. What are the implications of these metaphors? Can they be related to Rebecca's association with wild flowers, sunlight, and the open window?

8. Rosmer's ideal is defined as "bringing liberalism" to men. What does Rosmer mean by "freedom"? How does he expect to achieve his ideal? Does the play take another, more complex view of this ideal? Who is "free" in *Rosmersholm*? Is freedom possible in the world of *Rosmersholm*? Does the truth set men free here? What is Brendel's role in developing this theme?

9. What does Rosmer mean when he says on page 142: "There is no judge over us, so we ourselves must see that justice is done"? How does Rebecca misunderstand him? Trace the misunderstandings that have run as an underlying design through *Rosmersholm*. How do they contribute to the meaning of Ibsen's drama?

10. Dramatic structure is more than a division of a play into acts; it is the significant ordering of the dramatic events. The four-act structure of *Rosmersholm* offers Ibsen many opportunities to give thematic implications to his design. His first draft opens in wintry mid-afternoon with the sun streaming in the windows. The final version opens in the gathering darkness of a summer evening and ends late at night, with Acts Two and Three set in the morning. What is suggested? What other significant moments of symmetry can be discovered?

11. In *The Devil's Disciple* Anderson moves from Puritan to Diabolonian. Does Rosmer? Is Rebecca a Shavian diabolonian heroine?

12. A traditional question much debated about *Rosmersholm* is whether it is Rosmer's tragedy or Rebecca's. Is the question valid?

13. One recent critic of Ibsen takes this view of Rosmer's end: "But Rosmer fails ultimately because his age is hostile to the ideal claims of man. Throughout the course of the drama we see him slowly disintegrating, gradually losing his solid core, a victim of attrition. As we observe Rosmer at the end, clinging to illusions, being pushed willy-nilly toward utter defeat, a sacrifice on the altar of natural forces, we see this once noble figure, who governed his life according to his own choice and the dictates of his own moral conscience, end as a pathetic nobody, deprived of those qualities which make for true tragic greatness."[14] Discuss.

---

[14] Sverre Arestad, "Ibsen's Concept of Tragedy," *PMLA*, LXXIV (June, 1959), 292.

EUGENE O'NEILL

Desire under the Elms

Biography

EUGENE O'NEILL (1888-1953), son of the distinguished actor James O'Neill, was born in New York City; his birthplace, appropriately, was on Broadway. After accompanying his family on their theatrical tours and attending various boarding schools, he studied at Princeton for a year (1906); his suspension there ended his formal education. He worked for a time in a mail-order house, got married, and then set off in 1909 for Honduras in search of gold; the following year he shipped on a freighter destined for Buenos Aires. Returning to New York after a voyage to South Africa, he lived for a time in a waterfront dive called "Jimmy the Priest's." In December, 1912, after he had worked for a few months as a reporter in New London, he was ordered to a sanatorium for the treatment of tuberculosis. In that year, too, O'Neill was divorced. His experiences as an ordinary seaman, his association with stevedores and outcasts, and his rough-and-tumble life as a vagabond are reflected in many of his plays.

O'Neill's decision in 1913 to become a dramatist marked a turning point in his life. His need for help on technical matters led him to attend Professor George Pierce Baker's famous drama workshop at Harvard in 1913-1914. Although he received encouragement, he became bored with the routine and his classmates and soon left. After spending the winter of 1915-1916 in Greenwich Village, O'Neill became associated with the Provincetown Players, who produced many of his early plays on Cape Cod. By 1920 he was through experimenting with one-act plays, which he felt were too limited in scope, and had produced his first full-length drama, *Beyond the Horizon,* which established him as a successful dramatist and won him his first Pulitzer Prize. *Anna Christie* and *Strange Interlude* were also awarded this prize, and in 1936 O'Neill received the Nobel Prize for Literature.

Whatever the final critical estimate of O'Neill may be, it cannot be denied that he was America's outstanding dramatist during the nineteen-twenties and thirties. When O'Neill began writing, he reflected the contemporary American mood of frustration and rebellion against existing dramatic conventions in much the same way that Ibsen and Shaw had rebelled against the conventions of Continental and English drama toward

153

the end of the nineteenth century. O'Neill brought to the American stage not only an intensity of feeling and language previously unknown in native drama, but also types of characters totally neglected by earlier playwrights—prostitutes, drunken sailors, derelicts, waterfront parasites—all in the violent throes of personal agony and, often, fated for sudden death.

Moreover, O'Neill was an inveterate experimenter in the theater; his style has ranged from realism to naturalism to expressionism to impressionism. As though trying the resources of the modern theater to their limits, he has played with masks, puppets, a chorus, rapidly shifting scenes, and double speeches to reflect a character's inner consciousness. Not content with writing drama of conventional length, he wrote plays so long it was necessary to begin the performance in the afternoon, recess for dinner, and resume in the evening. In his last years he began a monumental cycle of nine plays as a chronicle of American life and society, but illness forced him to abandon this ambitious project. Entitled *A Tale of Possessors Self-Dispossessed,* the plays traced what O'Neill described as "a far from model American family" through the whole course of American history. The central theme was the malevolent and destructive effect of possessions on their possessors. *A Touch of the Poet,* one of the two surviving plays in the cycle, was produced posthumously in 1958; the other, *More Stately Mansions,* in 1962.

Strangely, most of O'Neill's technical innovations have not been adopted by younger playwrights. Although they are indebted to him for helping to liberate the American stage from outworn dramatic conventions, they have not been interested in the philosophical and metaphysical concerns which governed his stylistic experiments. But it would be an error to regard O'Neill primarily as a dramatic technician, for no man in the modern theater has struggled harder to dramatize the philosophical problems of life as he saw them. "Even in his metaphysical flight O'Neill has caught the reality of common people living on sea or land," writes John Gassner; "he has presented humanity struggling against inherited or acquired limitations and facing racial prejudice, poverty, the hardness of a stony soil, the frustrations of puritanism, and the effects of a materialistic world which thwarts or perverts the spirit."[1] The recurrent theme in O'Neill's work is man's frustration in his search for happiness in a modern world where religion and traditional moral values have failed to provide him with insight into the meaning of his physical, natural life. For O'Neill, value lies, not in the powers of the intellect, but in man's struggle to live both emotionally and physically. That the struggle will probably be unsuccessful because of the immensity of the social and cosmic forces working against him is not important; the crucial thing

---

[1] John Gassner, *Masters of the Drama* (New York, 1954), p. 641.

is the fight itself, an exciting, terrible, but not frightening adventure at the end of which await, inevitably, death and freedom.

It may well be that in none of O'Neill's plays is there an artistic unity of dramatic technique and philosophical content; O'Neill may be, after all, the most imperfect of the theater's great writers. Nonetheless, we must acknowledge in his dramatizing of modern man's grappling with forces in himself, or in society, or in the universe itself, an intensity and a compelling excitement that must be reckoned with.

Principal Plays

Bound East for Cardiff (1916)
The Long Voyage Home (1917)
'Ile (1917)
The Moon of the Caribbees (1918)
Beyond the Horizon (1920)
The Emperor Jones (1920)
Gold (1921)
Anna Christie (1921)
The Hairy Ape (1922)
The First Man (1922)
All God's Chillun Got Wings (1924)
Welded (1924)
Desire under the Elms (1924)
The Fountain (1925)
The Great God Brown (1926)

Lazarus Laughed (1926)
Marco Millions (1928)
Strange Interlude (1928)
Dynamo (1929)
Mourning Becomes Electra (1931)
Ah, Wilderness! (1933)
Days Without End (1934)
The Iceman Cometh (1946)
A Moon for the Misbegotten (1947)
Long Day's Journey into Night (1956)
A Touch of the Poet (1958)
Hughie (1958)
More Stately Mansions (1962)

Selected Descriptive Bibliography

Alexander, Doris, *The Tempering of Eugene O'Neill*, New York, 1962.
This volume presents the people and literary forces which helped shape the playwright up to the age of thirty-two.

Bentley, Eric, *In Search of Theater*, New York, 1953.
Bentley's chapter "Trying to Like O'Neill" is one of the most stimulating of the attacks upon the playwright.

Boulton, Agnes, *Part of a Long Story*, New York, 1958.
A personal, romanticized account of the early years of their marriage by the second Mrs. O'Neill.

Bowen, Croswell, *The Curse of the Misbegotten*, New York, 1959.
An investigation into the lives of the O'Neill family that emphasizes their many tragic or sensational moments, but that fails to establish significant relationships between O'Neill's life and his work.

Bryer, Jackson R., "Forty Years of O'Neill Criticism: a Selected Bibliography," *Modern Drama*, IV (September, 1961), 196-216.
A selected compilation of the most significant articles and books on O'Neill.

Cargill, Oscar, ed., *O'Neill and His Plays*, New York, 1962.
Reviews, articles, and discussions covering O'Neill's whole career. Extended Bibliography.

Clark, Barrett H., *Eugene O'Neill, the Man and His Plays*, London, 1933; rev. ed., 1947.
One of the earliest studies of O'Neill which combines biography with brief critical comments about O'Neill's early plays.

Falk, Doris V., *Eugene O'Neill and the Tragic Tension*, New Brunswick, N.J., 1958.
Miss Falk sensitively uses a Jungian psychological approach to O'Neill characters. An excellent study, one of the best on O'Neill.

Flexner, Eleanor, *American Playwrights*, 1918-1938, New York, 1938.
Miss Flexner attacks O'Neill for viewing his materials from too limited a perspective and ignoring social implications in his drama.

Gelb, Arthur and Barbara, *O'Neill*, New York, 1962.
The most nearly definitive life of O'Neill yet written.

Modern Drama, III (December, 1960).
A special issue on O'Neill. See especially Sophus Keith Winther's fine study, "Desire under the Elms: A Modern Tragedy."

Racey, Edgar, F., Jr., "Myth as Tragic Structure in *Desire under the Elms*," *Modern Drama*, V (May, 1962), 42-46.
Racey points out the Hebraic and Greek myths that underlie the play.

Skinner, Richard Dana, *Eugene O'Neill: A Poet's Quest*, New York, 1935.
One of the first critical studies of the "inner continuity" of O'Neill's plays, the book is of limited value today because it does not have the perspective of O'Neill's entire dramatic career. Skinner seems often to superimpose his own mystical views upon O'Neill.

Winther, Sophus Keith, *Eugene O'Neill: A Critical Study*, New York, 1934.
Along with Barrett Clark's study, the standard early work on O'Neill. The book has a thematic organization and does not attempt systematic critical analysis of the plays.

Desire under the Elms EUGENE O'NEILL

CHARACTERS

EPHRAIM CABOT

SIMEON
PETER } *His sons*
EBEN

ABBIE PUTNAM

Young Girl, Two Farmers, The Fiddler, A Sheriff, and other folk from the neighboring farms.

The action of the entire play takes place in, and immediately outside of, the Cabot farmhouse in New England, in the year 1850. The south end of the house faces front to a stone wall with a wooden gate at center opening on a country road. The house is in good condition but in need of paint. Its walls are a sickly grayish, the green of the shutters faded. Two enormous elms are on each side of the house. They bend their trailing branches down over the roof. They appear to protect and at the same time subdue. There is a sinister maternity in their aspect, a crushing, jealous absorption. They have developed from their intimate contact with the life of man in the house an appalling humaneness. They brood oppressively over the house. They are like exhausted women resting their sagging breasts and hands and hair on its roof, and when it rains their tears trickle down monotonously and rot on the shingles.

There is a path running from the gate around the right corner of the house to the front door. A narrow porch is on this side. The end wall facing us has two windows in its upper story, two larger ones on the floor below. The two upper are those of the father's bedroom and that of the brothers. On the left, ground floor, is the kitchen—on the right, the parlor, the shades of which are always drawn down.

Desire under the Elms was first produced at the Greenwich Village Theatre in New York City on November 11, 1924.

Desire under the Elms *Copyright 1924 and renewed in 1952 by Eugene O'Neill. Reprinted by permission of Random House, Inc.*

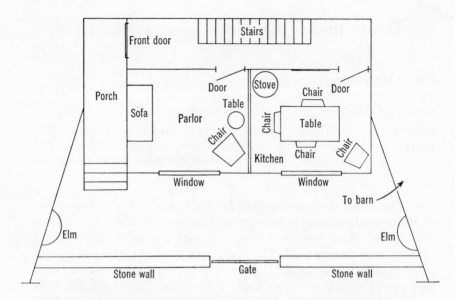

DESIRE UNDER THE ELMS • YARD AND FIRST FLOOR

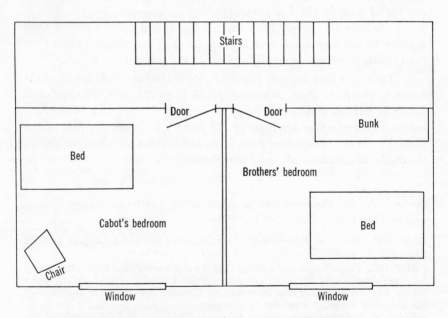

DESIRE UNDER THE ELMS • SECOND FLOOR

Part One

SCENE ONE

Exterior of the farmhouse. It is sunset of a day at the beginning of summer in the year 1850. There is no wind and everything is still. The sky above the roof is suffused with deep colors, the green of the elm glows, but the house is in shadow, seeming pale and washed out by contrast.

A door opens and EBEN CABOT *comes to the end of the porch and stands looking down the road to the right. He has a large bell in his hand and this he swings mechanically, awakening a deafening clangor. Then he puts his hands on his hips and stares up at the sky. He sighs with a puzzled awe and blurts out with halting appreciation.*

EBEN: God! Purty! (*His eyes fall and he stares about him frowningly. He is twenty-five, tall and sinewy. His face is well-formed, good-looking, but its expression is resentful and defensive. His defiant, dark eyes remind one of a wild animal's in captivity. Each day is a cage in which he finds himself trapped but inwardly unsubdued. There is a fierce repressed vitality about him. He has black hair, mustache, a thin curly trace of beard. He is dressed in rough farm clothes.*

He spits on the ground with intense disgust, turns and goes back into the house.

SIMEON *and* PETER *come in from their work in the fields. They are tall men, much older than their half-brother* [SIMEON *is thirty-nine and* PETER *thirty-seven*], *built on a squarer, simpler model, fleshier in body, more bovine and homelier in face, shrewder and more practical. Their shoulders stoop a bit from years of farm work. They clump heavily along in their clumsy thick-soled boots caked with earth. Their clothes, their faces, hands, bare arms and throats are earth-stained. They smell of earth. They stand together for a moment in front of the house and, as if with the one impulse, stare dumbly up at the sky, leaning on their hoes. Their faces have a compressed, unresigned expression. As they look upward, this softens.*)

SIMEON (*grudgingly*): Purty.

PETER: Ay-eh.

SIMEON (*suddenly*): Eighteen years ago.

PETER: What?

SIMEON: Jenn. My woman. She died.

PETER: I'd fergot.

SIMEON: I rec'lect—now an' agin. Makes it lonesome. She'd hair long's a hoss' tail—an' yaller like gold!

PETER: Waal—she's gone. (*This with indifferent finality—then after a pause*) They's gold in the West, Sim.

SIMEON (*still under the influence of sunset—vaguely*): In the sky!

PETER: Waal—in a manner o' speakin'—thar's the promise. (*Growing excited*) Gold in the sky—in the West—Golden Gate—Californi-a!—Goldest West!—fields o' gold!

SIMEON (*excited in his turn*): Fortunes layin' just atop o' the ground waitin' t' be picked! Solomon's mines,[2] they says! (*For a moment they continue looking up at the sky—then their eyes drop.*)

PETER (*with sardonic bitterness*): Here—it's stones atop o' the ground— stones atop o' stones—makin' stone walls—year atop o' year—him 'n' yew 'n' me 'n' then Eben—makin' stone walls fur him to fence us in!

SIMEON: We've wuked. Give our strength. Give our years. Plowed 'em under in the ground,—(*he stamps rebelliously*)—rottin'—makin' soil for his crops! (*A pause*) Waal—the farm pays good for hereabouts.

PETER: If we plowed in Californi-a, they'd be lumps o' gold in the furrow!

SIMEON: Californi-a's t'other side o' earth, a'most. We got t' calc'late—

PETER (*after a pause*): 'Twould be hard fur me, too, to give up what we've 'arned here by our sweat. (*A pause. EBEN sticks his head out of the dining-room window, listening.*)

SIMEON: Ay-eh. (*A pause*) Mebbe—he'll die soon.

PETER (*doubtfully*): Mebbe.

SIMEON: Mebbe—fur all we knows—he's dead now.

PETER: Ye'd need proof.

SIMEON: He's been gone two months—with no word.

PETER: Left us in the fields an evenin' like this. Hitched up an' druv off into the West. That's plum onnateral. He hain't never been off this farm 'ceptin' t' the village in thirty year or more, not since he married Eben's maw. (*A pause. Shrewdly*) I calc'late we might git him declared crazy by the court.

SIMEON: He skinned 'em too slick. He got the best o' all on 'em. They'd never b'lieve him crazy. (*A pause*) We got t' wait—till he's under ground.

EBEN (*with a sardonic chuckle*): Honor thy father! (*They turn, startled, and stare at him. He grins, then scowls*) I pray he's died. (*They stare at him. He continues matter-of-factly*) Supper's ready.

SIMEON *and* PETER (*together*): Ay-eh.

EBEN (*gazing up at the sky*): Sun's downin' purty.

SIMEON *and* PETER (*together*): Ay-eh. They's gold in the West.

EBEN: Ay-eh. (*Pointing*) Yonder atop o' the hill pasture, ye mean?

SIMEON *and* PETER (*together*): In Californi-a!

EBEN: Hunh? (*Stares at them indifferently for a second, then drawls*) Waal— supper's gittin' cold. (*He turns back into kitchen.*)

---

[2] Solomon, the son of David, reigned in Israel from about 974 B.C. to 937 B.C. He devoted himself lavishly to building, commerce, and mining for gold and silver.

SIMEON (*startled—smacks his lips*) : I air hungry!

PETER (*sniffing*) : I smells bacon!

SIMEON (*with hungry appreciation*) : Bacon's good!

PETER (*in same tone*) : Bacon's bacon! (*They turn, shouldering each other, their bodies bumping and rubbing together as they hurry clumsily to their food, like two friendly oxen toward their evening meal. They disappear around the right corner of house and can be heard entering the door.*)

(*The Curtain Falls.*)

SCENE TWO

The color fades from the sky. Twilight begins. The interior of the kitchen is now visible. A pine table is at center, a cookstove in the right rear corner, four rough wooden chairs, a tallow candle on the table. In the middle of the rear wall is fastened a big advertising poster with a ship in full sail and the word "California" in big letters. Kitchen utensils hang from nails. Everything is neat and in order but the atmosphere is of a men's camp kitchen rather than that of a home.

Places for three are laid. EBEN *takes boiled potatoes and bacon from the stove and puts them on the table, also a loaf of bread and a crock of water.* SIMEON *and* PETER *shoulder in, slump down in their chairs without a word.* EBEN *joins them. The three eat in silence for a moment, the two elder as naturally unrestrained as beasts of the field,* EBEN *picking at his food without appetite, glancing at them with a tolerant dislike.*

SIMEON (*suddenly turns to* EBEN) : Looky here! Ye'd oughtn't t' said that, Eben.

PETER : 'Twa'n't righteous.

EBEN : What?

SIMEON : Ye prayed he'd died.

EBEN : Waal—don't yew pray it? (*A pause.*)

PETER : He's our Paw.

EBEN (*violently*) : Not mine!

SIMEON (*dryly*) : Ye'd not let no one else say that about yer Maw! Ha! (*He gives one abrupt sardonic guffaw.* PETER *grins.*)

EBEN (*very pale*) : I meant—I hain't his'n—I hain't like him—he hain't me!

PETER (*dryly*) : Wait till ye've growed his age!

EBEN (*intensely*) : I'm Maw—every drop o' blood! (*A pause. They stare at him with indifferent curiosity.*)

PETER (*reminiscently*) : She was good t' Sim 'n' me. A good step-maw's scurse.

SIMEON : She was good t' everyone.

EBEN (*greatly moved, gets to his feet and makes an awkward bow to each of them—stammering*) : I be thankful t' ye. I'm her—her heir. (*He sits down in confusion.*)

PETER (*after a pause—judicially*) : She was good even t' him.

EBEN (*fiercely*): An' fur thanks he killed her!

SIMEON (*after a pause*): No one never kills nobody. It's allus some thin'. That's the murderer.

EBEN: Didn't he slave Maw t' death?

PETER: He's slaved himself t' death. He's slaved Sim 'n' me 'n' yew t' death —on'y none o' us hain't died—yit.

SIMEON: It's somethin'—drivin' him—t' drive us!

EBEN (*vengefully*): Waal—I hold him t' jedgment! (*Then scornfully*) Somethin'! What's somethin'?

SIMEON: Dunno.

EBEN (*sardonically*): What's drivin' yew to Californi-a, mebbe? (*They look at him in surprise*) Oh, I've heerd ye! (*Then, after a pause*) But ye'll never go t' the gold fields!

PETER (*assertively*): Mebbe!

EBEN: Whar'll ye git the money?

PETER: We kin walk. It's an a'mighty ways—Californi-a—but if yew was t' put all the steps we've walked on this farm end t' end we'd be in the moon!

EBEN: The Injuns'll skulp ye on the plains.

SIMEON (*with grim humor*): We'll mebbe make 'em pay a hair fur a hair!

EBEN (*decisively*): But 'tain't that. Ye won't never go because ye'll wait here fur yer share o' the farm, thinkin' allus he'll die soon.

SIMEON (*after a pause*): We've a right.

PETER: Two-thirds belong t' us.

EBEN (*jumping to his feet*): Ye've no right! She wa'n't yewr Maw! It was her farm! Didn't he steal it from her? She's dead. It's my farm.

SIMEON (*sardonically*): Tell that t' Paw—when he comes! I'll bet ye a dollar he'll laugh—fur once in his life. Ha! (*He laughs himself in one single mirthless bark.*)

PETER (*amused in turn, echoes his brother*): Ha!

SIMEON (*after a pause*): What've ye got held agin us, Eben? Year arter year it's skulked in yer eye—somethin'.

PETER: Ay-eh.

EBEN: Ay-eh. They's somethin'. (*Suddenly exploding*) Why didn't ye never stand between him 'n' my Maw when he was slavin' her to her grave— t' pay her back fur the kindness she done t' yew? (*There is a long pause. They stare at him in surprise.*)

SIMEON: Waal—the stock's got t' be watered.

PETER: 'R they was woodin' t' do.

SIMEON: 'R plowin'.

PETER: 'R hayin'.

SIMEON: 'R spreadin' manure.

PETER: 'R weedin'.

SIMEON: 'R prunin'.

PETER: 'R milkin'.

EBEN (*breaking in harshly*): An' makin' walls—stone atop o' stone—makin' walls till yer heart's a stone ye heft up out o' the way o' growth onto a stone wall t' wall in yer heart!

SIMEON (*matter-of-factly*) : We never had no time t' meddle.

PETER (*to* EBEN) : Yew was fifteen afore yer Maw died—an' big fur yer age. Why didn't ye never do nothin'?

EBEN (*harshly*) : They was chores t' do, wa'n't they? (*A pause—then slowly*) It was on'y arter she died I come to think o' it. Me cookin'— doin' her work—that made me know her, suffer her sufferin'—she'd come back t' help—come back t' bile potatoes—come back t' fry bacon—come back t' bake biscuits—come back all cramped up t' shake the fire, an' carry ashes, her eyes weepin' an' bloody with smoke an' cinders same's they used t' be. She still comes back—stands by the stove thar in the evenin'—she can't find it nateral sleepin' an' restin' in peace. She can't git used t' bein' free—even in her grave.

SIMEON : She never complained none.

EBEN : She'd got too tired. She'd got too used t' bein' too tired. That was what he done. (*With vengeful passion*) An' sooner'r later, I'll meddle. I'll say the thin's I didn't say then t' him! I'll yell 'em at the top o' my lungs. I'll see t' it my Maw gits some rest an' sleep in her grave! (*He sits down again, relapsing into a brooding silence. They look at him with a queer indifferent curiosity.*)

PETER (*after a pause*) : Whar in tarnation d'ye s'pose he went, Sim?

SIMEON : Dunno. He druv off in the buggy, all spick an' span, with the mare all breshed an' shiny, druv off clackin' his tongue an' wavin' his whip. I remember it right well. I was finishin' plowin', it was spring an' May an' sunset, an' gold in the West, an' he druv off into it. I yells "Whar ye goin', Paw?" an' he hauls up by the stone wall a jiffy. His old snake's eyes was glitterin' in the sun like he'd been drinkin' a jugful an' he says with a mule's grin : "Don't ye run away till I come back!"

PETER : Wonder if he knowed we was wantin' fur Californi-a?

SIMEON : Mebbe. I didn't say nothin' and he says, lookin' kinder queer an' sick : "I been hearin' the hens cluckin' an' the roosters crowin' all the durn day. I been listenin' t' the cows lowin' an' everythin' else kickin' up till I can't stand it no more. It's spring an' I'm feelin' damned," he says. "Damned like an old bare hickory tree fit on'y fur burnin'," he says. An' then I calc'late I must've looked a mite hopeful, fur he adds real spry and vicious : "But don't git no fool idee I'm dead. I've sworn t' live a hundred an' I'll do it, if on'y t' spite yer sinful greed! An' now I'm ridin' out t' learn God's message t' me in the spring, like the prophets done. An' yew git back t' yer plowin'," he says. An' he druv off singin' a hymn. I thought he was drunk—'r I'd stopped him goin'.

EBEN (*scornfully*) : No, ye wouldn't! Ye're scared o' him. He's stronger— inside—than both o' ye put together!

PETER (*sardonically*) : An' yew—be yew Samson?

EBEN : I'm gittin' stronger. I kin feel it growin' in me—growin' an' growin'— till it'll bust out—! (*He gets up and puts on his coat and a hat. They watch him, gradually breaking into grins.* EBEN *avoids their eyes sheepishly*) I'm goin' out fur a spell—up the road.

PETER : T' the village?

SIMEON : T' see Minnie?

EBEN (*defiantly*) : Ay-eh!

PETER (*jeeringly*) : The Scarlet Woman!

SIMEON : Lust—that's what's growin' in ye!

EBEN : Waal—she's purty!

PETER : She's been purty fur twenty year!

SIMEON : A new coat o' paint'll make a heifer out of forty.

EBEN : She hain't forty!

PETER : If she hain't, she's teeterin' on the edge.

EBEN (*desperately*) : What d'yew know—

PETER : All they is . . . Sim knew her—an' then me arter—

SIMEON : An' Paw kin tell yew somethin' too! He was fust!

EBEN : D'ye mean t' say he . . . ?

SIMEON (*with a grin*) : Ay-eh! We air his heirs in everythin'!

EBEN (*intensely*) : That's more to it! That grows on it! It'll bust soon! (*Then violently*) I'll go smash my fist in her face! (*He pulls open the door in rear violently.*)

SIMEON (*with a wink at* PETER—*drawlingly*) : Mebbe—but the night's wa'm —purty—by the time ye git thar mebbe ye'll kiss her instead!

PETER : Sart'n he will! (*They both roar with coarse laughter.* EBEN *rushes out and slams the door—then the outside front door—comes around the corner of the house and stands still by the gate, staring up at the sky.*)

SIMEON (*looking after him*) : Like his Paw.

PETER : Dead spit an' image!

SIMEON : Dog'll eat dog!

PETER : Ay-eh. (*Pause. With yearning*) Mebbe a year from now we'll be in Californi-a.

SIMEON : Ay-eh. (*A pause. Both yawn*) Let's git t' bed. (*He blows out the candle. They go out door in rear.* EBEN *stretches his arms up to the sky— rebelliously.*)

EBEN : Waal—thar's a star, an' somewhar's they's him, an' here's me, an' thar's Min up the road—in the same night. What if I does kiss her? She's like t'night, she's soft 'n' wa'm, her eyes kin wink like a star, her mouth's wa'm, her arms're wa'm, she smells like a wa'm plowed field, she's purty . . . Ay-eh! By God A'mighty she's purty, an' I don't give a damn how many sins she's sinned afore mine or who she's sinned 'em with, my sin's as purty as any one of 'em! (*He strides off down the road to the left.*)

(*The Curtain Falls.*)

SCENE THREE

It is the pitch darkness just before dawn. EBEN comes in from the left and goes around to the porch, feeling his way, chuckling bitterly and cursing half-aloud to himself.

EBEN : The cussed old miser! (*He can be heard going in the front door. There is a pause as he goes upstairs, then a loud knock on the bedroom door of the brothers*) Wake up!

SIMEON (*startedly*) : Who's thar?

EBEN (*pushing open the door and coming in, a lighted candle in his hand. The bedroom of the brothers is revealed. Its ceiling is the sloping roof. They can stand upright only close to the center dividing wall of the upstairs.* SIMEON *and* PETER *are in a double bed, front.* EBEN'S *cot is to the rear.* EBEN *has a mixture of silly grin and vicious scowl on his face*) : I be!

PETER (*angrily*) : What in hell's-fire . . . ?

EBEN: I got news fur ye! Ha! (*He gives one abrupt sardonic guffaw.*)

SIMEON (*angrily*) : Couldn't ye hold it 'til we'd got our sleep?

EBEN: It's nigh sunup. (*Then explosively*) He's gone an' married agen!

SIMEON *and* PETER (*explosively*) : Paw?

EBEN: Got himself hitched to a female 'bout thirty-five—an' purty, they says . . .

SIMEON (*aghast*) : It's a durn lie!

PETER: Who says?

SIMEON: They been stringin' ye!

EBEN: Think I'm a dunce, do ye? The hull village says. The preacher from New Dover, he brung the news—told it t' our preacher—New Dover, that's whar the old loon got himself hitched—that's whar the woman lived—

PETER (*no longer doubting—stunned*) : Waal . . . !

SIMEON (*the same*) : Waal . . . !

EBEN (*sitting down on a bed—with vicious hatred*) : Ain't he a devil out o' hell? It's jest t' spite us—the damned old mule!

PETER (*after a pause*) : Everythin'll go t' her now.

SIMEON: Ay-eh. (*A pause—dully*) Waal—if it's done—

PETER: It's done us. (*Pause—then persuasively*) They's gold in the fields o' Californi-a, Sim. No good a-stayin' here now.

SIMEON: Jest what I was a-thinkin'. (*Then with decision*) S'well fust' last! Let's light out and git this mornin'.

PETER: Suits me.

EBEN: Ye must like walkin'.

SIMEON (*sardonically*) : If ye'd grow wings on us we'd fly thar!

EBEN: Ye'd like ridin' better—on a boat, wouldn't ye? (*Fumbles in his pocket and takes out a crumpled sheet of foolscap*[3]) Waal, if ye sign this ye kin ride on a boat. I've had it writ out an' ready in case ye'd ever go. It says fur three hundred dollars t' each ye agree yewr shares o' the farm is sold t' me. (*They look suspiciously at the paper. A pause.*)

SIMEON (*wonderingly*) : But if he's hitched agen—

PETER: An' whar'd yew git that sum o' money, anyways?

EBEN (*cunningly*) : I know whar it's hid. I been waitin'—Maw told me. She knew whar it lay fur years, but she was waitin' . . . It's her'n—the money he hoarded from her farm an' hid from Maw. It's my money by rights now.

PETER: Whar's it hid?

EBEN (*cunningly*) : Whar yew won't never find it without me. Maw spied

---

[3] A sheet of paper approximately 13 x 16 inches.

on him—'r she'd never knowed. (*A pause. They look at him suspiciously, and he at them*) Waal, is it fa'r trade?

SIMEON: Dunno.

PETER: Dunno.

SIMEON (*looking at window*): Sky's grayin'.

PETER: Ye better start the fire, Eben.

SIMEON: An' fix some vittles.

EBEN: Ay-eh. (*Then with a forced jocular heartiness*) I'll git ye a good one. If ye're startin' t' hoof it t' Californi-a ye'll need somethin' that'll stick t' yer ribs. (*He turns to the door, adding meaningly*) But ye kin ride on a boat if ye'll swap. (*He stops at the door and pauses. They stare at him.*)

SIMEON (*suspiciously*): Whar was ye all night?

EBEN (*defiantly*): Up t' Min's. (*Then slowly*) Walkin' thar, fust I felt 's if I'd kiss her; then I got a-thinkin' o' what ye'd said o' him an' her an' I says, I'll bust her nose fur that! Then I got t' the village an' heerd the news an' I got madder'n hell an' run all the way t' Min's not knowin' what I'd do— (*He pauses—then sheepishly but more defiantly*) Waal— when I seen her, I didn't hit her—nor I didn't kiss her nuther—I begun t' beller like a calf an' cuss at the same time, I was so durn mad—an' she got scared—an' I jest grabbed holt an' tuk her! (*Proudly*) Yes, sirree! I tuk her. She may've been his'n—an' your'n, too—but she's mine now!

SIMEON (*dryly*): In love, air yew?

EBEN (*with lofty scorn*): Love! I don't take no stock in sech slop!

PETER (*winking at* SIMEON): Mebbe Eben's aimin' t' marry, too.

SIMEON: Min'd make a true faithful he'pmeet! (*They snicker.*)

EBEN: What do I care fur her—'ceptin' she's round an' wa'm? The p'int is she was his'n—an' now she b'longs t' me! (*He goes to the door—then turns —rebelliously*) An' Min hain't sech a bad un. They's worse'n Min in the world, I'll bet ye! Wait'll we see this cow the Old Man's hitched t'! She'll beat Min, I got a notion! (*He starts to go out.*)

SIMEON (*suddenly*): Mebbe ye'll try t' make her your'n, too?

PETER: Ha! (*He gives a sardonic laugh of relish at this idea.*)

EBEN (*spitting with disgust*): Her—here—sleepin' with him—stealin' my Maw's farm! I'd as soon pet a skunk 'r kiss a snake! (*He goes out. The two stare after him suspiciously. A pause. They listen to his steps receding.*)

PETER: He' startin' the fire.

SIMEON: I'd like t' ride t' Californi-a—but—

PETER: Min might o' put some scheme in his head.

SIMEON: Mebbe it's all a lie 'bout Paw marryin'. We'd best wait an' see the bride.

PETER: An' don't sign nothin' till we does!

SIMEON: Nor till we've tested it's good money! (*Then with a grin*) But if Paw's hitched we'd be sellin' Eben somethin' we'd never git nohow!

PETER: We'll wait an' see. (*Then with sudden vindictive anger*) An' till he comes, let's yew 'n' me not wuk a lick, let Eben tend to thin's if he's a mind t', let's us jest sleep an' eat an' drink likker an' let the hull damned farm go t' blazes!

SIMEON (*excitedly*): By God, we've 'arned a rest! We'll play rich fur a change. I hain't a-going to stir outa bed till breakfast's ready.

PETER: An' on the table!

SIMEON (*after a pause—thoughtfully*): What d'ye calc'late she'll be like— our new Maw? Like Eben thinks?

PETER: More'n' likely.

SIMEON (*vindictively*): Waal—I hope she's a she-devil that'll make him wish he was dead an' livin' in the pit o' hell fur comfort!

PETER (*fervently*): Amen!

SIMEON (*imitating his father's voice*): "I'm ridin' out t' learn God's message t' me in the spring like the prophets done," he says. I'll bet right then an' thar he knew plumb well he was goin' whorin', the stinkin' old hypocrite!

(*The Curtain Falls.*)

SCENE FOUR

Same as scene two—shows the interior of the kitchen with a lighted candle on table. It is gray dawn outside. SIMEON *and* PETER *are just finishing their breakfast.* EBEN *sits before his plate of untouched food, brooding frowningly.*

PETER (*glancing at him rather irritably*): Lookin' glum don't help none.

SIMEON (*sarcastically*): Sorrowin' over his lust o' the flesh!

PETER (*with a grin*): Was she yer fust?

EBEN (*angrily*): None o' yer business. (*A pause*) I was thinkin' o' him. I got a notion he's gittin' near—I kin feel him comin' on like yew kin feel malaria chill afore it takes ye.

PETER: It's too early yet.

SIMEON: Dunno. He'd like t' catch us nappin'—jest t' have somethin' t' hoss us 'round over.

PETER (*mechanically gets to his feet.* SIMEON *does the same*): Waal—let's git t' wuk. (*They both plod mechanically toward the door before they realize. Then they stop short.*)

SIMEON (*grinning*): Ye're a cussed fool, Pete—and I be wuss! Let him see we hain't wukin'! We don't give a durn!

PETER (*as they go back to the table*): Not a damned durn! It'll serve t' show him we're done with him. (*They sit down again.* EBEN *stares from one to the other with surprise.*)

SIMEON (*grins at him*): We're aimin' t' start bein' lilies o' the field.

PETER: Nary a toil 'r spin 'r lick o' wuk do we put in!

SIMEON: Ye're sole owner—till he comes—that's what ye wanted. Waal, ye got t' be sole hand, too.

PETER: The cows air bellerin'. Ye better hustle at the milkin'.

EBEN (*with excited joy*): Ye mean ye'll sign the paper?

SIMEON (*dryly*): Mebbe.

PETER: Mebbe.

SIMEON: We're considerin'. (*Peremptorily*) We better git t' wuk.

EBEN (*with queer excitement*): It's Maw's farm agen! It's my farm! Them's my cows! I'll milk my durn fingers off fur cows o' mine! (*He goes out door in rear; they stare after him indifferently.*)

SIMEON: Like his Paw.

PETER: Dead spit 'n' image!

SIMEON: Waal—let dog eat dog! (EBEN *comes out of front door and around the corner of the house. The sky is beginning to grow flushed with sunrise.* EBEN *stops by the gate and stares around him with glowing, possessive eyes. He takes in the whole farm with his embracing glance of desire.*)

EBEN: It's purty! It's damned purty! It's mine! (*He suddenly throws his head back boldly and glares with hard, defiant eyes at the sky*) Mine, d'ye hear? Mine! (*He turns and walks quickly off left, rear, toward the barn. The two brothers light their pipes.*)

SIMEON (*putting his muddy boots up on the table, tilting back his chair, and puffing defiantly*): Waal—this air solid comfort—fur once.

PETER: Ay-eh. (*He follows suit. A pause. Unconsciously they both sigh.*)

SIMEON (*suddenly*): He never was much o' a hand at milkin', Eben wa'n't.

PETER (*with a snort*): His hands air like hoofs! (*A pause.*)

SIMEON: Reach down the jug thar! Let's take a swaller. I'm feelin' kind o' low.

PETER: Good idee! (*He does so—gets two glasses—they pour out drinks of whisky*) Here's t' the gold in Californi-a!

SIMEON: An' luck t' find it! (*They drink—puff resolutely—sigh—take their feet down from the table.*)

PETER: Likker don't 'pear t' sot right.

SIMEON: We hain't used t' it this early. (*A pause. They become very restless.*)

PETER: Gittin' close in this kitchen.

SIMEON (*with immense relief*): Let's git a breath o' air. (*They arise briskly and go out rear—appear around house and stop by the gate. They stare up at the sky with a numbed appreciation.*)

PETER: Purty!

SIMEON: Ay-eh. Gold's t' the East now.

PETER: Sun's startin' with us fur the Golden West.

SIMEON (*staring around the farm, his compressed face tightened, unable to conceal his emotion*): Waal—it's our last mornin'—mebbe.

PETER (*the same*): Ay-eh.

SIMEON (*stamps his foot on the earth and addresses it desperately*): Waal—ye've thirty year o' me buried in ye—spread out over ye—blood an' bone an' sweat—rotted away—fertilizin' ye—richin' yer soul—prime manure, by God, that's what I been t' ye!

PETER: Ay-eh! An' me!

SIMEON: An' yew, Peter. (*He sighs—then spits*) Waal—no use 'n cryin' over spilt milk.

PETER: They's gold in the West—an' freedom, mebbe. We been slaves t' stone walls here.

SIMEON (*defiantly*): We hain't nobody's slaves from this out—nor no thin's slaves nuther. (*A pause—restlessly*) Speakin' o' milk, wonder how Eben's managin'?

PETER: I s'pose he's managin'.

SIMEON: Mebbe we'd ought t' help—this once.

PETER: Mebbe. The cows knows us.

SIMEON: An' likes us. They don't know him much.

PETER: An' the hosses, an' pigs, an' chickens. They don't know him much.

SIMEON: They knows us like brothers—an' likes us! (*Proudly*) Hain't we raised 'em t' be fust-rate, number one prize stock?

PETER: We hain't—not no more.

SIMEON (*dully*): I was fergittin'. (*Then resignedly*) Waal, let's go help Eben a spell an' git waked up.

PETER: Suits me. (*They are starting off down left, rear, for the barn when* EBEN *appears from there hurrying toward them, his face excited.*)

EBEN (*breathlessly*): Waal—thar they be! The old mule an' the bride! I seen 'em from the barn down below at the turnin'.

PETER: How could ye tell that far?

EBEN: Hain't I as far-sight as he's near-sight? Don't I know the mare 'n' buggy, an' two people settin' in it? Who else . . .? An' I tell ye I kin feel 'em a-comin', too! (*He squirms as if he had the itch.*)

PETER (*beginning to be angry*): Waal—let him do his own unhitchin'!

SIMEON (*angry in his turn*): Let's hustle in an' git our bundles an' be a-goin' as he's a-comin'. I don't want never t' step inside the door agen arter he's back. (*They both start back around the corner of the house.* EBEN *follows them.*)

EBEN (*anxiously*): Will ye sign it afore ye go?

PETER: Let's see the color o' the old skinflint's money an' we'll sign. (*They disappear left. The two brothers clump upstairs to get their bundles.* EBEN *appears in the kitchen, runs to window, peers out, comes back and pulls up a strip of flooring in under stove, takes out a canvas bag and puts it on table, then sets the floorboard back in place. The two brothers appear a moment after. They carry old carpetbags.*)

EBEN (*puts his hand on bag guardingly*): Have ye signed?

SIMEON (*shows paper in his hand*): Ay-eh. (Greedily) Be that the money?

EBEN (*opens bag and pours out pile of twenty-dollar gold pieces*): Twenty-dollar pieces—thirty of 'em. Count 'em. (*Peter does so, arranging them in stacks of five, biting one or two to test them.*)

PETER: Six hundred. (*He puts them in bag and puts it inside his shirt carefully.*)

SIMEON (*handing paper to* EBEN): Har ye be.

EBEN (*after a glance, folds it carefully and hides it under his shirt—gratefully*): Thank yew.

PETER: Thank yew fur the ride.

SIMEON: We'll send ye a lump o' gold fur Christmas. (*A pause.* EBEN *stares at them and they at him.*)

PETER (*awkwardly*): Waal—we're a-goin'.

SIMEON: Comin' out t' the yard?

EBEN: No. I'm waitin' in here a spell. (*Another silence. The brothers edge awkwardly to door in rear—then turn and stand.*)

SIMEON: Waal—good-by.

PETER: Good-by.

EBEN: Good-by. (*They go out. He sits down at the table, faces the stove and pulls out the paper. He looks from it to the stove. His face, lighted up by the shaft of sunlight from the window, has an expression of trance. His lips move. The two brothers come out to the gate.*)

PETER (*looking off toward barn*): Thar he be—unhitchin'.

SIMEON (*with a chuckle*): I'll bet ye he's riled!

PETER: An' thar she be.

SIMEON: Let's wait 'n' see what our new Maw looks like.

PETER (*with a grin*): An' give him our partin' cuss!

SIMEON (*grinning*): I feel like raisin' fun. I feel light in my head an' feet.

PETER: Me, too. I feel like laffin' till I'd split up the middle.

SIMEON: Reckon it's the likker?

PETER: No. My feet feel itchin' t' walk an' walk—an' jump high over thin's —an'. . . .

SIMEON: Dance? (*A pause.*)

PETER (*puzzled*): It's plumb onnateral.

SIMEON (*a light coming over his face*): I calc'late it's 'cause school's out. It's holiday. Fur once we're free!

PETER (*dazedly*): Free?

SIMEON: The halter's broke—the harness is busted—the fence bars is down— the stone walls air crumblin' an' tumblin'! We'll be kickin' up an' tearin' away down the road!

PETER (*drawing a deep breath—oratorically*): Anybody that wants this stinkin' old rock-pile of a farm kin hev it. 'Tain't our'n, no sirree!

SIMEON (*takes the gate off its hinges and puts it under his arm*): We harby 'bolishes shet gates, an' open gates, an' all gates, by thunder!

PETER: We'll take it with us fur luck an' let 'er sail free down some river.

SIMEON (*as a sound of voices comes from left, rear*): Har they comes! (*The two brothers congeal into two stiff, grim-visaged statues.* EPHRAIM CABOT *and* ABBIE PUTNAM *come in.* CABOT *is seventy-five, tall and gaunt, with great, wiry, concentrated power, but stoop-shouldered from toil. His face is as hard as if it were hewn out of a boulder, yet there is a weakness in it, a petty pride in its own narrow strength. His eyes are small, close together, and extremely near-sighted, blinking continually in the effort to focus on objects, their stare having a straining, ingrowing quality. He is dressed in his dismal black Sunday suit.* ABBIE *is thirty-five, buxom, full of vitality. Her round face is pretty but marred by its rather gross sensuality. There is strength and obstinacy in her jaw, a hard determination in her eyes, and about her whole personality the same unsettled, untamed, desperate quality which is so apparent in* EBEN.)

CABOT (*as they enter—a queer strangled emotion in his dry cracking voice*): Har we be t' hum, Abbie.

ABBIE (*with lust for the word*): Hum! (*Her eyes gloating on the house without seeming to see the two stiff figures at the gate*) It's purty—purty! I can't b'lieve it's r'ally mine.

CABOT (*sharply*): Yewr'n? Mine! (*He stares at her penetratingly, she stares back. He adds relentingly*) Our'n—mebbe! It was lonesome too long. I was growin' old in the spring. A hum's got t' hev a woman.

ABBIE (*her voice taking possession*) : A woman's got t' hev a hum!

CABOT (*nodding uncertainly*) : Ay-eh. (*Then irritably*) Whar be they? Ain't thar nobody about—'r wukin'—'r nothin'?

ABBIE (*sees the brothers. She returns their stare of cold appraising contempt with interest—slowly*) : Thar's two men loafin' at the gate an' starin' at me like a couple o' strayed hogs.

CABOT (*straining his eyes*) : I kin see 'em—but I can't make out. . . .

SIMEON : It's Simeon.

PETER : It's Peter.

CABOT (*exploding*) : Why hain't ye wukin'?

SIMEON (*dryly*) : We're waitin' t' welcome ye hum—yew an' the bride!

CABOT (*confusedly*) : Huh? Waal—this be yer new Maw, boys. (*She stares at them and they at her.*)

SIMEON (*turns away and spits contemptuously*) : I see her!

PETER (*spits also*) : An' I see her!

ABBIE (*with the conqueror's conscious superiority*) : I'll go in an' look at my house. (*She goes slowly around to porch.*)

SIMEON (*with a snort*) : *Her* house!

PETER (*calls after her*) : Ye'll find Eben inside. Ye better not tell him it's *yewr* house.

ABBIE (*mouthing the name*) : Eben. (*Then quietly*) I'll tell Eben.

CABOT (*with a contemptuous sneer*) : Ye needn't heed Eben. Eben's a dumb fool—like his Maw—soft an' simple!

SIMEON (*with his sardonic burst of laughter*) : Ha! Eben's a chip o' yew—spit 'n' image—hard 'n' bitter's a hickory tree! Dog'll eat dog. He'll eat ye yet, old man!

CABOT (*commandingly*) : Ye git t' wuk!

SIMEON (*as ABBIE disappears in house—winks at PETER and says tauntingly*) : So that thar's our new Maw, be it? Whar in hell did ye dig her up? (*He and PETER laugh.*)

PETER : Ha! Ye'd better turn her in the pen with the other sows. (*They laugh uproariously, slapping their thighs.*)

CABOT (*so amazed at their effrontery that he stutters in confusion*) : Simeon! Peter! What's come over ye? Air ye drunk?

SIMEON : We're free, old man—free o' yew an' the hull damned farm! (*They grow more and more hilarious and excited.*)

PETER : An' we're startin' out fur the gold fields o' Californi-a!

SIMEON : Ye kin take this place an' burn it!

PETER : An' bury it—fur all we cares!

SIMEON : We're free, old man! (*He cuts a caper.*)

PETER : Free! (*He gives a kick in the air.*)

SIMEON (*in a frenzy*) : Whoop!

PETER : Whoop! (*They do an absurd Indian war dance about the old man, who is petrified between rage and the fear that they are insane.*)

SIMEON : We're free as Injuns! Lucky we don't skulp ye!

PETER: An' burn yer barn an' kill the stock!

SIMEON: An' rape yer new woman! Whoop! (*He and* PETER *stop their dance, holding their sides, rocking with wild laughter.*)

CABOT (*edging away*): Lust fur gold—fur the sinful, easy gold o' Californi-a! It's made ye mad!

SIMEON (*tauntingly*): Wouldn't ye like us to send ye back some sinful gold, ye old sinner?

PETER: They's gold besides what's in Californi-a! (*He retreats back beyond the vision of the old man and takes the bag of money and flaunts it in the air above his head, laughing.*)

SIMEON: And sinfuller, too!

PETER: We'll be voyagin' on the sea! Whoop! (*He leaps up and down.*)

SIMEON: Livin' free! Whoop! (*He leaps in turn.*)

CABOT (*suddenly roaring with rage*): My cuss on ye!

SIMEON: Take our'n in trade fur it! Whoop!

CABOT: I'll hev ye both chained up in the asylum!

PETER: Ye old skinflint! Good-by!

SIMEON: Ye old blood sucker! Good-by!

CABOT: Go afore I . . . !

PETER: Whoop! (*He picks a stone from the road.* SIMEON *does the same.*)

SIMEON: Maw'll be in the parlor.

PETER: Ay-eh! One! Two!

CABOT (*frightened*): What air ye . . . ?

PETER: Three! (*They both throw, the stones hitting the parlor window with a crash of glass, tearing the shade.*)

SIMEON: Whoop!

PETER: Whoop!

CABOT (*in a fury now, rushing toward them*): If I kin lay hands on ye— I'll break yer bones fur ye! (*But they beat a capering retreat before him,* SIMEON *with the gate still under his arm.* CABOT *comes back, panting with impotent rage. Their voices as they go off take up the song of the gold-seekers to the old tune of "Oh, Susannah!"*)

> "I jumped aboard the Liza ship,
> And traveled on the sea,
> And every time I thought of home
> I wished it wasn't me!
> Oh! Californi-a,
> That's the land fur me!
> I'm off to Californi-a!
> With my wash bowl on my knee."

In the meantime, the window of the upper bedroom on right is raised and ABBIE *sticks her head out. She looks down at* CABOT—*with a sigh of relief.*)

ABBIE: Waal—that's the last o' them two, hain't it? (*He doesn't answer. Then in possessive tones*) This here's a nice bedroom, Ephraim. It's a r'al nice bed. Is it my room, Ephraim?

CABOT (*grimly—without looking up*): Our'n! (*She cannot control a grimace of aversion and pulls back her head slowly and shuts the window. A sudden horrible thought seems to enter* CABOT's *head*) They been up to somethin'! Mebbe—mebbe they've pizened the stock—'r somethin'! (*He almost runs off down toward the barn. A moment later the kitchen door is slowly pushed open and* ABBIE *enters. For a moment she stands looking at* EBEN. *He does not notice her at first. Her eyes take him in penetratingly with a calculating appraisal of his strength as against hers. But under this her desire is dimly awakened by his youth and good looks. Suddenly he becomes conscious of her presence and looks up. Their eyes meet. He leaps to his feet, glowering at her speechlessly.*)

ABBIE (*in her most seductive tones which she uses all through this scene*): Be you—Eben? I'm Abbie— (*She laughs*) I mean, I'm yer new Maw.

EBEN (*viciously*): No, damn ye!

ABBIE (*as if she hadn't heard—with a queer smile*): Yer Paw's spoke a lot o' yew. . . .

EBEN: Ha!

ABBIE: Ye mustn't mind him. He's an old man. (*A long pause. They stare at each other*) I don't want t' pretend playin' Maw t' ye, Eben. (*Admiringly*) Ye're too big an' too strong fur that. I want t' be frens with ye. Mebbe with me fur a fren ye'd find ye'd like livin' here better. I kin make it easy fur ye with him, mebbe. (*With a scornful sense of power*) I calc'late I kin git him t' do most anythin' fur me.

EBEN (*with bitter scorn*): Ha! (*They stare again,* EBEN *obscurely moved, physically attracted to her—in forced stilted tones*): Yew kin go t' the devil!

ABBIE (*calmly*): If cussin' me does ye good, cuss all ye've a mind t'. I'm all prepared t' have ye agin me—at fust. I don't blame ye nuther. I'd feel the same at any stranger comin' t' take my Maw's place. (*He shudders. She is watching him carefully*) Yew must've cared a lot fur yewr Maw, didn't ye? My Maw died afore I'd growed. I don't remember her none. (*A pause*) But yew won't hate me long, Eben. I'm not the wust in the world—an' yew an' me've got a lot in common. I kin tell that by lookin' at ye. Waal—I've had a hard life, too—oceans o' trouble an' nuthin' but wuk fur reward. I was a orphan early an' had t' wuk fur others in other folks' hums. Then I married an' he turned out a drunken spreer an' so he had to wuk fur others an' me too agen in other folks' hums, an' the baby died, an' my husband got sick an' died too, an' I was glad sayin' now I'm free fur once, on'y I diskivered right away all I was free fur was t' wuk agen in other folks' hums, doin' other folks' wuk till I'd most give up hope o' ever doin' my own wuk in my own hum, an' then yewr Paw come. . . . (CABOT *appears returning from the barn. He comes to the gate and looks down the road the brothers have gone. A faint strain of their retreating voices is heard: "Oh, Californi-a! That's the place for me." He stands glowering, his fist clenched, his face grim with rage.*)

EBEN (*fighting against his growing attraction and sympathy—harshly*): An' bought yew—like a harlot! (*She is stung and flushes angrily. She has been sincerely moved by the recital of her troubles. He adds furiously*) An' the price he's payin' ye—this farm—was my Maw's, damn ye!—an' mine now!

ABBIE (*with a cool laugh of confidence*): Yewr'n? We'll see 'bout that! (*Then strongly*) Waal—what if I did need a hum? What else'd I marry an old man like him fur?

EBEN (*maliciously*): I'll tell him ye said that!

ABBIE (*smiling*): I'll say ye're lyin' a-purpose—an' he'll drive ye off the place!

EBEN: Ye devil!

ABBIE (*defying him*): This be my farm—this be my hum—this be my kitchen—!

EBEN (*furiously, as if he were going to attack her*): Shut up, damn ye!

ABBIE (*walks up to him—a queer coarse expression of desire in her face and body—slowly*): An' upstairs—that be my bedroom—an' my bed! (*He stares into her eyes, terribly confused and torn. She adds softly*) I hain't bad nor mean—'ceptin' fur an enemy—but I got t' fight fur what's due me out o' life, if I ever 'spect t' git it. (*Then putting her hand on his arm—seductively*) Let's yew 'n' me be frens, Eben.

EBEN (*stupidly—as if hypnotized*): Ay-eh. (*Then furiously flinging off her arm*) No, ye durned old witch! I hate ye! (*He rushes out the door.*)

ABBIE (*looks after him smiling satisfiedly—then half to herself, mouthing the word*): Eben's nice. (*She looks at the table, proudly*) I'll wash up *my* dishes now. (EBEN *appears outside, slamming the door behind him. He comes around corner, stops on seeing his father, and stands staring at him with hate.*)

CABOT (*raising his arms to heaven in the fury he can no longer control*): Lord God o' Hosts, smite the undutiful sons with Thy wust cuss!

EBEN (*breaking in violently*): Yew 'n' yewr God! Allus cussin' folks—allus naggin' 'em!

CABOT (*oblivious to him—summoningly*): God o' the old! God o' the lonesome!

EBEN (*mockingly*): Naggin' His sheep t' sin! T' hell with yewr God! (CABOT *turns. He and* EBEN *glower at each other.*)

CABOT (*harshly*): So it's yew. I might've knowed it. (*Shaking his finger threateningly at him*) Blasphemin' fool! (*Then quickly*) Why hain't ye t' wuk?

EBEN: Why hain't yew? They've went. I can't wuk it all alone.

CABOT (*contemptuously*): Nor noways! I'm wuth ten o' ye yit, old's I be! Ye'll never be more'n half a man! (*Then, matter-of-factly*) Waal—let's git t' the barn. (*They go. A last faint note of the "Californi-a" song is heard from the distance.* ABBIE *is washing her dishes.*)

(*The Curtain Falls.*)

Part Two

SCENE ONE

The exterior of the farmhouse, as in Part One—a hot Sunday afternoon two months later. ABBIE, *dressed in her best, is discovered sitting in a rocker at the end of the porch. She rocks listlessly, enervated by the heat, staring in front of her with bored, half-closed eyes.*

EBEN *sticks his head out of his bedroom window. He looks around furtively and tries to see—or hear—if anyone is on the porch, but although he has been careful to make no noise,* ABBIE *has sensed his movement. She stops rocking, her face grows animated and eager, she waits attentively.* EBEN *seems to feel her presence, he scowls back his thoughts of her and spits with exaggerated disdain—then withdraws back into the room.* ABBIE *waits, holding her breath as she listens with passionate eagerness for every sound within the house.*

EBEN *comes out. Their eyes meet. His falter, he is confused, he turns away and slams the door resentfully. At this gesture,* ABBIE *laughs tantalizingly, amused but at the same time piqued and irritated. He scowls, strides off the porch to the path and starts to walk past her to the road with a grand swagger of ignoring her existence. He is dressed in his store suit, spruced up, his face shines from soap and water.* ABBIE *leans forward on her chair, her eyes hard and angry now, and, as he passes her, gives a sneering, taunting chuckle.*

EBEN *(stung—turns on her furiously)* : What air yew cacklin' 'bout?
ABBIE *(triumphant)* : Yew!
EBEN : What about me?
ABBIE : Ye look all slicked up like a prize bull.
EBEN *(with a sneer)* : Waal—ye hain't so durned purty yerself, be ye? *(They stare into each other's eyes, his held by hers in spite of himself, hers glowingly possessive. Their physical attraction becomes a palpable force quivering in the hot air.)*
ABBIE *(softly)* : Ye don't mean that, Eben. Ye may think ye mean it, mebbe, but ye don't. Ye can't. It's agin nature, Eben. Ye been fightin' yer nature ever since the day I come—tryin' t' tell yerself I hain't purty t'ye. *(She laughs a low humid laugh without taking her eyes from his. A pause—her body squirms desirously—she murmurs languorously)* Hain't the sun strong an' hot? Ye kin feel it burnin' into the earth—Nature—makin' thin's grow —bigger 'n' bigger—burnin' inside ye—makin' ye want t' grow—into somethin' else—till ye're jined with it—an' it's your'n—but it owns ye, too—an' makes ye grow bigger—like a tree—like them elums— *(She laughs again*

softly, holding his eyes. He takes a step toward her, compelled against his will) Nature'll beat ye, Eben. Ye might's well own up t' it fust 's last.

EBEN *(trying to break from her spell—confusedly)* : If Paw'd hear ye goin' on. . . . *(Resentfully)* But ye've made such a damned idjit out o' the old devil . . . ! *(*ABBIE *laughs.)*

ABBIE: Waal—hain't it easier fur yew with him changed softer?

EBEN *(defiantly)* : No. I'm fightin' him—fightin' yew—fightin' fur Maw's rights t' her hum! *(This breaks her spell for him. He glowers at her)* An' I'm onto ye. Ye hain't foolin' me a mite. Ye're aimin' t' swaller up every-thin' an' make it your'n. Waal, you'll find I'm a heap sight bigger hunk nor yew kin chew! *(He turns from her with a sneer.)*

ABBIE *(trying to regain her ascendancy—seductively)* : Eben!

EBEN: Leave me be! *(He starts to walk away.)*

ABBIE *(more commandingly)* : Eben!

EBEN *(stops—resentfully)* : What d'ye want?

ABBIE *(trying to conceal a growing excitement)* : Whar air ye goin'?

EBEN *(with malicious nonchalance)* : Oh—up the road a spell.

ABBIE: T' the village?

EBEN *(airily)* : Mebbe.

ABBIE *(excitedly)* : T' see that Min, I s'pose?

EBEN: Mebbe.

ABBIE *(weakly)* : What d'ye want t' waste time on her fur?

EBEN *(revenging himself now—grinning at her)* : Ye can't beat Nature, didn't ye say? *(He laughs and again starts to walk away.)*

ABBIE *(bursting out)* : An ugly old hake!

EBEN *(with a tantalizing sneer)* : She's purtier'n yew be!

ABBIE: That every wuthless drunk in the country has. . . .

EBEN *(tauntingly)* : Mebbe—but she's better'n yew. She owns up fa'r 'n' squar' t' her doin's.

ABBIE *(furiously)* : Don't ye dare compare. . . .

EBEN: She don't go sneakin' an' stealin'—what's mine.

ABBIE *(savagely seizing on his weak point)* : Your'n? Yew mean—my farm?

EBEN: I mean the farm yew sold yerself fur like any other old whore—my farm!

ABBIE *(stung—fiercely)* : Ye'll never live t' see the day when even a stinkin' weed on it 'll belong t' ye! *(Then in a scream)* Git out o' my sight! Go on t' yer slut—disgracin' yer Paw 'n' me! I'll git yer Paw t' horsewhip ye off the place if I want t'! Ye're only livin' here 'cause I tolerate ye! Git along! I hate the sight o' ye! *(She stops panting and glaring at him.)*

EBEN *(returning her glance in kind)* : An' I hate the sight o' yew! *(He turns and strides off up the road. She follows his retreating figure with concen-trated hate. Old* CABOT *appears coming up from the barn. The hard, grim expression of his face has changed. He seems in some queer way softened, mellowed. His eyes have taken on a strange, incongruous dreamy quality. Yet there is no hint of physical weakness about him—rather he looks more robust and younger.* ABBIE *sees him and turns away quickly with uncon-cealed aversion. He comes slowly up to her.)*

CABOT (*mildly*) : War yew an' Eben quarrelin' agen?

ABBIE (*shortly*) : No.

CABOT: Ye was talkin' a'mighty loud. (*He sits down on the edge of porch.*)

ABBIE (*snappishly*) : If ye heerd us they hain't no need askin' questions.

CABOT: I didn't hear what ye said.

ABBIE (*relieved*) : Waal—it wa'n't nothin' t' speak on.

CABOT (*after a pause*) : Eben's queer.

ABBIE (*bitterly*) : He's the dead spit 'n' image o' yew!

CABOT (*queerly interested*): D'ye think so, Abbie? (*After a pause, ruminatingly*) Me 'n' Eben's allus fit 'n' fit. I never could b'ar him noways. He's so thunderin' soft—like his Maw.

ABBIE (*scornfully*) : Ay-eh! 'Bout as soft as yew be!

CABOT (*as if he hadn't heard*) : Mebbe I been too hard on him.

ABBIE (*jeeringly*) : Waal—ye're gittin' soft now—soft as slop! That's what Eben was sayin'.

CABOT (*his face instantly grim and ominous*) : Eben was sayin'? Waal, he'd best not do nothin' t' try me 'r he'll soon diskiver. . . . (*A pause. She keeps her face turned away. His gradually softens. He stares up at the sky*) Purty, hain't it?

ABBIE (*crossly*) : I don't see nothin' purty.

CABOT: The sky. Feels like a wa'm field up thar.

ABBIE (*sarcastically*) : Air yew aimin' t' buy up over the farm too? (*She snickers contemptuously.*)

CABOT (*strangely*) : I'd like t' own my place up thar. (*A pause*) I'm gittin' old, Abbie. I'm gittin' ripe on the bough. (*A pause. She stares at him mystified. He goes on*) It's allus lonesome cold in the house—even when it's bilin' hot outside. Hain't yew noticed?

ABBIE: No.

CABOT: It's wa'm down t'the barn—nice smellin' an' wa'm—with the cows. (*A pause*) Cows is queer.

ABBIE: Like yew?

CABOT: Like Eben. (*A pause*) I'm gittin' t' feel resigned t' Eben—jest as I got t' feel 'bout his Maw. I'm gittin' t' learn to b'ar his softness—jest like her'n. I calc'late I c'd a'most take t' him—if he wa'n't sech a dumb fool! (*A pause*) I s'pose it's old age a'creepin' in my bones.

ABBIE (*indifferently*) : Waal—ye hain't dead yet.

CABOT (*roused*) : No, I hain't, yew bet—not by a hell of a sight—I'm sound 'n' tough as hickory! (*Then moodily*) But arter three score and ten the Lord warns ye t' prepare. (*A pause*) That's why Eben's come in my head. Now that his cussed sinful brothers is gone their path t' hell, they's no one left but Eben.

ABBIE (*resentfully*) : They's me, hain't they? (*Agitatedly*) What's all this sudden likin' ye've tuk to Eben? Why don't ye say nothin' 'bout me? Hain't I yer lawful wife?

CABOT (*simply*) : Ay-eh. Ye be. (*A pause—he stares at her desirously—his eyes grow avid—then with a sudden movement he seizes her hands and squeezes them, declaiming in a queer camp-meeting preacher's tempo*) Yew air my Rose o' Sharon! Behold, yew air fair; yer eyes air doves; yer lips air like scarlet; yer two breasts air like two fawns; yer navel be like a round goblet; yer belly be like a heap o' wheat. . . .[4] (*He covers her hand with kisses. She does not seem to notice. She stares before her with hard angry eyes.*)

ABBIE (*jerking her hands away—harshly*): So ye're plannin' t' leave the farm t' Eben, air ye?

CABOT (*dazedly*): Leave . . . ? (*Then with resentful obstinacy*) I hain't a-givin' it t' no one!

ABBIE (*remorselessly*): Ye can't take it with ye.

CABOT (*thinks a moment—then reluctantly*): No, I calc'late not. (*After a pause—with a strange passion*) But if I could, I would, by the Etarnal! 'R if I could, in my dyin' hour, I'd set it afire an' watch it burn—this house an' every ear o' corn an' every tree down t' the last blade o' hay! I'd sit an' know it was all a-dying with me an' no one else'd ever own what was mine, what I'd made out o' nothin' with my own sweat 'n' blood! (*A pause—then he adds with a queer affection*) 'Ceptin' the cows. Them I'd turn free.

ABBIE (*harshly*): An' me?

CABOT (*with a queer smile*): Ye'd be turned free, too.

ABBIE (*furiously*): So that's the thanks I git fur marryin' ye—t' have ye change kind to Eben who hates ye, an' talk o' turnin' me out in the road.

CABOT (*hastily*): Abbie! Ye know I wa'n't. . . .

ABBIE (*vengefully*): Just let me tell ye a thing or two 'bout Eben! Whar's he gone? T' see that harlot, Min! I tried fur t' stop him. Disgracin' yew an' me—on the Sabbath, too!

CABOT (*rather guiltily*): He's a sinner—nateral-born. It's lust eatin' his heart.

ABBIE (*enraged beyond endurance—wildly vindictive*): An' his lust fur me! Kin ye find excuses fur that?

CABOT (*stares at her—after a dead pause*): Lust—fur yew?

ABBIE (*defiantly*): He was tryin' t' make love t' me—when ye heerd us quarrelin'.

CABOT (*stares at her—then a terrible expression of rage comes over his face—he springs to his feet shaking all over*): By the A'mighty God—I'll end him!

ABBIE (*frightened now for* EBEN): No! Don't ye!

CABOT (*violently*): I'll git the shotgun an' blow his soft brains t' the top o' them elums!

ABBIE (*throwing her arms around him*): No, Ephraim!

CABOT (*pushing her away violently*): I will, by God!

ABBIE (*in a quieting tone*): Listen, Ephraim. 'Twa'n't nothin' bad—on'y a boy's foolin'—'twa'n't meant serious—jest jokin' an' teasin'. . . .

---

[4] Cabot is misquoting fragments from The Song of Solomon 4 and 7:

"Behold, thou art fair, my love; thou hast doves' eyes within thy locks. . . . Thy lips are like a thread of scarlet. . . . Thy two breasts are like two young roes that are twins, which feed among the lilies. (4:1, 3, 5)

"Thy navel is like a round goblet, which wanteth not liquor: thy belly is like a heap of wheat set about with lilies." (7:2)

CABOT: Then why did ye say—lust?

ABBIE: It must hev sounded wusser'n I meant. An' I was mad at thinkin'—ye'd leave him the farm.

CABOT (*quieter but still grim and cruel*): Waal then, I'll horsewhip him off the place if that much'll content ye.

ABBIE (*reaching out and taking his hand*): No. Don't think o' me! Ye mustn't drive him off. 'Tain't sensible. Who'll ye get to help ye on the farm? They's no one hereabouts.

CABOT (*considers this—then nodding his appreciation*): Ye got a head on ye. (*Then irritably*) Waal, let him stay. (*He sits down on the edge of the porch. She sits beside him. He murmurs contemptuously*) I oughtn't t' git riled so—at that 'ere fool calf. (*A pause*) But har's the p'int. What son o' mine'll keep on here t' the farm—when the Lord does call me? Simeon an' Peter air gone t' hell—an' Eben's follerin' 'em.

ABBIE: They's me.

CABOT: Ye're on'y a woman.

ABBIE: I'm yewr wife.

CABOT: That hain't me. A son is me—my blood—mine. Mine ought t' git mine. An' then it's still mine—even though I be six foot under. D'ye see?

ABBIE (*giving him a look of hatred*): Ay-eh. I see. (*She becomes very thoughtful, her face growing shrewd, her eyes studying* CABOT *craftily.*)

CABOT: I'm gittin' old—ripe on the bough. (*Then with a sudden forced reassurance*) Not but what I hain't a hard nut t' crack even yet—an' fur many a year t' come! By the Etarnal, I kin break most o' the young fellers' backs at any kind o' work any day o' the year!

ABBIE (*suddenly*): Mebbe the Lord'll give *us* a son.

CABOT (*turns and stares at her eagerly*): Ye mean—a son—t' me 'n' yew?

ABBIE (*with a cajoling smile*): Ye're a strong man yet, hain't ye? 'Tain't noways impossible, be it? We know that. Why d'ye stare so? Hain't ye never thought o' that afore? I been thinkin' o' it all along. Ay-eh—an' I been prayin' it'd happen, too.

CABOT (*his face growing full of joyous pride and a sort of religious ecstasy*): Ye been prayin', Abbie?—fur a son?—t' us?

ABBIE: Ay-eh. (*With a grim resolution*) I want a son now.

CABOT (*excitedly clutching both of her hands in his*): It'd be the blessin' o' God, Abbie—the blessin' o' God A'mighty on me—in my old age—in my lonesomeness! They hain't nothin' I wouldn't do fur ye then, Abbie. Ye'd hev on'y t' ask it—anythin' ye'd a mind t'!

ABBIE (*interrupting*): Would ye will the farm t' me then—t' me an' it . . . ?

CABOT (*vehemently*): I'd do anythin' ye axed, I tell ye! I swar it! May I be everlastin' damned t' hell if I wouldn't! (*He sinks to his knees pulling her down with him. He trembles all over with the fervor of his hopes*) Pray t' the Lord agen, Abbie. It's the Sabbath! I'll jine ye! Two prayers air better nor one. "An' God hearkened unto Rachel"![5] An' God hearkened

---

[5] Rachel was the wife of Jacob. After many years of marriage she bore him a son but died in childbirth. (Gen. 35:16-19)

unto Abbie! Pray, Abbie! Pray fur him to hearken! (*He bows his head, mumbling. She pretends to do likewise but gives him a side glance of scorn and triumph.*)

(*The Curtain Falls.*)

SCENE TWO

About eight in the evening. The interior of the two bedrooms on the top floor is shown. EBEN *is sitting on the side of his bed in the room on the left. On account of the heat he has taken off everything but his undershirt and pants. His feet are bare. He faces front, brooding moodily, his chin propped on his hands, a desperate expression on his face.*

In the other room CABOT *and* ABBIE *are sitting side by side on the edge of their bed, an old four-poster with feather mattress. He is in his night shirt, she in her nightdress. He is still in the queer, excited mood into which the notion of a son has thrown him. Both rooms are lighted dimly and flickeringly by tallow candles.*

CABOT: The farm needs a son.

ABBIE: I need a son.

CABOT: Ay-eh. Sometimes ye air the farm an' sometimes the farm be yew. That's why I clove t' ye in my lonesomeness. (*A pause. He pounds his knee with his fist*) Me an' the farm has got t' beget a son!

ABBIE: Ye'd best go t' sleep. Ye're gittin' thin's all mixed.

CABOT (*with an impatient gesture*): No, I hain't. My mind's clear's a well. Ye don't know me, that's it. (*He stares hopelessly at the floor.*)

ABBIE (*indifferently*): Mebbe. (*In the next room* EBEN *gets up and paces up and down distractedly.* ABBIE *hears him. Her eyes fasten on the intervening wall with concentrated attention.* EBEN *stops and stares. Their hot glances seem to meet through the wall. Unconsciously he stretches out his arms for her and she half rises. Then aware, he mutters a curse at himself and flings himself face downward on the bed, his clenched fists above his head, his face buried in the pillow.* ABBIE *relaxes with a faint sigh but her eyes remain fixed on the wall; she listens with all her attention for some movement from* EBEN.)

CABOT (*suddenly raises his head and looks at her—scornfully*): Will ye ever know me—'r will any man 'r woman? (*Shaking his head*) No. I calc'late 't wa'n't t' be. (*He turns away.* ABBIE *looks at the wall. Then, evidently unable to keep silent about his thoughts without looking at his wife, he puts out his hand and clutches her knee. She starts violently, looks at him, sees he is not watching her, concentrates again on the wall and pays no attention to what he says*) Listen, Abbie. When I come here fifty odd year ago—I was jest twenty an' the strongest an' hardest ye ever seen— ten times as strong an' fifty times as hard as Eben. Waal—this place was nothin' but fields o' stones. Folks laughed when I tuk it. They couldn't know what I knowed. When ye kin make corn sprout out o' stones, God's livin' in yew! They wa'n't strong enuf fur that! They reckoned God was easy. They laughed. They don't laugh no more. Some died hereabouts. Some went West an' died. They're all under ground—fur follerin' arter an easy God. God hain't easy. (*He shakes his head slowly*) An' I growed hard. Folks kept allus sayin' he's a hard man like 'twas sinful t' be hard, so's at last I said back at 'em: Waal then, by thunder, ye'll git me hard an' see how ye like it! (*Then suddenly*) But I give in t' weakness once. 'Twas arter I'd been here two year. I got weak—despairful—they was so many stones. They was a party leavin', givin' up, goin' West. I jined 'em. We tracked on 'n' on. We come t' broad medders, plains, whar the soil was black an' rich as gold. Nary a stone. Easy. Ye'd on'y to plow an' sow an' then set an' smoke yer pipe an' watch thin's grow. I could o' been a rich man—but somethin' in me fit me an' fit me—the voice o' God sayin': "This hain't wuth nothin' t' Me. Git ye back t' hum!" I got afeerd o' that voice an' I lit out back t' hum here, leavin' my claim an' crops t' who-ever'd a mind t' take 'em. Ay-eh. I actoolly give up what was rightful mine! God's hard, not easy! God's in the stones! Build my church on a rock—out o' stones an' I'll be in them! That's what He meant t' Peter![6] (*He sighs heavily—a pause*) Stones. I picked 'em up an' piled 'em into walls. Ye kin read the years o' my life in them walls, every day a hefted stone, climbin' over the hills up and down, fencin' in the fields that was mine, whar I'd made thin's grow out o' nothin'—like the will o' God, like the servant o' His hand. It wa'n't easy. It was hard an' He made me hard fur it. (*He pauses*) All the time I kept gittin' lonesomer. I tuk a wife. She bore Simeon an' Peter. She was a good woman. She wuked hard. We was married twenty year. She never knowed me. She helped but she never knowed what she was helpin'. I was allus lonesome. She died. After that it wa'n't so lonesome fur a spell. (*A pause*) I lost count o' the years. I had no time t' fool away countin' 'em. Sim an' Peter helped. The farm growed. It was all mine! When I thought o' that I didn't feel lonesome. (*A pause*) But ye can't hitch yer mind t' one thin' day an' night. I tuk another wife—Eben's Maw. Her folks was contestin' me at law over my deeds t' the farm—my farm! That's why Eben keeps a-talkin' his fool talk o' this bein' his Maw's farm. She bore Eben. She was purty—but soft. She tried t' be hard. She couldn't. She never knowed me nor nothin'. It was lonesomer 'n hell with her. After a matter o' sixteen odd years, she died. (*A pause*) I lived with the boys. They hated me 'cause I was hard. I hated them 'cause they was soft. They coveted the farm without knowin' what it meant. It made me bitter 'n wormwood. It aged me—them covet-ing what I'd made fur mine. Then this spring the call come—the voice o' God cryin' in my wilderness, in my lonesomeness—t' go out an' seek an' find! (*Turning to her with strange passion*) I sought ye an' I found ye! Yew air my Rose o' Sharon! Yer eyes air like. . . . (*She has turned a blank*

---

[6] "And I say also unto thee, That thou art Peter, and upon this rock I will build my church; and the gates of hell shall not prevail against it." (Matt. 16:18). It is not surprising that Cabot should name one son Peter, meaning *rock*, and an-other Eben, meaning *little stone of help*.

face, resentful eyes to his. He stares at her for a moment—then harshly) Air ye any the wiser fur all I've told ye?

ABBIE (*confusedly*) : Mebbe.

CABOT (*pushing her away from him—angrily*) : Ye don't know nothin'— nor never will. If ye don't hev a son t' redeem ye. . . . (*This in a tone of cold threat.*)

ABBIE (*resentfully*) : I've prayed, hain't I?

CABOT (*bitterly*) : Pray agen—fur understandin'!

ABBIE (*a veiled threat in her tone*) : Ye'll have a son out o' me, I promise ye.

CABOT: How kin ye promise?

ABBIE: I got second-sight mebbe. I kin foretell. (*She gives a queer smile.*)

CABOT: I believe ye have. Ye give me the chills sometimes. (*He shivers*) It's cold in this house. It's oneasy. They's thin's pokin' about in the dark— in the corners. (*He pulls on his trousers, tucking in his night shirt, and pulls on his boots.*)

ABBIE (*surprised*) : Whar air ye goin'?

CABOT (*queerly*) : Down whar it's restful—whar it's warm down t' the barn. (*Bitterly*) I kin talk t' the cows. They know. They know the farm an' me. They'll give me peace. (*He turns to go out the door.*)

ABBIE (*a bit frightenedly*) : Air ye ailin' tonight, Ephraim?

CABOT: Growin'. Growin' ripe on the bough. (*He turns and goes, his boots clumping down the stairs.* EBEN *sits up with a start, listening.* ABBIE *is conscious of his movement and stares at the wall.* CABOT *comes out of the house around the corner and stands by the gate, blinking at the sky. He stretches up his hands in a tortured gesture*) God A'mighty, call from the dark! (*He listens as if expecting an answer. Then his arms drop, he shakes his head and plods off toward the barn.* EBEN *and* ABBIE *stare at each other through the wall.* EBEN *sighs heavily and* ABBIE *echoes it. Both become terribly nervous, uneasy. Finally* ABBIE *gets up and listens, her ear to the wall. He acts as if he saw every move she was making, he becomes resolutely still. She seems driven into a decision—goes out the door in rear determinedly. His eyes follow her. Then as the door of his room is opened softly, he turns away, waits in an attitude of strained fixity.* ABBIE *stands for a second staring at him, her eyes burning with desire. Then with a little cry she runs over and throws her arms about his neck, she pulls his head back and covers his mouth with kisses. At first, he submits dumbly; then he puts his arms about her neck and returns her kisses, but finally, suddenly aware of his hatred, he hurls her away from him, springing to his feet. They stand speechless and breathless, panting like two animals.*)

ABBIE (*at last—painfully*) : Ye shouldn't, Eben—ye shouldn't—I'd make ye happy!

EBEN (*harshly*) : I don't want t' be happy—from yew!

ABBIE (*helplessly*) : Ye do, Eben! Ye do! Why d'ye lie?

EBEN (*viciously*) : I don't take t'ye, I tell ye! I hate the sight o' ye!

ABBIE (*with an uncertain troubled laugh*) : Waal, I kissed ye anyways—an' ye kissed back—yer lips was burnin'—ye can't lie 'bout that! (*Intensely*) If ye don't care, why did ye kiss me back—why was yer lips burnin'?

EBEN (*wiping his mouth*) : It was like pizen on 'em. (*Then tauntingly*) When I kissed ye back, mebbe I thought 'twas someone else.

ABBIE (*wildly*) : Min?

EBEN : Mebbe.

ABBIE (*torturedly*) : Did ye go t' see her? Did ye r'ally go? I thought ye mightn't. Is that why ye throwed me off jest now?

EBEN (*sneeringly*) : What if it be?

ABBIE (*raging*) : Then ye're a dog, Eben Cabot!

EBEN (*threateningly*) : Ye can't talk that way t' me!

ABBIE (*with a shrill laugh*) : Can't I? Did ye think I was in love with ye— a weak thin' like yew? Not much! I on'y wanted ye fur a purpose o' my own—an' I'll hev ye fur it yet 'cause I'm stronger'n yew be!

EBEN (*resentfully*) : I knowed well it was on'y part o' yer plan t' swaller everythin'!

ABBIE (*tauntingly*) : Mebbe!

EBEN (*furious*) : Git out o' my room!

ABBIE : This air my room an' ye're on'y hired help!

EBEN (*threateningly*) : Git out afore I murder ye!

ABBIE (*quite confident now*) : I hain't a mite afeerd. Ye want me, don't ye? Yes, ye do! An' yer Paw's son'll never kill what he wants! Look at yer eyes! They's lust fur me in 'em, burnin' 'em up! Look at yer lips now! They're tremblin' an' longin' t' kiss me, an' yer teeth t' bite! (*He is watching her now with a horrible fascination. She laughs a crazy triumphant laugh*) I'm a-goin' t' make all o' this hum my hum! They's one room hain't mine yet, but it's a-goin' t' be tonight. I'm a-goin' down now an' light up! (*She makes him a mocking bow*) Won't ye come courtin' me in the best parlor, Mister Cabot?

EBEN (*staring at her—horribly confused—dully*) : Don't ye dare! It hain't been opened since Maw died an' was laid out thar! Don't ye . . . ! (*But her eyes are fixed on his so burningly that his will seems to wither before hers. He stands swaying toward her helplessly.*)

ABBIE (*holding his eyes and putting all her will into her words as she backs out the door*) : I'll expect ye afore long, Eben.

EBEN (*stares after her for a while, walking toward the door. A light appears in the parlor window. He murmurs*) : In the parlor? (*This seems to arouse connotations for he comes back and puts on his white shirt, collar, half ties the tie mechanically, puts on coat, takes his hat, stands barefooted looking about him in bewilderment, mutters wonderingly*) Maw! Whar air yew? (*Then goes slowly toward the door in rear.*)

(*The Curtain Falls.*)

SCENE THREE

A few minutes later. The interior of the parlor is shown. A grim, repressed room like a tomb in which the family has been interred alive. ABBIE *sits on the edge of the horsehair soft. She has lighted all the candles and the room is revealed in all its preserved ugliness. A change has come over the woman. She looks awed and frightened now, ready to run away.*

The door is opened and EBEN *appears. His face wears an expression of obsessed confusion. He stands staring at her, his arms hanging disjointedly from his shoulders, his feet bare, his hat in his hand.*

ABBIE (*after a pause—with a nervous, formal politeness*) : Won't ye set?

EBEN (*dully*) : Ay-eh. (*Mechanically he places his hat carefully on the floor near the door and sits stiffly beside her on the edge of the sofa. A pause. They both remain rigid, looking straight ahead with eyes full of fear.*)

ABBIE : When I fust come in—in the dark—they seemed somethin' here.

EBEN (*simply*) : Maw.

ABBIE : I kin still feel—somethin'. . . .

EBEN : It's Maw.

ABBIE : At fust I was feered o' it. I wanted t' yell an' run. Now—since yew come—seems like it's growin' soft an' kind t' me. (*Addressing the air—queerly*) Thank yew.

EBEN : Maw allus loved me.

ABBIE : Mebbe it knows I love yew, too. Mebbe that makes it kind t' me.

EBEN (*dully*) : I dunno. I should think she'd hate ye.

ABBIE (*with certainty*) : No. I kin feel it don't—not no more.

EBEN : Hate ye fur stealin' her place—here in her hum—settin' in her parlor whar she was laid— (*He suddenly stops, staring stupidly before him.*)

ABBIE : What is it, Eben?

EBEN (*in a whisper*) : Seems like Maw didn't want me t' remind ye.

ABBIE (*excitedly*) : I knowed, Eben! It's kind t' me! It don't b'ar me no grudges fur what I never knowed an' couldn't help!

EBEN : Maw b'ars him a grudge.

ABBIE : Waal, so does all o' us.

EBEN : Ay-eh. (*With passion*) I does, by God!

ABBIE (*taking one of his hands in hers and patting it*) : Thar! Don't git riled thinkin' o' him. Think o' yer Maw who's kind t' us. Tell me about yer Maw, Eben.

EBEN : They hain't nothin' much. She was kind. She was good.

ABBIE (*putting one arm over his shoulder. He does not seem to notice—passionately*) : I'll be kind an' good t' ye!

EBEN : Sometimes she used t' sing fur me.

ABBIE : I'll sing fur ye!

EBEN : This was her hum. This was her farm.

ABBIE : This is my hum! This is my farm!

EBEN : He married her t' steal 'em. She was soft an' easy. He couldn't 'preciate her.

ABBIE : He can't 'preciate me!

EBEN : He murdered her with his hardness.

ABBIE : He's murderin' me!

EBEN : She died. (*A pause*) Sometimes she used to sing fur me. (*He bursts into a fit of sobbing.*)

ABBIE (*both her arms around him—with wild passion*) : I'll sing fur ye! I'll die fur ye! (*In spite of her overwhelming desire for him, there is a sincere maternal love in her manner and voice—a horribly frank mixture of lust and mother love*) Don't cry, Eben! I'll take yer Maw's place! I'll be everythin' she was t' ye! Let me kiss ye, Eben! (*She pulls his head around. He makes a bewildered pretense of resistance. She is tender*) Don't be afeered! I'll kiss ye pure, Eben—same 's if I was a Maw t' ye— an' ye kin kiss me back 's if yew was my son—my boy—sayin' good-night t' me! Kiss me, Eben. (*They kiss in restrained fashion. Then suddenly wild passion overcomes her. She kisses him lustfully again and again and he flings his arms about her and returns her kisses. Suddenly, as in the bedroom, he frees himself from her violently and springs to his feet. He is trembling all over, in a strange state of terror.* ABBIE *strains her arms toward him with fierce pleading*) Don't ye leave me, Eben! Can't ye see it hain't enuf—lovin' ye like a Maw—can't ye see it's got t' be that an' more—much more—a hundred times more—fur me t' be happy—fur yew t' be happy?

EBEN (*to the presence he feels in the room*) : Maw! Maw! What d'ye want? What air ye tellin' me?

ABBIE : She's tellin' ye t' love me. She knows I love ye an' I'll be good t' ye. Can't ye feel it? Don't ye know? She's tellin' ye t' love me, Eben!

EBEN : Ay-eh. I feel—mebbe she—but—I can't figger out—why—when ye've stole her place—here in her hum—in the parlor whar she was—

ABBIE (*fiercely*) : She knows I love ye!

EBEN (*his face suddenly lighting up with a fierce, triumphant grin*) : I see it! I see why. It's her vengeance on him—so's she kin rest quiet in her grave!

ABBIE (*wildly*) : Vengeance o' God on the hull o' us! What d'we give a durn? I love ye, Eben! God knows I love ye! (*She stretches out her arms for him.*)

EBEN (*throws himself on his knees beside the sofa and grabs her in his arms —releasing all his pent-up passion*) : An' I love yew, Abbie!—now I kin say it! I been dyin' fur want o' ye—every hour since ye come! I love ye! (*Their lips meet in a fierce, bruising kiss.*)

(*The Curtain Falls.*)

SCENE FOUR

Exterior of the farmhouse. It is just dawn. The front door at right is opened and EBEN *comes out and walks around to the gate. He is dressed in his working clothes. He seems changed. His face wears a bold and confident expression, he is grinning to himself with evident satisfaction. As he gets near the gate, the window of the parlor is heard opening and the shutters are flung back and* ABBIE *sticks her head out. Her hair tumbles over her shoulders in disarray, her face is flushed, she looks at* EBEN *with tender, languorous eyes and calls softly.*

ABBIE: Eben. (*As he turns—playfully*) Jest one more kiss afore ye go. I'm goin' to miss ye fearful all day.

EBEN: An' me yew, ye kin bet! (*He goes to her. They kiss several times. He draws away, laughingly*) Thar. That's enuf, hain't it? Ye won't hev none left fur next time.

ABBIE: I got a million o' 'em left fur yew! (*Then a bit anxiously*) D'ye r'ally love me, Eben?

EBEN (*emphatically*): I like ye better'n any gal I ever knowed! That's gospel!

ABBIE: Likin' hain't lovin'.

EBEN: Waal then—I love ye. Now air yew satisfied?

ABBIE: Ay-eh, I be. (*She smiles at him adoringly.*)

EBEN: I better git t' the barn. The old critter's liable t' suspicion an' come sneakin' up.

ABBIE (*with a confident laugh*): Let him! I kin allus pull the wool over his eyes. I'm goin' t' leave the shutters open and let in the sun 'n' air. This room's been dead long enuf. Now it's goin' t' be my room!

EBEN (*frowning*): Ay-eh.

ABBIE (*hastily*): I meant—our room.

EBEN: Ay-eh.

ABBIE: We made it our'n last night, didn't we? We give it life—our lovin' did. (*A pause.*)

EBEN (*with a strange look*): Maw's gone back t' her grave. She kin sleep now.

ABBIE: May she rest in peace! (*Then tenderly rebuking*) Ye oughtn't t' talk o' sad thin's—this mornin'.

EBEN: It jest come up in my mind o' itself.

ABBIE: Don't let it. (*He doesn't answer. She yawns*) Waal, I'm a-goin' t' steal a wink o' sleep. I'll tell the Old Man I hain't feelin' pert. Let him git his own vittles.

EBEN: I see him comin' from the barn. Ye better look smart an' git upstairs.

ABBIE: Ay-eh. Good-by. Don't ferget me. (*She throws him a kiss. He grins— then squares his shoulders and awaits his father confidently.* CABOT *walks slowly up from the left, staring up at the sky with a vague face.*)

EBEN (*jovially*): Mornin', Paw. Star-gazin' in daylight?

CABOT: Purty, hain't it?

EBEN (*looking around him possessively*): It's a durned purty farm.

CABOT: I mean the sky.

EBEN (*grinning*): How d'ye know? Them eyes o' your'n can't see that fur. (*This tickles his humor and he slaps his thigh and laughs*) Ho-ho! That's a good un!

CABOT (*grimly sarcastic*): Ye're feelin' right chipper, hain't ye? Whar'd ye steal the likker?

EBEN (*good-naturedly*): 'Tain't likker. Jest life. (*Suddenly holding out his hand—soberly*) Yew 'n' me is quits. Let's shake hands.

CABOT (*suspiciously*): What's come over ye?

EBEN: Then don't. Mebbe it's jest as well. (*A moment's pause*) What's come over me? (*Queerly*) Didn't ye feel her passin'—goin' back t' her grave?

CABOT (*dully*) : Who?

EBEN : Maw. She kin rest now an' sleep content. She's quit with ye.

CABOT (*confusedly*) : I rested. I slept good—down with the cows. They know how t' sleep. They're teachin' me.

EBEN (*suddenly jovial again*) : Good fur the cows! Waal—ye better git t' work.

CABOT (*grimly amused*) : Air ye bossin' me, ye calf?

EBEN (*beginning to laugh*) : Ay-eh! I'm bossin' yew! Ha-ha-ha! See how ye like it! Ha-ha-ha! I'm the prize rooster o' this roost. Ha-ha-ha! (*He goes off toward the barn laughing.*)

CABOT (*looks after him with scornful pity*) : Soft-headed. Like his Maw. Dead spit 'n' image. No hope in him! (*He spits with contemptuous disgust*) A born fool! (*Then matter-of-factly*) Waal—I'm gittin' peckish. (*He goes toward door.*)

   (*The Curtain Falls.*)

Part Three

SCENE ONE

   A night in late spring the following year. The kitchen and the two bedrooms upstairs are shown. The two bedrooms are dimly lighted by a tallow candle in each. EBEN *is sitting on the side of the bed in his room, his chin propped on his fists, his face a study of the struggle he is making to understand his conflicting emotions. The noisy laughter and music from below where a kitchen dance is in progress annoy and distract him. He scowls at the floor.*

   In the next room a cradle stands beside the double bed.

   In the kitchen all is festivity. The stove has been taken down to give more room to the dancers. The chairs, with wooden benches added, have been pushed back against the walls. On these are seated, squeezed in tight against one another, farmers and their wives and their young folks of both sexes from the neighboring farms. They are all chattering and laughing loudly. They evidently have some secret joke in common. There is no end of winking, of nudging, of meaning nods of the head toward CABOT, *who, in a state of extreme hilarious excitement increased by the amount he has drunk, is standing near the rear door where there is a small keg of whisky and serving drinks to all the men. In the left corner, front, dividing the attention with her husband,* ABBIE *is sitting in a rocking chair, a shawl wrapped about her shoulders. She is very pale, her face is thin and drawn, her eyes are fixed anxiously on the open door in rear as if waiting for someone.*

The musician is tuning up his fiddle, seated in the far right corner. He is a lanky young fellow with a long, weak face. His pale eyes blink incessantly and he grins about him slyly with a greedy malice.

ABBIE (*suddenly turning to a young girl on her right*) : Whar's Eben?

YOUNG GIRL (*eying her scornfully*): I dunno, Mrs. Cabot. I hain't seen Eben in ages. (*Meaningly*) Seems like he's spent most o' his time t' hum since yew come.

ABBIE (*vaguely*) : I tuk his Maw's place.

YOUNG GIRL: Ay-eh. So I've heerd. (*She turns away to retail this bit of gossip to her mother sitting next to her.* ABBIE *turns to her left to a big stoutish middle-aged man whose flushed face and starting eyes show the amount of "likker" he has consumed.*)

ABBIE: Ye hain't seen Eben, hev ye?

MAN: No, I hain't. (*Then he adds with a wink*) If yew hain't, who would?

ABBIE: He's the best dancer in the county. He'd ought t' come an' dance.

MAN (*with a wink*): Mebbe he's doin' the dutiful an' walkin' the kid t' sleep. It's a boy, hain't it?

ABBIE (*nodding vaguely*): Ay-eh—born two weeks back—purty's a picter.

MAN: They all is—t' their Maws. (*Then in a whisper, with a nudge and a leer*) Listen, Abbie—if ye ever git tired o' Eben, remember me! Don't fergit now! (*He looks at her uncomprehending face for a second—then grunts disgustedly*) Waal—guess I'll likker agin. (*He goes over and joins* CABOT, *who is arguing noisily with an old farmer over cows. They all drink.*)

ABBIE (*this time appealing to nobody in particular*): Wonder what Eben's a-doin'? (*Her remark is repeated down the line with many a guffaw and titter until it reaches the* FIDDLER. *He fastens his blinking eyes on* ABBIE.)

FIDDLER (*raising his voice*): Bet I kin tell ye, Abbie, what Eben's doin'! He's down t' the church offerin' up prayers o' thanksgivin'. (*They all titter expectantly.*)

A MAN: What fur? (*Another titter.*)

FIDDLER: 'Cause unto him a— (*He hesitates just long enough*) brother is born! (*A roar of laughter. They all look from* ABBIE *to* CABOT. *She is oblivious, staring at the door.* CABOT, *although he hasn't heard the words, is irritated by the laughter and steps forward, glaring about him. There is an immediate silence.*)

CABOT: What're ye all bleatin' about—like a flock o' goats? Why don't ye dance, damn ye? I axed ye here t' dance—t' eat, drink an' be merry—an' thar ye set cacklin' like a lot o' wet hens with the pip! Ye've swilled my likker an' guzzled my vittles like hogs, hain't ye? Then dance fur me, can't ye? That's fa'r an' squar', hain't it? (*A grumble of resentment goes around but they are all evidently in too much awe of him to express it openly.*)

FIDDLER (*slyly*) : We're waitin' fur Eben. (*A suppressed laugh.*)

CABOT (*with a fierce exultation*): T'hell with Eben! Eben's done fur now! I got a new son! (*His mood switching with drunken suddenness*) But ye needn't t' laugh at Eben, none o' ye! He's my blood, if he be a dumb fool. He's better nor any o' yew! He kin do a day's work a'most up t' what I kin—an' that'd put any o' yew pore critters t' shame!

FIDDLER: An' he kin do a good night's work too! (*A roar of laughter.*)

CABOT: Laugh, ye damn fools! Ye're right jist the same, Fiddler. He kin work day an' night too, like I kin, if need be!

OLD FARMER (*from behind the keg where he is weaving drunkenly back and forth—with great simplicity*): They hain't many t' touch ye, Ephraim— a son at seventy-six. That's a hard man fur ye! I be on'y sixty-eight an' I couldn't do it. (*A roar of laughter in which* CABOT *joins uproariously.*)

CABOT (*slapping him on the back*): I'm sorry fur ye, Hi. I'd never suspicion sech weakness from a boy like yew!

OLD FARMER: An' I never reckoned yew had it in ye nuther, Ephraim. (*There is another laugh.*)

CABOT (*suddenly grim*): I got a lot in me—a hell of a lot—folks don't know on. (*Turning to the* FIDDLER) Fiddle 'er up, durn ye! Give 'em somethin' t' dance t'! What air ye, an ornament? Hain't this a celebration? Then grease yer elbow an' go it!

FIDDLER (*seizes a drink which the* OLD FARMER *holds out to him and downs it*): Here goes! (*He starts to fiddle "Lady of the Lake." Four young fellows and four girls form in two lines and dance a square dance. The* FIDDLER *shouts directions for the different movements, keeping his words in the rhythm of the music and interspersing them with jocular personal remarks to the dancers themselves. The people seated along the walls stamp their feet and clap their hands in unison.* CABOT *is especially active in this respect. Only* ABBIE *remains apathetic, staring at the door as if she were alone in a silent room.*)

FIDDLER: Swing your partner t' the right! That's it, Jim! Give her a b'ar hug! Her Maw hain't lookin'. (*Laughter*) Change partners! That suits ye, don't it, Essie, now ye got Reub afore ye? Look at her redden up, will ye? Waal, life is short an' so's love, as the feller says. (*Laughter.*)

CABOT (*excitedly, stamping his foot*): Go it, boys! Go it, gals!

FIDDLER (*with a wink at the others*): Ye're the spryest seventy-six ever I sees, Ephraim! Now if ye'd on'y good eyesight . . . ! (*Suppressed laughter. He gives* CABOT *no chance to retort but roars*) Promenade! Ye're walkin' like a bride down the aisle, Sarah! Waal, while they's life they's allus hope, I've heerd tell. Swing your partner to the left! Gosh A'mighty, look at Johnny Cook high-steppin'! They hain't goin' t'be much strength left fur howin' in the corn lot t'morrow. (*Laughter.*)

CABOT: Go it! Go it! (*Then suddenly, unable to restrain himself any longer, he prances into the midst of the dancers, scattering them, waving his arms about wildly*) Ye're all hoofs! Git out o' my road! Give me room!

I'll show ye dancin'. Ye're all too soft! (*He pushes them roughly away. They crowd back toward the walls, muttering, looking at him resentfully.*)

FIDDLER (*jeeringly*): Go it, Ephraim! Go it! (*He starts "Pop Goes the Weasel," increasing the tempo with every verse until at the end he is fiddling crazily as fast as he can go.*)

CABOT (*starts to dance, which he does very well and with tremendous vigor. Then he begins to improvise, cuts incredibly grotesque capers, leaping up and cracking his heels together, prancing around in a circle with body bent in an Indian war dance, then suddenly straightening up and kicking as high as he can with both legs. He is like a monkey on a string. And all the while he intersperses his antics with shouts and derisive comments*): Whoop! Here's dancin' fur ye! Whoop! See that! Seventy-six, if I'm a day! Hard as iron yet! Beatin' the young 'uns like I allus done! Look at me! I'd invite ye t' dance on my hundredth birthday on'y ye'll all be dead by then. Ye're a sickly generation! Yer hearts air pink, not red! Yer veins is full o' mud an' water! I be the on'y man in the county! Whoop! See that! I'm a Injun! I've killed Injuns in the West afore ye was born—an' skulped 'em too! They's a arrer wound on my backside I c'd show ye! The hull tribe chased me. I outrun 'em all—with the arrer stuck in me! An' I tuk vengeance on 'em. Ten eyes fur an eye, that was my motter! Whoop! Look at me! I kin kick the ceilin' off the room! Whoop!

FIDDLER (*stops playing—exhaustedly*): God A'mighty, I got enuf. Ye got the devil's strength in ye.

CABOT (*delightedly*): Did I beat yew, too? Waal, ye played smart. Hev a swig. (*He pours whisky for himself and* FIDDLER. *They drink. The others watch* CABOT *silently with cold, hostile eyes. There is a dead pause. The* FIDDLER *rests.* CABOT *leans against the keg, panting, glaring around him confusedly. In the room above,* EBEN *gets to his feet and tiptoes out the door in rear, appearing a moment later in the other bedroom. He moves silently, even frightenedly, toward the cradle and stands there looking down at the baby. His face is as vague as his reactions are confused, but there is a trace of tenderness, of interested discovery. At the same moment that he reaches the cradle,* ABBIE *seems to sense something. She gets up weakly and goes to* CABOT.)

ABBIE: I'm goin' up t' the baby.

CABOT (*with real solicitation*): Air ye able fur the stairs? D'ye want me t' help ye, Abbie?

ABBIE: No. I'm able. I'll be down agen soon.

CABOT: Don't ye git wore out! He needs ye, remember—our son does! (*He grins affectionately, patting her on the back. She shrinks from his touch.*)

ABBIE (*dully*): Don't—tech me. I'm goin'—up. (*She goes.* CABOT *looks after her. A whisper goes around the room.* CABOT *turns. It ceases. He wipes his forehead streaming with sweat. He is breathing pantingly.*)

CABOT: I'm a-goin' out t' git fresh air. I'm feelin' a mite dizzy. Fiddle up thar! Dance, all o' ye! Here's likker fur them as wants it. Enjoy yerselves. I'll be back. (*He goes, closing the door behind him.*)

FIDDLER (*sarcastically*): Don't hurry none on our account! (*A suppressed laugh. He imitates* ABBIE) Whar's Eben? (*More laughter.*)

A WOMAN (*loudly*): What's happened in this house is plain as the nose on yer face! (ABBIE *appears in the doorway upstairs and stands looking in surprise and adoration at* EBEN, *who does not see her.*)

A MAN: Ssshh! He's li'ble t'be listenin' at the door. That'd be like him. (*Their voices die to an intensive whispering. Their faces are concentrated on this gossip. A noise as of dead leaves in the wind comes from the room.* CABOT *has come out from the porch and stands by the gate, leaning on it, staring at the sky blinkingly.* ABBIE *comes across the room silently.* EBEN *does not notice her until quite near.*)

EBEN (*starting*): Abbie!

ABBIE: Ssshh! (*She throws her arms around him. They kiss—then bend over the cradle together*) Ain't he purty?—dead spit 'n' image o' yew!

EBEN (*pleased*): Air he? I can't tell none.

ABBIE: E-zactly like!

EBEN (*frowningly*): I don't like this. I don't like lettin' on what's mine's his'n. I been doin' that all my life. I'm gittin' t' the end o' b'arin' it!

ABBIE (*putting her finger on his lips*): We're doin' the best we kin. We got t' wait. Somethin's bound t' happen. (*She puts her arms around him*) I got t' go back.

EBEN: I'm goin' out. I can't b'ar it with the fiddle playin' an' the laughin'.

ABBIE: Don't git feelin' low. I love ye, Eben. Kiss me. (*He kisses her. They remain in each other's arms.*)

CABOT (*at the gate, confusedly*): Even the music can't drive it out—somethin'. Ye kin feel it droppin' off the elums, climbin' up the roof, sneakin' down the chimney, pokin' in the corners! They's no peace in houses, they's no rest livin' with folks. Somethin's always livin' with ye. (*With a deep sigh*) I'll go t' the barn an' rest a spell. (*He goes wearily toward the barn.*)

FIDDLER (*tuning up*): Let's celebrate the old skunk gittin' fooled! We kin have some fun now he's went. (*He starts to fiddle "Turkey in the Straw." There is real merriment now. The young folks get up to dance.*)

(*The Curtain Falls.*)

SCENE TWO

*A half hour later—Exterior—*EBEN *is standing by the gate looking up at the sky, an expression of dumb pain bewildered by itself on his face.* CABOT *appears, returning from the barn, walking wearily, his eyes on the ground. He sees* EBEN *and his whole mood immediately changes. He becomes excited, a cruel, triumphant grin comes to his lips, he strides up and slaps* EBEN *on the back. From within comes the whining of the fiddle and the noise of stamping feet and laughing voices.*

CABOT: So har ye be!

EBEN (*startled, stares at him with hatred for a moment—then dully*): Ay-eh.

CABOT (*surveying him jeeringly*): Why hain't ye been in t' dance? They was all axin' fur ye.

EBEN: Let 'em ax!

CABOT: They's a hull passel o' purty gals.

EBEN: T' hell with 'em!

CABOT: Ye'd ought t' be marryin' one o' 'em soon.

EBEN: I hain't marryin' no one.

CABOT: Ye might 'arn a share o' a farm that way.

EBEN (*with a sneer*): Like yew did, ye mean? I hain't that kind.

CABOT (*stung*): Ye lie! 'Twas yer Maw's folks aimed t' steal my farm from me.

EBEN: Other folks don't say so. (*After a pause—defiantly*) An' I got a farm, anyways!

CABOT (*derisively*): Whar?

EBEN (*stamps a foot on the ground*): Har!

CABOT (*throws his head back and laughs coarsely*): Ho-ho! Ye hev, hev ye? Waal, that's a good un!

EBEN (*controlling himself—grimly*): Ye'll see!

CABOT (*stares at him suspiciously, trying to make him out—a pause—then with scornful confidence*): Ay-eh. I'll see. So'll ye. It's ye that's blind—blind as a mole underground. (EBEN *suddenly laughs, one short sardonic bark: "Ha." A pause.* CABOT *peers at him with renewed suspicion*) What air ye hawin' 'bout? (EBEN *turns away without answering.* CABOT *grows angry*) God A'mighty, yew air a dumb dunce! They's nothin' in that thick skull o' your'n but noise—like a empty keg it be! (EBEN *doesn't seem to hear.* CABOT's *rage grows*) Yewr farm! God A'mighty! If ye wa'n't a born donkey ye'd know ye'll never own stick nor stone on it, specially now arter him bein' born. It's his'n, I tell ye—his'n arter I die—but I'll live a hundred jest t' fool ye all—an' he'll be growed then—yewr age a'most! (EBEN *laughs again his sardonic "Ha." This drives* CABOT *into a fury*) Ha? Ye think ye kin git 'round that someways, do ye? Waal, it'll be her'n, too—Abbie's—ye won't git 'round her—she knows yer tricks—she'll be too much fur ye—she wants the farm her'n—she was afeerd o' ye—she told me ye was sneakin' 'round tryin' t' make love t' her t' git her on yer side . . . ye . . . ye mad fool, ye! (*He raises his clenched fists threateningly.*)

EBEN (*is confronting him choking with rage*): Ye lie, ye old skunk! Abbie never said no sech thing!

CABOT (*suddenly triumphant when he sees how shaken* EBEN *is*): She did. An' I says, I'll blow his brains t' the top o' them elums—an' she says no, that hain't sense, who'll ye git t'help ye on the farm in his place—an' then she says yew'n me ought t' have a son—I know we kin, she says—an' I says, if we do, ye kin have anythin' I've got ye've a mind t'. An' she says, I wants Eben cut off so's this farm'll be mine when ye die! (*With terrible gloating*) An' that's what's happened, hain't it? An' the farm's her'n! An' the dust o' the road—that's your'n! Ha! Now who's hawin'?

EBEN (*has been listening, petrified with grief and rage—suddenly laughs wildly and brokenly*): Ha-ha-ha! So that's her sneakin' game—all along! —like I suspicioned at fust—t'swaller it all—an' me, too . . . ! (*Madly*) I'll murder her! (*He springs toward the porch but* CABOT *is quicker and gets in between.*)

CABOT: No, ye don't!

EBEN: Git out o' my road! (*He tries to throw* CABOT *aside. They grapple in what becomes immediately a murderous struggle. The old man's concentrated strength is too much for* EBEN. CABOT *gets one hand on his throat and presses him back across the stone wall. At the same moment,* ABBIE *comes out on the porch. With a stifled cry she runs toward them.*)

ABBIE: Eben! Ephraim! (*She tugs at the hand on* EBEN'S *throat*) Let go, Ephraim! Ye're chokin' him!

CABOT (*removes his hand and flings* EBEN *sideways full length on the grass, gasping and choking. With a cry,* ABBIE *kneels beside him, trying to take his head on her lap, but he pushes her away.* CABOT *stands looking down with fierce triumph*): Ye needn't t've fret, Abbie, I wa'n't aimin' t' kill him. He hain't wuth hangin' fur—not by a hell of a sight! (*More and more triumphantly*) Seventy-six an' him not thirty yit—an' look whar he be fur thinkin' his Paw was easy! No, by God, I hain't easy! An' him upstairs, I'll raise him t' be like me! (*He turns to leave them*) I'm goin' in an' dance!—sing an' celebrate! (*He walks to the porch—then turns with a great grin*) I don't calc'late it's left in him, but if he gits pesky, Abbie, ye jest sing out. I'll come a-runnin' an' by the Etarnal, I'll put him across my knee an' birch him! Ha-ha-ha! (*He goes into the house laughing. A moment later his loud "whoop" is heard.*)

ABBIE (*tenderly*): Eben. Air ye hurt? (*She tries to kiss him but he pushes her violently away and struggles to a sitting position.*)

EBEN (*gaspingly*): T' hell—with ye!

ABBIE (*not believing her ears*): It's me, Eben—Abbie—don't ye know me?

EBEN (*glowering at her with hatred*): Ay-eh—I know ye—now! (*He suddenly breaks down, sobbing weakly.*)

ABBIE (*fearfully*): Eben—what's happened t' ye—why did ye look at me 's if ye hated me?

EBEN (*violently, between sobs and gasps*): I do hate ye! Ye're a whore—a damn trickin' whore!

ABBIE (*shrinking back horrified*): Eben! Ye don't know what ye're sayin'!

EBEN (*scrambling to his feet and following her—accusingly*): Ye're nothin' but a stinkin' passel o' lies! Ye've been lyin' t' me every word ye spoke, day an' night, since we fust—done it. Ye've kept sayin' ye loved me. . . .

ABBIE (*frantically*): I do love ye! (*She takes his hand but he flings hers away.*)

EBEN (*unheeding*): Ye've made a fool o' me—a sick, dumb fool—a-purpose! Ye've been on'y playin' yer sneakin', stealin' game all along—gittin' me t' lie with ye so's ye'd hev a son he'd think was his'n, an' makin' him promise he'd give ye the farm and let me eat dust, if ye did git him a son! (*Staring at her with anguished, bewildered eyes*) They must be a devil livin' in ye! 'Tain't human t' be as bad as that be!

ABBIE (*stunned—dully*): He told yew . . . ?

EBEN: Hain't it true? It hain't no good in yew lyin'.

ABBIE (*pleadingly*): Eben, listen—ye must listen—it was long ago—afore we done nothin'—yew was scornin' me—goin' t' see Min—when I was lovin' ye—an' I said it t' him t' git vengeance on ye!

EBEN (*unheedingly. With tortured passion*): I wish ye was dead! I wish I was dead along with ye afore this come! (*Ragingly*) But I'll git my vengeance too! I'll pray Maw t' come back t' help me—t' put her cuss on yew an' him!

ABBIE (*brokenly*): Don't ye, Eben! Don't ye! (*She throws herself on her knees before him, weeping*) I didn't mean t' do bad t' ye! Fergive me, won't ye?

EBEN (*not seeming to hear her—fiercely*): I'll git squar' with the old skunk—an' yew! I'll tell him the truth 'bout the son he's so proud o'! Then I'll leave ye here t' pizen each other—with Maw comin' out o' her grave at nights—an' I'll go t' the gold fields o' Californi-a whar Sim an' Peter be!

ABBIE (*terrified*): Ye won't—leave me? Ye can't!

EBEN (*with fierce determination*): I'm a-goin', I tell ye! I'll git rich thar an' come back an' fight him fur the farm he stole—an' I'll kick ye both out in the road—t' beg an' sleep in the woods—an' yer son along with ye— t' starve an' die! (*He is hysterical at the end.*)

ABBIE (*with a shudder—humbly*): He's yewr son, too, Eben.

EBEN (*torturedly*): I wish he never was born! I wish he'd die this minit! I wish I'd never sot eyes on him! It's him—yew havin' him—a-purpose t' steal—that's changed everythin'!

ABBIE (*gently*): Did ye believe I loved ye—afore he come?

EBEN: Ay-eh—like a dumb ox!

ABBIE: An' ye don't believe no more?

EBEN: B'lieve a lyin' thief! Ha!

ABBIE (*shudders—then humbly*): An' did ye r'ally love me afore?

EBEN (*brokenly*): Ay-eh—an' ye was trickin' me!

ABBIE: An' ye don't love me now!

EBEN (*violently*): I hate ye, I tell ye!

ABBIE: An' ye're truly goin' West—goin' t' leave me—all account o' him being born?

EBEN: I'm a-goin' in the mornin'—or may God strike me t' hell!

ABBIE (*after a pause—with a dreadful cold intensity—slowly*): If that's what his comin's done t'me—killin' yewr love—takin' yew away—my on'y joy— the on'y joy I ever knowed—like heaven t' me—purtier'n heaven—then I hate him, too, even if I be his Maw!

EBEN (*bitterly*): Lies! Ye love him! He'll steal the farm fur ye! (*Brokenly*) But 'tain't the farm so much—not no more—it's yew foolin' me—gittin' me t' love ye—lyin' yew loved me—jest t' git a son t' steal!

ABBIE (*distractedly*): He won't steal! I'd kill him fust! I do love ye! I'll prove t' ye . . . !

EBEN (*harshly*): 'Tain't no use lyin' no more. I'm deaf t' ye! (*He turns away*) I hain't seein' ye agen. Good-by!

ABBIE (*pale with anguish*): Hain't ye even goin' t' kiss me—not once—arter all we loved?

EBEN (*in a hard voice*): I hain't wantin' t' kiss ye never agen! I'm wantin' t' forgit I ever sot eyes on ye!

ABBIE: Eben!—ye mustn't—wait a spell—I want t' tell ye. . . .

EBEN: I'm a-goin' in t' git drunk. I'm a-goin' t' dance.

ABBIE (*clinging to his arm—with passionate earnestness*): If I could make it—'s if he'd never come up between us—if I could prove t' ye I wa'n't schemin' t' steal from ye—so's everythin' could be jest the same with us, lovin' each other jest the same, kissin' an' happy the same's we've been happy afore he come—if I could do it—ye'd love me agen, wouldn't ye? Ye'd kiss me agen? Ye wouldn't never leave me, would ye?

EBEN (*moved*): I calc'late not. (*Then shaking her hand off his arm—with a bitter smile*) But ye hain't God, be ye?

ABBIE (*exultantly*): Remember ye've promised! (*Then with strange intensity*) Mebbe I kin take back one thin' God does!

EBEN (*peering at her*): Ye're gittin' cracked, hain't ye? (*Then going towards door*) I'm a-goin' t' dance.

ABBIE (*calls after him intensely*): I'll prove t' ye! I'll prove I love ye better'n. . . . (*He goes in the door, not seeming to hear. She remains standing where she is, looking after him—then she finishes desperately*) Better'n everythin' else in the world!

(*The Curtain Falls.*)

SCENE THREE

Just before dawn in the morning—shows the kitchen and CABOT'S *bedroom. In the kitchen, by the light of a tallow candle on the table,* EBEN *is sitting, his chin propped on his hands, his drawn face blank and expressionless. His carpetbag is on the floor beside him. In the bedroom, dimly lighted by a small whale-oil lamp,* CABOT *lies asleep.* ABBIE *is bending over the cradle, listening, her face full of terror yet with an undercurrent of desperate triumph. Suddenly, she breaks down and sobs, appears about to throw herself on her knees beside the cradle; but the old man turns restlessly, groaning in his sleep, and she controls herself, and, shrinking away from the cradle with a gesture of horror, backs swiftly toward the door in rear and goes out. A moment later she comes into the kitchen and, running to* EBEN, *flings her arms about his neck and kisses him wildly. He hardens himself, he remains unmoved and cold, he keeps his eyes straight ahead.*

ABBIE (*hysterically*): I done it, Eben! I told ye I'd do it! I've proved I love ye—better'n everythin'—so's ye can't never doubt me no more!

EBEN (*dully*): Whatever ye done, it hain't no good now.

ABBIE (*wildly*): Don't ye say that! Kiss me, Eben, won't ye? I need ye t' kiss me arter what I done! I need ye t' say ye love me!

EBEN (*kisses her without emotion—dully*): That's fur goodby. I'm a-goin' soon.

ABBIE: No! No! Ye won't go—not now!

EBEN (*going on with his own thoughts*): I been a-thinkin'—an' I hain't goin' t' tell Paw nothin'. I'll leave Maw t' take vengeance on ye. If I told him, the old skunk'd jest be stinkin' mean enuf to take it out on that baby. (*His voice showing emotion in spite of him*) An' I don't want nothin' bad t' happen t' him. He hain't t' blame fur yew. (*He adds with a certain queer pride*) An' he looks like me! An' by God, he's mine! An' some day I'll be a-comin' back an' ... !

ABBIE (*too absorbed in her own thoughts to listen to him—pleadingly*): They's no cause fur ye t' go now—they's no sense—it's all the same's it was —they's nothin' come b'tween us now—arter what I done!

EBEN (*something in her voice arouses him. He stares at her a bit frightenedly*): Ye look mad, Abbie. What did ye do?

ABBIE: I—I killed him, Eben.

EBEN (*amazed*): Ye killed him?

ABBIE (*dully*): Ay-eh.

EBEN (*recovering from his astonishment—savagely*): An' serves him right! But we got t' do somethin' quick t' make it look 's if the old skunk'd killed himself when he was drunk. We kin prove by 'em all how drunk he got.

ABBIE (*wildly*): No! No! Not him! (*Laughing distractedly*) But that's what I ought t' done, hain't it? I oughter killed him instead! Why didn't ye tell me?

EBEN (*appalled*): Instead? What d'ye mean?

ABBIE: Not him.

EBEN (*his face grown ghastly*): Not—not that baby!

ABBIE (*dully*): Ah-eh!

EBEN (*falls to his knees as if he'd been struck—his voice trembling with horror*): Oh, God A'mighty! A'mighty God! Maw, whar was ye, why didn't ye stop her?

ABBIE (*simply*): She went back t' her grave that night we fust done it, remember? I hain't felt her about since. (*A pause. EBEN hides his head in his hands, trembling all over as if he had the ague. She goes on dully*) I left the piller over his little face. Then he killed himself. He stopped breathin'. (*She begins to weep softly.*)

EBEN (*rage beginning to mingle with grief*): He looked like me. He was mine, damn ye!

ABBIE (*slowly and brokenly*): I didn't want t' do it. I hated myself fur doin' it. I loved him. He was so purty—dead spit 'n' image o' yew. But I loved yew more—an' yew was goin' away—far off whar I'd never see ye agen, never kiss ye, never feel ye pressed agin me agen—an' ye said ye hated me fur havin' him—ye said ye hated him an' wished he was dead—ye said if it hadn't been fur him comin' it'd be the same's afore between us.

EBEN (*unable to endure this, springs to his feet in a fury, threatening her, his twitching fingers seeming to reach out for her throat*): Ye lie! I never said—I never dreamed ye'd—I'd cut off my head afore I'd hurt his finger!

ABBIE (*piteously, sinking on her knees*): Eben, don't ye look at me like that —hatin' me—not after what I done fur ye—fur us—so's we could be happy agen—

EBEN (*furiously now*): Shut up, or I'll kill ye! I see yer game now—the same old sneakin' trick—ye're aimin' t' blame me fur the murder ye done!

ABBIE (*moaning—putting her hands over her ears*): Don't ye, Eben! Don't ye! (*She grasps his legs.*)

EBEN (*his mood suddenly changing to horror, shrinks away from her*):
Don't ye tech me! Ye're pizen! How could ye—t' murder a pore little
critter— Ye must've swapped yer soul t' hell! (*Suddenly raging*) Ha! I
kin see why ye done it! Not the lies ye jest told—but 'cause ye wanted t'
steal agen—steal the last thin' ye'd left me—my part o' him—no, the hull
o' him—ye saw he looked like me—ye knowed he was all mine—an' ye
couldn't b'ar it—I know ye! Ye killed him fur bein' mine! (*All this has
driven him almost insane. He makes a rush past her for the door—then
turns—shaking both fists at her, violently*) But I'll take vengeance now!
I'll git the Sheriff! I'll tell him everythin'! Then I'll sing "I'm off
to Californi-a!" an' go—gold—Golden Gate—gold sun—fields o' gold
in the West! (*This last he half shouts, half croons incoherently, suddenly
breaking off passionately*) I'm a-goin' fur the Sheriff t' come an' git ye!
I want ye tuk away, locked up from me! I can't stand t' luk at ye!
Murderer an' thief 'r not, ye still tempt me! I'll give ye up t' the Sheriff!
(*He turns and runs out, around the corner of house, panting and sobbing,
and breaks into a swerving sprint down the road.*)
ABBIE (*struggling to her feet, runs to the door, calling after him*): I love ye,
Eben! I love ye! (*She stops at the door weakly, swaying, about to fall*)
I don't care what ye do—if ye'll on'y love me agen—(*She falls limply to
the floor in a faint.*)

(*The Curtain Falls.*)

SCENE FOUR

About an hour later. Same as scene three. Shows the kitchen and
CABOT's *bedroom. It is after dawn. The sky is brilliant with the sunrise. In
the kitchen,* ABBIE *sits at the table, her body limp and exhausted, her head
bowed down over her arms, her face hidden. Upstairs,* CABOT *is still asleep
but awakens with a start. He looks toward the window and gives a snort
of surprise and irritation—throws back the covers and begins hurriedly
pulling on his clothes. Without looking behind him, he begins talking to*
ABBIE, *whom he supposes beside him.*

CABOT: Thunder 'n' lightnin', Abbie! I hain't slept this late in fifty year!
Looks 's if the sun was full riz a'most. Must've been the dancin' an' likker.
Must be gittin' old. I hope Eben's t' wuk. Ye might've tuk the trouble t'
rouse me, Abbie. (*He turns—sees no one there—surprised*) Waal—whar air
she? Gittin' vittles, I calc'late. (*He tiptoes to the cradle and peers down—
proudly*) Mornin', sonny. Purty's a picture! Sleepin' sound. He don't
beller all night like most o' 'em. (*He goes quietly out the door in rear—
a few moments later enters kitchen—sees* ABBIE—*with satisfaction*) So thar
ye be. Ye got any vittles cooked?
ABBIE (*without moving*): No.
CABOT (*coming to her, almost sympathetically*): Ye feelin' sick?
ABBIE: No.

CABOT (*pats her on shoulder. She shudders*): Ye'd best lie down a spell. (*Half jocularly*) Yer son'll be needin' ye soon. He'd ought t' wake up with a gnashin' appetite, the sound way he's sleepin'.

ABBIE (*shudders—then in a dead voice*): He hain't never goin' t' wake up.

CABOT (*jokingly*): Takes after me this mornin'. I hain't slept so late in . . .

ABBIE: He's dead.

CABOT (*stares at her—bewilderedly*): What. . . .

ABBIE: I killed him.

CABOT (*stepping back from her—aghast*): Air ye drunk—'r crazy—'r . . . !

ABBIE (*suddenly lifts her head and turns on him—wildly*): I killed him, I tell ye! I smothered him. Go up an' see if ye don't b'lieve me! (CABOT *stares at her a second, then bolts out the rear door—can be heard bounding up the stairs—and rushes into the bedroom and over to the cradle.* ABBIE *has sunk back lifelessly into her former position.* CABOT *puts his hand down on the body in the crib. An expression of fear and horror comes over his face.*)

CABOT (*shrinking away—tremblingly*): God A'mighty! God A'mighty. (*He stumbles out the door—in a short while returns to the kitchen—comes to* ABBIE, *the stunned expression still on his face—hoarsely*) Why did ye do it? Why? (*As she doesn't answer, he grabs her violently by the shoulder and shakes her*) I ax ye why ye done it! Ye'd better tell me 'r . . . !

ABBIE (*gives him a furious push which sends him staggering back and springs to her feet—with wild rage and hatred*): Don't ye dare tech me! What right hev ye t' question me 'bout him? He wa'n't yewr son! Think I'd have a son by yew? I'd die fust! I hate the sight o' ye an' allus did! It's yew I should've murdered, if I'd had good sense! I hate ye! I love Eben. I did from the fust. An' he was Eben's son—mine an' Eben's—not your'n!

CABOT (*stands looking at her dazedly—a pause—finding his words with an effort—dully*): That was it—what I felt—pokin' round the corners—while ye lied—holdin' yerself from me—sayin' ye'd a'ready conceived— (*He lapses into crushed silence—then with a strange emotion*) He's dead, sart'n. I felt his heart. Pore little critter! (*He blinks back one tear, wiping his sleeve across his nose.*)

ABBIE (*hysterically*): Don't ye! Don't ye! (*She sobs unrestrainedly.*)

CABOT (*with a concentrated effort that stiffens his body into a rigid line and hardens his face into a stony mask—through his teeth to himself*): I got t' be—like a stone—a rock o' jedgment! (*A pause. He gets complete control over himself—harshly*) If he was Eben's, I be glad he air gone! An' mebbe I suspicioned it all along. I felt they was somethin' onnateral—somewhars—the house got so lonesome—an' cold—drivin' me down t' the barn—t' the beasts o' the field. . . . Ay-eh. I must've suspicioned—somethin'. Ye didn't fool me—not altogether, leastways—I'm too old a bird—growin' ripe on the bough. . . . (*He becomes aware he is wandering, straightens again, looks at* ABBIE *with a cruel grin*) So ye'd like t' hev murdered me 'stead o' him, would ye? Waal, I'll live to a hundred! I'll live t' see ye hung! I'll deliver ye up t' the jedgment o' God an' the law! I'll git the Sheriff now. (*Starts for the door.*)

ABBIE (*dully*): Ye needn't. Eben's gone fur him.

CABOT (*amazed*) : Eben—gone fur the Sheriff?

ABBIE: Ay-eh.

CABOT: T' inform agen ye?

ABBIE: Ay-eh.

CABOT (*considers this—a pause—then in a hard voice*) : Waal, I'm thankful fur him savin' me the trouble. I'll git t' wuk. (*He goes to the door—then turns—in a voice full of strange emotion*) He'd ought t' been my son, Abbie. Ye'd ought t' loved me. I'm a man. If ye'd loved me, I'd never told no Sheriff on ye no matter what ye did, if they was t' brile me alive!

ABBIE (*defensively*) : They's more to it nor yew know, makes him tell.

CABOT (*dryly*) : Fur yewr sake, I hope they be. (*He goes out—comes around to the gate—stares up at the sky. His control relaxes. For a moment he is old and weary. He murmurs despairingly*) God A'mighty, I be lone-somer'n ever! (*He hears running footsteps from the left, immediately is himself again.* EBEN *runs in, panting exhaustedly, wild-eyed and mad looking. He lurches through the gate.* CABOT *grabs him by the shoulder.* EBEN *stares at him dumbly*) Did ye tell the Sheriff?

EBEN (*nodding stupidly*) : Ay-eh.

CABOT (*gives him a push away that sends him sprawling—laughing with withering contempt*) : Good fur ye! A prime chip o' yer Maw ye be! (*He goes toward the barn, laughing harshly.* EBEN *scrambles to his feet. Suddenly* CABOT *turns—grimly threatening*) Git off this farm when the Sheriff takes her—or, by God, he'll have t' come back an' git me fur murder, too! (*He stalks off.* EBEN *does not appear to have heard him. He runs to the door and comes into the kitchen.* ABBIE *looks up with a cry of anguished joy.* EBEN *stumbles over and throws himself on his knees beside her—sobbing brokenly.*)

EBEN: Fergive me!

ABBIE (*happily*) : Eben! (*She kisses him and pulls his head over against her breast.*)

EBEN: I love ye! Fergive me!

ABBIE (*ecstatically*) : I'd fergive ye all the sins in hell fur sayin' that! (*She kisses his head, pressing it to her with a fierce passion of possession.*)

EBEN (*brokenly*) : But I told the Sheriff. He's comin' fur ye!

ABBIE: I kin b'ar what happens t' me—now!

EBEN: I woke him up. I told him. He says, wait 'til I git dressed. I was waitin'. I got to thinkin' o' yew. I got to thinkin' how I'd loved ye. It hurt like somethin' was bustin' in my chest an' head. I got t' cryin'. I knowed sudden I loved ye yet, an' allus would love ye!

ABBIE (*caressing his hair—tenderly*) : My boy, hain't ye?

EBEN: I begun t' run back. I cut across the fields an' through the woods. I thought ye might have time t' run away—with me—an' . . .

ABBIE (*shaking her head*) : I got t' take my punishment—t' pay fur my sin.

EBEN: Then I want t' share it with ye.

ABBIE: Ye didn't do nothin'.

EBEN: I put it in yer head. I wisht he was dead! I as much as urged ye t' do it!

ABBIE: No. It was me alone!

EBEN: I'm as guilty as yew be! He was the child o' our sin.

ABBIE (*lifting her head as if defying God*) : I don't repent that sin! I hain't askin' God t' fergive that!

EBEN: Nor me—but it led up t' the other—an' the murder ye did, ye did 'count o' me—an' it's my murder, too, I'll tell the Sheriff—an' if ye deny it, I'll say we planned it t'gether—an' they'll all b'lieve me, fur they suspicion everythin' we've done, an' it'll seem likely an' true to 'em. An' it is true—way down. I did help ye—somehow.

ABBIE (*laying her head on his—sobbing*) : No! I don't want yew t' suffer!

EBEN: I got t' pay fur my part o' the sin! An' I'd suffer wust leavin' ye, goin' West, thinkin' o' ye day an' night, bein' out when yew was in— (*Lowering his voice*) 'r bein' alive when yew was dead. (*A pause*) I want t' share with ye, Abbie—prison 'r death 'r hell 'r anythin'! (*He looks into her eyes and forces a trembling smile*) If I'm sharin' with ye, I won't feel lonesome, leastways.

ABBIE (*weakly*) : Eben! I won't let ye! I can't let ye!

EBEN (*kissing her—tenderly*) : Ye can't he'p yerself. I got ye beat fur once!

ABBIE (*forcing a smile—adoringly*) : I hain't beat—s'long's I got ye!

EBEN (*hears the sound of feet outside*) : Ssshh! Listen! They've come t' take us!

ABBIE: No, it's him. Don't give him no chance to fight ye, Eben. Don't say nothin'—no matter what he says. An' I won't neither. (*It is* CABOT. *He comes up from the barn in a great state of excitement and strides into the house and then into the kitchen.* EBEN *is kneeling beside* ABBIE, *his arm around her, hers around him. They stare straight ahead.*)

CABOT (*stares at them, his face hard. A long pause—vindictively*) : Ye make a slick pair o' murderin' turtle doves! Ye'd ought t' be both hung on the same limb an' left thar t' swing in the breeze an' rot—a warnin' t' old fools like me t' b'ar their lonesomeness alone—an' fur young fools like ye t' hobble their lust. (*A pause. The excitement returns to his face, his eyes snap, he looks a bit crazy*) I couldn't wuk today. I couldn't take no interest. T' hell with the farm! I'm leavin' it! I've turned the cows an' other stock loose! I've druv 'em into the woods whar they kin be free! By freein' 'em, I'm freein' myself! I'm quittin' here today! I'll set fire t' house an' barn an' watch 'em burn, an' I'll leave yer Maw t' haunt the ashes, an' I'll will the fields back t' God, so that nothin' human kin never touch 'em! I'll be a-goin' to Californi-a—t' jine Simeon an' Peter—true sons o' mine if they be dumb fools—an' the Cabots'll find Solomon's Mines t'gether! (*He suddenly cuts a mad caper*) Whoop! What was the song they sung? "Oh, Californi-a! That's the land fur me." (*He sings this—then gets on his knees by the floor-board under which the money was hid*) An' I'll sail thar on one o' the finest clippers I kin find! I've got the money! Pity ye didn't know whar this was hidden so's ye could steal. . . . (*He has pulled up the board. He stares—feels—stares again. A pause of dead silence. He slowly turns, slumping into a sitting position on the floor, his eyes like those of a dead fish, his face the sickly green of an attack of nausea. He swallows painfully several times—forces a weak smile at last*) So—ye did steal it!

EBEN (*emotionlessly*): I swapped it t' Sim an' Peter fur their share o' the farm—t' pay their passage t' Californi-a.

CABOT (*with one sardonic*): Ha! (*He begins to recover. Gets slowly to his feet—strangely*) I calc'late God give it to 'em—not yew! God's hard, not easy! Mebbe they's easy gold in the West but it hain't God's gold. It hain't fur me. I kin hear His voice warnin' me agen t' be hard an' stay on my farm. I kin see His hand usin' Eben t' steal t' keep me from weakness. I kin feel I be in the palm o' His hand, His fingers guidin' me. (*A pause— then he mutters sadly*) It's a-goin' t' be lonesomer now than ever it war afore—an' I'm gittin' old, Lord—ripe on the bough. . . . (*Then stiffening*) Waal—what d'ye want? God's lonesome, hain't He? God's hard an' lonesome! (*A pause. The* SHERIFF *with two men comes up the road from the left. They move cautiously to the door. The* SHERIFF *knocks on it with the butt of his pistol.*)

SHERIFF: Open in the name o' the law! (*They start.*)

CABOT: They've come fur ye. (*He goes to the rear door*) Come in, Jim! (*The three men enter.* CABOT *meets them in doorway*) Jest a minit, Jim. I got 'em safe here. (*The* SHERIFF *nods. He and his companions remain in the doorway.*)

EBEN (*suddenly calls*): I lied this mornin', Jim. I helped her to do it. Ye kin take me, too.

ABBIE (*brokenly*): No!

CABOT: Take 'em both. (*He comes forward—stares at* EBEN *with a trace of grudging admiration*) Purty good—fur yew! Waal, I got t' round up the stock. Good-by.

EBEN: Good-by.

ABBIE: Good-by. (CABOT *turns and strides past the men—comes out and around the corner of the house, his shoulders squared, his face stony, and stalks grimly toward the barn. In the meantime the* SHERIFF *and men have come into the room.*)

SHERIFF (*embarrassedly*): Waal—we'd best start.

ABBIE: Wait. (*Turns to* EBEN) I love ye, Eben.

EBEN: I love ye, Abbie. (*They kiss. The three men grin and shuffle embarrassedly.* EBEN *takes* ABBIE'S *hand. They go out the door in rear, the men following, and come from the house, walking hand in hand to the gate.* EBEN *stops there and points to the sunrise sky*) Sun's a-rizin'. Purty, hain't it?

ABBIE: Ay-eh. (*They both stand for a moment looking up raptly in attitudes strangely aloof and devout.*)

SHERIFF (*looking around at the farm enviously—to his companion*): It's a jim-dandy farm, no denyin'. Wished I owned it!

(*The Curtain Falls.*)

Commentary

Rosmersholm and *Desire under the Elms* are, in one sense, studies in crime and punishment. With Ibsen the focus is upon punishment, and as Rebecca and Rosmer come to realize their guilt, they come to understand themselves as human beings. Ibsen is here more interested in the moral and psychological consequences of an act than in the act itself; hence in *Rosmersholm* only by subtle hints and veiled innuendoes do we gain an intimation that behind the dignified serenity of Rosmersholm may lie adultery, illegitimacy, incest, insanity, as well as a suicide which has an aura of murder about it. O'Neill's drama, on the other hand, explodes with violence, passionate hate, greed, revenge, pride, and the most horrible of crimes—infanticide, incest, attempted patricide, adultery. O'Neill cuts through the veneer of man's civilized and social conduct to reveal a primordial, pagan pattern of behavior, elemental in its savagery. One question which must be faced in evaluating *Desire under the Elms* is whether the play goes beyond the sensationalism and brutality of its narrative. Is the violence meaningful?

O'Neill's set foreshadows the thematic and symbolic implications underlying the violence of his drama. The dramatic tension revealed in the scenery is much greater than anything seen as the curtain goes up on Rosmersholm. The elms shadowing the Cabot farmhouse are more crucial to the meaning of O'Neill's drama than is the avenue of tall old trees leading up to Rosmer's home. They are beautiful and frightening. They protect and subdue. As a kind of primordial fertility symbol of motherhood, they are "sinister" in their "crushing, jealous absorption." Note how each of these words echoes through the play in action and emotion. Yet if maternity is sinister, what can be said of paternity in *Desire under the Elms*? "Brooding oppressively over the house," the elms suggest the power of Eben's mother as well as her exhaustion and grief—"they are like exhausted women resting their sagging breasts and hands and hair on its roof, and when it rains their tears trickle down monotonously and rot on the shingles." Yet as the curtain rises on five different scenes, it is Eben who is seen brooding, more than once with his chin propped on his hands—a gesture which imitates the bending of the branches over him. What is O'Neill suggesting?

The conflicts inherent in the elms are everywhere in the opening moments. The beauty of the sunset and the glowing green of the elms contrast with the shadowy house, "sickly grayish" and in need of paint. Eben's handsome face sets off a "resentful and defensive" expression. He and his stepbrothers are men described either as wild animals trapped in captivity or as cows and friendly oxen. The stillness of the summer evening is shattered by the "deafening clangor" of the dinner bell. Eben, deeply moved by the grandeur of the sunset, cries "God! Purty!" and then spits on the ground in intense disgust. Such an action would be incredible at Rosmersholm, where the conflicts are expressed largely in rhetorical terms, but at the Cabot farm it is only an ironic foreshadowing of the bitter hatred inside the house: father against son, sons against each other, son against stepmother, husband against wife.

Rosmersholm and Desire under the Elms are dramas about home, but neither playwright calls upon the usual stereotypes of life on the old homestead. O'Neill experiments with the theatrical innovation of presenting the whole Cabot farmhouse with the front sliced away. What dramatic and ironic effects can be achieved through the use of the disappearing wall? Would such a device have worked as well in Rosmersholm? By cutting into the heart of this home, O'Neill prepares for his theme of desire which lies at the heart of each of his characters. The tragedy works out numerous variations on the title. The play opens with Peter and Simeon dreaming of the fields of gold beckoning in California, an exciting contrast to the rocky soil of their New England home. The desire for gold and freedom sends them on their way, no longer "slaves t' stone walls here" (p. 168), and Simeon punctuates Peter's declaration by wrenching the gate off its hinges. Eben's first words to his brothers are an ominous prayer for his father's death. His passions for Min and for the farm are expressed in identical terms: ". . . my sin's as purty as any one of 'em!" (p. 164); "he takes in the whole farm with his embracing glance of desire: 'It's purty! It's damned purty! It's mine!'" (p. 168). What is O'Neill's point? And why should this same thought and passion be given to Abbie as she first comes on stage: "(with lust for the word): 'Hum!' (Her eyes gloating on the house without seeming to see the two stiff figures at the gate) 'It's purty—purty! I can't b'lieve it's r'ally mine'" (p. 170). Is O'Neill suggesting some affinity between Abbie and Eben, or is he planting the seeds for future conflict? Eben desires possession of the farm because he believes it was his mother's. Why is Abbie determined to have it as her own? What is each ready to do to achieve his desire?

O'Neill pushes his theme beyond a romantic love of land or a modern search for security. For Ephraim the farm, rocky and barren as it is, is the means by which he defines himself. It is his way of life and his god: "God's hard, not easy! God's in the stones! . . . Stones. I picked 'em up an' piled 'em into walls. Ye kin read the years o' my life in them walls . . ." (p. 181). When Abbie tells him the baby is not his, Cabot replies "with a concentrated effort that stiffens his body into a rigid line and hardens his face into a stony mask . . . , 'I got t'be—like a stone— a rock o' jedgment!'" (p. 198). Throughout the play we see a stone wall, a monument to the Cabot way of life, running across the front of the stage. Ephraim had once gone through its gate to the rich plains of the Midwest, but a life of prosperous ease was not for him. Two wives he had worked to an early death; two sons he has now driven away as he returns home with a third bride to ease the lonesomeness which he discovers at the end of the play is to be worse than ever before. What does Ephraim mean when he says he is lonesome? Ironically he was more "lonesome" while his first two wives were living than after they are dead. Of his first wife he says: "She helped but she never knowed what she was helpin'. I was allus lonesome" (p. 181); and of Eben's mother: "She never knowed me nor nothin'. It was lonesomer'n hell with her" (p. 181). Now he tells Abbie, "Ye don't know nothin'," and goes out to the barn to sleep—"Down whar it's restful—whar it's warm down t' the barn. (*Bitterly*) I kin talk t' the cows. They know. They know the farm an' me. They'll give me peace" (p. 182). Since it is a stifling hot night, why should Ephraim complain of the cold in the house? Is Ephraim's remark merely O'Neill's contrived way of allowing Abbie and Eben a chance to be alone? What does Ephraim mean by "know"? Is there a touch of self-pity here? Why should he be more at home with the cows in the barn than with his wife or with his neighbors at the end of Part Three, scene two? Why is he more concerned with the freedom of his cows than with that of his wives and sons? Cabot accuses his sons of coveting the farm "without knowin' what it meant" (p. 181). What does it mean to Cabot and to Abbie and his sons? How do these different attitudes toward the farm help precipitate the explosive conflicts?

One of the most difficult questions to confront in *Desire under the Elms* is whether Ephraim or Eben is the tragic hero. This question leads to the larger one: is *Desire under the Elms* a tragedy? And how can one define, or even describe, modern tragedy without dogmatically asserting a series of hard and fast rules? In ancient Greek tragedy the hero is often guilty of *hubris*—arrogance or pride—in violating the divine will of the gods, thus bringing about his own destruction. In Elizabethan and Shakespearean tragedy the emphasis shifts from the hero's conflict with an external Destiny to his conflict with facets of his own character (his "tragic flaw," as it has been called), or with other men, or with his world. Rather than emphasizing the humanistic concern for man's free will, modern tragedy more often concentrates upon man's struggle with the forces of heredity and environment. Both Greek and Elizabethan tragedy have as protagonist a man of heroic stature, often of royal blood, whose defeat means not only his own self-destruction but somehow involves the fate of mankind so that the audience might well say with pity and terror, "If a man of such strength of character can be destroyed, what hope is there for me?" or "There but for the grace of God go I." It is not necessary for us, however, to attempt to identify ourselves with the tragic protagonist, for he may, as in the case of Sophocles' Oedipus, who stands as O'Neill's archetype in *Desire under the Elms,* commit acts more monstrous than anything we are capable of. But it is good for us to know such a tragic hero. Tragedy usually involves the hero's coming to realize his own responsibility for his defeat, thus gaining new insight into his moral nature, often at a terrible price. Tragedy almost invariably has ethical or moral significance; in a sense, the moral order of the universe should be involved in the fate of the tragic protagonist, and the outcome, although it may bring about his downfall or death, must seem to be just and inevitable. This is not to say, however, that virtue must be rewarded and evil punished.

It is precisely over these larger issues in *Desire under the Elms* that O'Neill's critics divide most sharply. John Gassner argues that the play is

> true tragedy; the power of the passions, the impressiveness of the charac-
> ters, and the timelessness of the inner struggle between a son and a father
> ensure tragic elevation.[7]

Alan Reynolds Thompson argues, on the other hand, that O'Neill is unable to resolve these tragic issues which he starts out to dramatize:

> *Desire under the Elms* . . . starts as a study of greed, with tough, relent-
> less old Cabot as a worthy protagonist—worthy because, though possessed
> as he is by lust of possession, he is a man of will. But, halfway through,
> the play turns off into the more alluring theme of sexual lust; old Cabot
> gets thrust into the background; and the ending asks us to feel sorry for
> Eben and Abbie, paramours and infanticides, because they have found
> spiritual love at last and are ready to take their medicine. This ending,
> though affecting, is trite and dangerously close to sentimentality, and it
> does not follow from the premises. The play falls in two.[8]

How valid is Thompson's judgment of the structure of the drama?

For Kenneth Thorpe Rowe the ending, far from destroying the play, exalts it to the level of tragedy:

> Eben and Abbie are comparatively weak people with spiritual lives stunted
> and warped by environment. In a relation founded in lust and greed
> they grow into love for each other, inchoate, distrusting. That which is
> spiritually best in them, their love, produces the crime of Abbie's killing
> of their child. Out of their crime they grope forward in spiritual growth
> to a moment when they stand together at the end of the play in clarity
> of love which embraces suffering and transcends the future before them
> of trial for murder. The future may destroy them. They are limited in
> strength, in intelligence, in foundations of spiritual experience. The play
> achieves the catharsis of tragedy, pale, but assured. The moment of spir-
> itual awareness may be only a moment, but by being enclosed within a
> work of dramatic art it is indestructible.[9]

---

[7] Gassner, p. 651.

[8] Alan Reynolds Thompson, *The Anatomy of Drama* (Berkeley and Los Angeles, 1942), p. 303.

[9] Kenneth Thorpe Rowe, *A Theater in Your Head* (New York, 1960), pp. 143-144.

Father Matthew T. Conlin, who also employs Rowe's moral standard of judgment, arrives at a completely opposite conclusion:

> Tragedy should evoke pity but Abbie and Eben are too defiant to be pitied and Ephraim is too self-sufficient. Their final predicament fails to break their spirits in any agony of entanglement. . . . In the final analysis it may be O'Neill's attitude toward incest which keeps his play from reaping the harvest of tragedy. Coleridge praised Shakespeare's view of life for giving us "no innocent adulteries, no interesting incests," no vice that "walks as in twilight." We are moved to a catharsis of pity and terror for Abbie and the Cabots only if we are pleased to see vice "walking in twilight." The better tragedians have always presumed that their audiences would not want to see vice so walking even if, as in *Desire under the Elms,* it is walking off to jail to satisfy human justice.[10]

Divided though they are over the tragic implications of O'Neill's ending, both Rowe and Father Conlin see Eben and Abbie as the protagonists. Richard Dana Skinner argues that in the final scene Eben emerges as tragic hero:

> In many respects, *Desire under the Elms* is unlike all O'Neill's other plays in its complete absorption in the sins of lust, and in its description of those sins—proudly unrepented to the end. In this lies its sense of almost overwhelming defeat. Using the incest symbol of old mythology and tragedy to describe the first battle of youth against the ties of childhood, it describes a battle without an outcome. Eben is victorious in only one thing—a final acceptance of one responsibility of manhood. But he goes off to prison with Abbie, still loving her—the person who has symbolized his mother in his antagonism to his father.[11]

Barrett H. Clark would disagree with Thompson that the play is a failure structurally and with Skinner that it is the tragedy of a young man growing up. For Clark it is Abbie who unifies the play:

> In arousing the repressed passion of Eben she has forgotten, or perhaps never known, that the sex instinct cannot easily be controlled; she has depended on her own craftiness to see her machinations through in cold blood to the end. Then suddenly she finds herself caught in her own trap.[12]

Sophus Keith Winther is forthright in his rejection of both Eben and Abbie as being in any way strong enough to be considered tragic:

> Eben is a complex of delicate and sentimental love for the memory of his dead mother. Mixed with this emotion is a passion for the farm which

---

[10] Matthew T. Conlin, O.F.M., "The Tragic Effect in *Autumn Fire* and *Desire under the Elms,*" *Modern Drama,* I (Spring, 1959), 235.

[11] Richard Dana Skinner, *Eugene O'Neill: A Poet's Quest* (New York, 1935), p. 154.

[12] Barrett H. Clark, *Eugene O'Neill: The Man and His Plays* (London, 1933), p. 136.

is nothing more than a superficial attitude learned from his father. He will steal in the name of his mother to acquire his brothers' rights to the land. He will desecrate her love in the company of a whore; he will commit incest and console himself with the thought that the restless spirit of his mother finds peace at last in the approval of his action. Abbie has no fixed value by which she can live. Greed, ambition, power and carnal love are so mixed in her behavior that she never finds a principle by which she can reconcile her practice with a fixed standard of conduct.[13]

Unlike Kenneth Rowe, Winther finds nothing tragic in the lovers' conduct at the conclusion of the play:

> The lovers in their attempt to destroy Ephraim destroy themselves. Their end is ignominious defeat. Their actions are ignorant and cowardly. Their cringing acceptance of their fate deserves the towering contempt of Ephraim.[14]

Winther, however, does not agree with either Alan Thompson or Father Conlin that the ending of *Desire under the Elms* fails as tragedy. For Winther the play is Ephraim's:

> In his futile battle to know God's way and be like God he is doomed to defeat; in his determination never to submit or yield, he is heroic. In this struggle that has dominated his life he can never win. At the age of seventy-five, he walks out into the stony fields, into the beauty of dawn.[15]

Winther argues that the Greek *hubris* is not Ephraim's "tragic flaw" but rather the key to his tragic greatness:

> It is pride that sustains him, it is by pride that he has endured his failures, it has strengthened him in his search for God. Not through humility but by pride does man attain his true humanity as a being that measures the extent of his universe and develops the courage to face his doom. Ephraim's exit is heroic.[16]

Clearly the judgments of all of O'Neill's critics cannot be reconciled. Who is right? When the opinions of professional critics seem only to cancel each other out, what is the reader to do? Is it possible to achieve a synthesis of the perspectives recorded here which will provide other illuminating insights into the tragic issues dramatized in O'Neill's play? One might take as his point of departure Eben's last words in the play as he gazes at the sunrise—"Purty, hain't it?"—for they return us to the sunset of the preceding summer and his first words—"God! Purty!"— where one must begin his discovery of the tragic implications of *Desire under the Elms*.

---

[13] Sophus Keith Winther, "*Desire under the Elms:* A Modern Tragedy," *Modern Drama,* III (December, 1960), 329.
[14] *Ibid.,* p. 331.
[15] *Ibid.,* p. 332.
[16] *Ibid.,* p. 332.

Questions and Problems

1. *The Devil's Disciple* and *Desire under the Elms* are both studies of New England Puritanism. Define the concept in each play. What differences are noteworthy? How is its effect felt in each play? What attitudes does each playwright invite us to take toward Puritanism?

2. Shaw's use of animal imagery to describe Christy is done with playful intent. What more serious comment does O'Neill make describing his characters in the same metaphors?

3. In a tragic plot the action is inevitable; in a melodramatic plot it is accidental. In tragedy escape is impossible; in melodrama it is inevitable. Discuss the differences between *The Devil's Disciple* and *Desire under the Elms* in terms of these distinctions.

4. What motivates this "desire" under the elms? What does each character hate and why? Are Eben and Abbie victims of environmental forces over which they have little control? To what extent can they be held morally responsible for their actions?

5. One of O'Neill's critics challenges the validity of the climax of *Desire under the Elms:* "Now I do not believe that Abbie would deliberately murder her baby. I believe she would have killed Ephraim, and I think that that is what she ought to have done in the play."[17] Is this assumption tenable? What would the effect have been if O'Neill had decided upon the murder of Ephraim?

6. Both Abbie and Rebecca want control over a man. Why? Both are defeated. How? What are the differences between the forces which trap them? Both women are prepared to make a sacrifice when the men they love demand proof of their affection. Is there any similarity in the impact this knowledge makes upon Eben and Rosmer? Are the two men capable of an act of self-sacrifice? What are Ibsen and O'Neill suggesting about the nature of love? Do both plays end with the hint of a larger victory wrenched from obvious defeat, or are the endings ambiguous and ironical?

7. Eben insists that "I'm Maw—every drop o' blood" (p. 161), but his half-brothers call him the "dead spit an' image" of his father (p. 164). O'Neill reiterates this apparent contradiction at later moments in the play. Where? In what ways are both positions accurate? Is Eben ever able to achieve a harmony between these conflicting forces within him? Does the same conflict exist in Abbie? What does Ephraim mean when he asserts "I'm a man" (p. 199)? Does his "manhood" differ from Eben's? What lies behind his grudging praise of Eben at the end: "Purty good—fur yew!" (p. 201)?

8. What is our final view of Ephraim, Eben, and Abbie to be?

9. Rosmer and Rebecca acknowledge their guilt and attempt to atone for their sins. How does O'Neill treat the problem of guilt and atonement? What does Eben mean by "I got t' pay fur my part o' the sin!"? Since he feels no remorse

---

[17] Clark, p. 137.

for his adultery, why should he accept punishment for a murder he did not commit? Has justice been done?

10. Neither Shaw, Ibsen, nor O'Neill concludes his play in a manner we might expect. The superficial similarity of the endings—Mrs. Anderson and Dick shaking hands, Rebecca and Rosmer, Abbie and Eben hand in hand—suggests reconciliation or harmony, a bond between each couple. What is it that draws each pair together? Does each ending seem an integral part of its play and an appropriate ending for it? How do the ironic disparities in the tone and meaning of these endings dramatize the differences in each playwright's view of his material?

11. What is O'Neill suggesting by the Sheriff's tag line: "It's a jim-dandy farm, no denyin'. Wished I owned it!"? Does the remark suggest that the play is about to start on another cycle of possessive greed since the forces which have exploded on the Cabot farm reside in all men, or is it only a casually innocent statement which takes on tragically ironic overtones in the light of all that has preceded it?

TENNESSEE WILLIAMS

The Glass Menagerie

Biography

ONE OF THE most outstanding dramatists to appear on the American theatrical scene since World War II is Tennessee Williams (1914-), who won five major playwriting awards in the first decade after *The Glass Menagerie* appeared on Broadway. Born Thomas Lanier Williams, he adopted his college nickname "Tennessee" because he came from pioneer Tennessee ancestry. His father was a traveling shoe salesman; his mother, a member of the southern aristocracy. It was his maternal grandfather, an Episcopalian rector, who influenced the boy's literary development. A few years after his family moved to St. Louis from Mississippi, Williams entered the University of Missouri, but because he spent more time on his own writing than on his studies (he failed the ROTC course), his father insisted that he go to work in a shoe factory. For two years he worked all day at a job he hated (although he admitted later he gained "valuable insight into the monotony of the white collar worker's life") and stayed up writing most of the night until he finally collapsed under the strain. Upon his recovery he returned to college, studying first at Washington University in St. Louis and then at the University of Iowa, from which he was graduated in 1938. Traveling restlessly all over the country on a roving writing career after graduation, he held every conceivable kind of job—he was a bellhop, a teletypist, a theater usher, a warehouse handyman, and a reciter of verses in a Greenwich Village night club.

By 1939 Williams' one-act plays were becoming known in theatrical circles. His full-length play *Battle of Angels,* produced in 1940, infuriated a Boston audience with its theme of violence, sex, and decadence; it collapsed in failure, but after seventeen years of stubborn revision it was successfully produced as *Orpheus Descending.* The year 1943 found Williams trying to write scripts for MGM, but his distaste for assignments to provide dialogue for Lana Turner and Margaret O'Brien soon terminated his career in Hollywood, although in recent years he has written movie scripts for most of his major plays as well as for his film *Baby Doll.* With the enthusiastic reception accorded *The Glass Menagerie* in 1945, Williams won acclaim. The honors heaped on that play have been showered on its successors with amazing regularity. *The Glass Menagerie* won the New York Drama Critics' Circle Award, as did *A Streetcar Named Desire* and *Cat on a Hot Tin Roof;* the latter two plays also won Pulitzer Prizes and have helped make Williams one of the most respected figures writing for the theater today.

Works

PLAYS

Battle of Angels (1940)
The Glass Menagerie (1944)
27 Wagons Full of Cotton and
Other One-Act Plays (1946)
A Streetcar Named Desire (1947)
American Blues (five short plays) (1948)
Summer and Smoke (1948)
The Rose Tattoo (1951)
Camino Real (1953)

Cat on a Hot Tin Roof (1955)
Orpheus Descending (1957)
Suddenly Last Summer (1958)
Sweet Bird of Youth (1959)
Period of Adjustment (1960)
Night of the Iguana (1961)
The Milk Train Doesn't Stop Here Any More (1962)
The Mutilated (1962)

NOVELS AND SHORT STORIES

One Arm, and Other Stories (1948)
The Roman Spring of Mrs. Stone (1950)

Hard Candy, a Book of Stories (1954)

POEMS

In the Winter of Cities (1956)

Selected Descriptive Bibliography

Dony, Nadine, "Tennessee Williams: A Selected Bibliography," *Modern Drama,* I (December, 1958), 181-191. Addenda: Carpenter, Charles A. and Elizabeth Cook, *Modern Drama,* II (December, 1959), 220-223.
   The most complete Bibliography of Williams through 1959.
Falk, Signi, *Tennessee Williams,* New York, 1961.
   A largely unsympathetic study of Williams' achievement. Extensive plot paraphrasing. Good descriptive Bibliography.
_____, "The Profitable World of Tennessee Williams," *Modern Drama,* I (December, 1958), 172-180.
   A criticism of Williams' characters as sentimental and tawdry.

Ganz, Arthur, "The Desperate Morality of the Plays of Tennessee Williams," *American Scholar*, XXXI (Spring, 1962), 278-294.
Ganz argues that Williams' strength lies not in his powers of characterization but in the strength of his moral vision.

Gassner, John, "Tennessee Williams: Dramatist of Frustration," *College English*, X (October, 1948), 1-7.
The salient points of Gassner's article have been incorporated in an updated study of Williams in Theatre at the Crossroads.

Jones, Robert Emmet, "Tennessee Williams' Early Heroines," *Modern Drama*, II (December, 1959), 211-219.
Jones's analysis of the social forces which destroy Williams' early heroines is least successful with Amanda. No mention is made of Laura.

Moor, Paul, "A Mississippian Named Tennessee," *Harper's* CXXXVII (July, 1948), 63-71.
An early biographical account of Williams' development as a playwright.

Nelson, Benjamin, *Tennessee Williams: The Man and His Work*, New York, 1961.
The best of the full-length studies of Williams. Nelson avoids the danger of substituting a paraphrase of sensational plots for literary criticism. His judgments are thoughtful and fair.

Popkin, Henry, "The Plays of Tennessee Williams," *Tulane Drama Review*, IV (March, 1960), 45-64.
An excellent, tightly written comparative study of Williams' plays with illuminating commentary on their worlds, characters, themes, symbols, and structure.

Sharp, William, "An Unfashionable View of Tennessee Williams," *Tulane Drama Review*, VI (March, 1962), 160-171.
A criticism of some currently popular opinions about Williams' characters and themes. Sharp argues that Williams is a writer of tragedy.

Tischler, Nancy M., *Tennessee Williams: Rebellious Puritan*, New York, 1961.
Studying the plays in the context of Williams' biography, Mrs. Tischler focuses upon sexual themes in his dramas.

Vowles, Richard B., "Tennessee Williams: The World of His Imagery," *Tulane Drama Review*, III (December, 1958), 51-56.
Interesting, but occasionally far-fetched, speculation about Williams' "liquid" imagery.

Williams, Tennessee, "Tennessee Williams on the Past, the Present and the Perhaps," *New York Times*, March 17, 1957, Sec. 2, pp. 1, 3.
Williams' lively account of his early career before achieving success as a playwright.

Production Notes for *The Glass Menagerie*

The reader of The Glass Menagerie *has the advantage, denied the theater-goer, of having at hand Tennessee Williams' revealing production notes, prepared for the published version of the play. These notes, which follow, shed light on the author's interpretation of the unusual theatrical devices he employs; but more than that, Williams' commentary provides an insight into the theory of dramatic art upon which his plays are constructed.*

Being a "memory play," *The Glass Menagerie* can be presented with unusual freedom of convention. Because of its considerably delicate or tenuous material, atmospheric touches and subtleties of direction play a particularly important part. Expressionism and all other unconventional techniques in drama have only one valid aim, and that is a closer approach to truth. When a play employs unconventional techniques, it is not, or certainly shouldn't be, trying to escape its responsibility of dealing with reality, or interpreting experience, but is actually or should be attempting to find a closer approach, a more penetrating and vivid expression of things as they are. The straight realistic play with its genuine frigidaire and authentic ice-cubes, its characters that speak exactly as its audience speaks, corresponds to the academic landscape and has the same virtue of a photographic likeness. Everyone should know nowadays the unimportance of the photographic in art: that truth, life, or reality is an organic thing which the poetic imagination can represent or suggest, in essence, only through transformation, through changing into other forms than those which were merely present in appearance.

These remarks are not meant as a preface only to this particular play. They have to do with a conception of a new, plastic theatre which must take the place of the exhausted theatre of realistic conventions if the theatre is to resume vitality as a part of our culture.

THE SCREEN DEVICE

There is *only one important difference between the original and acting version of the play* and that is the *omission* in the latter of the device which I tentatively included in my *original* script. This device was the use of a screen on which were projected magic-lantern slides bearing images or titles. I do not regret the omission of this device from the present Broadway production. The extraordinary power of Miss Taylor's[1] performance made it suitable to have the utmost simplicity in the physical production. But I think it may be interesting to some readers to see how this device was conceived. So I am putting it into the published manu-

---

[1] Laurette Taylor (1884-1946) was a distinguished American actress who came out of retirement to play Amanda, her last role.

script. These images and legends, projected from behind, were cast on a section of wall between the front-room and dining-room areas, which should be indistinguishable from the rest when not in use.

The purpose of this will probably be apparent. It is to give accent to certain values in each scene. Each scene contains a particular point (or several) which is structurally the most important. In an episodic play, such as this, the basic structure or narrative line may be obscured from the audience; the effect may seem fragmentary rather than architectural. This may not be the fault of the play so much as a lack of attention in the audience. The legend or image upon the screen will strengthen the effect of what is merely allusion in the writing and allow the primary point to be made more simply and lightly than if the entire responsibility were on the spoken lines. Aside from this structural value, I think the screen will have a definite emotional appeal, less definable but just as important. An imaginative producer or director may invent many other uses for this device than those indicated in the present script. In fact the possibilities of the device seem much larger to me than the instance of this play can possibly utilize.

THE MUSIC

Another extra-literary accent in this play is provided by the use of music. A single recurring tune, "The Glass Menagerie," is used to give emotional emphasis to suitable passages. This tune is like circus music, not when you are on the grounds or in the immediate vicinity of the parade, but when you are at some distance and very likely thinking of something else. It seems under those circumstances to continue almost interminably and it weaves in and out of your preoccupied consciousness; then it is the lightest, most delicate music in the world and perhaps the saddest. It expresses the surface vivacity of life with the underlying strain of immutable and inexpressible sorrow. When you look at a piece of delicately spun glass you think of two things: how beautiful it is and how easily it can be broken. Both of those ideas should be woven into the recurring tune, which dips in and out of the play as if it were carried on a wind that changes. It serves as a thread of connection and allusion between the narrator with his separate point in time and space and the subject of his story. Between each episode it returns as reference to the emotion, nostalgia, which is the first condition of the play. It is primarily Laura's music and therefore comes out most clearly when the play focuses upon her and the lovely fragility of glass which is her image.

THE LIGHTING

The lighting in the play is not realistic. In keeping with the atmosphere of memory, the stage is dim. Shafts of light are focused on selected areas or actors, sometimes in contradistinction to what is the apparent center. For instance, in the quarrel scene between Tom and Amanda, in which Laura has no active part, the clearest pool of light is on her figure.

This is also true of the supper scene, when her silent figure on the sofa should remain the visual center. The light upon Laura should be distinct from the others, having a peculiar pristine clarity such as light used in early religious portraits of female saints or madonnas. A certain correspondence to light in religious paintings, such as El Greco's,[2] where the figures are radiant in an atmosphere that is relatively dusky, could be effectively used throughout the play. (It will also permit a more effective use of the screen.) A free, imaginative use of light can be of enormous value in giving a mobile, plastic quality to plays of a more or less static nature.

---

[2] El Greco (c. 1542-1614), Spanish painter, architect, and sculptor, is famous for his work in Toledo, Spain. His paintings are often cold and ashen in coloring, and his restless figures are gaunt, startlingly elongated, and distorted.

The Glass Menagerie TENNESSEE WILLIAMS

CHARACTERS

AMANDA WINGFIELD (*the mother*), *a little woman of great but confused vitality clinging frantically to another time and place. Her characterization must be carefully created, not copied from type. She is not paranoiac, but her life is paranoia. There is much to admire in Amanda, and as much to love and pity as there is to laugh at. Certainly she has endurance and a kind of heroism, and though her foolishness makes her unwittingly cruel at times, there is tenderness in her slight person.*

LAURA WINGFIELD (*her daughter*). *Amanda, having failed to establish contact with reality, continues to live vitally in her illusions, but Laura's situation is even graver. A childhood illness has left her crippled, one leg slightly shorter than the other, and held in a brace. This defect need not be more than suggested on the stage. Stemming from this, Laura's separation increases till she is like a piece of her own glass collection, too exquisitely fragile to move from the shelf.*

TOM WINGFIELD (*her son and the narrator of the play*). *A poet with a job in a warehouse. His nature is not remorseless, but to escape from a trap he has to act without pity.*

JIM O'CONNOR (*the gentleman caller*), *a nice, ordinary, young man.*

SCENE: *An Alley in St. Louis.*
TIME: *Now and the Past.*

The Glass Menagerie was first produced at the Civic Theater, Chicago, Illinois, on December 26, 1944, and then at the Playhouse Theater, New York City, on March 31, 1945.

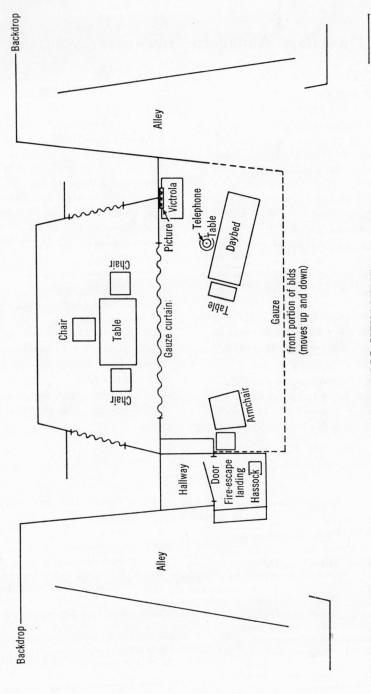

THE GLASS MENAGERIE

Scene One

The Wingfield apartment is in the rear of the building, one of those vast hive-like conglomerations of cellular living-units that flower as warty growths in overcrowded urban centers of lower middle-class population and are symptomatic of the impulse of this largest and fundamentally enslaved section of American society to avoid fluidity and differentiation and to exist and function as one interfused mass of automatism.

The apartment faces an alley and is entered by a fire-escape, a structure whose name is a touch of accidental poetic truth, for all of these huge buildings are always burning with the slow and implacable fires of human desperation. The fire-escape is included in the set—that is, the landing of it and steps descending from it.

The scene is memory and is therefore nonrealistic. Memory takes a lot of poetic license. It omits some details; others are exaggerated, according to the emotional value of the articles it touches, for memory is seated predominantly in the heart. The interior is therefore rather dim and poetic.

At the rise of the curtain, the audience is faced with the dark, grim rear wall of the Wingfield tenement. This building, which runs parallel to the footlights, is flanked on both sides by dark, narrow alleys which run into murky canyons of tangled clotheslines, garbage cans and the sinister latticework of neighboring fire-escapes. It is up and down these side alleys that exterior entrances and exits are made, during the play. At the end of TOM'S *opening commentary, the dark tenement wall slowly reveals (by means of a transparency) the interior of the ground floor Wingfield apartment.*

Downstage is the living room, which also serves as a sleeping room for LAURA, *the sofa unfolding to make her bed. Upstage, center, and divided by a wide arch or second proscenium with transparent faded portieres (or second curtain), is the dining room. In an old-fashioned whatnot in the living room are seen scores of transparent glass animals. A blown-up photograph of the father hangs on the wall of the living room, facing the audience, to the left of the archway. It is the face of a very handsome young man in a doughboy's First World War cap. He is gal-*

lantly smiling, ineluctably smiling, as if to say, "I will be smiling forever."

The audience hears and sees the opening scene in the dining room through both the transparent fourth wall of the building and the transparent gauze portieres of the dining-room arch. It is during this revealing scene that the fourth wall slowly ascends, out of sight. This transparent exterior wall is not brought down again until the very end of the play, during TOM's *final speech.*

The narrator is an undisguised convention of the play. He takes whatever license with dramatic convention as is convenient to his purposes.

TOM *enters dressed as a merchant sailor from alley, stage left, and strolls across the front of the stage to the fire-escape. There he stops and lights a cigarette. He addresses the audience.*

TOM: Yes, I have tricks in my pocket, I have things up my sleeve. But I am the opposite of a stage magician. He gives you illusion that has the appearance of truth. I give you truth in the pleasant disguise of illusion.

To begin with, I turn back time. I reverse it to that quaint period, the thirties, when the huge middle class of America was matriculating in a school for the blind. Their eyes had failed them, or they had failed their eyes, and so they were having their fingers pressed forcibly down on the fiery Braille alphabet of a dissolving economy.

In Spain there was revolution. Here there was only shouting and confusion.

In Spain there was Guernica. Here there were disturbances of labor, sometimes pretty violent, in otherwise peaceful cities such as Chicago, Cleveland, Saint Louis. . . .

This is the social background of the play. (*Music*)

The play is memory.

Being a memory play, it is dimly lighted, it is sentimental, it is not realistic.

In memory everything seems to happen to music. That explains the fiddle in the wings.

I am the narrator of the play, and also a character in it.

The other characters are my mother, Amanda, my sister, Laura, and a gentleman caller who appears in the final scenes.

He is the most realistic character in the play, being an emissary from a world of reality that we were somehow set apart from.

But since I have a poet's weakness for symbols, I am using this character also as a symbol; he is the long delayed but always expected something that we live for.

There is a fifth character in the play who doesn't appear except in this larger-than-life-size photograph over the mantel.

This is our father who left us a long time ago.

He was a telephone man who fell in love with long distances; he gave up his job with the telephone company and skipped the light fantastic out of town. . . .

The last we heard of him was a picture post-card from Mazatlan, on the Pacific coast of Mexico, containing a message of two words—
"Hello— Good-bye!" and no address.
I think the rest of the play will explain itself. . . .

(AMANDA's *voice becomes audible through the portieres.* LEGEND ON SCREEN: "OÙ SONT LES NEIGES?"[3] *He divides the portieres and enters the upstage area.* AMANDA *and* LAURA *are seated at a drop-leaf table. Eating is indicated by gestures without food or utensils.* AMANDA *faces the audience,* TOM *and* LAURA *are seated in profile. The interior has lit up softly and through the scrim we see* AMANDA *and* LAURA *seated at the table in the upstage area.*)

AMANDA (*calling*) : Tom?

TOM: Yes, Mother.

AMANDA: We can't say grace until you come to the table!

TOM: Coming, Mother. (*He bows slightly and withdraws, reappearing a few moments later in his place at the table.*)

AMANDA (*to her son*) : Honey, don't *push* with your *fingers.* If you have to push with something, the thing to push with is a crust of bread. And chew —chew! Animals have sections in their stomachs which enable them to digest food without mastication, but human beings are supposed to chew their food before they swallow it down. Eat food leisurely, son, and really enjoy it. A well-cooked meal has lots of delicate flavors that have to be held in the mouth for appreciation. So chew your food and give your salivary glands a chance to function!

(TOM *deliberately lays his imaginary fork down and pushes his chair back from the table.*)

TOM: I haven't enjoyed one bite of this dinner because of your constant directions on how to eat it. It's you that make me rush through meals with your hawk-like attention to every bite I take. Sickening—spoils my appetite—all this discussion of—animals' secretion—salivary glands—mastication!

AMANDA (*lightly*) : Temperament like a Metropolitan star! (*He rises and crosses downstage*) You're not excused from the table.

TOM: I'm getting a cigarette.

AMANDA: You smoke too much.

(LAURA *rises.*)

LAURA: I'll bring in the blanc mange.

(*He remains standing with his cigarette by the portieres during the following.*)

AMANDA (*rising*) : No, sister, no, sister—you be the lady this time and I'll be the darky.

LAURA: I'm already up.

AMANDA: Resume your seat, little sister—I want you to stay fresh and pretty —for gentlemen callers!

LAURA: I'm not expecting any gentlemen callers.

---

[3] "Where are the snows of yesteryear?"—the famous tribute to beautiful women written by the fifteenth-century lyric poet François Villon.

AMANDA (*crossing out to kitchenette. Airily*): Sometimes they come when they are least expected! Why, I remember one Sunday afternoon in Blue Mountain—(*Enters kitchenette.*)

TOM: I know what's coming!

LAURA: Yes. But let her tell it.

TOM: Again?

LAURA: She loves to tell it.

(AMANDA *returns with bowl of dessert.*)

AMANDA: One Sunday afternoon in Blue Mountain—your mother received— *seventeen!*—gentlemen callers! Why, sometimes there weren't chairs enough to accommodate them all. We had to send the nigger over to bring in folding chairs from the parish house.

TOM (*remaining at portieres*): How did you entertain those gentlemen callers?

AMANDA: I understood the art of conversation!

TOM: I bet you could talk.

AMANDA: Girls in those days *knew* how to talk, I can tell you.

TOM: Yes?

(IMAGE: AMANDA AS A GIRL ON A PORCH, GREETING CALLERS.)

AMANDA: They knew how to entertain their gentlemen callers. It wasn't enough for a girl to be possessed of a pretty face and a graceful figure— although I wasn't slighted in either respect. She also needed to have a nimble wit and a tongue to meet all occasions.

TOM: What did you talk about?

AMANDA: Things of importance going on in the world! Never anything coarse or common or vulgar. (*She addresses* TOM *as though he were seated in the vacant chair at the table though he remains by portieres. He plays this scene as though he held the book*) My callers were gentlemen—all! Among my callers were some of the most prominent young planters of the Mississippi Delta—planters and sons of planters! (TOM *motions for music and a spot of light on* AMANDA. *Her eyes lift, her face glows, her voice becomes rich and elegiac.* SCREEN LEGEND: "OÙ SONT LES NEIGES?")

There was young Champ Laughlin, who later became vice-president of the Delta Planters Bank.

Hadley Stevenson, who was drowned in Moon Lake and left his widow one hundred and fifty thousand in Government bonds.

There were the Cutrere brothers, Wesley and Bates. Bates was one of my bright particular beaux! He got in a quarrel with that wild Wainwright boy. They shot it out on the floor of Moon Lake Casino. Bates was shot through the stomach. Died in the ambulance on his way to Memphis. His widow was also well-provided for, came into eight or ten thousand acres, that's all. She married him on the rebound—never loved her—carried my picture on him the night he died!

And there was that boy that every girl in the Delta had set her cap for! That beautiful, brilliant young Fitzhugh boy from Greene County!

TOM: What did he leave his widow?

AMANDA: He never married! Gracious, you talk as though all of my old admirers had turned up their toes to the daisies!

TOM: Isn't this the first you've mentioned that still survives?

AMANDA: That Fitzhugh boy went North and made a fortune—came to be known as the Wolf of Wall Street! He had the Midas touch, whatever he touched turned to gold!

And I could have been Mrs. Duncan J. Fitzhugh, mind you! But—I picked your *father!*

LAURA (*rising*): Mother, let me clear the table.

AMANDA: No, dear, you go in front and study your typewriter chart. Or practice your shorthand a little. Stay fresh and pretty!—It's almost time for our gentlemen callers to start arriving. (*She flounces girlishly toward the kitchenette*) How many do you suppose we're going to entertain this afternoon?

(TOM *throws down the paper and jumps up with a groan.*)

LAURA (*alone in the dining room*): I don't believe we're going to receive any, Mother.

AMANDA (*reappearing, airily*): What? No one—not one? You must be joking! (LAURA *nervously echoes her laugh. She slips in a fugitive manner through the half-open portieres and draws them gently behind her. A shaft of very clear light is thrown on her face against the faded tapestry of the curtains.* MUSIC: "THE GLASS MENAGERIE" UNDER FAINTLY. *Lightly*) Not one gentleman caller? It can't be true! There must be a flood, there must have been a tornado!

LAURA: It isn't a flood, it's not a tornado, Mother. I'm just not popular like you were in Blue Mountain. . . . (TOM *utters another groan.* LAURA *glances at him with a faint, apologetic smile. Her voice catching a little*) Mother's afraid I'm going to be an old maid.

(*The Scene Dims Out with "Glass Menagerie" Music.*)

Scene Two

LEGEND: "LAURA, HAVEN'T YOU EVER LIKED SOME BOY?"

On the dark stage the screen is lighted with the image of blue roses. Gradually LAURA'S *figure becomes apparent and the screen goes out. The music subsides.*

LAURA *is seated in the delicate ivory chair at the small clawfoot table.*

She wears a dress of soft violet material for a kimono—her hair tied back from her forehead with a ribbon.

She is washing and polishing her collection of glass.

AMANDA *appears on the fire-escape steps. At the sound of her ascent,* LAURA *catches her breath, thrusts the bowl of ornaments away and seats herself stiffly before the diagram of the typewriter keyboard as though it held her spellbound.*

Something has happened to AMANDA. *It is written in her face as she climbs to the landing: a look that is grim and hopeless and a little absurd.*

She has on one of those cheap or imitation velvety-looking cloth coats with imitation fur collar. Her hat is five or six years old, one of those dreadful cloche hats that were worn in the late twenties and she is clasping an enormous black patent-leather pocketbook with nickel clasps and initials. This is her full-dress outfit, the one she usually wears to the D.A.R.[4]

Before entering she looks through the door.

She purses her lips, opens her eyes very wide, rolls them upward and shakes her head.

Then she slowly lets herself in the door. Seeing her mother's expression LAURA *touches her lips with a nervous gesture.*

LAURA: Hello, Mother, I was— (*She makes a nervous gesture toward the chart on the wall.* AMANDA *leans against the shut door and stares at* LAURA *with a martyred look.*)
AMANDA: Deception? Deception? (*She slowly removes her hat and gloves, continuing the sweet suffering stare. She lets the hat and gloves fall on the floor—a bit of acting.*)
LAURA (*shakily*): How was the D.A.R. meeting? (AMANDA *slowly opens her purse and removes a dainty white handkerchief which she shakes out delicately and delicately touches to her lips and nostrils*) Didn't you go to the D.A.R. meeting, Mother?
AMANDA (*faintly, almost inaudibly*): —No.—No. (*Then more forcibly*) I did not have the strength—to go to the D.A.R. In fact, I did not have the courage! I wanted to find a hole in the ground and hide myself in it forever! (*She crosses slowly to the wall and removes the diagram of the typewriter keyboard. She holds it in front of her for a second, staring at it sweetly and sorrowfully—then bites her lips and tears it in two pieces.*)
LAURA (*faintly*): Why did you do that, Mother? (AMANDA *repeats the same procedure with the chart of the Gregg Alphabet*[5]) Why are you—
AMANDA: Why? Why? How old are you, Laura?
LAURA: Mother, you know my age.
AMANDA: I thought that you were an adult; it seems that I was mistaken. (*She crosses slowly to the sofa and sinks down and stares at* LAURA.)
LAURA: Please don't stare at me, Mother.
(AMANDA *closes her eyes and lowers her head. Count ten.*)

---

[4] The Daughters of the American Revolution, an organization of American women whose ancestors fought in the American Revolution.
[5] A commonly used shorthand alphabet.

AMANDA: What are we going to do, what is going to become of us, what is the future?

(*Count ten.*)

LAURA: Has something happened, Mother? (AMANDA *draws a long breath and takes out the handkerchief again. Dabbing process*) Mother, has—something happened?

AMANDA: I'll be all right in a minute, I'm just bewildered—(*Count five*)—by life. . . .

LAURA: Mother, I wish that you would tell me what's happened!

AMANDA: As you know, I was supposed to be inducted into my office at the D.A.R. this afternoon. (IMAGE: A SWARM OF TYPEWRITERS) But I stopped off at Rubicam's Business College to speak to your teachers about your having a cold and ask them what progress they thought you were making down there.

LAURA: Oh. . . .

AMANDA: I went to the typing instructor and introduced myself as your mother. She didn't know who you were. Wingfield, she said. We don't have any such student enrolled at the school!

I assured her she did, that you had been going to classes since early in January.

"I wonder," she said, "if you could be talking about that terribly shy little girl who dropped out of school after only a few days' attendance?"

"No," I said, "Laura, my daughter, has been going to school every day for the past six weeks!"

"Excuse me," she said. She took the attendance book out and there was your name, unmistakably printed, and all the dates you were absent until they decided that you had dropped out of school.

I still said, "No, there must have been some mistake! There must have been some mix-up in the records!"

And she said, "No—I remember her perfectly now. Her hands shook so that she couldn't hit the right keys! The first time we gave a speed-test, she broke down completely—was sick at the stomach and almost had to be carried into the wash-room! After that morning she never showed up any more. We phoned the house but never got any answer"—while I was working at Famous and Barr, I suppose, demonstrating those— Oh!

I felt so weak I could barely keep on my feet!

I had to sit down while they got me a glass of water!

Fifty dollars' tuition, all of our plans—my hopes and ambitions for you—just gone up the spout, just gone up the spout like that. (LAURA *draws a long breath and gets awkwardly to her feet. She crosses to the victrola and winds it up*) What are you doing?

LAURA: Oh! (*She releases the handle and returns to her seat.*)

AMANDA: Laura, where have you been going when you've gone out pretending that you were going to business college?

LAURA: I've just been going out walking.

AMANDA: That's not true.

LAURA: It is. I just went walking.

AMANDA: Walking? Walking? In winter? Deliberately courting pneumonia in that light coat? Where did you walk to, Laura?

LAURA: All sorts of places—mostly in the park.

AMANDA: Even after you'd started catching that cold?

LAURA: It was the lesser of two evils, Mother. (IMAGE: WINTER SCENE IN PARK) I couldn't go back up. I—threw up—on the floor!

AMANDA: From half past seven till after five every day you mean to tell me you walked around in the park, because you wanted to make me think that you were still going to Rubicam's Business College?

LAURA: It wasn't as bad as it sounds. I went inside places to get warmed up.

AMANDA: Inside where?

LAURA: I went in the art museum and the bird-houses at the Zoo. I visited the penguins every day! Sometimes I did without lunch and went to the movies. Lately I've been spending most of my afternoons in the Jewel-box, that big glass house where they raise the tropical flowers.

AMANDA: You did all this to deceive me, just for deception? (LAURA looks down) Why?

LAURA: Mother, when you're disappointed, you get that awful suffering look on your face, like the picture of Jesus' mother in the museum!

AMANDA: Hush!

LAURA: I couldn't face it.

(*Pause. A whisper of strings.* LEGEND: "THE CRUST OF HUMILITY.")

AMANDA (*hopelessly fingering the huge pocketbook*): So what are we going to do the rest of our lives? Stay home and watch the parades go by? Amuse ourselves with the glass menagerie, darling? Eternally play those worn-out phonograph records your father left as a painful reminder of him?

We won't have a business career—we've given that up because it gave us nervous indigestion! (*Laughs wearily*) What is there left but dependency all our lives? I know so well what becomes of unmarried women who aren't prepared to occupy a position. I've seen such pitiful cases in the South—barely tolerated spinsters living upon the grudging patronage of sister's husband or brother's wife!—stuck away in some little mouse-trap of a room—encouraged by one in-law to visit another—little birdlike women without any nest—eating the crust of humility all their life!

Is that the future that we've mapped out for ourselves?

I swear it's the only alternative I can think of!

It isn't a very pleasant alternative, is it?

Of course—some girls *do marry.* (LAURA *twists her hands nervously*) Haven't you ever liked some boy?

LAURA: Yes. I liked one once. (*Rises*) I came across his picture a while ago.

AMANDA (*with some interest*): He gave you his picture?

LAURA: No, it's in the year-book.

AMANDA (*disappointed*): Oh—a high-school boy.

(SCREEN IMAGE: JIM AS HIGH-SCHOOL HERO BEARING A SILVER CUP.)

LAURA: Yes. His name was Jim. (LAURA *lifts the heavy annual from the claw-foot table*) Here he is in *The Pirates of Penzance.*

AMANDA (*absently*): The what?

LAURA: The operetta the senior class put on. He had a wonderful voice and we sat across the aisle from each other Mondays, Wednesdays and Fridays in the Aud. Here he is with the silver cup for debating! See his grin?

AMANDA *(absently)* : He must have had a jolly disposition.

LAURA: He used to call me—Blue Roses.

(IMAGE: BLUE ROSES.)

AMANDA: Why did he call you such a name as that?

LAURA: When I had that attack of pleurosis—he asked me what was the matter when I came back. I said pleurosis—he thought that I said Blue Roses! So that's what he always called me after that. Whenever he saw me, he'd holler, "Hello, Blue Roses!" I didn't care for the girl that he went out with. Emily Meisenbach. Emily was the best-dressed girl at Soldan. She never struck me, though, as being sincere . ... It says in the Personal Section—they're engaged. That's—six years ago! They must be married by now.

AMANDA: Girls that aren't cut out for business careers usually wind up married to some nice man. *(Gets up with a spark of revival)* Sister, that's what you'll do!

(LAURA *utters a startled, doubtful laugh. She reaches quickly for a piece of glass.*)

LAURA: But, Mother—

AMANDA: Yes? *(Crossing to photograph.)*

LAURA *(in a tone of frightened apology)* : I'm—crippled!

(IMAGE: SCREEN.)

AMANDA: Nonsense! Laura, I've told you never, never to use that word. Why, you're not crippled, you just have a little defect—hardly noticeable, even! When people have some slight disadvantage like that, they cultivate other things to make up for it—develop charm—and vivacity—and—*charm!* That's all you have to do! *(She turns again to the photograph)* One thing your father had *plenty of*—was *charm!*

(TOM *motions to the fiddle in the wings.*)

(The Scene Fades Out with Music.)

Scene Three

LEGEND ON SCREEN: "AFTER THE FIASCO—"

TOM *speaks from the fire-escape landing.*

TOM: After the fiasco at Rubicam's Business College, the idea of getting a gentleman caller for Laura began to play a more and more important part in Mother's calculations.

It became an obsession. Like some archetype of the universal unconscious, the image of the gentleman caller haunted our small apartment. ... (IMAGE: YOUNG MAN AT DOOR WITH FLOWERS)

An evening at home rarely passed without some allusion to this image, this spectre, this hope. . . .

Even when he wasn't mentioned, his presence hung in Mother's preoccupied look and in my sister's frightened, apologetic manner—hung like a sentence passed upon the Wingfields!

Mother was a woman of action as well as words.

She began to take logical steps in the planned direction.

Late that winter and in the early spring—realizing that extra money would be needed to properly feather the nest and plume the bird—she conducted a vigorous campaign on the telephone, roping in subscribers to one of those magazines for matrons called *The Homemaker's Companion,* the type of journal that features the serialized sublimations of ladies of letters who think in terms of delicate cuplike breasts, slim, tapering waists, rich, creamy thighs, eyes like wood-smoke in autumn, fingers that soothe and caress like strains of music, bodies as powerful as Etruscan sculpture. (SCREEN IMAGE: GLAMOR MAGAZINE COVER. AMANDA *enters with phone on long extension cord. She is spotted in the dim stage.*)

AMANDA: Ida Scott? This is Amanda Wingfield!

We *missed* you at the D.A.R. last Monday!

I said to myself: She's probably suffering with that sinus condition! How is that sinus condition?

Horrors! Heaven have mercy!—You're a Christian martyr, yes, that's what you are, a Christian martyr!

Well, I just now happened to notice that your subscription to the *Companion's* about to expire! Yes, it expires with the next issue, honey!—just when that wonderful new serial by Bessie Mae Hopper is getting off to such an exciting start. Oh, honey, it's something that you can't miss! You remember how *Gone With the Wind* took everybody by storm? You simply couldn't go out if you hadn't read it. All everybody *talked* was Scarlett O'Hara. Well, this is a book that critics already compare to *Gone With the Wind.* It's the *Gone With the Wind* of the post-World War generation!— What?—Burning?—Oh, honey, don't let them burn, go take a look in the oven and I'll hold the wire! Heavens—I think she's hung up!

Dim Out

(LEGEND ON SCREEN: "YOU THINK I'M IN LOVE WITH CONTINENTAL SHOE-MAKERS?" *Before the stage is lighted, the violent voices of* TOM *and* AMANDA *are heard. They are quarreling behind the portieres. In front of them stands* LAURA *with clenched hands and panicky expression. A clear pool of light on her figure throughout this scene.*)

TOM: What in Christ's name am I—

AMANDA (*shrilly*) : Don't you use that—

TOM: Supposed to do!

AMANDA: Expression! Not in my—

TOM: Ohhh!

AMANDA: Presence! Have you gone out of your senses?

TOM: I have, that's true, *driven* out!

AMANDA: What is the matter with you, you—big—big—IDIOT!

TOM: Look!—I've got *no thing,* no single thing—

AMANDA: Lower your voice!

TOM: In my life here that I can call my own! Everything is—

AMANDA: Stop that shouting!

TOM: Yesterday you confiscated my books! You had the nerve to—

AMANDA: I took that horrible novel back to the library—yes! That hideous book by that insane Mr. Lawrence. (TOM *laughs wildly*) I cannot control the output of diseased minds or people who cater to them— (TOM *laughs still more wildly*) BUT I WON'T ALLOW SUCH FILTH BROUGHT INTO MY HOUSE! No, no, no, no, no!

TOM: House, house! Who pays rent on it, who makes a slave of himself to—

AMANDA (*fairly screeching*): Don't you DARE to—

TOM: No, no, *I* mustn't say things! *I've* got to just—

AMANDA: Let me tell you—

TOM: I don't want to hear any more! (*He tears the portieres open. The upstage area is lit with a turgid smoky red glow.*)

(AMANDA'S *hair is in metal curlers and she wears a very old bathrobe, much too large for her slight figure, a relic of the faithless Mr. Wingfield. An upright typewriter and a wild disarray of manuscripts is on the drop-leaf table. The quarrel was probably precipitated by* AMANDA'S *interruption of his creative labor. A chair lying overthrown on the floor. Their gesticulating shadows are cast on the ceiling by the fiery glow.*)

AMANDA: You *will* hear more, you—

TOM: No, I won't hear more, I'm going out!

AMANDA: You come right back in—

TOM: Out, out, out! Because I'm—

AMANDA: Come back here, Tom Wingfield! I'm not through talking to you!

TOM: Oh, go—

LAURA (*desperately*): —Tom!

AMANDA: You're going to listen, and no more insolence from you! I'm at the end of my patience!

(*He comes back toward her.*)

TOM: What do you think I'm at? Aren't I supposed to have any patience to reach the end of, Mother? I know, I know. It seems unimportant to you, what I'm *doing*—what I *want* to do—having a little *difference* between them! You don't think that—

AMANDA: I think you've been doing things that you're ashamed of. That's why you act like this. I don't believe that you go every night to the movies. Nobody goes to the movies night after night. Nobody in their right minds goes to the movies as often as you pretend to. People don't go to the movies at nearly midnight, and movies don't let out at two A.M. Come in stumbling. Muttering to yourself like a maniac! You get three hours' sleep and then go to work. Oh, I can picture the way you're doing down there. Moping, doping, because you're in no condition.

TOM (*wildly*): No, I'm in no condition!

AMANDA: What right have you got to jeopardize your job? Jeopardize the security of us all? How do you think we'd manage if you were—

TOM: Listen! You think I'm crazy *about the warehouse?* (*He bends fiercely toward her slight figure*) You think I'm in love with the Continental

Shoemakers? You think I want to spend fifty-five *years* down there in that —*celotex interior!* with—*fluorescent—tubes!* Look! I'd rather somebody picked up a crowbar and battered out my brains—than go back mornings! I *go!* Every time you come in yelling that God damn *"Rise and Shine!" "Rise and Shine!"* I say to myself, "How *lucky dead* people are!" But I get up. I *go!* For sixty-five dollars a month I give up all that I dream of doing and being ever! And you say self—*self's* all I ever think of. Why, listen, if self is what I thought of, Mother, I'd be where he is—GONE! (*Pointing to father's picture*) As far as the system of transportation reaches! (*He starts past her. She grabs his arm*) Don't grab at me, Mother!

AMANDA: Where are you going?

TOM: I'm going to the *movies!*

AMANDA: I don't believe that lie!

TOM (*crouching toward her, overtowering her tiny figure. She backs away, gasping*): I'm going to opium dens! Yes, opium dens, dens of vice and criminals' hang-outs, Mother. I've joined the Hogan gang,[6] I'm a hired assassin, I carry a tommy-gun in a violin case! I run a string of cat-houses in the Valley! They call me Killer, Killer Wingfield, I'm leading a double-life, a simple, honest warehouse worker by day, by night a dynamic *czar* of the *underworld, Mother.* I go to gambling casinos, I spin away fortunes on the roulette table! I wear a patch over one eye and a false mustache, sometimes I put on green whiskers. On those occasions they call me—*El Diablo!* Oh, I could tell you things to make you sleepless! My enemies plan to dynamite this place. They're going to blow us all sky-high some night! I'll be glad, very happy, and so will you! You'll go up, up on a broomstick, over Blue Mountain with seventeen gentlemen callers! You ugly—babbling old—*witch.* . . . (*He goes through a series of violent, clumsy movements, seizing his overcoat, lunging to the door, pulling it fiercely open. The women watch him, aghast. His arm catches in the sleeve of the coat as he struggles to pull it on. For a moment he is pinioned by the bulky garment. With an outraged groan he tears the coat off again, splitting the shoulder of it, and hurls it across the room. It strikes against the shelf of* LAURA'S *glass collection, there is a tinkle of shattering glass.* LAURA *cries out as if wounded.* MUSIC. LEGEND:* "THE GLASS MENAGERIE.")

LAURA (*shrilly*): My glass!—menagerie. . . . (*She covers her face and turns away.*)

(*But* AMANDA *is still stunned and stupefied by the "ugly witch" so that she barely notices this occurrence. Now she recovers her speech.*)

AMANDA (*in an awful voice*): I won't speak to you—until you apologize! (*She crosses through portieres and draws them together behind her.* TOM *is left with* LAURA. LAURA *clings weakly to the mantel with her face averted.* TOM *stares at her stupidly for a moment. Then he crosses to shelf.*

---

[6] "Dapper Danny" Hogan was the leader of the underworld in St. Paul, Minnesota, during the 1920s.

Drops awkwardly on his knees to collect the fallen glass, glancing at LAURA *as if he would speak but couldn't.*)

(*"The Glass Menagerie" steals in as*
The Scene Dims Out.)

Scene Four

The interior is dark. Faint light in the alley.

A deep-voiced bell in a church is tolling the hour of five as the scene commences.

TOM *appears at the top of the alley. After each solemn boom of the bell in the tower, he shakes a little noise-maker or rattle as if to express the tiny spasm of man in contrast to the sustained power and dignity of the Almighty. This and the unsteadiness of his advance make it evident that he has been drinking.*

As he climbs the few steps to the fire-escape landing light steals up inside. LAURA *appears in night-dress, observing* TOM'S *empty bed in the front room.*

TOM *fishes in his pockets for door-key, removing a motley assortment of articles in the search, including a perfect shower of movie-ticket stubs and an empty bottle. At last he finds the key, but just as he is about to insert it, it slips from his fingers. He strikes a match and crouches below the door.*

TOM (*bitterly*) : One crack—and it falls through!
(LAURA *opens the door.*)
LAURA: Tom, Tom, what are you doing?
TOM: Looking for a door-key.
LAURA: Where have you been all this time?
TOM: I have been to the movies.
LAURA: All this time at the movies?
TOM: There was a very long program. There was a Garbo[7] picture and a Mickey Mouse and a travelogue and a newsreel and a preview of coming

---

[7] Greta Garbo (1905-   ), an American motion picture actress of Swedish descent, achieved great popularity in the 1930s for her roles in *Camille* and *Anna Karenina*.

attractions. And there was an organ solo and a collection for the milk-fund—simultaneously—which ended up in a terrible fight between a fat lady and an usher!

LAURA (*innocently*) : Did you have to stay through everything?

TOM: Of course! And, oh, I forgot! There was a big stage show! The head-liner on this stage show was Malvolio the Magician. He performed wonderful tricks, many of them, such as pouring water back and forth between pitchers. First it turned to wine and then it turned to beer and then it turned to whiskey. I know it was whiskey it finally turned into because he needed somebody to come up out of the audience to help him, and I came up—both shows! It was Kentucky Straight Bourbon. A very generous fellow, he gave souvenirs. (*He pulls from his back pocket a shimmering rainbow-colored scarf*) He gave me this. This is his magic scarf. You can have it, Laura. You wave it over a canary cage and you get a bowl of gold-fish. You wave it over the gold-fish bowl and they fly away canaries. . . . But the wonderfullest trick of all was the coffin trick. We nailed him into a coffin and he got out of the coffin without removing one nail. (*He has come inside*) There is a trick that would come in handy for me—get me out of this 2 by 4 situation! (*Flops onto bed and starts removing shoes.*)

LAURA: Tom—Shhh!

TOM: What're you shushing me for?

LAURA: You'll wake up Mother.

TOM: Goody, goody! Pay 'er back for all those "Rise an' Shines." (*Lies down, groaning*) You know it don't take much intelligence to get yourself into a nailed-up coffin, Laura. But who in hell ever got himself out of one without removing one nail?

(*As if in answer, the father's grinning photograph lights up.*)

    Scene Dims Out

(*Immediately following: The church bell is heard striking six. At the sixth stroke the alarm clock goes off in* AMANDA'S *room, and after a few moments we hear her calling: "Rise and Shine! Rise and Shine! Laura, go tell your brother to rise and shine!"*)

TOM (*sitting up slowly*) : I'll rise—but I won't shine.

(*The light increases.*)

AMANDA: Laura, tell your brother his coffee is ready.

(LAURA *slips into front room.*)

LAURA: Tom!—It's nearly seven. Don't make Mother nervous. (*He stares at her stupidly. Beseechingly*) Tom, speak to Mother this morning. Make up with her, apologize, speak to her!

TOM: She won't to me. It's her that started not speaking.

LAURA: If you just say you're sorry she'll start speaking.

TOM: Her not speaking—is that such a tragedy?

LAURA: Please—please!

AMANDA (*calling from kitchenette*) : Laura, are you going to do what I asked you to do, or do I have to get dressed and go out myself?

LAURA: Going, going—soon as I get on my coat! (*She pulls on a shapeless felt hat with nervous, jerky movement, pleadingly glancing at* TOM.

Rushes awkwardly for coat. The coat is one of AMANDA'S, *inaccurately made-over, the sleeves too short for* LAURA) Butter and what else?

AMANDA (*entering upstage*) : Just butter. Tell them to charge it.

LAURA: Mother, they make such faces when I do that.

AMANDA: Sticks and stones can break our bones, but the expression on Mr. Garfinkel's face won't harm us! Tell your brother his coffee is getting cold.

LAURA (*at door*) : Do what I asked you, will you, will you, Tom?

(*He looks sullenly away.*)

AMANDA: Laura, go now or just don't go at all!

LAURA (*rushing out*) : Going—going! (*A second later she cries out.* TOM *springs up and crosses to door.* AMANDA *rushes anxiously in.* TOM *opens the door.*)

TOM: Laura?

LAURA: I'm all right. I slipped, but I'm all right.

AMANDA (*peering anxiously after her*) : If anyone breaks a leg on those fire-escape steps, the landlord ought to be sued for every cent he possesses! (*She shuts door. Remembers she isn't speaking and returns to other room.*)

(*As* TOM *enters listlessly for his coffee, she turns her back to him and stands rigidly facing the window on the gloomy gray vault of the areaway. Its light on her face with its aged but childish features is cruelly sharp, satirical as a Daumier[8] print.* MUSIC UNDER: "AVE MARIA."

TOM *glances sheepishly but sullenly at her averted figure and slumps at the table. The coffee is scalding hot; he sips it and gasps and spits it back in the cup. At his gasp,* AMANDA *catches her breath and half turns. Then catches herself and turns back to window.*

TOM *blows on his coffee, glancing sidewise at his mother. She clears her throat.* TOM *clears his. He starts to rise. Sinks back down again, scratches his head, clears his throat again.* AMANDA *coughs.* TOM *raises his cup in both hands to blow on it, his eyes staring over the rim of it at his mother for several moments. Then he slowly sets the cup down and awkwardly and hesitantly rises from the chair.*)

TOM (*hoarsely*) : Mother. I—I apologize, Mother. (AMANDA *draws a quick, shuddering breath. Her face works grotesquely. She breaks into childlike tears*) I'm sorry for what I said, for everything that I said, I didn't mean it.

AMANDA (*sobbingly*) : My devotion has made me a witch and so I make myself hateful to my children!

TOM: *No,* you *don't.*

AMANDA: I worry so much, don't sleep, it makes me nervous!

TOM (*gently*) : I understand that.

AMANDA: I've had to put up a solitary battle all these years. But you're my right-hand bower![9] Don't fall down, don't fail!

---

[8] Honoré Daumier (1808–1879) was a French caricaturist and painter. His famous lithographs hold the foibles of a bourgeois society up to ridicule.

[9] In the card games of euchre and five hundred, the highest card, the jack of trumps, is called the right bower.

TOM (*gently*) : I'll try, Mother.

AMANDA (*with great enthusiasm*): Try and you will SUCCEED! (*The notion makes her breathless*) Why, you—you're just *full* of natural endowments! Both my children—they're *unusual* children! Don't you think I know it? I'm so—*proud!* Happy and—feel I've—so much to be thankful for but— Promise me one thing, Son!

TOM: What, Mother?

AMANDA: Promise, son, you'll—never be a drunkard!

TOM (*turns to her grinning*) : I will never be a drunkard, Mother.

AMANDA: That's what frightened me so, that you'd be drinking! Eat a bowl of Purina!

TOM: Just coffee, Mother.

AMANDA: Shredded wheat biscuit?

TOM: No. No, Mother, just coffee.

AMANDA: You can't put in a day's work on an empty stomach. You've got ten minutes—don't gulp! Drinking too-hot liquids makes cancer of the stomach. . . . Put cream in.

TOM: No, thank you.

AMANDA: To cool it.

TOM: No! No, thank you, I want it black.

AMANDA: I know, but it's not good for you. We have to do all that we can to build ourselves up. In these trying times we live in, all that we have to cling to is—each other. . . . That's why it's so important to— Tom, I— I sent out your sister so I could discuss something with you. If you hadn't spoken I would have spoken to you. (*Sits down.*)

TOM (*gently*) : What is it, Mother, that you want to discuss?

AMANDA: *Laura!*

(TOM *puts his cup down slowly.* LEGEND ON SCREEN: "LAURA." MUSIC: "THE GLASS MENAGERIE.")

TOM: —Oh.—Laura. . . .

AMANDA (*touching his sleeve*) : You know how Laura is. So quiet but—still water runs deep! She notices things and I think she—broods about them. (TOM *looks up*) A few days ago I came in and she was crying.

TOM: What about?

AMANDA: You.

TOM: Me?

AMANDA: She has an idea that you're not happy here.

TOM: What gave her that idea?

AMANDA: What gives her any idea? However, you do act strangely. I—I'm not criticizing, understand *that!* I know your ambitions do not lie in the warehouse, that like everybody in the whole wide world—you've had to— make sacrifices, but—Tom—Tom—life's not easy, it calls for—Spartan endurance! There's so many things in my heart that I cannot describe to you! I've never told you but I—*loved* your father. . . .

TOM (*gently*) : I know that, Mother.

AMANDA: And you—when I see you taking after his ways! Staying out late— and—well, you *had* been drinking the night you were in that—terrifying condition! Laura says that you hate the apartment and that you go out nights to get away from it! Is that true, Tom?

TOM: No. You say there's so much in your heart that you can't describe to me. That's true of me, too. There's so much in my heart that I can't describe to *you!* So let's respect each other's—

AMANDA: But, why—*why*, Tom—are you always so *restless?* Where do you *go* to, nights?

TOM: I—go to the movies.

AMANDA: Why do you go to the movies so much, Tom?

TOM: I go to the movies because—I like adventure. Adventure is something I don't have much of at work, so I go to the movies.

AMANDA: But, Tom, you go to the movies *entirely* too *much!*

TOM: I like a lot of adventure.

(AMANDA *looks baffled, then hurt. As the familiar inquisition resumes he becomes hard and impatient again.* AMANDA *slips back into her querulous attitude toward him.* IMAGE ON SCREEN: SAILING VESSEL WITH JOLLY ROGER.[10])

AMANDA: Most young men find adventure in their careers.

TOM: Then most young men are not employed in a warehouse.

AMANDA: The world is full of young men employed in warehouses and offices and factories.

TOM: Do all of them find adventure in their careers?

AMANDA: They do or they do without it! Not everybody has a craze for adventure.

TOM: Man is by instinct a lover, a hunter, a fighter, and none of those instincts are given much play at the warehouse!

AMANDA: Man is by instinct! Don't quote instinct to me! Instinct is something that people have got away from! It belongs to animals! Christian adults don't want it!

TOM: What do Christian adults want, then, Mother?

AMANDA: Superior things! Things of the mind and the spirit! Only animals have to satisfy instincts! Surely your aims are somewhat higher than theirs! Than monkeys—pigs—

TOM: I reckon they're not.

AMANDA: You're joking! However, that isn't what I wanted to discuss.

TOM (*rising*): I haven't much time.

AMANDA (*pushing his shoulders*): Sit down.

TOM: You want me to punch in red at the warehouse, Mother?

AMANDA: You have five minutes. I want to talk about Laura.

(LEGEND: "PLANS AND PROVISIONS.")

TOM: All right! What about Laura?

AMANDA: We have to be making some plans and provisions for her. She's older than you, two years, and nothing has happened. She just drifts along doing nothing. It frightens me terribly how she just drifts along.

TOM: I guess she's the type that people call home girls.

---

[10] A black pirate flag with white skull and crossbones.

AMANDA: There's no such type, and if there is, it's a pity! That is unless the home is hers, with a husband!

TOM: What?

AMANDA: Oh, I can see the handwriting on the wall as plain as I see the nose in front of my face! It's terrifying!

More and more you remind me of your father! He was out all hours without explanation!—Then *left! Good-bye!*

And me with the bag to hold. I saw that letter you got from the Merchant Marine. I know what you're dreaming of. I'm not standing here blindfolded.

Very well, then. Then *do* it!

But not till there's somebody to take your place.

TOM: What do you mean?

AMANDA: I mean that as soon as Laura has got somebody to take care of her, married, a home of her own, independent—why, then you'll be free to go wherever you please, on land, on sea, whichever way the wind blows you!

But until that time you've got to look out for your sister. I don't say me because I'm old and don't matter! I say for your sister because she's young and dependent.

I put her in business college—a dismal failure! Frightened her so it made her sick at the stomach.

I took her over to the Young People's League at the church. Another fiasco. She spoke to nobody, nobody spoke to her. Now all she does is fool with those pieces of glass and play those worn-out records. What kind of a life is that for a girl to lead?

TOM: What can I do about it?

AMANDA: Overcome selfishness!

Self, self, self is all that you ever think of! (TOM *springs up and crosses to get his coat. It is ugly and bulky. He pulls on a cap with earmuffs*) Where is your muffler? Put your wool muffler on! (*He snatches it angrily from the closet and tosses it around his neck and pulls both ends tight*) Tom! I haven't said what I had in mind to ask you.

TOM: I'm too late to—

AMANDA (*catching his arm—very importunately. Then shyly*): Down at the warehouse, aren't there some—nice young men?

TOM: No!

AMANDA: There *must* be—*some. . . .*

TOM: Mother—(*Gesture.*)

AMANDA: Find out one that's clean-living—doesn't drink and—ask him out for sister!

TOM: What?

AMANDA: For *sister!* To *meet!* Get *acquainted!*

TOM (*stamping to door*): Oh, my go-osh!

AMANDA: Will you? (*He opens door. Imploringly*) Will you? (*He starts down*) Will you? *Will* you, dear?

TOM (*calling back*): YES!

(AMANDA *closes the door hesitantly and with a troubled but faintly hope-*

ful expression. SCREEN IMAGE: GLAMOR MAGAZINE COVER. *Spot* AMANDA *at phone.*)

AMANDA: Ella Cartwright? This is Amanda Wingfield!

How are you, honey?

How is that kidney condition? (*Count five*)

Horrors! (*Count five*)

You're a Christian martyr, yes, honey, that's what you are, a Christian martyr!

Well, I just now happened to notice in my little red book that your subscription to the *Companion* has just run out! I knew that you wouldn't want to miss out on the wonderful serial starting in this new issue. It's by Bessie Mae Hopper, the first thing she's written since *Honeymoon for Three.*

Wasn't that a strange and interesting story? Well, this one is even lovelier, I believe. It has a sophisticated, society background. It's all about the horsey set on Long Island!

(*Fade Out.*)

Scene Five

LEGEND ON SCREEN: "ANNUNCIATION."[11] *Fade with music.*

It is early dusk of a spring evening. Supper has just been finished in the Wingfield apartment. AMANDA *and* LAURA *in light-colored dresses are removing dishes from the table, in the upstage area, which is shadowy, their movements formalized almost as a dance or ritual, their moving forms as pale and silent as moths.*

TOM, *in white shirt and trousers, rises from the table and crosses toward the fire-escape.*

AMANDA (*as he passes her*): Son, will you do me a favor?

TOM: What?

AMANDA: Comb your hair! You look so pretty when your hair is combed! (TOM *slouches on sofa with evening paper. Enormous caption "Franco Triumphs"*) There is only one respect in which I would like you to emulate your father.

TOM: What respect is that?

---

[11] The actual moment of the Incarnation, when the angel announced to the Virgin Mary that God the Son was to be born to her (Luke 1:26-28).

AMANDA: The care he aways took of his appearance. He never allowed himself to look untidy. (*He throws down the paper and crosses to fire-escape*) Where are you going?

TOM: I'm going out to smoke.

AMANDA: You smoke too much. A pack a day at fifteen cents a pack. How much would that amount to in a month? Thirty times fifteen is how much, Tom? Figure it out and you will be astounded at what you could save. Enough to give you a night-school course in accounting at Washington U! Just think what a wonderful thing that would be for you, Son! (TOM *is unmoved by the thought.*)

TOM: I'd rather smoke. (*He steps out on landing, letting the screen door slam.*)

AMANDA (*sharply*): I know! That's the tragedy of it. . . . (*Alone, she turns to look at her husband's picture.*)

(DANCE MUSIC: "ALL THE WORLD IS WAITING FOR THE SUNRISE!")

TOM (*to the audience*): Across the alley from us was the Paradise Dance Hall. On evenings in spring the windows and doors were open and the music came outdoors. Sometimes the lights were turned out except for a large glass sphere that hung from the ceiling. It would turn slowly about and filter the dusk with delicate rainbow colors. Then the orchestra played a waltz or a tango, something that had a slow and sensuous rhythm. Couples would come outside, to the relative privacy of the alley. You could see them kissing behind ash-pits and telephone poles.

This was the compensation for lives that passed like mine, without any change or adventure.

Adventure and change were imminent in this year. They were waiting around the corner for all these kids.

Suspended in the mist over Berchtesgaden, caught in the folds of Chamberlain's umbrella—

In Spain there was Guernica!

But here there was only hot swing music and liquor, dance halls, bars, and movies, and sex that hung in the gloom like a chandelier and flooded the world with brief, descriptive rainbows. . . .

All the world was waiting for bombardments!

(AMANDA *turns from the picture and comes outside.*)

AMANDA (*sighing*): A fire-escape landing's a poor excuse for a porch. (*She spreads a newspaper on a step and sits down, gracefully and demurely as if she were settling into a swing on a Mississippi veranda*) What are you looking at?

TOM: The moon.

AMANDA: Is there a moon this evening?

TOM: It's rising over Garfinkel's Delicatessen.

AMANDA: So it is! A little silver slipper of a moon. Have you made a wish on it yet?

TOM: Um-hum.

AMANDA: What did you wish for?

TOM: That's a secret.

AMANDA: A secret, huh? Well, I won't tell mine either. I will be just as mysterious as you.

TOM: I bet I can guess what yours is.

AMANDA: Is my head so transparent?

TOM: You're not a sphinx.

AMANDA: No, I don't have secrets. I'll tell you what I wished for on the moon. Success and happiness for my precious children! I wish for that whenever there's a moon, and when there isn't a moon, I wish for it, too.

TOM: I thought perhaps you wished for a gentleman caller.

AMANDA: Why do you say that?

TOM: Don't you remember asking me to fetch one?

AMANDA: I remember suggesting that it would be nice for your sister if you brought home some nice young man from the warehouse. I think that I've made that suggestion more than once.

TOM: Yes, you have made it repeatedly.

AMANDA: Well?

TOM: We are going to have one.

AMANDA: *What?*

TOM: A gentleman caller!

(THE ANNUNCIATION IS CELEBRATED WITH MUSIC. AMANDA *rises*. IMAGE ON SCREEN: CALLER WITH BOUQUET.)

AMANDA: You mean you have asked some nice young man to come over?

TOM: Yep. I've asked him to dinner.

AMANDA: You really did?

TOM: I did!

AMANDA: You did, and did he—*accept?*

TOM: He did!

AMANDA: Well, well—well, well! That's—lovely!

TOM: I thought that you would be pleased.

AMANDA: It's definite, then?

TOM: Very definite.

AMANDA: Soon?

TOM: Very soon.

AMANDA: For heaven's sake, stop putting on and tell me some things, will you?

TOM: What things do you want me to tell you?

AMANDA: *Naturally* I would like to know when he's *coming!*

TOM: He's coming tomorrow.

AMANDA: *Tomorrow?*

TOM: Yep. Tomorrow.

AMANDA: But, Tom!

TOM: Yes, Mother?

AMANDA: Tomorrow gives me no time!

TOM: Time for what?

AMANDA: Preparations! Why didn't you phone me at once, as soon as you asked him, the minute that he accepted? Then, don't you see, I could have been getting ready!

TOM: You don't have to make any fuss.

AMANDA: Oh, Tom, Tom, Tom, of course I have to make a fuss! I want things nice, not sloppy! Not thrown together. I'll certainly have to do some fast thinking, won't I?

TOM: I don't see why you have to think at all.

AMANDA: You just don't know. We can't have a gentleman caller in a pigsty! All my wedding silver has to be polished, the monogrammed table linen ought to be laundered! The windows have to be washed and fresh curtains put up. And how about clothes? We have to *wear* something, don't we?

TOM: Mother, this boy is no one to make a fuss over!

AMANDA: Do you realize he's the first young man we've introduced to your sister?

It's terrible, dreadful, disgraceful that poor little sister has never received a single gentleman caller! Tom, come inside! (*She opens the screen door.*)

TOM: What for?

AMANDA: I want to ask you some things.

TOM: If you're going to make such a fuss, I'll call it off, I'll tell him not to come!

AMANDA: You certainly won't do anything of the kind. Nothing offends people worse than broken engagements. It simply means I'll have to work like a Turk! We won't be brilliant, but we will pass inspection. Come on inside. (TOM *follows, groaning*) Sit down.

TOM: Any particular place you would like me to sit?

AMANDA: Thank heavens I've got that new sofa! I'm also making payments on a floor lamp I'll have sent out! And put the chintz covers on, they'll brighten things up! Of course I'd hoped to have these walls re-papered. . . . What is the young man's name?

TOM: His name is O'Connor.

AMANDA: That, of course, means fish—tomorrow is Friday! I'll have that salmon loaf—with Durkee's dressing! What does he do? He works at the warehouse?

TOM: Of course! How else would I—

AMANDA: Tom, he—doesn't drink?

TOM: Why do you ask me that?

AMANDA: Your father *did!*

TOM: Don't get started on that!

AMANDA: He *does* drink, then?

TOM: Not that I know of!

AMANDA: Make sure, be certain! The last thing I want for my daughter's a boy who drinks!

TOM: Aren't you being a little bit premature? Mr. O'Connor has not yet appeared on the scene!

AMANDA: But will tomorrow. To meet your sister, and what do I know about his character? Nothing! Old maids are better off than wives of drunkards!

TOM: Oh, my God!

AMANDA: Be still!

TOM (*leaning forward to whisper*) : Lots of fellows meet girls whom they don't marry!

AMANDA: Oh, talk sensibly, Tom—and don't be sarcastic! (*She has gotten a hairbrush.*)

TOM: What are you doing?

AMANDA: I'm brushing that cow-lick down!

What is this young man's position at the warehouse?

TOM (*submitting grimly to the brush and the interrogation*) : This young man's position is that of a shipping clerk, Mother.

AMANDA: Sounds to me like a fairly responsible job, the sort of a job *you* would be in if you just had more *get-up*.

What is his salary? Have you any idea?

TOM: I would judge it to be approximately eighty-five dollars a month.

AMANDA: Well—not princely, but—

TOM: Twenty more than I make.

AMANDA: Yes, how well I know! But for a family man, eighty-five dollars a month is not much more than you can just get by on. . . .

TOM: Yes, but Mr. O'Connor is not a family man.

AMANDA: He might be, mightn't he? Some time in the future?

TOM: I see. Plans and provisions.

AMANDA: You are the only young man that I know of who ignores the fact that the future becomes the present, the present the past, and the past turns into everlasting regret if you don't plan for it!

TOM: I will think that over and see what I can make of it.

AMANDA: Don't be supercilious with your mother! Tell me some more about this—what do you call him?

TOM: James D. O'Connor. The D. is for Delaney.

AMANDA: Irish on *both* sides! *Gracious!* And doesn't drink?

TOM: Shall I call him up and ask him right this minute?

AMANDA: The only way to find out about those things is to make discreet inquiries at the proper moment. When I was a girl in Blue Mountain and it was suspected that a young man drank, the girl whose attentions he had been receiving, if any girl *was*, would sometimes speak to the minister of his church, or rather her father would if her father was living, and sort of feel him out on the young man's character. That is the way such things are discreetly handled to keep a young woman from making a tragic mistake!

TOM: Then how did you happen to make a tragic mistake?

AMANDA: That innocent look of your father's had everyone fooled!

He *smiled*—the world was *enchanted!*

No girl can do worse than put herself at the mercy of a handsome appearance!

I hope that Mr. O'Connor is not too good-looking.

TOM: No, he's not too good-looking. He's covered with freckles and hasn't too much of a nose.

AMANDA: He's not right-down homely, though?

TOM: Not right-down homely. Just medium homely, I'd say.

AMANDA: Character's what to look for in a man.

TOM: That's what I've always said, Mother.

AMANDA: You've never said anything of the kind and I suspect you would never give it a thought.

TOM: Don't be so suspicious of me.

AMANDA: At least I hope he's the type that's up and coming.

TOM: I think he really goes in for self-improvement.

AMANDA: What reason have you to think so?

TOM: He goes to night school.

AMANDA (*beaming*): Splendid! What does he do, I mean study?

TOM: Radio engineering and public speaking!

AMANDA: Then he has visions of being advanced in the world!

Any young man who studies public speaking is aiming to have an executive job some day!

And radio engineering? A thing for the future!

Both of these facts are very illuminating. Those are the sort of things that a mother should know concerning any young man who comes to call on her daughter. Seriously or—not.

TOM: One little warning. He doesn't know about Laura. I didn't let on that we had dark ulterior motives. I just said, why don't you come and have dinner with us? He said okay and that was the whole conversation.

AMANDA: I bet it was! You're eloquent as an oyster.

However, he'll know about Laura when he gets here. When he sees how lovely and sweet and pretty she is, he'll thank his lucky stars he was asked to dinner.

TOM: Mother, you mustn't expect too much of Laura.

AMANDA: What do you mean?

TOM: Laura seems all those things to you and me because she's ours and we love her. We don't even notice she's crippled any more.

AMANDA: Don't say crippled! You know that I never allow that word to be used!

TOM: But face facts, Mother. She is and—that's not all—

AMANDA: What do you mean "not all"?

TOM: Laura is very different from other girls.

AMANDA: I think the difference is all to her advantage.

TOM: Not quite all—in the eyes of others—strangers—she's terribly shy and lives in a world of her own and those things make her seem a little peculiar to people outside the house.

AMANDA: Don't say peculiar.

TOM: Face the facts. She is.

(THE DANCE-HALL MUSIC CHANGES TO A TANGO THAT HAS A MINOR AND SOMEWHAT OMINOUS TONE.)

AMANDA: In what way is she peculiar—may I ask?

TOM (*gently*): She lives in a world of her own—a world of—little glass ornaments, Mother. . . . (*Gets up.* AMANDA *remains holding brush, looking at him, troubled*) She plays old phonograph records and—that's about all— (*He glances at himself in the mirror and crosses to door.*)

AMANDA (*sharply*): Where are you going?

TOM: I'm going to the movies. (*Out screen door.*)

AMANDA: Not to the movies, every night to the movies! (*Follows quickly to screen door*) I don't believe you always go to the movies! (*He is gone.* AMANDA *looks worriedly after him for a moment. Then vitality and optimism return and she turns from the door. Crossing to portieres*) Laura! Laura! (LAURA *answers from kitchenette.*)

LAURA: Yes, Mother.

AMANDA: Let those dishes go and come in front! (LAURA *appears with dish towel. Gaily*) Laura, come here and make a wish on the moon!
(SCREEN IMAGE: MOON.)

LAURA: (*entering*): Moon—moon?

AMANDA: A little silver slipper of a moon.
   Look over your left shoulder, Laura, and make a wish! (LAURA *looks faintly puzzled as if called out of sleep.* AMANDA *seizes her shoulders and turns her at an angle by the door*)
   Now!
   Now, darling, *wish!*

LAURA: What shall I wish for, Mother?

AMANDA (*her voice trembling and her eyes suddenly filling with tears*): Happiness! Good fortune!
(*The violin rises and the stage dims out.*)

   (*The Curtain Falls.*)

Scene Six

IMAGE: HIGH SCHOOL HERO.

TOM: And so the following evening I brought Jim home to dinner. I had known Jim slightly in high school. In high school Jim was a hero. He had tremendous Irish good nature and vitality with the scrubbed and polished look of white chinaware. He seemed to move in a continual spotlight. He was a star in basketball, captain of the debating club, president of the senior class and the glee club and he sang the male lead in the annual light operas. He was always running or bounding, never just walking. He seemed always at the point of defeating the law of gravity. He was shooting with such velocity through his adolescence that you would logically expect him to arrive at nothing short of the White House by the time he was thirty. But Jim apparently ran into more interference after his graduation from Soldan. His speed had definitely slowed. Six years after he left high school he was holding a job that wasn't much better than mine. (IMAGE: CLERK)

He was the only one at the warehouse with whom I was on friendly terms. I was valuable to him as someone who could remember his former glory, who had seen him win basketball games and the silver cup in debating. He knew of my secret practice of retiring to a cabinet of the washroom to work on poems when business was slack in the warehouse. He called me Shakespeare. And while the other boys in the warehouse regarded me with suspicious hostility, Jim took a humorous attitude toward me. Gradually his attitude affected the others, their hostility wore off and they also began to smile at me as people smile at an oddly fashioned dog who trots across their path at some distance.

I knew that Jim and Laura had known each other at Soldan, and I had heard Laura speak admiringly of his voice. I didn't know if Jim remembered her or not. In high school Laura had been as unobtrusive as Jim had been astonishing. If he did remember Laura, it was not as my sister, for when I asked him to dinner, he grinned and said, "You know, Shakespeare, I never thought of you as having folks!"

He was about to discover that I did. . . .

(LIGHT UP STAGE. LEGEND ON SCREEN: "THE ACCENT OF A COMING FOOT." *Friday evening. It is about five o'clock of a late spring evening which comes "scattering poems in the sky." A delicate lemony light is in the Wingfield apartment.* AMANDA *has worked like a Turk in preparation for the gentleman caller. The results are astonishing. The new floor lamp with its rose-silk shade is in place, a colored paper lantern conceals the broken light fixture in the ceiling, new billowing white curtains are at the windows, chintz covers are on chairs and sofa, a pair of new sofa pillows make their initial appearance. Open boxes and tissue paper are scattered on the floor.* LAURA *stands in the middle with lifted arms while* AMANDA *crouches before her, adjusting the hem of the new dress, devout and ritualistic. The dress is colored and designed by memory. The arrangement of* LAURA'S *hair is changed; it is softer and more becoming. A fragile, unearthly prettiness has come out in* LAURA: *she is like a piece of translucent glass touched by light, given a momentary radiance, not actual, not lasting.*)

AMANDA (*impatiently*): Why are you trembling?

LAURA: Mother, you've made me so nervous!

AMANDA: How have I made you nervous?

LAURA: By all this fuss! You make it seem so important!

AMANDA: I don't understand you, Laura. You couldn't be satisfied with just sitting home, and yet whenever I try to arrange something for you, you seem to resist it. (*She gets up*)

Now take a look at yourself.

No, wait! Wait just a moment—I have an idea!

LAURA: What is it now?

(AMANDA *produces two powder puffs which she wraps in handkerchiefs and stuffs in* LAURA'S *bosom.*)

LAURA: Mother, what are you doing?

AMANDA: They call them "Gay Deceivers"!

LAURA: I won't wear them!

AMANDA: You will!

LAURA: Why should I?

AMANDA: Because, to be painfully honest, your chest is flat.

LAURA: You made it seem like we were setting a trap.

AMANDA: All pretty girls are a trap, a pretty trap, and men expect them to be. (LEGEND: "A PRETTY TRAP")

Now look at yourself, young lady. This is the prettiest you will ever be!

I've got to fix myself now! You're going to be surprised by your mother's appearance! (*She crosses through portieres, humming gaily.*)

(LAURA *moves slowly to the long mirror and stares solemnly at herself. A wind blows the white curtains inward in a slow, graceful motion and with a faint, sorrowful sighing.*)

AMANDA (*off stage*): It isn't dark enough yet. (LAURA *turns slowly before the mirror with a troubled look.*)

(LEGEND ON SCREEN: "THIS IS MY SISTER: CELEBRATE HER WITH STRINGS!" MUSIC.)

AMANDA (*laughing, off*): I'm going to show you something. I'm going to make a spectacular appearance!

LAURA: What is it, Mother?

AMANDA: Possess your soul in patience—you will see!

Something I've resurrected from that old trunk! Styles haven't changed so terribly much after all. . . . (*She parts the portieres*)

Now just look at your mother! (*She wears a girlish frock of yellowed voile with a blue silk sash. She carries a bunch of jonquils—the legend of her youth is nearly revived. Feverishly*)

This is the dress in which I led the cotillion. Won the cakewalk twice at Sunset Hill, wore one spring to the Governor's ball in Jackson!

See how I sashayed around the ballroom, Laura? (*She raises her skirt and does a mincing step around the room*)

I wore it on Sundays for my gentlemen callers! I had it on the day I met your father—

I had malaria fever all that spring. The change of climate from East Tennessee to the Delta—weakened resistance—I had a little temperature all the time—not enough to be serious—just enough to make me restless and giddy!—Invitations poured in—parties all over the Delta!—"Stay in bed," said Mother, "you have fever!"—but I just wouldn't.—I took quinine but kept on going, going!—Evenings, dances!—Afternoons, long, long rides! Picnics—lovely!—So lovely, that country in May.—All lacy with dogwood, literally flooded with jonquils!—That was the spring I had the craze for jonquils. Jonquils became an absolute obsession. Mother said, "Honey, there's no more room for jonquils." And still I kept on bringing in more jonquils. Whenever, wherever I saw them, I'd say, "Stop! Stop! I see jonquils!" I made the young men help me gather the jonquils! It was a joke, Amanda and her jonquils! Finally there were no more vases to hold them, every available space was filled with jonquils. No vases to hold them? All right, I'll hold them myself! And then I—(*She stops in front of the picture.* MUSIC) met your father!

Malaria fever and jonquils and then—this—boy. . . . (*She switches on the rose-colored lamp*)

I hope they get here before it starts to rain. (*She crosses upstage and places the jonquils in bowl on table*)

I gave your brother a little extra change so he and Mr. O'Connor could take the service car home.

LAURA (*with altered look*) : What did you say his name was?

AMANDA: O'Connor.

LAURA: What is his first name?

AMANDA: I don't remember. Oh, yes, I do. It was—Jim!

(LAURA *sways slightly and catches hold of a chair.* LEGEND ON SCREEN: "NOT JIM!")

LAURA (*faintly*) : Not—Jim!

AMANDA: Yes, that was it, it was Jim! I've never known a Jim that wasn't nice!

(MUSIC: OMINOUS.)

LAURA: Are you sure his name is Jim O'Connor?

AMANDA: Yes. Why?

LAURA: Is he the one that Tom used to know in high school?

AMANDA: He didn't say so. I think he just got to know him at the warehouse.

LAURA: There was a Jim O'Connor we both knew in high school—(*Then, with effort*) If that is the one that Tom is bringing to dinner—you'll have to excuse me, I won't come to the table.

AMANDA: What sort of nonsense is this?

LAURA: You asked me once if I'd ever liked a boy. Don't you remember I showed you this boy's picture?

AMANDA: You mean the boy you showed me in the year book?

LAURA: Yes, that boy.

AMANDA: Laura, Laura, were you in love with that boy?

LAURA: I don't know, Mother. All I know is I couldn't sit at the table if it was him!

AMANDA: It won't be him! It isn't the least bit likely. But whether it is or not, you will come to the table. You will not be excused.

LAURA: I'll have to be, Mother.

AMANDA: I don't intend to humor your silliness, Laura. I've had too much from you and your brother, both!

So just sit down and compose yourself till they come. Tom has forgotten his key so you'll have to let them in, when they arrive.

LAURA (*panicky*) : Oh, Mother—*you* answer the door!

AMANDA (*lightly*) : I'll be in the kitchen—busy!

LAURA: Oh, Mother, please answer the door, don't make me do it!

AMANDA (*crossing into kitchenette*) : I've got to fix the dressing for the salmon. Fuss, fuss—silliness!—over a gentleman caller!

(*Door swings shut.* LAURA *is left alone.* LEGEND: "TERROR!" *She utters a low moan and turns off the lamp—sits stiffly on the edge of the sofa, knotting her fingers together.* LEGEND ON SCREEN: "THE OPENING OF A DOOR!" TOM *and* JIM *appear on the fire-escape steps and climb to land-*

ing. Hearing their approach, LAURA *rises with a panicky gesture. She retreats to the portieres. The doorbell.* LAURA *catches her breath and touches her throat. Low drums.*)

AMANDA (*calling*) : Laura, sweetheart! The door!

(LAURA *stares at it without moving.*)

JIM: I think we just beat the rain.

TOM: Uh-huh. (*He rings again, nervously.* JIM *whistles and fishes for a cigarette.*)

AMANDA (*very, very gaily*) : Laura, that is your brother and Mr. O'Connor! Will you let them in, darling?

(LAURA *crosses toward kitchenette door.*)

LAURA (*breathlessly*) : Mother—you go to the door!

(AMANDA *steps out of kitchenette and stares furiously at* LAURA. *She points imperiously at the door.*)

LAURA: Please, please!

AMANDA (*in a fierce whisper*) : What is the matter with you, you silly thing?

LAURA (*desperately*) : Please, you answer it, *please!*

AMANDA: I told you I wasn't going to humor you, Laura. Why have you chosen this moment to lose your mind?

LAURA: Please, please, please, you go!

AMANDA: You'll have to go to the door because I can't!

LAURA (*despairingly*) : I can't either!

AMANDA: *Why?*

LAURA: I'm *sick!*

AMANDA: I'm sick, too—of your nonsense! Why can't you and your brother be normal people? Fantastic whims and behavior! (TOM *gives a long ring*)

Preposterous goings on! Can you give me one reason—(*Calls out lyrically*) COMING! JUST ONE SECOND!—why you should be afraid to open a door? Now you answer it, Laura!

LAURA: Oh, oh, oh . . . (*She returns through the portieres. Darts to the victrola and winds it frantically and turns it on.*)

AMANDA: Laura Wingfield, you march right to that door!

LAURA: Yes—yes, Mother!

(*A faraway, scratchy rendition of "Dardanella" softens the air and gives her strength to move through it. She slips to the door and draws it cautiously open.* TOM *enters with the caller,* JIM O'CONNOR.)

TOM: Laura, this is Jim. Jim, this is my sister, Laura.

JIM (*stepping inside*) : I didn't know that Shakespeare had a sister!

LAURA (*retreating stiff and trembling from the door*) : How—how do you do?

JIM (*heartily extending his hand*) : Okay!

(LAURA *touches it hesitantly with hers.*)

JIM: Your hand's *cold,* Laura!

LAURA: Yes, well—I've been playing the victrola. . . .

JIM: Must have been playing classical music on it! You ought to play a little hot swing music to warm you up!

LAURA: Excuse me—I haven't finished playing the victrola. . . .

(*She turns awkwardly and hurries into the front room. She pauses a second by the victrola. Then catches her breath and darts through the portieres like a frightened deer.*)

JIM (*grinning*): What was the matter?

TOM: Oh—with Laura? Laura is—terribly shy.

JIM: Shy, huh? It's unusual to meet a shy girl nowadays. I don't believe you ever mentioned you had a sister.

TOM: Well, now you know. I have one. Here is the *Post Dispatch*. You want a piece of it?

JIM: Uh-huh.

TOM: What piece? The comics?

JIM: Sports! (*Glances at it*) Ole Dizzy Dean is on his bad behavior.

TOM (*disinterest*): Yeah? (*Lights cigarette and crosses back to fire-escape door.*)

JIM: Where are *you* going?

TOM: I'm going out on the terrace.

JIM (*goes after him*): You know, Shakespeare—I'm going to sell you a bill of goods!

TOM: What goods?

JIM: A course I'm taking.

TOM: Huh?

JIM: In public speaking! You and me, we're not the warehouse type.

TOM: Thanks—that's good news. But what has public speaking got to do with it?

JIM: It fits you for—executive positions!

TOM: Awww.

JIM: I tell you it's done a helluva lot for me.

(IMAGE: EXECUTIVE AT DESK.)

TOM: In what respect?

JIM: In every! Ask yourself what is the difference between you an' me and men in the office down front? Brains?—No!—Ability?—No! Then what? Just one little thing—

TOM: What is that one little thing?

JIM: Primarily it amounts to—social poise! Being able to square up to people and hold your own on any social level!

AMANDA (*off stage*): Tom?

TOM: Yes, Mother?

AMANDA: Is that you and Mr. O'Connor?

TOM: Yes, Mother.

AMANDA: Well, you just make yourselves comfortable in there.

TOM: Yes, Mother.

AMANDA: Ask Mr. O'Connor if he would like to wash his hands.

JIM: Aw, no—no—thank you—I took care of that at the warehouse. Tom—

TOM: Yes?

JIM: Mr. Mendoza was speaking to me about you.

TOM: Favorably?

JIM: What do you think?

TOM: Well—

JIM: You're going to be out of a job if you don't wake up.

TOM: I am waking up—

JIM: You show no signs.

TOM: The signs are interior.

(IMAGE ON SCREEN: THE SAILING VESSEL WITH JOLLY ROGER AGAIN.)

TOM: I'm planning to change. (*He leans over the rail speaking with quiet exhilaration. The incandescent marquees and signs of the first-run movie houses light his face from across the alley. He looks like a voyager*) I'm right at the point of committing myself to a future that doesn't include the warehouse and Mr. Mendoza or even a night-school course in public speaking.

JIM: What are you gassing about?

TOM: I'm tired of the movies.

JIM: Movies!

TOM: Yes, movies! Look at them— (*A wave toward the marvels of Grand Avenue*) All of those glamorous people—having adventures—hogging it all, gobbling the whole thing up! You know what happens? People go to the *movies* instead of *moving!* Hollywood characters are supposed to have all the adventures for everybody in America, while everybody in America sits in a dark room and watches them have them! Yes, until there's a war. That's when adventure becomes available to the masses! *Everyone's* dish, not only Gable's! Then the people in the dark room come out of the dark room to have some adventures themselves—Goody, goody!—It's our turn now, to go to the South Sea Islands—to make a safari—to be exotic, far-off!—But I'm not patient. I don't want to wait till then. I'm tired of the *movies* and I am *about* to move!

JIM (*incredulously*): Move?

TOM: Yes.

JIM: When?

TOM: Soon!

JIM: Where? Where?

(THEME THREE MUSIC SEEMS TO ANSWER THE QUESTION, WHILE TOM THINKS IT OVER. HE SEARCHES AMONG HIS POCKETS.)

TOM: I'm starting to boil inside. I know I seem dreamy, but inside—well, I'm boiling!—Whenever I pick up a shoe, I shudder a little thinking how short life is and what I am doing!—Whatever that means, I know it doesn't mean shoes—except as something to wear on a traveler's feet! (*Finds paper*) Look—

JIM: What?

TOM: I'm a member.

JIM (*reading*): The Union of Merchant Seamen.

TOM: I paid my dues this month, instead of the light bill.

JIM: You will regret it when they turn the lights off.

TOM: I won't be here.

JIM: How about your mother?

TOM: I'm like my father. The bastard son of a bastard! See how he grins? And he's been absent going on sixteen years!

JIM: You're just talking, you drip. How does your mother feel about it?

TOM: Shhh!—Here comes Mother! Mother is not acquainted with my plans!

AMANDA (*enters portieres*): Where are you all?

TOM: On the terrace, Mother.

(*They start inside. She advances to them.* TOM *is distinctly shocked at her appearance. Even* JIM *blinks a little. He is making his first contact with girlish Southern vivacity and in spite of the night-school course in public speaking is somewhat thrown off the beam by the unexpected outlay of social charm. Certain responses are attempted by* JIM *but are swept aside by* AMANDA'S *gay laughter and chatter.* TOM *is embarrassed but after the first shock* JIM *reacts very warmly. Grins and chuckles, is altogether won over.* IMAGE: AMANDA AS A GIRL.)

AMANDA (*coyly smiling, shaking her girlish ringlets*): Well, well, well, so this is Mr. O'Connor. Introductions entirely unnecessary. I've heard so much about you from my boy. I finally said to him, Tom—good gracious! —why don't you bring this paragon to supper? I'd like to meet this nice young man at the warehouse!—Instead of just hearing him sing your praises so much!

I don't know why my son is so stand-offish—that's not Southern behavior!

Let's sit down and—I think we could stand a little more air in here! Tom, leave the door open. I felt a nice fresh breeze a moment ago. Where has it gone to?

Mmm, so warm already! And not quite summer, even. We're going to burn up when summer really gets started.

However, we're having—we're having a very light supper. I think light things are better fo' this time of year. The same as light clothes are. Light clothes an' light food are what warm weather calls fo'. You know our blood gets so thick during th' winter—it takes a while fo' us to *adjust* ou'selves!—when the season changes. . . .

It's come so quick this year. I wasn't prepared. All of a sudden— heavens! Already summer!—I ran to the trunk an' pulled out this light dress— Terribly old! Historical almost! But feels so good—so good an' co-ol, y' know. . . .

TOM: Mother—

AMANDA: Yes, honey?

TOM: How about—supper?

AMANDA: Honey, you go ask Sister if supper is ready! You know that Sister is in full charge of supper!

Tell her you hungry boys are waiting for it. (*To* JIM) Have you met Laura?

JIM: She—

AMANDA: Let you in? Oh, good, you've met already! It's rare for a girl as sweet an' pretty as Laura to be domestic! But Laura is, thank heavens, not only pretty but also very domestic. I'm not at all. I never was a bit. I never could make a thing but angel-food cake. Well, in the South we had so many servants. Gone, gone, gone. All vestige of gracious living! Gone completely! I wasn't prepared for what the future brought me. All of my gentlemen callers were sons of planters and so of course I assumed that I would be married to one and raise my family on a large piece of land with plenty of servants. But man proposes—and woman accepts the proposal!—To vary that old, old saying a little bit—I married no planter! I married a man who worked for the telephone company!—That gallantly smiling gentleman over there! (*Points to the picture*) A telephone man who—fell in love with long-distance!—Now he travels and I don't even know where!—But what am I going on for about my—tribulations?

Tell me yours—I hope you don't have any!

Tom?

TOM (*returning*): Yes, Mother?

AMANDA: Is supper nearly ready?

TOM: It looks to me like supper is on the table.

AMANDA: Let me look— (*She rises prettily and looks through portieres*) Oh, lovely!—But where is Sister?

TOM: Laura is not feeling well and she says that she thinks she'd better not come to the table.

AMANDA: What?—Nonsense!—Laura? Oh, Laura!

LAURA (*off stage, faintly*): Yes, Mother.

AMANDA: You really must come to the table. We won't be seated until you come to the table!

Come in, Mr. O'Connor. You sit over there, and I'll—

Laura? Laura Wingfield!

You're keeping us waiting, honey! We can't say grace until you come to the table!

(*The back door is pushed weakly open and* LAURA *comes in. She is obviously quite faint, her lips trembling, her eyes wide and staring. She moves unsteadily toward the table.* LEGEND: "TERROR!" *Outside a summer storm is coming abruptly. The white curtains billow inward at the windows and there is a sorrowful murmur and deep blue dusk.* LAURA *suddenly stumbles —she catches at a chair with a faint moan.*)

TOM: Laura!

AMANDA: Laura! (*There is a clap of thunder.* LEGEND: "AH!" *Despairingly*) Why, Laura, you *are* sick, darling! Tom, help your sister into the living room, dear!

Sit in the living room, Laura—rest on the sofa.

Well! (*To the gentleman caller*)

Standing over the hot stove made her ill!—I told her that it was just too warm this evening, but—(TOM *comes back in.* LAURA *is on the sofa*)

Is Laura all right now?

TOM: Yes.

AMANDA: What *is* that? Rain? A nice cool rain has come up! (*She gives the gentleman caller a frightened look*)

I think we may—have grace—now. . . . (TOM *looks at her stupidly*)

Tom, honey—you say grace!

TOM: Oh . . .

"For these and all thy mercies—" (*They bow their heads,* AMANDA *stealing a nervous glance at* JIM. *In the living room* LAURA, *stretched on the sofa, clenches her hand to her lips, to hold back a shuddering sob*) God's Holy Name be praised—

(*The Scene Dims Out.*)

Scene Seven

A Souvenir.

Half an hour later. Dinner is just being finished in the up-stage area which is concealed by the drawn portieres.

As the curtain rises, LAURA *is still huddled upon the sofa, her feet drawn under her, her head resting on a pale blue pillow, her eyes wide and mysteriously watchful. The new floor lamp with its shade of rose-colored silk gives a soft, becoming light to her face, bringing out the fragile, unearthly prettiness which usually escapes attention. There is a steady murmur of rain, but it is slackening and stops soon after the scene begins; the air outside becomes pale and luminous as the moon breaks out.*

A moment after the curtain rises, the lights in both rooms flicker and go out.

JIM: Hey, there, Mr. Light Bulb!
(AMANDA *laughs nervously.* LEGEND: "SUSPENSION OF A PUBLIC SERVICE.")
AMANDA: Where was Moses when the lights went out? Ha-ha. Do you know the answer to that one, Mr. O'Connor?
JIM: No, Ma'am, what's the answer?
AMANDA: In the dark! (JIM *laughs appreciatively*)
Everybody sit still. I'll light the candles. Isn't it lucky we have them on the table? Where's a match? Which of you gentlemen can provide a match?
JIM: Here.
AMANDA: Thank you, sir.
JIM: Not at all, Ma'am!
AMANDA: I guess the fuse has burnt out. Mr. O'Connor, can you tell a burnt-out fuse? I know I can't and Tom is a total loss when it comes to mechanics. (SOUND: GETTING UP: VOICES RECEDE A LITTLE TO KITCHEN-ETTE)

Oh, be careful you don't bump into something. We don't want our gentleman caller to break his neck. Now wouldn't that be a fine howdy-do?

JIM: Ha-ha! Where is the fuse-box?

AMANDA: Right here next to the stove. Can you see anything?

JIM: Just a minute.

AMANDA: Isn't electricity a mysterious thing?

Wasn't it Benjamin Franklin who tied a key to a kite?

We live in such a mysterious universe, don't we? Some people say that science clears up all the mysteries for us. In my opinion it only creates more!

Have you found it yet?

JIM: No Ma'am. All these fuses look okay to me.

AMANDA: Tom!

TOM: Yes, Mother?

AMANDA: That light bill I gave you several days ago. The one I told you we got the notices about?

(LEGEND: "HA!")

TOM: Oh.—Yeah.

AMANDA: You didn't neglect to pay it by any chance?

TOM: Why, I—

AMANDA: Didn't! I might have known it!

JIM: Shakespeare probably wrote a poem on that light bill, Mrs. Wingfield.

AMANDA: I might have known better than to trust him with it! There's such a high price for negligence in this world!

JIM: Maybe the poem will win a ten-dollar prize.

AMANDA: We'll just have to spend the remainder of the evening in the nineteenth century, before Mr. Edison made the Mazda lamp!

JIM: Candlelight is my favorite kind of light.

AMANDA: That shows you're romantic! But that's no excuse for Tom.

Well, we got through dinner. Very considerate of them to let us get through dinner before they plunged us into everlasting darkness, wasn't it, Mr. O'Connor?

JIM: Ha-ha!

AMANDA: Tom, as a penalty for your carelessness you can help me with the dishes.

JIM: Let me give you a hand.

AMANDA: Indeed you will not!

JIM: I ought to be good for something.

AMANDA: Good for something? (Her tone is rhapsodic)

You? Why, Mr. O'Connor, nobody, nobody's given me this much entertainment in years—as you have!

JIM: Aw, now, Mrs. Wingfield!

AMANDA: I'm not exaggerating, not one bit! But Sister is all by her lonesome. You go keep her company in the parlor!

I'll give you this lovely old candelabrum that used to be on the altar at the church of the Heavenly Rest. It was melted a little out of shape when the church burnt down. Lightning struck it one spring. Gypsy Jones was holding a revival at the time and he intimated that the church was destroyed because the Episcopalians gave card parties.

JIM: Ha-ha!

AMANDA: And how about you coaxing Sister to drink a little wine? I think it would be good for her! Can you carry both at once?

JIM: Sure. I'm Superman!

AMANDA: Now, Thomas, get into this apron!

(*The door of kitchenette swings closed on* AMANDA'S *gay laughter; the flickering light approaches the portieres.* LAURA *sits up nervously as he enters. Her speech at first is low and breathless from the almost intolerable strain of being alone with a stranger.* THE LEGEND: "I DON'T SUPPOSE YOU REMEMBER ME AT ALL!" *In her first speeches in this scene, before* JIM'S *warmth overcomes her paralyzing shyness,* LAURA'S *voice is thin and breathless as though she has just run up a steep flight of stairs.* JIM'S *attitude is gently humorous. In playing this scene it should be stressed that while the incident is apparently unimportant, it is to* LAURA *the climax of her secret life.*)

JIM: Hello, there, Laura.

LAURA (*faintly*): Hello. (*She clears her throat.*)

JIM: How are you feeling now? Better?

LAURA: Yes. Yes, thank you.

JIM: This is for you. A little dandelion wine. (*He extends it toward her with extravagant gallantry.*)

LAURA: Thank you.

JIM: Drink it—but don't get drunk! (*He laughs heartily.* LAURA *takes the glass uncertainly; laughs shyly*) Where shall I set the candles?

LAURA: Oh—oh, anywhere. . . .

JIM: How about here on the floor? Any objections?

LAURA: No.

JIM: I'll spread a newspaper under to catch the drippings. I like to sit on the floor. Mind if I do?

LAURA: Oh, no.

JIM: Give me a pillow?

LAURA: What?

JIM: A pillow!

LAURA: Oh . . . (*Hands him one quickly.*)

JIM: How about you? Don't you like to sit on the floor?

LAURA: Oh—yes.

JIM: Why don't you, then?

LAURA: I—will.

JIM: Take a pillow! (LAURA *does. Sits on the other side of the candelabrum.* JIM *crosses his legs and smiles engagingly at her*) I can't hardly see you sitting way over there.

LAURA: I can—see you.

JIM: I know, but that's not fair, I'm in the limelight. (LAURA *moves her pillow closer*) Good! Now I can see you! Comfortable?

LAURA: Yes.

JIM: So am I. Comfortable as a cow! Will you have some gum?

LAURA: No, thank you.

JIM: I think that I will indulge, with your permission. (*Musingly unwraps it and holds it up*) Think of the fortune made by the guy that invented the first piece of chewing gum. Amazing, huh? The Wrigley Building is one of the sights of Chicago.—I saw it summer before last when I went up to the Century of Progress. Did you take in the Century of Progress?

LAURA: No, I didn't.

JIM: Well, it was quite a wonderful exposition. What impressed me most was the Hall of Science. Gives you an idea of what the future will be in America, even more wonderful than the present time is! (*Pause. Smiling at her*) Your brother tells me you're shy. Is that right, Laura?

LAURA: I—don't know.

JIM: I judge you to be an old-fashioned type of girl. Well, I think that's a pretty good type to be. Hope you don't think I'm being too personal— do you?

LAURA (*hastily, out of embarrassment*): I believe I *will* take a piece of gum, if you—don't mind. (*Clearing her throat*) Mr. O'Connor, have you—kept up with your singing?

JIM: Singing? Me?

LAURA: Yes. I remember what a beautiful voice you had.

JIM: When did you hear me sing?

(VOICE OFF STAGE IN THE PAUSE.)

VOICE (*off stage*):

> O blow, ye winds, heigh-ho,
> A-roving I will go!
> I'm off to my love
> With a boxing glove—
> Ten thousand miles away!

JIM: You say you've heard me sing?

LAURA: Oh, yes! Yes, very often. . . . I—don't suppose—you remember me— at all?

JIM (*smiling doubtfully*): You know I have an idea I've seen you before. I had that idea soon as you opened the door. It seemed almost like I was about to remember your name. But the name that I started to call you— wasn't a name! And so I stopped myself before I said it.

LAURA: Wasn't it—Blue Roses?

JIM (*springs up. Grinning*): Blue Roses!—My gosh, yes—Blue Roses! That's what I had on my tongue when you opened the door!

Isn't it funny what tricks your memory plays? I didn't connect you with high school somehow or other.

But that's where it was; it was high school. I didn't even know you were Shakespeare's sister!

Gosh, I'm sorry.

LAURA: I didn't expect you to. You—barely knew me!

JIM: But we did have a speaking acquaintance, huh?

LAURA: Yes, we—spoke to each other.

JIM: When did you recognize me?

LAURA: Oh, right away!

JIM: Soon as I came in the door?

LAURA: When I heard your name I thought it was probably you. I knew that Tom used to know you a little in high school. So when you came in the door—

Well, then I was—sure.

JIM: Why didn't you *say* something, then?

LAURA (*breathlessly*): I didn't know what to say, I was—too surprised!

JIM: For goodness' sakes! You know, this sure is funny!

LAURA: Yes! Yes, isn't it, though. . . .

JIM: Didn't we have a class in something together?

LAURA: Yes, we did.

JIM: What class was that?

LAURA: It was—singing—Chorus!

JIM: Aw!

LAURA: I sat across the aisle from you in the Aud.

JIM: Aw.

LAURA: Mondays, Wednesdays and Fridays.

JIM: Now I remember—you always came in late.

LAURA: Yes, it was so hard for me, getting upstairs. I had that brace on my leg—it clumped so loud!

JIM: I never heard any clumping.

LAURA (*wincing at the recollection*): To me it sounded like—thunder!

JIM: Well, well, well, I never even noticed.

LAURA: And everybody was seated before I came in. I had to walk in front of all those people. My seat was in the back row. I had to go clumping all the way up the aisle with everyone watching!

JIM: You shouldn't have been self-conscious.

LAURA: I know, but I was. It was always such a relief when the singing started.

JIM: Aw, yes, I've placed you now! I used to call you Blue Roses. How was it that I got started calling you that?

LAURA: I was out of school a little while with pleurosis. When I came back you asked me what was the matter. I said I had pleurosis—you thought I said Blue Roses. That's what you always called me after that!

JIM: I hope you didn't mind.

LAURA: Oh, no—I liked it. You see, I wasn't acquainted with many— people. . . .

JIM: As I remember you sort of stuck by yourself.

LAURA: I—I—never have had much luck at—making friends.

JIM: I don't see why you wouldn't.

LAURA: Well, I—started out badly.

JIM: You mean being—

LAURA: Yes, it sort of—stood between me—

JIM: You shouldn't have let it!

LAURA: I know, but it did, and—

JIM: You were shy with people!

LAURA: I tried not to be but never could—

JIM: Overcome it?

LAURA: No, I—I never could!

JIM: I guess being shy is something you have to work out of kind of gradually.

LAURA (*sorrowfully*): Yes—I guess it—

JIM: Takes time!

LAURA: Yes.

JIM: People are not so dreadful when you know them. That's what you have to remember! And everybody has problems, not just you, but practically everybody has got some problems.

You think of yourself as having the only problems, as being the only one who is disappointed. But just look around you and you will see lots of people as disappointed as you are. For instance, I hoped when I was going to high school that I would be further along at this time, six years later, than I am now— You remember that wonderful write-up I had in *The Torch*?

LAURA: Yes! (*She rises and crosses to table.*)

JIM: It said I was bound to succeed in anything I went into! (LAURA *returns with the annual*) Holy Jeez! *The Torch*! (*He accepts it reverently. They smile across it with mutual wonder.* LAURA *crouches beside him and they begin to turn through it.* LAURA's *shyness is dissolving in his warmth.*)

LAURA: Here you are in *The Pirates of Penzance*!

JIM (*wistfully*): I sang the baritone lead in that operetta.

LAURA (*raptly*): So—*beautifully*!

JIM (*protesting*): Aw—

LAURA: Yes, yes—beautifully—beautifully!

JIM: You heard me?

LAURA: All three times!

JIM: No!

LAURA: Yes!

JIM: All three performances?

LAURA (*looking down*): Yes.

JIM: Why?

LAURA: I—wanted to ask you to—autograph my program.

JIM: Why didn't you ask me to?

LAURA: You were always surrounded by your own friends so much that I never had a chance to.

JIM: You should have just—

LAURA: Well, I—thought you might think I was—

JIM: Thought I might think you was—what?

LAURA: Oh—

JIM (*with reflective relish*): I was beleaguered by females in those days.

LAURA: You were terribly popular!

JIM: Yeah—

LAURA: You had such a—friendly way—

JIM: I was spoiled in high school.

LAURA: Everybody—liked you!

JIM: Including you?

LAURA: I—yes, I—I did, too— (*She gently closes the book in her lap.*)

JIM: Well, well, well!—Give me that program, Laura. (*She hands it to him. He signs it with a flourish*) There you are—better late than never!

LAURA: Oh, I—what a—surprise!

JIM: My signature isn't worth very much right now.

But some day—maybe—it will increase in value!

Being disappointed is one thing and being discouraged is something else. I am disappointed but I am not discouraged.

I'm twenty-three years old.

How old are you?

LAURA: I'll be twenty-four in June.

JIM: That's not old age!

LAURA: No, but—

JIM: You finished high school?

LAURA (*with difficulty*): I didn't go back.

JIM: You mean you dropped out?

LAURA: I made bad grades in my final examinations. (*She rises and replaces the book and the program. Her voice strained*) How is—Emily Meisenbach getting along?

JIM: Oh, that kraut-head!

LAURA: Why do you call her that?

JIM: That's what she was.

LAURA: You're not still—going with her?

JIM: I never see her.

LAURA: It said in the Personal Section that you were—engaged!

JIM: I know, but I wasn't impressed by that—propaganda!

LAURA: It wasn't—the truth?

JIM: Only in Emily's optimistic opinion!

LAURA: Oh—

(LEGEND: "WHAT HAVE YOU DONE SINCE HIGH SCHOOL?" JIM *lights a cigarette and leans indolently back on his elbows smiling at* LAURA *with a warmth and charm which lights her inwardly with altar candles. She remains by the table and turns in her hands a piece of glass to cover her tumult.*)

JIM (*after several reflective puffs on a cigarette*): What have you done since high school? (*She seems not to hear him*) Huh? (LAURA *looks up*) I said what have you done since high school, Laura?

LAURA: Nothing much.

JIM: You must have been doing something these six long years.

LAURA: Yes.

JIM: Well, then, such as what?

LAURA: I took a business course at business college—

JIM: How did that work out?

LAURA: Well, not very—well—I had to drop out, it gave me—indigestion— (JIM *laughs gently.*)

JIM: What are you doing now?

LAURA: I don't do anything—much. Oh, please don't think I sit around doing nothing! My glass collection takes up a good deal of time. Glass is something you have to take good care of.

JIM: What did you say—about glass?

LAURA: Collection I said—I have one— (*She clears her throat and turns away again, acutely shy.*)

JIM (*abruptly*): You know what I judge to be the trouble with you?

Inferiority complex! Know what that is? That's what they call it when someone low-rates himself!

I understand it because I had it, too. Although my case was not so aggravated as yours seems to be. It had it until I took up public speaking, developed my voice, and learned that I had an aptitude for science. Before that time I never thought of myself as being outstanding in any way whatsoever!

Now I've never made a regular study of it, but I have a friend who says I can analyze people better than doctors that make a profession of it. I don't claim that to be necessarily true, but I can sure guess a person's psychology. Laura! (*Takes out his gum*) Excuse me, Laura. I always take it out when the flavor is gone. I'll use this scrap of paper to wrap it in. I know how it is to get it stuck on a shoe.

Yep—that's what I judge to be your principal trouble. A lack of confidence in yourself as a person. You don't have the proper amount of faith in yourself. I'm basing that fact on a number of your remarks and also on certain observations I've made. For instance that clumping you thought was so awful in high school. You say that you even dreaded to walk into class. You see what you did? You dropped out of school, you gave up an education because of a clump, which as far as I know was practically non-existent! A little physical defect is what you have. Hardly noticeable even! Magnified thousands of times by imagination!

You know what my strong advice to you is? Think of yourself as *superior* in some way!

LAURA: In what way would I think?

JIM: Why, man alive, Laura! Just look about you a little. What do you see? A world full of common people! All of 'em born and all of 'em going to die!

Which of them has one-tenth of your good points! Or mine! Or anyone else's, as far as that goes—Gosh!

Everybody excels in some one thing. Some in many! (*Unconsciously glances at himself in the mirror*)

All you've got to do is discover in *what!*

Take me, for instance. (*He adjusts his tie at the mirror*)

My interest happens to lie in electro-dynamics. I'm taking a course in radio engineering at night school, Laura, on top of a fairly responsible job at the warehouse. I'm taking that course and studying public speaking.

LAURA: Ohhhh.

JIM: Because I believe in the future of television! (*Turning back to her*)

I wish to be ready to go up right along with it. Therefore I'm planning to get in on the ground floor. In fact I've already made the right connections and all that remains is for the industry itself to get under way! Full steam—(*His eyes are starry*)

Knowledge—Zzzzzp! Money—Zzzzzzp!—Power!

That's the cycle democracy is built on! (*His attitude is convincingly dynamic.* LAURA *stares at him, even her shyness eclipsed in her absolute wonder. He suddenly grins*)

I guess you think I think a lot of myself!

LAURA: No—o-o-o, I—

JIM: Now how about you? Isn't there something you take more interest in than anything else?

LAURA: Well, I do—as I said—have my—glass collection—

(*A peal of girlish laughter from the kitchen.*)

JIM: I'm not right sure I know what you're talking about.

What kind of glass is it?

LAURA: Little articles of it, they're ornaments mostly!

Most of them are little animals made out of glass, the tiniest little animals in the world. Mother calls them a glass menagerie!

Here's an example of one, if you'd like to see it!

This one is one of the oldest. It's nearly thirteen. (MUSIC: "THE GLASS MENAGERIE." *He stretches out his hand*) Oh, be careful—if you breathe, it breaks!

JIM: I'd better not take it. I'm pretty clumsy with things.

LAURA: Go on, I trust you with him! (*Places it in his palm*)

There now—you're holding him gently!

Hold him over the light, he loves the light! You see how the light shines through him?

JIM: It sure does shine!

LAURA: I shouldn't be partial, but he is my favorite one.

JIM: What kind of a thing is this one supposed to be?

LAURA: Haven't you noticed the single horn on his forehead?

JIM: A unicorn, huh?

LAURA: Mmm-hmmm!

JIM: Unicorns, aren't they extinct in the modern world?

LAURA: I know!

JIM: Poor little fellow, he must feel sort of lonesome.

LAURA (*smiling*): Well, if he does he doesn't complain about it. He stays on a shelf with some horses that don't have horns and all of them seem to get along nicely together.

JIM: How do you know?

LAURA (*lightly*): I haven't heard any arguments among them!

JIM (*grinning*): No arguments, huh? Well, that's a pretty good sign! Where shall I set him?

LAURA: Put him on the table. They all like a change of scenery once in a while!

JIM (*stretching*): Well, well, well, well—

Look how big my shadow is when I stretch!

LAURA: Oh, oh, yes—it stretches across the ceiling!

JIM (*crossing to door*): I think it's stopped raining. (*Opens fire-escape door*) Where does the music come from?

LAURA: From the Paradise Dance Hall across the alley.

JIM: How about cutting the rug a little, Miss Wingfield?

LAURA: Oh, I—

JIM: Or is your program filled up? Let me have a look at it. (*Grasps imaginary card*) Why, every dance is taken! I'll just have to scratch some out. (WALTZ MUSIC: "LA GOLONDRINA") Ahhh, a waltz! (*He executes some sweeping turns by himself then holds his arms toward* LAURA.)

LAURA (*breathlessly*): I—can't dance!

JIM: There you go, that inferiority stuff!

LAURA: I've never danced in my life!

JIM: Come on, try!

LAURA: Oh, but I'd step on you!

JIM: I'm not made out of glass.

LAURA: How—how—how do we start?

JIM: Just leave it to me. You hold your arms out a little.

LAURA: Like this?

JIM: A little bit higher. Right. Now don't tighten up, that's the main thing about it—relax.

LAURA (*laughing breathlessly*): It's hard not to.

JIM: Okay.

LAURA: I'm afraid you can't budge me.

JIM: What do you bet I can't. (*He swings her into motion.*)

LAURA: Goodness, yes, you can!

JIM: Let yourself go, now, Laura, just let yourself go.

LAURA: I'm—

JIM: Come on!

LAURA: Trying!

JIM: Not so stiff— Easy does it!

LAURA: I know but I'm—

JIM: Loosen th' backbone! There now, that's a lot better.

LAURA: Am I?

JIM: Lots, lots better! (*He moves her about the room in a clumsy waltz.*)

LAURA: Oh, my!

JIM: Ha-ha!

LAURA: Oh, my goodness!

JIM: Ha-ha-ha! (*They suddenly bump into the table.* JIM *stops*) What did we hit on?

LAURA: Table.

JIM: Did something fall off it? I think—

LAURA: Yes.

JIM: I hope it wasn't the little glass horse with the horn!

LAURA: Yes.

JIM: Aw, aw, aw. Is it broken?

LAURA: Now it is just like all the other horses.

JIM: It's lost its—

LAURA: Horn!

It doesn't matter. Maybe it's a blessing in disguise.

JIM: You'll never forgive me. I bet that that was your favorite piece of glass.

LAURA: I don't have favorites much. It's no tragedy, Freckles. Glass breaks so easily. No matter how careful you are. The traffic jars the shelves and things fall off them.

JIM: Still I'm awfully sorry that I was the cause.

LAURA (*smiling*): I'll just imagine he had an operation.

The horn was removed to make him feel less—freakish! (*They both laugh*)

Now he will feel more at home with the other horses, the ones that don't have horns. . . .

JIM: Ha-ha, that's very funny! (*Suddenly serious*)

I'm glad to see that you have a sense of humor.

You know—you're—well—very different!

Surprisingly different from anyone else I know! (*His voice becomes soft and hesitant with a genuine feeling*)

Do you mind me telling you that? (LAURA *is abashed beyond speech*)

I mean it in a nice way. . . . (LAURA *nods shyly, looking away*)

You make me feel sort of—I don't know how to put it!

I'm usually pretty good at expressing things, but—

This is something that I don't know how to say! (LAURA *touches her throat and clears it—turns the broken unicorn in her hands. Even softer*) Has anyone ever told you that you were pretty? (PAUSE: MUSIC. LAURA *looks up slowly, with wonder, and shakes her head*)

Well, you are! In a very different way from anyone else.

And all the nicer because of the difference, too. (*His voice becomes low and husky.* LAURA *turns away, nearly faint with the novelty of her emotions*)

I wish that you were my sister. I'd teach you to have some confidence in yourself. The different people are not like other people, but being different is nothing to be ashamed of. Because other people are not such wonderful people. They're one hundred times one thousand. You're one times one! They walk all over the earth. You just stay here. They're common as—weeds, but—you—well, you're—*Blue Roses!* (IMAGE ON SCREEN: BLUE ROSES. MUSIC CHANGES.)

LAURA: But blue is wrong for—roses. . . .

JIM: It's right for you!—You're—pretty!

LAURA: In what respect am I pretty?

JIM: In all respects—believe me! Your eyes—your hair—are pretty! Your hands are pretty! (*He catches hold of her hand*)

You think I'm making this up because I'm invited to dinner and have to be nice. Oh, I could do that! I could put on an act for you, Laura, and say lots of things without being very sincere. But this time I am. I'm talking to you sincerely. I happened to notice you had this inferiority complex that keeps you from feeling comfortable with people.

Somebody needs to build your confidence up and make you proud instead of shy and turning away and—blushing—

Somebody—ought to—

Ought to—*kiss* you, Laura! (*His hand slips slowly up her arm to her shoulder.* MUSIC SWELLS TUMULTUOUSLY. *He suddenly turns her about and kisses her on the lips. When he releases her,* LAURA *sinks on the sofa with a bright, dazed look.* JIM *backs away and fishes in his pocket for a cigarette.* LEGEND ON SCREEN: "SOUVENIR")

Stumble-john! (*He lights the cigarette, avoiding her look. There is a peal of girlish laughter from* AMANDA *in the kitchen.* LAURA *slowly raises and opens her hand. It still contains the little broken glass animal. She looks at it with a tender, bewildered expression*)

Stumble-john!

I shouldn't have done that— That was way off the beam. You don't smoke, do you?

(*She looks up, smiling, not hearing the question. He sits beside her a little gingerly. She looks at him speechlessly—waiting. He coughs decorously and moves a little farther aside as he considers the situation and senses her feelings, dimly, with perturbation. Gently*) Would you—care for a— mint? (*She doesn't seem to hear him but her look grows brighter even*)

Peppermint—Life-Saver?

My pocket's a regular drug store—wherever I go. . . . (*He pops a mint in his mouth. Then gulps and decides to make a clean breast of it. He speaks slowly and gingerly*)

Laura, you know, if I had a sister like you, I'd do the same thing as Tom. I'd bring out fellows and—introduce her to them. The right type of boys of a type to—appreciate her.

Only—well—he made a mistake about me.

Maybe I've got no call to be saying this. That may not have been the idea in having me over. But what if it was?

There's nothing wrong about that. The only trouble is that in my case—I'm not in a situation to—do the right thing.

I can't take down your number and say I'll phone.

I can't call up next week and—ask for a date.

I thought I had better explain the situation in case you—misunderstood it and—hurt your feelings. . . .

(*Pause. Slowly, very slowly,* LAURA'S *look changes, her eyes returning slowly from his to the ornament in her palm.* AMANDA *utters another gay laugh in the kitchen.*)

LAURA (*faintly*): You—won't—call again?

JIM: No, Laura, I can't. (*He rises from the sofa*)

As I was just explaining, I've—got strings on me.

Laura, I've—been going steady!

I go out all of the time with a girl named Betty. She's a homegirl like you, and Catholic, and Irish, and in a great many ways we—get along fine.

I met her last summer on a moonlight boat trip up the river to Alton, on the *Majestic.*

Well—right away from the start it was—love! (LEGEND: LOVE! LAURA *sways slightly forward and grips the arm of the sofa. He fails to notice, now enrapt in his own comfortable being*)

Being in love has made a new man of me! (*Leaning stiffly forward, clutching the arm of the sofa,* LAURA *struggles visibly with her storm. But* JIM *is oblivious, she is a long way off*)

The power of love is really pretty tremendous!

Love is something that—changes the whole world, Laura! (*The storm abates a little and* LAURA *leans back. He notices her again*)

It happened that Betty's aunt took sick, she got a wire and had to go to Centralia. So Tom—when he asked me to dinner—I naturally just accepted the invitation, not knowing that you—that he—that I—(*He stops awkwardly*)

Huh—I'm a stumble-john! (*He flops back on the sofa. The holy candles in the altar of* LAURA's *face have been snuffed out. There is a look of almost infinite desolation.* JIM *glances at her uneasily*)

I wish that you would—say something. (*She bites her lip which was trembling and then bravely smiles. She opens her hand again on the broken glass ornament. Then she gently takes his hand and raises it level with her own. She carefully places the unicorn in the palm of his hand, then pushes his fingers closed upon it*) What are you—doing that for? You want me to have him?—Laura? (*She nods*) What for?

LAURA: A—souvenir. . . . (*She rises unsteadily and crouches beside the victrola to wind it up.* LEGEND ON SCREEN: "THINGS HAVE A WAY OF TURNING OUT SO BADLY!" OR IMAGE: "GENTLEMAN CALLER WAVING GOOD-BYE!—GAILY." *At this moment* AMANDA *rushes brightly back in the front room. She bears a pitcher of fruit punch in an old-fashioned cut-glass pitcher and a plate of macaroons. The plate has a gold border and poppies painted on it.*)

AMANDA: Well, well, well! Isn't the air delightful after the shower? I've made you children a little liquid refreshment. (*Turns gaily to the gentleman caller*)

Jim, do you know that song about lemonade?

"Lemonade, lemonade
Made in the shade and stirred with a spade—
Good enough for any old maid!"

JIM (*uneasily*): Ha-ha! No—I never heard it.

AMANDA: Why, Laura! You look so serious!

JIM: We were having a serious conversation.

AMANDA: Good! Now you're better acquainted!

JIM (*uncertainly*): Ha-ha! Yes.

AMANDA: You modern young people are much more serious-minded than my generation. I was so gay as a girl!

JIM: You haven't changed, Mrs. Wingfield.

AMANDA: Tonight I'm rejuvenated! The gaiety of the occasion, Mr. O'Connor! (*She tosses her head with a peal of laughter. Spills lemonade*) Oooo! I'm baptizing myself!

JIM: Here—let me—

AMANDA (*setting the pitcher down*): There now. I discovered we had some maraschino cherries. I dumped them in, juice and all!

JIM: You shouldn't have gone to that trouble, Mrs. Wingfield.

AMANDA: Trouble, trouble? Why, it was loads of fun!

Didn't you hear me cutting up in the kitchen? I bet your ears were burning! I told Tom how outdone with him I was for keeping you to himself so long a time! He should have brought you over much, much sooner! Well, now that you've found your way, I want you to be a very frequent caller! Not just occasional but all the time.

Oh, we're going to have a lot of gay times together! I see them coming!

Mmm, just breathe that air! So fresh, and the moon's so pretty!

I'll skip back out—I know where my place is when young folks are having a—serious conversation!

JIM: Oh, don't go out, Mrs. Wingfield. The fact of the matter is I've got to be going.

AMANDA: Going, now? You're joking! Why, it's only the shank of the evening, Mr. O'Connor!

JIM: Well, you know how it is.

AMANDA: You mean you're a young workingman and have to keep workingmen's hours. We'll let you off early tonight. But only on the condition that next time you stay later.

What's the best night for you? Isn't Saturday night the best night for you workingmen?

JIM: I have a couple of time-clocks to punch, Mrs. Wingfield. One at morning, another one at night!

AMANDA: My, but you *are* ambitious! You work at night, too?

JIM: No, Ma'am, not work but—Betty! (*He crosses deliberately to pick up his hat. The band at the Paradise Dance Hall goes into a tender waltz.*)

AMANDA: Betty? Betty? Who's—Betty?

(*There is an ominous cracking sound in the sky.*)

JIM: Oh, just a girl. The girl I go steady with! (*He smiles charmingly. The sky falls.*)

(LEGEND: "THE SKY FALLS.")

AMANDA (*a long-drawn exhalation*): Ohhhh . . . Is it a serious romance, Mr. O'Connor?

JIM: We're going to be married the second Sunday in June.

AMANDA: Ohhhh—how nice!

Tom didn't mention that you were engaged to be married.

JIM: The cat's not out of the bag at the warehouse yet.

You know how they are. They call you Romeo and stuff like that. (*He stops at the oval mirror to put on his hat. He carefully shapes the brim and the crown to give a discreetly dashing effect*)

It's been a wonderful evening, Mrs. Wingfield. I guess this is what they mean by Southern hospitality.

AMANDA: It really wasn't anything at all.

JIM: I hope it don't seem like I'm rushing off. But I promised Betty I'd pick her up at the Wabash depot, an' by the time I get my jalopy down there her train'll be in. Some women are pretty upset if you keep 'em waiting.

AMANDA: Yes, I know— The tyranny of women! (*Extends her hand*) Good-bye, Mr. O'Connor.

I wish you luck—and happiness—and success! All three of them, and so does Laura!—Don't you, Laura?

LAURA: Yes!

JIM (*taking her hand*): Good-bye, Laura. I'm certainly going to treasure that souvenir. And don't you forget the good advice I gave you. (*Raises his voice to a cheery shout*)

So long, Shakespeare!

Thanks again, ladies— Good night! (*He grins and ducks jauntily out. Still bravely grimacing,* AMANDA *closes the door on the gentleman caller. Then she turns back to the room with a puzzled expression. She and* LAURA *don't dare to face each other.* LAURA *crouches beside the victrola to wind it.*)

AMANDA (*faintly*): Things have a way of turning out so badly.

I don't believe that I would play the victrola.

Well, well—well—

Our gentleman caller was engaged to be married!

Tom!

TOM (*from back*): Yes, Mother?

AMANDA: Come in here a minute. I want to tell you something awfully funny.

TOM (*enters with macaroon and a glass of the lemonade*): Has the gentleman caller gotten away already?

AMANDA: The gentleman caller has made an early departure.

What a wonderful joke you played on us!

TOM: How do you mean?

AMANDA: You didn't mention that he was engaged to be married.

TOM: Jim? Engaged?

AMANDA: That's what he just informed us.

TOM: I'll be jiggered! I didn't know about that.

AMANDA: That seems very peculiar.

TOM: What's peculiar about it?

AMANDA: Didn't you call him your best friend down at the warehouse?

TOM: He is, but how did I know?

AMANDA: It seems extremely peculiar that you wouldn't know your best friend was going to be married!

TOM: The warehouse is where I work, not where I know things about people!

AMANDA: You don't know things anywhere! You live in a dream; you manufacture illusions! (*He crosses to door*) Where are you going?

TOM: I'm going to the movies.

AMANDA: That's right, now that you've had us make such fools of ourselves.

The effort, the preparations, all the expense! The new floor lamp, the rug, the clothes for Laura! All for what? To entertain some other girl's fiancé!

Go to the movies, go! Don't think about us, a mother deserted, an unmarried sister who's crippled and has no job! Don't let anything interfere with your selfish pleasure!

Just go, go, go—to the movies!

TOM: All right, I will! The more you shout about my selfishness to me the quicker I'll go, and I won't go to the movies!

AMANDA: Go, then! Then go to the moon—you selfish dreamer!

(TOM *smashes his glass on the floor. He plunges out on the fire-escape, slamming the door.* LAURA *screams—cut by door. Dance-hall music up.* TOM *goes to the rail and grips it desperately, lifting his face in the chill white moonlight penetrating the narrow abyss of the alley.* LEGEND ON SCREEN: "AND SO GOOD-BYE . . ." TOM'S *closing speech is timed with the interior pantomime. The interior scene is played as though viewed through soundproof glass.* AMANDA *appears to be making a comforting speech to* LAURA, *who is huddled upon the sofa. Now that we cannot hear the mother's speech, her silliness is gone and she has dignity and tragic beauty.* LAURA'S *dark hair hides her face until at the end of the speech she lifts it to smile at her mother.* AMANDA'S *gestures are slow and graceful, almost dancelike, as she comforts the daughter. At the end of her speech she glances a moment at the father's picture—then withdraws through the portieres. At close of* TOM'S *speech,* LAURA *blows out the candles, ending the play.*)

TOM: I didn't go to the moon, I went much further—for time is the longest distance between two places—

Not long after that I was fired for writing a poem on the lid of a shoe-box.

I left Saint Louis. I descended the steps of this fire-escape for a last time and followed, from then on, in my father's footsteps, attempting to find in motion what was lost in space—

I traveled around a great deal. The cities swept about me like dead leaves, leaves that were brightly colored but torn away from the branches.

I would have stopped, but I was pursued by something.

It always came upon me unawares, taking me altogether by surprise. Perhaps it was a familiar bit of music. Perhaps it was only a piece of transparent glass—

Perhaps I am walking along a street at night, in some strange city, before I have found companions. I pass the lighted window of a shop where perfume is sold. The window is filled with pieces of colored glass, tiny transparent bottles in delicate colors, like bits of a shattered rainbow.

Then all at once my sister touches my shoulder. I turn around and look into her eyes. . . .

Oh, Laura, Laura, I tried to leave you behind me, but I am more faithful than I intended to be!

I reach for a cigarette, I cross the street, I run into the movies or a bar, I buy a drink, I speak to the nearest stranger—anything that can blow your candles out! (LAURA *bends over the candles*)—for nowadays the world is lit by lightning! Blow out your candles, Laura—and so good-bye. . . .

(*She blows the candles out.*)

(*The Scene Dissolves.*)

Commentary

It would be futile to seek the literary value or dramatic appeal of *The Glass Menagerie* in a paraphrase of a plot in which the most important event is the arrival of a guest for dinner. Although only a few seemingly trivial moments in the lives of the Wingfields are dramatized, Williams constantly makes us aware of a larger world of objective reality by his allusions to contemporary events and names. (What is the meaning of each of these: Guernica, "Franco Triumphs," Berchtesgaden, Chamberlain's umbrella, Ole Dizzy Dean, Century of Progress?) Hence the restlessness, frustrations, and despair in the lives of Williams' characters seem all the more poignant when pictured against the backdrop of a sick and insecure world poised on the brink of a catastrophic war.

Although this play lacks the brutality and violence of *Desire under the Elms,* the Cabots and the Wingfields confront similar problems and react with similar emotions, whether in New England in 1850, or in St. Louis in 1938. For both families there is a loneliness tinged with desperation and defeat. The urgent necessity for escape sends Peter and Simeon Cabot careening drunkenly through the open gate and beyond the confines of the intolerable stone wall to a romantic dream of gold and freedom in the hills of California. Tom Wingfield also is to follow a dream of adventure by giving up the vicarious excitement of the movies and joining the merchant marine. For him the fire escape is his avenue to freedom, although in retrospect his sense of guilty responsibility for abandoning Laura makes that freedom only physical. For Amanda the fire escape is also a means of fleeing from an intolerable reality; although it is "a poor excuse for a porch," she sits on it "gracefully and demurely as if she were settling into a swing on a Mississippi veranda" (p. 240) to await the arrival of 17 gentlemen callers. For Laura with her physical disability and her psychological isolation, there is no romantic escape into memory. Unlike Amanda she has no past, and unlike Tom no future.

To achieve "a closer approach to truth" in dramatizing the unhappy, disappointed lives of the Wingfields, Williams employs many unconventional theatrical techniques in a revolt against what he calls "the exhausted theatre of realistic conventions" of plays like *Rosmersholm,* as earlier Shaw in *The Devil's Disciple* had turned in parody on the outworn and stereotyped techniques of nineteenth-century melodrama. Novelty or originality are meaningless in the theater unless they are made a part of the unity of a drama. A technique which simply calls attention to itself as a violation of usual dramatic conventions destroys any unified effect; it must instead serve a specific purpose better perhaps than any traditional dramatic resources that the playwright could call upon. Williams' magic-lantern slides projected on a screen are a good case in point. Eddie Dowling did not use this device in his Broadway production, and Tennessee Williams made no objection because Laurette Taylor's magnificent performance made simplicity desirable. Clearly, then, the device is not integral to the structural unity of the play. The question is thus raised whether it is only a nonessential theater trick. In his production notes Williams gives reasons for including the slides; but one critic, commenting on the published stage directions, calls the technique "redundant and rather precious; the young playwright was straining for effect, perhaps without realizing how well he had succeeded in making his simple tale hauntingly self-sufficient."[12] Whose point of view seems the more convincing?

But if the screen is controversial, many of Williams' ~~other~~ theatrical devices are of the first importance in establishing character and tone. The set itself, for example, is functional: its great depth—the living room *kitchen*, the ~~dining~~ *bed* room, the ~~fire-escape~~ *staircase*, and the ~~alleys on either side of the tenement appear~~—permits different actions to take place simultaneously. By using transparencies, the dramatist can have visible either the ~~exterior~~ *outer room* of the ~~Wingfield~~ apartment (as at the rise of the curtain) or the interior. *inner room* The first scene, which takes place in a soft light behind the transparent portieres, stresses the words of Tom, the narrator: "Being a memory play, it is dimly lighted, it is sentimental, it is not realistic" (p. 222).

Because the living room is downstage, the important glass menagerie and the father's picture are visible throughout the play. The symbolism of the menagerie, Laura's primary means of escape from a realistic world she cannot understand, is obvious. The victrola is a second way of escape for her. For example, when Amanda takes Laura to task for deceiving her about her attendance at the business college, Laura instinctively goes to wind the victrola, trying to escape her mother's cruel words by drowning them out with music. On what other occasions does she turn to this source of comfort? During her conversation with Jim in which she loses

---

12 John Gassner, *Theatre at the Crossroads* (New York, 1960), p. 84.

some of her shy self-consciousness, she shows him her glass menagerie and allows him to hold her choicest possession, the lonely and unique unicorn, a symbol of herself. When she gives him the broken unicorn, Jim is unaware that the souvenir which he has unintentionally made "less freakish" and "more at home" is the Laura that might have been. Why is it appropriate that Jim should be given the unicorn? What other points of resemblance are there between Laura and the creatures of her menagerie? How does Williams succeed here in transforming symbol into a theatrically exciting scene?

By contrast, the typewriter, another important prop in the living room, is for Laura an instrument of torture, reminding her of her unbearable experience at the business college. In Scene Two, when she hears Amanda approaching, Laura leaves her glass collection and "seats herself stiffly before the diagram of the typewriter keyboard" (p. 226). But for Tom, who is frustrated both at home and at work, the typewriter is an instrument of creative expression: in Scene Three it is surrounded by "a wild disarray of manuscripts." The quarrel between Amanda and Tom "was probably precipitated by Amanda's interruption of his creative labor" (p. 231).

Wingfield's picture makes him a silent but forcible character. Both Amanda and Tom speak of him often and glance at his photograph, exaggerated in size because of its emotional value. For Amanda, this picture brings forth memories of her days in Blue Mountain when (according to her stories) she could have had her choice of numerous suitors, all potentially successful men. She cannot forget her youth, when she was gay, pretty, and sought after. Talking nostalgically about the "good old days" in Blue Mountain is for her a form of escape from her present miserable circumstances. Like Laura, she too has her glass menagerie, but her collection is one of memories that grow brighter with the passing years. In an effort to forget her ruinous mistake in marrying Wingfield, she talks constantly of her numerous "gentlemen callers." The picture of his smiling father, which even lights up on occasion, reminds Tom that one man has escaped and gone to faraway places in search of the adventure that he himself can have only vicariously, through the movies. He realizes that his father wronged his family, yet he knows all too well the strong desires that led him to abandon them: "I'm like my father. The bastard son of a bastard! See how he grins? And he's been absent going on sixteen years!" (p. 251). Tom's glass menagerie is the movie house; as he says while looking at the flashing marquees on Grand Avenue: "People go to the *movies* instead of *moving!* Hollywood characters are supposed to have all the adventures for everybody in America, while everybody in America sits in a dark room and watches them have them!" (p. 251). Later he makes his escape a reality by leaving to become a seaman, yet in his own words, "Oh, Laura, Laura, I tried to leave you behind me, but I am more faithful than I intended to be!" (p. 269). Unlike his father, Tom is not the mere "selfish dreamer" his mother accuses him of being.

In addition to the menagerie, typewriter, unicorn, and picture there is one other important symbol—Jim. Not just a guest coming to dinner, he is a "Gentleman Caller" and all that this means in the play. For Amanda and Laura "he is the long delayed but always expected something that we live for" (p. 222). Amanda firmly believes that he will solve her problem of what to do about Laura, and for a few moments even Laura thinks that he will become a part of her life. In the words of the narrator, "He is . . . an emissary from a world of reality that we were somehow set apart from" (p. 222). Yet all the preparations and expense come to naught, and Jim returns to his world of reality and Betty, affected by his experience with Laura, yet not comprehending how he has increased the pathos of her situation.

The use of Tom as narrator gives the drama a double focus and a complex and delicate tone. He is both a detached commentator speaking in the present and a sympathetic participant in the pathetic loneliness of Laura's world from which he cannot escape altogether. It is Tom who justifies Williams' "memory devices," for although this is Laura's play, it is Tom's memory which etches these remembrances with poignancy and colors them with nostalgia.

In addition to the skillful use of the spotlight and the dim stage to create this atmosphere of memory, lighting intensifies such scenes as the emotionally charged one in which Amanda and Tom quarrel violently. In contrast to the "clear pool of light" that falls on Laura, desperate and panic-stricken, "the upstage area is lit with a turgid smoky red glow," reflecting the fiery rage of mother and son, as it casts their angry gestures on the ceiling (pp. 230-231). On another occasion the marquee lights shining during Tom's rebellious speech to Jim give dramatic impact to his words. Why? Just before the dinner in Scene Six, the sudden summer storm heightens the mood. Laura is sick and faint at the thought of the meal with Jim. "The white curtains billow inward at the windows and there is a sorrowful murmur and deep blue dusk" (p. 253). A clap of thunder underscores the cries of Tom and Amanda—"Laura!"—when they see that she is ill. The symbolism of the storm within Laura is obvious. During the dinner the central figure, that of Laura huddled on the sofa, is bathed in "a soft, becoming light" that reveals a prettiness not usually apparent. Then the lights go out, and the dinner is finished in candlelight, just as Amanda might really wish it to be. (Is the history of the "lovely old candelabrum" just another piece of Amanda's social chatter?) Such a light is most suitable for the scene between Jim and Laura, for it is romantic, soft, and flattering. During this scene, too, the storm has ended, and "the air outside becomes pale and luminous as the moon breaks out" (p. 254). Candlelight is stressed again in a metaphor describing the joyous radiance in Laura's face. After Jim's revelation about his fiancée, "The holy candles in the altar of Laura's face have been snuffed out. There is a look of almost infinite desolation" (p. 266). The final words of the play resolve the candle-motif, for Tom, bathed "in the chill white moonlight," says, "—for nowadays the world is lit by lightning! Blow out your candles, Laura—and so goodbye . . ." (p. 270). She blows out the candles, and the scene, like a memory, "dissolves."

The Glass Menagerie begins in the evening and ends in darkness. The "dark, grim rear wall of the Wingfield tenement" (p. 221), which was raised in Scene One, slowly falls as Amanda attempts to comfort Laura. The storm of that evening moves outward to ignite the world in the conflagration of World War II, but Amanda and Laura remain shrouded in darkness. If anything, their plight is worse than when the play began. For them there has been no moment of illumination. Unlike Beate and Rosmer in *Rosmersholm,* they have gained no self-knowledge; clinging pathetically to their illusions, they have in fact feared and even fiercely resisted the truth. Even Tom, who sees his family with compassionate insight yet knows that only through revolt can he save himself, for a time accepts the ironic illusion that he can find himself in the wartime adventures of the merchant marine: "It's our turn now, to go to the South Sea Islands—to make a safari—to be exotic, far-off!" (p. 251). But from his vantage point in time at the end of the play he recognizes that he has not discovered "in motion what was lost in space—" (p. 269). Laura's touch is upon his shoulder, and he cannot avoid her eyes. The play itself, Tom's memory, is proof of that.

Questions and Problems

1. Timothy Dudgeon in *The Devil's Disciple,* Beate in *Rosmersholm,* Eben's mother in *Desire under the Elms,* and Mr. Wingfield are characters out of the past who never appear on stage but whose influence is felt in their former homes. How? Compare the power they wield and its consequences. Beate and Wingfield foreshadow the direction the hero is to take at the close of the play. What similar functions do any two of these characters have? How do remarks made about them create an impression of four marriages which, before the plays begin, have ended in separation or death?

2. The playwright has created an elaborate set which is an integral part of his total effect. What is the function of the lighted movie marquees across the alley? The dining room? The Paradise Dance Hall? How does the set resemble that of *Desire under the Elms?*

3. Early in the play the audience, like Amanda, scarcely believes that Tom can possibly go to the movies as much as he says he does. What proof is there that he is telling the truth?

4. Why should D. H. Lawrence be a favorite author of Tom's? Why would his works be calculated to drive Amanda to a fury?

5. What ironic significance does Tom's recital of grace have at the end of Scene Six?

6. How is Jim's analysis of Laura on page 261 a revelation of his own character? How does he differ from the other characters?

7. What connotations do "blue roses" take on in the play? How is the phrase related to other symbols?

8. What is the significance of Amanda's calling Laura "crippled" on page 269?

9. Discuss the importance of costumes in establishing character in *The Glass Menagerie.*

10. Williams has given his reader a thumbnail sketch of his four characters. Develop each into a full-length portrait, citing evidence to substantiate each trait. What is our final attitude toward each of the characters?

11. Analyze the extraordinary complexity of tone in *The Glass Menagerie,* showing how the various moods are created.

12. Williams generalizes about the importance of music in establishing the mood of his play. Establish the specific effects created each time there is an offstage melody.

13. What is the function of humor in this play about pathetic and lonely individuals? Since even Amanda's laughter lacks spontaneity, how does the playwright achieve the comic? Is Amanda as ridiculous a mother as Mrs. Dudgeon in *The Devil's Disciple?*

14. What ironies are achieved between what Williams on page 217 calls the "apparent center" and the "visual center" in a scene? The author says that "each scene contains a particular point (or several) which is structurally the most important." Find the place in each scene. In an episodic drama there is the danger that the total design may be loose or incoherent. How does Williams avoid the difficulty? What is his principle of selection underlying these apparently disconnected moments? How does he keep the action moving toward the catastrophe of the final scene?

15. At the end of the film version of *The Glass Menagerie* Laura greets a new gentleman caller. Does the play support the validity of such a conclusion?

16. What are the underlying causes for the plight of the Wingfield family? Does Williams suggest any answers? Would Amanda be happier if she abandoned her illusions? Is Tom's solution of running away from home justified? Do Jim's plans for the future offer more hope of successful fulfillment?

ANTON CHEKHOV

The Cherry Orchard

a comedy in four acts

Translated by Avrahm Yarmolinsky

Biography

ANTON CHEKHOV was born in the old Black Sea port of Taganrog on January 17, 1860. His unhappy boyhood was spent helping his large poverty-stricken family. After graduating from high school at Taganrog, he entered the University of Moscow as a medical student; at the same time, in order to support himself, he wrote a large number of short stories and sketches of Russian life. In 1884 he received his degree as doctor of medicine, although by then he was writing professionally. With the publication of his first collection of short stories in 1887, his talent was immediately recognized.

Chekhov's interest in the drama was aroused at an early age, and he wrote and produced plays (none of which was a success) for at least ten years before the Moscow Art Theater was established. In fact, at the time of his death he was better known as the author of several hundred short stories and sketches than as a playwright. His first minor success was *Ivanov,* produced at Korsh's Theater in Moscow in November, 1887.

Seriously ill of tuberculosis, Chekhov retired in 1890 to the Crimea, where he spent most of his remaining years, making frequent trips to Moscow to superintend the production of his four important plays at the Moscow Art Theater. Even though in bad health himself, he continued his work as a country doctor, helping the poor without remuneration and risking his own life to fight the cholera epidemic of 1892. At the first performance of *The Cherry Orchard,* his last play, Chekhov was feted as one of Russia's greatest dramatists, primarily because of his skill in recreating the atmosphere of the Russia of his day. Only a few months afterward Chekhov died in a little German village in the Black Forest, where he had gone in a futile attempt to recover his health.

Chekhov was by temperament a twentieth-century figure. Perhaps his own disease, which prematurely cut short his life, and his career as a doctor helped to give him a deep sympathy with a generation of Russians living in a disintegrating world. He perceived acutely the cultural and social dilemma of a country with a demoralized intelligentsia and an ignorant, poverty-stricken, and despairing peasantry—a country that was soon to be torn apart by a political revolution which was violently to transform its character.

Principal Works

PLAYS

Ivanov (1887)
The Bear (1888)
The Swan Song (1889)
The Proposal (1889)
The Wood Demon (1889)

The Sea Gull (1898)
Uncle Vanya (1899)
The Three Sisters (1901)
The Cherry Orchard (1904)

NOVELS AND SHORT STORY COLLECTIONS

Tales of Melpomene (1884)
Twilight, and Other Stories (1887)
Gloomy People (1890)
The Duel (1891)

Ward Number Six (1892)
Variegated Tales (1894)
My Life (1896)

Selected Descriptive Bibliography

Bruford, W. H., *Anton Chekhov*, New Haven, 1957.
> *A monograph on Chekhov's short stories and plays, too brief to discuss any in depth. Good for arriving at a general first impression of Chekhov's creative output.*

_____, *Chekhov and His Russia*, New York, 1948.
> *A sociological study that views Chekhov as a product of late nineteenth-century Russia.*

Chekhov, Anton, *The Personal Papers of Anton Chekhov*, New York, 1948.
> *The volume, with an Introduction by Matthew Josephson, contains Chekhov's curious little notebook of anecdotes and observations, translated by S. S. Koteliansky and Leonard Woolf, and selections from Chekhov's letters, translated by Constance Garnett.*

Chukovsky, Kornei, *Chekhov the Man*, trans. Pauline Rose, London, 1945.
> *A brief, informal biography, more concerned with a portrayal of character than with the facts of a career.*

Deer, Irving, "Speech as Action in Chekhov's *The Cherry Orchard*," *Educational Theatre Journal*, X (March, 1958), 30-34.
> *Deer argues perceptively that Chekhov's dialogue provides "a perfect means of making objective the constant struggle his characters have between their desire to act realistically in order to solve their problems and their desire to daydream . . . in order to avoid their problems."*

Fergusson, Francis, *The Idea of a Theater* (New York, 1953), pp. 174-190.
> *A difficult, but highly rewarding study of Chekhov's craft in* The Cherry Orchard.

Gerhardi, William, *Anton Chehov: a Critical Study,* London, 1923; rev. ed., 1949.
Impressionistic and often unreliable in its judgments. Little comment on the plays.

Hellman, Lillian, ed., *The Selected Letters of Anton Chekhov,* trans. Sidonie Lederer, New York, 1955.
One of the best ways to know Chekhov the man is to read his letters. Miss Hellman has written a lively and pertinent Introduction to this fine collection.

Hingley, Ronald, *Chekhov: a Biographical and Critical Study,* London, 1950.
One of the best efforts at blending Chekhov's biography with a literary evaluation of his work.

Latham, Jacqueline E. M., *"The Cherry Orchard* as Comedy," *Educational Theatre Journal,* X (March, 1958), 21-29.
An intelligent defense of Chekhov's position that The Cherry Orchard *is a comedy.*

Magarshack, David, *Chekhov: a Life,* New York, 1953.
The standard biography of Chekhov. Fully detailed, it draws heavily upon Chekhov's correspondence.

————, *Chekhov the Dramatist,* New York, 1952.
Magarshack traces the development of Chekhov's dramatic art. He argues vigorously for taking The Cherry Orchard *as a comedy.*

Nemirovsky, Irene, *A Life of Chekhov,* trans. Erik De Mauny, London, 1950.
A highly colored and romantic portrayal of Chekhov.

Silverstein, Norman, "Chekhov's Comic Spirit and *The Cherry Orchard,"* *Modern Drama,* I (September, 1958), 91-100.
A helpful analysis of the interplay of farce and pathos in The Cherry Orchard.

Yermilov, Vladimir, *A. P. Chekhov,* trans. Ivy Litvinov, Moscow, n.d.
Interesting primarily because it provides a Communist view of Chekhov's life and work.

A Note on *The Cherry Orchard*

The Cherry Orchard is a play which takes place around the turn of the century and deals with the disintegration of the Russian aristocracy following the breakup of the Russian feudal system in 1861. A comparable period in our own history would be the days of the Reconstruction in the South. The cleavage between the old agrarian and the new industrial orders can be seen in the social positions of all the characters.

The Cherry Orchard ANTON CHEKHOV

Translated by Avrahm Yarmolinsky

CHARACTERS

LUBOV ANDREYEVNA RANEVSKAYA, *a landowner*

ANYA, *her seventeen-year-old daughter*

VARYA, *her adopted daughter, twenty-two years old*

LEONID ANDREYEVICH GAYEV, MME. RANEVSKAYA'S *brother*

YERMOLAY ALEXEYEVICH LOPAHIN, *a merchant*

PYOTR SERGEYEVICH TROFIMOV, *a student*

SIMEONOV-PISHCHIK, *a landowner*

CHARLOTTA IVANOVNA, *a governess*

SEMYON YEPIHODOV, *a clerk*

DUNYASHA, *a maid*

FIRS (*pronounced "fierce"*), *a man-servant, aged eighty-seven*

YASHA, *a young valet*

A TRAMP

STATIONMASTER, POST OFFICE CLERK, GUESTS, SERVANTS

The action takes place on MME. RANEVSKAYA'S *estate.*

The Cherry Orchard was first performed at the Moscow Art Theater on January 17, 1904.

The Cherry Orchard *from* The Portable Chekhov, *translated by Avrahm Yarmolinsky. Copyright 1947 by The Viking Press, Inc. Reprinted by their permission.*

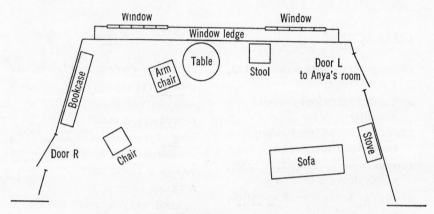

THE CHERRY ORCHARD • ACTS I AND IV

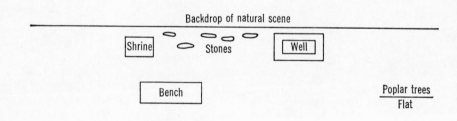

THE CHERRY ORCHARD • ACT II

Act One

A room that is still called the nursery. One of the doors leads into ANYA'S *room. Dawn, the sun will soon rise. It is May, the cherry trees are in blossom, but it is cold in the orchard; there is a morning frost. The windows are shut. Enter* DUNYASHA *with a candle, and* LOPAHIN *with a book in his hand.*

LOPAHIN: The train is in, thank God. What time is it?

DUNYASHA: Nearly two. (*Puts out the candle*) It's light already.

LOPAHIN: How late is the train, anyway? Two hours at least. (*Yawns and stretches*) I'm a fine one! What a fool I've made of myself! I came here on purpose to meet them at the station, and then I went and overslept. I fell asleep in my chair. How annoying! You might have waked me. . . .

DUNYASHA: I thought you'd left. (*Listens*) I think they're coming!

LOPAHIN (*listens*): No, they've got to get the luggage, and one thing and another. . . . (*Pause*) Lubov Andreyevna spent five years abroad, I don't know what she's like now. . . . She's a fine person—lighthearted, simple. I remember when I was a boy of fifteen, my poor father—he had a shop here in the village then—punched me in the face with his fist and made my nose bleed. We'd come into the yard, I don't know what for, and he'd had a drop too much. Lubov Andreyevna, I remember her as if it were yesterday—she was still young and so slim—led me to the wash-basin, in this very room . . . in the nursery. "Don't cry, little peasant," she said, "it'll heal in time for your wedding. . . ." (*Pause*) Little peasant . . . my father was a peasant, it's true, and here I am in a white waistcoat and yellow shoes. A pig in a pastry shop, you might say. It's true I'm rich, I've got a lot of money. . . . But when you look at it closely, I'm a peasant through and through. (*Pages the book*) Here I've been reading this book and I didn't understand a word of it. . . . I was reading it and fell asleep. . . . (*Pause.*)

DUNYASHA: And the dogs were awake all night; they feel that their masters are coming.

LOPAHIN: Dunyasha, why are you so—

DUNYASHA: My hands are trembling. I'm going to faint.

LOPAHIN: You're too soft, Dunyasha. You dress like a lady, and look at the way you do your hair. That's not right. One should remember one's place. (*Enter* YEPIHODOV *with a bouquet; he wears a jacket and highly polished boots that squeak badly. He drops the bouquet as he comes in.*)

YEPIHODOV (*picking up the bouquet*) : Here, the gardener sent these, said you're to put them in the dining room. (*Hands the bouquet to* DUNYASHA.)

LOPAHIN: And bring me some kvass.[1]

DUNYASHA: Yes, sir. (*Exits.*)

YEPIHODOV: There's a frost this morning—three degrees below—and yet the cherries are all in blossom. I cannot approve of our climate. (*Sighs*) I cannot. Our climate does not activate properly. And, Yermolay Alexeyevich, allow me to make a further remark. The other day I bought myself a pair of boots, and I make bold to assure you, they squeak so that it is really intolerable. What should I grease them with?

LOPAHIN: Oh, get out! I'm fed up with you.

YEPIHODOV: Every day I meet with misfortune. And I don't complain, I've got used to it, I even smile.

(DUNYASHA *enters, hands* LOPAHIN *the kvass.*)

YEPIHODOV: I am leaving. (*Stumbles against a chair, which falls over*) There! (*Triumphantly, as it were*) There again, you see what sort of circumstance, pardon the expression. . . . It is absolutely phenomenal! (*Exits.*)

DUNYASHA: You know, Yermolay Alexeyevich, I must tell you, Yepihodov has proposed to me.

LOPAHIN: Ah!

DUNYASHA: I simply don't know . . . he's a quiet man, but sometimes when he starts talking, you can't make out what he means. He speaks nicely—and it's touching—but you can't understand it. I sort of like him though, and he is crazy about me. He's an unlucky man . . . every day something happens to him. They tease him about it here . . . they call him Two-and-Twenty Troubles.

LOPAHIN (*listening*) : There! I think they're coming.

DUNYASHA: They *are* coming! What's the matter with me? I feel cold all over.

LOPAHIN: They really are coming. Let's go and meet them. Will she recognize me? We haven't seen each other for five years.

DUNYASHA (*in a flutter*) : I'm going to faint this minute. . . . Oh, I'm going to faint!

(*Two carriages are heard driving up to the house.* LOPAHIN *and* DUNYASHA *go out quickly. The stage is left empty. There is a noise in the adjoining rooms.* FIRS, *who had driven to the station to meet* LUBOV ANDREYEVNA RANEVSKAYA, *crosses the stage hurriedly, leaning on a stick. He is wearing an old-fashioned livery and a tall hat. He mutters to himself indistinctly. The hubbub off-stage increases.* A VOICE: "Come, let's go this way." Enter LUBOV ANDREYEVNA, ANYA *and* CHARLOTTA IVANOVNA, *with a pet dog on a leash, all in traveling dresses;* VARYA, *wearing a coat and kerchief;* GAYEV, SIMEONOV-PISHCHIK, LOPAHIN, DUNYASHA *with a bag and an umbrella, servants with luggage. All walk across the room.*)

ANYA: Let's go this way. Do you remember what room this is, mamma?

MME. RANEVSKAYA (*joyfully, through her tears*) : The nursery!

---

[1] Russian beer made from malt, barley, and rye.

VARYA: How cold it is! My hands are numb. (*To* MME. RANEVSKAYA) Your rooms are just the same as they were, mamma, the white one and the violet.

MME. RANEVSKAYA: The nursery! My darling, lovely room! I slept here when I was a child. . . . (*Cries*) And here I am, like a child again! (*Kisses her brother and* VARYA, *and then her brother again*) Varya's just the same as ever, like a nun. And I recognized Dunyasha. (*Kisses* DUN-YASHA.)

GAYEV: The train was two hours late. What do you think of that? What a way to manage things!

CHARLOTTA (*to* PISHCHIK): My dog eats nuts, too.

PISHCHIK (*in amazement*): You don't say so!

(*All go out, except* ANYA *and* DUNYASHA.)

DUNYASHA: We've been waiting for you for hours. (*Takes* ANYA'S *hat and coat.*)

ANYA: I didn't sleep on the train for four nights and now I'm frozen. . . .

DUNYASHA: It was Lent when you left; there was snow and frost, and now . . . My darling! (*Laughs and kisses her*) I have been waiting for you, my sweet, my darling! But I must tell you something. . . . I can't put it off another minute. . . .

ANYA (*listlessly*): What now?

DUNYASHA: The clerk, Yepihodov, proposed to me, just after Easter.

ANYA: There you are, at it again. . . . (*Straightening her hair*) I've lost all my hairpins. . . . (*She is staggering with exhaustion.*)

DUNYASHA: Really, I don't know what to think. He loves me—he loves me so!

ANYA (*looking towards the door of her room, tenderly*): My own room, my windows, just as though I'd never been away. I'm home! Tomorrow morning I'll get up and run into the orchard. Oh, if I could only get some sleep. I didn't close my eyes during the whole journey—I was so anxious.

DUNYASHA: Pyotr Sergeyevich came the day before yesterday.

ANYA (*joyfully*): Petya!

DUNYASHA: He's asleep in the bath-house. He has settled there. He said he was afraid of being in the way. (*Looks at her watch*) I should wake him, but Miss Varya told me not to. "Don't you wake him," she said.

(*Enter* VARYA *with a bunch of keys at her belt.*)

VARYA: Dunyasha, coffee, and be quick. . . . Mamma's asking for coffee.

DUNYASHA: In a minute. (*Exits.*)

VARYA: Well, thank God, you've come. You're home again. (*Fondling* ANYA) My darling is here again. My pretty one is back.

ANYA: Oh, what I've been through!

VARYA: I can imagine.

ANYA: When we left, it was Holy Week, it was cold then, and all the way Charlotta chattered and did her tricks. Why did you have to saddle me with Charlotta?

VARYA: You couldn't have traveled all alone, darling—at seventeen!

ANYA: We got to Paris, it was cold there, snowing. My French is dreadful.

Mamma lived on the fifth floor; I went up there, and found all kinds of Frenchmen, ladies, an old priest with a book. The place was full of tobacco smoke, and so bleak. Suddenly I felt sorry for mamma, so sorry, I took her head in my arms and hugged her and couldn't let go of her. Afterwards mamma kept fondling me and crying. . . .

VARYA (*through tears*): Don't speak of it . . . don't.

ANYA: She had already sold her villa at Mentone, she had nothing left, nothing. I hadn't a kopeck[2] left either, we had only just enough to get home. And mamma wouldn't understand! When we had dinner at the stations, she always ordered the most expensive dishes, and tipped the waiters a whole ruble. Charlotta, too. And Yasha kept ordering, too—it was simply awful. You know Yasha's mamma's footman now, we brought him here with us.

VARYA: Yes, I've seen the blackguard.

ANYA: Well, tell me—have you paid the interest?

VARYA: How could we?

ANYA: Good heavens, good heavens!

VARYA: In August the estate will be put up for sale.

ANYA: My God!

(LOPAHIN *peeps in at the door and bleats.*)

LOPAHIN: Meh-h-h. (*Disappears.*)

VARYA (*through tears*): What I couldn't do to him! (*Shakes her fist threateningly.*)

ANYA (*embracing* VARYA, *gently*): Varya, has he proposed to you? (VARYA *shakes her head*) But he loves you. Why don't you come to an understanding? What are you waiting for?

VARYA: Oh, I don't think anything will ever come of it. He's too busy, he has no time for me . . . pays no attention to me. I've washed my hands of him—I can't bear the sight of him. They all talk about our getting married, they all congratulate me—and all the time there's really nothing to it—it's all like a dream. (*In another tone*) You have a new brooch—like a bee.

ANYA (*sadly*): Mamma bought it. (*She goes into her own room and speaks gaily like a child*) And you know, in Paris I went up in a balloon.

VARYA: My darling's home, my pretty one is back! (DUNYASHA *returns with the coffee-pot and prepares coffee.* VARYA *stands at the door of* ANYA's *room*) All day long, darling, as I go about the house, I keep dreaming. If only we could marry you off to a rich man, I should feel at ease. Then I would go into a convent, and afterwards to Kiev, to Moscow. . . . I would spend my life going from one holy place to another. . . . I'd go on and on. . . . What a blessing that would be!

ANYA: The birds are singing in the orchard. What time is it?

VARYA: It must be after two. Time you were asleep, darling. (*Goes into* ANYA's *room*) What a blessing that would be!

(YASHA *enters with a plaid and a traveling bag, crosses the stage.*)

---

[2] A copper coin, one hundredth of a ruble, the equivalent of about half a cent in Chekhov's time.

YASHA (*finically*) : May I pass this way, please?

DUNYASHA: A person could hardly recognize you, Yasha. Your stay abroad has certainly done wonders for you.

YASHA: Hm-m . . . and who are you?

DUNYASHA: When you went away I was that high—(*indicating with her hand*) I'm Dunyasha—Fyodor Kozoyedev's daughter. Don't you remember?

YASHA: Hm! What a peach! (*He looks round and embraces her. She cries out and drops a saucer.* YASHA *leaves quickly.*)

VARYA (*in the doorway, in a tone of annoyance*) : What's going on here?

DUNYASHA (*through tears*) : I've broken a saucer.

VARYA: Well, that's good luck.

ANYA (*coming out of her room*) : We ought to warn mamma that Petya's here.

VARYA: I left orders not to wake him.

ANYA (*musingly*) : Six years ago father died. A month later brother Grisha was drowned in the river. . . . Such a pretty little boy he was—only seven. It was more than mamma could bear, so she went away, went away without looking back. . . . (*Shudders*) How well I understand her, if she only knew! (*Pauses*) And Petya Trofimov was Grisha's tutor, he may remind her of it all. . . .

(*Enter* FIRS, *wearing a jacket and a white waistcoat. He goes up to the coffee-pot.*)

FIRS (*anxiously*) : The mistress will have her coffee here. (*Puts on white gloves*) Is the coffee ready? (*Sternly, to* DUNYASHA) Here, you! And where's the cream?

DUNYASHA: Oh, my God! (*Exits quickly.*)

FIRS (*fussing over the coffee-pot*) : Hah! the addlehead![3] (*Mutters to himself*) Home from Paris. And the old master used to go to Paris too . . . by carriage. (*Laughs.*)

VARYA: What is it, Firs?

FIRS: What is your pleasure, Miss? (*Joyfully*) My mistress has come home, and I've seen her at last! Now I can die. (*Weeps with joy.*)

(*Enter* MME. RANEVSKAYA, GAYEV, *and* SIMEONOV-PISHCHIK. *The latter is wearing a tight-waisted, pleated coat of fine cloth, and full trousers.* GAYEV, *as he comes in, goes through the motions of a billiard player with his arms and body.*)

MME. RANEVSKAYA: Let's see, how does it go? Yellow ball in the corner! Bank shot in the side pocket!

GAYEV: I'll tip it in the corner! There was a time, sister, when you and I used to sleep in this very room, and now I'm fifty-one, strange as it may seem.

LOPAHIN: Yes, time flies.

GAYEV: Who?

---

[3] Firs's habitual phrase, and perhaps his own epitaph, in Russian is literally "half-chopped," a word brought into common usage by Chekhov in this play. Our colloquialism "half-baked" is perhaps its nearest equivalent.

LOPAHIN: I say, time flies.

GAYEV: It smells of patchouli[4] here.

ANYA: I'm going to bed. Good night, mamma. (*Kisses her mother.*)

MME. RANEVSKAYA: My darling child! (*Kisses her hands*) Are you happy to be home? I can't come to my senses.

ANYA: Good night, uncle.

GAYEV (*kissing her face and hands*): God bless you, how like your mother you are! (*To his sister*) At her age, Luba, you were just like her. (ANYA *shakes hands with* LOPAHIN *and* PISHCHIK, *then goes out, shutting the door behind her.*)

MME. RANEVSKAYA: She's very tired.

PISHCHIK: Well, it was a long journey.

VARYA (*to* LOPAHIN *and* PISHCHIK): How about it, gentlemen? It's past two o'clock—isn't it time for you to go?

MME. RANEVSKAYA (*laughs*): You're just the same as ever, Varya. (*Draws her close and kisses her*) I'll have my coffee and then we'll all go. (FIRS *puts a small cushion under her feet*) Thank you, my dear. I've got used to coffee. I drink it day and night. Thanks, my dear old man. (*Kisses him.*)

VARYA: I'd better see if all the luggage has been brought in. (*Exits.*)

MME. RANEVSKAYA: Can it really be I sitting here? (*Laughs*) I feel like dancing, waving my arms about. (*Covers her face with her hands*) But maybe I am dreaming! God knows I love my country, I love it tenderly; I couldn't look out of the window in the train, I kept crying so. (*Through tears*) But I must have my coffee. Thank you, Firs, thank you, dear old man. I'm so happy that you're still alive.

FIRS: Day before yesterday.

GAYEV: He's hard of hearing.

LOPAHIN: I must go soon, I'm leaving for Kharkov about five o'clock. How annoying! I'd like to have a good look at you, talk to you. . . . You're just as splendid as ever.

PISHCHIK (*breathing heavily*): She's even better-looking. . . . Dressed in the latest Paris fashion. . . . Perish my carriage and all its four wheels. . . .

LOPAHIN: Your brother, Leonid Andreyevich, says I'm a vulgarian and an exploiter. But it's all the same to me—let him talk. I only want you to trust me as you used to. I want you to look at me with your touching, wonderful eyes, as you used to. Dear God! My father was a serf of your father's and grandfather's, but you, you yourself, did so much for me once . . . so much . . . that I've forgotten all about that; I love you as though you were my sister—even more.

MME. RANEVSKAYA: I can't sit still, I simply can't. (*Jumps up and walks about in violent agitation*) This joy is too much for me. . . . Laugh at me, I'm silly! My own darling bookcase! My darling table! (*Kisses it.*)

GAYEV: While you were away, nurse died.

---

[4] A mint from which a strong perfume is derived. Lopahin apparently drenches himself in some sort of after-shave lotion.

MME. RANEVSKAYA (*sits down and takes her coffee*) : Yes, God rest her soul; they wrote me about it.

GAYEV: And Anastasy is dead. Petrushka Kossoy has left me and has gone into town to work for the police inspector. (*Takes a box of sweets out of his pocket and begins to suck one.*)

PISHCHIK: My daughter Dashenka sends her regards.

LOPAHIN: I'd like to tell you something very pleasant—cheering. (*Glancing at his watch*) I am leaving directly. There isn't much time to talk. But I will put it in a few words. As you know, your cherry orchard is to be sold to pay your debts. The sale is to be on the twenty-second of August; but don't you worry, my dear, you may sleep in peace; there is a way out. Here is my plan. Give me your attention! Your estate is only fifteen miles from the town; the railway runs close by it; and if the cherry orchard and the land along the river bank were cut up into lots and these leased for summer cottages, you would have an income of at least 25,000 rubles[5] a year out of it.

GAYEV: Excuse me. . . . What nonsense.

MME. RANEVSKAYA: I don't quite understand you, Yermolay Alexeyevich.

LOPAHIN: You will get an annual rent of at least ten rubles per acre, and if you advertise at once, I'll give you any guarantee you like that you won't have a square foot of ground left by autumn, all the lots will be snapped up. In short, congratulations, you're saved. The location is splendid—by that deep river. . . . Only, of course, the ground must be cleared . . . all the old buildings, for instance, must be torn down, and this house, too, which is useless, and, of course, the old cherry orchard must be cut down.

MME. RANEVSKAYA: Cut down? My dear, forgive me, but you don't know what you're talking about. If there's one thing that's interesting—indeed, remarkable—in the whole province, it's precisely our cherry orchard.

LOPAHIN: The only remarkable thing about this orchard is that it's a very large one. There's a crop of cherries every other year, and you can't do anything with them; no one buys them.

GAYEV: This orchard is even mentioned in the Encyclopedia.

LOPAHIN (*glancing at his watch*): If we can't think of a way out, if we don't come to a decision, on the twenty-second of August the cherry orchard and the whole estate will be sold at auction. Make up your minds! There's no other way out—I swear. None, none.

FIRS: In the old days, forty or fifty years ago, the cherries were dried, soaked, pickled, and made into jam, and we used to—

GAYEV: Keep still, Firs.

FIRS: And the dried cherries would be shipped by the cartload. It meant a lot of money! And in those days the dried cherries were soft and juicy, sweet, fragrant. . . . They knew the way to do it, then.

MME. RANEVSKAYA: And why don't they do it that way now?

FIRS: They've forgotten. Nobody remembers it.

---

[5] A Russian silver coin, equal to 100 kopecks, and then worth about 50 cents.

PISHCHIK (*to* MME. RANEVSKAYA): What's doing in Paris? Eh? Did you eat frogs there?

MME. RANEVSKAYA: I ate crocodiles.

PISHCHIK: Just imagine!

LOPAHIN: There used to be only landowners and peasants in the country, but now these summer people have appeared on the scene. . . . All the towns, even the small ones, are surrounded by these summer cottages; and in another twenty years, no doubt, the summer population will have grown enormously. Now the summer resident only drinks tea on his porch, but maybe he'll take to working his acre, too, and then your cherry orchard will be a rich, happy, luxuriant place.

GAYEV (*indignantly*): Poppycock!

(*Enter* VARYA *and* YASHA.)

VARYA: There are two telegrams for you, mamma dear. (*Picks a key from the bunch at her belt and noisily opens an old-fashioned bookcase*) Here they are.

MME. RANEVSKAYA: They're from Paris. (*Tears them up without reading them*) I'm through with Paris.

GAYEV: Do you know, Luba, how old this bookcase is? Last week I pulled out the bottom drawer and there I found the date burnt in it. It was made exactly a hundred years ago. Think of that! We could celebrate its centenary. True, it's an inanimate object, but nevertheless, a bookcase. . . .

PISHCHIK (*amazed*): A hundred years! Just imagine!

GAYEV: Yes. (*Tapping it*) That's something. . . . Dear, honored bookcase, hail to you who for more than a century have served the glorious ideals of goodness and justice! Your silent summons to fruitful toil has never weakened in all those hundred years (*through tears*), sustaining, through successive generations of our family, courage and faith in a better future, and fostering in us ideals of goodness and social consciousness. . . . (*Pauses.*)

LOPAHIN: Yes. . . .

MME. RANEVSKAYA: You haven't changed a bit, Leonid.

GAYEV (*somewhat embarrassed*): I'll play it off the red in the corner! Tip it in the side pocket!

LOPAHIN (*looking at his watch*): Well, it's time for me to go. . . .

YASHA (*handing a pill box to* MME. RANEVSKAYA): Perhaps you'll take your pills now.

PISHCHIK: One shouldn't take medicines, dearest lady; they do neither harm nor good. . . . Give them here, my valued friend. (*Takes the pill box, pours the pills into his palm, blows on them, puts them in his mouth, and washes them down with some kvass*) There!

MME. RANEVSKAYA (*frightened*): You must be mad!

PISHCHIK: I've taken all the pills.

LOPAHIN: What a glutton!

(*All laugh.*)

FIRS: The gentleman visited us in Easter week, ate half a bucket of pickles, he did. . . . (*Mumbles.*)

MME. RANEVSKAYA: What's he saying?

VARYA: He's been mumbling like that for the last three years—we're used to it.

YASHA: His declining years!

(CHARLOTTA IVANOVNA *very thin, tightly laced, dressed in white, a lorgnette at her waist, crosses the stage.*)

LOPAHIN: Forgive me, Charlotta Ivanovna, I've not had time to greet you. (*Tries to kiss her hand.*)

CHARLOTTA (*pulling away her hand*): If I let you kiss my hand, you'll be wanting to kiss my elbow next, and then my shoulder.

LOPAHIN: I've no luck today. (*All laugh*) Charlotta Ivanovna, show us a trick.

MME. RANEVSKAYA: Yes, Charlotta, do a trick for us.

CHARLOTTA: I don't see the need. I want to sleep. (*Exits.*)

LOPAHIN: In three weeks we'll meet again. (*Kisses* MME. RANEVSKAYA'S *hand*) Good-by till then. Time's up. (*To* GAYEV) Bye-bye. (*Kisses* PISHCHIK) Bye-bye. (*Shakes hands with* VARYA, *then with* FIRS *and* YASHA) I hate to leave. (*To* MME. RANEVSKAYA) If you make up your mind about the cottages, let me know; I'll get you a loan of 50,000 rubles. Think it over seriously.

VARYA (*crossly*): Will you never go!

LOPAHIN: I'm going, I'm going. (*Exits.*)

GAYEV: The vulgarian. But, excuse me . . . Varya's going to marry him, he's Varya's fiancé.

VARYA: You talk too much, uncle dear.

MME. RANEVSKAYA: Well, Varya, it would make me happy. He's a good man.

PISHCHIK: Yes, one must admit, he's a most estimable man. And my Dashenka . . . She too says that . . . she says . . . lots of things. (*Snores; but wakes up at once*) All the same, my valued friend, could you oblige me . . . with a loan of 240 rubles? I must pay the interest on the mortgage tomorrow.

VARYA (*alarmed*): We can't, we can't!

MME. RANEVSKAYA: I really haven't any money.

PISHCHIK: It'll turn up. (*Laughs*) I never lose hope, I thought everything was lost, that I was done for, when lo and behold, the railway ran through my land . . . and I was paid for it. . . . And something else will turn up again, if not today, then tomorrow. . . . Dashenka will win two hundred thousand . . . she's got a lottery ticket.

MME. RANEVSKAYA: I've had my coffee, now let's go to bed.

FIRS (*brushes off* GAYEV; *admonishingly*): You've got the wrong trousers on again. What am I to do with you?

VARYA (*softly*): Anya's asleep. (*Gently opens the window*) The sun's up now, it's not a bit cold. Look, mamma dear, what wonderful trees. And heavens, what air! The starlings are singing!

GAYEV (*opens the other window*): The orchard is all white. You've not forgotten it, Luba? That's the long alley that runs straight, straight as an arrow; how it shines on moonlight nights, do you remember? You've not forgotten?

MME. RANEVSKAYA (*looking out of the window into the orchard*): Oh, my childhood, my innocent childhood. I used to sleep in this nursery—I used to look out into the orchard, happiness waked with me every morning, the orchard was just the same then . . . nothing has changed. (*Laughs with joy*) All, all white! Oh, my orchard! After the dark, rainy autumn and the cold winter, you are young again, and full of happiness, the heavenly angels have not left you. . . . If I could free my chest and my shoulders from this rock that weighs on me, if I could only forget the past!

GAYEV: Yes, and the orchard will be sold to pay our debts, strange as it may seem. . . .

MME. RANEVSKAYA: Look! There is our poor mother walking in the orchard . . . all in white. . . . (*Laughs with joy*) It is she!

GAYEV: Where?

VARYA: What are you saying, mamma dear!

MME. RANEVSKAYA: There's no one there, I just imagined it. To the right, where the path turns towards the arbor, there's a little white tree, leaning over, that looks like a woman. . . .

(TROFIMOV *enters, wearing a shabby student's uniform and spectacles.*)

MME. RANEVSKAYA: What an amazing orchard! White masses of blossom, the blue sky. . . .

TROFIMOV: Lubov Andreyevna! (*She looks round at him*) I just want to pay my respects to you, then I'll leave at once. (*Kisses her hand ardently*) I was told to wait until morning, but I hadn't the patience. . . . (MME. RANEVSKAYA *looks at him, perplexed.*)

VARYA (*through tears*): This is Petya Trofimov.

TROFIMOV: Petya Trofimov, formerly your Grisha's tutor. . . . Can I have changed so much? (MME. RANEVSKAYA *embraces him and weeps quietly.*)

GAYEV (*embarrassed*): Don't, don't, Luba.

VARYA (*crying*): I told you, Petya, to wait until tomorrow.

MME. RANEVSKAYA: My Grisha . . . my little boy . . . Grisha . . . my son.

VARYA: What can one do, mamma dear, it's God's will.

TROFIMOV (*softly, through tears*): There . . . there.

MME. RANEVSKAYA (*weeping quietly*): My little boy was lost . . . drowned. Why? Why, my friend? (*More quietly*) Anya's asleep in there, and here I am talking so loudly . . . making all this noise. . . . But tell me, Petya, why do you look so badly? Why have you aged so?

TROFIMOV: A mangy master, a peasant woman in the train called me.

MME. RANEVSKAYA: You were just a boy then, a dear little student, and now your hair's thin—and you're wearing glasses! Is it possible you're still a student? (*Goes towards the door.*)

TROFIMOV: I suppose I'm a perpetual student.

MME. RANEVSKAYA (*kisses her brother, then* VARYA): Now, go to bed . . . You have aged, too, Leonid.

PISHCHIK (*follows her*): So now we turn in. Oh, my gout! I'm staying the night here. . . . Lubov Andreyevna, my angel, tomorrow morning. . . . I do need 240 rubles.

GAYEV: He keeps at it.

PISHCHIK: I'll pay it back, dear . . . it's a trifling sum.

MME. RANEVSKAYA: All right, Leonid will give it to you. Give it to him, Leonid.

GAYEV: Me give it to him! That's a good one!

MME. RANEVSKAYA: It can't be helped. Give it to him! He needs it. He'll pay it back.

(MME. RANEVSKAYA, TROFIMOV, PISHCHIK, *and* FIRS *go out;* GAYEV, VARYA, *and* YASHA *remain.*)

GAYEV: Sister hasn't got out of the habit of throwing money around. (*To* YASHA) Go away, my good fellow, you smell of the barnyard.

YASHA (*with a grin*): And you, Leonid Andreyevich, are just the same as ever.

GAYEV: Who? (*To* VARYA) What did he say?

VARYA (*to* YASHA): Your mother's come from the village; she's been sitting in the servants' room since yesterday, waiting to see you.

YASHA: Botheration!

VARYA: You should be ashamed of yourself!

YASHA: She's all I needed! She could have come tomorrow. (*Exits.*)

VARYA: Mamma is just the same as ever; she hasn't changed a bit. If she had her own way, she'd keep nothing for herself.

GAYEV: Yes . . . (*Pauses*) If a great many remedies are offered for some disease, it means it is incurable; I keep thinking and racking my brains; I have many remedies, ever so many, and that really means none. It would be fine if we came in for a legacy; it would be fine if we married off our Anya to a very rich man; or we might go to Yaroslavl and try our luck with our aunt, the Countess. She's very, very rich, you know. . . .

VARYA (*weeping*): If only God would help us!

GAYEV: Stop bawling. Aunt's very rich, but she doesn't like us. In the first place, sister married a lawyer who was no nobleman. . . . (ANYA *appears in the doorway*) She married beneath her, and it can't be said that her behavior has been very exemplary. She's good, kind, sweet, and I love her, but no matter what extenuating circumstances you may adduce, there's no denying that she has no morals. You sense it in her least gesture.

VARYA (*in a whisper*): Anya's in the doorway.

GAYEV: Who? (*Pauses*) It's queer, something got into my right eye—my eyes are going back on me. . . . And on Thursday, when I was in the circuit court—

(*Enter* ANYA.)

VARYA: Why aren't you asleep, Anya?

ANYA: I can't get to sleep, I just can't.

GAYEV: My little pet! (*Kisses* ANYA's *face and hands*) My child! (*Weeps*) You are not my niece, you're my angel! You're everything to me. Believe me, believe—

ANYA: I believe you, uncle. Everyone loves you and respects you . . . but, uncle dear, you must keep still. . . . You must. What were you saying just now about my mother? Your own sister? What made you say that?

GAYEV: Yes, yes. . . . (*Covers his face with her hand*) Really, that was awful! Good God! Heaven help me! Just now I made a speech to the bookcase . . . so stupid! And only after I was through, I saw how stupid it was.

VARYA: It's true, uncle dear, you ought to keep still. Just don't talk, that's all.

ANYA: If you could only keep still, it would make things easier for you too.

GAYEV: I'll keep still. (*Kisses* ANYA's *and* VARYA's *hands*) I will. But now about business. On Thursday I was in court; well, there were a number of us there, and we began talking of one thing and another, and this and that, and do you know, I believe it will be possible to raise a loan on a promissory note, to pay the interest at the bank.

VARYA: If only God would help us!

GAYEV: On Tuesday I'll go and see about it again. (*To* VARYA) Stop bawling. (*To* ANYA) Your mamma will talk to Lopahin, and he, of course, will not refuse her . . . and as soon as you're rested, you'll go to Yaroslavl to the Countess, your great-aunt. So we'll be working in three directions at once, and the thing is in the bag. We'll pay the interest—I'm sure of it. (*Puts a candy in his mouth*) I swear on my honor, I swear by anything you like, the estate shan't be sold. (*Excitedly*) I swear by my own happiness! Here's my hand on it, you can call me a swindler and a scoundrel if I let it come to an auction! I swear by my whole being.

ANYA (*relieved and quite happy again*): How good you are, uncle, and how clever! (*Embraces him*) Now I'm at peace, quite at peace, I'm happy.
(*Enter* FIRS.)

FIRS (*reproachfully*): Leonid Andreyevich, have you no fear of God? When are you going to bed?

GAYEV: Directly, directly. Go away, Firs, I'll . . . yes, I will undress myself. Now, children, 'nightie-'nightie. We'll consider details tomorrow, but now go to sleep. (*Kisses* ANYA *and* VARYA) I am a man of the 'Eighties; they have nothing good to say of that period nowadays. Nevertheless, in the course of my life I have suffered not a little for my convictions. It's not for nothing that the peasant loves me; one should know the peasant; one should know from which—

ANYA: There you go again, uncle.

VARYA: Uncle dear, be quiet.

FIRS (*angrily*): Leonid Andreyevich!

GAYEV: I'm coming, I'm coming! Go to bed! Double bank shot in the side pocket! Here goes a clean shot. . . .
(*Exits,* FIRS *hobbling after him.*)

ANYA: I am at peace now. I don't want to go to Yaroslavl—I don't like my great-aunt, but still, I am at peace, thanks to uncle. (*Sits down.*)

VARYA: We must get some sleep. I'm going now. While you were away something unpleasant happened. In the old servants' quarters there are only the old people, as you know; Yefim, Polya, Yevstigney, and Karp, too. They began letting all sorts of rascals in to spend the night. . . . I didn't say anything. Then I heard they'd been spreading a report that I gave them nothing but dried peas to eat—out of stinginess, you know . . . and it was all Yevstigney's doing. . . . All right, I thought, if that's how it is, I thought, just wait. I sent for Yevstigney. . . . (*Yawns*) He comes.

. . . "How's this, Yevstigney?" I say, "You fool. . . ." (*Looking at* ANYA) Anichka! (*Pauses*) She's asleep. (*Puts her arm around* ANYA) Come to your little bed. . . . Come. . . . (*Leads her*) My darling has fallen asleep. . . . Come.

(*They go out. Far away beyond the orchard a shepherd is piping.* TROFI-MOV *crosses the stage and, seeing* VARYA *and* ANYA, *stands still.*)

VARYA: Sh! She's asleep . . . asleep . . . Come, darling.

ANYA (*softly, half-asleep*): I'm so tired. Those bells . . . uncle . . . dear. . . . Mamma and uncle. . . .

VARYA: Come, my precious, come along. (*They go into* ANYA'S *room.*)

TROFIMOV (*with emotion*): My sunshine, my spring!

(*The Curtain Falls.*)

Act Two

A meadow. An old, long-abandoned, lopsided little chapel; near it, a well, large slabs, which had apparently once served as tombstones, and an old bench. In the background, the road to the Gayev estate. To one side poplars loom darkly, where the cherry orchard begins. In the distance a row of telegraph poles, and far off, on the horizon, the faint outline of a large city which is seen only in fine, clear weather. The sun will soon be setting. CHARLOTTA, YASHA, *and* DUNYASHA *are seated on the bench.* YEPIHODOV *stands near and plays a guitar. All are pensive.* CHARLOTTA *wears an old peaked cap. She has taken a gun from her shoulder and is straightening the buckle on the strap.*

CHARLOTTA (*musingly*): I haven't a real passport, I don't know how old I am, and I always feel that I am very young. When I was a little girl, my father and mother used to go from fair to fair and give performances, very good ones. And I used to do the *salto mortale,*[6] and all sorts of other tricks. And when papa and mamma died, a German lady adopted me and began to educate me. Very good. I grew up and became a governess. But where I come from and who I am, I don't know. . . . Who were my parents? Perhaps they weren't even married. . . . I don't know. . . . (*Takes a cucumber out of her pocket and eats it*) I don't know a thing. (*Pause*) One wants so much to talk, and there isn't anyone to talk to. . . . I haven't anybody.

---

[6] The leap of death (Italian).

YEPIHODOV (*plays the guitar and sings*): "What care I for the jarring world? What's friend or foe to me? . . ." How agreeable it is to play the mandolin.

DUNYASHA: That's a guitar, not a mandolin. (*Looks in a hand mirror and powders her face.*)

YEPIHODOV: To a madman in love it's a mandolin. (*Sings*) "Would that the heart were warmed by the fire of mutual love!" (YASHA *joins in.*)

CHARLOTTA: How abominably these people sing. Pfui! Like jackals!

DUNYASHA (*to* YASHA): How wonderful it must be though to have stayed abroad!

YASHA: Ah, yes, of course, I cannot but agree with you there. (*Yawns and lights a cigar.*)

YEPIHODOV: Naturally. Abroad, everything has long since achieved full perplexion.

YASHA: That goes without saying.

YEPIHODOV: I'm a cultivated man, I read all kinds of remarkable books. And yet I can never make out what direction I should take, what is it that I want, properly speaking. Should I live, or should I shoot myself, properly speaking? Nevertheless, I always carry a revolver about me. . . . Here it is. . . . (*Shows revolver.*)

CHARLOTTA: I've finished. I'm going. (*Puts the gun over her shoulder*) You are a very clever man, Yepihodov, and a very terrible one; women must be crazy about you. Br-r-r! (*Starts to go*) These clever men are all so stupid; there's no one for me to talk to . . . always alone, alone, I haven't a soul . . . and who I am, and why I am, nobody knows. (*Exits unhurriedly.*)

YEPIHODOV: Properly speaking and letting other subjects alone, I must say regarding myself, among other things, that fate treats me mercilessly, like a storm treats a small boat. If I am mistaken, let us say, why then do I wake up this morning, and there on my chest is a spider of enormous dimensions . . . like this . . . (*indicates with both hands*). Again, I take up a pitcher of kvass to have a drink, and in it there is something unseemly to the highest degree, something like a cockroach. (*Pause*) Have you read Buckle[7]? (*Pause*) I wish to have a word with you, Avdotya Fyodorovna, if I may trouble you.

DUNYASHA: Well, go ahead.

YEPIHODOV: I wish to speak with you alone. (*Sighs.*)

DUNYASHA (*embarrassed*): Very well. Only first bring me my little cape. You'll find it near the wardrobe. It's rather damp here.

YEPIHODOV: Certainly, ma'am; I will fetch it, ma'am. Now I know what to do with my revolver. (*Takes the guitar and goes off playing it.*)

YASHA: Two-and-Twenty Troubles! An awful fool, between you and me. (*Yawns.*)

DUNYASHA: I hope to God he doesn't shoot himself! (*Pause*) I've become so nervous, I'm always fretting. I was still a little girl when I was taken

---

[7] Henry Buckle (1821-1862), English historian interested in the effects of physical conditions such as climate and soil upon a nation's history.

into the big house, I am quite unused to the simple life now, and my hands are white, as white as a lady's. I've become so soft, so delicate, so refined, I'm afraid of everything. It's so terrifying; and if you deceive me, Yasha, I don't know what will happen to my nerves. (YASHA *kisses her.*)

YASHA: You're a peach! Of course, a girl should never forget herself; and what I dislike more than anything is when a girl don't behave properly.

DUNYASHA: I've fallen passionately in love with you; you're educated—you have something to say about everything. (*Pause.*)

YASHA (*yawns*): Yes, ma'am. Now the way I look at it, if a girl loves someone, it means she is immoral. (*Pause*) It's agreeable smoking a cigar in the fresh air. (*Listens*) Someone's coming this way. . . . It's our madam and the others. (DUNYASHA *embraces him impulsively*) You go home, as though you'd been to the river to bathe; go by the little path, or else they'll run into you and suspect me of having arranged to meet you here. I can't stand that sort of thing.

DUNYASHA (*coughing softly*): Your cigar's made my head ache. (*Exits.* YASHA *remains standing near the chapel. Enter* MME. RANEVSKAYA, GAYEV, *and* LOPAHIN.)

LOPAHIN: You must make up your mind once and for all—there's no time to lose. It's quite a simple question, you know. Do you agree to lease your land for summer cottages or not? Answer in one word, yes or no; only one word!

MME. RANEVSKAYA: Who's been smoking such abominable cigars here? (*Sits down.*)

GAYEV: Now that the railway line is so near, it's made things very convenient. (*Sits down*) Here we've been able to have lunch in town. Yellow ball in the side pocket! I feel like going into the house and playing just one game.

MME. RANEVSKAYA: You can do that later.

LOPAHIN: Only one word! (*Imploringly*) Do give me an answer!

GAYEV (*yawning*): Who?

MME. RANEVSKAYA (*looks into her purse*): Yesterday I had a lot of money and now my purse is almost empty. My poor Varya tries to economize by feeding us just milk soup; in the kitchen the old people get nothing but dried peas to eat, while I squander money thoughtlessly. (*Drops the purse, scattering gold pieces*) You see there they go. . . . (*Shows vexation.*)

YASHA: Allow me—I'll pick them up. (*Picks up the money.*)

MME. RANEVSKAYA: Be so kind, Yasha. And why did I go to lunch in town? That nasty restaurant, with its music and the tablecloth smelling of soap . . . Why drink so much, Leonid? Why eat so much? Why talk so much? Today again you talked a lot, and all so inappropriately about the 'Seventies, about the decadents. And to whom? Talking to waiters about decadents!

LOPAHIN: Yes.

GAYEV (*waving his hand*): I'm incorrigible; that's obvious. (*Irritably, to* YASHA) Why do you keep dancing about in front of me?

YASHA (*laughs*): I can't hear your voice without laughing—

GAYEV: Either he or I—

MME. RANEVSKAYA: Go away, Yasha; run along.

YASHA (*handing* MME. RANEVSKAYA *her purse*): I'm going, at once. (*Hardly able to suppress his laughter*) This minute. (*Exits.*)

LOPAHIN: That rich man, Deriganov, wants to buy your estate. They say he's coming to the auction himself.

MME. RANEVSKAYA: Where did you hear that?

LOPAHIN: That's what they are saying in town.

GAYEV: Our aunt in Yaroslavl has promised to help; but when she will send the money, and how much, no one knows.

LOPAHIN: How much will she send? A hundred thousand? Two hundred?

MME. RANEVSKAYA: Oh, well, ten or fifteen thousand; and we'll have to be grateful for that.

LOPAHIN: Forgive me, but such frivolous people as you are, so queer and unbusinesslike—I never met in my life. One tells you in plain language that your estate is up for sale, and you don't seem to take it in.

MME. RANEVSKAYA: What are we to do? Tell us what to do.

LOPAHIN: I do tell you, every day; every day I say the same thing! You must lease the cherry orchard and the land for summer cottages, you must do it and as soon as possible—right away. The auction is close at hand. Please understand! Once you've decided to have the cottages, you can raise as much money as you like, and you're saved.

MME. RANEVSKAYA: Cottages—summer people—forgive me, but it's all so vulgar.

GAYEV: I agree with you absolutely.

LOPAHIN: I shall either burst into tears or scream or faint! I can't stand it! You've worn me out! (*To* GAYEV) You're an old woman!

GAYEV: Who?

LOPAHIN: An old woman! (*Gets up to go.*)

MME. RANEVSKAYA (*alarmed*): No, don't go! Please stay, I beg you, my dear. Perhaps we shall think of something.

LOPAHIN: What is there to think of?

MME. RANEVSKAYA: Don't go, I beg you. With you here it's more cheerful anyway. (*Pause*) I keep expecting something to happen; it's as though the house were going to crash about our ears.

GAYEV (*in deep thought*): Bank shot in the corner. . . ˙. Three cushions in the side pocket. . . .

MME. RANEVSKAYA: We have been great sinners. . . .

LOPAHIN: What sins could you have committed?

GAYEV (*putting a candy in his mouth*): They say I've eaten up my fortune in candy! (*Laughs.*)

MME. RANEVSKAYA: Oh, my sins! I've squandered money away recklessly, like a lunatic, and I married a man who made nothing but debts. My husband drank himself to death on champagne, he was a terrific drinker. And then, to my sorrow, I fell in love with another man, and I lived with him. And just then—that was my first punishment—a blow on the head: my little boy was drowned here in the river. And I went abroad, went away forever . . . never to come back, never to see this river again. . . . I closed my eyes and ran, out of my mind. . . . But he followed me, pitiless, brutal. I bought a villa near Mentone, because he fell ill there; and for three years, day and night, I knew no peace, no rest. The sick man wore me out, he sucked my soul dry. Then last year, when the villa was sold to pay my debts, I went to Paris, and there he robbed me, abandoned me, took up with another woman; I tried to poison myself—it was stupid, so shameful—and then suddenly I felt drawn back to Russia, back to my own country, to my little girl. (*Wipes her tears away*) Lord, Lord! Be merciful, forgive me my sins—don't punish me any more! (*Takes a telegram out of her pocket*) This came today from Paris—he begs me to forgive him, implores me to go back. . . . (*Tears up the telegram*) Do I hear music? (*Listens.*)

GAYEV: That's our famous Jewish band, you remember? Four violins, a flute, and a double bass.

MME. RANEVSKAYA: Does it still exist? We ought to send for them some evening and have a party.

LOPAHIN (*listens*): I don't hear anything. (*Hums softly*) "The Germans for a fee will Frenchify a Russian." (*Laughs*) I saw a play at the theater yesterday—awfully funny.

MME. RANEVSKAYA: There was probably nothing funny about it. You shouldn't go to see plays, you should look at yourselves more often. How drab your lives are—how full of unnecessary talk.

LOPAHIN: That's true; come to think of it, we do live like fools. (*Pause*) My pop was a peasant, an idiot; he understood nothing, never taught me anything, all he did was beat me when he was drunk, and always with a stick. Fundamentally, I'm just the same kind of blockhead and idiot. I was never taught anything—I have a terrible handwriting; I write so that I feel ashamed before people, like a pig.

MME. RANEVSKAYA: You should get married, my friend.

LOPAHIN: Yes . . . that's true.

MME. RANEVSKAYA: To our Varya, she's a good girl.

LOPAHIN: Yes.

MME. RANEVSKAYA: She's a girl who comes of simple people, she works all day long; and above all, she loves you. Besides, you've liked her for a long time now.

LOPAHIN: Well, I've nothing against it. She's a good girl. (*Pause.*)

GAYEV: I've been offered a place in the bank—6,000 a year. Have you heard?

MME. RANEVSKAYA: You're not up to it. Stay where you are.

(FIRS *enters, carrying an overcoat.*)

FIRS (*to* GAYEV): Please put this on, sir, it's damp.

GAYEV (*putting it on*): I'm fed up with you, brother.

FIRS: Never mind. This morning you drove off without saying a word. (*Looks him over.*)

MME. RANEVSKAYA: How you've aged, Firs.

FIRS: I beg your pardon?

LOPAHIN: The lady says you've aged.

FIRS: I've lived a long time; they were arranging my wedding and your papa wasn't born yet. (*Laughs*) When freedom came I was already head footman. I wouldn't consent to be set free then; I stayed on with the master. . . . (*Pause*) I remember they were all very happy, but why they were happy, they didn't know themselves.

LOPAHIN: It was fine in the old days! At least there was flogging!

FIRS (*not hearing*) : Of course. The peasants kept to the masters, the masters kept to the peasants; but now they've all gone their own ways, and there's no making out anything.

GAYEV: Be quiet, Firs. I must go to town tomorrow. They've promised to introduce me to a general who might let us have a loan.

LOPAHIN: Nothing will come of that. You won't even be able to pay the interest, you can be certain of that.

MME. RANEVSKAYA: He's raving, there isn't any general. (*Enter* TROFIMOV, ANYA, *and* VARYA.)

GAYEV: Here come our young people.

ANYA: There's mamma, on the bench.

MME. RANEVSKAYA (*tenderly*) : Come here, come along, my darlings. (*Embraces* ANYA *and* VARYA) If you only knew how I love you both! Sit beside me—there, like that. (*All sit down.*)

LOPAHIN: Our perpetual student is always with the young ladies.

TROFIMOV: That's not any of your business.

LOPAHIN: He'll soon be fifty, and he's still a student!

TROFIMOV: Stop your silly jokes.

LOPAHIN: What are you so cross about, you queer bird?

TROFIMOV: Oh, leave me alone.

LOPAHIN (*laughs*) : Allow me to ask you, what do you think of me?

TROFIMOV: What I think of you, Yermolay Alexeyevich, is this: you are a rich man who will soon be a millionaire. Well, just as a beast of prey, which devours everything that comes in its way, is necessary for the process of metabolism to go on, so you too are necessary. (*All laugh.*)

VARYA: Better tell us something about the planets, Petya.

MME. RANEVSKAYA: No, let's go on with yesterday's conversation.

TROFIMOV: What was it about?

GAYEV: About man's pride.

TROFIMOV: Yesterday we talked a long time, but we came to no conclusion. There is something mystical about man's pride in your sense of the word. Perhaps you're right, from your own point of view. But if you reason simply, without going into subtleties, then what call is there for pride? Is there any sense in it, if man is so poor a thing physiologically, and if, in the great majority of cases, he is coarse, stupid, and profoundly unhappy? We should stop admiring ourselves. We should work, and that's all.

GAYEV: You die, anyway.

TROFIMOV: Who knows? And what does it mean—to die? Perhaps man has a hundred senses, and at his death only the five we know perish, while the other ninety-five remain alive.

MME. RANEVSKAYA: How clever you are, Petya!

LOPAHIN (*ironically*) : Awfully clever!

TROFIMOV: Mankind goes forward, developing its powers. Everything that is now unattainable for it will one day come within man's reach and be clear to him; only we must work, helping with all our might those who seek the truth. Here among us in Russia only the very few work as yet. The great majority of the intelligentsia, as far as I can see, seek nothing, do nothing, are totally unfit for work of any kind. They call themselves the intelligentsia, yet they are uncivil to their servants, treat the peasants like animals, are poor students, never read anything serious, do absolutely nothing at all, only talk about science, and have little appreciation of the arts. They are all solemn, have grim faces, they all philosophize and talk of weighty matters. And meanwhile the vast majority of us, ninety-nine out of a hundred, live like savages. At the least provocation—a punch in the jaw, and curses. They eat disgustingly, sleep in filth and stuffiness, bedbugs everywhere, stench and damp and moral slovenliness. And obviously, the only purpose of all our fine talk is to hoodwink ourselves and others. Show me where the public nurseries are that we've heard so much about, and the libraries. We read about them in novels, but in reality they don't exist; there is nothing but dirt, vulgarity, and Asiatic backwardness. I don't like very solemn faces, I'm afraid of them, I'm afraid of serious conversations. We'd do better to keep quiet for a while.

LOPAHIN: Do you know, I get up at five o'clock in the morning, and I work from morning till night; and I'm always handling money, my own and other people's, and I see what people around me are really like. You've only to start doing anything to see how few honest, decent people there are. Sometimes when I lie awake at night, I think: "Oh, Lord, thou hast given us immense forests, boundless fields, the widest horizons, and living in their midst, we ourselves ought really to be giants."

MME. RANEVSKAYA: Now you want giants! They're only good in fairy tales; otherwise they're frightening.

(YEPIHODOV *crosses the stage at the rear, playing the guitar.*)

MME. RANEVSKAYA (*pensively*): There goes Yepihodov.

ANYA (*pensively*): There goes Yepihodov.

GAYEV: Ladies and gentlemen, the sun has set.

TROFIMOV: Yes.

GAYEV (*in a low voice, declaiming as it were*): Oh, Nature, wondrous Nature, you shine with eternal radiance, beautiful and indifferent! You, whom we call our mother, unite within yourself life and death! You animate and destroy!

VARYA (*pleadingly*): Uncle dear!

ANYA: Uncle, again!

TROFIMOV: You'd better bank the yellow ball in the side pocket.

GAYEV: I'm silent, I'm silent. . . .

(*All sit plunged in thought. Stillness reigns. Only* FIRS'S *muttering is audible. Suddenly a distant sound is heard, coming from the sky as it were, the sound of a snapping string, mournfully dying away.*)

MME. RANEVSKAYA: What was that?

LOPAHIN: I don't know. Somewhere far away, in the pits, a bucket's broken loose; but somewhere very far away.

GAYEV: Or it might be some sort of bird, perhaps a heron.

TROFIMOV: Or an owl. . . .

MME. RANEVSKAYA (*shudders*) : It's weird, somehow. (*Pause.*)

FIRS: Before the calamity the same thing happened—the owl screeched, and the samovar hummed all the time.

GAYEV: Before what calamity?

FIRS: Before the Freedom. (*Pause.*)

MME. RANEVSKAYA: Come, my friends, let's be going. It's getting dark. (*To* ANYA) You have tears in your eyes. What is it, my little one? (*Embraces her.*)

ANYA: I don't know, mamma; it's nothing.

TROFIMOV: Somebody's coming.

(*A* TRAMP *appears, wearing a shabby white cap and an overcoat. He is slightly drunk.*)

TRAMP: Allow me to inquire, will this short-cut take me to the station?

GAYEV: It will. Just follow that road.

TRAMP: My heartfelt thanks. (*Coughing*) The weather is glorious. (*Recites*) "My brother, my suffering brother . . . Go down to the Volga! Whose groans . . . ?" (*To* VARYA) Mademoiselle, won't you spare 30 kopecks for a hungry Russian?

(VARYA, *frightened, cries out.*)

LOPAHIN (*angrily*) : Even panhandling has its proprieties.

MME. RANEVSKAYA (*scared*) : Here, take this. (*Fumbles in her purse*) I haven't any silver . . . never mind, here's a gold piece.

TRAMP: My heartfelt thanks. (*Exits. Laughter.*)

VARYA (*frightened*) : I'm leaving, I'm leaving . . . Oh, mamma dear, at home the servants have nothing to eat, and you gave him a gold piece!

MME. RANEVSKAYA: What are you going to do with me? I'm such a fool. When we get home, I'll give you everything I have. Yermolay Alexeyevich, you'll lend me some more. . . .

LOPAHIN: Yes, ma'am.

MME. RANEVSKAYA: Come, ladies and gentlemen, it's time to be going. Oh! Varya, we've settled all about your marriage. Congratulations!

VARYA (*through tears*) : Really, mamma, that's not a joking matter.

LOPAHIN: "Aurelia, get thee to a nunnery, go . . ."

GAYEV: And do you know, my hands are trembling: I haven't played billiards in a long time.

LOPAHIN: "Aurelia, nymph, in your orisons, remember me!"[8]

MME. RANEVSKAYA: Let's go, it's almost suppertime.

VARYA: He frightened me! My heart's pounding.

LOPAHIN: Let me remind you, ladies and gentlemen, on the 22nd of August the cherry orchard will be up for sale. Think about that! Think!

(*All except* TROFIMOV *and* ANYA *go out.*)

---

[8] Lopahin has apparently heard someone quote from Shakespeare's *Hamlet* (III, i) :
The fair Ophelia!—Nymph, in thy orisons
Be all my sins remembered.

ANYA (*laughs*): I'm grateful to that tramp; he frightened Varya and so we're alone.

TROFIMOV: Varya's afraid we'll fall in love with each other all of a sudden. She hasn't left us alone for days. Her narrow mind can't grasp that we're above love. To avoid the petty and illusory, everything that prevents us from being free and happy—that is the goal and meaning of our life. Forward! Do not fall behind, friends!

ANYA (*strikes her hands together*): How well you speak! (*Pause*) It's wonderful here today.

TROFIMOV: Yes, the weather's glorious.

ANYA: What have you done to me, Petya? Why don't I love the cherry orchard as I used to? I loved it so tenderly. It seemed to me there was no spot on earth lovelier than our orchard.

TROFIMOV: All Russia is our orchard. Our land is vast and beautiful, there are many wonderful places in it. (*Pause*) Think of it, Anya, your grandfather, your great-grandfather and all your ancestors were serf-owners, owners of living souls, and aren't human beings looking at you from every tree in the orchard, from every leaf, from every trunk? Don't you hear voices? Oh, it's terrifying! Your orchard is a fearful place, and when you pass through it in the evening or at night, the old bark on the trees gleams faintly, and the cherry trees seem to be dreaming of things that happened a hundred, two hundred years ago and to be tormented by painful visions. What is there to say? We're at least two hundred years behind, we've really achieved nothing yet, we have no definite attitude to the past, we only philosophize, complain of the blues, or drink vodka. It's all so clear: in order to live in the present, we should first redeem our past, finish with it, and we can expiate it only by suffering, only by extraordinary, unceasing labor. Realize that, Anya.

ANYA: The house in which we live has long ceased to be our own, and I will leave it, I give you my word.

TROFIMOV: If you have the keys, fling them into the well and go away. Be free as the wind.

ANYA (*in ecstasy*): How well you put that!

TROFIMOV: Believe me, Anya, believe me! I'm not yet thirty, I'm young, I'm still a student—but I've already suffered so much. In winter I'm hungry, sick, harassed, poor as a beggar, and where hasn't Fate driven me? Where haven't I been? And yet always, every moment of the day and night, my soul is filled with inexplicable premonitions. . . . I have a premonition of happiness, Anya. . . . I see it already!

ANYA (*pensively*): The moon is rising.

(YEPIHODOV *is heard playing the same mournful tune on the guitar. The moon rises. Somewhere near the poplars* VARYA *is looking for* ANYA *and calling* "Anya, where are you?")

TROFIMOV: Yes, the moon is rising. (*Pause*) There it is, happiness, it's approaching, it's coming nearer and nearer, I can already hear its footsteps. And if we don't see it, if we don't know it, what does it matter? Others will!

VARYA'S *voice*: "Anya! Where are you?"
TROFIMOV: That Varya again! (*Angrily*) It's revolting!
ANYA: Never mind, let's go down to the river. It's lovely there.
TROFIMOV: Come on. (*They go.*)
VARYA'S *voice*: "Anya! Anya!"

(*The Curtain Falls.*)

Act Three

A drawing-room separated by an arch from a ballroom. Evening.
Chandelier burning. The Jewish band is heard playing in the anteroom. In
the ballroom they are dancing the Grand Rond. PISHCHIK is heard calling,
"Promenade à une paire."[9] PISHCHIK *and* CHARLOTTA, TROFIMOV *and*
MME. RANEVSKAYA, ANYA *and the* POST OFFICE CLERK, VARYA *and the*
STATIONMASTER, *and others, enter the drawing-room in couples.* DUN-
YASHA *is in the last couple.* VARYA *weeps quietly, wiping her tears as she
dances. All parade through drawing-room.* PISHCHIK *calling* "Grand
rond, balancez!" *and* "Les cavaliers à genoux et remerciez vos dames!"[10]
FIRS, *wearing a dress-coat, brings in soda-water on a tray.* PISHCHIK *and*
TROFIMOV *enter the drawing-room.*

PISHCHIK: I'm a full-blooded man; I've already had two strokes. Dancing's
hard work for me; but as they say, "If you run with the pack, you can
bark or not, but at least wag your tail." Still, I'm as strong as a horse.
My late lamented father, who would have his joke, God rest his soul, used
to say, talking about our origin, that the ancient line of the Simeonov-
Pishchiks was descended from the very horse that Caligula[11] had made a
senator. (*Sits down*) But the trouble is, I have no money. A hungry dog
believes in nothing but meat. (*Snores and wakes up at once*) It's the same
with me—I can think of nothing but money.
TROFIMOV: You know, there *is* something equine about your figure.
PISHCHIK: Well, a horse is a fine animal—one can sell a horse.
(*Sound of billiards being played in an adjoining room.* VARYA *appears in
the archway.*)

---

[9] Walk in pairs (French).
[10] Large circle, swing! Gentlemen kneel and thank your ladies (French).
[11] Mad Roman emperor (A.D. 38-41), who proposed that his horse be elected to
the consulship of Rome.

TROFIMOV (*teasing her*): Madam Lopahina! Madam Lopahina!

VARYA (*angrily*): Mangy master!

TROFIMOV: Yes, I am a mangy master and I'm proud of it.

VARYA (*reflecting bitterly*): Here we've hired musicians, and what shall we pay them with? (*Exits.*)

TROFIMOV (*to* PISHCHIK): If the energy you have spent during your lifetime looking for money to pay interest had gone into something else, in the end you could have turned the world upside down.

PISHCHIK: Nietzsche,[12] the philosopher, the greatest, most famous of men, that colossal intellect, says in his works, that it is permissible to forge banknotes.

TROFIMOV: Have you read Nietzsche?

PISHCHIK: Well . . . Dashenka told me . . . And now I've got to the point where forging banknotes is about the only way out for me. . . . The day after tomorrow I have to pay 310 rubles—I already have 130. . . . (*Feels in his pockets. In alarm*) The money's gone! I've lost my money! (*Through tears*) Where's my money? (*Joyfully*) Here it is! Inside the lining. . . . I'm all in a sweat. . . .

(*Enter* MME. RANEVSKAYA *and* CHARLOTTA.)

MME. RANEVSKAYA (*hums the "Lezginka"*[13]): Why isn't Leonid back yet? What is he doing in town? (*To* DUNYASHA) Dunyasha, offer the musicians tea.

TROFIMOV: The auction hasn't taken place, most likely.

MME. RANEVSKAYA: It's the wrong time to have the band, and the wrong time to give a dance. Well, never mind. (*Sits down and hums softly.*)

CHARLOTTA (*hands* PISHCHIK *a pack of cards*): Here is a pack of cards. Think of any card you like.

PISHCHIK: I've thought of one.

CHARLOTTA: Shuffle the pack now. That's right. Give it here, my dear Mr. Pishchik. *Ein, zwei, drei!*[14] Now look for it—it's in your side pocket.

PISHCHIK (*taking the card out of his pocket*): The eight of spades! Perfectly right! Just imagine!

CHARLOTTA (*holding pack of cards in her hands. To* TROFIMOV): Quickly, name the top card.

TROFIMOV: Well, let's see—the queen of spades.

CHARLOTTA: Right! (*To* PISHCHIK) Now name the top card.

PISHCHIK: The ace of hearts.

CHARLOTTA: Right! (*Claps her hands and the pack of cards disappears*) Ah, what lovely weather it is today! (*A mysterious feminine voice which seems to come from under the floor, answers her*) "Oh, yes, it's magnificent weather, madam."

CHARLOTTA: You are my best ideal.

VOICE: "And I find you pleasing too, madam."

---

[12] Friedrich Nietzsche (1844-1900), German philosopher who held Christian ideals in contempt.

[13] A lively Caucasian dance in two-four time.

[14] One, two, three (German).

STATIONMASTER (*applauding*) : The lady ventriloquist, bravo!

PISHCHIK (*amazed*) : Just imagine! Enchanting Charlotta Ivanovna, I'm simply in love with you.

CHARLOTTA: In love? (*Shrugs her shoulders*) Are you capable of love? *Guter Mensch, aber schlechter Musikant!*[15]

TROFIMOV (*claps* PISHCHIK *on the shoulder*) : You old horse, you!

CHARLOTTA: Attention please! One more trick! (*Takes a plaid from a chair*) Here is a very good plaid; I want to sell it. (*Shaking it out*) Does anyone want to buy it?

PISHCHIK (*in amazement*) : Just imagine!

CHARLOTTA: *Ein, zwei, drei!* (*Raises the plaid quickly; behind it stands* ANYA. *She curtsies, runs to her mother, embraces her, and runs back into the ballroom, amidst general enthusiasm.*)

MME. RANEVSKAYA (*applauds*) : Bravo! Bravo!

CHARLOTTA: Now again! *Ein, zwei, drei!* (*Lifts the plaid; behind it stands* VARYA *bowing.*)

PISHCHIK (*running after her*) : The rascal! What a woman, what a woman! (*Exits.*)

MME. RANEVSKAYA: And Leonid still isn't here. What is he doing in town so long? I don't understand. It must be all over by now. Either the estate has been sold, or the auction hasn't taken place. Why keep us in suspense so long?

VARYA (*trying to console her*) : Uncle's bought it, I feel sure of that.

TROFIMOV (*mockingly*) : Oh, yes!

VARYA: Great-aunt sent him an authorization to buy it in her name, and to transfer the debt. She's doing it for Anya's sake. And I'm sure that God will help us, and uncle will buy it.

MME. RANEVSKAYA: Great-aunt sent fifteen thousand to buy the estate in her name; she doesn't trust us, but that's not even enough to pay the interest. (*Covers her face with her hands*) Today my fate will be decided, my fate—

TROFIMOV (*teasing* VARYA) : Madam Lopahina!

VARYA (*angrily*) : Perpetual student! Twice already you've been expelled from the university.

MME. RANEVSKAYA: Why are you so cross, Varya? He's teasing you about Lopahin. Well, what of it? If you want to marry Lopahin, go ahead. He's a good man, and interesting; if you don't want to, don't. Nobody's compelling you, my pet!

VARYA: Frankly, mamma dear, I take this thing seriously; he's a good man and I like him.

MME. RANEVSKAYA: All right then, marry him. I don't know what you're waiting for.

VARYA: But, mamma, I can't propose to him myself. For the last two years everyone's been talking to me about him—talking. But he either keeps silent, or else cracks jokes. I understand; he's growing rich, he's absorbed

---

[15] A better man, but a worse musician (German).

in business—he has no time for me. If I had money, even a little, say, 100 rubles, I'd throw everything up and go far away—I'd go into a nunnery.

TROFIMOV: What a blessing. . . .

VARYA: A student ought to be intelligent. (*Softly, with tears in her voice*) How homely you've grown, Petya! How old you look! (*To* MME. RANEVSKAYA, *with dry eyes*) But I can't live without work, mamma dear; I must keep busy every minute.

(*Enter* YASHA.)

YASHA (*hardly restraining his laughter*): Yepihodov has broken a billiard cue! (*Exits.*)

VARYA: Why is Yepihodov here? Who allowed him to play billiards? I don't understand these people! (*Exits.*)

MME. RANEVSKAYA: Don't tease her, Petya. She's unhappy enough without that.

TROFIMOV: She bustles so—and meddles in other people's business. All summer long she's given Anya and me no peace. She's afraid of a love-affair between us. What business is it of hers? Besides, I've given no grounds for it, and I'm far from such vulgarity. We are above love.

MME. RANEVSKAYA: And I suppose I'm beneath love? (*Anxiously*) What can be keeping Leonid? If I only knew whether the estate has been sold or not. Such a calamity seems so incredible to me that I don't know what to think—I feel lost. . . . I could scream. . . . I could do something stupid. . . . Save me, Petya, tell me something, talk to me!

TROFIMOV: Whether the estate is sold today or not, isn't it all one? That's all done with long ago—there's no turning back, the path is overgrown. Calm yourself, my dear. You mustn't deceive yourself. For once in your life you must face the truth.

MME. RANEVSKAYA: What truth? You can see the truth, you can tell it from falsehood, but I seem to have lost my eyesight, I see nothing. You settle every great problem so boldly, but tell me, my dear boy, isn't it because you're young, because you don't yet know what one of your problems means in terms of suffering? You look ahead fearlessly, but isn't it because you don't see and don't expect anything dreadful, because life is still hidden from your young eyes? You're bolder, more honest, more profound than we are, but think hard, show just a bit of magnanimity, spare me. After all, I was born here, my father and mother lived here, and my grandfather; I love this house. Without the cherry orchard, my life has no meaning for me, and if it really must be sold, then sell me with the orchard. (*Embraces* TROFIMOV, *kisses him on the forehead*) My son was drowned here. (*Weeps*) Pity me, you good, kind fellow!

TROFIMOV: You know, I feel for you with all my heart.

MME. RANEVSKAYA: But that should have been said differently, so differently! (*Takes out her handkerchief—a telegram falls on the floor*) My heart is so heavy today—you can't imagine! The noise here upsets me— my inmost being trembles at every sound—I'm shaking all over. But I can't go into my own room; I'm afraid to be alone. Don't condemn me, Petya. . . . I love you as though you were one of us, I would gladly let you marry Anya—I swear I would—only, my dear boy, you must study—you must take your degree—you do nothing, you let yourself be tossed by Fate from place to place—it's so strange. It's true, isn't it? And you should do something about your beard, to make it grow somehow! (*Laughs*) You're so funny!

TROFIMOV (*picks up the telegram*): I've no wish to be a dandy.

MME. RANEVSKAYA: That's a telegram from Paris. I get one every day. One yesterday and one today. That savage is ill again—he's in trouble again. He begs forgiveness, implores me to go to him, and really I ought to go to Paris to be near him. Your face is stern, Petya; but what is there to do, my dear boy? What am I to do? He's ill, he's alone and unhappy, and who is to look after him, who is to keep him from doing the wrong thing, who is to give him his medicine on time? And why hide it or keep still about it—I love him! That's clear. I love him, love him! He's a millstone round my neck, he'll drag me to the bottom, but I love that stone, I can't live without it. (*Presses* TROFIMOV's *hand*) Don't think badly of me, Petya, and don't say anything, don't say. . . .

TROFIMOV (*through tears*): Forgive me my frankness in heaven's name; but, you know, he robbed you!

MME. RANEVSKAYA: No, no, no, you mustn't say such things! (*Covers her ears.*)

TROFIMOV: But he's a scoundrel! You're the only one who doesn't know it. He's a petty scoundrel—a nonentity!

MME. RANEVSKAYA (*controlling her anger*): You are twenty-six or twenty-seven years old, but you're still a schoolboy.

TROFIMOV: That may be.

MME. RANEVSKAYA: You should be a man at your age. You should understand people who love—and ought to be in love yourself. You ought to fall in love! (*Angrily*) Yes, yes! And it's not purity in you, it's prudishness, you're simply a queer fish, a comical freak!

TROFIMOV (*horrified*): What is she saying?

MME. RANEVSKAYA: "I am above love!" You're not above love, but simply, as our Firs says, you're an addlehead. At your age not to have a mistress!

TROFIMOV (*horrified*): This is frightful! What is she saying! (*Goes rapidly into the ballroom, clutching his head*) It's frightful—I can't stand it, I won't stay! (*Exits, but returns at once*) All is over between us! (*Exits into anteroom.*)

MME. RANEVSKAYA (*shouts after him*): Petya! Wait! You absurd fellow, I was joking. Petya!

(*Sound of somebody running quickly downstairs and suddenly falling down with a crash.* ANYA *and* VARYA *scream. Sound of laughter a moment later.*)

MME. RANEVSKAYA: What's happened?

(ANYA *runs in.*)

ANYA (*laughing*): Petya's fallen downstairs! (*Runs out.*)

MME. RANEVSKAYA: What a queer bird that Petya is!

(STATIONMASTER, *standing in the middle of the ballroom, recites Alexey*

Tolstoy's "Magdalene,"[16] *to which all listen, but after a few lines, the sound of a waltz is heard from the anteroom and the reading breaks off. All dance.* TROFIMOV, ANYA, VARYA, *and* MME. RANEVSKAYA *enter from the anteroom.*)

MME. RANEVSKAYA: Petya, you pure soul, please forgive me. . . . Let's dance. (*Dances with* PETYA. ANYA *and* VARYA *dance.* FIRS *enters, puts his stick down by the side door.* YASHA *enters from the drawing-room and watches the dancers.*)

YASHA: Well, grandfather?

FIRS: I'm not feeling well. In the old days it was generals, barons, and admirals that were dancing at our balls, and now we have to send for the Post Office clerk and the Stationmaster, and even they aren't too glad to come. I feel kind of shaky. The old master that's gone, their grandfather, dosed everyone with sealing-wax, whatever ailed 'em. I've been taking sealing-wax every day for twenty years or more. Perhaps that's what's kept me alive.

YASHA: I'm fed up with you, grandpop. (*Yawns*) It's time you croaked.

FIRS: Oh, you addlehead! (*Mumbles.*)

(TROFIMOV *and* MME. RANEVSKAYA *dance from the ballroom into the drawing-room.*)

MME. RANEVSKAYA: *Merci.* I'll sit down a while. (*Sits down*) I'm tired. (*Enter* ANYA.)

ANYA (*excitedly*): There was a man in the kitchen just now who said the cherry orchard was sold today.

MME. RANEVSKAYA: Sold to whom?

ANYA: He didn't say. He's gone. (*Dances off with* TROFIMOV.)

YASHA: It was some old man gabbing, a stranger.

FIRS: And Leonid Andreyevich isn't back yet; he hasn't come. And he's wearing his lightweight between-season overcoat; like enough, he'll catch cold. Ah, when they're young they're green.

MME. RANEVSKAYA: This is killing me. Go, Yasha, find out to whom it has been sold.

YASHA: But the old man left long ago. (*Laughs.*)

MME. RANEVSKAYA: What are you laughing at? What are you pleased about?

YASHA: That Yepihodov is such a funny one. A funny fellow, Two-and-Twenty Troubles!

MME. RANEVSKAYA: Firs, if the estate is sold, where will you go?

FIRS: I'll go where you tell me.

MME. RANEVSKAYA: Why do you look like that? Are you ill? You ought to go to bed.

FIRS: Yes! (*With a snigger*) Me go to bed, and who's to hand things round? Who's to see to things? I'm the only one in the whole house.

YASHA (*to* MME. RANEVSKAYA): Lubov Andreyevna, allow me to ask a

---

[16] Count Leo Tolstoy (1828-1910), famous Russian novelist and author of *War and Peace*. Chekhov's choice of this poem is not entirely accidental.

favor of you, be so kind! If you go back to Paris, take me with you, I beg you. It's positively impossible for me to stay here. (*Looking around; sotto voce*[17]) What's the use of talking? You see for yourself, it's an uncivilized country, the people have no morals, and then the boredom! The food in the kitchen's revolting, and besides there's this Firs wanders about mumbling all sorts of inappropriate words. Take me with you, be so kind!

(*Enter* PISHCHIK.)

PISHCHIK: May I have the pleasure of a waltz with you, charming lady? (MME. RANEVSKAYA *accepts*) All the same, enchanting lady, you must let me have 180 rubles. . . . You must let me have (*dancing*) just one hundred and eighty rubles. (*They pass into the ballroom.*)

YASHA (*hums softly*): "Oh, wilt thou understand the tumult in my soul?" (*In the ballroom a figure in a gray top hat and checked trousers is jumping about and waving its arms; shouts:* "Bravo, Charlotta Ivanovna!")

DUNYASHA (*stopping to powder her face; to* FIRS): The young miss has ordered me to dance. There are so many gentlemen and not enough ladies. But dancing makes me dizzy, my heart begins to beat fast, Firs Nikolayevich. The Post Office clerk said something to me just now that quite took my breath away. (*Music stops.*)

FIRS: What did he say?

DUNYASHA: "You're like a flower," he said.

YASHA (*yawns*): What ignorance. (*Exits.*)

DUNYASHA: "Like a flower!" I'm such a delicate girl. I simply adore pretty speeches.

FIRS: You'll come to a bad end.

(*Enter* YEPIHODOV.)

YEPIHODOV (*to* DUNYASHA): You have no wish to see me, Avdotya Fyodorovna . . . as though I was some sort of insect. (*Sighs*) Ah, life!

DUNYASHA: What is it you want?

YEPIHODOV: Indubitably you may be right. (*Sighs*) But of course, if one looks at it from the point of view, if I may be allowed to say so, and apologizing for my frankness, you have completely reduced me to a state of mind. I know my fate. Every day some calamity befalls me, and I grew used to it long ago, so that I look upon my fate with a smile. You gave me your word, and though I—

DUNYASHA: Let's talk about it later, please. But just now leave me alone, I am daydreaming. (*Plays with a fan.*)

YEPIHODOV: A misfortune befalls me every day; and if I may be allowed to say so, I merely smile, I even laugh.

(*Enter* VARYA.)

VARYA (*to* YEPIHODOV): Are you still here? What an impertinent fellow you are really! Run along, Dunyasha. (*To* YEPIHODOV) Either you're playing billiards and breaking a cue, or you're wandering about the drawing-room as though you were a guest.

---

[17] In an undertone (Italian).

YEPIHODOV: You cannot, permit me to remark, penalize me.

VARYA: I'm not penalizing you; I'm just telling you. You merely wander from place to place, and don't do your work. We keep you as a clerk, but Heaven knows what for.

YEPIHODOV (*offended*): Whether I work or whether I walk, whether I eat or whether I play billiards, is a matter to be discussed only by persons of understanding and of mature years.

VARYA (*enraged*): You dare say that to me—you dare? You mean to say I've no understanding? Get out of here at once! This minute!

YEPIHODOV (*scared*): I beg you to express yourself delicately.

VARYA (*beside herself*): Clear out this minute! Out with you!

(YEPIHODOV *goes towards the door,* VARYA *following.*)

VARYA: Two-and-Twenty Troubles! Get out—don't let me set eyes on you! (*Exit* YEPIHODOV. *His voice is heard behind the door:* "I shall lodge a complaint against you!")

VARYA: Oh, you're coming back? (*She seizes the stick left near door by* FIRS) Well, come then . . . come . . . I'll show you . . . Ah, you're coming? You're coming? . . . Come. . . . (*Swings the stick just as* LOPAHIN *enters.*)

LOPAHIN: Thank you kindly.

VARYA (*angrily and mockingly*): I'm sorry.

LOPAHIN: It's nothing. Thank you kindly for your charming reception.

VARYA: Don't mention it. (*Walks away, looks back and asks softly*) I didn't hurt you, did I?

LOPAHIN: Oh, no, not at all. I shall have a large bump, though.

(*Voices from the ballroom:* "Lopahin is here! Lopahin!" *Enter* PISH-CHIK.)

PISHCHIK: My eyes do see, my ears do hear! (*Kisses* LOPAHIN.)

LOPAHIN: You smell of cognac, my dear friends. And we've been celebrating here, too.

(*Enter* MME. RANEVSKAYA.)

MME. RANEVSKAYA: Is that you, Yermolay Alexeyevich? What kept you so long? Where's Leonid?

LOPAHIN: Leonid Andreyevich arrived with me. He's coming.

MME. RANEVSKAYA: Well, what happened? Did the sale take place? Speak!

LOPAHIN (*embarrassed, fearful of revealing his joy*): The sale was over at four o'clock. We missed the train—had to wait till half past nine. (*Sighing heavily*) Ugh. I'm a little dizzy.

(*Enter* GAYEV. *In his right hand he holds parcels, with his left he is wiping away his tears.*)

MME. RANEVSKAYA: Well, Leonid? What news? (*Impatiently, through tears*) Be quick, for God's sake!

GAYEV (*not answering, simply waves his hand. Weeping, to* FIRS): Here, take these; anchovies, Kerch herrings. . . . I haven't eaten all day. What I've been through! (*The click of billiard balls comes through the open door of the billiard room and* YASHA'S *voice is heard:* "Seven and eighteen!" GAYEV'S *expression changes, he no longer weeps*) I'm terribly tired. Firs, help me change. (*Exits, followed by* FIRS.)

PISHCHIK: How about the sale? Tell us what happened.

MME. RANEVSKAYA: Is the cherry orchard sold?

LOPAHIN: Sold.

MME. RANEVSKAYA: Who bought it?

LOPAHIN: I bought it.

(*Pause.* MME. RANEVSKAYA *is overcome. She would fall to the floor, were it not for the chair and table near which she stands.* VARYA *takes the keys from her belt, flings them on the floor in the middle of the drawing-room and goes out.*)

LOPAHIN: I bought it. Wait a bit, ladies and gentlemen, please, my head is swimming, I can't talk. (*Laughs*) We got to the auction and Deriganov was there already. Leonid Andreyevich had only 15,000 and straight off Deriganov bid 30,000 over and above the mortgage. I saw how the land lay, got into the fight, bid 40,000. He bid 45,000. I bid fifty-five. He kept adding five thousands, I ten. Well . . . it came to an end. I bid ninety above the mortgage and the estate was knocked down to me. Now the cherry orchard's mine! Mine! (*Laughs uproariously*) Lord! God in Heaven! The cherry orchard's mine! Tell me that I'm drunk—out of my mind—that it's all a dream. (*Stamps his feet*) Don't laugh at me! If my father and my grandfather could rise from their graves and see all that has happened—how their Yermolay, who used to be flogged, their half-literate Yermolay, who used to run about barefoot in winter, how that very Yermolay has bought the most magnificent estate in the world. I bought the estate where my father and grandfather were slaves, where they weren't even allowed to enter the kitchen. I'm asleep—it's only a dream—I only imagine it. . . . It's the fruit of your imagination, wrapped in the darkness of the unknown! (*Picks up the keys, smiling genially*) She threw down the keys, wants to show she's no longer mistress here. (*Jingles keys*) Well, no matter. (*The band is heard tuning up*) Hey, musicians! Strike up! I want to hear you! Come, everybody, and see how Yermolay Lopahin will lay the ax to the cherry orchard and how the trees will fall to the ground. We will build summer cottages there, and our grandsons and great-grandsons will see a new life here. Music! Strike up!

(*The band starts to play.* MME. RANEVSKAYA *has sunk into a chair and is weeping bitterly.*)

LOPAHIN (*reproachfully*): Why, why didn't you listen to me? My dear friend, my poor friend, you can't bring it back now. (*Tearfully*) Oh, if only this were over quickly! Oh, if only our wretched, disordered life were changed!

PISHCHIK (*takes him by the arm; sotto voce*): She's crying. Let's go into the ballroom. Let her be alone. Come. (*Takes his arm and leads him into the ballroom.*)

LOPAHIN: What's the matter? Musicians, play so I can hear you! Let me have things the way I want them. (*Ironically*) Here comes the new master, the owner of the cherry orchard. (*Accidentally he trips over a little table, almost upsetting the candelabra*) I can pay for everything.

(*Exits with* PISHCHIK. MME. RANEVSKAYA, *alone, sits huddled up, weeping bitterly. Music plays softly. Enter* ANYA *and* TROFIMOV *quickly.* ANYA *goes to her mother and falls on her knees before her.* TROFIMOV *stands in the doorway.*)

ANYA: Mamma, mamma, you're crying! Dear, kind, good mamma, my precious, I love you, I bless you! The cherry orchard is sold, it's gone, that's true, quite true. But don't cry, mamma, life is still before you, you still have your kind, pure heart. Let us go, let us go away from here, darling. We will plant a new orchard, even more luxuriant than this one. You will see it, you will understand, and like the sun at evening, joy— deep, tranquil joy—will sink into your soul, and you will smile, mamma. Come, darling, let us go.

(*The Curtain Falls.*)

Act Four

Scene as in Act One. No window curtains or pictures, only a little furniture, piled up in a corner, as if for sale. A sense of emptiness. Near the outer door and at the back, suitcases, bundles, etc., are piled up. A door open on the left and the voices of VARYA *and* ANYA *are heard.* LOPAHIN *stands waiting.* YASHA *holds a tray with glasses full of champagne.* YEPI- HODOV *in the anteroom is tying up a box. Behind the scene a hum of voices: peasants have come to say good-by. Voice of* GAYEV: *"Thanks, brothers, thank you."*

YASHA: The country folk have come to say good-by. In my opinion, Yermo- lay Alexeyevich, they are kindly souls, but there's nothing in their heads. (*The hum dies away. Enter* MME. RANEVSKAYA *and* GAYEV. *She is not crying, but is pale, her face twitches and she cannot speak.*)

GAYEV: You gave them your purse, Luba. That won't do! That won't do!

MME. RANEVSKAYA: I couldn't help it! I couldn't! (*They go out.*)

LOPAHIN (*calls after them*): Please, I beg you, have a glass at parting. I didn't think of bringing any champagne from town and at the station I could find only one bottle. Please, won't you? (*Pause*) What's the matter, ladies and gentlemen, don't you want any? (*Moves away from the door*) If I'd known, I wouldn't have bought it. Well, then I won't drink any, either. (YASHA *carefully sets the tray down on a chair*) At least you have a glass, Yasha.

YASHA: Here's to the travelers! And good luck to those that stay! (*Drinks*) This champagne isn't the real stuff, I can assure you.

LOPAHIN: Eight rubles a bottle. (*Pause*) It's devilishly cold here.

YASHA: They didn't light the stoves today—it wasn't worth it, since we're leaving. (*Laughs.*)

LOPAHIN: Why are you laughing?

YASHA: It's just that I'm pleased.

LOPAHIN: It's October, yet it's as still and sunny as though it were summer. Good weather for building. (*Looks at his watch, and speaks off*) Bear in mind, ladies and gentlemen, the train goes in forty-seven minutes, so you ought to start for the station in twenty minutes. Better hurry up!

(*Enter* TROFIMOV *wearing an overcoat.*)

TROFIMOV: I think it's time to start. The carriages are at the door. The devil only knows what's become of my rubbers; they've disappeared. (*Calling off*) Anya! My rubbers are gone. I can't find them.

LOPAHIN: I've got to go to Kharkov. I'll take the same train you do. I'll spend the winter in Kharkov. I've been hanging round here with you, till I'm worn out with loafing. I can't live without work—I don't know what to do with my hands, they dangle as if they didn't belong to me.

TROFIMOV: Well, we'll soon be gone; then you can go on with your useful labors again.

LOPAHIN: Have a glass.

TROFIMOV: No, I won't.

LOPAHIN: So you're going to Moscow now?

TROFIMOV: Yes. I'll see them into town, and tomorrow I'll go on to Moscow.

LOPAHIN: Well, I'll wager the professors aren't giving any lectures; they're waiting for you to come.

TROFIMOV: That's none of your business.

LOPAHIN: Just how many years have you been at the university?

TROFIMOV: Can't you think of something new? Your joke's stale and flat. (*Looking for his rubbers*) We'll probably never see each other again, so allow me to give you a piece of advice at parting: don't wave your hands about! Get out of the habit. And another thing: building bungalows, figuring that summer residents will eventually become small farmers, figuring like that is just another form of waving your hands about. . . . Never mind, I love you anyway; you have fine, delicate fingers, like an artist; you have a fine, delicate soul.

LOPAHIN (*embracing him*): Good-by, my dear fellow. Thank you for everything. Let me give you some money for the journey, if you need it.

TROFIMOV: What for? I don't need it.

LOPAHIN: But you haven't any.

TROFIMOV: Yes, I have, thank you. I got some money for a translation—here it is in my pocket. (*Anxiously*) But where are my rubbers?

VARYA (*from the next room*): Here! Take the nasty things. (*Flings a pair of rubbers onto the stage.*)

TROFIMOV: What are you so cross about, Varya? Hm . . . and these are not my rubbers.

LOPAHIN: I sowed three thousand acres of poppies in the spring, and now I've made 40,000 on them, clear profit; and when my poppies were in bloom, what a picture it was! So, as I say, I made 40,000; and I am offering you a loan because I can afford it. Why turn up your nose at it? I'm a peasant—I speak bluntly.

TROFIMOV: Your father was a peasant, mine was a druggist—that proves absolutely nothing whatever. (LOPAHIN *takes out his wallet*) Don't, put that away! If you were to offer me two hundred thousand I wouldn't take it. I'm a free man. And everything that all of you, rich and poor alike, value so highly and hold so dear, hasn't the slightest power over me. It's like so much fluff floating in the air. I can get on without you, I can pass you by, I'm strong and proud. Mankind is moving towards the highest truth, towards the highest happiness possible on earth, and I am in the front ranks.

LOPAHIN: Will you get there?

TROFIMOV: I will. (*Pause*) I will get there, or I will show others the way to get there.

(*The sound of axes chopping down trees is heard in the distance.*)

LOPAHIN: Well, good-by, my dear fellow. It's time to leave. We turn up our noses at one another, but life goes on just the same. When I'm working hard, without resting, my mind is easier, and it seems to me that I too know why I exist. But how many people are there in Russia, brother, who exist nobody knows why? Well, it doesn't matter. That's not what makes the wheels go round. They say Leonid Andreyevich has taken a position in the bank, 6,000 rubles a year. Only, of course, he won't stick to it, he's too lazy. . . .

ANYA (*in the doorway*): Mamma begs you not to start cutting down the cherry trees until she's gone.

TROFIMOV: Really, you should have more tact! (*Exits.*)

LOPAHIN: Right away—right away! Those men. . . . (*Exits.*)

ANYA: Has Firs been taken to the hospital?

YASHA: I told them this morning. They must have taken him.

ANYA (*to* YEPIHODOV, *who crosses the room*): Yepihodov, please find out if Firs has been taken to the hospital.

YASHA (*offended*): I told Yegor this morning. Why ask a dozen times?

YEPIHODOV: The aged Firs, in my definitive opinion, is beyond mending. It's time he was gathered to his fathers. And I can only envy him. (*Puts a suitcase down on a hat-box and crushes it*) There now, of course. I knew it! (*Exits.*)

YASHA (*mockingly*): Two-and-Twenty Troubles!

VARYA (*through the door*): Has Firs been taken to the hospital?

ANYA: Yes.

VARYA: Then why wasn't the note for the doctor taken too?

ANYA: Oh! Then someone must take it to him. (*Exits.*)

VARYA (*from adjoining room*): Where's Yasha? Tell him his mother's come and wants to say good-by.

YASHA (*waves his hand*): She tries my patience.

(DUNYASHA *has been occupied with the luggage. Seeing* YASHA *alone, she goes up to him.*)

DUNYASHA: You might just give me one little look, Yasha. You're going away. . . . You're leaving me. . . . (*Weeps and throws herself on his neck.*)

YASHA: What's there to cry about? (*Drinks champagne*) In six days I shall be in Paris again. Tomorrow we get into an express train and off we go, that's the last you'll see of us. . . . I can scarcely believe it. *Vive la*

France! It don't suit me here, I just can't live here. That's all there is to it. I'm fed up with the ignorance here, I've had enough of it. (*Drinks champagne*) What's there to cry about? Behave yourself properly, and you'll have no cause to cry.

DUNYASHA (*powders her face, looking in pocket mirror*): Do send me a letter from Paris. You know I loved you, Yasha, how I loved you! I'm a delicate creature, Yasha.

YASHA: Somebody's coming! (*Busies himself with the luggage; hums softly.*) (*Enter* MME. RANEVSKAYA, GAYEV, ANYA, *and* CHARLOTTA.)

GAYEV: We ought to be leaving. We haven't much time. (*Looks at* YASHA) Who smells of herring?

MME. RANEVSKAYA: In about ten minutes we should be getting into the carriages. (*Looks around the room*) Good-by, dear old home, good-by, grandfather. Winter will pass, spring will come, you will no longer be here, they will have torn you down. How much these walls have seen! (*Kisses* ANYA *warmly*) My treasure, how radiant you look! Your eyes are sparkling like diamonds. Are you glad? Very?

ANYA (*gaily*): Very glad. A new life is beginning, mamma.

GAYEV: Well, really, everything is all right now. Before the cherry orchard was sold, we all fretted and suffered; but afterwards, when the question was settled finally and irrevocably, we all calmed down, and even felt quite cheerful. I'm a bank employee now, a financier. The yellow ball in the side pocket! And anyhow, you are looking better, Luba; there's no doubt of that.

MME. RANEVSKAYA: Yes, my nerves are better, that's true. (*She is handed her hat and coat*) I sleep well. Carry out my things, Yasha. It's time. (*To* ANYA) We shall soon see each other again, my little girl. I'm going to Paris, I'll live there on the money your great-aunt sent us to buy the estate with—long live Auntie! But that money won't last long.

ANYA: You'll come back soon, soon, mamma, won't you? Meanwhile I'll study, I'll pass my high school examination, and then I'll go to work and help you. We'll read all kinds of books together, mamma, won't we? (*Kisses her mother's hands*) We'll read in the autumn evenings, we'll read lots of books, and a new wonderful world will open up before us. (*Falls into a revery*) Mamma, do come back.

MME. RANEVSKAYA: I will come back, my precious. (*Embraces her daughter. Enter* LOPAHIN *and* CHARLOTTA, *who is humming softly.*)

GAYEV: Charlotta's happy: she's singing.

CHARLOTTA (*picks up a bundle and holds it like a baby in swaddling-clothes*): Bye, baby, bye. (*A baby is heard crying* "Wah! Wah!") Hush, hush, my pet, my little one. "Wah! Wah!" I'm so sorry for you! (*Throws the bundle down*) You will find me a position, won't you? I can't go on like this.

LOPAHIN: We'll find one for you, Charlotta Ivanovna, don't worry.

GAYEV: Everyone's leaving us. Varya's going away. We've suddenly become of no use.

CHARLOTTA: There's no place for me to live in town; I must go away. (*Hums.*)

(*Enter* PISHCHIK.)

LOPAHIN: There's nature's masterpiece!

PISHCHIK (*gasping*): Oh . . . let me get my breath . . . I'm in agony. . . . Esteemed friends . . . Give me a drink of water. . . .

GAYEV: Wants some money, I suppose. No, thank you . . . I'll keep out of harm's way. (*Exits.*)

PISHCHIK: It's a long while since I've been to see you, most charming lady. (*To* LOPAHIN) So you are here . . . glad to see you, you intellectual giant . . . There. . . . (*Gives* LOPAHIN *money*) Here's 400 rubles, and I still owe you 840.

LOPAHIN (*shrugging his shoulders in bewilderment*): I must be dreaming. . . . Where did you get it?

PISHCHIK: Wait a minute. . . . It's hot. . . . A most extraordinary event! Some Englishmen came to my place and found some sort of white clay on my land. . . . (*To* MME. RANEVSKAYA) And 400 for you . . . most lovely . . . most wonderful. . . . (*Hands her the money*) The rest later. (*Drinks water*) A young man in the train was telling me just now that a great philosopher recommends jumping off roofs. "Jump!" says he; "that's the long and the short of it!" (*In amazement*) Just imagine! Some more water!

LOPAHIN: What Englishmen?

PISHCHIK: I leased them the tract with the clay on it for twenty-four years. . . . And now, forgive me, I can't stay. . . . I must be dashing on. . . . I'm going over to Znoikov . . . to Kardamanov. . . . I owe them all money. . . . (*Drinks water*) Good-by, everybody. . . . I'll look in on Thursday. . . .

MME. RANEVSKAYA: We're just moving into town; and tomorrow I go abroad.

PISHCHIK (*upset*): What? Why into town? That's why the furniture is like that . . . and the suitcases. . . . Well, never mind! (*Through tears*) Never mind. . . . Men of colossal intellect, these Englishmen. . . . Never mind. . . . Be happy. God will come to your help. . . . Never mind. . . . Everything in this world comes to an end. (*Kisses* MME. RANEVSKAYA'S *hand*) If the rumor reaches you that it's all up with me, remember this old . . . horse, and say: Once there lived a certain . . . Simeonov-Pishchik . . . the kingdom of Heaven be his . . . Glorious weather! . . . Yes. . . . (*Exits, in great confusion, but at once returns and says in the doorway*) My daughter Dashenka sends her regards. (*Exit.*)

MME. RANEVSKAYA: Now we can go. I leave with two cares weighing on me. The first is poor old Firs. (*Glancing at her watch*) We still have about five minutes.

ANYA: Mamma, Firs has already been taken to the hospital. Yasha sent him there this morning.

MME. RANEVSKAYA: My other worry is Varya. She's used to getting up early and working; and now, with no work to do, she is like a fish out of water. She has grown thin and pale, and keeps crying, poor soul. (*Pause*) You know this very well, Yermolay Alexeyevich; I dreamed of seeing her married to you, and it looked as though that's how it would be. (*Whispers to* ANYA, *who nods to* CHARLOTTA, *and both go out*) She loves you. You find her attractive. I don't know, I don't know why it is you seem to avoid each other; I can't understand it.

LOPAHIN: To tell you the truth, I don't understand it myself. It's all a puzzle. If there's still time, I'm ready now, at once. Let's settle it straight off, and have done with it! Without you, I feel I'll never be able to propose.

MME. RANEVSKAYA: That's splendid. After all, it will only take a minute. I'll call her at once. . . .

LOPAHIN: And luckily, here's champagne too. (*Looks at the glasses*) Empty! Somebody's drunk it all. (YASHA *coughs*) That's what you might call guzzling. . . .

MME. RANEVSKAYA (*animatedly*): Excellent! We'll go and leave you alone. Yasha, *allez!*[18] I'll call her. (*At the door*) Varya, leave everything and come here. Come! (*Exits with* YASHA.)

LOPAHIN (*looking at his watch*): Yes. . . . (*Pause behind the door, smothered laughter and whispering; at last, enter* VARYA.)

VARYA (*looking over the luggage in leisurely fashion*): Strange, I can't find it. . . .

LOPAHIN: What are you looking for?

VARYA: Packed it myself, and I don't remember. . . . (*Pause.*)

LOPAHIN: Where are you going now, Varya?

VARYA: I? To the Ragulins'. I've arranged to take charge there—as housekeeper, if you like.

LOPAHIN: At Yashnevo? About fifty miles from here. (*Pause*) Well, life in this house is ended!

VARYA (*examining luggage*): Where is it? Perhaps I put it in the chest. Yes, life in this house is ended. . . . There will be no more of it.

LOPAHIN: And I'm just off to Kharkov—by this next train. I've a lot to do there. I'm leaving Yepihodov here. . . . I've taken him on.

VARYA: Oh!

LOPAHIN: Last year at this time it was snowing, if you remember, but now it's sunny and there's no wind. It's cold, though. . . . It must be three below.

VARYA: I didn't look. (*Pause*) And besides, our thermometer's broken. (*Pause. Voice from the yard:* "Yermolay Alexeyevich!")

LOPAHIN (*as if he had been waiting for the call*): This minute! (*Exit quickly.* VARYA *sits on the floor and sobs quietly, her head on a bundle of clothes. Enter* MME. RANEVSKAYA *cautiously.*)

MME. RANEVSKAYA: Well? (*Pause*) We must be going.

VARYA (*wiping her eyes*): Yes, it's time, mamma dear. I'll be able to get to the Ragulins' today, if only we don't miss the train.

MME. RANEVSKAYA (*at the door*): Anya, put your things on. (*Enter* ANYA, GAYEV, CHARLOTTA. GAYEV *wears a heavy overcoat with a hood. Enter servants and coachmen.* YEPIHODOV *bustles about the luggage.*)

MME. RANEVSKAYA: Now we can start on our journey.

ANYA (*joyfully*): On our journey!

---

[18] Go (French).

GAYEV: My friends, my dear, cherished friends, leaving this house forever, can I be silent? Can I at leave-taking refrain from giving utterance to those emotions that now fill my being?

ANYA (*imploringly*): Uncle!

VARYA: Uncle, uncle dear, don't.

GAYEV (*forlornly*): I'll bank the yellow in the side pocket. . . . I'll be silent. . . .

(*Enter* TROFIMOV, *then* LOPAHIN.)

TROFIMOV: Well, ladies and gentlemen, it's time to leave.

LOPAHIN: Yepihodov, my coat.

MME. RANEVSKAYA: I'll sit down just a minute. It seems as though I'd never before seen what the walls of this house were like, the ceilings, and now I look at them hungrily, with such tender affection.

GAYEV: I remember when I was six years old sitting on that window sill on Whitsunday,[19] watching my father going to church.

MME. RANEVSKAYA: Has everything been taken?

LOPAHIN: I think so. (*Putting on his overcoat*) Yepihodov, see that everything's in order.

YEPIHODOV (*in a husky voice*): You needn't worry, Yermolay Alexeyevich.

LOPAHIN: What's the matter with your voice?

YEPIHODOV: I just had a drink of water. I must have swallowed something.

YASHA (*contemptuously*): What ignorance!

MME. RANEVSKAYA: When we're gone, not a soul will be left here.

LOPAHIN: Until the spring.

(VARYA *pulls an umbrella out of a bundle, as though about to hit someone with it.* LOPAHIN *pretends to be frightened.*)

VARYA: Come, come, I had no such idea!

TROFIMOV: Ladies and gentlemen, let's get into the carriages—it's time. The train will be in directly.

VARYA: Petya, there they are, your rubbers, by that trunk. (*Tearfully*) And what dirty old things they are!

TROFIMOV (*puts on rubbers*): Let's go, ladies and gentlemen.

GAYEV (*greatly upset, afraid of breaking down*): The train . . . the station. . . . Three cushions in the side pocket, I'll bank this one in the corner. . . .

MME. RANEVSKAYA: Let's go.

LOPAHIN: Are we all here? No one in there? (*Locks the side door on the left*) There are some things stored here, better lock up. Let us go!

ANYA: Good-by, old house! Good-by, old life!

TROFIMOV: Hail to you, new life!

(*Exit with* ANYA. VARYA *looks round the room and goes out slowly.* YASHA *and* CHARLOTTA *with her dog go out.*)

LOPAHIN: And so, until the spring. Go along, friends. . . . 'Bye-'bye! (*Exits.*)

(MME. RANEVSKAYA *and* GAYEV *remain alone. As though they had been waiting for this, they throw themselves on each other's necks, and break into subdued, restrained sobs, afraid of being overheard.*)

---

[19] The seventh Sunday after Easter, or Pentecost. A Christian festival which celebrates the descent of the Holy Spirit on the Apostles.

GAYEV (*in despair*): My sister! My sister!

MME. RANEVSKAYA: Oh, my orchard—my dear, sweet, beautiful orchard! My life, my youth, my happiness—good-by! Good-by! (*Voice of* ANYA, *gay and summoning:* "Mamma!" *Voice of* TROFIMOV, *gay and excited:* "Halloo!")

MME. RANEVSKAYA: One last look at the walls, at the windows. . . . Our poor mother loved to walk about this room. . . .

GAYEV: My sister, my sister! (*Voice of* ANYA: "Mamma!" *Voice of* TROFIMOV: "Halloo!")

MME. RANEVSKAYA: We're coming.

(*They go out. The stage is empty. The sound of doors being locked, of carriages driving away. Then silence. In the stillness is heard the muffled sound of the ax striking a tree, a mournful, lonely sound.*

Footsteps are heard. FIRS *appears in the doorway on the right. He is dressed as usual in a jacket and white waistcoat and wears slippers. He is ill.*)

FIRS (*goes to the door, tries the handle*): Locked! They've gone. . . . (*Sits down on the sofa*) They've forgotten me. . . . Never mind. . . . I'll sit here a bit. . . . I'll wager Leonid Andreyevich hasn't put his fur coat on; he's gone off in his light overcoat. . . . (*Sighs anxiously*) I didn't keep an eye on him. . . . Ah, when they're young, they're green. . . . (*Mumbles something indistinguishable*) Life has gone by as if I had never lived. (*Lies down*) I'll lie down a while. . . . There's no strength left in you, old fellow; nothing is left, nothing. Ah, you addlehead! (*Lies motionless. A distant sound is heard coming from the sky as it were, the sound of a snapping string mournfully dying away. All is still again, and nothing is heard but the strokes of the ax against a tree far away in the orchard.*)

(*The Curtain Falls.*)

Commentary

Reading Shaw, we perceive that the dramatist is firmly convinced of the right answers to the moral problems he presents, even if his characters are not. In Chekhov there is no sense of assurance. Like the world of Ibsen's *Rosmersholm*, the world Chekhov creates is so psychologically complex that one wonders if there *are* any final answers. If there are, Chekhov makes no claims to knowing them, but instead seems only to say, "This is what it feels like to live in this kind of world; this is the way these people are."

Nor does Chekhov use plot for Shavian comic intrigue or for Ibsen's and O'Neill's character entanglements. It is as difficult to define the plot conflict of *The Cherry Orchard* as it is that of *The Glass Menagerie,* a play which resembles Chekhov's drama in many ways. Virtually no suspense is created. The answer to the question "Will the cherry orchard be sold?" is obviously "Yes." Mme. Ranevskaya and Gayev absolutely refuse to consider Lopahin's proposal, which is the only possible solution. "Poppycock!" exclaims Gayev indignantly (p. 292), and Mme. Ranevskaya considers cottages and summer people "so vulgar" (p. 300). Indeed they accept the sale as inevitable when in the first act (p. 294) Gayev says, "Yes, and the orchard will be sold to pay our debts, strange as it may seem. . . ." Nor are the love affairs getting anywhere at all. Lopahin simply refuses to the very end to pop the long awaited question to Varya. Trofimov repeatedly announces, "We're above love" (pp. 305 and 309). Dunyasha, whom Yepihodov wants to marry, confesses that she is passionately in love with Yasha, but he retorts, ". . . if a girl loves someone, it means she is immoral" (p. 299). Francis Fergusson defines Chekhov's plot technique as a selection of ". . . only those incidents, those moments in his characters' lives, between their rationalized efforts, when they sense their situation and destiny most directly. So he contrives to show the action of the play as a whole—the unsuccessful attempt to cling to the cherry orchard—in many diverse reflectors and without propounding any thesis about it."[20]

Chekhov implies that the self-absorption and impracticality of the old order, symbolized by the cherry orchard, have doomed it to destruction in the face of cultural and economic changes that the aristocracy can cope with no longer. Trapped in the decaying way of life that produced them, the charming Mme. Ranevskaya and the utterly impractical Gayev hope that the impossible will occur to save them: "It would be fine if we came in for a legacy; it would be fine if we married off our Anya to a very rich man; or we might go to Yaroslavl and try our luck with our aunt, the Countess" (p. 295). Yet they both realize that these dreams are merely wishful thinking, and so they passively await the inevitable.

The structural unity of *The Cherry Orchard* is stronger and more significant than that of the conventionally realistic narrative plot. The play is a drama of conflicting attitudes toward the central symbol, the cherry orchard. "Each character," as Fergusson says, "sees some value in it—economic, sentimental, social, cultural—which he wishes to keep."[21] Hence the orchard is not simply a piece of property around which cluster nostalgic memories; it is a symbol of various ways of life. As the focal center of the play, it brings into coherence the sharp split between the

---

[20] Francis Fergusson, *The Idea of a Theater* (New York, 1953), p. 175.
[21] *Ibid.,* p. 176.

old attitudes toward life, primarily cultural and sentimental, and the new economic and social values replacing them. The play opens with the new order, best seen in Lopahin. He is acutely aware of his peasant upbringing and his newly acquired position as a wealthy merchant, yet, he says, "I am a peasant through and through" (p. 285). Later he points out the recent change in the class structure of this society and optimistically predicts a future in which villa residents will prosperously cultivate their small plots of land. The housemaid Dunyasha is also affecting upper-class ways. Lopahin chides her for dressing above her station in life. She puts on the grand act of a refined and sensitive lady whenever the occasion presents itself, as, for example, when she flutters, "I'm going to faint this minute," until she realizes that Lopahin has gone to greet Mme. Ranevskaya and will not catch her if she collapses. Firs, on the other hand, reminisces in a world of his own about his life as head footman before the emancipation, which he calls "the calamity."

The clashing ways of life in a changing society, first dramatized by the contrast between Firs on the one hand and Lopahin and Dunyasha on the other, can be seen in all the characters. Yasha and Trofimov also are members of the new order. Yasha, who repudiates his mother, begs Mme. Ranevskaya to take him back to the gaiety of Paris because he cannot tolerate the dullness and barbarism of Russian society. Trofimov is shocked at the brutal treatment the serfs received and summarizes his position clearly (p. 305): "We're at least two hundred years behind, we've really achieved nothing yet, we have no definite attitude to the past, we only philosophize, complain of the blues, or drink vodka. It's all so clear: in order to live in the present, we should first redeem our past, finish with it. . . ." Along with Firs, Mme. Ranevskaya and her brother Gayev best represent the old order now in decay. Dreaming of a dead past, both are incapable of positive action to prevent the destruction of the last remnants of their life. Gayev calls himself a man of the 80s and maintains *noblesse oblige* as his standard of political conduct. Nor can Varya face the world realistically; she dreams of marrying Anya off to some rich man so that she may travel blissfully through Russia, visiting holy shrines. Pishchik can do nothing but hope that miracles will continue to save him from ruin. Yepihodov cannot decide whether to live or to shoot himself and so carries a revolver around with him to be ready for any contingency. Anya is the only hope of this decadent society, for she has confidence in the future. On page 305 she says to Trofimov: "The house in which we live has long ceased to be our own, and I will leave it, I give you my word," and in Act Four she tells her mother that she is very happy because a new life is beginning for them.

It would grossly distort the subtle fabric of Chekhov's play to emphasize too sharply this cleavage between old and new, past and future. Because *The Cherry Orchard*, like *The Glass Menagerie*, is a play of delicate shadings and nuances of mood, not a drama of ideas, Chekhov has not hesitated to sacrifice realism in order to focus attention on atmosphere. Note, for example, his symbolic stage direction on page 303: "Suddenly a distant sound is heard, coming from the sky as it were, the sound of a snapping string, mournfully dying away." Like Williams, Chekhov uses original theatrical effects to heighten the emotional qualities, the symbolic implications, the inner essence of a scene. Note especially the dramatic contribution made in both plays by lighting and music.

The complex and ambivalent moods are quickly established by Mme. Ranevskaya's arrival home. Her first line is spoken "joyfully, through her tears" (p. 286). Throughout, characters laugh and weep simultaneously. But it is important not to overlook the subtitle: *A Comedy in Four Acts*. Chekhov himself, upset when the Moscow Art Theater emphasized the tragic, wrote the director's wife, Mme. Stanislavsky, that *The Cherry Orchard* was "not a drama, but a comedy, sometimes even a farce. . . . The last act is gay, the whole play is gay, light." Yepihodov's entrance on page 285, for instance, is burlesqued: he comes squeaking noisily into the room, dropping his nosegay as he does so. He finds his misfortunes "absolutely phenomenal" and triumphantly proves his point by accidentally crashing into a chair. Many stage directions are sheer vaudeville. Mme. Ranevskaya's grand entrance is straight out of the circus. With tremendous furor she and her entourage come parading onto the stage complete with luggage, bag, umbrella, and dog. Charlotta's first remark to Pishchik — "My dog eats nuts, too" — continues the comic tone, as does the cordial greeting Yasha gives Dunyasha. Lopahin's bleat shatters the pathos that is beginning to develop in the first act. His way of making love is pure farce. Pishchik's falling asleep and snoring in the middle of his remarks, his gulping down all of Mme. Ranevskaya's pills with a swallow of beer, and Gayev's dramatic speech in honor of the centennial of the bookcase are just three more ways of establishing the comedy of Act One.

On the other hand, the tears must not be overlooked. Sentimental as she may seem, Mme. Ranevskaya is genuinely glad to return to her home. Her homesickness has been acute. Firs is deeply moved that he may again serve his beloved mistress before he dies. The first indication of a serious turn to Act One comes with Lopahin's announcement that the date of the sale of the orchard has been fixed. Later, as Varya, Mme. Ranevskaya, and Gayev look out upon the orchard in full bloom, the vague, romantic atmosphere and their nostalgia and sentimentality make for quiet melancholy. Trofimov's entrance adds a note of pathos because he reminds them all of the untimely death of little Grisha. The act draws to a close at a slow, drowsy pace.

The second act begins with a tone of meditation, which is given an amusing twist when Charlotta begins to munch on her cucumber. The self-centeredness of the characters is clearly seen here, for all the conversations are soliloquies. The people seem to talk in parallel lines, never getting their discussions onto the same topic or paying the slightest attention to what anyone else is saying. Such a tendency was earlier dramatized by the deaf Firs, whose answers are usually far afield of the topic under discussion (p. 290):

MME. RANEVSKAYA: I'm so happy that you're still alive.
FIRS: Day before yesterday.

Act Two moves toward a melancholy ending with the distant sound of the breaking string. The long silences effectively contribute to this mood. The atmosphere found at the end of Act One is again felt here, as indeed it is in the final moments of each act. The comedy is played down, and a calm, pensive mood is achieved with Yepihodov's playing a mournful song on his guitar as the moon rises over the horizon. Against this setting of quiet romantic beauty, Trofimov sees happiness only as an ideal.

In the beginning of Act Three the mood shifts again to the comic. The fact that Mme. Ranevskaya picks the day of the sale to hold her dance shows how little she really understands what is happening to her way of life. At first the sale is treated very casually. Anya announces that somebody in the kitchen has said the cherry orchard has been sold, but she has forgotten to ask to whom; and then she blithely dances out of the room. When Gayev comes in, he is interested only in his anchovies and Kerch herrings, and he departs without having responded to his sister's impatient pleadings. (Point out in this act repeated use of the techniques of burlesque encountered early in Act One.) Charlotta's magic and ventriloquist acts, the stationmaster's interrupted recitation of a poem by Tolstoy, and, most important, the background music and dancing all contribute to the gaiety and pleasant excitement. With the crushing realization that Lopahin has bought the orchard, Mme. Ranevskaya nearly collapses with grief. The dance music from the drawing room plays softly in ironic counterpoint to her bitter weeping as Anya naively and touchingly consoles her mother.

In Act Four comedy is played down but not eliminated, for Yepihodov, true to form, manages to crush a bandbox, Yasha downs the entire supply of champagne, and Lopahin squirms out of a marital trap carefully laid by Mme. Ranevskaya. Also both Gayev and his sister admit that, now their fate has irrevocably been decided, they are much calmer and happier. The audience genuinely regrets their sorrow and defeat — an attitude made even more intense by the highly effective and symbolic curtain scene. The cold, dark, empty stage picks up the lonely echoes of the axe and the mournful sound of the breaking string as the old order makes way for the new. Forgotten because of the thoughtless bungling of those to whom he is most devoted, Firs, too, prepares for the future.

Although Chekhov's attitude is a subtle blend of pity and amusement over the Russian character and his country's social and economic changes, he is still coolly objective in his portrayal of character. Consequently, the failings of each person are exposed and laughed at good-naturedly. Even Trofimov, who does say some things that Chekhov would probably agree with, tends at times to be a caricature. His rhetorical outbursts on the doctrine of work cannot be taken too seriously because the man has never worked in his life, whereas his theory on man with a hundred senses is utter nonsense. Lopahin, the practical businessman, with his comic bleat and his terror of matrimony, is also laughed at. Absorbed in themselves, unable to fit into the practical world, the muddled, silly, good-humored aristocrats both irritate and amuse us. They are ridiculous people with highly romantic egos and extremely volatile moods. Gayev, with his billiard routine and candy-munching, is just one example. His love for the histrionic leads him into some absurd performances, such as his declamation on nature and his final farewell to the old homestead. Yet he engages our affections because he, like Mme. Ranevskaya, is aware of his foibles. He admits with embarrassment the stupidity of his speech over a bookcase. Chekhov does, however, show a sympathetic understanding of his characters' problems. Even Trofimov succumbs when Mme. Ranevskaya entreats, ". . . show just a bit of magnanimity, spare me. After all, I was born here, my father and mother lived here, and my grandfather; I love this house. Without the cherry orchard, my life has no meaning for me . . ." (p. 309).

What life without the cherry orchard will be, Chekhov does not say, for the action of his drama is complete. All efforts to save the orchard have been doomed to failure from the beginning, and the characters arrive only to depart. Have they learned from suffering? Have they come to a new awareness of themselves, or their society, or their future? Do they recognize their responsibility for the fate that has befallen them? Like all great art, *The Cherry Orchard* provides, in T. S. Eliot's words, only "hints and guesses, hints followed by guesses"; the rest is hidden in the inscrutable silences that pervade Chekhov's masterpiece.

Questions and Problems

1. How are Lopahin's stick and watch symbols of two facets of his personality? What does Gayev's fondness for candy and billiards tell us about him? What facets of other characters are illuminated through the use of props?
2. What make-up should Trofimov wear? How would you costume the characters?

3. How do the pace at the opening of Act Two and the props of the cucumber and the revolver contribute to the mood?

4. The characters in *The Cherry Orchard* are extraordinarily aware of words, voices, and talking. Trace this poetic motif from the final moments of Act One through Act Two. What is Chekhov suggesting by such a pattern of language?

5. Since Chekhov leaves the arrangement of the set in Act Three almost completely up to the director, how would you set the stage for this act? Draw ground plans for the act.

6. Chekhov often presents moments of great emotion indirectly through the exchange of trivia and irrelevant small talk. Analyze the final conversation between Lopahin and Varya as one example. What similar moments are there in the play?

7. Take any minor character, such as Yasha, and discuss (1) what he contributes to the play; and (2) how you would play the part, particularly when you have nothing to say.

8. Analyze in detail the pace and tempo of each act of *The Cherry Orchard,* accounting for all significant changes.

9. Evaluate in detail the final moments of the play, beginning with Lubov and Gayev's farewell, as an example of Chekhov's brilliant use of symbol, pace, character, setting, dialogue, and tone. How does the family's failure to remember Firs bring to a final focus our ambivalent attitudes toward them? Why is it dramatically appropriate that the old retainer should be left behind, alone and forgotten? Does he die?

10. To what extent is Jim O'Connor in *The Glass Menagerie* like Lopahin?

11. One critic says that a theme of *The Cherry Orchard* is "the destruction of beauty by those who are utterly blind to it."[22] Discuss. Does this idea occur also in *The Glass Menagerie?*

12. Most of the characters in *The Cherry Orchard* are daydreamers. What do their dreams reveal about themselves and their view of the world as it ought to be? Mme. Ranevskaya, like Amanda in *The Glass Menagerie,* longs for an idealized, dreamlike past. What do their vanished worlds have in common?

13. It has been suggested that the structure of each act is built on some sort of social ceremony. What is it? What is Chekhov's artistic purpose in making use of such an organization? How does the structure of *The Glass Menagerie* bear a resemblance to that of *The Cherry Orchard?* Why is it appropriate that it should?

---

[22] David Magarshack, *Chekhov the Dramatist* (London, 1952), p. 274.

ARTHUR MILLER

A View from the Bridge

Biography

ARTHUR MILLER was born in New York City in 1915, the son of a prosperous manufacturer who had come to the United States from Austria as a young boy. "I passed through the public school system unscathed," he has said. After graduating from a Brooklyn high school in 1932, he worked during the depression in a Tenth Avenue warehouse in Manhattan. Riding to work on the subway, he read Dostoyevski's *The Brothers Karamazov*, "a book that changed my life." It was then that Miller decided that he would become a writer, and he entered the University of Michigan in 1934. While there, he was awarded the Avery Hopwood Prize for his play *The Grass Still Grows* and in 1938 the Theatre Guild National Award. During the years following graduation from college he wrote radio script for the Federal Theatre Project. Rejected for military service in World War II for physical reasons, Miller worked for a time in the Brooklyn Navy Yard.

Miller's first play on Broadway, *The Man Who Had All the Luck*, appeared in 1944, but despite the title the playwright had none. Three years later, however, *All My Sons* received the Drama Critics' Circle Award and the Pulitzer Prize, honors again won in 1949 by *Death of a Salesman*. *A View from the Bridge*, which failed on Broadway in 1955 as a one-act drama, was extensively revised and had a successful run in London in 1957 as a full-length play. All of Miller's major plays have been made into movies. *The Crucible* was adapted in a French version by Jean-Paul Sartre, and *A View from the Bridge* was produced by a French motion picture company in 1962. Miller wrote the screenplay of his second book, *The Misfits*, which was Clark Gable's last movie and co-starred Marilyn Monroe, Miller's former wife. The title came from his introduction to the original version of *A View from the Bridge*, published in 1955: "Our society — and I am speaking of every industrialized society in the world — is so complex, each person being so specialized an integer, that the moment any individual is dramatically characterized and set forth as a hero, our common sense reduces him to the size of a complainer, a misfit."[1]

Influenced by Ibsen and O'Neill, as well as by Dostoyevski, Miller

---

[1] Arthur Miller, *A View from the Bridge* (New York, 1955), p. 8.

331

is often called the foremost writer of social drama today. For Miller social drama is "the drama of the whole man. It seeks to deal with his differences from others not *per se,* but toward the end that, if only through drama, we may know how much the same we are, for if we lose that knowledge we shall have nothing left at all. The social drama to me is only incidentally an arraignment of society." Social drama, writes Miller, must ultimately concern itself with the ancient question, "how are we to live?"[2]

Works

PLAYS

All My Sons (1947)

Death of a Salesman (1949)

An Enemy of the People (1950)
  (an adaptation from Ibsen)

The Crucible (1953)

A Memory of Two Mondays (1955)

A View from the Bridge (1955)

NOVELS

Focus (1945)

The Misfits (a revision of a screenplay) (1961)

REPORTAGE

Situation Normal (1944)

Selected Descriptive Bibliography

Driver, Tom F., "Strength and Weakness in Arthur Miller," *Tulane Drama Review,* IV (May, 1960), 45-52.
    Driver presents his view of Miller's psychological and social strengths and his ontological weaknesses by discussing Miller's Introduction to his Collected Plays.

Eissenstat, Martha Turnquist, "Arthur Miller: A Bibliography," *Modern Drama,* V (May, 1962), 93-106.
    The most extensive Bibliography compiled on Miller.

---

[2] *Ibid.,* p. 7.

Miller, Arthur, *Collected Plays*, New York, 1957.
Miller's Introduction provides both significant comment on his plays and interesting views on the nature of modern drama.

————, "The Family in Modern Drama," *The Atlantic*, CXCVII (April, 1956), 35-41.
Miller evaluates the place of realism in modern drama.

————, "Morality and Modern Drama," *Educational Theatre Journal*, X (October, 1958), 190-202.
The transcript of an unrehearsed radio interview in which Miller asserts the moral affirmations in modern drama.

————, "On Social Plays," *A View from the Bridge* (New York, 1955), pp. 1-15.
This Introduction to the original version of A View from the Bridge *is one of the most important of Miller's essays, arguing that a dramatist must be aware of the moral and social problems of his time.*

————, "The Playwright and the Atomic World," *Tulane Drama Review*, V (June, 1961), 3-20.
Miller surveys American cultural attitudes from an international perspective, but there is more here about the atomic world than about the playwright.

————, "The Shadow of the Gods," *Harper's*, CCXVII (August, 1958), 35-43.
Miller discusses the impact of his reading during the depression and comments on the limitations of much of today's drama.

Popkin, Henry, "Arthur Miller: the Strange Encounter," *Sewanee Review*, LXVIII (Winter, 1960), 34-60.
Popkin analyzes with penetrating insight some of the recurrent themes in Miller's dramas.

Welland, Dennis, *Arthur Miller*, New York, 1962.
A helpful little biography with a survey of Miller's literary output.

Wiegand, William, "Arthur Miller and the Man Who Knows," *The Western Review*, XXI (Winter, 1957), 85-102.
Wiegand traces the later development of several of Miller's major themes out of his earliest works.

A View from the Bridge ARTHUR MILLER

CHARACTERS

LOUIS
MIKE } *longshoremen*

ALFIERI, *a lawyer*

EDDIE CARBONE, *a longshoreman*

CATHERINE, *his niece*

BEATRICE, *his wife*

MARCO, *Beatrice's cousin*

TONY, *a longshoreman*

RODOLPHO, *Marco's young brother*

FIRST IMMIGRATION OFFICER

SECOND IMMIGRATION OFFICER

MR. LIPARI, *the neighborhood butcher*

MRS. LIPARI, *his wife*

TWO "SUBMARINES"

NEIGHBORS

The New York première of *A View from the Bridge* was held at the Coronet Theatre on September 29, 1955; the London première on October 11, 1956.

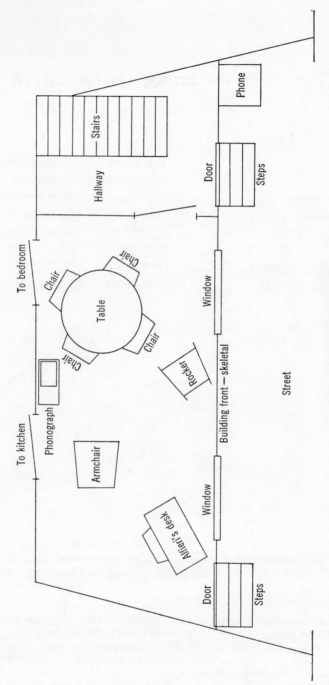

A VIEW FROM THE BRIDGE

Act One

*The street and house front of a tenement building. The front is
skeletal entirely. The main acting area is the living room-dining room of*
EDDIE's *apartment. It is a worker's flat, clean, sparse, homely. There is
a rocker down front; a round dining table at center, with chairs; and a
portable phonograph.*

*At back are a bedroom door and an opening to the kitchen; none
of these interiors are seen.*

At the right, forestage, a desk. This is MR. ALFIERI's *law office.*

*There is also a telephone booth. This is not used until the last scenes,
so it may be covered or left in view.*

*A stairway leads up to the apartment, and then farther up to the
next story, which is not seen.*

Ramps, representing the street, run upstage and off to right and left.

As the curtain rises, LOUIS *and* MIKE, *longshoremen, are pitching
coins against the building at left.*

A distant foghorn blows.

Enter ALFIERI, *a lawyer in his fifties turning gray; he is portly, good-
humored, and thoughtful. The two pitchers nod to him as he passes. He
crosses the stage to his desk, removes his hat, runs his fingers through his
hair, and grinning, speaks to the audience.*

ALFIERI: You wouldn't have known it, but something amusing has just
happened. You see how uneasily they nod to me? That's because I am
a lawyer. In this neighborhood to meet a lawyer or a priest on the street
is unlucky. We're only thought of in connection with disasters, and they'd
rather not get too close.

I often think that behind that suspicious little nod of theirs lie three
thousand years of distrust. A lawyer means the law, and in Sicily, from
where their fathers came, the law has not been a friendly idea since the
Greeks were beaten.

I am inclined to notice the ruins in things, perhaps because I was
born in Italy. . . . I only came here when I was twenty-five. In those

days, Al Capone,[3] the greatest Carthaginian of all, was learning his trade on these pavements, and Frankie Yale[4] himself was cut precisely in half by a machine gun on the corner of Union Street, two blocks away. Oh, there were many here who were justly shot by unjust men. Justice is very important here.

But this is Red Hook, not Sicily. This is the slum that faces the bay on the seaward side of Brooklyn Bridge. This is the gullet of New York swallowing the tonnage of the world. And now we are quite civilized, quite American. Now we settle for half, and I like it better. I no longer keep a pistol in my filing cabinet.

And my practice is entirely unromantic.

My wife has warned me, so have my friends; they tell me the people in this neighborhood lack elegance, glamour. After all, who have I dealt with in my life? Longshoremen and their wives, and fathers and grandfathers, compensation cases, evictions, family squabbles — the petty troubles of the poor — and yet . . . every few years there is still a case, and as the parties tell me what the trouble is, the flat air in my office suddenly washes in with the green scent of the sea, the dust in this air is blown away and the thought comes that in some Caesar's year, in Calabria[5] perhaps or on the cliff at Syracuse,[6] another lawyer, quite differently dressed, heard the same complaint and sat there as powerless as I, and watched it run its bloody course.

(EDDIE *has appeared and has been pitching coins with the men and is highlighted among them. He is forty — a husky, slightly overweight longshoreman*)

This one's name was Eddie Carbone, a longshoreman working the docks from Brooklyn Bridge to the breakwater where the open sea begins.

(ALFIERI *walks into darkness.*)

EDDIE (*moving up steps into doorway*) : Well, I'll see ya, fellas.

(CATHERINE *enters from kitchen, crosses down to window, looks out.*)

LOUIS : You workin' tomorrow?

EDDIE : Yeah, there's another day yet on that ship. See ya, Louis.

(EDDIE *goes into the house, as light rises in the apartment.* CATHERINE *is waving to* LOUIS *from the window and turns to him.*)

CATHERINE : Hi, Eddie!

(EDDIE *is pleased and therefore shy about it; he hangs up his cap and jacket.*)

EDDIE : Where you goin' all dressed up?

CATHERINE (*running her hands over her skirt*) : I just got it. You like it?

EDDIE : Yeah, it's nice. And what happened to your hair?

---

[3] Al ("Scarface Al") Capone (1899-1947) was the head of the Torrio gang in Chicago during the late 1920s and the 1930s.

[4] Frankie Yale (or Uale) was a Brooklyn underworld leader who was shot to death on July 1, 1928. He was buried in a silver casket after a funeral which cost $52,000.

[5] Territory in the southern extremity of Italy. Its fertile coastal strip produces wine, olive oil, oranges, lemons, and figs.

[6] A city situated on the east coast of Sicily.

CATHERINE: You like it? I fixed it different. (*Calling to kitchen*) He's here, B.!

EDDIE: Beautiful. Turn around, lemme see in the back. (*She turns for him*) Oh, if your mother was alive to see you now! She wouldn't believe it.

CATHERINE: You like it, huh?

EDDIE: You look like one of them girls that went to college. Where you goin'?

CATHERINE (*taking his arm*): Wait'll B. comes in, I'll tell you something. Here, sit down. (*She is walking him to the armchair. Calling offstage*) Hurry up, will you, B.?

EDDIE (*sitting*): What's goin' on?

CATHERINE: I'll get you a beer, all right?

EDDIE: Well, tell me what happened. Come over here, talk to me.

CATHERINE: I want to wait till B. comes in. (*She sits on her heels beside him*) Guess how much we paid for the skirt.

EDDIE: I think it's too short, ain't it?

CATHERINE (*standing*): No! not when I stand up.

EDDIE: Yeah, but you gotta sit down sometimes.

CATHERINE: Eddie, it's the style now. (*She walks to show him*) I mean, if you see me walkin' down the street—

EDDIE: Listen, you been givin' me the willies the way you walk down the street, I mean it.

CATHERINE: Why?

EDDIE: Catherine, I don't want to be a pest, but I'm tellin' you you're walkin' wavy.

CATHERINE: I'm walkin' wavy?

EDDIE: Now don't aggravate me, Katie, you are walkin' wavy! I don't like the looks they're givin' you in the candy store. And with them new high heels on the sidewalk — clack, clack, clack. The heads are turnin' like windmills.

CATHERINE: But those guys look at all the girls, you know that.

EDDIE: You ain't "all the girls."

CATHERINE (*almost in tears because he disapproves*): What do you want me to do? You want me to —

EDDIE: Now don't get mad, kid.

CATHERINE: Well, I don't know what you want from me.

EDDIE: Katie, I promised your mother on her deathbed. I'm responsible for you. You're a baby, you don't understand these things. I mean like when you stand here by the window, wavin' outside.

CATHERINE: I was wavin' to Louis!

EDDIE: Listen, I could tell you things about Louis which you wouldn't wave to him no more.

CATHERINE (*trying to joke him out of his warning*): Eddie, I wish there was one guy you couldn't tell me things about!

EDDIE: Catherine, do me a favor, will you? You're gettin' to be a big girl now, you gotta keep yourself more, you can't be so friendly, kid. (*Calls*) Hey, B., what're you doin' in there? (*To* CATHERINE) Get her in here, will you? I got news for her.

CATHERINE (*starting out*) : What?

EDDIE : Her cousins landed.

CATHERINE (*clapping her hands together*): No! (*She turns instantly and starts for the kitchen*) B.! Your cousins!

(BEATRICE *enters, wiping her hands with a towel.*)

BEATRICE (*in the face of* CATHERINE'S *shout*) : What?

CATHERINE: Your cousins got in!

BEATRICE (*astounded, turns to* EDDIE) : What are you talkin' about? Where?

EDDIE: I was just knockin' off work before and Tony Bereli come over to me; he says the ship is in the North River.

BEATRICE (*Her hands are clasped at her breast; she seems half in fear, half in unutterable joy*) : They're all right?

EDDIE: He didn't see them yet, they're still on board. But as soon as they get off he'll meet them. He figures about ten o'clock they'll be here.

BEATRICE (*sits, almost weak from tension*) : And they'll let them off the ship all right? That's fixed, heh?

EDDIE: Sure, they give them regular seamen papers and they walk off with the crew. Don't worry about it, B., there's nothin' to it. Couple of hours they'll be here.

BEATRICE: What happened? They wasn't supposed to be till next Thursday.

EDDIE: I don't know; they put them on any ship they can get them out on. Maybe the other ship they was supposed to take there was some danger— What you cryin' about?

BEATRICE (*astounded and afraid*) : I'm— I just—I can't believe it! I didn't even buy a new tablecloth; I was gonna wash the walls—

EDDIE: Listen, they'll think it's a millionaire's house compared to the way they live. Don't worry about the walls. They'll be thankful. (*To* CATHERINE) Whyn't you run down buy a tablecloth. Go ahead, here. (*He is reaching into his pocket.*)

CATHERINE: There's no stores open now.

EDDIE (*to* BEATRICE) : You was gonna put a new cover on the chair.

BEATRICE: I know—well, I thought it was gonna be next week! I was gonna clean the walls, I was gonna wax the floors. (*She stands disturbed.*)

CATHERINE (*pointing upward*) : Maybe Mrs. Dondero upstairs—

BEATRICE (*of the tablecloth*) : No, hers is worse than this one. (*Suddenly*) My God, I don't even have nothin' to eat for them! (*She starts for the kitchen.*)

EDDIE (*reaching out and grabbing her arm*) : Hey, hey! Take it easy.

BEATRICE: No, I'm just nervous, that's all. (*To* CATHERINE) I'll make the fish.

EDDIE: You're savin' their lives, what're you worryin' about the tablecloth? They probably didn't see a tablecloth in their whole life where they come from.

BEATRICE (*looking into his eyes*) : I'm just worried about you, that's all I'm worried.

EDDIE: Listen, as long as they know where they're gonna sleep.

BEATRICE: I told them in the letters. They're sleepin' on the floor.

EDDIE: Beatrice, all I'm worried about is you got such a heart that I'll end up on the floor with you, and they'll be in our bed.

BEATRICE: All right, stop it.

EDDIE: Because as soon as you see a tired relative, I end up on the floor.

BEATRICE: When did you end up on the floor?

EDDIE: When your father's house burned down I didn't end up on the floor?

BEATRICE: Well, their house burned down!

EDDIE: Yeah, but it didn't keep burnin' for two weeks!

BEATRICE: All right, look, I'll tell them to go someplace else. (*She starts into the kitchen.*)

EDDIE: Now wait a minute. Beatrice! (*She halts. He goes to her*) I just don't want you bein' pushed around, that's all. You got too big a heart. (*He touches her hand*) What're you so touchy?

BEATRICE: I'm just afraid if it don't turn out good you'll be mad at me.

EDDIE: Listen, if everybody keeps his mouth shut, nothin' can happen. They'll pay for their board.

BEATRICE: Oh, I told them.

EDDIE: Then what the hell. (*Pause. He moves*) It's an honor, B. I mean it. I was just thinkin' before, comin' home, suppose my father didn't come to this country, and I was starvin' like them over there . . . and I had people in America could keep me a couple of months? The man would be honored to lend me a place to sleep.

BEATRICE (*There are tears in her eyes. She turns to* CATHERINE): You see what he is? (*She turns and grabs* EDDIE'S *face in her hands*) Mmm! You're an angel! God'll bless you. (*He is gratefully smiling*) You'll see, you'll get a blessing for this!

EDDIE (*laughing*): I'll settle for my own bed.

BEATRICE: Go, Baby, set the table.

CATHERINE: We didn't tell him about me yet.

BEATRICE: Let him eat first, then we'll tell him. Bring everything in. (*She hurries* CATHERINE *out.*)

EDDIE (*sitting at the table*): What's all that about? Where's she goin'?

BEATRICE: Noplace. It's very good news, Eddie. I want you to be happy.

EDDIE: What's goin' on?

(CATHERINE *enters with plates, forks.*)

BEATRICE: She's got a job.

(*Pause.* EDDIE *looks at* CATHERINE, *then back to* BEATRICE.)

EDDIE: What job? She's gonna finish school.

CATHERINE: Eddie, you won't believe it—

EDDIE: No—no, you gonna finish school. What kinda job, what do you mean? All of a sudden you—

CATHERINE: Listen a minute, it's wonderful.

EDDIE: It's not wonderful. You'll never get nowheres unless you finish school. You can't take no job. Why didn't you ask me before you take a job?

BEATRICE: She's askin' you now, she didn't take nothin' yet.

CATHERINE: Listen a minute! I came to school this morning and the principal called me out of the class, see? To go to his office.

EDDIE: Yeah?

CATHERINE: So I went in and he says to me he's got my records, y'know? And there's a company wants a girl right away. It ain't exactly a secretary, it's a stenographer first, but pretty soon you get to be secretary. And he says to me that I'm the best student in the whole class—

BEATRICE: You hear that?

EDDIE: Well why not? Sure she's the best.

CATHERINE: I'm the best student, he says, and if I want, I should take the job and the end of the year he'll let me take the examination and he'll give me the certificate. So I'll save practically a year!

EDDIE (*strangely nervous*): Where's the job? What company?

CATHERINE: It's a big plumbing company over Nostrand Avenue.

EDDIE: Nostrand Avenue and where?

CATHERINE: It's someplace by the Navy Yard.

BEATRICE: Fifty dollars a week, Eddie.

EDDIE (*to* CATHERINE, *surprised*): Fifty?

CATHERINE: I swear.

(*Pause.*)

EDDIE: What about all the stuff you wouldn't learn this year, though?

CATHERINE: There's nothin' more to learn, Eddie, I just gotta practice from now on. I know all the symbols and I know the keyboard. I'll just get faster, that's all. And when I'm workin' I'll keep gettin' better and better, you see?

BEATRICE: Work is the best practice anyway.

EDDIE: That ain't what I wanted, though.

CATHERINE: Why! It's a great big company—

EDDIE: I don't like that neighborhood over there.

CATHERINE: It's a block and half from the subway, he says.

EDDIE: Near the Navy Yard plenty can happen in a block and a half. And a plumbin' company! That's one step over the water front. They're practically longshoremen.

BEATRICE: Yeah, but she'll be in the office, Eddie.

EDDIE: I know she'll be in the office, but that ain't what I had in mind.

BEATRICE: Listen, she's gotta go to work sometime.

EDDIE: Listen, B., she'll be with a lotta plumbers? And sailors up and down the street? So what did she go to school for?

CATHERINE: But it's fifty a week, Eddie.

EDDIE: Look, did I ask you for money? I supported you this long I support you a little more. Please, do me a favor, will ya? I want you to be with different kind of people. I want you to be in a nice office. Maybe a lawyer's office someplace in New York in one of them nice buildings. I mean if you're gonna get outa here then get out; don't go practically in the same kind of neighborhood.

(*Pause.* CATHERINE *lowers her eyes.*)

BEATRICE: Go, Baby, bring in the supper. (CATHERINE *goes out*) Think about it a little bit, Eddie. Please. She's crazy to start work. It's not a little shop, it's a big company. Some day she could be a secretary. They picked her out of the whole class. (*He is silent, staring down at the tablecloth, fingering the pattern*) What are you worried about? She could take care of herself. She'll get out of the subway and be in the office in two minutes.

EDDIE (*somehow sickened*) : I know that neighborhood, B., I don't like it.

BEATRICE : Listen, if nothin' happened to her in this neighborhood it ain't gonna happen noplace else. (*She turns his face to her*) Look, you gotta get used to it, she's no baby no more. Tell her to take it. (*He turns his head away*) You hear me? (*She is angering*) I don't understand you; she's seventeen years old, you gonna keep her in the house all her life?

EDDIE (*insulted*) : What kinda remark is that?

BEATRICE (*with sympathy but insistent force*) : Well, I don't understand when it ends. First it was gonna be when she graduated high school, so she graduated high school. Then it was gonna be when she learned stenographer, so she learned stenographer. So what're we gonna wait for now? I mean it, Eddie, sometimes I don't understand you; they picked her out of the whole class, it's an honor for her.

(CATHERINE *enters with food, which she silently sets on the table. After a moment of watching her face,* EDDIE *breaks into a smile, but it almost seems that tears will form in his eyes.*)

EDDIE : With your hair that way you look like a madonna, you know that? You're the madonna type. (*She doesn't look at him, but continues ladling out food onto the plates*) You wanna go to work, heh, Madonna?

CATHERINE (*softly*) : Yeah.

EDDIE (*with a sense of her childhood, her babyhood, and the years*) : All right, go to work. (*She looks at him, then rushes and hugs him*) Hey, hey! Take it easy! (*He holds her face away from him to look at her*) What're you cryin' about? (*He is affected by her, but smiles his emotion away.*)

CATHERINE (*sitting at her place*) : I just—(*Bursting out*) I'm gonna buy all new dishes with my first pay! (*They laugh warmly*) I mean it. I'll fix up the whole house! I'll buy a rug!

EDDIE : And then you'll move away.

CATHERINE : No, Eddie!

EDDIE (*grinning*) : Why not? That's life. And you'll come visit on Sundays, then once a month, then Christmas and New Year's, finally.

CATHERINE (*grasping his arm to reassure him and to erase the accusation*) : No, please!

EDDIE (*smiling but hurt*) : I only ask you one thing—don't trust nobody. You got a good aunt but she's got too big a heart, you learned bad from her. Believe me.

BEATRICE : Be the way you are, Katie, don't listen to him.

EDDIE (*to* BEATRICE—*strangely and quickly resentful*) : You lived in a house all your life, what do you know about it? You never worked in your life.

BEATRICE : She likes people. What's wrong with that?

EDDIE : Because most people ain't people. She's goin' to work; plumbers; they'll chew her to pieces if she don't watch out. (*To* CATHERINE) Believe me, Katie, the less you trust, the less you be sorry.

(EDDIE *crosses himself and the women do the same, and they eat.*)

CATHERINE : First thing I'll buy is a rug, heh, B.?

BEATRICE : I don't mind. (*To* EDDIE) I smelled coffee all day today. You unloadin' coffee today?

EDDIE : Yeah, a Brazil ship.

CATHERINE: I smelled it too. It smelled all over the neighborhood.

EDDIE: That's one time, boy, to be a longshoreman is a pleasure. I could work coffee ships twenty hours a day. You go down in the hold, y'know? It's like flowers, that smell. We'll bust a bag tomorrow, I'll bring you some.

BEATRICE: Just be sure there's no spiders in it, will ya? I mean it. (*She directs this to* CATHERINE, *rolling her eyes upward*) I still remember that spider coming out of that bag he brung home. I nearly died.

EDDIE: You call that a spider? You oughta see what comes outa the bananas sometimes.

BEATRICE: Don't talk about it!

EDDIE: I seen spiders could stop a Buick.

BEATRICE (*clapping her hands over her ears*): All right, shut up!

EDDIE (*laughing and taking a watch out of his pocket*): Well, who started with spiders?

BEATRICE: All right, I'm sorry, I didn't mean it. Just don't bring none home again. What time is it?

EDDIE: Quarter nine. (*Puts watch back in his pocket.*)

(*They continue eating in silence.*)

CATHERINE: He's bringin' them ten o'clock, Tony?

EDDIE: Around, yeah. (*He eats.*)

CATHERINE: Eddie, suppose somebody asks if they're livin' here. (*He looks at her as though already she had divulged something publicly. Defensively*) I mean if they ask.

EDDIE: Now look, Baby, I can see we're gettin' mixed up again here.

CATHERINE: No, I just mean . . . people'll see them goin' in and out.

EDDIE: I don't care who sees them goin' in and out as long as you don't see them goin' in and out. And this goes for you too, B. You don't see nothin' and you don't know nothin'.

BEATRICE: What do you mean? I understand.

EDDIE: You don't understand; you still think you can talk about this to somebody just a little bit. Now lemme say it once and for all, because you're makin' me nervous again, both of you. I don't care if somebody comes in the house and sees them sleepin' on the floor, it never comes out of your mouth who they are or what they're doin' here.

BEATRICE: Yeah, but my mother'll know—

EDDIE: Sure she'll know, but just don't you be the one who told her, that's all. This is the United States government you're playin' with now, this is the Immigration Bureau. If you said it you knew it, if you didn't say it you didn't know it.

CATHERINE: Yeah, but Eddie, suppose somebody—

EDDIE: I don't care what question it is. You—don't—know—nothin'. They got stool pigeons all over this neighborhood they're payin' them every week for information, and you don't know who they are. It could be your best friend. You hear? (*To* BEATRICE) Like Vinny Bolzano, remember Vinny?

BEATRICE: Oh, yeah. God forbid.

EDDIE: Tell her about Vinny. (*To* CATHERINE) You think I'm blowin' steam here? (*To* BEATRICE) Go ahead, tell her. (*To* CATHERINE) You was a baby then. There was a family lived next door to her mother, he was about sixteen—

BEATRICE: No, he was no more than fourteen, 'cause I was to his confirmation in Saint Agnes. But the family had an uncle that they were hidin' in the house, and he snitched to the Immigration.

CATHERINE: The kid snitched?

EDDIE: On his own uncle!

CATHERINE: What, was he crazy?

EDDIE: He was crazy after, I tell you that, boy.

BEATRICE: Oh, it was terrible. He had five brothers and the old father. And they grabbed him in the kitchen and pulled him down the stairs—three flights his head was bouncin' like a coconut. And they spit on him in the street, his own father and his brothers. The whole neighborhood was cryin'.

CATHERINE: Ts! So what happened to him?

BEATRICE: I think he went away. (*To* EDDIE) I never seen him again, did you?

EDDIE (*rises during this, taking out his watch*): Him? You'll never see him no more, a guy do a thing like that? How's he gonna show his face? (*To* CATHERINE, *as he gets up uneasily*) Just remember, kid, you can quicker get back a million dollars that was stole than a word that you gave away. (*He is standing now, stretching his back.*)

CATHERINE: Okay, I won't say a word to nobody, I swear.

EDDIE: Gonna rain tomorrow. We'll be slidin' all over the decks. Maybe you oughta put something on for them, they be here soon.

BEATRICE: I only got fish, I hate to spoil it if they ate already. I'll wait, it only takes a few minutes; I could broil it.

CATHERINE: What happens, Eddie, when that ship pulls out and they ain't on it, though? Don't the captain say nothin'?

EDDIE (*slicing an apple with his pocket knife*): Captain's pieced off, what do you mean?

CATHERINE: Even the captain?

EDDIE: What's the matter, the captain don't have to live? Captain gets a piece, maybe one of the mates, piece for the guy in Italy who fixed the papers for them, Tony here'll get a little bite. . . .

BEATRICE: I just hope they get work here, that's all I hope.

EDDIE: Oh, the syndicate'll fix jobs for them; till they pay 'em off they'll get them work every day. It's after the pay-off, then they'll have to scramble like the rest of us.

BEATRICE: Well, it be better than they got there.

EDDIE: Oh sure, well, listen. So you gonna start Monday, heh, Madonna?

CATHERINE (*embarrassed*): I'm supposed to, yeah.

(EDDIE *is standing facing the two seated women. First* BEATRICE *smiles, then* CATHERINE, *for a powerful emotion is on him, a childish one and a knowing fear, and the tears show in his eyes—and they are shy before the avowal.*)

EDDIE (*sadly smiling, yet somehow proud of her*): Well . . . I hope you have good luck. I wish you the best. You know that, kid.

CATHERINE (*rising, trying to laugh*) : You sound like I'm goin' a million miles!

EDDIE: I know. I guess I just never figured on one thing.

CATHERINE (*smiling*) : What?

EDDIE: That you would ever grow up. (*He utters a soundless laugh at himself, feeling his breast pocket of his shirt*) I left a cigar in my other coat, I think. (*He starts for the bedroom.*)

CATHERINE: Stay there! I'll get it for you.

(*She hurries out. There is a slight pause, and* EDDIE *turns to* BEATRICE, *who has been avoiding his gaze.*)

EDDIE: What are you mad at me lately?

BEATRICE: Who's mad? (*She gets up, clearing the dishes*) I'm not mad. (*She picks up the dishes and turns to him*) You're the one is mad. (*She turns and goes into the kitchen as* CATHERINE *enters from the bedroom with a cigar and a pack of matches.*)

CATHERINE: Here! I'll light it for you! (*She strikes a match and holds it to his cigar. He puffs. Quietly*) Don't worry about me, Eddie, heh?

EDDIE: Don't burn yourself. (*Just in time she blows out the match*) You better go in help her with the dishes.

CATHERINE (*turns quickly to the table, and, seeing the table cleared, she says, almost guiltily*) : Oh! (*She hurries into the kitchen, and as she exits there*) I'll do the dishes, B.!

(*Alone,* EDDIE *stands looking toward the kitchen for a moment. Then he takes out his watch, glances at it, replaces it in his pocket, sits in the armchair, and stares at the smoke flowing out of his mouth.*

The lights go down, then come up on ALFIERI, *who has moved onto the forestage.*)

ALFIERI: He was as good a man as he had to be in a life that was hard and even. He worked on the piers when there was work, he brought home his pay, and he lived. And toward ten o'clock of that night, after they had eaten, the cousins came.

(*The lights fade on* ALFIERI *and rise on the street. Enter* TONY, *escorting* MARCO *and* RODOLPHO, *each with a valise.* TONY *halts, indicates the house. They stand for a moment looking at it.*)

MARCO (*He is a square-built peasant of thirty-two, suspicious, tender, and quiet-voiced*) : Thank you.

TONY: You're on your own now. Just be careful, that's all. Ground floor.

MARCO: Thank you.

TONY (*indicating the house*) : I'll see you on the pier tomorrow. You'll go to work.

(MARCO *nods.* TONY *continues on walking down the street.*)

RODOLPHO: This will be the first house I ever walked into in America! Imagine! She said they were poor!

MARCO: Ssh! Come. (*They go to door.*)

(MARCO *knocks. The lights rise in the room.* EDDIE *goes and opens the door. Enter* MARCO *and* RODOLPHO, *removing their caps.* BEATRICE *and* CATHERINE *enter from the kitchen. The lights fade in the street.*)

EDDIE: You Marco?

MARCO: Marco.

EDDIE: Come on in! (*He shakes* MARCO'S *hand.*)

BEATRICE: Here, take the bags!

MARCO (*nods, looks to the women and fixes on* BEATRICE. *Crosses to* BEA-TRICE): Are you my cousin?

(*She nods. He kisses her hand.*)

BEATRICE (*above the table, touching her chest with her hand*): Beatrice. This is my husband, Eddie. (*All nod*) Catherine, my sister Nancy's daughter. (*The brothers nod.*)

MARCO (*indicating* RODOLPHO): My brother. Rodolpho. (RODOLPHO *nods.* MARCO *comes with a certain formal stiffness to* EDDIE) I want to tell you now Eddie—when you say go, we will go.

EDDIE: Oh, no . . . (*Takes* MARCO'S *bag.*)

MARCO: I see it's a small house, but soon, maybe, we can have our own house.

EDDIE: You're welcome, Marco, we got plenty of room here. Katie, give them supper, heh? (*Exits into bedroom with their bags.*)

CATHERINE: Come here, sit down. I'll get you some soup.

MARCO (*as they go to the table*): We ate on the ship. Thank you. (*To* EDDIE, *calling off to bedroom*) Thank you.

BEATRICE: Get some coffee. We'll all have coffee. Come sit down.

(RODOLPHO *and* MARCO *sit, at the table.*)

CATHERINE (*wondrously*): How come he's so dark and you're so light, Rodolpho?

RODOLPHO (*ready to laugh*): I don't know. A thousand years ago, they say, the Danes invaded Sicily.

(BEATRICE *kisses* RODOLPHO. *They laugh as* EDDIE *enters.*)

CATHERINE (*to* BEATRICE): He's practically blond!

EDDIE: How's the coffee doin'?

CATHERINE (*brought up*): I'm gettin' it. (*She hurries out to kitchen.*)

EDDIE (*sits on his rocker*): Yiz have a nice trip?

MARCO: The ocean is always rough. But we are good sailors.

EDDIE: No trouble gettin' here?

MARCO: No. The man brought us. Very nice man.

RODOLPHO (*to* EDDIE): He says we start to work tomorrow. Is he honest?

EDDIE (*laughing*): No. But as long as you owe them money, they'll get you plenty of work. (*To* MARCO) Yiz ever work on the piers in Italy?

MARCO: Piers? Ts!—no.

RODOLPHO (*smiling at the smallness of his town*): In our town there are no piers, only the beach, and little fishing boats.

BEATRICE: So what kinda work did yiz do?

MARCO (*shrugging shyly, even embarrassed*): Whatever there is, anything.

RODOLPHO: Sometimes they build a house, or if they fix the bridge—Marco is a mason and I bring him the cement. (*He laughs*) In harvest time we work in the fields . . . if there is work. Anything.

EDDIE: Still bad there, heh?

MARCO: Bad, yes.

RODOLPHO (*laughing*): It's terrible! We stand around all day in the piazza listening to the fountain like birds. Everybody waits only for the train.

BEATRICE: What's on the train?

RODOLPHO: Nothing. But if there are many passengers and you're lucky you make a few lire[7] to push the taxi up the hill.

(*Enter* CATHERINE; *she listens.*)

BEATRICE: You gotta push a taxi?

RODOLPHO (*laughing*): Oh, sure! It's a feature in our town. The horses in our town are skinnier than goats. So if there are too many passengers we help to push the carriages up to the hotel. (*He laughs*) In our town the horses are only for show.

CATHERINE: Why don't they have automobile taxis?

RODOLPHO: There is one. We push that too. (*They laugh*) Everything in our town, you gotta push!

BEATRICE (*to* EDDIE): How do you like that!

EDDIE (*to* MARCO): So what're you wanna do, you gonna stay here in this country or you wanna go back?

MARCO (*surprised*): Go back?

EDDIE: Well, you're married, ain't you?

MARCO: Yes. I have three children.

BEATRICE: Three! I thought only one.

MARCO: Oh, no. I have three now. Four years, five years, six years.

BEATRICE: Ah . . . I bet they're cryin' for you already, heh?

MARCO: What can I do? The older one is sick in his chest. My wife—she feeds them from her own mouth. I tell you the truth, if I stay there they will never grow up. They eat the sunshine.

BEATRICE: My God. So how long you want to stay?

MARCO: With your permission, we will stay maybe a—

EDDIE: She don't mean in this house, she means in the country.

MARCO: Oh. Maybe four, five, six years, I think.

RODOLPHO (*smiling*): He trusts his wife.

BEATRICE: Yeah, but maybe you'll get enough, you'll be able to go back quicker.

MARCO: I hope. I don't know. (*To* EDDIE) I understand it's not so good here either.

EDDIE: Oh, you guys'll be all right—till you pay them off, anyway. After that, you'll have to scramble, that's all. But you'll make better here than you could there.

RODOLPHO: How much? We hear all kinds of figures. How much can a man make? We work hard, we'll work all day, all night—

(MARCO *raises a hand to hush him.*)

EDDIE (*He is coming more and more to address* MARCO *only*): On the average a whole year? Maybe—well, it's hard to say, see. Sometimes we lay off, there's no ships three four weeks.

---

[7] The monetary unit and a coin of Italy, equal to 100 centesimi, and valued at less than a cent.

MARCO: Three, four weeks!—Ts!

EDDIE: But I think you could probably—thirty, forty a week, over the whole twelve months of the year.

MARCO (*rises, crosses to* EDDIE): Dollars.

EDDIE: Sure dollars.

(MARCO *puts an arm round* RODOLPHO *and they laugh.*)

MARCO: If we can stay here a few months, Beatrice—

BEATRICE: Listen, you're welcome, Marco—

MARCO: Because I could send them a little more if I stay here.

BEATRICE: As long as you want, we got plenty a room.

MARCO (*His eyes are showing tears*): My wife— (*To* EDDIE) My wife—I want to send right away maybe twenty dollars—

EDDIE: You could send them something next week already.

MARCO (*He is near tears*): Eduardo . . . (*He goes to* EDDIE, *offering his hand.*)

EDDIE: Don't thank me. Listen, what the hell, it's no skin off me. (*To* CATHERINE) What happened to the coffee?

CATHERINE: I got it on. (*To* RODOLPHO) You married too? No.

RODOLPHO (*rises*): Oh, no . . .

BEATRICE (*to* CATHERINE): I told you he—

CATHERINE: I know, I just thought maybe he got married recently.

RODOLPHO: I have no money to get married. I have a nice face, but no money. (*He laughs.*)

CATHERINE (*to* BEATRICE): He's a real blond!

BEATRICE (*to* RODOLPHO): You want to stay here too, heh? For good?

RODOLPHO: Me? Yes, forever! Me, I want to be an American. And then I want to go back to Italy when I am rich, and I will buy a motorcycle. (*He smiles.* MARCO *shakes him affectionately.*)

CATHERINE: A motorcycle!

RODOLPHO: With a motorcycle in Italy you will never starve any more.

BEATRICE: I'll get you coffee. (*She exits to the kitchen.*)

EDDIE: What you do with a motorcycle?

MARCO: He dreams, he dreams.

RODOLPHO (*to* MARCO): Why? (*To* EDDIE) Messages! The rich people in the hotel always need someone who will carry a message. But quickly, and with a great noise. With a blue motorcycle I would station myself in the courtyard of the hotel, and in a little while I would have messages.

MARCO: When you have no wife you have dreams.

EDDIE: Why can't you just walk, or take a trolley or sump'm?

(*Enter* BEATRICE *with coffee.*)

RODOLPHO: Oh, no, the machine, the machine is necessary. A man comes into a great hotel and says, I am a messenger. Who is this man? He disappears walking, there is no noise, nothing. Maybe he will never come back, maybe he will never deliver the message. But a man who rides up on a great machine, this man is responsible, this man exists. He will be given messages. (*He helps* BEATRICE *set out the coffee things*) I am also a singer, though.

EDDIE: You mean a regular—?

RODOLPHO: Oh, yes. One night last year Andreola got sick. Baritone. And I took his place in the garden of the hotel. Three arias I sang without a mistake! Thousand-lire notes they threw from the tables, money was falling like a storm in the treasury. It was magnificent. We lived six months on that night, eh, Marco?

(MARCO *nods doubtfully.*)

MARCO: Two months.

(EDDIE *laughs.*)

BEATRICE: Can't you get a job in that place?

RODOLPHO: Andreola got better. He's a baritone, very strong.

(BEATRICE *laughs.*)

MARCO (*regretfully, to* BEATRICE): He sang too loud.

RODOLPHO: Why too loud?

MARCO: Too loud. The guests in that hotel are all Englishmen. They don't like too loud.

RODOLPHO (*to* CATHERINE): Nobody ever said it was too loud!

MARCO: I say. It was too loud. (*To* BEATRICE) I knew it as soon as he started to sing. Too loud.

RODOLPHO: Then why did they throw so much money?

MARCO: They paid for your courage. The English like courage. But once is enough.

RODOLPHO (*to all but* MARCO): I never heard anybody say it was too loud.

CATHERINE: Did you ever hear of jazz?

RODOLPHO: Oh, sure! I *sing* jazz.

CATHERINE (*rises*): You could sing jazz?

RODOLPHO: Oh, I sing Napolidan, jazz, bel canto[8]— I sing "Paper Doll," you like "Paper Doll"?

CATHERINE: Oh, sure, I'm crazy for "Paper Doll." Go ahead, sing it.

RODOLPHO (*takes his stance after getting a nod of permission from* MARCO, *and with a high tenor voice begins singing*):

"I'll tell you boys it's tough to be alone,
  And it's tough to love a doll that's not your own.
I'm through with all of them,
I'll never fall again,
Hey, boy, what you gonna do?
I'm gonna buy a paper doll that I can call my own,
A doll that other fellows cannot steal.

(EDDIE *rises and moves upstage*)

And then those flirty, flirty guys
With their flirty, flirty eyes
Will have to flirt with dollies that are real—

EDDIE: Hey, kid—hey, wait a minute—

CATHERINE (*enthralled*): Leave him finish, it's beautiful! (*To* BEATRICE) He's terrific! It's terrific, Rodolpho.

EDDIE: Look, kid; you don't want to be picked up, do ya?

---

[8] Literally, beautiful song (Italian). Rodolpho says he can sing with an emphasis on sweetness of tone rather than on volume.

MARCO: No—no! (*He rises.*)

EDDIE (*indicating the rest of the building*): Because we never had no singers here . . . and all of a sudden there's a singer in the house, y'know what I mean?

MARCO: Yes, yes. You'll be quiet, Rodolpho.

EDDIE (*He is flushed*): They got guys all over the place, Marco. I mean.

MARCO: Yes. He'll be quiet. (*To* RODOLPHO) You'll be quiet.

(RODOLPHO *nods.* EDDIE *has risen, with iron control, even a smile. He moves to* CATHERINE.)

EDDIE: What's the high heels for, Garbo?

CATHERINE: I figured for tonight—

EDDIE: Do me a favor, will you? Go ahead.

(*Embarrassed now, angered,* CATHERINE *goes out into the bedroom.* BEATRICE *watches her go and gets up; in passing, she gives* EDDIE *a cold look, restrained only by the strangers, and goes to the table to pour coffee.*)

EDDIE (*striving to laugh, and to* MARCO, *but directed as much to* BEATRICE): All actresses they want to be around here.

RODOLPHO (*happy about it*): In Italy too! All the girls.

(CATHERINE *emerges from the bedroom in low-heel shoes, comes to the table.* RODOLPHO *is lifting a cup.*)

EDDIE (*He is sizing up* RODOLPHO, *and there is a concealed suspicion*): Yeah, heh?

RODOLPHO: Yes! (*Laughs, indicating* CATHERINE) Especially when they are so beautiful!

CATHERINE: You like sugar?

RODOLPHO: Sugar? Yes! I like sugar very much!

(EDDIE *is downstage, watching as she pours a spoonful of sugar into his cup, his face puffed with trouble, and the room dies.*

Lights rise on ALFIERI.)

ALFIERI: Who can ever know what will be discovered? Eddie Carbone had never expected to have a destiny. A man works, raises his family, goes bowling, eats, gets old, and then he dies. Now, as the weeks passed, there was a future, there was a trouble that would not go away.

(*The lights fade on* ALFIERI, *then rise on* EDDIE *standing at the doorway of the house.* BEATRICE *enters on the street. She sees* EDDIE, *smiles at him. He looks away. She starts to enter the house when* EDDIE *speaks.*)

EDDIE: It's after eight.

BEATRICE: Well, it's a long show at the Paramount.

EDDIE: They must've seen every picture in Brooklyn by now. He's supposed to stay in the house when he ain't working. He ain't supposed to go advertising himself.

BEATRICE: Well that's his trouble, what do you care? If they pick him up they pick him up, that's all. Come in the house.

EDDIE: What happened to the stenography? I don't see her practice no more.

BEATRICE: She'll get back to it. She's excited, Eddie.

EDDIE: She tell you anything?

BEATRICE (*comes to him, now the subject is opened*): What's the matter with you? He's a nice kid, what do you want from him?

EDDIE: That's a nice kid? He gives me the heeby-jeebies.

BEATRICE (*smiling*) : Ah, go on, you're just jealous.

EDDIE : Of *him?* Boy, you don't think much of me.

BEATRICE : I don't understand you. What's so terrible about him?

EDDIE : You mean it's all right with you? That's gonna be her husband?

BEATRICE : Why? He's a nice fella, hard workin', he's a good-lookin' fella.

EDDIE : He sings on the ships, didja know that?

BEATRICE : What do you mean, he sings?

EDDIE : Just what I said, he sings. Right on the deck, all of a sudden, a whole song comes out of his mouth—with motions. You know what they're callin' him now? Paper Doll they're callin' him, Canary. He's like a weird. He comes out on the pier, one-two-three, it's a regular free show.

BEATRICE : Well, he's a kid; he don't know how to behave himself yet.

EDDIE : And with that wacky hair; he's like a chorus girl or sump'm.

BEATRICE : So he's blond, so—

EDDIE : I just hope that's his regular hair, that's all I hope.

BEATRICE : You crazy or sump'm? (*She tries to turn him to her.*)

EDDIE (*He keeps his head turned away*) : What's so crazy? I don't like his whole way.

BEATRICE : Listen, you never seen a blond guy in your life? What about Whitey Balso?

EDDIE (*turning to her victoriously*) : Sure, but Whitey don't sing; he don't do like that on the ships.

BEATRICE : Well, maybe that's the way they do in Italy.

EDDIE : Then why don't his brother sing? Marco goes around like a man; nobody kids Marco. (*He moves from her, halts. She realizes there is a campaign solidified in him*) I tell you the truth; I'm surprised I have to tell you all this. I mean I'm surprised, B.

BEATRICE (*She goes to him with purpose now*) : Listen, you ain't gonna start nothin' here.

EDDIE : I ain't startin' nothin', but I ain't gonna stand around lookin' at that. For that character I didn't bring her up. I swear, B., I'm surprised at you; I sit there waitin' for you to wake up but everything is great with you.

BEATRICE : No, everything ain't great with me.

EDDIE : No?

BEATRICE : No. But I got other worries.

EDDIE : Yeah. (*He is already weakening.*)

BEATRICE : Yeah, you want me to tell you?

EDDIE (*in retreat*) : Why? What worries you got?

BEATRICE : When am I gonna be a wife again, Eddie?

EDDIE : I ain't been feelin' good. They bother me since they came.

BEATRICE : It's almost three months you don't feel good; they're only here a couple of weeks. It's three months, Eddie.

EDDIE : I don't know, B. I don't want to talk about it.

BEATRICE : What's the matter, Eddie, you don't like me, heh?

EDDIE : What do you mean, I don't like you? I said I don't feel good, that's all.

BEATRICE : Well, tell me, am I doing something wrong? Talk to me.

EDDIE (*Pause. He can't speak, then*): I can't. I can't talk about it.

BEATRICE: Well, tell me what—

EDDIE: I got nothin' to say about it!

(*She stands for a moment; he is looking off; she turns to go into the house.*)

EDDIE: I'll be all right, B.; just lay off me, will ya? I'm worried about her.

BEATRICE: The girl is gonna be eighteen years old, it's time already.

EDDIE: B., he's taking her for a ride!

BEATRICE: All right, that's her ride. What're you gonna stand over her till she's forty? Eddie, I want you to cut it out now, you hear me? I don't like it! Now come in the house.

EDDIE: I want to take a walk, I'll be in right away.

BEATRICE: They ain't goin' to come any quicker if you stand in the street. It ain't nice, Eddie.

EDDIE: I'll be in right away. Go ahead. (*He walks off.*)

(*She goes into the house.* EDDIE *glances up the street, sees* LOUIS *and* MIKE *coming, and sits on an iron railing.* LOUIS *and* MIKE *enter.*)

LOUIS: Wanna go bowlin' tonight?

EDDIE: I'm too tired. Goin' to sleep.

LOUIS: How's your two submarines[9]?

EDDIE: They're okay.

LOUIS: I see they're gettin' work allatime.

EDDIE: Oh yeah, they're doin' all right.

MIKE: That's what we oughta do. We oughta leave the country and come in under the water. Then we get work.

EDDIE: You ain't kiddin'.

LOUIS: Well, what the hell. Y'know?

EDDIE: Sure.

LOUIS (*sits on railing beside* EDDIE): Believe me, Eddie, you got a lotta credit comin' to you.

EDDIE: Aah, they don't bother me, don't cost me nutt'n.

MIKE: That older one, boy, he's a regular bull. I seen him the other day liftin' coffee bags over the Matson Line. They leave him alone he woulda load the whole ship by himself.

EDDIE: Yeah, he's a strong guy, that guy. Their father was a regular giant, supposed to be.

LOUIS: Yeah, you could see. He's a regular slave.

MIKE (*grinning*): That blond one, though— (EDDIE *looks at him*) He's got a sense of humor. (LOUIS *snickers.*)

EDDIE (*searchingly*): Yeah. He's funny—

MIKE (*starting to laugh*): Well he ain't exackly funny, but he's always like makin' remarks like, y'know? He comes around, everybody's laughin'. (LOUIS *laughs.*)

EDDIE (*uncomfortably, grinning*): Yeah, well . . . he's got a sense of humor.

MIKE (*laughing*): Yeah, I mean, he's always makin' like remarks, like, y'know?

---

9 A slang expression for someone who illegally enters a country from a ship.

EDDIE: Yeah, I know. But he's a kid yet, y'know? He—he's just a kid, that's all.

MIKE (*getting hysterical with* LOUIS): I know. You take one look at him—everybody's happy. (LOUIS *laughs*) I worked one day with him last week over the Moore-MacCormack Line, I'm tellin' you they was all hysterical. (LOUIS *and he explode in laughter.*)

EDDIE: Why? What'd he do?

MIKE: I don't know . . . he was just humorous. You never can remember what he says, y'know? But it's the way he says it. I mean he gives you a look sometimes and you start laughin'!

EDDIE: Yeah. (*Troubled*) He's got a sense of humor.

MIKE (*gasping*): Yeah.

LOUIS (*rising*): Well, we see ya, Eddie.

EDDIE: Take it easy.

LOUIS: Yeah. See ya.

MIKE: If you wanna come bowlin' later we're goin' Flatbush Avenue.
(*Laughing, they move to exit, meeting* RODOLPHO *and* CATHERINE *entering on the street. Their laughter rises as they see* RODOLPHO, *who does not understand but joins in.* EDDIE *moves to enter the house as* LOUIS *and* MIKE *exit.* CATHERINE *stops him at the door.*)

CATHERINE: Hey, Eddie—what a picture we saw! Did we laugh!

EDDIE (*He can't help smiling at sight of her*): Where'd you go?

CATHERINE: Paramount. It was with those two guys, y'know? That—

EDDIE: Brooklyn Paramount?

CATHERINE (*with an edge of anger, embarrassed before* RODOLPHO): Sure, the Brooklyn Paramount. I told you we wasn't goin' to New York.

EDDIE (*retreating before the threat of her anger*): All right, I only asked you. (*To* RODOLPHO) I just don't want her hangin' around Times Square, see? It's full of tramps over there.

RODOLPHO: I would like to go to Broadway once, Eddie. I would like to walk with her once where the theaters are and the opera. Since I was a boy I see pictures of those lights.

EDDIE (*his little patience waning*): I want to talk to her a minute, Rodolpho. Go inside, will you?

RODOLPHO: Eddie, we only walk together in the streets. She teaches me.

CATHERINE: You know what he can't get over? That there's no fountains in Brooklyn!

EDDIE (*smiling unwillingly*): Fountains? (RODOLPHO *smiles at his own naïveté.*)

CATHERINE: In Italy he says, every town's got fountains, and they meet there. And you know what? They got oranges on the trees where he comes from, and lemons. Imagine—on the trees? I mean it's interesting. But he's crazy for New York.

RODOLPHO (*attempting familiarity*): Eddie, why can't we go once to Broadway—?

EDDIE: Look, I gotta tell her something—

RODOLPHO: Maybe you can come too. I want to see all those lights. (*He sees no response in* EDDIE's *face. He glances at* CATHERINE) I'll walk by the river before I go to sleep. (*He walks off down the street.*)

CATHERINE: Why don't you talk to him, Eddie? He blesses you, and you don't talk to him hardly.

EDDIE (*enveloping her with his eyes*): I bless you and you don't talk to me. (*He tries to smile.*)

CATHERINE: *I* don't talk to you? (*She hits his arm*) What do you mean?

EDDIE: I don't see you no more. I come home you're runnin' around some-place—

CATHERINE: Well, he wants to see everything, that's all, so we go. . . . You mad at me?

EDDIE: No. (*He moves from her, smiling sadly*) It's just I used to come home, you was always there. Now, I turn around, you're a big girl. I don't know how to talk to you.

CATHERINE: Why?

EDDIE: I don't know, you're runnin', you're runnin', Katie. I don't think you listening any more to me.

CATHERINE (*going to him*): Ah, Eddie, sure I am. What's the matter? You don't like him?

(*Slight pause.*)

EDDIE (*turns to her*): *You* like him, Katie?

CATHERINE (*with a blush but holding her ground*): Yeah. I like him.

EDDIE (*His smile goes*): You like him.

CATHERINE (*looking down*): Yeah. (*Now she looks at him for the conse- quences, smiling but tense. He looks at her like a lost boy*) What're you got against him? I don't understand. He only blesses you.

EDDIE (*turns away*): He don't bless me, Katie.

CATHERINE: He does! You're like a father to him!

EDDIE (*turns to her*): Katie.

CATHERINE: What, Eddie?

EDDIE: You gonna marry him?

CATHERINE: I don't know. We just been . . . goin' around, that's all. (*Turns to him*) What're you got against him, Eddie? Please, tell me. What?

EDDIE: He don't respect you.

CATHERINE: Why?

EDDIE: Katie . . . if you wasn't an orphan, wouldn't he ask your father's permission before he run around with you like this?

CATHERINE: Oh, well, he didn't think you'd mind.

EDDIE: He knows I mind, but it don't bother him if I mind, don't you see that?

CATHERINE: No, Eddie, he's got all kinds of respect for me. And you too! We walk across the street he takes my arm—he almost bows to me! You got him all wrong, Eddie; I mean it, you—

EDDIE: Katie, he's only bowin' to his passport.

CATHERINE: His passport!

EDDIE: That's right. He marries you he's got the right to be an American citizen. That's what's goin' on here. (*She is puzzled and surprised*) You understand what I'm tellin' you? The guy is lookin' for his break, that's all he's lookin' for.

CATHERINE (*pained*): Oh, no, Eddie, I don't think so

EDDIE: You don't think so! Katie, you're gonna make me cry here. Is that a workin' man? What does he do with his first money? A snappy new jacket he buys, records, a pointy pair new shoes and his brother's kids are starvin' over there with tuberculosis? That's a hit-and-run guy, baby; he's got bright lights in his head, Broadway. Them guys don't think of nobody but theirself! You marry him and the next time you see him it'll be for divorce!

CATHERINE (*steps toward him*): Eddie, he never said a word about his papers or—

EDDIE: You mean he's supposed to tell you that?

CATHERINE: I don't think he's even thinking about it.

EDDIE: What's better for him to think about! He could be picked up any day here and he's back pushin' taxis up the hill!

CATHERINE: No, I don't believe it.

EDDIE: Katie, don't break my heart, listen to me.

CATHERINE: I don't want to hear it.

EDDIE: Katie, listen . . .

CATHERINE: He loves me!

EDDIE (*with deep alarm*): Don't say that, for God's sake! This is the oldest racket in the country—

CATHERINE (*desperately, as though he had made his imprint*): I don't believe it! (*She rushes to the house.*)

EDDIE (*following her*): They been pullin' this since the Immigration Law was put in! They grab a green kid that don't know nothin' and they—

CATHERINE (*sobbing*): I don't believe it and I wish to hell you'd stop it!

EDDIE: Katie!

(*They enter the apartment. The lights in the living room have risen and* BEATRICE *is there. She looks past the sobbing* CATHERINE *at* EDDIE, *who in the presence of his wife, makes an awkward gesture of eroded command, indicating* CATHERINE.)

EDDIE: Why don't you straighten her out?

BEATRICE (*inwardly angered at his flowing emotion, which in itself alarms her*): When are you going to leave her alone?

EDDIE: B., the guy is no good!

BEATRICE (*suddenly, with open fright and fury*): You going to leave her alone? Or you gonna drive me crazy? (*He turns, striving to retain his dignity, but nevertheless in guilt walks out of the house, into the street and away.* CATHERINE *starts into a bedroom.*) Listen, Catherine. (CATHERINE *halts, turns to her sheepishly*) What are you going to do with yourself?

CATHERINE: I don't know.

BEATRICE: Don't tell me you don't know; you're not a baby any more, what are you going to do with yourself?

CATHERINE: He won't listen to me.

BEATRICE: I don't understand this. He's not your father, Catherine. I don't understand what's going on here.

CATHERINE (*as one who herself is trying to rationalize a buried impulse*): What am I going to do, just kick him in the face with it?

BEATRICE: Look, honey, you wanna get married, or don't you wanna get married? What are you worried about, Katie?

CATHERINE (*quietly, trembling*): I don't know, B. It just seems wrong if he's against it so much.

BEATRICE (*never losing her aroused alarm*): Sit down, honey, I want to tell you something. Here, sit down. Was there ever any fella he liked for you? There wasn't, was there?

CATHERINE: But he says Rodolpho's just after his papers.

BEATRICE: Look, he'll say anything. What does he care what he says? If it was a prince came here for you it would be no different. You know that, don't you?

CATHERINE: Yeah, I guess.

BEATRICE: So what does that mean?

CATHERINE (*slowly turns her head to* BEATRICE): What?

BEATRICE: It means you gotta be your own self more. You still think you're a little girl, honey. But nobody else can make up your mind for you any more, you understand? You gotta give him to understand that he can't give you orders no more.

CATHERINE: Yeah, but how am I going to do that? He thinks I'm a baby.

BEATRICE: Because *you* think you're a baby. I told you fifty times already, you can't act the way you act. You still walk around in front of him in your slip—

CATHERINE: Well I forgot.

BEATRICE: Well you can't do it. Or like you sit on the edge of the bathtub talkin' to him when he's shavin' in his underwear.

CATHERINE: When'd I do that?

BEATRICE: I seen you in there this morning.

CATHERINE: Oh . . . well, I wanted to tell him something and I—

BEATRICE: I know, honey. But if you act like a baby and he be treatin' you like a baby. Like when he comes home sometimes you throw yourself at him like when you was twelve years old.

CATHERINE: Well I like to see him and I'm happy so I—

BEATRICE: Look, I'm not tellin' you what to do honey, but—

CATHERINE: No, you could tell me, B.! Gee, I'm all mixed up. See, I— He looks so sad now and it hurts me.

BEATRICE: Well look Katie, if it's goin' to hurt you so much you're gonna end up an old maid here.

CATHERINE: No!

BEATRICE: I'm tellin' you. I'm not makin' a joke. I tried to tell you a couple of times in the last year or so. That's why I was so happy you were going to go out and get work, you wouldn't be here so much, you'd be a little more independent. I mean it. It's wonderful for a whole family to love each other, but you're a grown woman and you're in the same house with a grown man. So you'll act different now, heh?

CATHERINE: Yeah, I will. I'll remember.

BEATRICE: Because it ain't only up to him, Katie, you understand? I told him the same thing already.

CATHERINE (*quickly*): What?

BEATRICE: That he should let you go. But, you see, if only I tell him, he thinks I'm just bawlin' him out, or maybe I'm jealous or somethin', you know?

CATHERINE (*astonished*): He said you was jealous?

BEATRICE: No, I'm just sayin' maybe that's what he thinks. (*She reaches over to* CATHERINE'S *hand; with a strained smile*) You think I'm jealous of you, honey?

CATHERINE: No! It's the first I thought of it.

BEATRICE (*with a quiet sad laugh*): Well you should have thought of it before . . . but I'm not. We'll be all right. Just give him to understand; you don't have to fight, you're just— You're a woman, that's all, and you got a nice boy, and now the time came when you said good-by. All right?

CATHERINE (*strangely moved at the prospect*): All right. . . . If I can.

BEATRICE: Honey . . . you gotta.

(CATHERINE, *sensing now an imperious demand, turns with some fear, with a discovery, to* BEATRICE. *She is at the edge of tears, as though a familiar world had shattered.*)

CATHERINE: Okay.

(*Lights out on them and up on* ALFIERI, *seated behind his desk.*)

ALFIERI: It was at this time that he first came to me. I had represented his father in an accident case some years before, and I was acquainted with the family in a casual way. I remember him now as he walked through my doorway—(*Enter* EDDIE *down right ramp*) His eyes were like tunnels; my first thought was that he had committed a crime, (EDDIE *sits beside the desk, cap in hand, looking out*) but soon I saw it was only a passion that had moved into his body, like a stranger. (ALFIERI *pauses, looks down at his desk, then to* EDDIE *as though he were continuing a conversation with him*) I don't quite understand what I can do for you. Is there a question of law somewhere?

EDDIE: That's what I want to ask you.

ALFIERI: Because there's nothing illegal about a girl falling in love with an immigrant.

EDDIE: Yeah, but what about it if the only reason for it is to get his papers?

ALFIERI: First of all you don't know that.

EDDIE: I see it in his eyes; he's laughin' at her and he's laughin' at me.

ALFIERI: Eddie, I'm a lawyer. I can only deal in what's provable. You understand that, don't you? Can you prove that?

EDDIE: *I know what's in his mind, Mr. Alfieri!*

ALFIERI: Eddie, even if you could prove that—

EDDIE: Listen . . . will you listen to me a minute? My father always said you was a smart man. I want you to listen to me.

ALFIERI: I'm only a lawyer, Eddie.

EDDIE: Will you listen a minute? I'm talkin' about the law. Lemme just bring out what I mean. A man, which he comes into the country illegal, don't it stand to reason he's gonna take every penny and put it in the sock? Because they don't know from one day to another, right?

ALFIERI: All right.

EDDIE: He's spendin'. Records he buys now. Shoes. Jackets. Y'understand me? This guy ain't worried. This guy is *here*. So it must be that he's got it all laid out in his mind already—he's stayin'. Right?

ALFIERI: Well? What about it?

EDDIE: All right. (*He glances at* ALFIERI, *then down to the floor*) I'm talking to you confidential, ain't I?

ALFIERI: Certainly.

EDDIE: I mean it don't go no place but here. Because I don't like to say this about anybody. Even my wife I didn't exactly say this.

ALFIERI: What is it?

EDDIE (*takes a breath and glances briefly over each shoulder*): The guy ain't right, Mr. Alfieri.

ALFIERI: What do you mean?

EDDIE: I mean he ain't right.

ALFIERI: I don't get you.

EDDIE (*shifts to another position in the chair*): Dja ever get a look at him?

ALFIERI: Not that I know of, no.

EDDIE: He's a blond guy. Like . . . platinum. You know what I mean?

ALFIERI: No.

EDDIE: I mean if you close the paper fast—you could blow him over.

ALFIERI: Well that doesn't mean—

EDDIE: Wait a minute, I'm tellin' you sump'm. He sings, see. Which is— I mean it's all right, but sometimes he hits a note, see. I turn around. I mean—high. You know what I mean?

ALFIERI: Well, that's a tenor.

EDDIE: I know a tenor, Mr. Alfieri. This ain't no tenor. I mean if you came in the house and you didn't know who was singin', you wouldn't be lookin' for him you be lookin' for her.

ALFIERI: Yes, but that's not—

EDDIE: I'm tellin' you sump'm, wait a minute. Please, Mr. Alfieri. I'm tryin' to bring out my thoughts here. Couple of nights ago my niece brings out a dress which it's too small for her, because she shot up like a light this last year. He takes the dress, lays it on the table, he cuts it up; one-two-three, he makes a new dress. I mean he looked so sweet there, like an angel—you could kiss him he was so sweet.

ALFIERI: Now look, Eddie—

EDDIE: Mr. Alfieri, they're laughin' at him on the piers. I'm ashamed. Paper Doll they call him. Blondie now. His brother thinks it's because he's got a sense of humor, see—which he's got—but that ain't what they're laughin'. Which they're not goin' to come out with it because they know he's my relative, which they have to see me if they make a crack, y'know? But I know what they're laughin' at, and when I think of that guy layin' his hands on her I could—I mean it's eatin' me out, Mr. Alfieri, because I struggled for that girl. And now he comes in my house and—

ALFIERI: Eddie, look—I have my own children. I understand you. But the law is very specific. The law does not . . .

EDDIE (*with a fuller flow of indignation*): You mean to tell me that there's no law that a guy which he ain't right can go to work and marry a girl and—?

ALFIERI: You have no recourse in the law, Eddie.

EDDIE: Yeah, but if he ain't right, Mr. Alfieri, you mean to tell me—

ALFIERI: There is nothing you can do, Eddie, believe me.

EDDIE: Nothin'.

ALFIERI: Nothing at all. There's only one legal question here.

EDDIE: What?

ALFIERI: The manner in which they entered the country. But I don't think you want to do anything about that, do you?

EDDIE: You mean—?

ALFIERI: Well, they entered illegally.

EDDIE: Oh, Jesus, no, I wouldn't do nothin' about that, I mean—

ALFIERI: All right, then, let me talk now, eh?

EDDIE: Mr. Alfieri, I can't believe what you tell me. I mean there must be some kinda law which—

ALFIERI: Eddie, I want you to listen to me. (*Pause*) You know, sometimes God mixes up the people. We all love somebody, the wife, the kids— every man's got somebody that he loves, heh? But sometimes . . . there's too much. You know? There's too much, and it goes where it mustn't. A man works hard, he brings up a child, sometimes it's a niece, some- times even a daughter, and he never realizes it, but through the years— there is too much love for the daughter, there is too much love for the niece. Do you understand what I'm saying to you?

EDDIE (*sardonically*): What do you mean, I shouldn't look out for her good?

ALFIERI: Yes, but these things have to end, Eddie, that's all. The child has to grow up and go away, and the man has to learn to forget. Because after all, Eddie—what other way can it end? (*Pause*) Let her go. That's my advice. You did your job, now it's her life; wish her luck, and let her go. (*Pause*) Will you do that? Because there's no law, Eddie; make up your mind to it; the law is not interested in this.

EDDIE: You mean to tell me, even if he's a punk? If he's—

ALFIERI: There's nothing you can do.

(EDDIE *stands.*)

EDDIE: Well, all right, thanks. Thanks very much.

ALFIERI: What are you going to do?

EDDIE (*with a helpless but ironic gesture*): What can I do? I'm a patsy, what can a patsy[10] do? I worked like a dog twenty years so a punk could have her, so that's what I done. I mean, in the worst times, in the worst, when there wasn't a ship comin' in the harbor, I didn't stand around lookin' for relief—I hustled. When there was empty piers in Brooklyn I went to Hoboken, Staten Island, the West Side, Jersey, all over—because I made a promise. I took out of my own mouth to give to her. I took out of my wife's mouth. I walked hungry plenty days in this city! (*It begins to break through*) And now I gotta sit in my own house and look at a son-of-a-bitch punk like that—which he came out of nowhere! I give him my house to sleep! I take the blankets off my bed for him, and he takes and puts his dirty filthy hands on her like a goddam thief!

ALFIERI (*rising*): But, Eddie, she's a woman now.

---

[10] Slang for someone who has been easily and unwittingly duped or deceived by another person.

EDDIE: He's stealing from me!

ALFIERI: She wants to get married, Eddie. She can't marry you, can she?

EDDIE (*furiously*): What're you talkin' about, marry me! I don't know what the hell you're talkin' about!

(*Pause.*)

ALFIERI: I gave you my advice, Eddie. That's it.

(EDDIE *gathers himself. A pause.*)

EDDIE: Well, thanks. Thanks very much. It just—it's breakin' my heart, y'know. I—

ALFIERI: I understand. Put it out of your mind. Can you do that?

EDDIE: I'm—(*He feels the threat of sobs, and with a helpless wave*) I'll see you around. (*He goes out up the right ramp.*)

ALFIERI (*sits on desk*): There are times when you want to spread an alarm, but nothing has happened. I knew, I knew then and there—I could have finished the whole story that afternoon. It wasn't as though there was a mystery to unravel. I could see every step coming, step after step, like a dark figure walking down a hall toward a certain door. I knew where he was heading for, I knew where he was going to end. And I sat here many afternoons asking myself why, being an intelligent man, I was so powerless to stop it. I even went to a certain old lady in the neighborhood, a very wise old woman, and I told her, and she only nodded, and said, "Pray for him . . ." And so I—waited here.

(*As lights go out on* ALFIERI, *they rise in the apartment where all are finishing dinner.* BEATRICE *and* CATHERINE *are clearing the table.*)

CATHERINE: You know where they went?

BEATRICE: Where?

CATHERINE: They went to Africa once. On a fishing boat. (EDDIE *glances at her*) It's true, Eddie.

(BEATRICE *exits into the kitchen with dishes.*)

EDDIE: I didn't say nothin'. (*He goes to his rocker, picks up a newspaper.*)

CATHERINE: And I was never even in Staten Island.

EDDIE (*sitting with the paper*): You didn't miss nothin'. (*Pause.* CATHERINE *takes dishes out*) How long that take you, Marco—to get to Africa?

MARCO (*rising*): Oh . . . two days. We go all over.

RODOLPHO (*rising*): Once we went to Yugoslavia.

EDDIE (*to* MARCO): They pay all right on them boats?

(BEATRICE *enters. She and* RODOLPHO *stack the remaining dishes.*)

MARCO: If they catch fish they pay all right. (*Sits on a stool.*)

RODOLPHO: They're family boats, though. And nobody in our family owned one. So we only worked when one of the families was sick.

BEATRICE: Y'know, Marco, what I don't understand—there's an ocean full of fish and yiz are all starvin'.

EDDIE: They gotta have boats, nets, you need money.

(CATHERINE *enters.*)

BEATRICE: Yeah, but couldn't they like fish from the beach? You see them down Coney Island—

MARCO: Sardines.

EDDIE: Sure. (*Laughing*) How you gonna catch sardines on a hook?

BEATRICE: Oh, I didn't know they're sardines. (*To* CATHERINE) They're sardines!

CATHERINE: Yeah, they follow them all over the ocean, Africa, Yugoslavia . . . (*She sits and begins to look through a movie magazine.* RODOLPHO *joins her.*)

BEATRICE (*to* EDDIE): It's funny, y'know. You never think of it, that sardines are swimming in the ocean! (*She exits to kitchen with dishes.*)

CATHERINE: I know. It's like oranges and lemons on a tree. (*To* EDDIE) I mean you ever think of oranges and lemons on a tree?

EDDIE: Yeah, I know. It's funny. (*To* MARCO) I heard that they paint the oranges to make them look orange.

(BEATRICE *enters.*)

MARCO (*He has been reading a letter*): Paint?

EDDIE: Yeah, I heard that they grow like green.

MARCO: No, in Italy the oranges are orange.

RODOLPHO: Lemons are green.

EDDIE (*resenting his instruction*): I know lemons are green, for Christ's sake, you see them in the store they're green sometimes. I said oranges they paint, I didn't say nothin' about lemons.

BEATRICE (*sitting; diverting their attention*): Your wife is gettin' the money all right, Marco?

MARCO: Oh, yes. She bought medicine for my boy.

BEATRICE: That's wonderful. You feel better, heh?

MARCO: Oh, yes! But I'm lonesome.

BEATRICE: I just hope you ain't gonna do like some of them around here. They're here twenty-five years, some men, and they didn't get enough together to go back twice.

MARCO: Oh, I know. We have many families in our town, the children never saw the father. But I will go home. Three, four years, I think.

BEATRICE: Maybe you should keep more here. Because maybe she thinks it comes so easy you'll never get ahead of yourself.

MARCO: Oh, no, she saves. I send everything. My wife is very lonesome. (*He smiles shyly.*)

BEATRICE: She must be nice. She pretty? I bet, heh?

MARCO (*blushing*): No, but she understand everything.

RODOLPHO: Oh, he's got a clever wife!

EDDIE: I betcha there's plenty surprises sometimes when those guys get back there, heh?

MARCO: Surprises?

EDDIE (*laughing*): I mean, you know—they count the kids and there's a couple extra than when they left?

MARCO: No—no . . . The women wait, Eddie. Most. Most. Very few surprises.

RODOLPHO: It's more strict in our town. (EDDIE *looks at him now*) It's not so free.

EDDIE (*rises, paces up and down*): It ain't so free here either, Rodolpho, like you think. I seen greenhorns sometimes get in trouble that way—

they think just because a girl don't go around with a shawl over her head that she ain't strict, y'know? Girl don't have to wear black dress to be strict. Know what I mean?

RODOLPHO: Well, I always have respect—

EDDIE: I know, but in your town you wouldn't just drag off some girl without permission, I mean. (*He turns*) You know what I mean, Marco? It ain't that much different here.

MARCO (*cautiously*): Yes.

BEATRICE: Well, he didn't exactly drag her off though, Eddie.

EDDIE: I know, but I seen some of them get the wrong idea sometimes. (*To* RODOLPHO) I mean it might be a little more free here but it's just as strict.

RODOLPHO: I have respect for her, Eddie. I do anything wrong?

EDDIE: Look, kid, I ain't her father, I'm only her uncle—

BEATRICE: Well then, be an uncle then. (EDDIE *looks at her, aware of her criticizing force*) I mean.

MARCO: No, Beatrice, if he does wrong you must tell him. (*To* EDDIE) What does he do wrong?

EDDIE: Well, Marco, till he came here she was never out on the street twelve o'clock at night.

MARCO (*to* RODOLPHO): You come home early now.

BEATRICE (*to* CATHERINE): Well, you said the movie ended late, didn't you?

CATHERINE: Yeah.

BEATRICE: Well, tell him, honey. (*To* EDDIE) The movie ended late.

EDDIE: Look, B., I'm just sayin'—he thinks she always stayed out like that.

MARCO: You come home early now, Rodolpho.

RODOLPHO (*embarrassed*): All right, sure. But I can't stay in the house all the time, Eddie.

EDDIE: Look, kid, I'm not only talkin' about her. The more you run around like that the more chance you're takin'. (*To* BEATRICE) I mean suppose he gets hit by a car or something. (*To* MARCO) Where's his papers, who is he? Know what I mean?

BEATRICE: Yeah, but who is he in the daytime, though? It's the same chance in the daytime.

EDDIE (*holding back a voice full of anger*): Yeah, but he don't have to go lookin' for it, Beatrice. If he's here to work, then he should work; if he's here for a good time then he could fool around! (*To* MARCO) But I understood, Marco, that you was both comin' to make a livin' for your family. You understand me, don't you, Marco? (*He goes to his rocker.*)

MARCO: I beg your pardon, Eddie.

EDDIE: I mean, that's what I understood in the first place, see.

MARCO: Yes. That's why we came.

EDDIE (*sits on his rocker*): Well, that's all I'm askin'.

(EDDIE *reads his paper. There is a pause, an awkwardness. Now* CATHERINE *gets up and puts a record on the phonograph—"Paper Doll."*)

CATHERINE (*flushed with revolt*): You wanna dance, Rodolpho?

(EDDIE *freezes.*)

RODOLPHO (*in deference to* EDDIE): No, I—I'm tired.

BEATRICE: Go ahead, dance, Rodolpho.

CATHERINE: Ah, come on. They got a beautiful quartet, these guys. Come. (*She has taken his hand and he stiffly rises, feeling* EDDIE'S *eyes on his back, and they dance.*)

EDDIE (*to* CATHERINE): What's that, a new record?

CATHERINE: It's the same one. We bought it the other day.

BEATRICE (*to* EDDIE): They only bought three records. (*She watches them dance;* EDDIE *turns his head away.* MARCO *just sits there, waiting. Now* BEATRICE *turns to* EDDIE) Must be nice to go all over in one of them fishin' boats. I would like that myself. See all them other countries?

EDDIE: Yeah.

BEATRICE (*to* MARCO): But the women don't go along, I bet.

MARCO: No, not on the boats. Hard work.

BEATRICE: What're you got, a regular kitchen and everything?

MARCO: Yes, we eat very good on the boats—especially when Rodolpho comes along; everybody gets fat.

BEATRICE: Oh, he cooks?

MARCO: Sure, very good cook. Rice, pasta,[11] fish, everything. (EDDIE *lowers his paper.*)

EDDIE: He's a cook, too! (*Looking at* RODOLPHO) He sings, he cooks. . . . (RODOLPHO *smiles thankfully.*)

BEATRICE: Well it's good, he could always make a living.

EDDIE: It's wonderful. He sings, he cooks, he could make dresses. . . .

CATHERINE: They get some high pay, them guys. The head chefs in all the big hotels are men. You read about them.

EDDIE: That's what I'm sayin'. (CATHERINE *and* RODOLPHO *continue dancing.*)

CATHERINE: Yeah, well, I mean.

EDDIE (*to* BEATRICE): He's lucky, believe me. (*Slight pause. He looks away, then back to* BEATRICE) That's why the water front is no place for him. (*They stop dancing.* RODOLPHO *turns off phonograph*) I mean like me— I can't cook, I can't sing, I can't make dresses, so I'm on the water front. But if I could cook, if I could sing, if I could make dresses, I wouldn't be on the water front. (*He has been unconsciously twisting the newspaper into a tight roll. They are all regarding him now; he senses he is exposing the issue and he is driven on*) I would be someplace else. I would be like in a dress store. (*He has bent the rolled paper and it suddenly tears in two. He suddenly gets up and pulls his pants up over his belly and goes to* MARCO) What do you say, Marco, we go to the bouts next Saturday night. You never seen a fight, did you?

MARCO (*uneasily*): Only in the moving pictures.

EDDIE (*going to* RODOLPHO): I'll treat yiz. What do you say, Danish? You wanna come along? I'll buy the tickets.

RODOLPHO: Sure. I like to go.

CATHERINE (*goes to* EDDIE; *nervously happy now*): I'll make some coffee, all right?

---

[11] Macaroni or spaghetti (Italian).

EDDIE: Go ahead, make some! Make it nice and strong. (*Mystified, she smiles and exits to kitchen. He is weirdly elated, rubbing his fists into his palms. He strides to* MARCO) You wait, Marco, you see some real fights here. You ever do any boxing?

MARCO: No, I never.

EDDIE (*to* RODOLPHO): Betcha you have done some, heh?

RODOLPHO: No.

EDDIE: Well, come on, I'll teach you.

BEATRICE: What's he got to learn that for?

EDDIE: Ya can't tell, one a these days somebody's liable to step on his foot or sump'm. Come on, Rodolpho, I show you a couple a passes. (*He stands below table.*)

BEATRICE: Go ahead, Rodolpho. He's a good boxer, he could teach you.

RODOLPHO (*embarrassed*): Well, I don't know how to—(*He moves down to* EDDIE.)

EDDIE: Just put your hands up. Like this, see? That's right. That's very good, keep your left up, because you lead with the left, see, like this. (*He gently moves his left into* RODOLPHO's *face*) See? Now what you gotta do is you gotta block me, so when I come in like that you—(RODOLPHO *parries his left*) Hey, that's very good! (RODOLPHO *laughs*) All right, now come into me. Come on.

RODOLPHO: I don't want to hit you, Eddie.

EDDIE: Don't pity me, come on. Throw it, I'll show you how to block it. (RODOLPHO *jabs at him, laughing. The others join*) 'At's it. Come on again. For the jaw right here. (RODOLPHO *jabs with more assurance*) Very good!

BEATRICE (*to* MARCO): He's very good!

(EDDIE *crosses directly upstage of* RODOLPHO.)

EDDIE: Sure, he's great! Come on, kid, put sump'm behind it, you can't hurt me. (RODOLPHO, *more seriously, jabs at* EDDIE's *jaw and grazes it*) Attaboy. (CATHERINE *comes from the kitchen, watches*) Now I'm gonna hit you, so block me, see?

CATHERINE (*with beginning alarm*): What are they doin'?

(*They are lightly boxing now.*)

BEATRICE (*She senses only the comradeship in it now*): He's teachin' him; he's very good!

EDDIE: Sure, he's terrific! Look at him go! (RODOLPHO *lands a blow*) 'At's it! Now, watch out, here I come, Danish! (*He feints with his left hand and lands with his right. It mildly staggers* RODOLPHO. MARCO *rises.*)

CATHERINE (*rushing to* RODOLPHO): Eddie!

EDDIE: Why! I didn't hurt him. Did I hurt you, kid? (*He rubs the back of his hand across his mouth.*)

RODOLPHO: No, no, he didn't hurt me. (*To* EDDIE *with a certain gleam and a smile*) I was only surprised.

BEATRICE (*pulling* EDDIE *down into the rocker*): That's enough, Eddie; he did pretty good, though.

EDDIE: Yeah. (*Rubbing his fists together*) He could be very good, Marco. I'll teach him again.

(*Marco nods at him dubiously.*)

RODOLPHO: Dance, Catherine. Come. (*He takes her hand; they go to phonograph and start it. It plays "Paper Doll."*)

(RODOLPHO *takes her in his arms. They dance.* EDDIE *in thought sits in his chair, and* MARCO *takes a chair, places it in front of* EDDIE, *and looks down at it.* BEATRICE *and* EDDIE *watch him.*)

MARCO: Can you lift this chair?

EDDIE: What do you mean?

MARCO: From here. (*He gets on one knee with one hand behind his back, and grasps the bottom of one of the chair legs but does not raise it.*)

EDDIE: Sure, why not? (*He comes to the chair, kneels, grasps the leg, raises the chair one inch, but it leans over to the floor*) Gee, that's hard, I never knew that. (*He tries again, and again fails*) It's on an angle, that's why, heh?

MARCO: Here. (*He kneels, grasps, and with strain slowly raises the chair higher and higher, getting to his feet now.* RODOLPHO *and* CATHERINE *have stopped dancing as* MARCO *raises the chair over his head.*

  MARCO *is face to face with* EDDIE, *a strained tension gripping his eyes and jaw, his neck stiff, the chair raised like a weapon over* EDDIE'S *head—and he transforms what might appear like a glare of warning into a smile of triumph, and* EDDIE'S *grin vanishes as he absorbs his look.*)

(*The Curtain Falls.*)

Act Two

Light rises on ALFIERI *at his desk.*

ALFIERI: On the twenty-third of that December a case of Scotch whisky slipped from a net while being unloaded—as a case of Scotch whisky is inclined to do on the twenty-third of December on Pier Forty-one. There was no snow, but it was cold, his wife was out shopping. Marco was still at work. The boy had not been hired that day; Catherine told me later that this was the first time they had been alone together in the house.

(*Light is rising on* CATHERINE *in the apartment.* RODOLPHO *is watching as she arranges a paper pattern on cloth spread on the table.*)

CATHERINE: You hungry?

RODOLPHO: Not for anything to eat. (*Pause*) I have nearly three hundred dollars. Catherine?

CATHERINE: I heard you.

RODOLPHO: You don't like to talk about it any more?

CATHERINE: Sure, I don't mind talkin' about it.

RODOLPHO: What worries you, Catherine?

CATHERINE: I been wantin' to ask you about something. Could I?

RODOLPHO: All the answers are in my eyes, Catherine. But you don't look in my eyes lately. You're full of secrets. (*She looks at him. She seems withdrawn*) What is the question?

CATHERINE: Suppose I wanted to live in Italy.

RODOLPHO (*smiling at the incongruity*): You going to marry somebody rich?

CATHERINE: No, I mean live there—you and me.

RODOLPHO (*his smile vanishing*): When?

CATHERINE: Well . . . when we get married.

RODOLPHO (*astonished*): You want to be an Italian?

CATHERINE: No, but I could live there without being Italian. Americans live there.

RODOLPHO: Forever?

CATHERINE: Yeah.

RODOLPHO (*crosses to rocker*): You're fooling.

CATHERINE: No, I mean it.

RODOLPHO: Where do you get such an idea?

CATHERINE: Well, you're always saying it's so beautiful there, with the mountains and the ocean and all the—

RODOLPHO: You're fooling me.

CATHERINE: I mean it.

RODOLPHO (*goes to her slowly*): Catherine, if I ever brought you home with no money, no business, nothing, they would call the priest and the doctor and they would say Rodolpho is crazy.

CATHERINE: I know, but I think we would be happier there.

RODOLPHO: Happier! What would you eat? You can't cook the view!

CATHERINE: Maybe you could be a singer, like in Rome or—

RODOLPHO: Rome! Rome is full of singers.

CATHERINE: Well, I could work then.

RODOLPHO: Where?

CATHERINE: God, there must be jobs somewhere!

RODOLPHO: There's nothing! Nothing, nothing, nothing. Now tell me what you're talking about. How can I bring you from a rich country to suffer in a poor country? What are you talking about? (*She searches for words*) I would be a criminal stealing your face. In two years you would have an old, hungry face. When my brother's babies cry they give them water, water that boiled a bone. Don't you believe that?

CATHERINE (*quietly*): I'm afraid of Eddie here.

(*Slight pause.*)

RODOLPHO (*steps closer to her*): We wouldn't live here. Once I am a citizen I could work anywhere and I would find better jobs and we would have a house, Catherine. If I were not afraid to be arrested I would start to be something wonderful here!

CATHERINE (*steeling herself*): Tell me something. I mean just tell me, Rodolpho—would you still want to do it if it turned out we had to go live in Italy? I mean just if it turned out that way.

RODOLPHO: This is your question or his question?

CATHERINE: I would like to know, Rodolpho. I mean it.

RODOLPHO: To go there with nothing.

CATHERINE: Yeah.

RODOLPHO: No. (*She looks at him wide-eyed*) No.

CATHERINE: You wouldn't?

RODOLPHO: No; I will not marry you to live in Italy. I want you to be my wife, and I want to be a citizen. Tell him that, or I will. Yes. (*He moves about angrily*) And tell him also, and tell yourself, please, that I am not a beggar, and you are not a horse, a gift, a favor for a poor immigrant.

CATHERINE: Well, don't get mad!

RODOLPHO: I am furious! (*Goes to her*) Do you think I am so desperate? My brother is desperate, not me. You think I would carry on my back the rest of my life a woman I didn't love just to be an American? It's so wonderful? You think we have no tall buildings in Italy? Electric lights? No wide streets? No flags? No automobiles? Only work we don't have. I want to be an American so I can work, that is the only wonder here—work! How can you insult me, Catherine?

CATHERINE: I didn't mean that—

RODOLPHO: My heart dies to look at you. Why are you so afraid of him?

CATHERINE (*near tears*): I don't know!

RODOLPHO: Do you trust me, Catherine? You?

CATHERINE: It's only that I— He was good to me, Rodolpho. You don't know him; he was always the sweetest guy to me. Good. He razzes me all the time but he don't mean it. I know. I would—just feel ashamed if I made him sad. 'Cause I always dreamt that when I got married he would be happy at the wedding, and laughin'—and now he's—mad all the time and nasty— (*She is weeping*) Tell him you'd live in Italy—just tell him, and maybe he would start to trust you a little, see? Because I want him to be happy; I mean—I like him, Rodolpho—and I can't stand it!

RODOLPHO: Oh, Catherine—oh, little girl.

CATHERINE: I love you, Rodolpho, I love you.

RODOLPHO: Then why are you afraid? That he'll spank you?

CATHERINE: Don't, don't laugh at me! I've been here all my life. . . . Every day I saw him when he left in the morning and when he came home at night. You think it's so easy to turn around and say to a man he's nothin' to you no more?

RODOLPHO: I know, but—

CATHERINE: You don't know; nobody knows! I'm not a baby, I know a lot more than people think I know. Beatrice says to be a woman, but—

RODOLPHO: Yes.

CATHERINE: Then why don't she be a woman? If I was a wife I would make a man happy instead of goin' at him all the time. I can tell a block away when he's blue in his mind and just wants to talk to somebody quiet and nice. . . . I can tell when he's hungry or wants a beer before he even says anything. I know when his feet hurt him, I mean I *know* him and now I'm supposed to turn around and make a stranger out of him? I don't know why I have to do that, I mean.

RODOLPHO: Catherine. If I take in my hands a little bird. And she grows and wishes to fly. But I will not let her out of my hands because I love her so much, is that right for me to do? I don't say you must hate him; but anyway you must go, mustn't you? Catherine?

CATHERINE (*softly*): Hold me.

RODOLPHO (*clasping her to him*): Oh, my little girl.

CATHERINE: Teach me. (*She is weeping*) I don't know anything, teach me, Rodolpho, hold me.

RODOLPHO: There's nobody here now. Come inside. Come. (*He is leading her toward the bedrooms*) And don't cry any more.

(*Light rises on the street. In a moment* EDDIE *appears. He is unsteady, drunk. He mounts the stairs. He enters the apartment, looks around, takes out a bottle from one pocket, puts it on the table. Then another bottle from another pocket, and a third from an inside pocket. He sees the pattern and cloth, goes over to it and touches it, and turns toward upstage.*)

EDDIE: Beatrice? (*He goes to the open kitchen door and looks in*) Beatrice? Beatrice?

(CATHERINE *enters from bedroom; under his gaze she adjusts her dress.*)

CATHERINE: You got home early.

EDDIE: Knocked off for Christmas early. (*Indicating the pattern*) Rodolpho makin' you a dress?

CATHERINE: No. I'm makin' a blouse.

(RODOLPHO *appears in the bedroom doorway.* EDDIE *sees him and his arm jerks slightly in shock.* RODOLPHO *nods to him testingly.*)

RODOLPHO: Beatrice went to buy presents for her mother.

(*Pause.*)

EDDIE: Pack it up. Go ahead. Get your stuff and get outa here. (CATHERINE *instantly turns and walks toward the bedroom, and* EDDIE *grabs her arm*) Where you goin'?

CATHERINE (*trembling with fright*): I think I have to get out of here, Eddie.

EDDIE: No, you ain't goin' nowheres, he's the one.

CATHERINE: I think I can't stay here no more. (*She frees her arm, steps back toward the bedroom*) I'm sorry, Eddie. (*She sees the tears in his eyes*) Well, don't cry. I'll be around the neighborhood; I'll see you. I just can't stay here no more. You know I can't. (*Her sobs of pity and love for him break her composure*) Don't you know I can't? You know that, don't you? (*She goes to him*) Wish me luck. (*She clasps her hands prayerfully*) Oh, Eddie, don't be like that!

EDDIE: You ain't goin' nowheres.

CATHERINE: Eddie, I'm not gonna be a baby any more! You—

(*He reaches out suddenly, draws her to him, and as she strives to free herself he kisses her on the mouth.*)

RODOLPHO: Don't! (*He pulls on* EDDIE'S *arm*) Stop that! Have respect for her!

EDDIE (*spun round by* RODOLPHO): You want something?

RODOLPHO: Yes! She'll be my wife. That is what I want. My wife!

EDDIE: But what're you gonna be?

RODOLPHO: I show you what I be!

CATHERINE: Wait outside; don't argue with him!

EDDIE: Come on, show me! What're you gonna be? Show me!

RODOLPHO (*with tears of rage*): Don't say that to me! (RODOLPHO *flies at him in attack.* EDDIE *pins his arms, laughing, and suddenly kisses him.*)

CATHERINE: Eddie! Let go, ya hear me! I'll kill you! Leggo of him!

(*She tears at* EDDIE'S *face and* EDDIE *releases* RODOLPHO. EDDIE *stands there with tears rolling down his face as he laughs mockingly at* RODOLPHO. *She is staring at him in horror.* RODOLPHO *is rigid. They are like animals that have torn at one another and broken up without a decision, each waiting for the other's mood.*)

EDDIE (*to* CATHERINE): You see? (*To* RODOLPHO) I give you till tomorrow, kid. Get outa here. Alone. You hear me? Alone.

CATHERINE: I'm going with him, Eddie. (*She starts toward* RODOLPHO.)

EDDIE (*indicating* RODOLPHO *with his head*): Not with that. (*She halts, frightened. He sits, still panting for breath, and they watch him helplessly as he leans toward them over the table*) Don't make me do nuttin', Catherine. Watch your step, submarine. By rights they oughta throw you back in the water. But I got pity for you. (*He moves unsteadily toward the door, always facing* RODOLPHO) Just get outa here and don't lay another hand on her unless you wanna go out feet first. (*He goes out of the apartment.*)

(*The lights go down, as they rise on* ALFIERI.)

ALFIERI: On December twenty-seventh I saw him next. I normally go home well before six, but that day I sat around looking out my window at the bay, and when I saw him walking through my doorway, I knew why I had waited. And if I seem to tell this like a dream, it was that way. Several moments arrived in the course of the two talks we had when it occurred to me how—almost transfixed I had come to feel. I had lost my strength somewhere. (EDDIE *enters, removing his cap, sits in the chair, looks thoughtfully out*) I looked in his eyes more than I listened—in fact, I can hardly remember the conversation. But I will never forget how dark the room became when he looked at me; his eyes were like tunnels. I kept wanting to call the police, but nothing had happened. Nothing at all had really happened. (*He breaks off and looks down at the desk. Then he turns to* EDDIE) So in other words, he won't leave?

EDDIE: My wife is talkin' about renting a room upstairs for them. An old lady on the top floor is got an empty room.

ALFIERI: What does Marco say?

EDDIE: He just sits there. Marco don't say much.

ALFIERI: I guess they didn't tell him, heh? What happened?

EDDIE: I don't know; Marco don't say much.

ALFIERI: What does your wife say?

EDDIE (*unwilling to pursue this*): Nobody's talkin' much in the house. So what about that?

ALFIERI: But you didn't prove anything about him. It sounds like he just wasn't strong enough to break your grip.

EDDIE: I'm tellin' you I know—he ain't right. Somebody that don't want it can break it. Even a mouse, if you catch a teeny mouse and you hold it in your hand, that mouse can give you the right kind of fight. He didn't give me the right kind of fight, I know it, Mr. Alfieri, the guy ain't right.

ALFIERI: What did you do that for, Eddie?

EDDIE: To show her what he is! So she would see, once and for all! Her mother'll turn over in the grave! (*He gathers himself almost peremptorily*) So what do I gotta do now? Tell me what to do.

ALFIERI: She actually said she's marrying him?

EDDIE: She told me, yeah. So what do I do?

(*Slight pause.*)

ALFIERI: This is my last word, Eddie, take it or not, that's your business. Morally and legally you have no rights, you cannot stop it; she is a free agent.

EDDIE (*angering*): Didn't you hear what I told you?

ALFIERI (*with a tougher tone*): I heard what you told me, and I'm telling you what the answer is. I'm not only telling you now, I'm warning you—the law is nature. The law is only a word for what has a right to happen. When the law is wrong it's because it's unnatural, but in this case it is natural and a river will drown you if you buck it now. Let her go. And bless her. (*A phone booth begins to glow on the opposite side of the stage; a faint, lonely blue.* EDDIE *stands up, jaws clenched*) Somebody had to come for her, Eddie, sooner or later. (EDDIE *starts turning to go and* ALFIERI *rises with new anxiety*) You won't have a friend in the world, Eddie! Even those who understand will turn against you, even the ones who feel the same will despise you! (EDDIE *moves off*) Put it out of your mind! Eddie! (*He follows into the darkness, calling desperately.*)

(EDDIE *is gone. The phone is glowing in light now. Light is out on* ALFIERI. EDDIE *has at the same time appeared beside the phone.*)

EDDIE: Give me the number of the Immigration Bureau. Thanks. (*He dials*) I want to report something. Illegal immigrants. Two of them. That's right. Four-forty-one Saxon Street, Brooklyn, yeah. Ground floor. Heh? (*With greater difficulty*) I'm just around the neighborhood, that's all. Heh?

(*Evidently he is being questioned further, and he slowly hangs up. He leaves the phone just as* LOUIS *and* MIKE *come down the street.*)

LOUIS: Go bowlin', Eddie?

EDDIE: No, I'm due home.

LOUIS: Well, take it easy.

EDDIE: I'll see yiz.

(*They leave him, exiting right, and he watches them go. He glances about, then goes up into the house. The lights go on in the apartment.* BEATRICE *is taking down Christmas decorations and packing them in a box.*)

EDDIE: Where is everybody? (BEATRICE *does not answer*) I says where is everybody?

BEATRICE (*looking up at him, wearied with it, and concealing a fear of him*): I decided to move them upstairs with Mrs. Dondero.

EDDIE: Oh, they're all moved up there already?

BEATRICE: Yeah.

EDDIE: Where's Catherine? She up there?

BEATRICE: Only to bring pillow cases.

EDDIE: She ain't movin' in with them.

BEATRICE: Look, I'm sick and tired of it. I'm sick and tired of it!

EDDIE: All right, all right, take it easy.

BEATRICE: I don't wanna hear no more about it, you understand? Nothin'!

EDDIE: What're you blowin' off about? Who brought them in here?

BEATRICE: All right, I'm sorry; I wish I'd a drop dead before I told them to come. In the ground I wish I was.

EDDIE: Don't drop dead, just keep in mind who brought them in here, that's all. (*He moves about restlessly*) I mean I got a couple of rights here. (*He moves, wanting to beat down her evident disapproval of him*) This is my house here not their house.

BEATRICE: What do you want from me? They're moved out; what do you want now?

EDDIE: I want my respect!

BEATRICE: So I moved them out, what more do you want? You got your house now, you got your respect.

EDDIE (*He moves about biting his lip*): I don't like the way you talk to me, Beatrice.

BEATRICE: I'm just tellin' you I done what you want!

EDDIE: I don't like it! The way you talk to me and the way you look at me. This is my house. And she is my niece and I'm responsible for her.

BEATRICE: So that's why you done that to him?

EDDIE: I done what to him?

BEATRICE: What you done to him in front of her; you know what I'm talkin' about. She goes around shakin' all the time, she can't go to sleep! That's what you call responsible for her?

EDDIE (*quietly*): The guy ain't right, Beatrice. (*She is silent*) Did you hear what I said?

BEATRICE: Look, I'm finished with it. That's all. (*She resumes her work.*)

EDDIE (*helping her to pack the tinsel*): I'm gonna have it out with you one of these days, Beatrice.

BEATRICE: Nothin' to have out with me, it's all settled. Now we gonna be like it never happened, that's all.

EDDIE: I want my respect, Beatrice, and you know what I'm talkin' about.

BEATRICE: What?

(*Pause.*)

EDDIE (*Finally his resolution hardens*): What I feel like doin' in the bed and what I don't feel like doin'. I don't want no—

BEATRICE: When'd I say anything about that?

EDDIE: You said, you said, I ain't deaf. I don't want no more conversations about that, Beatrice. I do what I feel like doin' or what I don't feel like doin'.

BEATRICE: Okay.

(*Pause.*)

EDDIE: You used to be different, Beatrice. You had a whole different way.

BEATRICE: *I'm* no different.

EDDIE: You didn't used to jump me all the time about everything. The last year or two I come in the house I don't know what's gonna hit me. It's a shootin' gallery in here and I'm the pigeon.

BEATRICE: Okay, okay.

EDDIE: Don't tell me okay, okay, I'm tellin' you the truth. A wife is supposed to believe the husband. If I tell you that guy ain't right don't tell me he is right.

BEATRICE: But how do you know?

EDDIE: Because I know. I don't go around makin' accusations. He give me the heeby-jeebies the first minute I seen him. And I don't like you sayin' I don't want her marryin' anybody. I broke my back payin' her stenography lessons so she could go out and meet a better class of people. Would I do that if I didn't want her to get married? Sometimes you talk like I was a crazy man or sump'm.

BEATRICE: But she likes him.

EDDIE: Beatrice, she's a baby, how is she gonna know what she likes?

BEATRICE: Well, you kept her a baby, you wouldn't let her go out. I told you a hundred times.

(*Pause.*)

EDDIE: All right. Let her go out, then.

BEATRICE: She don't wanna go out now. It's too late, Eddie.

(*Pause.*)

EDDIE: Suppose I told her to go out. Suppose I—

BEATRICE: They're going to get married next week, Eddie.

EDDIE (*His head jerks around to her*): She said that?

BEATRICE: Eddie, if you want my advice, go to her and tell her good luck. I think maybe now that you had it out you learned better.

EDDIE: What's the hurry next week?

BEATRICE: Well, she's been worried about him bein' picked up; this way he could start to be a citizen. She loves him, Eddie. (*He gets up, moves about uneasily, restlessly*) Why don't you give her a good word? Because I still think she would like you to be a friend, y'know? (*He is standing, looking at the floor*) I mean like if you told her you'd go to the wedding.

EDDIE: She asked you that?

BEATRICE: I know she would like it. I'd like to make a party here for her. I mean there oughta be some kinda send-off. Heh? I mean she'll have trouble enough in her life, let's start it off happy. What do you say? 'Cause in her heart she still loves you, Eddie. I know it. (*He presses his fingers against his eyes*) What're you, cryin'? (*She goes to him, holds his face*) Go . . . whyn't you go tell her you're sorry? (CATHERINE *is seen on the upper landing of the stairway, and they hear her descending*) There . . . she's comin' down. Come on, shake hands with her.

EDDIE (*moving with suppressed suddenness*): No, I can't, I can't talk to her.

BEATRICE: Eddie, give her a break; a wedding should be happy!

EDDIE: I'm goin', I'm goin' for a walk.

(*He goes upstage for his jacket.* CATHERINE *enters and starts for the bedroom door.*)

BEATRICE: Katie? . . . Eddie, don't go, wait a minute. (*She embraces* EDDIE'S *arm with warmth*) Ask him, Katie. Come on, honey.

EDDIE: It's all right, I'm— (*He starts to go and she holds him.*)

BEATRICE: No, she wants to ask you. Come on, Katie, ask him. We'll have a party! What're we gonna do, hate each other? Come on!

CATHERINE: I'm gonna get married, Eddie. So if you wanna come, the wedding be on Saturday.

(*Pause.*)

EDDIE: Okay. I only wanted the best for you, Katie. I hope you know that.

CATHERINE: Okay. (*She starts out again.*)

EDDIE: Catherine? (*She turns to him*) I was just tellin' Beatrice . . . if you wanna go out, like . . . I mean I realize maybe I kept you home too much. Because he's the first guy you ever knew, y'know? I mean now that you got a job, you might meet some fellas, and you get a different idea, y'know? I mean you could always come back to him, you're still only kids, the both of yiz. What's the hurry? Maybe you'll get around a little bit, you grow up a little more, maybe you'll see different in a couple of months. I mean you be surprised, it don't have to be him.

CATHERINE: No, we made it up already.

EDDIE (*with increasing anxiety*): Katie, wait a minute.

CATHERINE: No, I made up my mind.

EDDIE: But you never knew no other fella, Katie! How could you make up your mind?

CATHERINE: 'Cause I did. I don't want nobody else.

EDDIE: But, Katie, suppose he gets picked up.

CATHERINE: That's why we gonna do it right away. Soon as we finish the wedding he's goin' right over and start to be a citizen. I made up my mind, Eddie. I'm sorry. (*To* BEATRICE) Could I take two more pillow cases for the other guys?

BEATRICE: Sure, go ahead. Only don't let her forget where they came from.

(CATHERINE *goes into a bedroom.*)

EDDIE: She's got other boarders up there?

BEATRICE: Yeah, there's two guys that just came over.

EDDIE: What do you mean, came over?

BEATRICE: From Italy. Lipari the butcher—his nephew. They come from Bari,[12] they just got here yesterday. I didn't even know till Marco and Rodolpho moved up there before. (CATHERINE *enters, going toward exit with two pillow cases*) It'll be nice, they could all talk together.

EDDIE: Catherine! (*She halts near the exit door. He takes in* BEATRICE *too*) What're you, got no brains? You put them up there with two other submarines?

CATHERINE: Why?

EDDIE (*in a driving fright and anger*): Why! How do you know they're not trackin' these guys? They'll come up for them and find Marco and Rodolpho! Get them out of the house!

BEATRICE: But they been here so long already—

---

[12] A town in southern Italy on the Adriatic Sea.

EDDIE: How do you know what enemies Lipari's got? Which they'd love to stab him in the back?

CATHERINE: Well what'll I do with them?

EDDIE: The neighborhood is full of rooms. Can't you stand to live a couple of blocks away from him? Get them out of the house!

CATHERINE: Well maybe tomorrow night I'll—

EDDIE: Not tomorrow, do it now. Catherine, you never mix yourself with somebody else's family! These guys get picked up, Lipari's liable to blame you or me and we got his whole family on our head. They got a temper, that family.

(*Two men in overcoats appear outside, start into the house.*)

CATHERINE: How'm I gonna find a place tonight?

EDDIE: Will you stop arguin' with me and get them out! You think I'm always tryin' to fool you or sump'm? What's the matter with you, don't you believe I could think of your good? Did I ever ask sump'm for myself? You think I got no feelin's? I never told you nothin' in my life that wasn't for your good. Nothin'! And look at the way you talk to me! Like I was an enemy! Like I— (*A knock on the door. His head swerves. They all stand motionless. Another knock.* EDDIE, *in a whisper, pointing upstage*) Go up the fire escape, get them out over the back fence.

(*Catherine stands motionless, uncomprehending.*)

FIRST OFFICER (*in the hall*): Immigration! Open up in there!

EDDIE: Go, go. Hurry up! (*She stands a moment staring at him in a realized horror*) Well, what're you lookin' at!

FIRST OFFICER: Open up!

EDDIE (*calling toward door*): Who's that there?

FIRST OFFICER: Immigration, open up.

(EDDIE *turns, looks at* BEATRICE. *She sits. Then he looks at* CATHERINE. *With a sob of fury* CATHERINE *streaks into a bedroom. Knock is repeated.*)

EDDIE: All right, take it easy, take it easy. (*He goes and opens the door.* THE OFFICER *steps inside*) What's all this?

FIRST OFFICER: Where are they?

(SECOND OFFICER *sweeps past and, glancing about, goes into the kitchen.*)

EDDIE: Where's who?

FIRST OFFICER: Come on, come on, where are they? (*He hurries into the bedrooms.*)

EDDIE: Who? We got nobody here. (*He looks at* BEATRICE, *who turns her head away. Pugnaciously, furious, he steps toward* BEATRICE) What's the matter with *you?*

(FIRST OFFICER *enters from the bedroom, calls to the kitchen.*)

FIRST OFFICER: Dominick?

(*Enter* SECOND OFFICER *from kitchen.*)

SECOND OFFICER: Maybe it's a different apartment.

FIRST OFFICER: There's only two more floors up there. I'll take the front, you go up the fire escape. I'll let you in. Watch your step up there.

SECOND OFFICER: Okay, right, Charley. (FIRST OFFICER *goes out apartment door and runs up the stairs*) This is Four-forty-one, isn't it?

EDDIE: That's right.

(SECOND OFFICER *goes out into the kitchen.* EDDIE *turns to* BEATRICE. *She looks at him now and sees his terror.*)

BEATRICE *(weakened with fear)* : Oh, Jesus, Eddie.

EDDIE: What's the matter with *you?*

BEATRICE *(pressing her palms against her face)* : Oh, my God, my God.

EDDIE: What're you, accusin' me?

BEATRICE *(Her final thrust is to turn toward him instead of running from him)* : My God, what did you do?

(*Many steps on the outer stair draw his attention. We see the* FIRST OFFICER *descending, with* MARCO, *behind him* RODOLPHO, *and* CATHERINE *and the two strange immigrants, followed by* SECOND OFFICER. BEATRICE *hurries to door.*)

CATHERINE *(backing down stairs, fighting with* FIRST OFFICER; *as they appear on the stairs)* : What do yiz want from them? They work, that's all. They're boarders upstairs, they work on the piers.

BEATRICE *(to* FIRST OFFICER*)* : Ah, Mister, what do you want from them, who do they hurt?

CATHERINE *(pointing to* RODOLPHO*)* : They ain't no submarines, he was born in Philadelphia.

FIRST OFFICER: Step aside, lady.

CATHERINE: What do you mean? You can't just come in a house and—

FIRST OFFICER: All right, take it easy. (*To* RODOLPHO) What street were you born in Philadelphia?

CATHERINE: What do you mean, what street? Could you tell me what street you were born?

FIRST OFFICER: Sure. Four blocks away, One-eleven Union Street. Let's go, fellas.

CATHERINE *(fending him off* RODOLPHO*)* : No, you can't! Now, get outa here!

FIRST OFFICER: Look, girlie, if they're all right they'll be out tomorrow. If they're illegal they go back where they came from. If you want, get yourself a lawyer, although I'm tellin' you now you're wasting your money. Let's get them in the car, Dom. (*To the men*) Andiamo,[13] Andiamo, let's go.

(*The men start, but* MARCO *hangs back.*)

BEATRICE *(from doorway)* : Who're they hurtin', for God's sake, what do you want from them? They're starvin' over there, what do you want! Marco!

(MARCO *suddenly breaks from the group and dashes into the room and faces* EDDIE; BEATRICE *and* FIRST OFFICER *rush in as* MARCO *spits into* EDDIE's *face.*

CATHERINE *runs into hallway and throws herself into* RODOLPHO's *arms.* EDDIE, *with an enraged cry, lunges for* MARCO.)

EDDIE: Oh, you mother's—!

(FIRST OFFICER *quickly intercedes and pushes* EDDIE *from* MARCO, *who stands there accusingly.*)

---

[13] Let's go (Italian).

FIRST OFFICER (*between them, pushing* EDDIE *from* MARCO): Cut it out!

EDDIE (*over the* FIRST OFFICER'S *shoulder, to* MARCO): I'll kill you for that, you son of a bitch!

FIRST OFFICER: Hey! (*Shakes him*) Stay in here now, don't come out, don't bother him. You hear me? Don't come out, fella.

(*For an instant there is silence. Then* FIRST OFFICER *turns and takes* MARCO'S *arm and then gives a last, informative look at* EDDIE. *As he and* MARCO *are going out into the hall,* EDDIE *erupts.*)

EDDIE: I don't forget that, Marco! You hear what I'm sayin'?

(*Out in the hall,* FIRST OFFICER *and* MARCO *go down the stairs. Now, in the street,* LOUIS, MIKE, *and several neighbors including the butcher,* LIPARI—*a stout, intense, middle-aged man—are gathering around the stoop.*

LIPARI, *the butcher, walks over to the two strange men and kisses them. His wife, keening, goes and kisses their hands.* EDDIE *is emerging from the house shouting after* MARCO. BEATRICE *is trying to restrain him.*)

EDDIE: That's the thanks I get? Which I took the blankets off my bed for yiz? You gonna apologize to me, Marco! *Marco!*

FIRST OFFICER (*in the doorway with* MARCO): All right, lady, let them go. Get in the car, fellas, it's over there.

(RODOLPHO *is almost carrying the sobbing* CATHERINE *off up the street, left.*)

CATHERINE: He was born in Philadelphia! What do you want from him?

FIRST OFFICER: Step aside, lady, come on now. . . .

(*The* SECOND OFFICER *has moved off with the two strange men.* MARCO, *taking advantage of the* FIRST OFFICER'S *being occupied with* CATHERINE, *suddenly frees himself and points back at* EDDIE.)

MARCO: That one! I accuse that one!

(EDDIE *brushes* BEATRICE *aside and rushes out to the stoop.*)

FIRST OFFICER (*grabbing him and moving him quickly off up the left street*): Come on!

MARCO (*as he is taken off, pointing back at* EDDIE): That one! He killed my children! That one stole the food from my children!

(MARCO *is gone. The crowd has turned to* EDDIE.)

EDDIE (*to* LIPARI *and wife*): He's crazy! I give them the blankets off my bed. Six months I kept them like my own brothers!

(LIPARI, *the butcher, turns and starts up left with his arm around his wife.*)

EDDIE: Lipari! (*He follows* LIPARI *up left*) For Christ's sake, I kept them, I give them the blankets off my bed!

(LIPARI *and wife exit.* EDDIE *turns and starts crossing down right to* LOUIS *and* MIKE.)

EDDIE: Louis! *Louis!*

(LOUIS *barely turns, then walks off and exits down right with* MIKE. *Only* BEATRICE *is left on the stoop.* CATHERINE *now returns, blank-eyed, from offstage and the car.* EDDIE *calls after* LOUIS *and* MIKE.)

EDDIE: He's gonna take that back. He's gonna take that back or I'll kill him! You hear me? I'll kill him! I'll kill him! (*He exits up street calling.*)

(*There is a pause of darkness before the lights rise, on the reception room of a prison.* MARCO *is seated;* ALFIERI, CATHERINE, *and* RODOLPHO *standing.*)

ALFIERI: I'm waiting, Marco, what do you say?

RODOLPHO: Marco never hurt anybody.

ALFIERI: I can bail you out until your hearing comes up. But I'm not going to do it, you understand me? Unless I have your promise. You're an honorable man, I will believe your promise. Now what do you say?

MARCO: In my country he would be dead now. He would not live this long.

ALFIERI: All right, Rodolpho—you come with me now.

RODOLPHO: No! Please, Mister. Marco—promise the man. Please, I want you to watch the wedding. How can I be married and you're in here? Please, you're not going to do anything; you know you're not.

(MARCO *is silent.*)

CATHERINE (*kneeling left of* MARCO): Marco, don't you understand? He can't bail you out if you're gonna do something bad. To hell with Eddie. Nobody is gonna talk to him again if he lives to a hundred. Everybody knows you spit in his face, that's enough, isn't it? Give me the satisfaction—I want you at the wedding. You got a wife and kids, Marco. You could be workin' till the hearing comes up, instead of layin' around here.

MARCO (*to* ALFIERI): I have no chance?

ALFIERI (*crosses to behind* MARCO): No, Marco. You're going back. The hearing is a formality, that's all.

MARCO: But him? There is a chance, eh?

ALFIERI: When she marries him he can start to become an American. They permit that, if the wife is born here.

MARCO (*looking at* RODOLPHO): Well—we did something. (*He lays a palm on* RODOLPHO'S *arm and* RODOLPHO *covers it.*)

RODOLPHO: Marco, tell the man.

MARCO (*pulling his hand away*): What will I tell him? He knows such a promise is dishonorable.

ALFIERI: To promise not to kill is not dishonorable.

MARCO (*looking at* ALFIERI): No?

ALFIERI: No.

MARCO (*gesturing with his head—this is a new idea*): Then what is done with such a man?

ALFIERI: Nothing. If he obeys the law, he lives. That's all.

MARCO (*rises, turns to* ALFIERI): The law? All the law is not in a book.

ALFIERI: Yes. In a book. There is no other law.

MARCO (*his anger rising*): He degraded my brother. My blood. He robbed my children, he mocks my work. I work to come here, mister!

ALFIERI: I know, Marco—

MARCO: There is no law for that? Where is the law for that?

ALFIERI: There is none.

MARCO (*shaking his head, sitting*): I don't understand this country.

ALFIERI: Well? What is your answer? You have five or six weeks you could work. Or else you sit here. What do you say to me?

MARCO (*lowers his eyes. It almost seems he is ashamed*): All right.

ALFIERI: You won't touch him. This is your promise.

(*Slight pause.*)

MARCO: Maybe he wants to apologize to me.

(MARCO *is staring away.* ALFIERI *takes one of his hands.*)

ALFIERI: This is not God, Marco. You hear? Only God makes justice.

MARCO: All right.

ALFIERI (*nodding, not with assurance*): Good! Catherine, Rodolpho, Marco, let us go.

(CATHERINE *kisses* RODOLPHO *and* MARCO, *then kisses* ALFIERI'S *hand.*)

CATHERINE: I'll get Beatrice and meet you at the church. (*She leaves quickly.*)

(MARCO *rises.* RODOLPHO *suddenly embraces him.* MARCO *pats him on the back and* RODOLPHO *exits after* CATHERINE. MARCO *faces* ALFIERI.)

ALFIERI: Only God, Marco.

(MARCO *turns and walks out.* ALFIERI *with a certain processional tread leaves the stage. The lights dim out.*

The lights rise in the apartment. EDDIE *is alone in the rocker, rocking back and forth in little surges. Pause. Now* BEATRICE *emerges from a bedroom. She is in her best clothes, wearing a hat.*)

BEATRICE (*with fear, going to* EDDIE): I'll be back in about an hour, Eddie. All right?

EDDIE (*quietly, almost inaudibly, as though drained*): What, have I been talkin' to myself?

BEATRICE: Eddie, for God's sake, it's her wedding.

EDDIE: Didn't you hear what I told you? You walk out that door to that wedding you ain't comin' back here, Beatrice.

BEATRICE: Why! What do you want?

EDDIE: I want my respect. Didn't you ever hear of that? From my wife?

(CATHERINE *enters from bedroom.*)

CATHERINE: It's after three; we're supposed to be there already, Beatrice. The priest won't wait.

BEATRICE: Eddie. It's her wedding. There'll be nobody there from her family. For my sister let me go. I'm goin' for my sister.

EDDIE (*as though hurt*): Look, I been arguin' with you all day already, Beatrice, and I said what I'm gonna say. He's gonna come here and apologize to me or nobody from this house is goin' into that church today. Now if that's more to you than I am, then go. But don't come back. You be on my side or on their side, that's all.

CATHERINE (*suddenly*): Who the hell do you think you are?

BEATRICE: Sssh!

CATHERINE: You got no more right to tell nobody nothin'! Nobody! The rest of your life, nobody!

BEATRICE: Shut up, Katie! (*She turns* CATHERINE *around.*)

CATHERINE: You're gonna come with me!

BEATRICE: I can't Katie, I can't. . . .

CATHERINE: How can you listen to him? This rat!

BEATRICE (*shaking* CATHERINE): Don't you call him that!

CATHERINE (*clearing from* BEATRICE): What're you scared of? He's a rat! He belongs in the sewer!

BEATRICE: Stop it!

CATHERINE (*weeping*): He bites people when they sleep! He comes when nobody's lookin' and poisons decent people. In the garbage he belongs! (EDDIE *seems about to pick up the table and fling it at her.*)

BEATRICE: No, Eddie! Eddie! (*To* CATHERINE) Then we all belong in the garbage. You, and me too. Don't say that. Whatever happened we all done it, and don't you ever forget it, Catherine. (*She goes to* CATHERINE) Now go, go to your wedding, Katie, I'll stay home. Go. God bless you, God bless your children.

(*Enter* RODOLPHO.)

RODOLPHO: Eddie?

EDDIE: Who said you could come in here? Get outa here!

RODOLPHO: Marco is coming, Eddie. (*Pause.* BEATRICE *raises her hands in terror*) He's praying in the church. You understand? (*Pause.* RODOLPHO *advances into the room*) Catherine, I think it is better we go. Come with me.

CATHERINE: Eddie, go away, please.

BEATRICE (*quietly*): Eddie. Let's go someplace. Come. You and me. (*He has not moved*) I don't want you to be here when he comes. I'll get your coat.

EDDIE: Where? Where am I goin'? This is my house.

BEATRICE (*crying out*): What's the use of it! He's crazy now, you know the way they get, what good is it! You got nothin' against Marco, you always liked Marco!

EDDIE: I got nothin' against Marco? Which he called me a rat in front of the whole neighborhood? Which he said I killed his children! Where you been?

RODOLPHO (*quite suddenly, stepping up to* EDDIE): It is my fault, Eddie. Everything. I wish to apologize. It was wrong that I do not ask your permission. I kiss your hand. (*He reaches for* EDDIE'S *hand, but* EDDIE *snaps it away from him.*)

BEATRICE: Eddie, he's apologizing!

RODOLPHO: I have made all our troubles. But you have insult me too. Maybe God understand why you did that to me. Maybe you did not mean to insult me at all—

BEATRICE: Listen to him! Eddie, listen what he's tellin' you!

RODOLPHO: I think, maybe when Marco comes, if we can tell him we are comrades now, and we have no more argument between us. Then maybe Marco will not—

EDDIE: Now, listen—

CATHERINE: Eddie, give him a chance!

BEATRICE: What do you want! Eddie, what do you want!

EDDIE: I want my name! He didn't take my name; he's only a punk. Marco's got my name—(*to* RODOLPHO) and you can run tell him, kid, that he's gonna give it back to me in front of this neighborhood, or we have it out. (*Hoisting up his pants*) Come on, where is he? Take me to him.

BEATRICE: Eddie, listen—

EDDIE: I heard enough! Come on, let's go!

BEATRICE: Only blood is good? He kissed your hand!

EDDIE: What he does don't mean nothin' to nobody! (*To* RODOLPHO) Come on!

BEATRICE (*barring his way to the stairs*): What's gonna mean somethin'? Eddie, listen to me. Who could give you your name? Listen to me, I love you, I'm talkin' to you, I love you; if Marco'll kiss your hand outside, if he goes on his knees, what is he got to give you? That's not what you want.

EDDIE: Don't bother me!

BEATRICE: You want somethin' else, Eddie, and you can never have her!

CATHERINE (*in horror*): B.!

EDDIE (*shocked, horrified, his fists clenching*): Beatrice!

(MARCO *appears outside, walking toward the door from a distant point.*)

BEATRICE (*crying out, weeping*): The truth is not as bad as blood, Eddie! I'm tellin' you the truth—tell her good-by forever!

EDDIE (*crying out in agony*): That's what you think of me—that I would have such a thought? (*His fists clench his head as though it will burst.*)

MARCO (*calling near the door outside*): Eddie Carbone!

(EDDIE *swerves about; all stand transfixed for an instant. People appear outside.*)

EDDIE (*as though flinging his challenge*): Yeah, Marco! Eddie Carbone. Eddie Carbone. Eddie Carbone. (*He goes up the stairs and emerges from the apartment.* RODOLPHO *streaks up and out past him and runs to* MARCO.)

RODOLPHO: No, Marco, please! Eddie, please, he has children! You will kill a family!

BEATRICE: Go in the house! Eddie, go in the house!

EDDIE (*He gradually comes to address the people*): Maybe he come to apologize to me. Heh, Marco? For what you said about me in front of the neighborhood? (*He is incensing himself and little bits of laughter even escape him as his eyes are murderous and he cracks his knuckles in his hands with a strange sort of relaxation*) He knows that ain't right. To do like that? To a man? Which I put my roof over their head and my food in their mouth? Like in the Bible? Strangers I never seen in my whole life? To come out of the water and grab a girl for a passport? To go and take from your own family like from the stable—and never a word to me? And now accusations in the bargain! (*Directly to* MARCO) Wipin' the neighborhood with my name like a dirty rag! I want my name, Marco. (*He is moving now, carefully, toward* MARCO) Now gimme my name and we go together to the wedding.

BEATRICE *and* CATHERINE (*keening*): Eddie! Eddie, don't! Eddie!

EDDIE: No, Marco knows what's right from wrong. Tell the people, Marco, tell them what a liar you are! (*He has his arms spread and* MARCO *is spreading his*) Come on, liar, you know what you done! (*He lunges for* MARCO *as a great hushed shout goes up from the people.* MARCO *strikes* EDDIE *beside the neck.*)

MARCO: Animal! You go on your knees to me!

(EDDIE *goes down with the blow and* MARCO *starts to raise a foot to stomp him when* EDDIE *springs a knife into his hand and* MARCO *steps back.* LOUIS *rushes in toward* EDDIE.)

LOUIS: Eddie, for Christ's sake!

(EDDIE *raises the knife and* LOUIS *halts and steps back.*)

EDDIE: You lied about me, Marco. Now say it. Come on now, say it!

MARCO: Anima-a-a-l!

(EDDIE *lunges with the knife.* MARCO *grabs his arm, turning the blade inward and pressing it home as the women and* LOUIS *and* MIKE *rush in and separate them, and* EDDIE, *the knife still in his hand, falls to his knees before* MARCO. *The two women support him for a moment, calling his name again and again.*)

CATHERINE: Eddie, I never meant to do nothing bad to you.

EDDIE: Then why— Oh, B.!

BEATRICE: Yes, yes!

EDDIE: My B.!

(*He dies in her arms, and* BEATRICE *covers him with her body.* ALFIERI, *who is in the crowd, turns out to the audience. The lights have gone down, leaving him in a glow, while behind him the dull prayers of the people and the keening of the women continue.*)

ALFIERI: Most of the time now we settle for half and I like it better. But the truth is holy, and even as I know how wrong he was, and his death useless, I tremble, for I confess that something perversely pure calls to me from his memory—not purely good, but himself purely, for he allowed himself to be wholly known and for that I think I will love him more than all my sensible clients. And yet, it is better to settle for half, it must be! And so I mourn him—I admit it—with a certain . . . alarm.

(*The Curtain Falls.*)

Commentary

Arthur Miller has said that *A View from the Bridge* "is not designed primarily to draw tears or laughter from an audience but to strike a particular note of astonishment at the way in which, and the reasons for which, a man will endanger and risk and lose his very life."[14] Miller achieves his purpose by combining the violence and savagery of *Desire under the Elms* with O'Neill's and Ibsen's interest in the psychology of why a man acts as he does. Ibsen's brilliant exposition of his characters'

---

[14] Miller, *A View from the Bridge*, p. 18.

motivations has won him Miller's admiration. In *Rosmersholm* the dramatic action begins very late in the total story of Rosmer and Rebecca, and much of the play is taken up with bringing the past into the present. Unlike many modern plays which, says Miller, present "a situation without roots," Ibsen's drama makes one constantly aware "of process, change, development . . . , of the process by which the present has become what it is."[15]

In order to provide his audience with a perspective and a frame of reference for the tragedy of Eddie Carbone, Miller has, like Williams, employed the device of a commentator. But although the action of both *The Glass Menagerie* and *A View from the Bridge* is told in retrospect as the commentator's memory, Alfieri is more detached from the events of the drama than is Tom, who both participates and comments. Alfieri is only casually acquainted with the Carbone family. Miller makes him a lawyer to establish a critical voice which is intelligent, reasonable, and articulate. Yet for all his compassionate understanding he is powerless to prevent the disaster; although Eddie and Marco seek his advice, neither follows it. With every premonition of the way the action will "run its bloody course" (p. 338) he does nothing more than consult "a very wise old woman" (p. 361) as though she were a soothsayer. Confirmed in his fears, he returns, like a Greek chorus, to await the inevitable. Why doesn't the playwright allow Alfieri a more active role? Why does Alfieri identify himself with another lawyer "in some Caesar's year, in Calabria perhaps or on the cliff at Syracuse" (p. 338)? Besides suggesting this larger perspective of time and space Alfieri provides a legal and a moral frame of reference. His discussion of the details of the United States Immigration Laws (pp. 359-360) moves to a profounder view of moral and psychological law: "the law is nature" (p. 371). What does he mean? Does he contradict himself when he argues with Marco later that "there is no other law" (p. 378) but legal statutes?

It is appropriate that the lawyer Alfieri should in his opening remarks set up one of the central themes of *A View from the Bridge*: "Justice is very important here." What does he mean when he continues, "Now we settle for half, and I like it better," an observation underscored by his repeating it at the close of the drama? Like *Rosmersholm* and *Desire under the Elms*, *A View from the Bridge* explores in its own terms the problems of punishment and justice. Eddie Carbone believes he is justified in turning Marco and Rodolpho in to the Immigration Bureau, and in a legal sense of course he is since they have entered the country without passports. But law enforcement is the last thing in Eddie's mind as he desperately plunges ahead on a course of action which will destroy him.

---

[15] Arthur Miller, *Arthur Miller's Collected Plays* (New York, 1959), p. 21.

Similarly, with a pride and a passion equal only to Eddie's, Marco ignores Alfieri's warning that "only God makes justice" (p. 379) and gains his revenge at the price of murder.

Whereas Ibsen is more interested in the moral and psychological consequences of action and O'Neill is largely concerned with the conflicts and events which produce an act of violence, Miller focuses upon the question of what drives a man to murder. The answer for Eddie Carbone is not at all what he thinks it is. In the hands of an accomplished dramatist like Miller one effective technique for establishing his hero's illusions is dramatic irony. Dramatic irony exists when the audience has more information than a character on stage possesses and hence can view the dramatic action with a double perspective. To enrich our response, a playwright can create layers upon layers of dramatic irony so that some characters know more than others but not so much as the audience. Knowledge in Miller's play is not so much an awareness of facts as it is psychological insight. Beatrice is the first to sense the dangerous conflicts in her husband. It is she who guides the audience to a deeper understanding of Eddie's incestuous feelings for his niece. Next Alfieri and finally Catherine and Rodolpho attain our level of perception, but the greatest irony is that the tragic hero himself dies ignorant of the mainsprings of his nature.

Thus the theme of guilt and punishment broadens in *A View from the Bridge* to one of failure of self-recognition. Since Eddie understands himself so little, he cannot tolerate the truth even when Beatrice and Alfieri confront him with it. Instead he attempts to justify his bitter resentment of Rodolpho, his unconscious rival, by questioning the young boy's manhood as well as his motives for wanting to marry Catherine. Eddie is convinced of the truth of the charges he levels against Rodolpho; this is no malicious effort to destroy the integrity of his wife's cousin. Using every shred of "evidence" to substantiate his assumptions, Eddie believes he is fully justified in turning Rodolpho and his brother over to the immigration authorities, and he goes to his death protesting the purity of his motives for this treacherous betrayal. Oblivious to the fact that he has attempted to destroy Rodolpho's name, Eddie turns his frustrated wrath on Marco and dies demanding that Marco apologize for the slur on his character: "I want my name" (p. 380). The knife which Eddie intends to use against Marco is, with a symbolic touch of ironic justice, turned inward, and Eddie dies by his own hand.

Six years before he created the character of Eddie Carbone, Miller wrote:

> . . . I think the tragic feeling is evoked in us when we are in the presence of a character who is ready to lay down his life, if need be, to secure one thing—his sense of personal dignity. . . .

> Tragedy, then, is the consequence of a man's total compulsion to evaluate himself justly.
>
> In the sense of having been initiated by the hero himself, the tale always reveals what has been called his "tragic flaw," a failing that is not peculiar to grand or elevated characters. Nor is it necessarily a weakness. The flaw, or crack in the character, is really nothing—and need be nothing, but his inherent unwillingness to remain passive in the face of what he conceives to be a challenge to his dignity, his image of his rightful status.[16]

The playwright's observations on the tragic hero in modern drama provide a pertinent gloss on the character of Eddie Carbone. Frustrated and defeated though he is, Eddie demands that he be recognized as a human being. Marco's insulting cry of "Animal!" drives Eddie to a murderous assault, although by the act he confirms the epithet. He has created the disaster which destroys him, but even in defeat, he compels our respect for his good name. As Miller argues,

> . . . however one might dislike this man, who does all sorts of frightful things, he possesses or exemplifies the wondrous and humane fact that he too can be driven to what in the last analysis is a sacrifice of himself for his conception, however misguided, of right, dignity, and justice.[17]

He has, Alfieri says as the curtain falls, "allowed himself to be wholly known." Yet the irony remains that he is wholly known to everyone except himself.

The discovery of the self is in *Rosmersholm* a private matter, and Rosmer and Rebecca take their knowledge with them to the millrace. The larger world of the town and Norway, suggested by Kroll, Brendel, and Mortensgard, helps to bring truth to Rosmersholm, but it does not share in the secret process. *A View from the Bridge,* on the other hand, is not a private drama. The society of the play is a significant part of its meaning, and the hero can be understood only in terms of it. Urging the need for as many extras as is economically possible in a production of his tragedy, Miller says of his revision of the play:

> . . . the betrayal achieves its true proportions as it flies in the face of the mores administrated by Eddie's conscience—which is also the conscience of his friends, co-workers, and neighbors and not just his own autonomous creation. Thus his "oddness" came to disappear as he was seen in context, as a creature of his environment as well as an exception to it; and where originally there had been only a removed sense of terror at the oncoming catastrophe, now there was pity and, I think, the kind

---

[16] Arthur Miller, "Tragedy and the Common Man," *New York Times,* Feb. 27, 1949, Sec. 2, p. 1.

[17] Miller, *Collected Plays,* p. 51.

of wonder which it had been my aim to create in the first place. It was finally possible to mourn this man.[18]

What are the mores which Eddie violates? Is there a moral order in the world of *A View from the Bridge* or only a social order—a rigid code of social conduct? Is there really a unified sense of community in Eddie's world, or are there two communities in conflict: the civilized official world of the Immigration Bureau and the courts and the primitive, private world of the immigrant, loyal only to its own laws and taboos? What is Alfieri's view? Are the forces which crush Eddie largely psychological or social and legal? Or is Eddie destroyed by some more complex interplay of man and his community? Why is it finally possible, if Miller is right, to mourn Eddie "with a certain . . . alarm"?

Questions and Problems

1. Quoted below are the final moments of the original version of *A View from the Bridge*.[19]

(RODOLPHO *enters the apartment. A pause.*)

EDDIE: Get outa here.

RODOLPHO: Marco is coming, Eddie. (*Pause.* BEATRICE *raises her hands*) He's praying in the church. You understand? (*Pause.*)

BEATRICE (*in terror*): Eddie. Eddie, get out.

EDDIE: What do you mean, get out?

BEATRICE: Eddie, you got kids, go 'way, go 'way from here! Get outa the house!

EDDIE: Me get outa the house? *Me* get outa the house?
What did I do that I gotta get outa the house?
That I wanted a girl not to turn into a tramp?
That I made a promise and I kept my promise
She should be sump'm in her life?
(CATHERINE *goes trembling to him.*)

CATHERINE: Eddie—

EDDIE: What do *you* want?

CATHERINE: Please, Eddie, go away. He's comin' for you.

EDDIE: What do you care? What do you care he's comin' for me?

CATHERINE (*weeping, she embraces him*): I never meant to do nothin' bad to you in my life, Eddie!

EDDIE (*with tears in his eyes*): Then who meant somethin' bad? How'd it get bad?

CATHERINE: I don't know, I don't know!

---

[18] Miller, *Collected Plays*, p. 52.
[19] From Arthur Miller's A View from the Bridge, Copyright © 1955 by Arthur Miller and reprinted by special permission from The Viking Press, Inc.

EDDIE (*pointing to* RODOLPHO *with the new confidence of the embrace*):
They made it bad! This one and his brother made it bad which they
came like thieves to rob, to rob! (*He grabs her arm and swings her behind
him so that he is between her and* RODOLPHO, *who is alone at the door*)
You go tell him to come and come quick.
You go tell him I'm waitin' here for him to apologize
For what he said to me in front of the neighborhood!
Now get goin'!

RODOLPHO (*starting around* EDDIE *toward* CATHERINE): Come, Catherine,
we—

EDDIE (*nearly throwing* RODOLPHO *out the door*): Get away from her!

RODOLPHO (*starting back in*): Catherine!

EDDIE (*turning on* CATHERINE): Tell him to get out! (*She stands par-
alyzed before him*) Katie! I'll do somethin' if he don't get outa here!

BEATRICE (*rushing to him, her open hands pressed together before him as
though in prayer*): Eddie, it's her husband, it's her husband! Let her go,
it's her husband!

(CATHERINE, *moaning, breaks for the door, and she and* RODOLPHO *start
down the stairs;* EDDIE *lunges and catches her; he holds her, and she weeps
up into his face. And he kisses her on the lips.*)

EDDIE (*like a lover, out of his madness*): It's me, ain't it?

BEATRICE (*hitting his body*): Eddie! God, Eddie!

EDDIE: Katie, it's me, ain't it? You know it's me!

CATHERINE: Please, please, Eddie, lemme go. Heh? Please? (*She moves
to go.*)

(MARCO *appears on the street.*)

EDDIE (*to* RODOLPHO): Punk! Tell her what you are! You know what you
are, you punk!

CATHERINE (*pulling* RODOLPHO *out the doorway*): Come on!

(EDDIE *rushes after them to the doorway.*)

EDDIE: Make him tell you what he is! Tell her, punk! (*He is on the stairway, calling down*) Why don't he answer me! Punk, answer me! (*He
rushes down the stairs,* BEATRICE *after him.*)

BEATRICE: Eddie, come back!

(*Outside,* RODOLPHO *sees* MARCO *and cries out,* "No, Marco, Marco, go
away, go away!" *But* MARCO *nears the stoop, looking up at the descending*
EDDIE.)

EDDIE (*emerging from the house*): Punk, what are you gonna do with a
girl! I'm waitin' for your answer, punk. Where's your—answer!

(*He sees* MARCO. *Two other neighbors appear on the street, stand and
watch.* BEATRICE *now comes in front of him.*)

BEATRICE: Go in the house, Eddie!

EDDIE (*pushing her aside, coming out challengingly on the stoop, and glaring
down at* MARCO): What do you mean, go in the house? Maybe he came
to apologize to me. (*To the people*)
Which I took the blankets off my bed for them;
Which I brought up a girl, she wasn't even my daughter,
And I took from my own kids to give to her—

And they took her like you take from a stable,
Like you go in and rob from your own family!
And never a word to me!
And now accusations in the bargain?
Makin' my name like a dirty rag?
(*He faces* MARCO *now, and moves toward him*)
You gonna take that back?

BEATRICE: Eddie! Eddie!

EDDIE: I want my good name, Marco! You took my name!

(BEATRICE *rushes past him to* MARCO *and tries to push him away.*)

BEATRICE: Go, go!

MARCO: Animal! You go on your knees to me!

(*He strikes* EDDIE *powerfully on the side of the head.* EDDIE *falls back and draws a knife.* MARCO *springs to a position of defense, both men circling each other.* EDDIE *lunges, and* MIKE, LOUIS, *and all the neighbors move in to stop them, and they fight up the steps of the stoop, and there is a wild scream—*BEATRICE'S—*and they all spread out, some of them running off.*

MARCO *is standing over* EDDIE, *who is on his knees, a bleeding knife in his hands.* EDDIE *falls forward on his hands and knees, and he crawls a yard to* CATHERINE. *She raises her face away—but she does not move as he reaches over and grasps her leg, and, looking up at her, he seems puzzled, questioning, betrayed.*)

EDDIE: Catherine—why—? (*He falls forward and dies.*)

(CATHERINE *covers her face and weeps. She sinks down beside the weeping* BEATRICE. *The lights fade, and* ALFIERI *is illuminated in his office.*)

ALFIERI: Most of the time now we settle for half,
And I like it better.
And yet, when the tide is right
And the green smell of the sea
Floats in through my window,
The waves of this bay
Are the waves against Siracusa,
And I see a face that suddenly seems carved;
The eyes look like tunnels
Leading back toward some ancestral beach
Where all of us once lived.

And I wonder at those times
How much of all of us
Really lives there yet,
And when we will truly have moved on,
On and away from that dark place,
That world that has fallen to stones?

This is the end of the story. Good night.

(*The Curtain Falls.*)

A comparative study of the original and revised endings will indicate many of the differences between the two versions as a whole and will demonstrate the direction of Miller's thinking in recasting his earlier script.
a. In the original text Beatrice urges Eddie to leave home for the sake of his children. Why have the children been dropped? Why does Beatrice urge that she and Eddie go together? b. In what ways has Beatrice been given a more important role in the revision? Why? c. What changes have been made in Catherine's and Rodolpho's parts? Why? d. What implications can be drawn from the changes in Eddie's questions? In his stage directions? Why are his taunts at Rodolpho eliminated? e. How does the revised description of the fight and Eddie's death underscore the changes Miller has made elsewhere in this last scene? Account for the differences in Eddie's dying words. f. Miller has almost completely rewritten Alfieri's final speech. What is the significance of the original? How has the dramatist shifted the emphasis in the revision? What is the difference in the mood of these two curtain speeches? Is the character of Alfieri changed as a result? g. In general, what kind of changes has Miller made? What is the total effect of these revisions?

2. Why does Miller call this play *A View from the Bridge*? What is viewed from the bridge? Does the title suggest a way of approaching the drama?

3. What is the function of Eddie's story about Vinny Bolzano?

4. Miller carefully develops his hero in the context of a series of interrelated themes, often differently interpreted by his characters. Trace, for example, the themes of a. the responsibility and loyalty to one's family; b. the search for freedom; c. the necessity of trust; d. the power of passion; e. the need for self-respect; f. the definition of manhood; g. the meaning of growing up; h. guilt, punishment, and justice. What contribution does each of these themes make to the tragedy?

5. The sets of *The Glass Menagerie* and *A View from the Bridge* provide more of a backdrop than is needed for the acting area. Why?

6. A common dramatic convention is the arrival of a visitor to upset the existing equilibrium. For what purposes do Ibsen, O'Neill, Williams, and Miller employ this device?

7. Discuss the contributions made by the phonograph in *A View from the Bridge* and *The Glass Menagerie*. Why is the popular song "Baby Doll" first sung by Rodolpho and later played on a record?

8. What contribution does dancing make in *Desire under the Elms, The Glass Menagerie, The Cherry Orchard,* and *A View from the Bridge*?

9. *Desire under the Elms* and *A View from the Bridge* are in dialect. In which are the problems of dialogue more competently handled? Why? Read aloud from each play before reaching a conclusion.

10. Compare the roles of the townspeople in *The Devil's Disciple* and the neighbors in *Desire under the Elms* and *A View from the Bridge*.

11. Miller calls Eddie Carbone "a creature of his environment as well as an exception to it." To what extent can any of the other heroes in this volume be similarly characterized?

12. If Eddie Carbone has "allowed himself to be wholly known," can the same assertion be made of Shaw's Dick Dudgeon, Ibsen's Rosmer, O'Neill's Eben, or Williams' Tom? Which of these characters allow themselves to be wholly known? Which come to know themselves wholly? Note how Chekhov ironically plays with this theme. Mme. Ranevskaya and Gayev know themselves perhaps altogether too well. Yet what are the consequences of self-knowledge for Chekhov's characters? For the other heroes mentioned here?

13. In what ways does Miller's view of the nature of tragedy and the concept of the tragic hero differ from Ibsen's and O'Neill's? Are they in apparent agreement at points?

T. S. ELIOT

Murder in the Cathedral

Biography

THOMAS STEARNS ELIOT was born in St. Louis, Missouri, on September 26, 1888. His ancestor Andrew Eliot was a member of the jury that heard the trial of the Salem witches presided over by one of Nathaniel Hawthorne's ancestors. Another ancestor, the Rev. Andrew Eliot, declined election as president of Harvard so that he could remain as pastor of the North Church in Cambridge. Eliot's grandfather founded Washington University in St. Louis and became its Chancellor in 1872.

After a year at Milton Academy, Eliot entered Harvard in the fall of 1906. He was an editor of *The Harvard Advocate,* the undergraduate literary magazine, in which he published his first poems. Irving Babbitt and George Santayana were two members of the Harvard faculty who had a strong influence on him. Eliot completed his studies in three years, and after a year of graduate study in philosophy, he went to Paris to read French literature and philosophy at the Sorbonne. Returning to the Harvard Graduate School in 1911, he spent the next three years studying metaphysics, logic, Indic philology, and Sanskrit. In 1913-1914 he taught philosophy at Harvard, and after a summer in Germany he read Greek philosophy at Merton College, Oxford. His first mature poem, "The Love Song of J. Alfred Prufrock," was published in *Poetry* in 1915.

After his marriage in 1915 Eliot taught for a time at the Highgate School near London, and then accepted a banking position with Lloyds Bank, Ltd. From 1917 to 1919 he was assistant editor of *The Egoist,* and in 1923 he became editor of *The Criterion,* a quarterly review, a position he held until World War II. The publication of *The Waste Land* in 1922 established his reputation as a poet. Since 1925 he has been a director of the London publishing house of Faber and Faber. In 1927 Eliot became a member of the Church of England and a British citizen. He has made a number of trips to the United States, once to accept appointment as Charles Eliot Norton Professor of Poetry at Harvard in 1932-1933, and again to teach at the University of Chicago. In 1947 Eliot was awarded the Order of Merit and the Nobel Prize for Literature.

Eliot's reputation as the most influential poet and critic of the twentieth century was already established before he began writing drama.

Although his plays have not commanded the attention paid his poems, his experimentations in verse drama are one of the most important developments in the modern theater.

Principal Works

POEMS

Prufrock (1917)
Poems (1920)
The Waste Land (1922)
The Hollow Men (1925)

Ash Wednesday (1930)
Collected Poems 1909-1935
Four Quartets (1943)

PLAYS

Sweeney Agonistes, Fragments of an
  Aristophanic Melodrama (1927)
The Rock, a Pageant Play (1934)
Murder in the Cathedral (1935)

The Family Reunion (1938)
The Cocktail Party (1950)
The Confidential Clerk (1953)
The Elder Statesman (1958)

ESSAYS AND CRITICISM

The Sacred Wood (1920)
Homage to John Dryden (1924)
For Lancelot Andrewes (1928)
Selected Essays (1932; revised 1951)
The Use of Poetry and the Use of
  Criticism (1933)

The Idea of a Christian Society
  (1940)
Notes Towards the Definition of Culture (1948)
Poetry and Drama (1951)
On Poetry and Poets (1956)

Selected Descriptive Bibliography

Blackmur, R. P., "T. S. Eliot: From 'Ash Wednesday' to *Murder in the Cathedral,*" *The Double Agent* (New York, 1935), pp. 184-218; reprinted in *T. S. Eliot: a Selected Critique,* ed. Leonard Unger (New York, 1948), pp. 236-262.
  Blackmur discusses Murder in the Cathedral *as a product of Eliot's Christian sensibility.*
Donoghue, Denis, *The Third Voice,* Princeton, 1959.
  In a chapter on Murder in the Cathedral *Donoghue criticizes the play as a failure in structure and language.*

Fergusson, Francis, *The Idea of a Theatre,* New York, 1953.
  Fergusson offers some intelligent commentary on the difficult climax at the end of Part One.

Gardner, Helen, *The Art of T. S. Eliot,* London, 1949.
  In one of the best studies of Eliot's poetry Miss Gardner has time for only a few pages on Eliot the dramatist. For her Thomas is unconvincing and the stature of Murder in the Cathedral *is achieved through the poetry of the choruses.*

Gerstenberger, Donna, "The Saint and the Circle," *Criticism,* II (Fall, 1960), 336-341.
  A brief but pertinent analysis of the image of the wheel in Murder in the Cathedral.

Jones, David E., *The Plays of T. S. Eliot,* London, 1960.
  Jones's extended analysis of Murder in the Cathedral *is one of the most useful and intelligent essays on the play.*

Kenner, Hugh, *The Invisible Poet: T. S. Eliot,* New York, 1959.
  A short chapter with flashes of incisive comment in a fine book on Eliot.

Martz, Louis, "The Wheel and the Point: Aspect of Imagery and Theme in Eliot's Later Poetry," *Sewanee Review,* LV (Winter, 1947), 126-147; reprinted in Unger, pp. 444-462.
  An excellent analysis of Murder in the Cathedral *that points up the relation of its themes and images to the larger body of Eliot's poetic achievement.*

Matthiessen, F. O., *The Achievement of T. S. Eliot,* 3rd ed., New York, 1958.
  Matthiessen's remarks on Eliot are always pertinent.

Peacock, Ronald, *The Poet in the Theatre,* London, 1946.
  One chapter on Murder in the Cathedral *and* The Family Reunion *compares Eliot's achievement with that of other writers in poetry and drama.*

Peter, John, "Murder in the Cathedral," *Sewanee Review,* LXI (Summer, 1953), 362-383.
  A helpful exegesis of the play. A good place to begin a study of the criticism of Murder in the Cathedral.

Smith, Grover, Jr., *T. S. Eliot's Poetry and Plays,* Chicago, 1956.
  In a chapter on Murder in the Cathedral *Smith explores the meaning of the theological paradoxes of action and suffering that he argues are at the heart of the drama.*

A Note on Thomas à Becket

Thomas à Becket (1118-1170) was chancellor of England and archbishop of Canterbury under Henry II. His father, a prosperous trader, moved to London from France before Becket was born. As a young man

Thomas served in the household of Theobald, the archbishop of Canterbury, and soon became the primate's confidant. In 1154 with the assistance of Theobald, Becket was appointed archdeacon of Canterbury and chancellor of England. In this capacity he became a close friend of Henry II, who was fifteen years younger than Becket. Active in diplomacy and on the battlefield, Becket organized the Toulouse campaign in 1159. He was always ready, when the occasion arose, to uphold royal authority over ecclesiastical claims.

In 1162 Henry's influence succeeded in getting Becket elected archbishop of Canterbury. Becket was reluctant to accept the position because he foresaw an inevitable conflict between ecclesiastical duty and royal will, but Henry was convinced that their cooperation and close friendship would continue. Becket surprised his king by at once resigning the chancellorship because he feared a conflict of interests. At the council of Westminster in 1163 Becket began to support the clergy on issues of canon law and to resist the king. Henry then tried to ruin Becket, who was forced to flee to France in November, 1164.

Becket spent six austere years of exile in French abbeys studying canon law and corresponding extensively. During these years Henry was unrelentingly vindictive, and Thomas was intransigent on matters of religious principle. Becket himself believed that only his death would resolve the impasse. In 1169 he excommunicated the bishops of London and Salisbury, and in 1170 Henry retaliated by having the archbishop of York crown the heir apparent, a deliberate infringement upon Becket's rights as archbishop of Canterbury. Pope Alexander III intervened to bring about an apparent, but obviously ineffectual, reconciliation between king and primate. Thomas thereupon suspended the bishops who had crowned the young king and then returned to England. On Christmas Day, 1170, he publicly excommunicated his enemies. Four days later four knights, loyal to Henry, murdered Becket in his cathedral church. In 1173 Thomas was canonized, and his shrine at Canterbury has long been famous.

Murder in the Cathedral T. S. ELIOT

CHARACTERS

A CHORUS OF WOMEN OF CANTER-
    BURY

THREE PRIESTS OF THE CATHEDRAL

A MESSENGER

ARCHBISHOP THOMAS BECKET

FOUR TEMPTERS

FOUR KNIGHTS

ATTENDANTS

PART ONE: *The scene is the Archbishop's Hall, on December 2nd, 1170.*

PART TWO: *The first scene is in the Archbishop's Hall; the second scene is in the Cathedral, on December 29th, 1170.*

Murder in the Cathedral was first performed in June, 1935 at the Canterbury Festival in Canterbury, England.

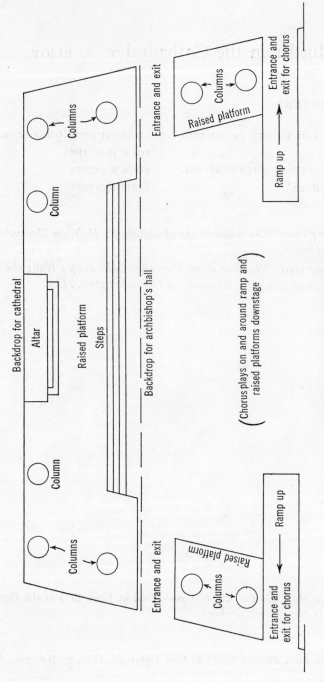

MURDER IN THE CATHEDRAL

Part One

CHORUS: Here let us stand, close by the cathedral. Here let us wait.
Are we drawn by danger? Is it the knowledge of safety, that draws our
   feet
Towards the cathedral? What danger can be
For us, the poor, the poor women of Canterbury? What tribulation
With which we are not already familiar? There is no danger
For us, and there is no safety in the cathedral. Some presage of an act
Which our eyes are compelled to witness, has forced our feet
Towards the cathedral. We are forced to bear witness.

Since golden October declined into somber November
And the apples were gathered and stored, and the land became brown
   sharp points of death in a waste of water and mud,
The New Year waits, breathes, waits, whispers in darkness.
While the laborer kicks off a muddy boot and stretches his hand to the
   fire,
The New Year waits, destiny waits for the coming.
Who has stretched out his hand to the fire and remembered the Saints at
   All Hallows,[1]
Remembered the martyrs and saints who wait? And who shall
Stretch out his hand to the fire, and deny his master? Who shall be warm
By the fire, and deny his master?

Seven years and the summer is over,
Seven years since the Archbishop left us,
He who was always kind to his people.
But it would not be well if he should return.
King rules or barons rule;
We have suffered various oppression,
But mostly we are left to our own devices,
And we are content if we are left alone.
We try to keep our households in order;
The merchant, shy and cautious, tries to compile a little fortune,
And the laborer bends to his piece of earth, earth-color, his own color,
Preferring to pass unobserved.

---

[1] November 1, All Saints Day, is the day of the feast to celebrate all Christian
saints.

Now I fear disturbance of the quiet seasons:
Winter shall come bringing death from the sea,
Ruinous spring shall beat at our doors,
Root and shoot shall eat our eyes and our ears,
Disastrous summer burn up the beds of our streams
And the poor shall wait for another decaying October.
Why should the summer bring consolation
For autumn fires and winter fogs?
What shall we do in the heat of summer
But wait in barren orchards for another October?
Some malady is coming upon us. We wait, we wait,
And the saints and martyrs wait, for those who shall be martyrs and
    saints.
Destiny waits in the hand of God, shaping the still unshapen:
I have seen these things in a shaft of sunlight.
Destiny waits in the hand of God, not in the hands of statesmen
Who do, some well, some ill, planning and guessing,
Having their aims which turn in their hands in the pattern of time.
Come, happy December, who shall observe you, who shall preserve you?
Shall the Son of Man be born again in the litter of scorn?
For us, the poor, there is no action,
But only to wait and to witness.
    (*Enter* PRIESTS.)
FIRST PRIEST: Seven years and the summer is over.
Seven years since the Archbishop left us.
SECOND PRIEST: What does the Archbishop do, and our Sovereign Lord the
    Pope
With the stubborn King and the French King
In ceaseless intrigue, combinations,
In conference, meetings accepted, meetings refused,
Meetings unended or endless
At one place or another in France?
THIRD PRIEST: I see nothing quite conclusive in the art of temporal govern-
    ment,
But violence, duplicity and frequent malversation.
King rules or barons rule:
The strong man strongly and the weak man by caprice.
They have but one law, to seize the power and keep it,
And the steadfast can manipulate the greed and lust of others,
The feeble is devoured by his own.
FIRST PRIEST: Shall these things not end
    Until the poor at the gate
    Have forgotten their friend, their Father in God, have forgotten
    That they had a friend?
    (*Enter* MESSENGER.)
MESSENGER: Servants of God, and watchers of the temple,
    I am here to inform you, without circumlocution:
    The Archbishop is in England, and is close outside the city.

I was sent before in haste
To give you notice of his coming, as much as was possible,
That you may prepare to meet him.
FIRST PRIEST: What, is the exile ended, is our Lord Archbishop
Reunited with the King? What reconciliation
Of two proud men?
THIRD PRIEST: What peace can be found
To grow between the hammer and the anvil?
SECOND PRIEST: Tell us,
Are the old disputes at an end, is the wall of pride cast down
That divided them? Is it peace or war?
FIRST PRIEST: Does he come
In full assurance, or only secure
In the power of Rome, the spiritual rule,
The assurance of right, and the love of the people?
MESSENGER: You are right to express a certain incredulity.
He comes in pride and sorrow, affirming all his claims,
Assured, beyond doubt, of the devotion of the people,
Who receive him with scenes of frenzied enthusiasm,
Lining the road and throwing down their capes,
Strewing the way with leaves and late flowers of the season.
The streets of the city will be packed to suffocation,
And I think that his horse will be deprived of its tail,
A single hair of which becomes a precious relic.
He is at one with the Pope, and with the King of France,
Who indeed would have liked to detain him in his kingdom:
But as for our King, that is another matter.
FIRST PRIEST: But again, is it war or peace?
MESSENGER: Peace, but not the kiss of peace.
A patched up affair, if you ask my opinion.
And if you ask me, I think the Lord Archbishop
Is not the man to cherish any illusions,
Or yet to diminish the least of his pretensions.
If you ask my opinion, I think that this peace
Is nothing like an end, or like a beginning.
It is common knowledge that when the Archbishop
Parted from the King, he said to the King,
My Lord, he said, I leave you as a man
Whom in this life I shall not see again.
I have this, I assure you, on the highest authority;
There are several opinions as to what he meant,
But no one considers it a happy prognostic. (*Exit.*)
FIRST PRIEST: I fear for the Archbishop, I fear for the Church,
I know that the pride bred of sudden prosperity
Was but confirmed by bitter adversity.
I saw him as Chancellor, flattered by the King,
Liked or feared by courtiers, in their overbearing fashion,
Despised and despising, always isolated,

Never one among them, always insecure;
His pride always feeding upon his own virtues,
Pride drawing sustenance from impartiality,
Pride drawing sustenance from generosity,
Loathing power given by temporal devolution,
Wishing subjection to God alone.
Had the King been greater, or had he been weaker
Things had perhaps been different for Thomas.

SECOND PRIEST: Yet our Lord is returned. Our Lord has come back to his
　　own again.
We have had enough of waiting, from December to dismal December.
The Archbishop shall be at our head, dispelling dismay and doubt.
He will tell us what we are to do, he will give us orders, instruct us.
Our Lord is at one with the Pope, and also the King of France.
We can lean on a rock, we can feel a firm foothold
Against the perpetual wash of tides of balance of forces of barons and
　　landholders.
The rock of God is beneath our feet. Let us meet the Archbishop with
　　cordial thanksgiving:
Our Lord, our Archbishop returns. And when the Archbishop returns
Our doubts are dispelled. Let us therefore rejoice,
I say rejoice, and show a glad face for his welcome.
I am the Archbishop's man. Let us give the Archbishop welcome!

THIRD PRIEST: For good or ill, let the wheel turn.
The wheel has been still, these seven years, and no good.
For ill or good, let the wheel turn.
For who knows the end of good or evil?
Until the grinders cease
And the door shall be shut in the street,
And all the daughters of music shall be brought low.

CHORUS: Here is no continuing city, here is no abiding stay.
Ill the wind, ill the time, uncertain the profit, certain the danger.
O late late late, late is the time, late too late, and rotten the year;
Evil the wind, and bitter the sea, and grey the sky, grey grey grey.
O Thomas, return, Archbishop; return, return to France.
Return. Quickly. Quietly. Leave us to perish in quiet.
You come with applause, you come with rejoicing, but you come bringing
　　death into Canterbury:
A doom on the house, a doom on yourself, a doom on the world.

We do not wish anything to happen.
Seven years we have lived quietly,
Succeeded in avoiding notice,
Living and partly living.
There have been oppression and luxury,
There have been poverty and license,
There has been minor injustice.
Yet we have gone on living,

Living and partly living.
Sometimes the corn has failed us,
Sometimes the harvest is good,
One year is a year of rain,
Another a year of dryness,
One year the apples are abundant,
Another year the plums are lacking.
Yet we have gone on living,
Living and partly living.
We have kept the feasts, heard the masses,
We have brewed beer and cider,
Gathered wood against the winter,
Talked at the corner of the fire,
Talked at the corners of streets,
Talked not always in whispers,
Living and partly living.
We have seen births, deaths and marriages,
We have had various scandals,
We have been afflicted with taxes,
We have had laughter and gossip,
Several girls have disappeared
Unaccountably, and some not able to.
We have all had our private terrors,
Our particular shadows, our secret fears.
But now a great fear is upon us, a fear not of one but of many,
A fear like birth and death, when we see birth and death alone
In a void apart. We
Are afraid in a fear which we cannot know, which we cannot face, which
none understands,
And our hearts are torn from us, our brains unskinned like the layers of
an onion, our selves are lost lost
In a final fear which none understands. O Thomas Archbishop,
O Thomas our Lord, leave us and leave us be, in our humble and tar-
nished frame of existence, leave us; do not ask us
To stand to the doom on the house, the doom on the Archbishop, the
doom on the world.
Archbishop, secure and assured of your fate, unaffrayed among the shades,
do you realize what you ask, do you realize what it means
To the small folk drawn into the pattern of fate, the small folk who live
among small things,
The strain on the brain of the small folk who stand to the doom of the
house, the doom of their lord, the doom of the world?
O Thomas, Archbishop, leave us, leave us, leave sullen Dover, and set sail
for France. Thomas our Archbishop still our Archbishop even in
France. Thomas Archbishop, set the white sail between the grey sky
and the bitter sea, leave us, leave us for France.

SECOND PRIEST: What a way to talk at such a juncture!
You are foolish, immodest and babbling women.

Do you not know that the good Archbishop
Is likely to arrive at any moment?
The crowds in the streets will be cheering and cheering,
You go on croaking like frogs in the treetops:
But frogs at least can be cooked and eaten.
Whatever you are afraid of, in your craven apprehension,
Let me ask you at the least to put on pleasant faces,
And give a hearty welcome to our good Archbishop.
(*Enter* THOMAS.)

THOMAS: Peace. And let them be, in their exaltation.
They speak better than they know, and beyond your understanding.
They know and do not know, what it is to act or suffer.
They know and do not know, that action is suffering
And suffering is action. Neither does the agent suffer
Nor the patient act. But both are fixed
In an eternal action, an eternal patience
To which all must consent that it may be willed
And which all must suffer that they may will it,
That the pattern may subsist, for the pattern is the action
And the suffering, that the wheel may turn and still
Be forever still.

SECOND PRIEST: O my Lord, forgive me, I did not see you coming,
Engrossed by the chatter of these foolish women.
Forgive us, my Lord, you would have had a better welcome
If we had been sooner prepared for the event.
But your Lordship knows that seven years of waiting,
Seven years of prayer, seven years of emptiness,
Have better prepared our hearts for your coming,
Than seven days could make ready Canterbury.
However, I will have fires laid in all your rooms
To take the chill off our English December,
Your Lordship now being used to a better climate.
Your Lordship will find your rooms in order as you left them.

THOMAS: And will try to leave them in order as I find them.
I am more than grateful for all your kind attentions.
These are small matters. Little rest in Canterbury
With eager enemies restless about us.
Rebellious bishops, York, London, Salisbury,
Would have intercepted our letters,
Filled the coast with spies and sent to meet me
Some who hold me in bitterest hate.
By God's grace aware of their prevision
I sent my letters on another day,
Had fair crossing, found at Sandwich
Broc, Warenne,[2] and the Sheriff of Kent,

---

[2] Ranulf de Broc and Reynold de Warenne were Becket's bitter enemies in his struggle with Henry II.

Those who had sworn to have my head from me
Only John, the Dean of Salisbury,
Fearing for the King's name, warning against treason,
Made them hold their hands. So for the time
We are unmolested.
FIRST PRIEST: But do they follow after?
THOMAS: For a little time the hungry hawk
  Will only soar and hover, circling lower,
  Waiting excuse, pretense, opportunity.
  End will be simple, sudden, God-given.
  Meanwhile the substance of our first act
  Will be shadows, and the strife with shadows.
  Heavier the interval than the consummation.
  All things prepare the event. Watch.
  (*Enter* FIRST TEMPTER.)
FIRST TEMPTER: You see, my Lord, I do not wait upon ceremony:
  Here I have come, forgetting all acrimony,
  Hoping that your present gravity
  Will find excuse for my humble levity
  Remembering all the good time past.
  Your Lordship won't despise an old friend out of favor?
  Old Tom, gay Tom, Becket of London,
  Your Lordship won't forget that evening on the river
  When the King, and you and I were all friends together?
  Friendship should be more than biting Time can sever.
  What, my Lord, now that you recover
  Favor with the King, shall we say that summer's over
  Or that the good time cannot last?
  Fluting in the meadows, viols in the hall,
  Laughter and apple-blossom floating on the water,
  Singing at nightfall, whispering in chambers,
  Fires devouring the winter season,
  Eating up the darkness, with wit and wine and wisdom!
  Now that the King and you are in amity,
  Clergy and laity may return to gaiety,
  Mirth and sportfulness need not walk warily.
THOMAS: You talk of seasons that are past. I remember
  Not worth forgetting.
TEMPTER: And of the new season.
  Spring has come in winter. Snow in the branches
  Shall float as sweet as blossoms. Ice along the ditches
  Mirror the sunlight. Love in the orchard
  Send the sap shooting. Mirth matches melancholy.
THOMAS: We do not know very much of the future
  Except that from generation to generation
  The same things happen again and again.
  Men learn little from others' experience.
  But in the life of one man, never

The same time returns. Sever
The cord, shed the scale. Only
The fool, fixed in his folly, may think
He can turn the wheel on which he turns.
TEMPTER: My Lord, a nod is as good as a wink.
A man will often love what he spurns.
For the good times past, that are come again
I am your man.
THOMAS: Not in this train
Look to your behavior. You were safer
Think of penitence and follow your master.
TEMPTER: Not at this gait!
If you go so fast, others may go faster.
Your Lordship is too proud!
The safest beast is not the one that roars most loud,
This was not the way of the King our master!
You were not used to be so hard upon sinners
When they were your friends. Be easy, man!
The easy man lives to eat the best dinners.
Take a friend's advice. Leave well alone,
Or your goose may be cooked and eaten to the bone.
THOMAS: You come twenty years too late.
TEMPTER: Then I leave you to your fate.
I leave you to the pleasures of your higher vices,
Which will have to be paid for at higher prices.
Farewell, my Lord, I do not wait upon ceremony,
I leave as I came, forgetting all acrimony,
Hoping that your present gravity
Will find excuse for my humble levity.
If you will remember me, my Lord, at your prayers,
I'll remember you at kissing-time below the stairs.
THOMAS: Leave-well-alone, the springtime fancy,
So one thought goes whistling down the wind.
The impossible is still temptation.
The impossible, the undesirable,
Voices under sleep, waking a dead world,
So that the mind may not be whole in the present.
(*Enter* SECOND TEMPTER.)
SECOND TEMPTER: Your Lordship has forgotten me, perhaps. I will remind
     you.
We met at Clarendon, at Northampton,
And last at Montmirail, in Maine. Now that I have recalled them,
Let us but set these not too pleasant memories
In balance against other, earlier
And weightier ones: those of the Chancellorship.
See how the late ones rise! You, master of policy
Whom all acknowledged, should guide the state again.
THOMAS: Your meaning?

TEMPTER: The Chancellorship that you resigned
When you were made Archbishop—that was a mistake
On your part—still may be regained. Think, my Lord,
Power obtained grows to glory,
Life lasting, a permanent possession.
A templed tomb, monument of marble.
Rule over men reckon no madness.

THOMAS: To the man of God what gladness?

TEMPTER: Sadness
Only to those giving love to God alone.
Shall he who held the solid substance
Wander waking with deceitful shadows?
Power is present. Holiness hereafter.

THOMAS: Who then?

TEMPTER: The Chancellor. King and Chancellor.
King commands. Chancellor richly rules.
This is a sentence not taught in the schools.
To set down the great, protect the poor,
Beneath the throne of God can man do more?
Disarm the ruffian, strengthen the laws,
Rule for the good of the better cause,
Dispensing justice make all even,
Is thrive on earth, and perhaps in heaven.

THOMAS: What means?

TEMPTER: Real power
Is purchased at price of a certain submission.
Your spiritual power is earthly perdition.
Power is present, for him who will wield.

THOMAS: Who shall have it?

TEMPTER: He who will come.

THOMAS: What shall be the month?

TEMPTER: The last from the first.

THOMAS: What shall we give for it?

TEMPTER: Pretense of priestly power.

THOMAS: Why should we give it?

TEMPTER: For the power and the glory.

THOMAS: No!

TEMPTER: Yes! Or bravery will be broken,
Cabined in Canterbury, realmless ruler,
Self-bound servant of a powerless Pope,
The old stag, circled with hounds.

THOMAS: No!

TEMPTER: Yes! men must manœuver. Monarchs also,
Waging war abroad, need fast friends at home.
Private policy is public profit;
Dignity still shall be dressed with decorum.

THOMAS: You forget the bishops
Whom I have laid under excommunication.

TEMPTER: Hungry hatred
  Will not strive against intelligent self-interest.
THOMAS: You forget the barons. Who will not forget
  Constant curbing of petty privilege.
TEMPTER: Against the barons
  Is King's cause, churl's cause, Chancellor's cause.
THOMAS: No! shall I, who keep the keys
  Of heaven and hell, supreme alone in England,
  Who bind and loose, with power from the Pope,
  Descend to desire a punier power?
  Delegate to deal the doom of damnation,
  To condemn kings, not serve among their servants,
  Is my open office. No! Go.
TEMPTER: Then I leave you to your fate.
  Your sin soars sunward, covering kings' falcons.
THOMAS: Temporal power, to build a good world,
  To keep order, as the world knows order.
  Those who put their faith in worldly order
  Not controlled by the order of God,
  In confident ignorance, but arrest disorder,
  Make it fast, breed fatal disease,
  Degrade what they exalt. Power with the King—
  I *was* the King, his arm, his better reason.
  But what was once exaltation
  Would now be only mean descent.
  (*Enter* THIRD TEMPTER.)
THIRD TEMPTER: I am an unexpected visitor.
THOMAS: I expected you.
TEMPTER: But not in this guise, or for my present purpose.
THOMAS: No purpose brings surprise.
TEMPTER: Well, my Lord,
  I am no trifler, and no politician.
  To idle or intrigue at court
  I have no skill. I am no courtier.
  I know a horse, a dog, a wench;
  I know how to hold my estates in order,
  A country-keeping lord who minds his own business.
  It is we country lords who know the country
  And we who know what the country needs.
  It is our country. We care for the country.
  We are the backbone of the nation.
  We, not the plotting parasites
  About the King. Excuse my bluntness:
  I am a rough straightforward Englishman.
THOMAS: Proceed straight forward.
TEMPTER: Purpose is plain.
  Endurance of friendship does not depend

Upon ourselves, but upon circumstance.
But circumstance is not undetermined.
Unreal friendship may turn to real
But real friendship, once ended, cannot be mended.
Sooner shall enmity turn to alliance.
The enmity that never knew friendship
Can sooner know accord.
THOMAS: For a countryman
You wrap your meaning in as dark generality
As any courtier.
TEMPTER: This is the simple fact!
You have no hope of reconciliation
With Henry the King. You look only
To blind assertion in isolation.
That is a mistake.
THOMAS: O Henry, O my King!
TEMPTER: Other friends
May be found in the present situation.
King in England is not all-powerful;
King is in France, squabbling in Anjou;
Round him waiting hungry sons.
We are for England. We are in England.
You and I, my Lord, are Normans.
England is a land for Norman
Sovereignty. Let the Angevin[3]
Destroy himself, fighting in Anjou.
He does not understand us, the English barons.
We are the people.
THOMAS: To what does this lead?
TEMPTER: To a happy coalition
Of intelligent interests.
THOMAS: But what have you—
If you do speak for barons—
TEMPTER: For a powerful party
Which has turned its eyes in your direction—
To gain from you, your Lordship asks.
For us, Church favor would be an advantage,
Blessing of Pope powerful protection
In the fight for liberty. You, my Lord,
In being with us, would fight a good stroke
At once, for England and for Rome,
Ending the tyrannous jurisdiction
Of king's court over bishop's court,
Of king's court over baron's court.

---

[3] An inhabitant of the old French territory of Anjou, now the department of Maine
et Loire in western France.

THOMAS: Which I helped to found.

TEMPTER: Which you helped to found.
But time past is time forgotten.
We expect the rise of a new constellation.

THOMAS: And if the Archbishop cannot trust the King,
How can he trust those who work for King's undoing?

TEMPTER: Kings will allow no power but their own;
Church and people have good cause against the throne.

THOMAS: If the Archbishop cannot trust the Throne,
He has good cause to trust none but God alone.
I ruled once as Chancellor
And men like you were glad to wait at my door.
Not only in the court, but in the field
And in the tilt-yard I made many yield.
Shall I who ruled like an eagle over doves
Now take the shape of a wolf among wolves?
Pursue your treacheries as you have done before:
No one shall say that I betrayed a king.

TEMPTER: Then, my Lord, I shall not wait at your door.
And I well hope, before another spring
The King will show his regard for your loyalty.

THOMAS: To make, then break, this thought has come before,
The desperate exercise of failing power.
Samson in Gaza did no more.⁴
But if I break, I must break myself alone.
(*Enter* FOURTH TEMPTER.)

FOURTH TEMPTER: Well done, Thomas, your will is hard to bend.
And with me beside you, you shall not lack a friend.

THOMAS: Who are you? I expected
Three visitors, not four.

TEMPTER: Do not be surprised to receive one more.
Had I been expected, I had been here before.
I always precede expectation.

THOMAS: Who are you?

TEMPTER: As you do not know me, I do not need a name,
And, as you know me, that is why I come.
You know me, but have never seen my face.
To meet before was never time or place.

THOMAS: Say what you come to say.

TEMPTER: It shall be said at last.
Hooks have been baited with morsels of the past.
Wantonness is weakness. As for the King,
His hardened hatred shall have no end.

---

⁴ The great Hebrew hero and enemy of the Philistines. After betraying the secret
of his great strength to Delilah, Samson was blinded by the Philistines and sent
in slavery to Gaza. He gained his revenge by pulling down the pillars of the
temple upon the Philistines.

You know truly, the King will never trust
Twice, the man who has been his friend.
Borrow use cautiously, employ
Your services as long as you have to lend.
You would wait for trap to snap
Having served your turn, broken and crushed.
As for barons, envy of lesser men
Is still more stubborn than king's anger.
Kings have public policy, barons private profit,
Jealousy raging possession of the fiend.
Barons are employable against each other;
Greater enemies must kings destroy.

THOMAS: What is your counsel?

TEMPTER: Fare forward to the end.
All other ways are closed to you
Except the way already chosen.
But what is pleasure, kingly rule,
Or rule of men beneath a king,
With craft in corners, stealthy stratagem,
To general grasp of spiritual power?
Man oppressed by sin, since Adam fell—
You hold the keys of heaven and hell.
Power to bind and loose: bind, Thomas, bind,
King and bishop under your heel.
King, emperor, bishop, baron, king:
Uncertain mastery of melting armies,
War, plague, and revolution,
New conspiracies, broken pacts;
To be master or servant within an hour,
This is the course of temporal power.
The Old King shall know it, when at last breath,
No sons, no empire, he bites broken teeth.
You hold the skein: wind, Thomas, wind
The thread of eternal life and death.
You hold this power, hold it.

THOMAS: Supreme, in this land?

TEMPTER: Supreme, but for one.

THOMAS: That I do not understand.

TEMPTER: It is not for me to tell you how this may be so;
I am only here, Thomas, to tell you what you know.

THOMAS: How long shall this be?

TEMPTER: Save what you know already, ask nothing of me.
But think, Thomas, think of glory after death.
When king is dead, there's another king,
And one more king is another reign.
King is forgotten, when another shall come:
Saint and Martyr rule from the tomb.

Think, Thomas, think of enemies dismayed,
Creeping in penance, frightened of a shade;
Think of pilgrims, standing in line
Before the glittering jewelled shrine,
From generation to generation
Bending the knee in supplication,
Think of the miracles, by God's grace,
And think of your enemies, in another place.

THOMAS: I have thought of these things.

TEMPTER: That is why I tell you.
Your thoughts have more power than kings to compel you.
You have also thought, sometimes at your prayers,
Sometimes hesitating at the angles of stairs,
And between sleep and waking, early in the morning,
When the bird cries, have thought of further scorning.
That nothing lasts, but the wheel turns,
The nest is rifled, and the bird mourns;
That the shrine shall be pillaged, and the gold spent,
The jewels gone for light ladies' ornament,
The sanctuary broken, and its stores
Swept into the laps of parasites and whores.
When miracles cease, and the faithful desert you,
And men shall only do their best to forget you.
And later is worse, when men will not hate you
Enough to defame or to execrate you,
But pondering the qualities that you lacked
Will only try to find the historical fact.
When men shall declare that there was no mystery
About this man who played a certain part in history.

THOMAS: But what is there to do? What is left to be done?
Is there no enduring crown to be won?

TEMPTER: Yes, Thomas, yes; you have thought of that too.
What can compare with glory of Saints
Dwelling forever in presence of God?
What earthly glory, of king or emperor,
What earthly pride, that is not poverty
Compared with richness of heavenly grandeur?
Seek the way of martyrdom, make yourself the lowest
On earth, to be high in heaven.
And see far off below you, where the gulf is fixed,
Your persecutors, in timeless torment,
Parched passion, beyond expiation.

THOMAS: No!
Who are you, tempting with my own desires?
Others have come, temporal tempters,
With pleasure and power at palpable price.
What do you offer? What do you ask?

TEMPTER: I offer what you desire. I ask
   What you have to give. Is it too much
   For such a vision of eternal grandeur?
THOMAS: Others offered real goods, worthless
   But real. You only offer
   Dreams to damnation.
TEMPTER: You have often dreamt them.
THOMAS: Is there no way, in my soul's sickness,
   Does not lead to damnation in pride?
   I well know that these temptations
   Mean present vanity and future torment.
   Can sinful pride be driven out
   Only by more sinful? Can I neither act nor suffer
   Without perdition?
TEMPTER: You know and do not know, what it is to act or suffer.
   You know and do not know, that action is suffering,
   And suffering action. Neither does the agent suffer
   Nor the patient act. But both are fixed
   In an eternal action, an eternal patience
   To which all must consent that it may be willed
   And which all must suffer that they may will it,
   That the pattern may subsist, that the wheel may turn and still
   Be forever still.
CHORUS: There is no rest in the house. There is no rest in the street.
   I hear restless movement of feet. And the air is heavy and thick.
   Thick and heavy the sky. And the earth presses up against our feet.
   What is the sickly smell, the vapor? The dark green light from a cloud
      on a withered tree? The earth is heaving to parturition of issue of hell.
   What is the sticky dew that forms on the back of my hand?
THE FOUR TEMPTERS: Man's life is a cheat and a disappointment;
   All things are unreal,
   Unreal or disappointing:
   The Catherine wheel,[5] the pantomime cat,
   The prizes given at the children's party,
   The prize awarded for the English Essay,
   The scholar's degree, the statesman's decoration.
   All things become less real, man passes
   From unreality to unreality.
   This man is obstinate, blind, intent
   On self-destruction.
   Passing from deception to deception,
   From grandeur to grandeur to final illusion,
   Lost in the wonder of his own greatness,
   The enemy of society, enemy of himself.
THE THREE PRIESTS: O Thomas my Lord, do not fight the intractable tide,

---

[5] A firework which rotates in the manner of a wheel.

Do not sail the irresistible wind; in the storm,
Should we not wait for the sea to subside, in the night
Abide the coming of day, when the traveller may find his way,
The sailor lay course by the sun?

(CHORUS, PRIESTS and TEMPTERS alternately.)

c.: Is it the owl that calls, or a signal between the trees?
p.: Is the window-bar made fast, is the door under lock and bolt?
t.: Is it rain that taps at the window, is it wind that pokes at the door?
c.: Does the torch flame in the hall, the candle in the room?
p.: Does the watchman walk by the wall?
t.: Does the mastiff prowl by the gate?
c.: Death has a hundred hands and walks by a thousand ways.
p.: He may come in the sight of all, he may pass unseen unheard.
t.: Come whispering through the ear, or a sudden shock on the skull.
c.: A man may walk with a lamp at night, and yet be drowned in a ditch.
p.: A man may climb the stair in the day, and slip on a broken step.
t.: A man may sit at meat, and feel the cold in his groin.

CHORUS: We have not been happy, my Lord, we have not been too happy.
We are not ignorant women, we know what we must expect and not
expect.
We know of oppression and torture,
We know of extortion and violence,
Destitution, disease,
The old without fire in winter,
The child without milk in summer,
Our labor taken away from us,
Our sins made heavier upon us.
We have seen the young man mutilated,
The torn girl trembling by the mill-stream.
And meanwhile we have gone on living,
Living and partly living,
Picking together the pieces,
Gathering faggots at nightfall,
Building a partial shelter,
For sleeping, and eating and drinking and laughter.

God gave us always some reason, some hope; but now a new terror has
soiled us, which none can avert, none can avoid, flowing under our
feet and over the sky;
Under doors and down chimneys, flowing in at the ear and the mouth
and the eye.
God is leaving us, God is leaving us, more pang, more pain than birth or
death.
Sweet and cloying through the dark air
Falls the stifling scent of despair;
The forms take shape in the dark air:
Puss-purr of leopard, footfall of padding bear,

Palm-pat of nodding ape, square hyaena waiting
For laughter, laughter, laughter. The Lords of Hell are here.
They curl round you, lie at your feet, swing and wing through the dark
air.
O Thomas Archbishop, save us, save us, save yourself that we may be
saved;
Destroy yourself and we are destroyed.

THOMAS: Now is my way clear, now is the meaning plain:
Temptation shall not come in this kind again.
The last temptation is the greatest treason:
To do the right deed for the wrong reason.
The natural vigor in the venial sin
Is the way in which our lives begin.
Thirty years ago, I searched all the ways
That lead to pleasure, advancement and praise.
Delight in sense, in learning and in thought,
Music and philosophy, curiosity,
The purple bullfinch in the lilac tree,
The tilt-yard skill, the strategy of chess,
Love in the garden, singing to the instrument,
Were all things equally desirable.
Ambition comes when early force is spent
And when we find no longer all things possible.
Ambition comes behind and unobservable.
Sin grows with doing good. When I imposed the King's law
In England, and waged war with him against Toulouse,[6]
I beat the barons at their own game. I
Could then despise the men who thought me most contemptible,
The raw nobility, whose manners matched their fingernails.
While I ate out of the King's dish
To become servant of God was never my wish.
Servant of God has chance of greater sin
And sorrow, than the man who serves a king.
For those who serve the greater cause may make the cause serve them,
Still doing right: and striving with political men
May make that cause political, not by what they do
But by what they are. I know
What yet remains to show you of my history
Will seem to most of you at best futility,
Senseless self-slaughter of a lunatic,
Arrogant passion of a fanatic.
I know that history at all times draws
The strangest consequence from remotest cause.
But for every evil, every sacrilege,

---

[6] As chancellor of England, Becket organized the Toulouse campaign in France
in 1159.

Crime, wrong, oppression and the axe's edge,
Indifference, exploitation, you, and you,
And you, must all be punished. So must you.
I shall no longer act or suffer, to the sword's end.
Now my good Angel, whom God appoints
To be my guardian, hover over the swords' points.

Interlude

THE ARCHBISHOP *preaches in the Cathedral on Christmas Morning, 1170:*
'Glory to God in the highest, and on earth peace to men of good will.'
The fourteenth verse of the second chapter of the Gospel according to Saint Luke. In the Name of the Father, and of the Son, and of the Holy Ghost. Amen.

Dear children of God, my sermon this Christmas morning will be a very short one. I wish only that you should meditate in your hearts the deep meaning and mystery of our masses of Christmas Day. For whenever Mass is said, we re-enact the Passion and Death of Our Lord; and on this Christmas Day we do this in celebration of His Birth. So that at the same moment we rejoice in His coming for the salvation of men, and offer again to God His Body and Blood in sacrifice, oblation and satisfaction for the sins of the whole world. It was in this same night that has just passed, that a multitude of the heavenly host appeared before the shepherds at Bethlehem, saying 'Glory to God in the highest, and on earth peace to men of good will'; at this same time of all the year that we celebrate at once the Birth of Our Lord and His Passion and Death upon the Cross. Beloved, as the World sees, this is to behave in a strange fashion. For who in the World will both mourn and rejoice at once and for the same reason? For either joy will be overborne by mourning, or mourning will be cast out by joy; so it is only in these our Christian mysteries that we can rejoice and mourn at once for the same reason. Now think for a moment about the meaning of this word 'peace.' Does it seem strange to you that the angels should have announced Peace, when ceaselessly the world has been stricken with War and the fear of War? Does it seem to you that the angelic voices were mistaken, and that the promise was a disappointment and a cheat?

Reflect now, how Our Lord Himself spoke of Peace. He said to His disciples, 'My peace I leave with you, my peace I give unto you.' Did He mean peace as we think of it: the kingdom of England at peace with its neighbors, the barons at peace with the King, the householder counting over his peaceful gains, the swept hearth, his best wine for a friend at the table, his wife singing to the children? Those men His disciples knew no such things: they went forth to journey afar, to suffer by land and sea, to know torture, imprisonment, disappointment, to suffer death by martyrdom. What then did He mean? If you ask that, remember then that He said also, 'Not as the world gives, give I unto you.' So then, He gave to His disciples peace, but not peace as the world gives.

Consider also one thing of which you have probably never thought. Not only do we at the feast of Christmas celebrate at once Our Lord's Birth and His Death: but on the next day we celebrate the martyrdom of His first martyr, the blessed Stephen. Is it an accident, do you think, that the day of the first martyr follows immediately the day of the Birth of Christ? By no means. Just as we rejoice and mourn at once, in the Birth and in the Passion of Our Lord; so also, in a smaller figure, we both rejoice and mourn in the death of martyrs. We mourn, for the sins of the world that has martyred them; we rejoice, that another soul is numbered among the Saints in Heaven, for the glory of God and for the salvation of men.

Beloved, we do not think of a martyr simply as a good Christian who has been killed because he is a Christian: for that would be solely to mourn. We do not think of him simply as a good Christian who has been elevated to the company of the Saints: for that would be simply to rejoice: and neither our mourning nor our rejoicing is as the world's is. A Christian martyrdom is never an accident, for Saints are not made by accident. Still less is a Christian martyrdom the effect of a man's will to become a Saint, as a man by willing and contriving may become a ruler of men. A martyrdom is always the design of God, for His love of men, to warn them and to lead them, to bring them back to His ways. It is never the design of man; for the true martyr is he who has become the instrument of God, who has lost his will in the will of God, and who no longer desires anything for himself, not even the glory of being a martyr. So thus as on earth the Church mourns and rejoices at once, in a fashion that the world cannot understand; so in Heaven the Saints are most high, having made themselves most low, and are seen, not as we see them, but in the light of the Godhead from which they draw their being.

I have spoken to you today, dear children of God, of the martyrs of the past, asking you to remember especially our martyr of Canterbury, the blessed Archbishop Elphege;[7] because it is fitting, on Christ's birthday, to remember what is that Peace which He brought; and because, dear children, I do not think I shall ever preach to you again; and because it is possible that in a short time you may have yet another martyr, and that one perhaps not the last. I would have you keep in your hearts these words that I say, and think of them at another time. In the Name of the Father, and of the Son, and of the Holy Ghost. Amen.

---

[7] St. Elphege (954-1012) became archbishop of Canterbury in 1006. In 1012, the year after Canterbury was burned by the Danes, Elphege died a martyr because he refused to allow his people to pay his ransom by sacrificing their property.

Part Two

CHORUS: Does the bird sing in the South?
  Only the sea-bird cries, driven inland by the storm.
  What sign of the spring of the year?
  Only the death of the old: not a stir, not a shoot, not a breath.
  Do the days begin to lengthen?
  Longer and darker the day, shorter and colder the night.
  Still and stifling the air: but a wind is stored up in the East.
  The starved crow sits in the field, attentive; and in the wood
  The owl rehearses the hollow note of death.
  What signs of a bitter spring?
  The wind stored up in the East.
  What, at the time of the birth of Our Lord, at Christmastide,
  Is there not peace upon earth, goodwill among men?
  The peace of this world is always uncertain, unless men keep the peace
    of God.
  And war among men defiles this world, but death in the Lord renews it,
  And the world must be cleaned in the winter, or we shall have only
  A sour spring, a parched summer, an empty harvest.
  Between Christmas and Easter what work shall be done?
  The ploughman shall go out in March and turn the same earth
  He has turned before, the bird shall sing the same song.
  When the leaf is out on the tree, when the elder and may
  Burst over the stream, and the air is clear and high,
  And voices trill at windows, and children tumble in front of the door,
  What work shall have been done, what wrong
  Shall the bird's song cover, the green tree cover, what wrong
  Shall the fresh earth cover? We wait, and the time is short
  But waiting is long.
  (*Enter the* FIRST PRIEST *with a banner of St. Stephen borne before him.*
  The lines sung are in italics.)
FIRST PRIEST: Since Christmas a day: and the day of St. Stephen, First
    Martyr.
  Princes moreover did sit, and did witness falsely against me.
  A day that was always most dear to the Archbishop Thomas.
  And he kneeled down and cried with a loud voice:
  Lord, lay not this sin to their charge.
  Princes moreover did sit.
  (*Introit of St. Stephen is heard. Enter the* SECOND PRIEST, *with a banner*
  of St. John the Apostle borne before him.)
SECOND PRIEST: Since St. Stephen a day: and the day of St. John the
    Apostle.
  In the midst of the congregation he opened his mouth.

That which was from the beginning, which we have heard,
Which we have seen with our eyes, and our hands have handled
Of the word of life; that which we have seen and heard
Declare we unto you.
In the midst of the congregation.
(*Introit of St. John is heard. Enter the* THIRD PRIEST, *with a banner of the Holy Innocents borne before him.*)
THIRD PRIEST: Since St. John the Apostle a day: and the day of the Holy
    Innocents.
Out of the mouth of very babes, O God.
As the voice of many waters, of thunder, of harps,
They sung as it were a new song.
The blood of thy saints have they shed like water,
And there was no man to bury them. Avenge, O Lord,
The blood of thy saints. In Rama, a voice heard, weeping.[8]
Out of the mouth of very babes, O God!
(THE PRIESTS *stand together with the banners behind them.*)
FIRST PRIEST: Since the Holy Innocents a day: the fourth day from Christ-
    mas.
THE THREE PRIESTS: *Rejoice we all, keeping holy day.*
FIRST PRIEST: As for the people, so also for himself, he offereth for sins.
    He lays down his life for the sheep.
THE THREE PRIESTS: *Rejoice we all, keeping holy day.*
FIRST PRIEST: Today?
SECOND PRIEST: Today, what is today? For the day is half gone.
FIRST PRIEST: Today, what is today? But another day, the dusk of the year.
SECOND PRIEST: Today, what is today? Another night, and another dawn.
THIRD PRIEST: What day is the day that we know that we hope for or fear
    for?
Every day is the day we should fear from or hope from. One moment
Weighs like another. Only in retrospection, selection,
We say, that was the day. The critical moment
That is always now, and here. Even now, in sordid particulars
The eternal design may appear.
(*Enter the* FOUR KNIGHTS. *The banners disappear.*)
FIRST KNIGHT: Servants of the King.
FIRST PRIEST: And known to us.
You are welcome. Have you ridden far?
FIRST KNIGHT: Not far today, but matters urgent
Have brought us from France. We rode hard,
Took ship yesterday, landed last night,
Having business with the Archbishop.
SECOND KNIGHT: Urgent business.
THIRD KNIGHT: From the King.

---

[8] Matthew 2:18. "In Rama was there a voice heard, lamentation, and weeping, and great mourning, Rachel weeping for her children, and would not be comforted, because they are not."

ѕᴇᴄᴏɴᴅ ᴋɴɪɢʜᴛ: By the King's order.
ꜰɪʀѕᴛ ᴋɴɪɢʜᴛ: Our men are outside.
ꜰɪʀѕᴛ ᴘʀɪᴇѕᴛ: You know the Archbishop's hospitality.
  We are about to go to dinner.
  The good Archbishop would be vexed
  If we did not offer you entertainment
  Before your business. Please dine with us.
  Your men shall be looked after also.
  Dinner before business. Do you like roast pork?
ꜰɪʀѕᴛ ᴋɴɪɢʜᴛ: Business before dinner. We will roast your pork
  First, and dine upon it after.
ѕᴇᴄᴏɴᴅ ᴋɴɪɢʜᴛ: We must see the Archbishop.
ᴛʜɪʀᴅ ᴋɴɪɢʜᴛ: Go, tell the Archbishop
  We have no need of his hospitality.
  We will find our own dinner.
ꜰɪʀѕᴛ ᴘʀɪᴇѕᴛ (*to* ᴀᴛᴛᴇɴᴅᴀɴᴛ): Go, tell His Lordship.
ꜰᴏᴜʀᴛʜ ᴋɴɪɢʜᴛ: How much longer will you keep us waiting?
  (*Enter* ᴛʜᴏᴍᴀѕ.)
ᴛʜᴏᴍᴀѕ (*to* ᴘʀɪᴇѕᴛѕ): However certain our expectation
  The moment foreseen may be unexpected
  When it arrives. It comes when we are
  Engrossed with matters of other urgency.
  On my table you will find
  The papers in order, and the documents signed.
  (*To* ᴋɴɪɢʜᴛѕ) You are welcome, whatever your business may be.
  You say, from the King?
ꜰɪʀѕᴛ ᴋɴɪɢʜᴛ: Most surely from the King.
  We must speak with you alone.
ᴛʜᴏᴍᴀѕ (*to* ᴘʀɪᴇѕᴛѕ):   Leave us then alone.
  Now what is the matter?
ꜰɪʀѕᴛ ᴋɴɪɢʜᴛ: This is the matter.
ᴛʜᴇ ᴛʜʀᴇᴇ ᴋɴɪɢʜᴛѕ: You are the Archbishop in revolt against the King;
    in rebellion to the King and the law of the land;
  You are the Archbishop who was made by the King; whom he set in
    your place to carry out his command.
  You are his servant, his tool, and his jack,
  You wore his favors on your back,
  You had your honors all from his hand; from him you had the power,
    the seal and the ring.
  This is the man who was the tradesman's son: the backstairs brat who
    was born in Cheapside;
  This is the creature that crawled upon the King; swollen with blood and
    swollen with pride.
  Creeping out of the London dirt,
  Crawling up like a louse on your shirt,
  The man who cheated, swindled, lied; broke his oath and betrayed his
    King.
ᴛʜᴏᴍᴀѕ: This is not true.

Both before and after I received the ring
I have been a loyal subject to the King.
Saving my order, I am at his command,
As his most faithful vassal in the land.
FIRST KNIGHT: Saving your order! let your order save you—
  As I do not think it is like to do.
  Saving your ambition is what you mean,
  Saving your pride, envy and spleen.
SECOND KNIGHT: Saving your insolence and greed.
  Won't you ask us to pray to God for you, in your need?
THIRD KNIGHT: Yes, we'll pray for you!
FIRST KNIGHT: Yes, we'll pray for you!
THE THREE KNIGHTS: Yes, we'll pray that God may help you!
THOMAS: But, gentlemen, your business
  Which you said so urgent, is it only
  Scolding and blaspheming?
FIRST KNIGHT: That was only
  Our indignation, as loyal subjects.
THOMAS: Loyal? To whom?
FIRST KNIGHT: To the King!
SECOND KNIGHT: The King!
THIRD KNIGHT: The King!
THE THREE KNIGHTS: God bless him!
THOMAS: Then let your new coat of loyalty be worn
  Carefully, so it get not soiled or torn.
  Have you something to say?
FIRST KNIGHT: By the King's command.
  Shall we say it now?
SECOND KNIGHT: Without delay,
  Before the old fox is off and away.
THOMAS: What you have to say
  By the King's command—if it be the King's command—
  Should be said in public. If you make charges,
  Then in public I will refute them.
FIRST KNIGHT: No! here and now!
  (*They make to attack him, but the* PRIESTS *and* ATTENDANTS *return and
  quietly interpose themselves.*)
THOMAS: Now and here!
FIRST KNIGHT: Of your earlier misdeeds I shall make no mention.
  They are too well known. But after dissension
  Had ended, in France, and you were endued
  With your former privilege, how did you show your gratitude?
  You had fled from England, not exiled
  Or threatened, mind you; but in the hope
  Of stirring up trouble in the French dominions.
  You sowed strife abroad, you reviled
  The King to the King of France, to the Pope,
  Raising up against him false opinions.

SECOND KNIGHT: Yet the King, out of his charity,
And urged by your friends, offered clemency,
Made a pact of peace, and all dispute ended
Sent you back to your See as you demanded.
THIRD KNIGHT: And burying the memory of your transgressions
Restored your honors and your possessions.
All was granted for which you sued:
Yet how, I repeat, did you show your gratitude?
FIRST KNIGHT: Suspending those who had crowned the young prince,
Denying the legality of his coronation.
SECOND KNIGHT: Binding with the chains of anathema.
THIRD KNIGHT: Using every means in your power to evince
The King's faithful servants, every one who transacts
His business in his absence, the business of the nation.
FIRST KNIGHT: These are the facts.
Say therefore if you will be content
To answer in the King's presence. Therefore were we sent.
THOMAS: Never was it my wish
To uncrown the King's son, or to diminish
His honor and power. Why should he wish
To deprive my people of me and keep me from my own
And bid me sit in Canterbury, alone?
I would wish him three crowns rather than one,
And as for the bishops, it is not my yoke
That is laid upon them, or mine to revoke.
Let them go to the Pope. It was he who condemned them.
FIRST KNIGHT: Through you they were suspended.
SECOND KNIGHT: By you be this amended.
THIRD KNIGHT: Absolve them.
FIRST KNIGHT: Absolve them.
THOMAS: I do not deny
That this was done through me. But it is not I
Who can loose whom the Pope has bound.
Let them go to him, upon whom redounds
Their contempt towards me, their contempt towards the Church shown.
FIRST KNIGHT: Be that as it may, here is the King's command:
That you and your servants depart from this land.
THOMAS: If that is the King's command, I will be bold
To say: seven years were my people without
My presence; seven years of misery and pain.
Seven years a mendicant on foreign charity
I lingered abroad: seven years is no brevity.
I shall not get those seven years back again.
Never again, you must make no doubt,
Shall the sea run between the shepherd and his fold.
FIRST KNIGHT: The King's justice, the King's majesty,
You insult with gross indignity;

Insolent madman, whom nothing deters
From attainting his servants and ministers.
THOMAS: It is not I who insult the King,
And there is higher than I or the King.
It is not I, Becket from Cheapside,
It is not against me, Becket, that you strive.
It is not Becket who pronounces doom,
But the Law of Christ's Church, the judgment of Rome.
FIRST KNIGHT: Priest, you have spoken in peril of your life.
SECOND KNIGHT: Priest, you have spoken in danger of the knife.
THIRD KNIGHT: Priest, you have spoken treachery and treason.
THE THREE KNIGHTS: Priest! traitor, confirmed in malfeasance.
THOMAS: I submit my cause to the judgment of Rome.
But if you kill me, I shall rise from my tomb
To submit my cause before God's throne. (*Exit.*)
FOURTH KNIGHT: Priest! monk! and servant! take, hold, detain,
Restrain this man, in the King's name.
FIRST KNIGHT: Or answer with your bodies.
SECOND KNIGHT: Enough of words.
THE FOUR KNIGHTS: We come for the King's justice, we come with swords.
(*Exeunt.*)
CHORUS: I have smelt them, the death-bringers, senses are quickened
By subtile forebodings; I have heard
Fluting in the night-time, fluting and owls, have seen at noon
Scaly wings slanting over, huge and ridiculous. I have tasted
The savor of putrid flesh in the spoon. I have felt
The heaving of earth at nightfall, restless, absurd. I have heard
Laughter in the noises of beasts that make strange noises: jackal, jackass,
    jackdaw; the scurrying noise of mouse and jerboa; the laugh of the
    loon, the lunatic bird. I have seen
Grey necks twisting, rat tails twining, in the thick light of dawn. I have
    eaten
Smooth creatures still living, with the strong salt taste of living things
    under sea; I have tasted
The living lobster, the crab, the oyster, the whelk and the prawn; and
    they live and spawn in my bowels, and my bowels dissolve in the light
    of dawn. I have smelt
Death in the rose, death in the hollyhock, sweet pea, hyacinth, primrose
    and cowslip. I have seen
Trunk and horn, tusk and hoof, in odd places;
I have lain on the floor of the sea and breathed with the breathing of
    the sea-anemone, swallowed with ingurgitation of the sponge. I have
    lain in the soil and criticized the worm. In the air
Flirted with the passage of the kite, I have plunged with the kite and
    cowered with the wren. I have felt
The horn of the beetle, the scale of the viper, the mobile hard insensitive
    skin of the elephant, the evasive flank of the fish. I have smelt

Corruption in the dish, incense in the latrine, the sewer in the incense,
   the smell of sweet soap in the woodpath, a hellish sweet scent in the
   woodpath, while the ground heaved. I have seen
Rings of light coiling downwards, descending
To the horror of the ape. Have I not known, not known
What was coming to be? It was here, in the kitchen, in the passage,
In the mews in the barn in the byre in the market place
In our veins our bowels our skulls as well
As well as in the plottings of potentates
As well as in the consultations of powers.
What is woven on the loom of fate
What is woven in the councils of princes
Is woven also in our veins, our brains,
Is woven like a pattern of living worms
In the guts of the women of Canterbury.

I have smelt them, the death-bringers; now is too late
For action, too soon for contrition.
Nothing is possible but the shamed swoon
Of those consenting to the last humiliation.
I have consented, Lord Archbishop, have consented.
Am torn away, subdued, violated,
United to the spiritual flesh of nature,
Mastered by the animal powers of spirit,
Dominated by the lust of self-demolition,
By the final utter uttermost death of spirit,
By the final ecstasy of waste and shame,
O Lord Archbishop, O Thomas Archbishop, forgive us, forgive us, pray
   for us that we may pray for you, out of our shame.
   (*Enter* THOMAS.)
THOMAS: Peace, and be at peace with your thoughts and visions.
   These things had to come to you and you to accept them.
   This is your share of the eternal burden,
   The perpetual glory. This is one moment,
   But know that another
   Shall pierce you with a sudden painful joy
   When the figure of God's purpose is made complete.
   You shall forget these things, toiling in the household,
   You shall remember them, droning by the fire,
   When age and forgetfulness sweeten memory
   Only like a dream that has often been told
   And often been changed in the telling. They will seem unreal.
   Human kind cannot bear very much reality.
   (*Enter* PRIESTS.)
PRIESTS (*severally*): My Lord, you must not stop here. To the minster.
   Through the cloister. No time to waste. They are coming back, armed.
   To the altar, to the altar.
THOMAS: All my life they have been coming, these feet. All my life

I have waited. Death will come only when I am worthy,
And if I am worthy, there is no danger.
I have therefore only to make perfect my will.

PRIESTS: My Lord, they are coming. They will break through presently.
You will be killed. Come to the altar.
Make haste, my Lord. Don't stop here talking. It is not right.
What shall become of us, my Lord, if you are killed; what shall become
of us?

THOMAS: Peace! be quiet! remember where you are, and what is happening;
No life here is sought for but mine,
And I am not in danger: only near to death.

PRIESTS: My Lord, to vespers! You must not be absent from vespers. You
must not be absent from the divine office. To vespers. Into the cathedral!

THOMAS: Go to vespers, remember me at your prayers.
They shall find the shepherd here; the flock shall be spared.
I have had a tremor of bliss, a wink of heaven, a whisper,
And I would no longer be denied; all things
Proceed to a joyful consummation.

PRIESTS: Seize him! force him! drag him!

THOMAS: Keep your hands off!

PRIESTS: To vespers! Hurry.

(*They drag him off. While the* CHORUS *speak, the scene is changed to
the cathedral.*)

CHORUS (*while a* Dies Iræ[9] *is sung in Latin by a choir in the distance*):
Numb the hand and dry the eyelid,
Still the horror, but more horror
Than when tearing in the belly.

Still the horror, but more horror
Than when twisting in the fingers,
Than when splitting in the skull.

More than footfall in the passage,
More than shadow in the doorway,
More than fury in the hall.

The agents of hell disappear, the human, they shrink and dissolve
Into dust on the wind, forgotten, unmemorable; only is here
The white flat face of Death, God's silent servant,
And behind the face of Death the Judgment
And behind the Judgment the Void, more horrid than active shapes of
hell;
Emptiness, absence, separation from God;
The horror of the effortless journey, to the empty land

---

[9] "Day of Wrath" (Latin), the opening words of a sequence in the Mass for the
Dead.

Which is no land, only emptiness, absence, the Void,
Where those who were men can no longer turn the mind
To distraction, delusion, escape into dream, pretense,
Where the soul is no longer deceived, for there are no objects, no tones,
No colors, no forms to distract, to divert the soul
From seeing itself, foully united forever, nothing with nothing,
Not what we call death, but what beyond death is not death,
We fear, we fear. Who shall then plead for me,
Who intercede for me, in my most need?

Dead upon the tree, my Savior,
Let not be in vain Thy labor;
Help me, Lord, in my last fear.

Dust I am, to dust am bending,
From the final doom impending
Help me, Lord, for death is near.
(*In the cathedral.* THOMAS *and* PRIESTS.)
PRIESTS: Bar the door. Bar the door.
   The door is barred.
   We are safe. We are safe.
   They dare not break in.
   They cannot break in. They have not the force.
   We are safe. We are safe.
THOMAS: Unbar the doors! throw open the doors!
   I will not have the house of prayer, the church of Christ,
   The sanctuary, turned into a fortress.
   The Church shall protect her own, in her own way, not
   As oak and stone; stone and oak decay,
   Give no stay, but the Church shall endure.
   The church shall be open, even to our enemies. Open the door!
PRIEST: My Lord! these are not men, these come not as men come, but
   Like maddened beasts. They come not like men, who
   Respect the sanctuary, who kneel to the Body of Christ,
   But like beasts. You would bar the door
   Against the lion, the leopard, the wolf or the boar,
   Why not more
   Against beasts with the souls of damned men, against men
   Who would damn themselves to beasts. My Lord! My Lord!
THOMAS: You think me reckless, desperate and mad.
   You argue by results, as this world does,
   To settle if an act be good or bad.
   You defer to the fact. For every life and every act
   Consequence of good and evil can be shown.
   And as in time results of many deeds are blended
   So good and evil in the end become confounded.
   It is not in time that my death shall be known;
   It is out of time that my decision is taken

If you call that decision
To which my whole being gives entire consent.
I give my life
To the Law of God above the Law of Man.
Unbar the door! unbar the door!
We are not here to triumph by fighting, by stratagem, or by resistance,
Not to fight with beasts as men. We have fought the beast
And have conquered. We have only to conquer
Now, by suffering. This is the easier victory.
Now is the triumph of the Cross, now
Open the door! I command it. OPEN THE DOOR!
(*The door is opened. The* KNIGHTS *enter, slightly tipsy.*)

PRIESTS: This way, my Lord! Quick. Up the stair. To the roof. To the crypt.
  Quick. Come. Force him.

KNIGHTS: Where is Becket, the traitor to the King?
  Where is Becket, the meddling priest?
  Come down Daniel to the lions' den,[10]
  Come down Daniel for the mark of the beast.

  Are you washed in the blood of the Lamb?
  Are you marked with the mark of the beast?
  Come down Daniel to the lions' den,
  Come down Daniel and join in the feast.

  Where is Becket the Cheapside brat?
  Where is Becket the faithless priest?
  Come down Daniel to the lions' den,
  Come down Daniel and join in the feast.

THOMAS: It is the just man who
  Like a bold lion, should be without fear.
  I am here.
  No traitor to the King. I am a priest,
  A Christian, saved by the blood of Christ,
  Ready to suffer with my blood.
  This is the sign of the Church always,
  The sign of blood. Blood for blood.
  His blood given to buy my life,
  My blood given to pay for His death,
  My death for His death.

FIRST KNIGHT: Absolve all those you have excommunicated.

SECOND KNIGHT: Resign the powers you have arrogated.

THIRD KNIGHT: Restore to the King the money you appropriated.

FIRST KNIGHT: Renew the obedience you have violated.

THOMAS: For my Lord I am now ready to die,

---

[10] Daniel 6:16-24. Cast into a lions' den by King Darius of Persia, Daniel was unharmed "because he believed in his God."

That His Church may have peace and liberty.
Do with me as you will, to your hurt and shame;
But none of my people, in God's name,
Whether layman or clerk, shall you touch.
This I forbid.

KNIGHTS: Traitor! traitor! traitor!

THOMAS: You, Reginald, three times traitor you:
Traitor to me as my temporal vassal,
Traitor to me as your spiritual lord,
Traitor to God in desecrating His Church.

FIRST KNIGHT: No faith do I owe to a renegade,
And what I owe shall now be paid.

THOMAS: Now to Almighty God, to the Blessed Mary ever Virgin, to the
blessed John the Baptist, the holy apostles Peter and Paul, to the blessed
martyr Denys,[11] and to all the Saints, I commend my cause and that of
the Church.

(*While the* KNIGHTS *kill him, we hear the* CHORUS.)

CHORUS: Clear the air! clean the sky! wash the wind! take stone from stone
and wash them.
The land is foul, the water is foul, our beasts and ourselves defiled with
blood.
A rain of blood has blinded my eyes. Where is England? Where is Kent?
Where is Canterbury?
O far far far far in the past; and I wander in a land of barren boughs:
if I break them, they bleed; I wander in a land of dry stones: if I
touch them they bleed.
How how can I ever return, to the soft quiet seasons?
Night stay with us, stop sun, hold season, let the day not come, let the
spring not come.
Can I look again at the day and its common things, and see them all
smeared with blood, through a curtain of falling blood?
We did not wish anything to happen.
We understood the private catastrophe,
The personal loss, the general misery,
Living and partly living;
The terror by night that ends in daily action,
The terror by day that ends in sleep;
But the talk in the market-place, the hand on the broom,
The night-time heaping of the ashes,
The fuel laid on the fire at daybreak,
These acts marked a limit to our suffering.
Every horror had its definition,
Every sorrow had a kind of end:
In life there is not time to grieve long.
But this, this is out of life, this is out of time,

---

[11] The patron saint of Paris (c. 250), Denys was one of seven bishops sent to
convert Gaul. After becoming bishop of Paris, he suffered martyrdom.

An instant eternity of evil and wrong.
We are soiled by a filth that we cannot clean, united to supernatural
vermin,
It is not we alone, it is not the house, it is not the city that is defiled,
But the world that is wholly foul.
Clear the air! clean the sky! wash the wind! take the stone from the stone,
take the skin from the arm, take the muscle from the bone, and wash
them. Wash the stone, wash the bone, wash the brain, wash the soul,
wash them wash them!

(*The* KNIGHTS, *having completed the murder, advance to the front of
the stage and address the audience.*)

FIRST KNIGHT: We beg you to give us your attention for a few moments.
We know that you may be disposed to judge unfavorably of our action.
You are Englishmen, and therefore you believe in fair play: and when
you see one man being set upon by four, then your sympathies are all with
the underdog. I respect such feelings, I share them. Nevertheless, I appeal
to your sense of honor. You are Englishmen, and therefore will not judge
anybody without hearing both sides of the case. That is in accordance
with our long-established principle of Trial by Jury. I am not myself
qualified to put our case to you. I am a man of action and not of words.
For that reason I shall do no more than introduce the other speakers,
who, with their various abilities, and different points of view, will be
able to lay before you the merits of this extremely complex problem. I
shall call upon our eldest member to speak first, my neighbor in the
country: Baron William de Traci.[12]

THIRD KNIGHT: I am afraid I am not anything like such an experienced
speaker as my old friend Reginald Fitz Urse would lead you to believe.
But there is one thing I should like to say, and I might as well say it at
once. It is this: in what we have done, and whatever you may think of
it, we have been perfectly disinterested. (*The other* KNIGHTS: 'Hear!
hear!') *We* are not getting anything out of this. We have much more to
lose than to gain. We are four plain Englishmen who put our country
first. I dare say that we didn't make a very good impression when we
came in just now. The fact is that we knew we had taken on a pretty
stiff job; I'll only speak for myself, but I had drunk a good deal—I am
not a drinking man ordinarily—to brace myself up for it. When you come
to the point, it does go against the grain to kill an Archbishop, especially
when you have been brought up in good Church traditions. So if we
seemed a bit rowdy, you will understand why it was; and for my part
I am awfully sorry about it. We realized this was our duty, but all the
same we had to work ourselves up to it. And, as I said, *we* are not getting
a penny out of this. We know perfectly well how things will turn out.
King Henry—God bless him—will have to say, for reasons of state, that
he never meant this to happen; and there is going to be an awful row;

---

[12] Tracy (d. 1173), Morville (d. 1200), and Brito were the historical murderers
of Becket. They had been loyal to him when he was Chancellor. After the murder
they escaped to Scotland and were later banished to the Holy Land by the Pope.

and at the best we shall have to spend the rest of our lives abroad. And even when reasonable people come to see that the Archbishop *had* to be put out of the way—and personally I had a tremendous admiration for him—you must have noticed what a good show he put up at the end— they won't give *us* any glory. No, we have done for ourselves, there's no mistake about that. So, as I said at the beginning, please give us at least the credit for being completely disinterested in this business. I think that is about all I have to say.

FIRST KNIGHT: I think we will all agree that William de Traci has spoken well and has made a very important point. The gist of his argument is this: that we have been completely disinterested. But our act itself needs more justification than that; and you must hear our other speakers. I shall next call upon Hugh de Morville, who has made a special study of statecraft and constitutional law. Sir Hugh de Morville.

SECOND KNIGHT: I should like first to recur to a point that was very well put by our leader, Reginald Fitz Urse: that you are Englishmen and therefore your sympathies are always with the underdog. It is the English spirit of fair play. Now the worthy Archbishop, whose good qualities I very much admired, has throughout been presented as the underdog. But is this really the case? I am going to appeal not to your emotions but to your reason. You are hard-headed sensible people, as I can see, and not to be taken in by emotional clap-trap. I therefore ask you to consider soberly: what were the Archbishop's aims? And what are King Henry's aims? In the answer to these questions lies the key to the problem.

The King's aim has been perfectly consistent. During the reign of the late Queen Matilda and the irruption of the unhappy usurper Stephen,[13] the kingdom was very much divided. Our King saw that the one thing needful was to restore order: to curb the excessive powers of local government, which were usually exercised for selfish and often for seditious ends, and to reform the legal system. He therefore intended that Becket, who had proved himself an extremely able administrator—no one denies that—should unite the offices of Chancellor and Archbishop. Had Becket concurred with the King's wishes, we should have had an almost ideal State: a union of spiritual and temporal administration, under the central government. I knew Becket well, in various official relations; and I may say that I have never known a man so well qualified for the highest rank of the Civil Service. And what happened? The moment that Becket, at the King's instance, had been made Archbishop, he resigned the office of Chancellor, he became more priestly than the priests, he ostentatiously and offensively adopted an ascetic manner of life, he affirmed immediately that there was a higher order than that which our King, and he as the King's servant, had for so many years striven to establish; and that—God knows why—the two orders were incompatible.

You will agree with me that such interference by an Archbishop

---

[13] Stephen (1097?-1154), king of England from 1135 to 1154, was the grandson of William the Conqueror and the nephew of Henry I. Matilda (1102-1167), daughter of Henry I and mother of Henry II, struggled for years with Stephen for the throne of England.

offends the instincts of a people like ours. So far, I know that I have your approval: I read it in your faces. It is only with the measures we have had to adopt, in order to set matters to rights, that you take issue. No one regrets the necessity for violence more than we do. Unhappily, there are times when violence is the only way in which social justice can be secured. At another time, you would condemn an Archbishop by vote of Parliament and execute him formally as a traitor, and no one would have to bear the burden of being called murderer. And at a later time still, even such temperate measures as these would become unnecessary. But, if you have now arrived at a just subordination of the pretensions of the Church to the welfare of the State, remember that it is we who took the first step. We have been instrumental in bringing about the state of affairs that you approve. We have served your interests; we merit your applause; and if there is any guilt whatever in the matter, you must share it with us.

FIRST KNIGHT: Morville has given us a great deal to think about. It seems to me that he has said almost the last word, for those who have been able to follow his very subtle reasoning. We have, however, one more speaker, who has I think another point of view to express. If there are any who are still unconvinced, I think that Richard Brito, coming as he does of a family distinguished for its loyalty to the Church, will be able to convince them. Richard Brito.

FOURTH KNIGHT: The speakers who have preceded me, to say nothing of our leader, Reginald Fitz Urse, have all spoken very much to the point. I have nothing to add along their particular lines of argument. What I have to say may be put in the form of a question: *Who killed the Archbishop?* As you have been eye-witnesses of this lamentable scene, you may feel some surprise at my putting it in this way. But consider the course of events. I am obliged, very briefly, to go over the ground traversed by the last speaker. While the late Archbishop was Chancellor, no one, under the King, did more to weld the country together, to give it the unity, the stability, order, tranquillity, and justice that it so badly needed. From the moment he became Archbishop, he completely reversed his policy; he showed himself to be utterly indifferent to the fate of the country, to be, in fact, a monster of egotism. This egotism grew upon him, until it became at last an undoubted mania. I have unimpeachable evidence to the effect that before he left France he clearly prophesied, in the presence of numerous witnesses, that he had not long to live, and that he would be killed in England. He used every means of provocation; from his conduct, step by step, there can be no inference except that he had determined upon a death by martyrdom. Even at the last, he could have given us reason: you have seen how he evaded our questions. And when he had deliberately exasperated us beyond human endurance, he could still have easily escaped; he could have kept himself from us long enough to allow our righteous anger to cool. That was just what he did not wish to happen; he insisted, while we were still inflamed with wrath, that the doors should be opened. Need I say more? I think, with these facts before you, you will unhesitatingly render a verdict of Suicide while of Unsound Mind. It is the only charitable verdict you can give, upon one who was, after all, a great man.

FIRST KNIGHT: Thank you, Brito, I think that there is no more to be said; and I suggest that you now disperse quietly to your homes. Please be careful not to loiter in groups at street corners, and do nothing that might provoke any public outbreak. (*Exeunt* KNIGHTS.)

FIRST PRIEST: O father, father, gone from us, lost to us,
How shall we find you, from what far place
Do you look down on us? You now in Heaven,
Who shall now guide us, protect us, direct us?
After what journey through what further dread
Shall we recover your presence? When inherit
Your strength? The Church lies bereft,
Alone, desecrated, desolated, and the heathen shall build on the ruins,
Their world without God. I see it. I see it.

THIRD PRIEST: No. For the Church is stronger for this action,
Triumphant in adversity. It is fortified
By persecution: supreme, so long as men will die for it.
Go, weak sad men, lost erring souls, homeless in earth or heaven.
Go where the sunset reddens the last grey rock
Of Brittany, or the Gates of Hercules.
Go venture shipwreck on the sullen coasts
Where blackamoors make captive Christian men;
Go to the northern seas confined with ice
Where the dead breath makes numb the hand, makes dull the brain;
Find an oasis in the desert sun,
Go seek alliance with the heathen Saracen,[14]
To share his filthy rites, and try to snatch
Forgetfulness in his libidinous courts,
Oblivion in the fountain by the date-tree;
Or sit and bite your nails in Aquitaine.[15]
In the small circle of pain within the skull
You still shall tramp and tread one endless round
Of thought, to justify your action to yourselves,
Weaving a fiction which unravels as you weave,
Pacing forever in the hell of make-believe
Which never is belief: this is your fate on earth
And we must think no further of you.

FIRST PRIEST: O my lord
The glory of whose new state is hidden from us,
Pray for us of your charity.

SECOND PRIEST: Now in the sight of God
Conjoined with all the saints and martyrs gone before you,
Remember us.

THIRD PRIEST: Let our thanks ascend
To God, who has given us another Saint in Canterbury.

---

[14] A Mohammedan or Moslem.
[15] The name of an ancient province in western France extending from the Loire River to the Pyrenees Mountains.

CHORUS (*while a* Te Deum[16] *is sung in Latin by a choir in the distance*):

We praise Thee, O God, for Thy glory displayed in all the creatures of the earth,

In the snow, in the rain, in the wind, in the storm; in all of Thy creatures, both the hunters and the hunted.

For all things exist only as seen by Thee, only as known by Thee, all things exist

Only in Thy light, and Thy glory is declared even in that which denies Thee; the darkness declares the glory of light.

Those who deny Thee could not deny, if Thou didst not exist; and their denial is never complete, for if it were so, they would not exist.

They affirm Thee in living; all things affirm Thee in living; the bird in the air, both the hawk and the finch; the beast on the earth, both the wolf and the lamb; the worm in the soil and the worm in the belly.

Therefore man, whom Thou hast made to be conscious of Thee, must consciously praise Thee, in thought and in word and in deed.

Even with the hand to the broom, the back bent in laying the fire, the knee bent in cleaning the hearth, we, the scrubbers and sweepers of Canterbury,

The back bent under toil, the knee bent under sin, the hands to the face under fear, the head bent under grief,

Even in us the voices of seasons, the snuffle of winter, the song of spring, the drone of summer, the voices of beasts and of birds, praise Thee.

We thank Thee for Thy mercies of blood, for Thy redemption by blood. For the blood of Thy martyrs and saints

Shall enrich the earth, shall create the holy places.

For wherever a saint has dwelt, wherever a martyr has given his blood for the blood of Christ,

There is holy ground, and the sanctity shall not depart from it

Though armies trample over it, though sightseers come with guide-books looking over it;

From where the western seas gnaw at the coast of Iona,[17]

To the death in the desert, the prayer in forgotten places by the broken imperial column,

From such ground springs that which forever renews the earth

Though it is forever denied. Therefore, O God, we thank Thee

Who hast given such blessing to Canterbury.

Forgive us, O Lord, we acknowledge ourselves as type of the common man,

Of the men and women who shut the door and sit by the fire;

Who fear the blessing of God, the loneliness of the night of God, the surrender required, the deprivation inflicted;

Who fear the injustice of men less than the justice of God;

---

16 "To you, O God" is an early Latin hymn to the Father and Son.

17 An island of the Inner Hebrides, a group of islands off the west coast of Scotland.

Who fear the hand at the window, the fire in the thatch, the fist in the
    tavern, the push into the canal,
Less than we fear the love of God.
We acknowledge our trespass, our weakness, our fault; we acknowledge
That the sin of the world is upon our heads; that the blood of the martyrs
    and the agony of the saints
Is upon our heads.
Lord, have mercy upon us.
Christ, have mercy upon us.
Lord, have mercy upon us.
Blessed Thomas, pray for us.

Commentary

Murder in the Cathedral has been called "the most sustained poetic
drama in English since *Samson Agonistes.*"[18] One could add that the
demands Eliot's play makes upon the reader are almost as great as those
made by its Miltonic predecessor. Unlike most of his contemporaries, Eliot
turns for his models not to Ibsen, Shaw, or Chekhov but to the tragedies
of Aeschylus and to the English morality play *Everyman.* Aware that
both Greek and English drama find their origins in religious celebration,
Eliot calls heavily upon Christian ritual and liturgy, and the formal design
of his play includes a sermon. *Murder in the Cathedral* was written for
performance at a religious festival before Christian pilgrims worshipping
at Becket's shrine in Canterbury. Some of the most effective productions
of this play are those performed in church where the audience is also a
congregation.

Unlike Ibsen, Williams, or Miller, for example, Eliot does not
present his characters in a social or psychological context, but rather in
a religious and moral one. In fact the *dramatis personae* are not individuals at all but embodiments of attitudes and ideas; and our interest in
them is not as people but as part of an intellectual, spiritual, and aesthetic
scheme. Eliot, furthermore, is not concerned with a biographical study
of the historical Thomas à Becket. Instead he explores dramatically the
meaning of an act—martyrdom. The play assumes our recognition of
Thomas' martyrdom—"Blessed Thomas, pray for us"—and then explores
the historical moment—December, 1170—and its spiritual significance

---

[18] F. O. Matthiessen, *The Achievement of T. S. Eliot,* 3rd ed. (New York, 1958),
p. 174.

both for its own and for all time. For this reason *Murder in the Cathedral* has no plot in the conventional sense, but only the expectation and ominous foreboding of violent death. The conflict essential for any drama is here not between characters nor between a character and his environment but instead within the character itself. This is the drama of a solitary man and the study of the greatness of the human spirit. But Eliot's concerns are not so remote from those of his contemporary playwrights as one would at first imagine. Like *A View from the Bridge, Murder in the Cathedral* is a play about "the way in which, and the reasons for which, a man will endanger and risk and lose his very life."[19] Different as the heroes of these plays are, Arthur Miller would argue that there is a bond of human passion between them because for Miller

> it matters not at all whether a modern play concerns itself with a grocer or a president if the intensity of the hero's commitment to his course is less than the maximum possible . . . ; if the intensity, the human passion to surpass his given bounds, the fanatic insistence upon his self-conceived role—if these are not present there can be only an outline of tragedy but no living thing.[20]

Eliot's play is about such a commitment, the implications of which involve not Becket alone but Canterbury and the Christian Church and us as well.

Because Eliot, like Shakespeare, uses no sets or scenery in *Murder in the Cathedral,* he must forego the dramatic advantages they would have afforded him. But what is lost visually is gained verbally, and through a study of the opening chorus we get both basic exposition and a feeling of what it is like to live in Eliot's Canterbury in December, 1170. Drawn almost against their will to the steps of the cathedral, the poor women of Canterbury can only stand and wait for an act which they cannot define but which they are "compelled to witness." Three times they mention the possibility of danger, but they see their role as only that of passive observers. Their eleven unanswered questions create a mood of uncertainty and apprehension. Expectancy and foreboding are reflected also in the atmosphere of their world where everything seems to be waiting: "The New Year waits, breathes, waits, whispers in darkness"; "destiny waits for the coming"; "who has remembered the martyrs and saints who wait?" But the chorus is not simply waiting for the coming of a new year nor for the hope of spring. Their world is more desolate than winter with "brown sharp points of death in a waste of water and mud"; it is a sterile wasteland and "the pattern of time" will not redeem it, for "ruinous spring" leads to "disastrous summer" and to only "another decaying October." To this barren world of suffering and death, the Archbishop returns after seven years of exile.

---

[19] Arthur Miller, *A View from the Bridge* (New York, 1955), p. 18.
[20] Miller, *Arthur Miller's Collected Plays* (New York, 1957), p. 33.

Since *Murder in the Cathedral* is not simply a dramatization of the murder of Thomas Becket but an exploration of the meaning of martyrdom, the main conflict in Part One is not an external one between Thomas and his enemies but an internal one between Thomas and his temptations, past and present. In the manner of a medieval morality play Eliot confronts his hero with his inner thoughts and desires (p. 405) :

> Meanwhile the substance of our first act
> Will be shadows, and the strife with shadows.

Who is the first tempter and what does he offer Thomas? Why is his speech filled with descriptions of meadows, apple blossoms and sunlit orchards? For what purpose is the chorus' earlier description of the seasons reworked here? How do the rhythms and rhymes of the first tempter help create his view of life? Why is the first temptation easily repudiated by Thomas?

The language of the second tempter offers a sharp contrast with its vigorous, pointed accents and short phrasings. Who is he? How does his choice of words differ from that of his predecessor? Why does Thomas first respond in a series of short questions and then after two explosive "No's!" begin to argue with the tempter? On what grounds does Thomas reject the proposition of the second tempter?

What do you make of the character of the third tempter and his proposal? When told to "proceed straightforward," why does he wrap his meaning "in as dark generality/ As any courtier"? What are his motives? Why does Thomas reject his suggestions? Which of these three temptations is it the easiest for Thomas to reject? The hardest?

The first three tempters have each offered Thomas an impossible course of action, and he now recognizes at the moment of the fourth tempter's arrival that he has reached an impasse. What then is he to do when "all other ways are closed"? The fourth tempter unexpectedly provides an answer which is for Thomas the only real and present temptation: "Seek the way of martyrdom . . ." (p. 412). In anguish Thomas acknowledges his spiritual pride and his "dreams to damnation" (p. 413). The first priest has foreshadowed this conflict when he portrayed Thomas as a hungrily proud man (p. 402) :

> His pride always feeding upon his own virtues,
> Pride drawing sustenance from impartiality,
> Pride drawing sustenance from generosity,
> Loathing power given by temporal devolution,
> Wishing subjection to God alone.

Actively to seek martyrdom would be to commit the sin of pride, the deadliest of sins, because Thomas would then be exalting his own will above the will of God. The martyrdom offered by the fourth tempter is not martyrdom at all but a promise of spiritual power and glory more insidious than the worldly renown insinuated by the second tempter. Thus the ~~fourth tempter~~ uses the same vocabulary of worldly power and the same arguments as the second tempter. In a moment of agonizing recognition that he is in danger of seeking "the greatest treason: / To do the right deed for the wrong reason" (p. 415), Thomas finds himself in an intolerable dilemma (p. 413):

> Is there no way, in my soul's sickness,
> Does not lead to damnation in pride?
> I well know that these temptations
> Mean present vanity and future torment.
> Can sinful pride be driven out
> Only by more sinful? Can I neither act nor suffer
> Without perdition?

With suave irony the fourth tempter tosses back into Thomas' face the very words he used to comfort the women of Canterbury upon his return from France (p. 404):

> You know and do not know, what it is to act or suffer.
> You know and do not know, that action is suffering,
> And suffering action. Neither does the agent suffer
> Nor the patient act. But both are fixed
> In an eternal action, an eternal patience
> To which all must consent that it may be willed
> And which all must suffer that they may will it,
> That the pattern may subsist, that the wheel may turn and still
> Be forever still.

In these paradoxes is stated one of the central themes of *Murder in the Cathedral*. Until this moment of confrontation Becket had understood their meaning only as an abstract intellectual proposition; he had not felt their emotional implications nor willed that his will be lost in the will of God. He had thought of himself only as the actor agreeing to undertake the suffering of martyrdom so that the women of Canterbury could be the passive recipients of the benefit of his act. The knowing and not knowing have been his as well as the women's. Now Thomas learns that he cannot will his own suffering; he must only consent to divine will and, as God's agent, patiently wait for the moment God elects to act through him. Eliot here is playing with the Latin roots of the verb *agere, to act,* from which *action* and *agent* are derived, and with the Latin verb *pati,* from which *patient* is derived and which means *to endure* as well as *to suffer* in the double sense of *to experience* and *to permit.* Thomas must be ready to endure pain for the love of God; he must consent, experience, and suffer for this act of the will. Only through selflessness can Thomas be an agent for and an expression of the pattern of God's perfect love and thereby bring good out of the evil of his murder.

As soon as Thomas perceives the danger of succumbing to the

fourth temptation, it ceases to be a temptation and is instead an instrument of suffering. Yet the moment of Thomas' transformation or conversion remains a mystery, for after Thomas cries out in despair, "Can I neither act nor suffer/Without perdition?" he falls silent. Since this is a play about a man's mind, why at the crucial moment should the hero stand in silence while the other actors in the drama intone a series of choral passages of despair, fear, and horror? Why should the revelation remain a mystery? Has Thomas undergone a mystical experience? Or does he hear the cry of the chorus (p. 415) :

O Thomas Archbishop, save us, save us, save yourself that we may be saved?

Is this crucial moral act of the purification of Becket's motives and will unspoken because it cannot be expressed in dramatic action or rational discourse? When Thomas again speaks, it is with assurance and purpose: "Now is my way clear, now is the meaning plain" (p. 415) ; his will has been swallowed up in the will of God, and he is ready to accept his destiny as a martyr without ulterior motive: "I shall no longer act or suffer, to the sword's end" (p. 416).

Becket's Christmas sermon, which binds the two parts of the drama in theme, symbol, and Christian tradition, is a rhetorical statement of his inner search for peace. The Interlude not only provides an insight into Thomas' new view of martyrdom but also looks forward to the murder which will occur four days later. When Becket asks us as audience and congregation to "think for a moment about the meaning of this word 'peace'" (p. 416), we may recall how the word was earlier used by the third priest (p. 401) :

What peace can be found
To grow between the hammer and the anvil?

No reconciliation is possible between men of iron will, and the messenger, announcing Becket's return to England, reveals the empty ring of the word: "Peace, but not the kiss of peace" (p. 401). Thomas' first word in the play is "Peace" (p. 404), but even at his return he seems less concerned with giving his blessing to the priests and the chorus than he is with quieting the second priest, who is angered by the "foolish, immodest and babbling women." In his sermon Thomas no longer thinks of peace "as the world gives," of a resolution of his struggle with Henry. His concern is now entirely with the angelic promise of peace given on the first Christmas and with the peace made possible by Christ's sacrifice. The rhythms of the sermon suggest the serenity of Thomas' state of mind as he completely accepts "the design of God," neither willing nor avoiding the martyrdom in which "in a smaller figure" he will re-enact Christ's sacrifice "for the glory of God and for the salvation of men." That Thomas has overcome all danger of yielding to the sin of pride is made explicit in his new understanding of the meaning of martyrdom: "It is never the design of man; for the true martyr is he who has become the instrument of God, who has lost his will in the will of God, and who no longer desires anything for himself, not even the glory of being a martyr." Thomas instructs us further in the emotions with which we should receive his death in Part Two: "we both rejoice and mourn in the death of martyrs."

By the end of Part One the play is virtually over, although so far there has been almost no dramatic action. In Part Two the anticipated result of the resolution of Becket's inward struggle is dramatized. The swift passing of the three days since Christmas and the nearness of martyrdom are suggested by the three priests, who parade colorfully across the stage carrying banners and chanting phrases from the Epistles for the feast days of St. Stephen, St. John the Apostle, and the Holy Innocents.) Eliot delays the moment of the murder by dividing Thomas' encounter with the knights. What is the advantage of this arrangement? What is the significance of their first confrontation? What are the differences between the two meetings? Why should Thomas re-enter with another invocation of peace: "Peace, and be at peace with your thoughts and visions" (p. 424)? How do the multiplying meanings which the play has given the word contribute here to our understanding of Thomas and the chorus?

(That Thomas is ready to suffer and with his "whole being gives entire consent" (p. 427) is dramatized by his refusal to yield to the quick and easy fear of the priests, who are concerned only with his physical safety. In contrast to the panic-stricken priests and the drunken knights, Thomas stands like the still point in a turning wheel, firm in the assurance of his cause and that of the Church, for he has had a "tremor of bliss."/What does he mean? How can "all things/Proceed to a joyful consummation" (p. 425) when an archbishop, unarmed and defenseless, is brutally struck down by drunken assailants in the sanctuary of his cathedral?

"The figure of God's purpose is made complete" (p. 424), and the ironic agents of the divine with Thomas' blood on their knives step out of the drama and come forward to address the audience. The shocking change in tone from poetry of high seriousness to colloquial prose seems to make a grotesque parody of the values for which Thomas has just died and thus has offended some critics. Is the knights' apologia relevant to the drama, or should Eliot have omitted it? What justification does each knight offer? How does the play defeat each feeble argument? Why does Eliot call attention now to our irrelevant roles as Englishmen who believe in fair play, as "hard-headed sensible people," as nationalists, as good sports, and perhaps even as Christians? What should our attitude be when the knights suddenly challenge us with commonplace, stereotyped attitudes and in the flat, conventional rhythms of everyday discourse? How are we involved in the drama just enacted before us? The knights argue that we have benefited by Thomas' death. To what extent are they correct?

Eliot's chief device for projecting the emotional consequences of Thomas' murder is the chorus, who mediates between the action and the audience. When we first see the poor women of Canterbury, they are annoyed that the everyday routine of their lives has been broken; they resent the necessity "to bear witness" (p. 399). They would have Becket return to France so that they could go on "living and partly living" (p. 402) in their "humble and tarnished frame of existence." They want in no way to be involved in any crisis between their archbishop and their king (p. 400):

> For us, the poor, there is no action,
> But only to wait and to witness.

They have only a fleeting intuition that the ominous event "waits in the hand of God," but ironically they keep reiterating the word *witness,* not knowing that *martyr* in Greek means *witness.* As the first tempter approaches, Thomas picks up this motif: "All things prepare the event. Watch" (p. 405). While witnessing Thomas' "strife with shadows," the chorus becomes aware that "a new terror has soiled us" (p. 414), and in panic that in the conflict God will abandon them, they cry out to Thomas to save them, acknowledging that their spiritual welfare depends upon their archbishop. No longer do they call, "O Thomas our Lord, leave us and leave us be" (p. 403).

Part Two begins, like Part One, with the chorus noting the portents of a storm and commenting upon the bleakness of winter. But how has the imagery of the seasons changed? How does this change reflect the new position of the chorus? Have they taken another attitude toward their waiting? After the departure of the four knights the chorus has a nightmarish vision of a world without order and out of time, a world in which they are a part of a chaotic, disordered nature. Yet because of a new recognition of their involvement and because of their capacity to attain this vision, they can now achieve salvation, for they admit their sins and cry to Thomas for absolution. Since the women of Canterbury have done nothing to prevent the imminent murder of their archbishop, they have by implication consented to it (p. 424):

> Nothing is possible but the shamed swoon
> Of those consenting to the last humiliation.

As the chorus acknowledges moral responsibility, the rhythms of the poetry grow certain and ordered like those of Thomas, who recognizes, as the chorus must, that

> These things had to come to you and you to accept them.
> This is your share of the eternal burden,
> The perpetual glory.

The chorus stands and waits, not as they did at the opening of the play, but as Becket now does, yielding their will to the divine purpose. In the moments before Becket's murder, the chorus sinks to the nadir of absolute negation, futility, and despair; they see the world as a meaningless void cut off eternally from God. In agony they turn to Christ, whose sacrifice is about to be renewed in Thomas' martyrdom. Their weakness and fallibility dramatize the fact that this vision of God's design is necessary to lead the chorus to a knowledge of themselves. At the moment of death the chorus sings a profoundly moving act of contrition into which are woven fragments of their earlier dialogues, now seen with deeper insight. What is achieved by this dramatic device? Although the chorus sees the world now "through a curtain of falling blood" (p. 428), their eyes are not so blinded as they think, for they recognize that it is not only they "but the world that is wholly foul." Thus the blood of Becket becomes not defilement but the means by which the world can be purified. This final illumination comes to the chorus after they have listened to the knights' irrelevant, shallow, and materialistic arguments. In a moment of triumphant exaltation, as the pealing of the organ and the strains of a magnificent hymn of praise are heard in the background, the chorus at last acknowledges that Thomas' sacrifice was made for them "as type of the common man." Echoing all the seasonal and natural imagery of the drama, they affirm the spiritual regeneration of the earth through "the blood of Thy martyrs and saints" (p. 433) :

> From such ground springs that which forever renews the earth
> Though it is forever denied.

And the play ends with the chorus quietly and humbly confessing their guilt and praying for the intercession of Saint Thomas. Thus the chorus has moved slowly and painfully from apathetic indifference and fearful evasion, as bystanders, to a recognition of their inevitable involvement in guilt and finally, as religious participants, to a humble belief in and an acceptance of the "eternal design."

Because *Murder in the Cathedral* is an effort to make complete "the figure of God's purpose" in both aesthetic and spiritual terms, the structural design of the play is a highly formal and brilliantly symmetrical emblem for its action and meaning, in part reflecting its dramatic origin in Christian liturgy and ritual. Part One deals with Thomas' inward victory over four tempters; Part Two dramatizes his outward triumph over four knights. Part One moves to a climactic act of will; Part Two, to a climax of theatrical action. The Interlude is the still point in the turning dramatic wheel. Becket's deliberately measured prose rhythms, suggesting his state of grace, contrast with the variety of rhythms of the tempters in Part One and the colloquial prose of the knights in Part Two. Death at the beginning reflects a spiritual wasteland in winter; at the end, salvation, redemption, and the renewal of nature in spring. Each part also has its own inner, fluid design as groups form, dissolve, and re-emerge around the figure of Thomas. Trace the contribution of the chorus as one of the significant parts of Eliot's structural design. What other elements of a formal symmetrical pattern are there?

Eliot's chief rhetorical device for establishing the interrelationship of form and content, of structure and theme, is the recurrent image of the still point at the center of the turning wheel. From the time that the third priest says, "For good or ill, let the wheel turn" (p. 402), the wheel develops as an image of the dramatic action. Thomas' submission of will and his martyrdom are accomplished so "that the wheel may turn and still/Be forever still" (p. 404). The wheel is seen by priest and tempter as only fortune's wheel, but by Thomas as a symbol for the martyr who has perfected his will and who is therefore at the center of a timeless moment in which his only act is the inaction of martyrdom. Thomas' realization that "for a little time the hungry hawk/Will only soar and hover, circling lower" (p. 405) and the second tempter's description of Becket as "the old stag, circled with hounds" (p. 407) prefigure the animal brutality of the knights as they circle Thomas and move in for the murder which will fulfill, not Henry's purposes as they suppose, but God's (p. 419):

> Even now, in sordid particulars
> The eternal design may appear.

Similarly, *Murder in the Cathedral* in its own artistic and theatrical design has brilliantly revealed "the critical moment/That is always now, and here."

Questions and Problems

1. Is the title of this play appropriate? What do you think of Eliot's original choice, *The Archbishop Murder Case*? He also considered *Fear in the Way* (read Eccl. 12:1-8). Why may he have rejected this title?

2. If Henry II is the antagonist, why does he never appear in *Murder in the Cathedral*?

3. What is the function of the priests? Why are the priests not given names whereas the knights are? Do the priests have any individuality?

4. What is the purpose of the speeches of the chorus, the tempters, and the priests on pages 413-415? Should Thomas be intently listening to them, or should he stand apart, lost in contemplation?

5. Why should Part One end with Thomas' reviewing the ambitions and accomplishments of his earlier career? What is their relevance for Thomas' present circumstances? Why does he conclude by addressing the audience as well as the chorus?

6. In some productions Becket swallows a sob as at the end of his sermon he says, ". . . and because, dear children, I do not think I shall ever preach to you again." What is the effect of such an interpretation? Is it justified?

7. There is a legend that a violent storm arose after Becket's murder. Why does Eliot treat the storm only symbolically through the imagery of the chorus and not dramatically?

8. What do the priests, the chorus, the knights, and Becket each "witness"? How does the act of witnessing differ for each?

9. Show how the images of the seasons and of the wheel work together in the design of the play.

10. Can a martyr be a tragic figure? Is Becket?

11. Tom in *The Glass Menagerie,* Alfieri in *A View from the Bridge,* and the chorus in *Murder in the Cathedral* comment upon, and in varying degrees participate in, the dramatic action of their plays. Compare their roles as narrators and participants.

12. Shaw has said that his hero Dick Dudgeon was ready, if necessary, to be a martyr and a saint. Compare Shaw's view of martyrdom with Eliot's.

13. *The Devil's Disciple, A View from the Bridge,* and *Murder in the Cathedral* are plays about a hero's commitment to a cause or to a course of action. Discuss the nature of these commitments and the motives behind them.

14. Ibsen once said of *Rosmersholm* that it dealt with the struggle which every serious-minded man must face in order to bring his life into harmony with his convictions. To what extent would this observation apply to *Murder in the Cathedral*?

JEAN ANOUILH

Becket or The Honor of God

Translated by Lucienne Hill

Biography

ONE OF THE MOST retiring of modern dramatists, Jean Anouilh
(pronounced Ahn-oo-ee) has been at great pains to keep secret the
details of his private life. When once asked for biographical information,
he wrote:

> I have no biography, and I am very glad of it. I was born in Bordeaux
> on the 23rd of June, 1910. I came to Paris when I was young and attended
> the Colbert Primary School and later Chaptal College. A year and a half
> at the Law Faculty in Paris, then two years in an advertising firm, where
> I learned to be ingenious and exact, lessons that for me took the place
> of studies in literature. After my play *L'Hermine* was produced I decided
> to live only by writing for the theatre, and a little for films. It was folly,
> but I did right to make that decision. I have managed never to touch
> journalism, and in films all I have on my conscience are one or two
> cheap farces and a few unsigned and now forgotten romantic melo-
> dramas. The rest of my life, and for as long as it pleases Heaven for it
> to be my private business, I shall keep the details to myself.[1]

While in the advertising business Anouilh met Monelle Valentin,
whom he married and in later years divorced. She played the roles of
many of his young heroines, including Antigone. In 1931 Anouilh took
a position with Louis Jouvet's theatrical company and was introduced to
the world of the theater. His first play *L'Hermine* was produced in
April, 1932, when he was twenty-two. Three years of poverty and disappointment were followed by the financial success of *Y'Avait un Prisonnier*
(*Once Was a Prisoner*), which was sold to Hollywood. Since 1937 almost
every theatrical season has seen the première of a new Anouilh play. The
production of *Antigone* in 1944 established Anouilh's reputation as one
of the leading dramatists in France, yet not until 1955 with *L'Alouette*
(*The Lark*), starring Julie Harris, did any play of his achieve popular
success on Broadway. In 1960 and 1961 productions of *Becket*, starring
Sir Laurence Olivier and Anthony Quinn, brought Anouilh his greatest
triumph to date in the United States and added further to his international prestige.

---

[1] Edward Owen Marsh, *Jean Anouilh* (London, 1953), p. 9.

Principal Works

(Titles in parentheses are those of the English translations.)

L'Hermine (The Ermine) (1932)

Y'Avait un Prisonnier (Once Was a Prisoner) (1935)

Le Voyageur sans bagage (Traveller without Luggage) (1937)

La Sauvage (Restless Heart) (1938)

Le Bal des voleurs (Thieves' Carnival) (1938)

Léocadia (Time Remembered) (1940)

Le Rendez-vous de Senlis (Dinner with the Family) (1941)

Eurydice (Point of Departure, or Legend of Lovers) (1942)

Antigone (Antigone) (1944)

Roméo et Jeannette (Fading Mansions) (1946)

L'Invitation au château (Ring Round the Moon) (1947)

Ardèle ou la Marguerite (Cry of the Peacock) (1948)

La Répétition ou l'amour puni (The Rehearsal) (1950)

Colombe (Mademoiselle Colombe) (1951)

La Valse des Toréadors (Waltz of the Toreadors) (1952)

Médée (Medea) (1953)

L'Alouette (The Lark) (1953)

Ornifle ou le courant d'air (1955)

Pauvre Bitos ou le diner de têtes (Poor Bitos) (1956)

L'Hurluberlu ou le réactionnaire amoureux (The Fighting Cock) (1959)

La Petite Molière (1959)

Becket ou l'honneur de Dieu (Becket or The Honor of God) (1959)

COLLECTED EDITIONS

Pièces noires (Black Plays) (1942)

Pièces roses (Rose Plays) (1942)

Nouvelles pièces noires (New Black Plays) (1946)

Pièces brillantes (Brilliant Plays) (1951)

Pièces grinçantes (Grating Plays) (1956)

Selected Descriptive Bibliography

Chiari, Joseph, *The Contemporary French Theatre*, New York, 1959.

Although Chiari's colorful chapter on Anouilh was written before the appearance of Becket, *it provides a good background for a study of the play.*

Fowlie, Wallace, *Dionysus in Paris*, New York, 1960.

In an excellent chapter on Anouilh, Fowlie establishes the central thematic conflicts underlying Anouilh's plays.

Gignoux, Hubert, *Jean Anouilh*, Paris, 1946.

A critical study, in French, of Anouilh's early plays.

Grossvogel, David I., *The Self-Conscious Stage in Modern French Drama*, New York, 1958.

In an extended chapter on Anouilh, Grossvogel provides a searching analysis of his characters.

Guicharnaud, Jacques (in collaboration with June Beckelman), *Modern French Theatre from Giraudoux to Beckett*, New Haven, 1961.

This intelligent discussion of the themes and techniques of modern French playwrights contains brief but relevant commentary on Becket.

Heiney, Donald, "Jean Anouilh: the Revival of Tragedy," *College English*, XVI (March, 1955), 331-335.

A brief study of Anouilh's tragic heroes and their antagonists.

Hobson, Harold, *The French Theatre of To-day*, London, 1953.

A short chapter on Anouilh as a moralist has little relevance for an understanding of Becket.

Marsh, Edward Owen, *Jean Anouilh: Poet of Pierrot and Pantaloon*, London, 1953.

An introductory and popularized study of the plays written during the first 20 years of Anouilh's career.

Pronko, Leonard Cabell, *The World of Jean Anouilh*, Berkeley and Los Angeles, 1961.

The most detailed and comprehensive study of Anouilh. Indispensable for an understanding of his themes, characters, and dramatic conventions.

Becket or The Honor of God JEAN ANOUILH

Translated by Lucienne Hill

CHARACTERS

HENRY II	1ST ENGLISH BARON
THOMAS BECKET	2ND ENGLISH BARON
ARCHBISHOP OF CANTERBURY	3RD ENGLISH BARON
GILBERT FOLLIOT	4TH ENGLISH BARON
BISHOP OF YORK	QUEEN MOTHER
SAXON PEASANT	THE QUEEN
HIS SON	LOUIS, KING OF FRANCE
GWENDOLEN	THE POPE

Becket was first presented at the Montparnasse-Gaston Baty Theater in Paris on October 8, 1959. Its American première was held at the St. James Theatre in New York City on October 5, 1960.

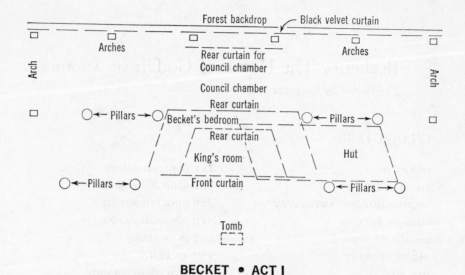

BECKET • ACT I

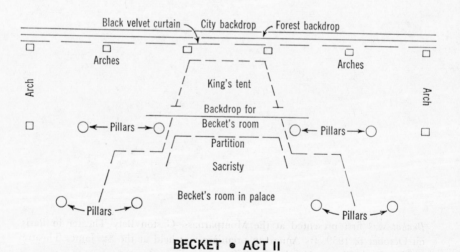

BECKET • ACT II

All ground plans for Becket *adapted from the original designs by Oliver Smith for the 1960 New York production.*

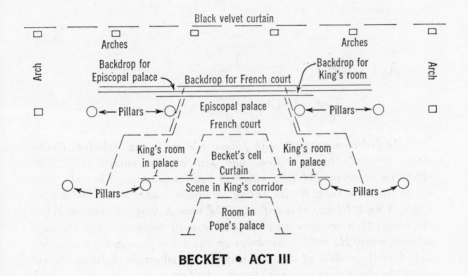

BECKET • ACT III

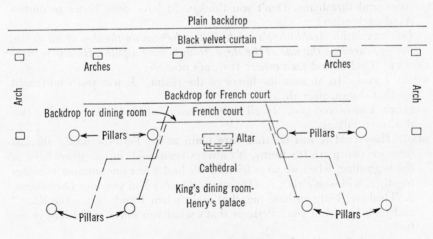

BECKET • ACT IV

Act One

An indeterminate set, with pillars. We are in the cathedral. Center stage: BECKET'S *tomb; a stone slab with a name carved on it. Two* SENTRIES *come in and take up their position upstage. Then the* KING *enters from the back. He is wearing his crown, and is naked under a big cloak. A* PAGE *follows at a distance. The* KING *hesitates a moment before the tomb; then removes his cloak with a swift movement and the* PAGE *takes it away. He falls to his knees on the stone floor and prays, alone, naked, in the middle of the stage. Behind the pillars, in the shadows, one senses the disquieting presence of unseen lookers-on.*

KING: Well, Thomas Becket, are you satisfied? I am naked at your tomb and your monks are coming to flog me. What an end to our story! You, rotting in this tomb, larded with my barons' dagger thrusts, and I, naked, shivering in the draughts, and waiting like an idiot for those brutes to come and thrash me. Don't you think we'd have done better to understand each other?

(BECKET *in his Archbishop's robes, just as he was on the day of his death, has appeared on the side of the stage, from behind a pillar. He says softly:*)

BECKET: Understand each other? It wasn't possible.

KING: I said, "In all save the honor of the realm." It was you who taught me that slogan, after all.

BECKET: I answered you, "In all save the honor of God." We were like two deaf men talking.

KING: How cold it was on that bare plain at La Ferté-Bernard,[2] the last time we two met! It's funny, it's always been cold, in our story. Save at the beginning, when we were friends. We had a few fine summer evenings together, with the girls. . . . (*He says suddenly*) Did you love Gwendolen, Archbishop? Did you hate me, that night when I said, "I am the King," and took her from you? Perhaps that's what you never could forgive me for?

BECKET (*quietly*): I've forgotten.

KING: Yet we were like two brothers, weren't we—you and I? That night it was a childish prank—a lusty lad shouting "I am the King!" . . . I was

---

[2] A town southwest of Paris where Henry II and Becket met on July 22, 1170, in a futile effort at reconciliation.

so young . . . And every thought in my head came from you, you know that.

BECKET (*gently, as if to a little boy*): Pray, Henry, and don't talk so much.

KING (*irritably*): If you think I'm in the mood for praying at the moment. . . . (BECKET *quietly withdraws into the darkness and disappears during the* KING'S *next speech*) I can see them through my fingers, spying on me from the aisles. Say what you like, they're an oafish lot, those Saxons of yours! To give oneself over naked to those ruffians! With my delicate skin. . . . Even you'd be afraid. Besides, I'm ashamed. Ashamed of this whole masquerade. I need them though, that's the trouble. I have to rally them to my cause, against my son, who'll gobble up my kingdom if I let him. So I've come to make my peace with their Saint. You must admit it's funny. You've become a Saint and here am I, the King, desperately in need of that great amorphous mass which could do nothing, up till now, save lie inert beneath its own enormous weight, cowering under blows, and which is all-powerful now. What use are conquests, when you stop to think? They are England now, because of their vast numbers, and the rate at which they breed—like rabbits, to make good the massacres. But one must always pay the price—that's another thing you taught me, Thomas Becket, when you were still advising me. . . . You taught me everything. . . . (*Dreamily*) Ah, those were happy times. . . . At the peep of dawn—well, our dawn that is, around noon, because we always went to bed very late—you'd come into my room, as I was emerging from the bathhouse, rested, smiling, debonair, as fresh as if we'd never spent the entire night drinking and whoring through the town. (*He says a little sourly*) That's another thing you were better at than me. . . .

(*The* PAGE *has come in. He wraps a white towel around the* KING *and proceeds to rub him down. Off stage is heard for the first time—we will hear it often—the gay, ironical Scottish marching song which* BECKET *is always whistling.*

The lighting changes. We are still in the empty cathedral. Then, a moment or so later, BECKET *will draw aside a curtain and reveal the* KING'S *room. Their manner, his and the* KING'S, *faraway at first, like a memory relived, will gradually become more real.*

THOMAS BECKET, *dressed as a nobleman, elegant, young, charming, in his short doublet and pointed, upturned shoes, comes in blithely and greets the* KING.)

BECKET: My respects, my Lord!

KING (*his face brightening*): Oh, Thomas . . . I thought you were still asleep.

BECKET: I've already been for a short gallop to Richmond and back, my Lord. There's a divine nip in the air.

KING (*his teeth chattering*): To think you actually like the cold! (*To the* PAGE) Rub harder, pig! (*Smiling,* BECKET *pushes the* PAGE *aside and proceeds to rub the* KING *himself. To the* PAGE) Throw a log on the fire and get out. Come back and dress me later.

BECKET: My prince, I shall dress you myself.

(*The* PAGE *goes.*)

KING: Nobody rubs me down the way you do. Thomas, what would I do without you? You're a nobleman, why do you play at being my valet? If I asked my barons to do this, they'd start a civil war!

BECKET (*smiling*): They'll come round to it in time, when Kings have learnt to play their role. I am your servant, my prince, that's all. Helping you to govern or helping you get warm again is part of the same thing to me. I like helping you.

KING (*with an affectionate little gesture*): My little Saxon! At the beginning, when I told them I was taking you into my service, do you know what they all said? They said you'd seize the chance to knife me in the back one day.

BECKET (*smiling as he dresses him*): Did you believe them, my prince?

KING: N . . . no. I was a bit scared at first. You know I scare easily . . . But you looked so well brought up, beside those brutes. However did you come to speak French without a trace of an English accent?

BECKET: My parents were able to keep their lands by agreeing to "collaborate," as they say, with the King your father. They sent me to France as a boy to acquire a good French accent.

KING: To France? Not to Normandy?

BECKET (*still smiling*): That was their one patriotic conceit. They loathed the Norman accent.

KING (*distinctly*): Only the accent?

BECKET (*lightly and inscrutably*): My father was a very severe man. I would never have taken the liberty of questioning him on his personal convictions while he was alive. And his death shed no light on them, naturally. He managed, by collaborating, to amass a considerable fortune. As he was also a man of rigid principles, I imagine he contrived to do it in accordance with his conscience. That's a little piece of sleight of hand that men of principle are very skillful at in troubled times.

KING: And you?

BECKET (*feigning not to understand the question*): I, my Lord?

KING (*putting a touch of contempt into his voice, for despite his admiration for Thomas or perhaps because of it, he would like to score a point against him occasionally*): The sleight of hand, were you adept at it too?

BECKET (*still smiling*): Mine was a different problem. I was a frivolous man, you'll agree? In fact, it never came up at all. I adore hunting and only the Normans and their protégés had the right to hunt. I adore luxury and luxury was Norman. I adore life and the Saxons' only birthright was slaughter. I'll add that I adore honor.

KING (*with faint surprise*): And was honor reconciled with collaboration too?

BECKET (*lightly*): I had the right to draw my sword against the first Norman nobleman who tried to lay hands on my sister. I killed him in single combat. It's a detail, but it has its points.

KING (*a little slyly*): You could always have slit his throat and fled into the forest, as so many did.

BECKET: That would have been uncomfortable, and not a lot of use. My sister would immediately have been raped by some other Norman baron,

like all the Saxon girls. Today, she is respected. (*Lightly*) My Lord, did
I tell you?—My new gold dishes have arrived from Florence. Will my
Liege do me the honor of christening them with me at my house?
KING: Gold dishes! You lunatic!
BECKET: I'm setting a new fashion.
KING: I'm your King and I eat off silver!
BECKET: My prince, your expenses are heavy and I have only my pleasures
to pay for. The trouble is I'm told they scratch easily. Still, we'll see. I
received two forks as well—
KING: Forks?
BECKET: Yes. It's a new instrument, a devilish little thing to look at—and
to use too. It's for pronging meat with and carrying it to your mouth.
It saves you dirtying your fingers.
KING: But then you dirty the fork?
BECKET: Yes. But it's washable.
KING: So are your fingers. I don't see the point.
BECKET: It hasn't any, practically speaking. But it's refined, it's subtle. It's
very un-Norman.
KING (*with sudden delight*): You must order me a dozen! I want to see my
great fat barons' faces, at the first court banquet, when I present them
with that! We won't tell them what they're for. We'll have no end of fun
with them.
BECKET (*laughing*): A dozen! Easy now, my Lord! Forks are very expensive,
you know! My prince, it's time for the Privy Council.
KING (*laughing too*): They won't make head nor tail of them! I bet you
they'll think they're a new kind of dagger. We'll have a hilarious time!
(*They go out, laughing, behind the curtain, which draws apart to reveal
the same set, with the pillars. The Council Chamber. The Councilors
stand waiting. The* KING *and* BECKET *come in, still laughing.*)
KING (*sitting in a chair*): Gentlemen, the Council is open. I have summoned you here today to deal with this refusal of the clergy to pay the
absentee tax. We really must come to an understanding about who rules
this kingdom, the Church—(*The Archbishop tries to speak*) just a moment, Archbishop!—or me! But before we quarrel, let us take the good
news first. I have decided to revive the office of Chancellor of England,
keeper of the Triple Lion Seal, and to entrust it to my loyal servant and
subject Thomas Becket.
(BECKET *rises in surprise, the color draining from his face.*)
BECKET: My Lord . . . !
KING (*roguishly*): What's the matter, Becket? Do you want to go and piss
already? True, we both had gallons to drink last night! (*He looks at him
with delight*) Well, that's good! I've managed to surprise you for once,
little Saxon.
BECKET (*dropping on one knee, says gravely*): My Liege, this is a token of
your confidence of which I fear I may not be worthy. I am very young,
frivolous perhaps—
KING: I'm young too. And you know more than all of us put together.
(*To the others*) He's read books, you know. It's amazing the amount he

knows. He'll checkmate the lot of you! Even the Archbishop! As for his frivolity, don't let him fool you! He drinks strong wine, he likes to enjoy himself, but he's a lad who thinks every minute of the time! Sometimes it embarrasses me to feel him thinking away beside me. Get up, Thomas. I never did anything without your advice anyway. Nobody knew it, now everybody will, that's all. (*He bursts out laughing, pulls something out of his pocket and gives it to* BECKET) There. That's the Seal. Don't lose it. Without the Seal, there's no more England and we'll all have to go back to Normandy. Now, to work!

(*The* ARCHBISHOP *rises, all smiles, now the first shock is over.*)

ARCHBISHOP: May I crave permission to salute, with my Lord's approval, my young and learned archdeacon here? For I was the first—I am weak enough to be proud of pointing it out—to notice him and take him under my wing. The presence at this Council, with the preponderant title of Chancellor of England, of one of our brethren—our spiritual son in a sense—is a guarantee for the Church of this country, that a new era of agreement and mutual understanding is dawning for us all and we must now, in a spirit of confident cooperation—

KING (*interrupting*): Etc., etc. . . . Thank you, Archbishop! I knew this nomination would please you. But don't rely too much on Becket to play your game. He is my man. (*He turns to* BECKET, *beaming*) Come to think of it, I'd forgotten you were a deacon, little Saxon.

BECKET (*smiling*): So had I, my prince.

KING: Tell me—I'm not talking about wenching, that's a venial sin—but on the odd occasions when I've seen you fighting, it seems to me you have a mighty powerful sword arm, for a priest! How do you reconcile that with the Church's commandment forbidding a priest to shed blood?

BISHOP OF OXFORD (*prudently*): Our young friend is only a deacon, he has not yet taken all his vows, my Lord. The Church in its wisdom knows that youth must have its day and that—under the sacred pretext of a war —a holy war, I mean, of course, young men are permitted to—

KING (*interrupting*): All wars are holy wars, Bishop! I defy you to find me a serious belligerent who doesn't have Heaven on his side, in theory. Let's get back to the point.

ARCHBISHOP: By all means, your Highness.

KING: Our customs demand that every landowner with sufficient acreage to maintain one must send a man-at-arms to the quarterly review of troops, fully armed and shield in hand, or pay a tax in silver. Where is my tax?

BISHOP OF OXFORD: *Distingo,* your Highness.

KING: Distinguish as much as you like. I've made up my mind. I want my money. My purse is open, just drop it in. (*He sprawls back in his chair and picks his teeth. To* BECKET) Thomas, I don't know about you, but I'm starving. Have them bring us something to eat.

(BECKET *makes a sign to the* SENTRY, *who goes out. A pause. The* ARCHBISHOP *rises.*)

ARCHBISHOP: A layman who shirks his duty to the State, which is to assist his Prince with arms, should pay the tax. Nobody will question that.

KING (*jovially*) : Least of all the clergy!

ARCHBISHOP (*continuing*) : A churchman's duty to the State is to assist his Prince in his prayers, and in his educational and charitable enterprises. He cannot therefore be liable to such a tax unless he neglects those duties.

BISHOP OF OXFORD: Have we refused to pray?

KING (*rising in fury*) : Gentlemen! Do you seriously think that I am going to let myself be swindled out of more than two thirds of my revenues with arguments of that sort? In the days of the Conquest, when there was booty to be had, our Norman abbots tucked up their robes all right. And lustily too! Sword in fist, hams in the saddle, at cockcrow or earlier! "Let's go to it, Sire! Out with the Saxon scum! It's God's will! It's God's will!" You had to hold them back then! And on the odd occasions when you wanted a little Mass, they never had the time. They'd mislaid their vestments, the churches weren't equipped—any excuse to put it off, for fear they'd miss some of the pickings while their backs were turned!

ARCHBISHOP: Those heroic days are over. It is peacetime now.

KING: Then pay up! I won't budge from that. (*Turning to* BECKET) Come on, Chancellor, say something! Has your new title caught your tongue?

BECKET: May I respectfully draw my Lord Archbishop's attention to one small point?

KING (*grunting*) : Respectfully, but firmly. You're the Chancellor now.

BECKET (*calmly and casually*) : England is a ship.

KING (*beaming*) : Why, that's neat! We must use that, sometime.

BECKET: In the hazards of seafaring, the instinct of self-preservation has always told men that there must be one and only one master on board ship. Mutinous crews who drown their captain always end up, after a short interval of anarchy, by entrusting themselves body and soul to one of their number, who then proceeds to rule over them, more harshly sometimes than their drowned captain.

ARCHBISHOP: My Lord Chancellor—my young friend—there is in fact a saying—the captain is sole master after God. (*He thunders suddenly, with a voice one did not suspect from that frail body*) After God! (*He crosses himself. All the* BISHOPS *follow suit. The wind of excommunication shivers through the Council. The* KING, *awed, crosses himself too and mumbles, a little cravenly.*)

KING: Nobody's trying to question God's authority, Archbishop.

BECKET (*who alone has remained unperturbed*) : God steers the ship by inspiring the captain's decisions. But I never heard tell that He gave His instructions directly to the helmsman.

(GILBERT FOLLIOT, *Bishop of London, rises. He is a thin-lipped, venomous man.*)

FOLLIOT: Our young Chancellor is only a deacon—but he is a member of the Church. The few years he has spent out in the tumult of the world cannot have made him forget so soon that it is through His Church Militant and more particularly through the intermediary of our Holy Father the Pope and his Bishops—his qualified representatives—that God dictates His decisions to men!

BECKET: There is a chaplain on board every ship, but he is not required to determine the size of the crew's rations, nor to take the vessel's bearings. My Reverend Lord the Bishop of London—who is the grandson of a sailor they tell me—cannot have forgotten that point either.

FOLLIOT (*yelping*): I will not allow personal insinuations to compromise the dignity of a debate of this importance! The integrity and honor of the Church of England are at stake!

KING (*cheerfully*): No big words, Bishop. You know as well as I do that all that's at stake is its money. I need money for my wars. Will the Church give me any, yes or no?

ARCHBISHOP (*cautiously*): The Church of England has always acknowledged that it was its duty to assist the King, to the best of its ability, in all his needs.

KING: There's a fine speech. But I don't like the past tense, Archbishop. There's something so nostalgic about it. I like the present. And the future. Are you going to pay up?

ARCHBISHOP: Your Highness, I am here to defend the privileges which your illustrious forefather William granted to the Church of England. Would you have the heart to tamper with your forefather's work?

KING: May he rest in peace. His work is inviolable. But where he is now he doesn't need money. I'm still on earth unfortunately, and I do.

FOLLIOT: Your Highness, this is a question of principle!

KING: I'm levying troops, Bishop! I have sent for 1,500 German foot soldiers, and three thousand Swiss infantry to help fight the King of France. And nobody has ever paid the Swiss with principles.

BECKET (*rises suddenly and says incisively*): I think, your Highness, that it is pointless to pursue a discussion in which neither speaker is listening to the other. The law and custom of the land give us the means of coercion. We will use them.

FOLLIOT (*beside himself*): Would you dare—you whom she raised from the obscurity of your base origins—to plunge a dagger in the bosom of your Mother Church?

BECKET: My Lord and King has given me his Seal with the Three Lions to guard. My mother is England now.

FOLLIOT (*frothing, and slightly ridiculous*): A deacon! A miserable deacon nourished in our bosom! Traitor! Little viper! Libertine! Sycophant! Saxon!

KING: My reverend friend, I suggest you respect my Chancellor, or else I'll call my guards. (*He has raised his voice a little toward the end of this speech. The* GUARDS *come in. Surprised*) Why, here they are! Oh, no, it's my snack. Excuse me, gentlemen, but around noon I need something to peck at or I tend to feel weak. And a King has no right to weaken, I needn't tell you that. I'll have it in my chapel; then I can pray directly afterwards. Come and sit with me, son.

(*He goes out taking* BECKET *with him. The three prelates have risen, deeply offended. They move away, murmuring to one another, with sidelong glances in the direction in which the* KING *went out.*)

FOLLIOT: We must appeal to Rome! We must take a firm line!

YORK: My Lord Archbishop, you are the Primate of England. Your person is inviolate and your decisions on all matters affecting the Church are law in this country. You have a weapon against such intransigence: excommunication.

BISHOP OF OXFORD: We must not use it save with a great deal of prudence, Reverend Bishop. The Church has always triumphed over the centuries, but it has triumphed prudently. Let us bide our time. The King's rages are terrible, but they don't last. They are fires of straw.

FOLLIOT: The little self-seeker he has at his elbow now will make it his business to kindle them. And I think, like the Reverend Bishop, that only the excommunication of that young libertine can reduce him to impotence.

(BECKET *comes in.*)

BECKET: My Lords, the King has decided to adjourn his Privy Council. He thinks that a night of meditation will inspire your Lordships with a wise and equitable solution—which he authorizes you to come and submit to him tomorrow.

FOLLIOT (*with a bitter laugh*): You mean it's time for the hunt.

BECKET (*smiling*): Yes, my Lord Bishop, to be perfectly frank with you, it is. Believe me, I am personally most grieved at this difference of opinion and the brutal form it has taken. But I cannot go back on what I said as Chancellor of England. We are all bound, laymen as well as priests, by the same feudal oath we took to the King as our Lord and Sovereign; the oath to preserve his life, limbs, dignity and honor. None of you, I think, has forgotten the words of that oath?

ARCHBISHOP (*quietly*): We have not forgotten it, my son. No more than the other oath we took, before that—the oath to God. You are young, and still uncertain of yourself, perhaps. Yet you have, in those few words, taken a resolution the meaning of which has not escaped me. Will you allow an old man, who is very close to death, and who, in this rather sordid argument, was defending more perhaps than you suspect—to hope, as a father, that you will never know the bitterness of realizing, one day, that you made a mistake. (*He holds out his ring and* BECKET *kisses it*) I give you my blessing, my son.

(BECKET *has knelt. Now he rises and says lightly:*)

BECKET: An unworthy son, Father, alas. But when is one worthy? And worthy of what? (*He pirouettes and goes out, insolent and graceful as a young boy.*)

FOLLIOT (*violently*): Such insults to your Grace cannot be tolerated! This young rake's impudence must be crushed!

ARCHBISHOP (*thoughtfully*): He was with me for a long time. His is a strange, elusive nature. Don't imagine he is the ordinary libertine that outward appearances would suggest. I've had plenty of opportunity to observe him, in the bustle of pleasure and daily living. He is as it were detached. As if seeking his real self.

FOLLIOT: Break him, my Lord, before he finds it! Or the clergy of this country will pay dearly.

ARCHBISHOP: We must be very circumspect. It is our task to see into the hearts of men. And I am not sure that this one will always be our enemy. (*The* ARCHBISHOP *and the three* BISHOPS *go out. The* KING *is heard calling off stage.*)

KING: Well, son, have they gone? Are you coming hunting?

(*Trees come down from the flies. The black velvet curtain at the back opens on a clear sky, transforming the pillars into the leafless trees of a forest in winter. Bugles. The lights have gone down. When they go up again, the* KING *and* BECKET *are on horseback, each with a hawk on his gauntleted wrist. Torrential rain is heard.*)

KING: Here comes the deluge. (*Unexpectedly*) Do you like hunting this way, with hawks?

BECKET: I don't much care to delegate my errands. I prefer to feel a wild boar on the end of my spear. When he turns and charges there's a moment of delicious personal contact when one feels, at last, responsible for oneself.

KING: It's odd, this craving for danger. Why are you all so hell-bent on risking your necks for the most futile reasons?

BECKET: One has to gamble with one's life to feel alive.

KING: Or dead! You make me laugh. (*To his hawk*) Quiet, my pretty, quiet! We'll take your hood off in a minute. You couldn't give much of a performance under all these trees. I'll tell you one creature that loves hawking anyway, and that's a hawk! It seems to me we've rubbed our backsides sore with three hours' riding, just to give them this royal pleasure.

BECKET (*smiling*): My Lord, these are Norman hawks. They belong to the master race. They have a right to it.

KING (*suddenly, as he reins his horse*): Do you love me, Becket?

BECKET: I am your servant, my prince.

KING: Did you love me when I made you Chancellor? I wonder sometimes if you're capable of love. Do you love Gwendolen?

BECKET: She is my mistress, my prince.

KING: Why do you put labels onto everything to justify your feelings?

BECKET: Because, without labels, the world would have no shape, my prince.

KING: Is it so important for the world to have a shape?

BECKET: It's essential, my prince, otherwise we can't know what we're doing. (*Bugles in the distance*) The rain is getting heavier, my Lord! Come, let us shelter in that hut over there.

(*He gallops off. After a second of confused indecision, the* KING *gallops after him, holding his hawk high and shouting:*)

KING: Becket! You didn't answer my question!

(*He disappears into the forest. Bugles again. The four* BARONS *cross the stage, galloping after them, and vanish into the forest. Thunder. Lightning. A hut has appeared to one side of the stage.* BECKET *is heard shouting:*)

BECKET: Hey there! You! Fellow! Can we put the horses under cover in your barn? Do you know how to rub down a horse? And have a look at the right forefoot of messire's horse. I think the shoe is loose. We'll sit out the storm under your roof.

(*After a second, the* KING *enters the hut, followed by a hairy Saxon who, cap in hand, bows repeatedly, in terrified silence.*)

KING (*shaking himself*) : What a soaking! I'll catch my death! (*He sneezes*) All this just to keep the hawks amused! (*Shouting at the man*) What are you waiting for? Light a fire, dog! It's freezing cold in this shack. (*The* MAN, *terror-stricken, does not move. The* KING *sneezes again. To* BECKET) What is he waiting for?

BECKET: Wood is scarce, my Lord. I don't suppose he has any left.

KING: What—in the middle of the forest?

BECKET: They are entitled to two measures of dead wood. One branch more and they're hanged.

KING (*astounded*) : Really? And yet people are always complaining about the amount of dead wood in the forests. Still, that's a problem for my intendants, not me. (*Shouting at the* MAN) Run and pick up all the wood you can carry and build us a roaring fire! We won't hang you this time, dog!

(*The peasant, terrified, dares not obey.* BECKET *says gently:*)

BECKET: Go, my son. Your King commands it. You've the right.

(*The* MAN *goes out, trembling, bowing to the ground, repeatedly.*)

KING: Why do you call that old man your son?

BECKET: Why not? You call him dog, my prince.

KING: It's a manner of speaking. Saxons are always called "dog." I can't think why, really. One could just as well have called them "Saxon"! But that smelly old ragbag your son! (*Sniffing*) What on earth can they eat to make the place stink so—dung?

BECKET: Turnips.

KING: Turnips—what are they?

BECKET: Roots.

KING (*amused*) : Do they eat roots?

BECKET: Those who live in the forests can't grow anything else.

KING: Why don't they move out into the open country then?

BECKET: They would be hanged if they left their area.

KING: Oh, I see. Mark you, that must make life a lot simpler, if you know you'll be hanged at the least show of initiative. You must ask yourself far fewer questions. They don't know their luck! But you still haven't told me why you called the fellow your son?

BECKET (*lightly*) : My prince, he is so poor and so bereft and I am so strong beside him, that he really is my son.

KING: We'd go a long way with that theory!

BECKET: Besides, my prince, you're appreciably younger than I am and you call me "son" sometimes.

KING: That's got nothing to do with it. It's because I love you.

BECKET: You are our King. We are all your sons and in your hands.

KING: What, Saxons too?

BECKET (*lightly, as he strips off his gloves*) : England will be fully built, my prince, on the day the Saxons are your sons as well.

KING: You are a bore today! I get the feeling that I'm listening to the Archbishop. And I'm dying of thirst. Hunt around and see if you can't find us something to drink. Go on, it's your son's house! (BECKET *starts looking, and leaves the room after a while. The* KING *looks around too, examining the hut with curiosity, touching things with grimaces of distaste. Suddenly he notices a kind of trap door at the foot of a wall. He opens it, thrusts his hand in and pulls out a terrified* GIRL. *He shouts*) Hey, Thomas! Thomas! (BECKET *comes in.*)

BECKET: Have you found something to drink, Lord?

KING (*holding the* GIRL *at arm's length*): No. Something to eat. What do you say to that, if it's cleaned up a bit?

BECKET (*coldly*): She's pretty.

KING: She stinks a bit, but we could wash her. Look, did you ever see anything so tiny? How old would you say it was—fifteen, sixteen?

BECKET (*quietly*): It can talk, my Lord. (*Gently, to the* GIRL) How old are you? (*The* GIRL *looks at them in terror and says nothing.*)

KING: You see? Of course it can't talk! (*The* MAN *has come back with the wood and stops in the doorway, terrified*) How old is your daughter, dog? (*The* MAN *trembles like a cornered animal and says nothing*) He's dumb as well, that son of yours. How did you get him—with a deaf girl? It's funny the amount of dumb people I meet the second I set foot out of my palace. I rule over a kingdom of the dumb. Can you tell me why?

BECKET: They're afraid, my prince.

KING: I know that. And a good thing too. The populace must live in fear, it's essential. The moment they stop being afraid they have only one thought in mind—to frighten other people instead. And they adore doing that! Just as much as we do! Give them a chance to do it and they catch up fast, those sons of yours! Did you never see a peasants' revolt? I did once, in my father's reign, when I was a child. It's not a pretty sight. (*He looks at the* MAN, *exasperated*) Look at it, will you? It's tongue-tied, it's obtuse, it stinks and the country is crawling with them! (*He seizes the* GIRL, *who was trying to run away*) Stay here, you! (*To* BECKET) I ask you, what use is it?

BECKET (*smiling*): It scratches the soil, it makes bread.

KING: Pooh, the English eat so little of it . . . At the French Court, yes, I daresay—they fairly stuff it down! But here!

BECKET (*smiling*): The troops have to be fed. For a King without troops. . . .

KING (*struck by this*): True enough! Yes, that makes sense. There must be some sort of reason in all these absurdities. Well well, you little Saxon philosopher, you! I don't know how you do it, but you'll turn me into an intelligent man yet! The odd thing is, it's so ugly and yet it makes such pretty daughters. How do you explain that, you who can explain it all?

BECKET: At twenty, before he lost his teeth and took on that indeterminate age the common people have, that man may have been handsome. He may have had one night of love, one minute when he too was a King, and shed his fear. Afterwards, his pauper's life went on, eternally the same. And he and his wife no doubt forgot it all. But the seed was sown.

KING (*dreamily*): You have such a way of telling things. . . . (*He looks at the* GIRL) Do you think she'll grow ugly too?

BECKET: For sure.

KING: If we made her a whore and kept her at the palace, would she stay pretty?

BECKET: Perhaps.

KING: Then we'd be doing her a service, don't you think?

BECKET (*coldly*): No doubt.

(*The* MAN *stiffens. The* GIRL *cowers, in terror. The* BROTHER *comes in, somber-faced, silent, threatening.*)

KING: Would you believe it? They understand every word, you know! Who's that one there?

BECKET (*taking in the situation at a glance*): The brother.

KING: How do you know?

BECKET: Instinct, my Lord. (*His hand moves to his dagger.*)

KING (*bawling suddenly*): Why are they staring at me like that? I've had enough of this! I told you to get something to drink, dog! (*Terrified, the* MAN *scuttles off.*)

BECKET: Their water will be brackish. I have a gourd of juniper juice in my saddlebag. (*To the* BROTHER) Come and give me a hand, you! My horse is restive.

(*He seizes the boy roughly by the arm and hustles him out into the forest, carelessly whistling his little marching song. Then, all of a sudden, he hurls himself onto him. A short silent struggle.* BECKET *gets the boy's knife away; he escapes into the forest.* BECKET *watches him go for a second, holding his wounded hand. Then he walks around the back of the hut. The* KING *has settled himself on a bench, with his feet up on another, whistling to himself. He lifts the* GIRL'S *skirts with his cane and examines her at leisure.*)

KING (*in a murmur*): All my sons! . . . (*He shakes himself*) That Becket! He wears me out. He keeps making me think! I'm sure it's bad for the health. (*He gets up;* BECKET *comes in followed by the* MAN) What about that water? How much longer do I have to wait?

BECKET: Here it is, my Lord. But it's muddy. Have some of this juniper juice instead.

KING: Drink with me. (*He notices* BECKET'S *hand, wrapped in a blood-stained cloth*) What's the matter? You're wounded!

BECKET (*hiding his hand*): No doubt about it, that horse of mine is a nervous brute. He can't bear his saddle touched. He bit me.

KING (*with a hearty, delighted laugh*): That's funny! Oh, that's very funny! Milord is the best rider in the Kingdom! Milord can never find a stallion with enough spirit for him! Milord makes us all look silly at the jousts, with his fancy horsemanship, and when he goes to open his saddlebags he gets himself bitten! Like a page! (*He is almost savagely gleeful. Then suddenly, his gaze softens*) You're white as a sheet, little Saxon . . . Why do I love you? . . . It's funny, I don't like to think of you in pain. Show me that hand. A horse bite can turn nasty. I'll put some of that juniper gin on it.

BECKET (*snatching his hand away*): I already have, my Lord; it's nothing.

KING: Then why do you look so pale? Show me your hand.

BECKET (*with sudden coldness*) : It's an ugly wound and you know you hate the sight of blood.

KING (*steps back a little, then exclaims with delight*) : All this just to fetch me a drink! Wounded in the service of the King! We'll tell the others you defended me against a wild boar and I'll present you with a handsome gift this evening. What would you like?

BECKET (*softly*) : This girl. (*He adds after a pause*) I fancy her. (*A pause.*)

KING (*his face clouding over*) : That's tiresome of you. I fancy her too. And where that's concerned, friendship goes by the board. (*A pause. His face takes on a cunning look*) All right, then. But favor for favor. You won't forget, will you?

BECKET: No, my prince.

KING: Favor for favor; do you give me your word as a gentleman?

BECKET: Yes, my prince.

KING (*draining his glass, suddenly cheerful*) : Done! She's yours. Do we take her with us or shall we have her sent?

BECKET: I'll send two soldiers to fetch her. Listen. The others have caught up.

(*A troop of men-at-arms have come riding up behind the shack during the end of the scene.*)

KING (*to the* MAN) : Wash your daughter, dog, and kill her fleas. She's going to the palace. For Milord here, who's a Saxon too. You're pleased about that, I hope? (*To* BECKET *as he goes*) Give him a gold piece. I'm feeling generous this morning. (*He goes out. The* MAN *looks at* BECKET *in terror.*)

BECKET: No one will come and take your daughter away. Keep her better hidden in future. And tell your son to join the others, in the forest; he'll be safer there, now. I think one of the soldiers saw us. Here!

(*He throws him a purse and goes out. When he has gone, the* MAN *snatches up the purse, then spits venomously, his face twisted with hate.*)

MAN: God rot your guts! Pig!

GIRL (*unexpectedly*) : He was handsome, that one. Is it true he's taking me to the palace?

MAN: You whore! You Norman's trollop!

(*He hurls himself onto her and beats her savagely. The* KING, BECKET *and the* BARONS *have galloped off, amid the sound of bugles. The hut and the forest backcloth disappear. We are in* BECKET'S *palace.*

FOOTMEN *push on a kind of low bed-couch, with cushions and some stools. Upstage, between two pillars, a curtain behind which can be seen the shadows of banqueting guests. Singing and roars of laughter. Downstage, curled up on the bed,* GWENDOLEN *is playing a string instrument. The curtain is drawn aside.* BECKET *appears. He goes to* GWENDOLEN *while the banqueting and the laughter, punctuated by hoarse incoherent snatches of song, go on upstage.* GWENDOLEN *stops playing.*)

GWENDOLEN: Are they still eating?

BECKET: Yes. They have an unimaginable capacity for absorbing food.

GWENDOLEN (*softly, beginning to play again*) : How can my Lord spend his days and a large part of his nights with such creatures?

BECKET (*crouching at her feet and caressing her*) : If he spent his time with learned clerics debating the sex of angels, your Lord would be even more bored, my kitten. They are as far from the true knowledge of things as mindless brutes.

GWENDOLEN (*gently, as she plays*) : I don't always understand everything my Lord condescends to say to me. . . . What I do know is that it is always very late when he comes to see me.

BECKET (*caressing her*) : The only thing I love is coming to you. Beauty is one of the few things which don't shake one's faith in God.

GWENDOLEN : I am my Lord's war captive and I belong to him body and soul. God has willed it so, since He gave the Normans victory over my people. If the Welsh had won the war I would have married a man of my own race, at my father's castle. God did not will it so.

BECKET (*quietly*) : That belief will do as well as any, my kitten. But, as I belong to a conquered race myself, I have a feeling that God's system is a little muddled. Go on playing.

(GWENDOLEN *starts to play again. Then she says suddenly:*)

GWENDOLEN : I'm lying. You are my Lord, God or no God. And if the Welsh had been victorious, you could just as easily have stolen me from my father's castle. I should have come with you. (*She says this gravely.* BECKET *rises abruptly and moves away. She looks up at him with anguished eyes and stops playing*) Did I say something wrong? What is the matter with my Lord?

BECKET : Nothing. I don't like being loved. I told you that.

(*The curtain opens. The* KING *appears.*)

KING (*a little drunk*) : Well, son, have you deserted us? It worked! I told you! They've tumbled to it! They're fighting with your forks! They've at last discovered that they're for poking one another's eyes out. They think it's a most ingenious little invention. You'd better go in, son, they'll break them in a minute. (BECKET *goes behind the curtain to quieten his guests. He can be heard shouting*) Gentlemen, gentlemen! No, no, they aren't little daggers. No, truly—they're for pronging meat. . . . Look, let me show you again.

(*Huge roars of laughter behind the curtain. The* KING *has moved over to* GWENDOLEN. *He stares at her.*)

KING : Was that you playing, while we were at table?

GWENDOLEN (*with a deep curtsy*) : Yes, my Lord.

KING : You have every kind of accomplishment, haven't you? Get up. (*He lifts her to her feet, caressing her as he does so. She moves away, ill at ease. He says with a wicked smile*) Have I frightened you, my heart? We'll soon put that right. (*He pulls the curtain aside*) Hey there, Becket! That's enough horseplay, my fat lads! Come and hear a little music. When the belly's full, it's good to elevate the mind a bit. (*To* GWENDOLEN) Play! (*The four* BARONS, *bloated with food and drink, come in with* BECKET. GWENDOLEN *has taken up her instrument again. The* KING *sprawls on the bed, behind her. The* BARONS, *with much sighing and puffing, unclasp their belts and sit down on stools, where they soon fall into a stupor.* BECKET *remains standing*) Tell her to sing us something

sad. I like sad music after dinner, it helps the digestion. (*He hiccups*)
You always feed us far too well, Thomas. Where did you steal that cook
of yours?

BECKET: I bought him, Sire. He's a Frenchman.

KING: Really? Aren't you afraid he might poison you? Tell me, how much
does one pay for a French cook?

BECKET: A good one, like him, costs almost as much as a horse, my Lord.

KING (*genuinely outraged*): It's outrageous! What is the country coming
to! No man is worth a horse! If I said "favor for favor"—remember?—
and I asked you to give him to me, would you?

BECKET: Of course, my Lord.

KING (*with a smile, gently caressing* GWENDOLEN): Well, I won't. I don't
want to eat too well every day; it lowers a man's morale. Sadder, sadder,
my little doe. (*He belches*) Oh, that venison! Get her to sing that lament
they composed for your mother, Becket. It's my favorite song.

BECKET: I don't like anyone to sing that lament, my Lord.

KING: Why not? Are you ashamed of being a Saracen girl's son? That's half
your charm, you fool! There must be some reason why you're more
civilized than all the rest of us put together! I adore that song. (GWEN-
DOLEN *looks uncertainly at* BECKET. *There is a pause. Then the* KING *says
coldly*) That's an order, little Saxon.

BECKET (*inscrutably, to* GWENDOLEN): Sing.

(*She strikes a few opening chords, while the* KING *makes himself comfortable beside her, belching contentedly. She begins.*)

GWENDOLEN (*singing*):

> Handsome Sir Gilbert
> Went to the war
> One fine morning in May
> To deliver the heart
> Of Lord Jesus our Savior,
> From the hands of the Saracens.
> Woe! Woe! Heavy is my heart
> At being without love!
> Woe! Woe! Heavy is my heart
> All the livelong day!

KING (*singing*):

> All the livelong day! Go on!

GWENDOLEN:

> As the battle raged
> He swung his mighty sword
> And many a Moor fell dead
> But his trusty charger
> Stumbled in the fray
> And Sir Gilbert fell.
> Woe! Woe! Heavy is my heart!
> At being without love!
> Woe! Woe! Heavy is my heart
> All the livelong day.

Wounded in the head
Away Gilbert was led
To the Algiers market
Chained hand and foot
And sold there as a slave.

KING (*singing, out of tune*):

All the livelong day!

GWENDOLEN:

A Saracen's daughter
Lovely as the night
Lost her heart to him
Swore to love him always
Vowed to be his wife.

Woe! Woe! Heavy is my heart
At being without love!
Woe! Woe! Heavy is my heart
All the livelong day—

KING (*interrupting*): It brings tears to my eyes, you know, that story. I look a brute but I'm soft as swansdown really. One can't change one's nature. I can't imagine why you don't like people to sing that song. It's wonderful to be a love child. When I look at my august parents' faces, I shudder to think what must have gone on. It's marvelous to think of your mother helping your father to escape and then coming to join him in London with you inside her. Sing us the end, girl. I adore the end.

GWENDOLEN (*softly*):

Then he asked the holy Father
For a priest to baptize her
And he took her as his wife
To cherish with his life
Giving her his soul
To love and keep alway.

Gay! Gay! Easy is my heart
At being full of love
Gay! Gay! Easy is my heart
To be loved alway.

KING (*dreamily*): Did he really love her all his life? Isn't it altered a bit in the song?

BECKET: No, my prince.

KING (*getting up, quite saddened*): Funny, it's the happy ending that makes me feel sad. . . . Tell me, do you believe in love, Thomas?

BECKET (*coldly*): For my father's love for my mother, Sire, yes.

(*The* KING *has moved over to the* BARONS, *who are now snoring on their stools. He gives them a kick as he passes.*)

KING: They've fallen asleep, the hogs. That's their way of showing their finer feelings. You know, my little Saxon, sometimes I have the impression that you and I are the only sensitive men in England. We eat with forks and we have infinitely distinguished sentiments, you and I. You've made a different man of me, in a way . . . What you ought to find me now, if you loved me, is a girl to give me a little polish. I've had enough of whores. (*He has come back to* GWENDOLEN. *He caresses her a little and then says suddenly*) Favor for favor—do you remember? (*A pause.*)

BECKET (*pale*): I am your servant, my prince, and all I have is yours. But you were also gracious enough to say I was your friend.

KING: That's what I mean! As one friend to another it's the thing to do! (*A short pause. He smiles maliciously, and goes on caressing* GWENDOLEN, *who cowers, terrified*) You care about her then? Can you care for something? Go on, tell me, tell me if you care about her? (BECKET *says nothing. The* KING *smiles*) You can't tell a lie. I know you. Not because you're afraid of lies—I think you must be the only man I know who isn't afraid of anything—not even Heaven—but because it's distasteful to you. You consider it inelegant. What looks like morality in you is nothing more than esthetics. Is that true or isn't it?

BECKET (*meeting his eyes, says softly*): It's true, my Lord.

KING: I'm not cheating if I ask for her, am I? I said "favor for favor" and I asked you for your word of honor.

BECKET (*icily*): And I gave it to you.

(*A pause. They stand quite still. The* KING *looks at* BECKET *with a wicked smile.* BECKET *does not look at him. Then the* KING *moves briskly away.*)

KING: Right. I'm off to bed. I feel like an early night tonight. Delightful evening, Becket. You're the only man in England who knows how to give your friends a royal welcome. (*He kicks the slumbering* BARONS) Call my guards and help me wake these porkers. (*The* BARONS *wake with sighs and belches as the* KING *pushes them about, shouting*) Come on, Barons, home! I know you're connoisseurs of good music, but we can't listen to music all night long. Happy evenings end in bed, eh Beçket?

BECKET (*stiffly*): May I ask your Highness for a brief moment's grace?

KING: Granted! Granted! I'm not a savage. I'll wait for you both in my litter. You can say good night to me downstairs.

(*He goes out, followed by the* BARONS. BECKET *stands motionless for a while under* GWENDOLEN's *steady gaze. Then he says quietly:*)

BECKET: You will have to go with him, Gwendolen.

GWENDOLEN (*composedly*): Did my Lord promise me to him?

BECKET: I gave him my word as a gentleman that I would give him anything he asked for. I never thought it would be you.

GWENDOLEN: If he sends me away tomorrow, will my Lord take me back?

BECKET: No.

GWENDOLEN: Shall I tell the girls to put my dresses in the coffer?

BECKET: He'll send over for it tomorrow. Go down. One doesn't keep the King waiting. Tell him I wish him a respectful good night.

GWENDOLEN (*laying her viol on the bed*): I shall leave my Lord my viol.

He can almost play it now. (*She asks, quite naturally*) My Lord cares for nothing, in the whole world, does he?

BECKET: No.

GWENDOLEN (*moves to him and says gently*): You belong to a conquered race too. But through tasting too much of the honey of life, you've forgotten that even those who have been robbed of everything have one thing left to call their own.

BECKET (*inscrutably*): Yes, I daresay I had forgotten. There is a gap in me where honor ought to be. Go now.

(GWENDOLEN *goes out.* BECKET *stands quite still. Then he goes to the bed, picks up the viol, looks at it, then throws it abruptly away. He pulls off the fur coverlet and starts to unbutton his doublet.*

A GUARD *comes in, dragging the* SAXON GIRL *from the forest, whom he throws down in the middle of the room. The* KING *appears.*)

KING (*hilariously*): Thomas, my son! You'd forgotten her! You see how careless you are! Luckily I think of everything. It seems they had to bully the father and the brother a tiny bit to get her, but anyway, here she is. You see?—I really am a friend to you, and you're wrong not to love me. You told me you fancied her. I hadn't forgotten that, you see. Sleep well, son!

(*He goes out, followed by the* GUARD. *The* GIRL, *still dazed, looks at* BECKET, *who has not moved. She recognizes him, gets to her feet and smiles at him. A long pause, then she asks with a kind of sly coquetry:*)

GIRL: Shall I undress, my Lord?

BECKET (*who has not moved*): Of course. (*The* GIRL *starts to undress.* BECKET *looks at her coldly, absent-mindedly whistling a few bars of his little march. Suddenly he stops, goes to the* GIRL, *who stands there dazed and half naked, and seizes her by the shoulders*) I hope you're full of noble feelings and that all this strikes you as pretty shabby?

(*A* SERVANT *runs in wildly and halts in the doorway speechless. Before he can speak, the* KING *comes stumbling in.*)

KING (*soberly*): I had no pleasure with her, Thomas. She let me lay her down in the litter, limp as a corpse, and then suddenly she pulled out a little knife from somewhere. There was blood everywhere. . . . I feel quite sick. (BECKET *has let go of the* GIRL. *The* KING *adds, haggard*) She could easily have killed me instead! (*A pause. He says abruptly*) Send that girl away. I'm sleeping in your room tonight. I'm frightened. (BECKET *motions to the* SERVANT, *who takes away the half-naked* GIRL. *The* KING *has thrown himself, fully dressed, onto the bed with an animal-like sigh*) Take half the bed.

BECKET: I'll sleep on the floor, my prince.

KING: No. Lie down beside me. I don't want to be alone tonight. (*He looks at him and murmurs*) You loathe me, I shan't even be able to trust you now. . . .

BECKET: You gave me your Seal to keep, my prince. And the Three Lions of England which are engraved on it keep watch over me too.

(*He snuffs out the candles, all save one. It is almost dark.*)

KING (*his voice already thick with sleep*) : I shall never know what you're thinking. . . .

(BECKET *has thrown a fur coverlet over the* KING. *He lies down beside him and says quietly:*)

BECKET: It will be dawn soon, my prince. You must sleep. Tomorrow we are crossing to the Continent. In a week we will face the King of France's army and there will be simple answers to everything at last.

(*He has lain down beside the* KING. *A pause, during which the* KING'S *snoring gradually increases. Suddenly, the* KING *moans and tosses in his sleep.*)

KING (*crying out*) : They're after me! They're after me! They're armed to the teeth! Stop them! Stop them!

(BECKET *sits up on one elbow. He touches the* KING, *who wakes up with a great animal cry.*)

BECKET: My prince . . . my prince . . . sleep in peace. I'm here.

KING: Oh . . . Thomas, it's you . . . They were after me.

(*He turns over and goes back to sleep with a sigh. Gradually he begins to snore again, softly.* BECKET *is still on one elbow. Almost tenderly, he draws the coverlet over the* KING.)

BECKET: My prince . . . If you were my true prince, if you were one of my race, how simple everything would be. How tenderly I would love you, my prince, in an ordered world. Each of us bound in fealty to the other, head, heart and limbs, with no further questions to ask of oneself, ever. (*A pause. The* KING'S *snores grow louder.* BECKET *sighs and says with a little smile*) But I cheated my way, a twofold bastard, into the ranks, and found a place among the conquerors. You can sleep peacefully though, my prince. So long as Becket is obliged to improvise his honor, he will serve you. And if one day, he meets it face to face. . . . (*A short pause*) But where is Becket's honor?

(*He lies down with a sigh, beside the* KING. *The* KING'S *snores grow louder still. The candle sputters. The lights grow even dimmer. . . .*)

(*The Curtain Falls.*)

Act Two

The curtain rises on the same set of arching pillars, which now represents a forest in France. The KING'S tent, not yet open for the day, is set up among the trees. A SENTRY stands some way off.

It is dawn. Crouched around a campfire, the four BARONS are having their morning meal, in silence. After a while, one of them says:

1ST BARON: This Becket then, who is he? (*A pause. All four are fairly slow in their reactions.*)

2ND BARON (*surprised at the question*): The Chancellor of England.

1ST BARON: I know that! But who is he, exactly?

2ND BARON: The Chancellor of England, I tell you! The Chancellor of England is the Chancellor of England! I don't see what else there is to inquire into on that score.

1ST BARON: You don't understand. Look, supposing the Chancellor of England were some other man. Me, for instance. . . .

2ND BARON: That's plain idiotic.

1ST BARON: I said supposing. Now, I would be Chancellor of England but I wouldn't be the same Chancellor of England as Becket is. You can follow that, can you?

2ND BARON (*guardedly*): Yes. . . .

1ST BARON: So, I *can* ask myself the question.

2ND BARON: What question?

1ST BARON: Who is this man Becket?

2ND BARON: What do you mean, who is this man Becket? He's the Chancellor of England.

1ST BARON: Yes. But what I'm asking myself is who is he, as a man?

2ND BARON (*looks at him and says sorrowfully*): Have you got a pain?

1ST BARON: No, why?

2ND BARON: A Baron who asks himself questions is a sick Baron. Your sword—what's that?

1ST BARON: My sword?

2ND BARON: Yes.

1ST BARON (*putting his hand to the hilt*): It's my sword! And anyone who thinks different—

2ND BARON: Right. Answered like a nobleman. We peers aren't here to ask questions. We're here to give answers.

1ST BARON: Right then. Answer me.

2ND BARON: Not to questions! To orders. You aren't asked to think in the army. When you're face to face with a French man-at-arms, do you ask yourself questions?

1ST BARON: No.

2ND BARON: Does he?

1ST BARON: No.

2ND BARON: You just fall to and fight. If you started asking each other questions like a pair of women, you might as well bring chairs onto the battlefield. If there are any questions to be asked you can be sure they've been asked already, higher up, by cleverer heads than yours.

1ST BARON (*vexed*): I meant I didn't like him, that's all.

2ND BARON: Why couldn't you say so then? That we'd have understood. You're entitled not to like him. I don't like him either, come to that. To begin with, he's a Saxon.

1ST BARON: To begin with!

3RD BARON: One thing you can't say though. You can't say he isn't a fighter. Yesterday when the King was in the thick of it, after his squire was killed, he cut his way right through the French, and he seized the King's banner and drew the enemy off and onto himself.

1ST BARON: All right! He's a good fighter!

3RD BARON (*to* 2ND BARON): Isn't he a good fighter?

2ND BARON (*stubbornly*): Yes. But he's a Saxon.

1ST BARON (*to the* 4TH BARON, *who has so far said nothing*): How about you, Regnault? What do you think of him?

4TH BARON (*placidly, swallowing his mouthful of food*): I'm waiting.

1ST BARON: Waiting for what?

4TH BARON: Till he shows himself. Some sorts of game are like that: you follow them all day through the forest, by sounds, or tracks, or smell. But it wouldn't do any good to charge ahead with drawn lance; you'd just spoil everything because you don't know for sure what sort of animal it is you're dealing with. You have to wait.

1ST BARON: What for?

4TH BARON: For whatever beast it is to show itself. And if you're patient it always does in the end. Animals know more than men do, nearly always, but a man has something in him that an animal hasn't got: he knows how to wait. With this man Becket—I'll wait.

1ST BARON: For what?

4TH BARON: For him to show himself. For him to break cover. (*He goes on eating*) The day he does, we'll know who he is.

(BECKET'S *little whistled march is heard off stage.* BECKET *comes in, armed.*)

BECKET: Good morning to you, Gentlemen. (*The four* BARONS *rise politely, and salute*) Is the King still asleep?

1ST BARON (*stiffly*): He hasn't called yet.

BECKET: Has the camp marshal presented his list of losses?

1ST BARON: No.

BECKET: Why not?

2ND BARON (*surlily*): He was part of the losses.

BECKET: Oh?

1ST BARON: I was nearby when it happened. A lance knocked him off his horse. Once on the ground, the foot soldiers dealt with him.

BECKET: Poor Beaumont. He was so proud of his new armor.

2ND BARON: There must have been a chink in it then. They bled him white. On the ground. French swine!

BECKET (*with a slight shrug*): That's war.

1ST BARON: War is a sport like any other. There are rules. In the old days, they took you for ransom. A Knight for a Knight. That was proper fighting!

BECKET (*smiling*): Since one has taken to sending the foot soldiery against the horses with no personal protection save a cutlass, they're a little inclined to seek out the chink in the armor of any Knight unwise enough to fall off his horse. It's repulsive, but I can understand them.

1ST BARON: If we start understanding the common soldiery war will be butchery plain and simple.

BECKET: The world is certainly tending towards butchery, Baron. The lesson of this battle, which has cost us far too much, is that we will have to form platoons of cutthroats too, that's all.

1ST BARON: And a soldier's honor, my Lord Chancellor, what of that?

BECKET (*dryly*): A soldier's honor, Baron, is to win victories. Let us not be hypocritical. The Norman nobility lost no time in teaching those they conquered that little point. I'll wake the King. Our entry into the city is timed for eight o'clock and the *Te Deum* in the cathedral for a quarter past nine. It would be bad policy to keep the French Bishop waiting. We want these people to collaborate with a good grace.

1ST BARON (*grunting*): In my day, we slaughtered the lot and marched in afterwards.

BECKET: Yes, into a dead city! I want to give the King living cities to increase his wealth. From eight o'clock this morning, I am the French people's dearest friend.

1ST BARON: What about England's honor, then?

BECKET (*quietly*): England's honor, Baron, in the final reckoning, has always been to succeed.

(*He goes into the* KING'S *tent smiling. The four* BARONS *look at each other, hostile.*)

1ST BARON (*muttering*): What a mentality!

4TH BARON (*sententiously*): We must wait for him. One day, he'll break cover.

(*The four* BARONS *move away.* BECKET *lifts the tent flap and hooks it back. The* KING *is revealed, in bed with a girl.*)

KING (*yawning*): Good morning, son. Did you sleep well?

BECKET: A little memento from the French on my left shoulder kept me awake, Sire. I took the opportunity to do some thinking.

KING (*worriedly*): You think too much. You'll suffer for it, you know! It's because people think that there are problems. One day, if you go on like this, you'll think yourself into a dilemma, your big head will present you with a solution and you'll jump feet first into a hopeless mess—which you'd have done far better to ignore, like the majority of fools, who know nothing and live to a ripe old age. What do you think of my little French girl? I must say, I adore France.

BECKET (*smiling*): So do I, Sire, like all Englishmen.

KING: The climate's warm, the girls are pretty, the wine is good. I intend to spend at least a month here every winter.

BECKET: The only snag is, it's expensive! Nearly 2,000 casualties yesterday.

KING: Has Beaumont made out his total?

BECKET: Yes. And he added himself to the list.

KING: Wounded? (BECKET *does not answer. The* KING *shivers. He says somberly*) I don't like learning that people I know have died. I've a feeling it may give Death ideas.

BECKET: My prince, shall we get down to work? We haven't dealt with yesterday's dispatches.

KING: Yesterday we were fighting! We can't do everything.

BECKET: That was a holiday! We'll have to work twice as hard today.

KING: Does it amuse you—working for the good of my people? Do you mean to say you love all those folk? To begin with they're too numerous. One can't love them, one doesn't know them. Anyway, you're lying, you don't love anything or anybody.

BECKET (*tersely*) : There's one thing I do love, my prince, and that I'm sure of. Doing what I have to do and doing it well.

KING (*grinning*) : Always the es—es. . . . What's your word again? I've forgotten it.

BECKET: Esthetics?

KING: Esthetics! Always the esthetic side, eh?

BECKET: Yes, my prince.

KING (*slapping the* GIRL'S *rump*) : And isn't that esthetic too? Some people go into ecstasies over cathedrals. But this is a work of art too! Look at that—round as an apple. . . . (*Quite naturally, as if he were offering him a sweetmeat*) Want her?

BECKET (*smiling*) : Business, my Lord!

KING (*pouting like a schoolboy*) : All right. Business. I'm listening. Sit down. (BECKET *sits down on the bed, beside the* KING, *with the* GIRL *like a fascinated rabbit in between them.*)

BECKET: The news is not good, my prince.

KING (*with a careless wave of the hand*) : News never is. That's a known fact. Life is one long web of difficulties. The secret of it—and there is one, brought to perfection by several generations of worldly-wise philosophers —is to give them no importance whatever. In the end one difficulty swallows up the other and you find yourself ten years later still alive with no harm done. Things always work out.

BECKET: Yes. But badly. My prince, when you play tennis, do you simply sit back and let things work out? Do you wait for the ball to hit your racket and say "It's bound to come this way eventually"?

KING: Ah, now just a minute. You're talking about things that matter. A game of tennis is important, it amuses me.

BECKET: And suppose I were to tell you that governing can be as amusing as a game of tennis? Are we going to let the others smash the ball into our court, my prince, or shall we try to score a point, both of us, like two good English sportsmen?

KING (*suddenly roused by his sporting instinct*) : The point, Begod, the point! You're right! On the court, I sweat and strain, I fall over my feet, I half kill myself, I'll cheat if need be, but I never give up the point!

BECKET: Well then, I'll tell you what the score is, so far. Piecing together all the information I have received from London since we've been on the Continent, one thing strikes me, and that is: that there exists in England a power which has grown until it almost rivals yours, my Lord. It is the power of your clergy.

KING: We did get them to pay the tax. That's something!

BECKET: Yes, it's a small sum of money. And they know that Princes can always be pacified with a little money. But those men are past masters at taking back with one hand what they were forced to give with the other. That's a little conjuring trick they've had centuries of practice in.

KING (*to the* GIRL): Pay attention, my little sparrow. Now's your chance to educate yourself. The gentleman is saying some very profound things!

BECKET (*in the same flippant way*): Little French sparrow, suppose you educate us instead. When you're married—if you do marry despite the holes in your virtue—which would you prefer, to be mistress in your own house or to have your village priest laying down the law there?

(*The* KING, *a little peeved, gets up on his knees on the bed and hides the bewildered* GIRL *under an eiderdown.*)

KING: Talk sense, Becket! Priests are always intriguing, I know that. But I also know that I can crush them any time I like.

BECKET: Talk sense, Sire. If you don't do the crushing now, in five years' time there will be two Kings in England, the Archbishop of Canterbury and you. And in ten years' time there will be only one.

KING (*a bit shamefaced*): And it won't be me?

BECKET (*coldly*): I rather fear not.

KING (*with a sudden shout*): Oh, yes, it will! We Plantagenets hold on to our own! To horse, Becket, to horse! For England's glory! War on the faithful! That will make a change for us!

(*The eiderdown starts to toss. The* GIRL *emerges, disheveled, and red in the face.*)

GIRL (*pleadingly*): My Lord! I can't breathe!

(*The* KING *looks at her in surprise. He had clearly forgotten her. He bursts out laughing.*)

KING: What are you doing there? Spying for the clergy? Be off. Put your clothes on and go home. Give her a gold piece, Thomas.

(*The* GIRL *picks up her rags and holds them up in front of her.*)

GIRL: Am I to come back to the camp tonight, my Lord?

KING (*exasperated*): Yes. No. I don't know! We're concerned with the Archbishop now, not you! Be off. (*The* GIRL *disappears into the back portion of the tent. The* KING *cries*) To horse, Thomas! For England's greatness! With my big fist and your big brain we'll do some good work, you and I! (*With sudden concern*) Wait a second. You can never be sure of finding another one as good in bed. (*He goes to the rear of the tent and cries*) Come back tonight, my angel! I adore you! You have the prettiest eyes in the world! (*He comes downstage and says confidentially to* BECKET) You always have to tell them that, even when you pay for it, if you want real pleasure with them. That's high politics, too! (*Suddenly anxious, as his childish fear of the clergy returns*) What will God say to it all, though? After all, they're *His* Bishops!

BECKET (*with an airy gesture*): We aren't children. You know one can always come to some arrangement with God, on this earth. Make haste and dress, my prince. We're going to be late.

KING (*hurrying out*): I'll be ready in a second. Do I have to shave?

BECKET (*smiling*): It might be as well, after two days' fighting.

KING: What a fuss for a lot of conquered Frenchmen! I wonder sometimes if you aren't a bit too finicky, Thomas.

(*He goes out.* BECKET *closes the tent just as two* SOLDIERS *bring on a* YOUNG MONK, *with his hands tied.*)

BECKET: What is it?

SOLDIER: We've just arrested this young monk, my Lord. He was loitering round the camp. He had a knife under his robe. We're taking him to the Provost.

BECKET: Have you got the knife? (*The* SOLDIER *hands it to him.* BECKET *looks at it, then at the little* MONK) What use do you have for this in your monastery?

MONK: I cut my bread with it!

BECKET (*amused*): Well, well. (*To the* SOLDIERS) Leave him to me. I'll question him.

SOLDIER: He's turbulent, my Lord. He struggled like a very demon. It took four of us to get his knife away and tie him up. He wounded the Sergeant. We'd have finished him there and then, only the Sergeant said there might be some information to be got out of him. That's why we're taking him to the Provost. (*He adds*) That's just to tell you he's a spiteful devil.

BECKET (*who has not taken his eyes off the little* MONK): Very well. Stand off. (*The* SOLDIERS *move out of earshot.* BECKET *goes on looking at the boy, and playing with the knife*) What are you doing in France? You're a Saxon.

MONK (*crying out despite himself*): How do you know?

BECKET: I can tell by your accent. I speak Saxon very well, as well as you speak French. Yes, you might almost pass for a Frenchman—to unpracticed ears. But I'd be careful. In your predicament, you'd do as well to be taken for a Frenchman as a Saxon. It's less unpopular. (*A pause.*)

MONK (*abruptly*): I'm prepared to die.

BECKET (*smiling*): After the deed. But before, you'll agree it's stupid. (*He looks at the knife which he is still holding between two fingers*) Where are you from?

MONK (*venomously*): Hastings![3]

BECKET: Hastings. And who was this kitchen implement intended for? (*No answer*) You couldn't hope to kill more than one man with a weapon of this sort. You didn't make the journey for the sake of an ordinary Norman soldier, I imagine. (*The little* MONK *does not answer. Tersely*) Listen to me, my little man. They're going to put you to the torture. Have you ever seen that? I'm obliged to attend professionally from time to time. You think you'll have the necessary strength of spirit, but they're terribly ingenious and they have a knowledge of anatomy that our imbecilic doctors would do well to emulate. One always talks. Believe me, I know. If I can vouch that you've made a full confession, it will go quicker for you. That's worth considering. (*The* MONK *does not answer*) Besides, there's an amusing detail to this affair. You are directly under my jurisdiction. The King gave me the deeds and livings of all the abbeys in Hastings when he made me Chancellor.

MONK (*stepping back*): Are you Becket?

BECKET: Yes. (*He looks at the knife with faint distaste*) You didn't only

---

[3] A town and county of Sussex, southeast of London. Here on October 14, 1066, the Normans under William the Conqueror defeated the Saxons.

use it to cut your bread. Your knife stinks of onion, like any proper little Saxon's knife. They're good, aren't they, the Hastings onions? (*He looks at the knife again with a strange smile*) You still haven't told me who it was for. (*The* MONK *says nothing*) If you meant it for the King, there was no sense in that, my lad. He has three sons. Kings spring up again like weeds! Did you imagine you could liberate your race single-handed?

MONK: No. (*He adds dully*) Not my race. Myself.

BECKET: Liberate yourself from what?

MONK: My shame.

BECKET (*with sudden gravity*): How old are you?

MONK: Sixteen.

BECKET (*quietly*): The Normans have occupied the island for a hundred years. Shame is an old vintage. Your father and your grandfather drank it to the dregs. The cup is empty now.

MONK (*shaking his head*): No.

(*A shadow seems to cross* BECKET'S *eyes. He goes on, quietly*:)

BECKET: So, one fine morning, you woke in your cell to the bell of the first offices, while it was still dark. And it was the bells that told you, a boy of sixteen, to take the whole burden of shame onto yourself?

MONK (*with the cry of a cornered animal*): Who told you that?

BECKET (*softly*): I told you I was a polyglot. (*Indifferently*) I'm a Saxon too, did you know that?

MONK (*stonily*): Yes.

BECKET (*smiling*): Go on. Spit. You're dying to.

(*The* MONK *looks at him, a little dazed, and then spits.*)

BECKET (*smiling*): That felt good, didn't it? (*Tersely*) The King is waiting. And this conversation could go on indefinitely. But I want to keep you alive, so we can continue it one of these days. (*He adds lightly*) It's pure selfishness, you know. Your life hasn't any sort of importance for me, obviously, but it's very rare for Fate to bring one face to face with one's own ghost, when young. (*Calling*) Soldier! (*The* SOLDIER *comes back and springs clanking to attention*) Fetch me the Provost. Run! (*The* SOLDIER *runs out.* BECKET *comes back to the silent* YOUNG MONK) Delightful day, isn't it? This early-morning sun, hot already under this light veil of mist . . . A beautiful place, France. But I'm like you, I prefer the solid mists of the Sussex downs. Sunshine is luxury. And we belong to a race which used to despise luxury, you and I. (*The* PROVOST MARSHAL *of the camp comes in, followed by the* SOLDIER. *He is an important personage, but* BECKET *is inaccessible, even for a* PROVOST MARSHAL, *and the man's behavior shows it*) Sir Provost, your men have arrested this monk who was loitering round the camp. He is a lay brother from the convent of Hastings and he is directly under my jurisdiction. You will make arrangements to have him sent back to England and taken to the convent, where his Abbot will keep him under supervision until my return. There is no specific charge against him, for the moment. I want him treated without brutality, but very closely watched. I hold you personally responsible for him.

PROVOST: Very good, my Lord.

(*He motions to the* SOLDIERS. *They surround the little* MONK *and take him away without a further glance from* BECKET. *Left alone,* BECKET *looks at the knife, smiles, wrinkles his nose and murmurs, with faint distaste:*)

BECKET: It's touching, but it stinks, all the same. (*He flings the knife away, and whistling his little march goes toward the tent. He goes in, calling out lightheartedly*) Well, my prince, have you put on your Sunday best? It's time to go. We mustn't keep the Bishop waiting!

(*A sudden joyful peal of bells. The tent disappears as soon as* BECKET *has gone in. The set changes. A backcloth representing a street comes down from the flies. The permanent pillars are there, but the* SOLDIERS *lining the route have decorated them with standards. The* KING *and* BECKET *advance into the city, on horseback, preceded by two* TRUMPET-ERS; *the* KING *slightly ahead of* BECKET *and followed by the four* BARONS. *Acclamations from the crowd. Bells, trumpets throughout the scene.*)

KING (*beaming as he waves*): Listen to that! They adore us, these French!

BECKET: It cost me quite a bit. I had money distributed among the populace this morning. The prosperous classes are at home, sulking, of course.

KING: Patriots?

BECKET: No. But they would have cost too much. There are also a certain number of your Highness' soldiers among the crowd, in disguise, to encourage any lukewarm elements.

KING: Why do you always make a game of destroying my illusions? I thought they loved me for myself! You're an amoral man, Becket. (*Anxiously*) Does one say amoral or immoral?

BECKET (*smiling*): It depends what one means.

KING: She's pretty, look—the girl on the balcony to the right there. Suppose we stopped a minute. . . .

BECKET: Impossible. The Bishop is waiting in the cathedral.

KING: It would be a lot more fun than going to see a Bishop!

BECKET: My Lord, do you remember what you have to say to him?

KING (*waving to the crowd*): Yes, yes, yes! As if it mattered what I say to a French Bishop, whose city I've just taken by force!

BECKET: It matters a great deal. For our future policy.

KING: Am I the strongest or am I not?

BECKET: You are, today. But one must never drive one's enemy to despair. It makes him strong. Gentleness is better politics. It saps virility. A good occupational force must not crush, it must corrupt.

KING (*waving graciously*): What about my pleasure then? Where does that enter into your scheme of things? Suppose I charged into this heap of frog-eaters now instead of acting the goat at their *Te Deum*? I can indulge in a bit of pleasure, can't I? I'm the conqueror.

BECKET: That would be a fault. Worse, a failing. One can permit oneself anything, Sire, but one must never indulge.

KING: Yes, Papa, right, Papa. What a bore you are today. Look at that little redhead there, standing on the fountain! Give orders for the procession to follow the same route back.

(*He rides on, turning his horse to watch the girl out of sight. They have gone by, the four* BARONS *bringing up the rear. Organ music. The stand-*

ards disappear, together with the SOLDIERS. *We are in the cathedral. The stage is empty.*

The organ is heard. Swelling chords. The organist is practicing in the empty cathedral. Then a sort of partition is pushed on, which represents the sacristy.

The KING, *attired for the ceremony, the* BARONS, *an unknown* PRIEST *and a* CHOIRBOY *come in. They seem to be waiting for something. The* KING *sits impatiently on a stool.*)

KING: Where's Becket? And what are we waiting for?

1ST BARON: He just said to wait, my Lord. It seems there's something not quite in order.

KING (*pacing about ill-humoredly*): What a lot of fuss for a French Bishop! What do I look like, I ask you, hanging about in this sacristy like a village bridegroom!

4TH BARON: I quite agree, my Lord! I can't think why we don't march straight in. After all, it's your cathedral now. (*Eagerly*) What do you say, my Lord? Shall we just draw our swords and charge?

KING (*going meekly back to his stool with a worried frown*): No. Becket wouldn't like it. And he's better than we are at knowing the right thing to do. If he told us to wait, there must be a good reason. (BECKET *hurries in*) Well, Becket, what's happening? We're freezing to death in here! What do the French think they're at, keeping us moldering in this sacristy?

BECKET: The order came from me, Sire. A security measure. My police are certain that a French rising was to break out during the ceremony.

(*The* KING *has risen. The* 2ND BARON *has drawn his sword. The other three follow suit.*)

2ND BARON: God's Blood!

BECKET: Put up your swords. The King is safe in here. I have put guards on all the doors.

2ND BARON: Have we your permission to go in and deal with it, my Lord? We'll make short work of it!

3RD BARON: Just say the word, Sire! Shall we go?

BECKET (*curtly*): I forbid you. There aren't enough of us. I am bringing fresh troops into the city and having the cathedral evacuated. Until that is done, the King's person is in your keeping, gentlemen. But sheathe your swords. No provocation, please. We are at the mercy of a chance incident and I still have no more than the fifty escort men-at-arms in the city.

KING (*tugging at* BECKET'S *sleeve*): Becket! Is that priest French?

BECKET: Yes. But he is part of the Bishop's immediate entourage. And the Bishop is our man.

KING: You know how reliable English Bishops are! So I leave you to guess how far we can trust a French one! That man has a funny look in his eyes.

BECKET: Who, the Bishop?

KING: No. That priest.

BECKET (*glances at the* PRIEST *and laughs*) : Of course, my prince, he squints! I assure you that's the only disturbing thing about him! It would be tactless to ask him to leave. Besides, even if he had a dagger, you have your coat of mail and four of your Barons. I must go and supervise the evacuation of the nave. (*He starts to go. The* KING *runs after him.*)

KING: Becket! (BECKET *stops*) The choirboy?

BECKET (*laughing*) : He's only so high!

KING: He may be a dwarf. You never know with the French. (*Drawing* BECKET *aside*) Becket, we talked a little flippantly this morning. Are you sure God isn't taking His revenge?

BECKET (*smiling*) : Of course not. I'm afraid it's simply my police force taking fright and being a little overzealous. Policemen have a slight tendency to see assassins everywhere. They only do it to make themselves important. Bah, what does it matter? We'll hear the *Te Deum* in a deserted church, that's all.

KING (*bitterly*) : And there was I thinking those folk adored me. Perhaps you didn't give them enough money.

BECKET: One can only buy those who are for sale, my prince. And those are just the ones who aren't dangerous. With the others, it's wolf against wolf. I'll come back straightaway and set your mind at rest.

(*He goes out. The* KING *darts anxious looks on the* PRIEST *as he paces up and down muttering his prayers.*)

KING: Baron!

(*The* 4TH BARON *is nearest the* KING. *He steps forward.*)

4TH BARON (*bellowing as usual*) : My Lord?

KING: Shush! Keep an eye on that man, all four of you, and at the slightest move, leap on him. (*There follows a little comic dumbshow by the* KING *and the* PRIEST, *who is beginning to feel uneasy too. A sudden violent knocking on the sacristy door. The* KING *starts*) Who is it? (*A* SOLDIER *comes in.*)

SOLDIER: A messenger from London, my Lord. They sent him on here from the camp. The message is urgent.

KING (*worried*) : I don't like it. Regnault, you go and see.

(*The* 4TH BARON *goes out and comes back again, reassured.*)

4TH BARON: It's William of Corbeil, my Lord. He has urgent letters.

KING: You're sure it *is* him? It wouldn't be a Frenchman in disguise? That's an old trick.

4TH BARON (*roaring with laughter*) : I know him, Sire! I've drained more tankards with him than there are whiskers on his face. And the old goat has plenty!

(*The* KING *makes a sign. The* 4TH BARON *admits the* MESSENGER, *who drops on one knee and presents his letters to the* KING.)

KING: Thank you. Get up. That's a fine beard you have, William of Corbeil. Is it well stuck on?

MESSENGER (*rising, bewildered*) : My beard, Sire?

(*The* 4TH BARON *guffaws and slaps him on the back.*)

4TH BARON: You old porcupine you!

(*The* KING *has glanced through the letters.*)

KING: Good news, gentlemen! We have one enemy less. (BECKET *comes in. The* KING *cries joyfully*) Becket!

BECKET: Everything is going according to plan, my prince. The troops are on their way. We've only to wait here quietly, until they arrive.

KING (*cheerfully*): You're right, Becket, everything is going according to plan. God isn't angry with us. He has just recalled the Archbishop.

BECKET (*in a murmur*): That little old man. . . . How could that feeble body contain so much strength?

KING: Now, now, now! Don't squander your sorrow, my son. I personally consider this an excellent piece of news!

BECKET: He was the first Norman who took an interest in me. He was a true father to me. God rest his soul.

KING: He will! After all the fellow did for Him, he's gone to Heaven, don't worry. Where he'll be definitely more use to God than he was to us. So it's definitely for the best. (*He pulls* BECKET *to him*) Becket! My little Becket, I think the ball's in our court now! This is the time to score a point. (*He seizes his arm, tense and quite transformed*) An extraordinary idea is just creeping into my mind, Becket. A master stroke! I can't think what's got into me this morning, but I suddenly feel extremely intelligent. It probably comes of making love with a French girl last night. I am subtle, Becket, I am profound! So profound it's making my head spin. Are you sure it isn't dangerous to think too hard? Thomas, my little Thomas! Are you listening to me?

BECKET (*smiling at his excitement*): Yes, my prince.

KING (*as excited as a little boy*): Are you listening carefully? Listen, Thomas! You told me once that the best ideas are the stupidest ones, but the clever thing is to think of them! Listen, Thomas! Tradition prevents me from touching the privileges of the Primacy. You follow me so far?

BECKET: Yes, my prince. . . .

KING: But what if the Primate is my man? If the Archbishop of Canterbury is for the King, how can his power possibly incommode me?

BECKET: That's an ingenious idea, my prince, but you forget that his election is a free one.

KING: No! You're forgetting the Royal Hand! Do you know what that is? When the candidate is displeasing to the Throne the King sends his Justicer to the Conclave of Bishops and it's the King who has the final say. That's an old custom too, and for once, it's in my favor! It's fully a hundred years since the Conclave of Bishops has voted contrary to the wishes of the King!

BECKET: I don't doubt it, my Lord. But we all know your Bishops. Which one of them could you rely on? Once the Primate's miter is on their heads, they grow dizzy with power.

KING: Are you asking me, Becket? I'll tell you. Someone who doesn't know what dizziness means. Someone who isn't even afraid of God. Thomas, my son, I need your help again and this time it's important. I'm sorry to deprive you of French girls and the fun of battle, my son, but pleasure will come later. You are going over to England.

BECKET: I am at your service, my prince.

KING: Can you guess what your mission will be?

(*A tremor of anguish crosses* BECKET'S *face at what is to come.*)

BECKET: No, my prince.

KING: You are going to deliver a personal letter from me to every Bishop in the land. And do you know what those letters will contain, my Thomas, my little brother? My royal wish to have you elected Primate of England.

(BECKET *has gone deathly white. He says with a forced laugh:*)

BECKET: You're joking, of course, my Lord. Just look at the edifying man, the saintly man whom you would be trusting with these holy functions! (*He has opened his fine coat to display his even finer doublet*) Why, my prince, you really fooled me for a second! (*The* KING *bursts out laughing.* BECKET *laughs too, rather too loudly in his relief*) A fine Archbishop I'd have made! Look at my new shoes! They're the latest fashion in Paris. Attractive, that little upturned toe, don't you think? Quite full of unction and compunction, isn't it, Sire?

KING (*suddenly stops laughing*): Shut up about your shoes, Thomas! I'm in deadly earnest. I shall write those letters before noon. You will help me.

(BECKET, *deathly pale, stammers:*)

BECKET: But my Lord, I'm not even a priest!

KING (*tersely*): You're a deacon. You can take your final vows tomorrow and be ordained in a month.

BECKET: But have you considered what the Pope will say?

KING (*brutally*): I'll pay the price!

(BECKET, *after an anguished pause, murmurs:*)

BECKET: My Lord, I see now that you weren't joking. Don't do this.

KING: Why not?

BECKET: It frightens me.

KING (*his face set and hard*): Becket, this is an order!

(BECKET *stands as if turned to stone. A pause. He murmurs:*)

BECKET (*gravely*): If I become Archbishop, I can no longer be your friend.

(*A burst of organ music in the cathedral. Enter an* OFFICER.)

OFFICER: The church is now empty, my Lord. The Bishop and his clergy await your Highness' good pleasure.

KING (*roughly to* BECKET): Did you hear that, Becket? Pull yourself together. You have an odd way of taking good news. Wake up! They say we can go in now.

(*The procession forms with the* PRIEST *and the* CHOIRBOY *leading.* BECKET *takes his place, almost reluctantly, a pace or so behind the* KING.)

BECKET (*in a murmur*): This is madness, my Lord. Don't do it. I could not serve both God and you.

KING (*looking straight ahead, says stonily*): You've never disappointed me, Thomas. And you are the only man I trust. You will leave tonight. Come, let's go in.

(*He motions to the* PRIEST. *The procession moves off and goes into the empty cathedral, as the organ swells.*

A moment's darkness. The organ continues to play. Then a dim light reveals BECKET'S *room. Open chests into which two* SERVANTS *are piling costly clothes.*)

2ND SERVANT (*who is the younger of the two*): The coat with the sable trimming as well?

1ST SERVANT: Everything! You heard what he said!

2ND SERVANT (*grumbling*): Sables! To beggars! Who'll give them alms if they beg with that on their backs! They'll starve to death!

1ST SERVANT (*cackling*): They'll eat the sables! Can't you understand, you idiot! He's going to sell all this and give them the money!

2ND SERVANT: But what will he wear himself? He's got nothing left at all!

(BECKET *comes in, wearing a plain gray dressing gown.*)

BECKET: Are the chests full? I want them sent over to the Jew before tonight. I want nothing left in this room but the bare walls. Gil, the fur coverlet!

1ST SERVANT (*regretfully*): My Lord will be cold at night.

BECKET: Do as I say. (*Regretfully, the* 1ST SERVANT *takes the coverlet and puts it in the chest*) Has the steward been told about tonight's meal? Supper for forty in the great hall.

1ST SERVANT: He says he won't have enough gold plate, my Lord. Are we to mix it with the silver dishes?

BECKET: Tell him to lay the table with the wooden platters and earthenware bowls from the kitchens. The plate has been sold. The Jew will send over for it late this afternoon.

1ST SERVANT (*dazed*): The earthenware bowls and the wooden platters. Yes, my Lord. And the steward says could he have your list of invitations fairly soon, my Lord. He only has three runners and he's afraid there won't be time to—

BECKET: There are no invitations. The great doors will be thrown open and you will go out into the street and tell the poor they are dining with me tonight.

1ST SERVANT (*appalled*): Very good, my Lord. (*He is about to go.* BECKET *calls him back.*)

BECKET: I want the service to be impeccable. The dishes presented to each guest first, with full ceremony, just as for princes. Go now. (*The two* SERVANTS *go out.* BECKET, *left alone, casually looks over one or two articles of clothing in the chests. He murmurs*) I must say it was all very pretty stuff. (*He drops the lid and bursts out laughing*) A prick of vanity! The mark of an upstart. A truly saintly man would never have done the whole thing in one day. Nobody will ever believe it's genuine. (*He turns to the jeweled crucifix above the bed and says simply*) I hope You haven't inspired me with all these holy resolutions in order to make me look ridiculous, Lord. It's all so new to me. I'm setting about it a little clumsily perhaps. (*He looks at the crucifix and with a swift gesture takes it off the wall*) And you're far too sumptuous too. Precious stones around your bleeding Body. . . . I shall give you to some poor village church. (*He lays the crucifix on the chest. He looks around the room, happy, lighthearted, and murmurs*) It's like leaving for a holiday. Forgive me,

Lord, but I never enjoyed myself so much in my whole life. I don't believe You are a sad God. The joy I feel in shedding all my riches must
be part of Your divine intentions. (*He goes behind the curtain into the
antechamber where he can be heard gaily whistling an old English marching song. He comes back a second later, his bare feet in sandals, and
wearing a monk's coarse woolen robe. He draws the curtain across again
and murmurs*) There. Farewell, Becket. I wish there had been something
I had regretted parting with, so I could offer it to You. (*He goes to the
crucifix and says simply*) Lord, are You sure You are not tempting me?
It all seems far too easy. (*He drops to his knees and prays.*)

(*The Curtain Falls.*)

Act Three

A room in the KING'S *palace. The two* QUEENS, *the* QUEEN MOTHER
and the YOUNG QUEEN, *are on stage, working at their tapestry. The* KING'S
two SONS, *one considerably older than the other, are playing in a corner,
on the floor. The* KING *is in another corner, playing at cup-and-ball. After
several unsuccessful attempts to catch the ball in the cup, he throws down
the toy and exclaims irritably:*

KING: Forty beggars! He invited forty beggars to dinner!

QUEEN MOTHER: The dramatic gesture, as usual! I always said you had
misplaced your confidence, my son.

KING (*pacing up and down*): Madam, I am very particular where I place
my confidence. I only ever did it once in my whole life and I am still
convinced I was right. But there's a great deal we don't understand!
Thomas is ten times more intelligent than all of us put together.

QUEEN MOTHER (*reprovingly*): You are talking about royalty, my son.

KING (*grunting*): What of it? Intelligence has been shared out on a different basis.

YOUNG QUEEN: It seems he has sold his gold plate and all his rich clothes
to a Jew. He wears an ordinary homespun habit now.

QUEEN MOTHER: I see that as a sign of ostentation, if nothing worse! One
can become a saintly man, certainly, but not in a single day. I've never
liked the man. You were insane to make him so powerful.

KING (*crying out*): He is my friend!

QUEEN MOTHER (*acidly*): More's the pity.

YOUNG QUEEN: He is your friend in debauchery. It was he who lured you away from your duty towards me. It was he who first took you to the whorehouses!

KING (*furious*): Rubbish, Madam! I didn't need anybody to lure me away from my duty towards you. I made you three children, very conscientiously. Phew! My duty is done for a while.

YOUNG QUEEN (*stung*): When that libertine loses the evil influence he has on you, you will come to appreciate the joys of family life again. Pray Heaven he disobeys you!

KING: The joys of family life are limited, Madam. To be perfectly frank, you bore me. You and your eternal backbiting, over your everlasting tapestry, the pair of you! That's no sustenance for a man! (*He trots about the room, furious, and comes to a halt behind their chairs*) If at least it had some artistic merit. My ancestress Mathilda, while she was waiting for her husband to finish carving out his kingdom, now *she* embroidered a masterpiece[4]—which they left behind in Bayeux, more's the pity. But that! It's beyond belief it's so mediocre.

YOUNG QUEEN (*nettled*): We can only use the gifts we're born with.

KING: Yes. And yours are meager. (*He glances out of the window once more to look at the time, and says with a sigh*) I've been bored to tears for a whole month. Not a soul to talk to. After his nomination, not wanting to seem in too indecent a hurry, I leave him alone to carry out his pastoral tour. Now, back he comes at last, I summon him to the palace and he's late. (*He looks out of the window again and exclaims*) Ah! Someone at the sentry post! (*He turns away, disappointed*) No, it's only a monk. (*He wanders about the room, aimlessly. He goes over to join the children, and watches them playing for a while. Sourly*) Charming babes. Men in the making. Sly and obtuse already. And to think one is expected to be dewy-eyed over creatures like that, merely because they aren't yet big enough to be hated or despised. Which is the elder of you two?

ELDER BOY (*rising*): I am, Sir.

KING: What's your name again?

ELDER BOY: Henry III.

KING (*sharply*): Not yet, Sir! Number II is in the best of health. (*To the* QUEEN) You've brought them up well! Do you think of yourself as Regent already? And you wonder that I shun your bedchamber? I don't care to make love with my widow.

(*An* OFFICER *comes in.*)

OFFICER: A messenger from the Archbishop, my Lord.

KING (*beside himself with rage*): A messenger! A messenger! I summoned the Archbishop Primate in person! (*He turns to the women, suddenly uneasy, almost touching*) Perhaps he's ill? That would explain everything.

QUEEN MOTHER (*bitterly*): That's too much to hope for.

KING (*raging*): You'd like to see him dead, wouldn't you, you females—

---

[4] The famous Bayeux tapestry, a band of linen 231 feet long, contains 72 scenes depicting the Norman conquest of England. Legend says that it was made about 1092 by Mathilda, wife of William the Conqueror.

because he loves me? If he hasn't come, it's because he's dying! Send the man in, quickly! O my Thomas. . . . (*The* OFFICER *goes and admits the* MONK. *The* KING *hurries over to him*) Who are you? Is Becket ill?

MONK (*falling on one knee*) : My Lord, I am William son of Etienne, secretary to his Grace the Archbishop.

KING: Is your master seriously ill?

MONK: No, my Lord. His Grace is in good health. He has charged me to deliver this letter with his deepest respects—and to give your Highness this. (*He bows lower and hands something to the* KING.)

KING (*stunned*) : The Seal? Why has he sent me back the Seal? (*He unrolls the parchment and reads it in silence. His face hardens. He says curtly, without looking at the* MONK) You have carried out your mission. Go. (*The* MONK *rises and turns to go.*)

MONK: Is there an answer from your Highness for his Grace the Archbishop?

KING (*harshly*) : No!

(*The* MONK *goes out. The* KING *stands still a moment, at a loss, then flings himself onto his throne, glowering. The women exchange a conspiratorial look. The* QUEEN MOTHER *rises and goes to him.*)

QUEEN MOTHER (*insidiously*) : Well, my son, what does your friend say in his letter?

KING (*bawling*) : Get out! Get out, both of you! And take your royal vermin with you! I am alone! (*Frightened, the* QUEENS *hurry out with the children. The* KING *stands there a moment, reeling a little, as if stunned by the blow. Then he collapses onto the throne and sobs like a child. Moaning*) O my Thomas! (*He remains a moment prostrate, then collects himself and sits up. He looks at the Seal in his hand and says between clenched teeth*) You've sent me back the Three Lions of England, like a little boy who doesn't want to play with me any more. You think you have God's honor to defend now! I would have gone to war with all England's might behind me, and against England's interests, to defend you, little Saxon. I would have given the honor of the Kingdom laughingly . . . for you. . . . Only I loved you and you didn't love me . . . that's the difference. (*His face hardens. He adds between clenched teeth*) Thanks all the same for this last gift as you desert me. I shall learn to be alone. (*He goes out. The lights dim.* SERVANTS *remove the furniture. When the lights go up again, the permanent set, with the pillars, is empty.*

A bare church; a man half hidden under a dark cloak is waiting behind a pillar. It is the KING. *Closing chords of organ music. Enter* GILBERT FOLLIOT, *Bishop of London, followed by his* CLERGY. *He has just said Mass. The* KING *goes to him*) Bishop. . . .

FOLLIOT (*stepping back*) : What do you want, fellow? (*His acolytes are about to step between them, when he exclaims*) The King!

KING: Yes.

FOLLIOT: Alone, without an escort, and dressed like a common squire?

KING: The King nevertheless. Bishop, I would like to make a confession.

FOLLIOT (*with a touch of suspicion*) : I am the Bishop of London. The

King has his own Confessor. That is an important Court appointment and it has its prerogatives.

KING: The choice of priest for Holy Confession is open, Bishop, even for a King. (FOLLIOT *motions to his* CLERGY, *who draw away*) Anyway, my confession will be short, and I'm not asking for absolution. I have something much worse than a sin on my conscience, Bishop: a mistake. A foolish mistake. (FOLLIOT *says nothing*) I ordered you to vote for Thomas Becket at the Council of Clarendon. I repent of it.

FOLLIOT (*inscrutably*): We bowed before the Royal Hand.

KING: Reluctantly, I know. It took me thirteen weeks of authority and patience to crush the small uncrushable opposition of which you were the head, Bishop. On the day the Council met you looked green. They told me you fell seriously ill afterwards.

FOLLIOT (*impenetrably*): God cured me.

KING: Very good of Him. But He is rather inclined to look after His own, to the exclusion of anyone else. He let me fall ill without lifting a finger! And I must cure myself without divine intervention. I have the Archbishop on my stomach. A big hard lump I shall have to vomit back. What does the Norman clergy think of him?

FOLLIOT (*reserved*): His Grace seems to have the reins of the Church of England well in hand. Those who are in close contact with him even say that he behaves like a holy man.

KING (*with grudging admiration*): It's a bit sudden, but nothing he does ever surprises me. God knows what the brute is capable of, for good or for evil. Bishop, let us be frank with each other. Is the Church very interested in holy men?

FOLLIOT (*with the ghost of a smile*): The Church has been wise for so long, your Highness, that she could not have failed to realize that the temptation of saintliness is one of the most insidious and fearsome snares the devil can lay for her priests. The administration of the realm of souls, with the temporal difficulties it carries with it, chiefly demands, as in all administrations, competent administrators. The Roman Catholic Church has its Saints, it invokes their benevolent intercession, it prays to them. But it has no need to create others. That is superfluous. And dangerous.

KING: You seem to be a man one can talk to, Bishop. I misjudged you. Friendship blinded me.

FOLLIOT (*still impenetrable*): Friendship is a fine thing.

KING (*suddenly hoarse*): It's a domestic animal, a living, tender thing. It seems to be all eyes, forever gazing at you, warming you. You don't see its teeth. But it's a beast with one curious characteristic. It is only after death that it bites.

FOLLIOT (*prudently*): Is the King's friendship for Thomas Becket dead, your Highness?

KING: Yes, Bishop. It died quite suddenly. A sort of heart failure.

FOLLIOT: A curious phenomenon, your Highness, but quite frequent.

KING (*taking his arm suddenly*): I hate Becket now, Bishop. There is nothing more in common between that man and me than this creature tearing at my guts. I can't bear it any more. I shall have to turn it loose on him. But I am the King; what they conventionally call my greatness stands in my way. I need somebody.

FOLLIOT (*stiffening*): I do not wish to serve anything but the Church.

KING: Let us talk like grown men, Bishop. We went in hand in hand to conquer, pillage and ransom England. We quarrel, we try to cheat each other of a penny or two, but Heaven and Earth still have one or two common interests. Do you know what I have just obtained from the Pope? His Blessing to go and murder Catholic Ireland, in the name of the Faith. Yes, a sort of crusade to impose Norman barons and clergy on the Irish, with our swords and standards solemnly blessed as if we were off to give the Turks a drubbing. The only condition: a little piece of silver per household per year, for St. Peter's pence, which the native clergy of Ireland is loath to part with and which I have undertaken to make them pay. It's a mere pittance. But at the end of the year it will add up to a pretty sum. Rome knows how to do her accounts.

FOLLIOT (*terror-stricken*): There are some things one should never say, your Highness: one should even try not to know about them, so long as one is not directly concerned with them.

KING (*smiling*): We are alone, Bishop, and the church is empty.

FOLLIOT: The church is never empty. A little red lamp burns in front of the High Altar.

KING (*impatiently*): Bishop, I like playing games, but only with boys of my own age! Do you take me for one of your sheep, holy pastor? The One whom that little red lamp honors read into your innermost heart and mine a long time ago. Of your cupidity and my hatred, He knows all there is to know. (FOLLIOT *withdraws into his shell. The* KING *cries irritably*) If that's the way you feel you must become a monk, Bishop! Wear a hair shirt on your naked back and go and hide yourself in a monastery to pray! The Bishopric of London, for the purehearted son of a Thames waterman, is too much, or too little! (*A pause.*)

FOLLIOT (*impassively*): If, as is my duty, I disregard my private feelings, I must admit that his Grace the Archbishop has so far done nothing which has not been in the interests of Mother Church.

KING (*eying him, says jovially*): I can see your game, my little friend. You mean to cost me a lot of money. But I'm rich—thanks to Becket, who has succeeded in making you pay the Absentee Tax. And it seems to me eminently ethical that a part of the Church's gold should find its way, via you, back to the Church. Besides, if we want to keep this on a moral basis, Holy Bishop, you can tell yourself that as the greatness of the Church and that of the State are closely linked, in serving me, you will in the long run be working for the consolidation of the Catholic Faith.

FOLLIOT (*contemplating him with curiosity*): I had always taken your Highness for a great adolescent lout who cared only for his pleasure.

KING: One can be wrong about people, Bishop. I made the same mistake. (*With a sudden cry*) O my Thomas. . . .

FOLLIOT (*fiercely*): You love him, your Highness! You still love him! You love that mitered hog, that impostor, that Saxon bastard, that little guttersnipe!

KING (*seizing him by the throat*): Yes, I love him! But that's my affair, priest! All I confided to you was my hatred. I'll pay you to rid me of him, but don't ever speak ill of him to me. Or we'll fight it out as man to man!

FOLLIOT: Highness, you're choking me!

KING (*abruptly releasing him*): We will meet again tomorrow, my Lord Bishop, and we'll go over the details of our enterprise together. You will be officially summoned to the palace on some pretext or other—my good works in your London Diocese, say—where I am your chief parishioner. But it won't be the poor and needy we'll discuss. My poor can wait. The Kingdom they pin their hopes on is eternal.

(*The* KING *goes out.* GILBERT FOLLIOT *remains motionless. His* CLERGY *join him timidly. He takes his crook and goes out with dignity, but not before one of his Canons has discreetly adjusted his miter, which was knocked askew in the recent struggle.*

They have gone out.

The lighting changes. Curtains between the pillars. The episcopal palace.

Morning. A PRIEST *enters, leading two* MONKS *and the* YOUNG MONK *from the convent of Hastings.*)

PRIEST: His Grace will receive you here.

(*The two* MONKS *are impressed. They push the* YOUNG MONK *about a little.*)

1ST MONK: Stand up straight. Kiss his Grace's ring and try to answer his questions with humility, or I'll tan your backside for you!

2ND MONK: I suppose you thought he'd forgotten all about you? The great never forget anything. And don't you act proud with him or you'll be sorry.

(*Enter* BECKET, *wearing a coarse monk's robe.*)

BECKET: Well, brothers, is it fine over in Hastings? (*He gives them his ring to kiss.*)

1ST MONK: Foggy, my Lord.

BECKET (*smiling*): Then it's fine in Hastings. We always think fondly of our Abbey there and we intend to visit it soon, when our new duties grant us a moment's respite. How has this young man been behaving? Has he given our Abbot much trouble?

2ND MONK: A proper mule, my Lord. Father Abbot tried kindness, as you recommended, but he soon had to have recourse to the dungeon and bread and water, and even to the whip. Nothing has any effect. The stubborn little wretch is just the same; all defiance and insults. He has fallen into the sin of pride. Nothing I know of will pull him out of that!

1ST MONK: Save a good kick in the rump perhaps—if your Grace will pardon the expression. (*To the boy*) Stand up straight.

BECKET (*to the boy*): Pay attention to your brother. Stand up straight. As a rule the sin of pride stiffens a man's back. Look me in the face. (*The*

YOUNG MONK *looks at him*) Good. (BECKET *looks at the boy for a while, then turns to the* MONKS) You will be taken to the kitchens where you can refresh yourselves before you leave, brothers. They have orders to treat you well. Don't spurn our hospitality; we relieve you, for today, of your vows of abstinence, and we fondly hope you will do honor to our bill of fare. Greet your father Abbot in Jesus on our behalf.

2ND MONK (*hesitantly*) : And the lad?

BECKET: We will keep him here.

1ST MONK: Watch out for him, your Grace. He's vicious.

BECKET (*smiling*) : We are not afraid. (*The* MONKS *go out.* BECKET *and the* YOUNG MONK *remain, facing each other*) Why do you hold yourself so badly?

YOUNG MONK: I don't want to look people in the face any more.

BECKET: I'll teach you. That will be your first lesson. Look at me. (*The boy gives him a sidelong glance*) Better than that. (*The boy looks at him*) Are you still bearing the full weight of England's shame alone? Is it that shame which bends your back like that?

YOUNG MONK: Yes.

BECKET: If I took over half of it, would it weigh less heavy? (*He motions to the* PRIEST) Show in their Lordships the Bishops. You'll soon see that being alone is not a privilege reserved entirely for you. (*The* BISHOPS *come in.* BECKET *leads the* YOUNG MONK *into a corner*) You stay here in the corner and hold my tablets. I ask only one thing. Don't leap at their throats; you'd complicate everything. (*He motions to the* BISHOPS, *who remain standing.*)

FOLLIOT: Your Grace, I am afraid this meeting may be a pointless one. You insisted—against our advice—on attacking the King openly. Even before the three excommunications which you asked us to sanction could be made public, the King has hit back. His Grand Justicer Richard de Lacy has just arrived in your antechamber and is demanding to see you in the name of the King. He is the bearer of an official order summoning you to appear before his assembled Council within twenty-four hours and there to answer the charges made against you.

BECKET: Of what is the King accusing me?

FOLLIOT: Prevarication. Following the examination of accounts by his Privy Council, his Highness demands a considerable sum still outstanding on your administration of the Treasury.

BECKET: When I resigned the Chancellorship I handed over my ledgers to the Grand Justicer, who acquitted me of all subsequent dues and claims. What does the King demand?

OXFORD: Forty thousand marks in fine gold.

BECKET (*smiling*) : I don't believe there was ever as much money in all the coffers of all England in all the time I was Chancellor. But a clever clerk can soon change that. . . . The King has closed his fist and I am like a fly inside it. (*He smiles and looks at him*) I have the impression, gentlemen, that you must be feeling something very akin to relief.

YORK: We advised you against open opposition.

BECKET: William of Aynsford, incited by the King, struck down the priest I had appointed to the Parish of his Lordship's See, on the pretext that his Highness disapproved of my choice. Am I to look on while my priests are murdered?

FOLLIOT: It is not for you to appoint a priest to a free fief! There is not a Norman, layman or cleric, who will ever concede that. It would mean reviewing the entire legal system of the Conquest. Everything can be called into question in England except the fact that it was conquered in 1066. England is the land of law and of the most scrupulous respect for the law; but the law begins at that date only, or England as such ceases to exist.

BECKET: Bishop, must I remind you that we are men of God and that we have an Honor to defend, which dates from all eternity?

OXFORD (quietly): This excommunication was bad policy, your Grace. William of Aynsford is a companion of the King.

BECKET (smiling): I know him very well. He's a charming man. I have drained many a tankard with him.

YORK (yelping): And his wife is my second cousin!

BECKET: That is a detail I deplore, my Lord Bishop, but he has killed one of my priests. If I do not defend my priests, who will? Gilbert of Clare has indicted before his court of justice a churchman who was under our exclusive jurisdiction.

YORK: An interesting victim I must say! He deserved the rope a hundred times over. The man was accused of rape and murder. Wouldn't it have been cleverer to let the wretch hang—and have peace?

BECKET: "I bring not peace but the sword." Your Lordship must I'm sure have read that somewhere. I am not interested in what this man is guilty of. If I allow my priests to be tried by a secular tribunal; if I let Robert de Vere abduct our tonsured clerics from our monasteries, as he has just done, on the grounds that the man was one of his serfs who had escaped land bondage, I don't give much for our freedom and our chances of survival in five years' time, my Lord. I have excommunicated Gilbert of Clare, Robert de Vere and William of Aynsford. The Kingdom of God must be defended like any other Kingdom. Do you think that Right has only to show its handsome face for everything to drop in its lap? Without Might, its old enemy, Right counts for nothing.

YORK: What Might? Let us not indulge in empty words. The King is Might and he is the law.

BECKET: He is the written law, but there is another, unwritten law, which always makes Kings bend the neck eventually. (He looks at them for a moment and smiles) I was a profligate, gentlemen, perhaps a libertine, in any case, a worldly man. I loved living and I laughed at all these things. But you passed the burden on to me and now I have to carry it. I have rolled up my sleeves and taken it on my back and nothing will ever make me set it down again. I thank your Lordships. The council is adjourned and I have made my decision. I shall stand by these three excommunications. I shall appear tomorrow before the King's supreme court of Justice. (*The* BISHOPS *look at one another in surprise, then bow and go out.* BECKET *turns to the* YOUNG MONK) Well, does the shame weigh less heavy now?

YOUNG MONK: Yes.

BECKET (*leading him off and laughing*) : Then stand up straight!
(*The drapes close. Distant trumpets. The* KING *comes out from behind the curtains and turns to peep through them at something. A pause. Then* GILBERT FOLLIOT *comes hurrying in.*)

KING: What's happening? I can't see a thing from up here.

FOLLIOT: Legal procedure is taking its course, your Highness. The third summons has been delivered. He has not appeared. In a moment he will be condemned in absentia. Once prevarication is established, our Dean the Bishop of Chichester will go to see him and communicate according to the terms of the ancient Charter of the Church of England, our corporated repudiation of allegiance, absolving us of obedience to him—and our intention to report him to our Holy Father the Pope. I shall then, as Bishop of London, step forward and publicly accuse Becket of having celebrated, in contempt of the King, a sacrilegious Mass at the instigation of the Evil Spirit.

KING (*anxiously*) : Isn't that going rather far?

FOLLIOT: Of course. It won't fool anyone, but it always works. The assembly will then go out to vote, in order of precedence, and return a verdict of imprisonment. The sentence is already drawn up.

KING: Unanimously?

FOLLIOT: We are all Normans. The rest is your Highness' concern. It will merely be a matter of carrying out the sentence.

KING (*staggering suddenly*) : O my Thomas!

FOLLIOT (*impassively*) : I can still stop the machine, your Highness.

KING (*hesitates a second then says*) : No. Go.
(FOLLIOT *goes out. The* KING *goes back to his place, behind the curtain. The two* QUEENS *come into the room, and join the* KING. *All three stand and peer through the curtain. A pause.*)

YOUNG QUEEN: He's doomed, isn't he?

KING (*dully*) : Yes.

YOUNG QUEEN: At last! (*The* KING *turns on her, his face twisted with hate.*)

KING: I forbid you to gloat!

YOUNG QUEEN: At seeing your enemy perish—why not?

KING (*frothing*) : Becket is my enemy, but in the human balance, bastard as he is, and naked as his mother made him, he weighs a hundred times more than you do, Madam, with your crown and all your jewels and your august father the Emperor into the bargain. Becket is attacking me and he has betrayed me. I am forced to fight him and crush him, but at least he gave me, with open hands, everything that is at all good in me. And you have never given me anything but your carping mediocrity, your everlasting obsession with your puny little person and what you thought was due to it. That is why I forbid you to smile as he lies dying!

YOUNG QUEEN: I gave you my youth! I gave you your children!

KING (*shouting*) : I don't like my children! And as for your youth—that dusty flower pressed in a hymnbook since you were twelve years old, with its watery blood and its insipid scent—you can say farewell to that without a tear. With age, bigotry and malice may perhaps give some spice to your character. Your body was an empty desert, Madam!—which duty forced me to wander in alone. But you have never been a wife to me! And Becket was my friend, red-blooded, generous and full of strength! (*He is shaken by a sob*) O my Thomas! (*The* QUEEN MOTHER *moves over to him.*)

QUEEN MOTHER (*haughtily*) : And I, my son, I gave you nothing either, I suppose?

KING (*recovers his composure, glares at her and says dully*) : Life. Yes. Thank you. But after that I never saw you save in a passage, dressed for a Ball, or in your crown and ermine mantle, ten minutes before official ceremonies, where you were forced to tolerate my presence. I have always been alone, and no one on this earth has ever loved me except Becket!

QUEEN MOTHER (*bitterly*) : Well, call him back! Absolve him, since he loves you! Give him supreme power then! But do something!

KING: I am. I'm learning to be alone again, Madam. As usual. (*A* PAGE *comes in, breathless*) Well? What's happening? How far have they got?

PAGE: My Liege, Thomas Becket appeared just when everyone had given him up; sick, deathly pale, in full pontifical regalia and carrying his own heavy silver cross. He walked the whole length of the hall without anyone daring to stop him, and when Robert Duke of Leicester, who was to read out his sentence, began the consecrated words, he stopped with a gesture and forbade him, in God's name, to pronounce judgment against him, his spiritual Father. Then he walked back through the crowd, which parted for him in silence. He has just left.

KING (*unable to hide his delight*) : Well played, Thomas! One point to you. (*He checks himself, embarrassed, and then says*) And what about my Barons?

PAGE: Their hands flew to their swords with cries of "Traitor! Perjurer! Arrest him! Miserable wretch! Hear your sentence!" But not one of them dared move, or touch the sacred ornaments.

KING (*with a roar*) : The fools! I am surrounded by fools and the only intelligent man in my Kingdom is against me!

PAGE (*continuing his story*) : Then, on the threshold, he turned, looked at them coldly as they shouted in their impotence, and he said that not so long ago he could have answered their challenge sword in hand. Now he could no longer do it, but he begged them to remember that there was a time when he met strength with strength.

KING (*jubilantly*) : He could beat them all! All, I tell you! On horseback, on foot, with a mace, with a lance, with a sword! In the lists they fell to him like ninepins!

PAGE: And his eyes were so cold, and so ironic—even though all he had in his hand was his episcopal crook—that one by one, they fell silent. Only then did he turn and go out. They say he has given orders to invite all the beggars of the city to sup at his house tonight.

KING (*somberly*): And what about the Bishop of London, who was going to reduce him to powder? What about my busy friend Gilbert Folliot?

PAGE: He had a horrible fit of rage trying to incite the crowd, he let out a screech of foul abuse and then he fainted. They are bringing him round now.

(*The* KING *suddenly bursts into a shout of irrepressible laughter, and, watched by the two outraged* QUEENS, *collapses into the* PAGE'S *arms, breathless and helpless with mirth.*)

KING: It's too funny! It's too funny!

QUEEN MOTHER (*coldly*): You will laugh less heartily tomorrow, my son. If you don't stop him, Becket will reach the coast tonight, ask asylum of the King of France and jeer at you, unpunished, from across the Channel. (*She sweeps out with the* YOUNG QUEEN. *Suddenly, the* KING *stops laughing and runs out.*

The light changes. Curtains part. We are at the Court of LOUIS, KING OF FRANCE.[5] *He is sitting in the middle of the courtroom, very erect on his throne. He is a burly man with intelligent eyes.*)

LOUIS (*to his* BARONS): Gentlemen, we are in France and the hell with England's King—as the song goes.

1ST BARON: Your Majesty cannot *not* receive his Ambassadors Extraordinary!

LOUIS: Ordinary, or extraordinary, I am at home to all ambassadors. It's my job. I shall receive them.

1ST BARON: They have been waiting in your Majesty's anteroom for over an hour, Sire.

LOUIS: Let them wait. That's *their* job. An ambassador is made for pacing about an antechamber. I know what they are going to ask me.

2ND BARON: The extradition of a felon is a courtesy due from one crowned head to another.

LOUIS: My dear man, crowned heads can play the little game of courtesy but nations owe each other none. My right to play the courteous gentleman stops where France's interests begin. And France's interests consist in making things as difficult as possible for England—a thing England never hesitates to do to us. The Archbishop is a millstone round Henry Plantagenet's neck. Long live the Archbishop! Anyway, I like the fellow.

2ND BARON: My gracious sovereign is master. And so long as our foreign policy permits us to expect nothing of King Henry—

LOUIS: For the time being, it is an excellent thing to stiffen our attitude. Remember the Montmirail affair.[6] We only signed the peace treaty with Henry on condition that he granted to spare the lives of the refugees from Brittany and Poitou whom he asked us to hand over to him. Two months later all of them had lost their heads. That directly touched my personal

---

[5] Louis VII (c. 1121-1180) married Eleanor of Bordeaux, heiress of William II, Duke of Aquitaine. After their divorce she married Henry II.

[6] On January 6, 1169, Louis and Henry met at Montmirail, near the frontier of Maine, to arrange a peace and to settle the question of Becket.

honor. I was not strong enough at the time, so I had to pretend I hadn't heard of these men's execution. And I continued to lavish smiles on my English cousin. But praise God our affairs have taken a turn for the better. And today *he* needs *us*. So I will now proceed to remember my honor. Show in the ambassadors.

(*Exit* 1ST BARON. *He comes back with* FOLLIOT *and the* DUKE OF ARUNDEL.)

1ST BARON: Permit me to introduce to your Majesty the two envoys extraordinary from his Highness Henry of England; his Grace the Bishop of London and the Duke of Arundel.

LOUIS (*with a friendly wave to the* DUKE): Greetings to you, Milord. I have not forgotten your amazing exploits at the last tournament at Calais. Do you still wield a lance as mightily as you did, Milord?

ARUNDEL (*with a gratified bow*): I hope so, Sire.

LOUIS: We hope that our friendly relations with your gracious master will allow us to appreciate your jousting skill again before long, on the occasion of the forthcoming festivities. (FOLLIOT *has unrolled a parchment*) Bishop, I see you have a letter for us from your master. We are listening.

FOLLIOT (*bows again and starts to read*): "To my Lord and friend Louis, King of the French; Henry, King of England, Duke of Normandy, Duke of Aquitaine and Count of Anjou: Learn that Thomas, former Archbishop of Canterbury, after a public trial held at my court by the plenary assembly of the Barons of my realm has been found guilty of fraud, perjury and treason towards me. He has forthwith fled my Kingdom as a traitor, and with evil intent. I therefore entreat you not to allow this criminal, nor any of his adherents, to reside upon your territories, nor to permit any of your vassals to give help, support or counsel to this my greatest enemy. For I solemnly declare that your enemies or those of your Realm would receive none from me or my subjects. I expect you to assist me in the vindication of my honor and the punishment of my enemy, as you would wish me to do for you, should the need arise."

(*A pause.* FOLLIOT *bows very low and hands the parchment to the* KING, *who rolls it up casually and hands it to one of the* BARONS.)

LOUIS: Gentlemen, we have listened attentively to our gracious cousin's request and we take good note of it. Our chancellery will draft a reply which will be sent to you tomorrow. All we can do at the moment, is express our surprise. No news had reached us of the presence of the Archbishop of Canterbury on our domains.

FOLLIOT (*tersely*): Sire, the former Archbishop has taken refuge at the Abbey of St. Martin, near Saint-Omer.

LOUIS (*still gracious*): My Lord Bishop, we flatter ourselves that there is some order in our Kingdom. If he were there, we would certainly have been informed. (*He makes a gesture of dismissal. The Ambassadors bow low and go out backwards, ushered out by the* 1ST BARON. *Immediately,* LOUIS *says to the* 2ND BARON) Show in Thomas Becket and leave us.

(*The* 2ND BARON *goes out and a second later admits* THOMAS, *dressed in a monk's robe.* THOMAS *drops onto one knee. The* BARON *goes out. Kindly*) Rise, Thomas Becket. And greet us as the Primate of England. The bow is enough—and if I know my etiquette, you are entitled to a slight nod of the head from me. There, that's done. I would even be required to kiss your ring, if your visit were an official one. But I have the impression that it isn't, am I right?

BECKET (*with a smile*) : No, Sire. I am only an exile.

LOUIS (*graciously*) : That too is an important title, in France.

BECKET: I am afraid it is the only one I have left. My property has been seized and distributed to those who served the King against me; letters have been sent to the Duke of Flanders and all his Barons enjoining them to seize my person. John, Bishop of Poitiers, who was suspected of wanting to grant me asylum, has just been poisoned.

LOUIS (*smiling*) : In fact you are a very dangerous man.

BECKET: I'm afraid so.

LOUIS (*unperturbed*) : We like danger, Becket. And if the King of France started being afraid of the King of England, there would be something sadly amiss in Europe. We grant you our royal protection on whichever of our domains it will please you to choose.

BECKET: I humbly thank your Majesty. I must, however, tell you that I cannot buy this protection with any act hostile to my country.

LOUIS: You do us injury. That was understood. You may be sure we are practiced enough in the task of Kingship not to make such gross errors in our choice of spies and traitors. The King of France will ask nothing of you. But. . . . There is always a but, as I'm sure you are aware, in politics. (BECKET *looks up. The* KING *rises heavily onto his fat legs, goes to him and says familiarly*) I am only responsible for France's interests, Becket. I really can't afford to shoulder those of Heaven. In a month or a year I can summon you back here and tell you, just as blandly, that my dealings with the King of England have taken a different turn and that I am obliged to banish you. (*He slaps him affably on the back, his eyes sparkling with intelligence and asks, with a smile*) I believe you have dabbled in politics too, Archbishop?

BECKET (*smiling*) : Yes, Sire. Not so very long ago.

LOUIS (*jovially*) : I like you very much. Mark you, had you been a French Bishop, I don't say I wouldn't have clapped you in prison myself. But in the present circumstances, you have a right to my royal protection. Do you value candor, Becket?

BECKET: Yes, Sire.

LOUIS: Then we are sure to understand each other. Do you intend to go to see the Holy Father?

BECKET: Yes, Sire, if you give me your safe conduct.

LOUIS: You shall have it. But a word in your ear—as a friend. (Keep this to yourself, won't you?—don't go and stir up trouble for me with Rome.) Beware of the Pope. He'll sell you for thirty pieces of silver. The man needs money.

(*The lights dim. A curtain closes. Two small rostrums, bearing the*

POPE[7] *and the* CARDINAL, *are pushed on stage, to a light musical accompaniment.*

The POPE *is a thin, fidgety little man with an atrocious Italian accent. The* CARDINAL *is swarthy, and his accent is even worse. The whole effect is a little grubby, among the gilded splendor.*)

POPE: I don't agree, Zambelli! I don't agree at all! It's a very bad plan altogether. We will forfeit our honor all for 3,000 silver marks.

CARDINAL: Holy Father, there is no question of forfeiting honor, but merely of taking the sum offered by the King of England and thereby gaining time. To lose that sum and give a negative answer right away would solve neither the problems of the Curia, nor those of Thomas Becket—nor even, I am afraid, those of the higher interests of the Church. To accept the money—the sum is meager, I agree, and cannot be viewed as a factor in our decision—is merely to make a gesture of appeasement in the interests of peace in Europe. Which has always been the supreme duty of the Holy See.

POPE (*concerned*): If we take money from the King, I cannot possibly receive the Archbishop, who has been waiting here in Rome for a whole month for me to grant him an audience.

CARDINAL: Receive the money from the King, Very Holy Father, and receive the Archbishop too. The one will neutralize the other. The money will remove all subversive taint from the audience you will grant the Archbishop and on the other hand, the reception of the Archbishop will efface whatever taint of humiliation there may have been in accepting the money.

POPE (*gloomily*): I don't want to receive him at all. I gather he is a sincere man. I am always disconcerted by people of that sort. They leave me with a bad taste in my mouth.

CARDINAL: Sincerity is a form of strategy, just like any other, Holy Father. In certain very difficult negotiations, when matters are not going ahead and the usual tactics cease to work, I have been known to use it myself. The great pitfall, of course, is if your opponent starts being sincere at the same time as you. Then the game becomes horribly confusing.

POPE: You know what they say Becket's been meaning to ask me?—in the month he's spent pacing about my antechamber?

CARDINAL (*innocently*): No, Holy Father.

POPE (*impatiently*): Zambelli! Don't play the fox with me! It was you who told me!

CARDINAL (*caught out*): I beg your pardon, Holy Father, I had forgotten. Or rather, as your Holiness asked me the question, I thought you had forgotten and so I took a chance and—

POPE (*irritably*): Zambelli, if we start outmaneuvering each other to no purpose, we'll be here all night!

CARDINAL (*in confusion*): Force of habit, your Holiness. Excuse me.

POPE: To ask me to relieve him of his rank and functions as Archbishop

---

[7] Alexander III, Pope from 1159 to 1181, steadily backed Becket in his struggle with Henry. Historians would not support Anouilh's caricature of him.

of Canterbury—that's the reason Becket is in Rome! And do you know why he wants to ask me that?

CARDINAL (*candidly for once*) : Yes, Holy Father.

POPE (*irritably*) : No, you do not know! It was your enemy Rapallo who told me!

CARDINAL (*modestly*) : Yes, but I knew it just the same, because I have a spy in Rapallo's palace.

POPE (*with a wink*) : Culograti?

CARDINAL : No. Culograti is only my spy in his master's eyes. By the man I have spying on Culograti.

POPE (*cutting short the digression*) : Becket maintains that the election of Clarendon was not a free one, that he owes his nomination solely to the royal whim and that consequently the honor of God, of which he has now decided he is the champion, does not allow him to bear this usurped title any longer. He wishes to be nothing more than an ordinary priest.

CARDINAL (*after a moment's thought*) : The man is clearly an abyss of ambition.

POPE : And yet he knows that we know that his title and functions are his only safeguard against the King's anger. I don't give much for his skin wherever he is, when he is no longer Archbishop!

CARDINAL (*thoughtfully*) : He's playing a deep game. But I have a plan. Your Holiness will pretend to believe in his scruples. You will receive him and relieve him of his titles and functions as Primate, then, immediately after, as a reward for his zeal in defending the Church of England, you will reappoint him Archbishop, in right and due form this time. We thus avert the danger, we score a point against him—and at the same time a point against the King.

POPE : That's a dangerous game. The King has a long arm.

CARDINAL : We can cover ourselves. We will send secret letters to the English court explaining that this new nomination is a pure formality and that we herewith rescind the excommunications pronounced by Becket; on the other hand, we will inform Becket of the existence of these secret letters, swearing him to secrecy and begging him to consider them as null and void.

POPE (*getting muddled*) : In that case, perhaps there isn't much point in the letters being secret?

CARDINAL : Yes, there is. Because that will allow us to maneuver with each of them as if the other was ignorant of the contents, while taking the precaution of making it known to them both. The main thing is for them not to know that we know they know. It's so simple a child of twelve could grasp it!

POPE : But Archbishop or no, what are we going to do with Becket?

CARDINAL (*with a lighthearted wave of his hand*) : We will send him to a convent. A French convent, since King Louis is protecting him—to the Cistercians say, at Pontigny. The monastic rule is a strict one. It will do that onetime dandy a world of good! Let him learn real poverty! That will teach him to be the comforter of the poor!

POPE : That sounds like good advice, Zambelli. Bread and water and noc-

turnal prayers are an excellent remedy for sincerity. (*He muses a moment*) The only thing that puzzles me, Zambelli, is why you should want to give me a piece of good advice. . . .
(*The* CARDINAL *looks a little embarrassed.*

The little rostra go as they came and the curtain opens revealing a small, bare cell, center stage.

BECKET *is praying before a humble wooden crucifix. Crouching in a corner, the* YOUNG MONK *is playing with a knife.*)

BECKET: Yet it would be simple enough. Too simple perhaps. Saintliness is a temptation too. Oh, how difficult it is to get an answer from You, Lord! I was slow in praying to You, but I cannot believe that others, worthier than I, who have spent years asking You questions, have been better than myself at deciphering Your real intentions. I am only a beginner and I must make mistake after mistake, as I did in my Latin translations as a boy, when my riotous imagination made the old priest roar with laughter. But I cannot believe that one learns Your language as one learns any human tongue, by hard studying, with a dictionary, a grammar and a set of idioms. I am sure that to the hardened sinner, who drops to his knees for the first time and murmurs Your name, marveling, You tell him all Your secrets, straightaway, and that he understands. I have served You like a dilettante, surprised that I could still find my pleasure in Your service. And for a long time I was on my guard because of it. I could not believe this pleasure would bring me one step nearer You. I could not believe that the road could be a happy one. Their hair shirts, their fasting, their bells in the small hours summoning one to meet You, on the icy paving stones, in the sick misery of the poor ill-treated human animal—I cannot believe that all these are anything but safeguards for the weak. In power and in luxury, and even in the pleasures of the flesh, I shall not cease to speak to You, I feel this now. You are the God of the rich man and the happy man too, Lord, and therein lies Your profound justice. You do not turn away Your eyes from the man who was given everything from birth. You have not abandoned him, alone in his ensnaring facility. And he may be Your true lost sheep. For Your scheme of things, which we mistakenly call Justice, is secret and profound and You plumb the hidden depths of poor men's puny frames as carefully as those of Kings. And beneath those outward differences, which blind us, but which to You are barely noticeable; beneath the diadem or the grime, You discern the same pride, the same vanity, the same petty, complacent preoccupation with oneself. Lord, I am certain now that You meant to tempt me with this hair shirt, object of so much vapid self-congratulation! this bare cell, this solitude, this absurdly endured winter-cold—and the conveniences of prayer. It would be too easy to buy You like this, at so low a price. I shall leave this convent, where so many precautions hem You round. I shall take up the miter and the golden cope again, and the great silver cross, and I shall go back and fight in the place and with the weapons it has pleased You to give me. It has pleased You to make me Archbishop and to set me, like a solitary pawn, face to face with the King, upon the chessboard. I shall go back to my

place, humbly, and let the world accuse me of pride, so that I may do
what I believe is my life's work. For the rest, Your will be done. (*He
crosses himself.*)

(*The* YOUNG MONK *is still playing with his knife. Suddenly he throws it
and watches as it quivers, embedded in the floor.*)

(*The Curtain Falls.*)

Act Four

The King of France's Court.

KING LOUIS *comes in, holding* BECKET *familiarly by the arm.*

LOUIS: I tell you, Becket, intrigue is an ugly thing. You keep the smell
about you for ages afterwards. There is a return of good understanding
between the Kingdom of England and Ourselves. Peace in that direction
assures me of a great advantage in the struggle which I will shortly have
to undertake against the Emperor. I must protect my rear by a truce
with Henry Plantagenet, before I march towards the East. And, needless
to say, you are one of the items on the King's bill of charges. I can even
tell you, that apart from yourself, his demands are negligible. (*Musingly*)
Curious man. England's best policy would have been to take advantage
of the Emperor's aggressive intentions and close the other jaw of the trap.
He is deliberately sacrificing this opportunity for the pleasure of seeing
you driven out. He really hates you, doesn't he?

BECKET (*simply*): Sire, we loved each other and I think he cannot forgive
me for preferring God to him.

LOUIS: Your King isn't doing his job properly, Archbishop. He is giving
way to passion. However! He has chosen to score a point against you,
instead of against me. You are on his bill; I have to pay his price and
banish you. I do not do so without a certain shame. Where are you
thinking of going?

BECKET: I am a shepherd who has remained too long away from his flock.
I intend to go back to England. I had already made my decision before
this audience with your Majesty.

LOUIS (*surprised*): You have a taste for martyrdom? You disappoint me.
I thought you more healthy-minded.

BECKET: Would it be healthy-minded to walk the roads of Europe, and beg
a refuge where my carcass would be safe? Besides, where would I be safe?

I am a Primate of England. That is a rather showy label on my back. The honor of God and common sense, which for once coincide, dictate that instead of risking the knife thrust of some hired assassin, on the highway, I should go and have myself killed—if killed I must be—clad in my golden cope, with my miter on my head and my silver cross in my hand, among my flock in my own cathedral. That place alone befits me. (*A pause.*)

LOUIS: I daresay you're right. (*He sighs*) Ah, what a pity it is to be a King, sometimes, when one has the surprise of meeting a man! You'll tell me, fortunately for me, that men are rare. Why weren't you born on this side of the Channel, Becket? (*He smiles*) True, you would no doubt have been a thorn in *my* side then! The honor of God is a very cumbersome thing. (*He muses for a moment and then says abruptly*) Who cares, I'll risk it! I like you too much. I'll indulge in a moment's humanity. I am going to try something, even if your master does seize on the chance to double his bill. After all, banishing you would merely have cost me a small slice of honor. . . . I am meeting Henry in a day or two, at La Ferté-Bernard, to seal our agreement. I shall try to persuade him to make his peace with you. Should he agree, will you be willing to talk with him?

BECKET: Sire, ever since we stopped seeing each other, I have never ceased to talk to him.

(*Blackout. Prolonged blare of trumpets. The set is completely removed. Nothing remains but the cyclorama around the bare stage. A vast, arid plain, lashed by the wind. Trumpets again.*

Two SENTRIES *are on stage, watching something in the distance.*)

SENTRY: Open those eyes of yours, lad! And drink it all in. You're new to the job, but you won't see something like this every day! This is a historic meeting!

YOUNG SENTRY: I daresay, but it's perishing cold! How long are they going to keep us hanging about?

SENTRY: We're sheltered by the wood here, but you can bet they're even colder than we are, out there in the plain.

YOUNG SENTRY: Look! They've come up to each other! I wonder what they're talking about?

SENTRY: What do you think they're talking about, mutton-head? Inquiring how things are at home? Complaining about their chilblains? The fate of the world, that's what they're arguing about! Things you and I won't ever understand. Even the words those bigwigs use—why, you wouldn't even know what they meant!

(*They go off. The lights go up.* BECKET *and the* KING, *on horseback, are alone in the middle of the plain, facing each other.*

Throughout the scene, the winter blizzard wails like a shrill dirge beneath their words. And during their silences, only the wind is heard.)

KING: You look older, Thomas.

BECKET: You too, Highness. Are you sure you aren't too cold?

KING: I'm frozen stiff. You love it of course! You're in your element, aren't you? And you're barefooted as well!

BECKET (*smiling*) : That's my latest affectation.

KING : Even with these fur boots on, my chilblains are killing me. Aren't yours, or don't you have any?

BECKET (*gently*) : Of course.

KING (*cackling*) : You're offering them up to God, I hope, holy monk?

BECKET (*gravely*) : I have better things to offer Him.

KING (*with a sudden cry*) : If we start straightaway, we're sure to quarrel! Let's talk about trivial things. You know my son is fourteen? He's come of age.

BECKET : Has he improved at all?

KING : He's a little idiot and sly like his mother. Becket, don't you ever marry!

BECKET (*smiling*) : The matter has been taken out of my hands. By you, Highness! It was you who had me ordained!

KING (*with a cry*) : Let's not start yet, I tell you! Talk about something else!

BECKET (*lightly*) : Has your Highness done much hunting lately?

KING (*snarling*) : Yes, every day! And it doesn't amuse me any more.

BECKET : Have you any new hawks?

KING (*furiously*) : The most expensive on the market! But they don't fly straight.

BECKET : And your horses?

KING : The Sultan sent me four superb stallions for the tenth anniversary of my reign. But they throw everyone! Nobody has managed to mount one of them, yet!

BECKET (*smiling*) : I must see what I can do about that some day.

KING : They'll throw you too! And we'll see your buttocks under your robe! At least, I hope so, or everything would be too dismal.

BECKET (*after a pause*) : Do you know what I miss most, Sire? The horses.

KING : And the women?

BECKET (*simply*) : I've forgotten.

KING : You hypocrite. You turned into a hypocrite when you became a priest. (*Abruptly*) Did you love Gwendolen?

BECKET : I've forgotten her too.

KING : You did love her! That's the only way I can account for it.

BECKET (*gravely*) : No, my prince, in my soul and conscience, I did not love her.

KING : Then you never loved anything, that's worse! (*Churlishly*) Why are you calling me your prince, like in the old days?

BECKET (*gently*) : Because you have remained my prince.

KING (*crying out*) : Then why are you doing me harm?

BECKET (*gently*) : Let's talk about something else.

KING : Well, what? I'm cold.

BECKET : I always told you, my prince, that one must fight the cold with the cold's own weapons. Strip naked and splash yourself with cold water every morning.

KING : I used to when you were there to force me into it. I never wash now. I stink. I grew a beard at one time. Did you know?

BECKET (*smiling*) : Yes. I had a hearty laugh over it.

KING : I cut it off because it itched. (*He cries out suddenly, like a lost child*) Becket, I'm bored!

BECKET (*gravely*) : My prince. I do so wish I could help you.

KING : Then what are you waiting for? You can see I'm dying for it!

BECKET (*quietly*) : I'm waiting for the honor of God and the honor of the King to become one.

KING : You'll wait a long time then!

BECKET : Yes. I'm afraid I will. (*A pause. Only the wind is heard.*)

KING (*suddenly*) : If we've nothing more to say to each other, we might as well go and get warm!

BECKET : We have everything to say to each other, my prince. The opportunity may not occur again.

KING : Make haste, then. Or there'll be two frozen statues on this plain making their peace in a frozen eternity! I am your King, Becket! And so long as we are on this earth you owe me the first move! I'm prepared to forget a lot of things but not the fact that I am King. You yourself taught me that.

BECKET (*gravely*) : Never forget it, my prince. Even against God. You have a different task to do. You have to steer the ship.

KING : And you—what do you have to do?

BECKET : Resist you with all my might, when you steer against the wind.

KING : Do you expect the wind to be behind me, Becket? No such luck! That's the fairy-tale navigation! God on the King's side? That's never happened yet! Yes, once in a century, at the time of the Crusades, when all Christendom shouts "It's God's will!" And even then! You know as well as I do what private greeds a Crusade covers up, in nine cases out of ten. The rest of the time, it's a head-on wind. And there must be somebody to keep the watch!

BECKET : And somebody else to cope with the absurd wind—and with God. The tasks have been shared out, once and for all. The pity of it is that it should have been between us two, my prince—who were friends.

KING (*crossly*) : The King of France—I still don't know what he hopes to gain by it—preached at me for three whole days for me to make my peace with you. What good would it do you to provoke me beyond endurance?

BECKET : None.

KING : You know that I am the King, and that I must act like a King! What do you expect of me? Are you hoping I'll weaken?

BECKET : No. That would prostrate me.

KING : Do you hope to conquer me by force then?

BECKET : You are the strong one.

KING : To win me round?

BECKET : No. Not that either. It is not for me to win you round. I have only to say no to you.

KING : But you must be logical, Becket!

BECKET : No. That isn't necessary, my Liege. We must only do—absurdly— what we have been given to do—right to the end.

KING : Yet I know you well enough, God knows. Ten years we spent together, little Saxon! At the hunt, at the whorehouse, at war; carousing all night long the two of us; in the same girl's bed, sometimes . . . and at work in the Council Chamber too. Absurdly. That word isn't like you.

BECKET: Perhaps. I am no longer like myself.

KING (*derisively*): Have you been touched by grace?

BECKET (*gravely*): Not by the one you think. I am not worthy of it.

KING: Did you feel the Saxon in you coming out, despite Papa's good collaborator's sentiments?

BECKET: No. Not that either.

KING: What then?

BECKET: I felt for the first time that I was being entrusted with something, that's all—there in that empty cathedral, somewhere in France, that day when you ordered me to take up this burden. I was a man without honor. And suddenly I found it—one I never imagined would ever become mine —the honor of God. A frail, incomprehensible honor, vulnerable as a boy-King fleeing from danger.

KING (*roughly*): Suppose we talked a little more precisely, Becket, with words I understand? Otherwise we'll be here all night. I'm cold. And the others are waiting for us on the fringes of this plain.

BECKET: I am being precise.

KING: I'm an idiot then! Talk to me like an idiot! That's an order. Will you lift the excommunication which you pronounced on William of Aynsford and others of my liegemen?

BECKET: No, Sire, because that is the only weapon I have to defend this child, who was given, naked, into my care.

KING: Will you agree to the twelve proposals which my Bishops have accepted in your absence at Northampton, and notably to forego the much-abused protection of Saxon clerics who get themselves tonsured to escape land bondage?

BECKET: No, Sire. My role is to defend my sheep. And they are my sheep. (*A pause*) Nor will I concede that the Bishops should forego the right to appoint priests in their own dioceses, nor that churchmen should be subject to any but the Church's jurisdiction. These are my duties as a pastor —which it is not for me to relinquish. But I shall agree to the nine other articles in a spirit of peace, and because I know that you must remain King—in all save the honor of God. (*A pause.*)

KING (*coldly*): Very well. I will help you defend your God, since that is your new vocation, in memory of the companion you once were to me— in all save the honor of the Realm. You may come back to England, Thomas.

BECKET: Thank you, my prince. I meant to go back in any case and give myself up to your power, for on this earth, you are my King. And in all that concerns this earth, I owe you obedience. (*A pause.*)

KING (*ill at ease*): Well, let's go back now. We've finished. I'm cold.

BECKET (*dully*): I feel cold too, now. (*Another pause. They look at each other. The wind howls.*)

KING (*suddenly*): You never loved me, did you, Becket?

BECKET: In so far as I was capable of love, yes, my prince, I did.

KING: Did you start to love God? (*He cries out*) You mule! Can't you ever answer a simple question?

BECKET (*quietly*) : I started to love the honor of God.

KING (*somberly*) : Come back to England. I give you my royal peace. May you find yours. And may you not discover you were wrong about yourself. This is the last time I shall come begging to you. (*He cries out*) I should never have seen you again! It hurts too much. (*His whole body is suddenly shaken by a sob.*)

BECKET (*goes nearer to him; moved*) : My prince—

KING (*yelling*) : No! No pity! It's dirty. Stand away from me! Go back to England! It's too cold out here!

(BECKET *turns his horse and moves nearer to the* KING.)

BECKET (*gravely*) : Farewell, my prince. Will you give me the kiss of peace?

KING: No! I can't bear to come near you! I can't bear to look at you! Later! Later! When it doesn't hurt any more!

BECKET: I shall set sail tomorrow. Farewell, my prince. I know I shall never see you again.

KING (*his face twisted with hatred*) : How dare you say that to me after I gave you my royal word? Do you take me for a traitor?

(BECKET *looks at him gravely for a second longer, with a sort of pity in his eyes. Then he slowly turns his horse and rides away. The wind howls.*)

KING: Thomas!

(*But* BECKET *has not heard. The* KING *does not call a second time. He spurs his horse and gallops off in the other direction. The lights fade. The wind howls.*

The lights change. Red curtains fall. BECKET'S *whistled march is heard off stage during the scene change.*

The curtains open. Royal music. King Henry's palace somewhere in England. The two QUEENS, *the* BARONS *and Henry's* SON *are standing around the dinner table, waiting. The* KING, *his eyes gleaming maliciously, looks at them and then exclaims:*)

KING: Today, gentlemen, I shall not be the first to sit down! (*To his* SON, *with a comic bow*) You are the King, Sir. The honor belongs to you. Take the high chair. Today I shall wait on *you!*

QUEEN MOTHER (*with slight irritation*) : My son!

KING: I know what I'm doing, Madam! (*With a sudden shout*) Go on, you great loon, look sharp! You're the King, but you're as stupid as ever! (*The boy flinches to avoid the blow he was expecting and goes to sit in the* KING's *chair, sly and rather ill at ease*) Take your places, gentlemen! I shall remain standing. Barons of England, here is your second King. For the good of our vast domains, a kingly colleague had become a necessity. Reviving an ancient custom, we have decided to have our successor crowned during our lifetime and to share our responsibilities with him. We ask you now to give him your homage and to honor him with the same title as Ourself. (*He makes a sign. Two* SERVANTS *have brought in a haunch of venison on a silver charger. The* KING *serves his* SON.)

YOUNG QUEEN (*to her* SON) : Sit up straight! And try to eat properly for once, now that you've been raised to glory!

KING (*grunting as he serves him*): He hasn't the face for it! He's a little slyboots and dim-witted at that. However, he'll be your King in good earnest one day, so you may as well get used to him. Besides, it's the best I had to offer.

QUEEN MOTHER (*indignantly*): Really, my son! This game is unworthy of you and of us. You insisted on it—against my advice—at least play it with dignity!

KING (*rounding on her in fury*): I'll play the games that amuse me, Madam, and I'll play them the way I choose! This mummery, gentlemen, which is, incidentally, without any importance at all—(if your new King fidgets, let me know; I'll give him a good kick up his train)—will at the very least have the appreciable result of showing our new friend, the Archbishop, that we can do without him. If there was one ancient privilege the Primacy clung to, tooth and nail, it was its exclusive right to anoint and consecrate the Kings of this realm. Well, it will be that old toad the Archbishop of York—with letters from the Pope authorizing him to do so—I paid the price!—who, tomorrow, will crown our son in the cathedral! What a joke that's going to be! (*He roars with laughter amid the general silence*) What a tremendous, marvelous joke! I'd give anything to see that Archbishop's face when he has to swallow that! (*To his* SON) Get down from there, you imbecile! Go back to the bottom of the table and take your victuals with you! You aren't officially crowned until tomorrow. (*The boy picks up his plate and goes back to his place, casting a cowed, smoldering look at his father. Watching him, says jovially*) What a look! Filial sentiments are a fine thing to see, gentlemen! You'd like to be the real King, wouldn't you, you young pig? You'd like that number III after your name, eh, with Papa good and stiff under his catafalque! You'll have to wait a bit! Papa is well. Papa is very well indeed!

QUEEN MOTHER: My son, God knows I criticized your attempts at reconciliation with that wretch, who has done us nothing but harm. . . . God knows I understand your hatred of him! But do not let it drag you into making a gesture you will regret, merely for the sake of wounding his pride. Henry is still a child. But you were not much older when you insisted on reigning by yourself, and in opposition to me. Ambitious self-seekers—and there is never any scarcity of those around Princes—can advise him, raise a faction against you and avail themselves of this hasty coronation to divide the Kingdom! Think it over, there is still time.

KING: We are still alive, Madam, and in control! And nothing can equal my pleasure in imagining my proud friend Becket's face when he sees the fundamental privilege of the Primacy whisked from under his nose! I let him cheat me out of one or two articles the other day, but I had something up my sleeve for him!

QUEEN MOTHER: Henry! I bore the weight of state affairs longer than you ever have. I have been your Queen and I am your mother. You are answerable for the interests of a great Kingdom, not for your moods. You already gave far too much away to the King of France, at La Ferté-Bernard. It is England you must think of, not your hatred—or disappointed love—for that man.

KING (*in a fury*): Disappointed love—disappointed love? What gives you the right, Madam, to meddle in my loves and hates?

QUEEN MOTHER: You have a rancor against the man which is neither healthy nor manly. The King your father dealt with his enemies faster and more summarily than that. He had them killed and said no more about it. If Thomas Becket were a faithless woman whom you still hankered after, you would act no differently. Sweet Jesu, tear him out of your heart once and for all! (*She bawls suddenly*) Oh, if I were a man!

KING (*grinning*): Thanks be to God, Madam, he gave you dugs. Which I never personally benefited from. I suckled a peasant girl.

QUEEN MOTHER (*acidly*): That is no doubt why you have remained so lumpish, my son.

YOUNG QUEEN: And haven't I a say in the matter? I tolerated your mistresses, Sir, but do you expect me to tolerate everything? Have you ever stopped to think what kind of woman I am? I am tired of having my life encumbered with this man. Becket! Always Becket! Nobody ever talks about anything else here! He was almost less of a hindrance when you loved him. I am a woman. I am your wife and your Queen. I refuse to be treated like this! I shall complain to my father, the Duke of Aquitaine! I shall complain to my uncle, the Emperor! I shall complain to all the Kings of Europe, my cousins! I shall complain to God!

KING (*shouting rather vulgarly*): I should start with God! Be off to your private chapel, Madam, and see if He's at home. (*He turns to his mother, fuming*) And you, the other Madam, away to your chamber with your secret councilors and go and spin your webs! Get out, both of you! I can't stand the sight of you! I retch with boredom whenever I set eyes on you! And young Henry III too! Go on, get out! (*He chases him out with kicks, yelling*) Here's my royal foot in your royal buttocks! And to the devil with my whole family, if he'll have you! Get out, all of you! Get out! Get out! Get out! (*The* QUEENS *scurry out, with a great rustling of silks. He turns to the* BARONS, *who all stand watching him, terror-stricken. More calmly*) Let us drink, gentlemen. That's about all one can do in your company. Let us get drunk, like men, all night; until we roll under the table, in vomit and oblivion. (*He fills their glasses and beckons them closer*) Ah, my four idiots! My faithful hounds! It's warm beside you, like being in a stable. Good sweat! Comfortable nothingness! (*He taps their skulls*) Not the least little glimmer inside to spoil the fun. And to think that before he came I was like you! A good fat machine for belching after drink, for pissing, for mounting girls and punching heads. What the devil did you put into it, Becket, to stop the wheels from going round? (*Suddenly to the* 2ND BARON) Tell me, do you think sometimes, Baron?

2ND BARON: Never, Sire. Thinking has never agreed with an Englishman. It's unhealthy. Besides, a gentleman has better things to do.

KING (*sitting beside them, suddenly quite calm*): Drink up, gentlemen. That's always been considered a healthy thing to do. (*He fills the goblets*) Has Becket landed? I'm told the sea has been too rough to cross these last few days.

1ST BARON (*somberly*): He has landed, Sire, despite the sea.

KING: Where?

1ST BARON: On a deserted stretch of coast, near Sandwich.

KING: So God did not choose to drown him?

1ST BARON: No.

KING (*he asks in his sly, brutish way*): Was nobody there waiting for him? There must be one or two men in England whom he can't call his friends!

1ST BARON: Yes. Gervase, Duke of Kent, Regnouf de Broc and Regnault de Garenne were waiting for him. Gervase had said that if he dared to land he'd cut off his head with his own hands. But the native Englishmen from all the coastal towns had armed themselves to form an escort for the Archbishop. And the Dean of Oxford went to meet the Barons and charged them not to cause bloodshed and make you look a traitor, seeing that you had given the Archbishop a safe conduct.

KING (*soberly*): Yes, I gave him a safe conduct.

1ST BARON: All along the road to Canterbury, the peasants, the artisans and the small shopkeepers came out to meet him, cheering him and escorting him from village to village. Not a single rich man, not a single Norman, showed his face.

KING: Only the Saxons?

1ST BARON: Poor people armed with makeshift shields and rusty lances. Riffraff. Swarms of them though, all camping around Canterbury, to protect him. (*Gloomily*) Who would have thought there were so many people in England!

(*The* KING *has remained prostrate without uttering a word. Now he suddenly jumps up and roars:*)

KING: A miserable wretch who ate my bread! A man I raised up from nothing! A Saxon! A man loved! (*Shouting like a madman*) I loved him! Yes, I loved him! And I believe I still do! Enough, O God! Enough! Stop, stop, O God, I've had enough! (*He flings himself down on the couch, sobbing hysterically; tearing at the horsehair mattress with his teeth, and eating it. The* BARONS, *stupefied, go nearer to him.*)

1ST BARON (*timidly*): Your Highness. . . .

KING (*moaning, with his head buried in the mattress*): I can do nothing! Nothing! I'm as limp and useless as a girl! So long as he's alive, I'll never be able to do a thing. I tremble before him astonished. And I am the King! (*With a sudden cry*) Will no one rid me of him? A priest! A priest who jeers at me and does me injury! Are there none but cowards like myself around me? Are there no men left in England? Oh, my heart! My heart is beating too fast to bear!

(*He lies, still as death on the torn mattress. The four* BARONS *stand around speechless. Suddenly, on a percussion instrument, there rises a rhythmic beating, a sort of muffled tom-tom which is at first only the agitated heartbeats of the* KING, *but which swells and grows more insistent. The four* BARONS *look at each other. Then they straighten, buckle their sword belts, pick up their helmets and go slowly out, leaving the* KING *alone with the muffled rhythm of the heartbeats, which will continue until the murder. The* KING *lies there prostrate, among the upturned benches, in the deserted hall. A torch splutters and goes out. He sits up,*) *looks around, sees they have gone and suddenly realizes why. A wild, lost look comes into his eyes. A moment's pause then he collapses on the bed with a long broken moan.)*

KING: O my Thomas!

(A second torch goes out. Total darkness. Only the steady throb of the heartbeats is heard. A dim light. The forest of pillars again. Canterbury Cathedral. Upstage a small altar, with three steps leading up to it, half screened by a grill. In a corner downstage BECKET, and the YOUNG MONK, who is helping him on with his vestments. Nearby, on a stool, the Archbishop's miter. The tall silver cross is leaning against a pillar.)

BECKET: I must look my best today. Make haste.

(The MONK fumbles with the vestments. The muffled tom-tom is heard distantly at first, then closer.)

MONK: It's difficult with all those little laces. It wants a girl's hands.

BECKET *(softly)*: A man's hands are better, today. Never mind the laces. The alb, quickly. And the stole. And then the cope.

MONK *(conscientiously)*: If it's worth doing it's worth doing well.

BECKET: You're quite right. If it's worth doing it's worth doing well. Do up all the little laces, every one of them. God will give us time. *(A pause. The boy struggles manfully on, putting out his tongue in concentration. The throbbing grows louder. Smiling)* Don't pull your tongue out like that! *(He watches the boy as he works away.)*

MONK *(sweating but content)*: There. That's all done. But I'd rather have cleaned out our pigsty at home! It's not half such hard work!

BECKET: Now the alb. *(A pause)* Were you fond of your pigs?

MONK *(his eyes lighting up)*: Yes, I was.

BECKET: At my father's house, we had some pigs too, when I was a child. *(Smiling)* We're two rough lads from Hastings, you and I! Give me the chasuble. *(BECKET kisses the chasuble and slips it over his head. He looks at the boy and says gently)* Do you miss your knife?

MONK: Yes. *(Pause)* Will it be today?

BECKET *(gravely)*: I think so, my son. Are you afraid?

MONK: Oh, no. Not if we have time to fight. All I want is the chance to strike a few blows first; so I shan't have done nothing but receive them all my life. If I can kill one Norman first—just one, I don't want much—one for one, that will seem fair and right enough to me.

BECKET *(with a kindly smile)*: Are you so very set on killing one?

MONK: One for one. After that, I don't much care if I *am* just a little grain of sand in the machine. Because I know that by putting more and more grains of sand in the machine, one day it will come grinding to a stop.

BECKET *(gently)*: And on that day, what then?

MONK: We'll set a fine, new, well-oiled machine in the place of the old one and this time we'll put the Normans into it instead. *(He asks, quite without irony)* That's what justice means, isn't it? *(BECKET smiles and does not answer him.)*

BECKET: Fetch me the miter. *(He says quietly, as the boy fetches it)* O Lord, You forbade Peter to strike a blow in the Garden of Olives. But

I shall not deprive him of that joy. He has had too few joys in his short span on earth. (*To the boy*) Now give me my silver cross. I must hold it.

MONK (*passing it to him*): Lord, it's heavy! A good swipe with that and they'd feel it! My word, I wish I could have it!

BECKET (*stroking his hair*): Lucky little Saxon! This black world will have been in order to the end, for you. (*He straightens, grave once more*) There. I'm ready, all adorned for Your festivities, Lord. Do not, in this interval of waiting, let one last doubt enter my soul.

(*During this scene, the throbbing has grown louder. Now it mingles with a loud knocking on the door. A* PRIEST *runs in wildly.*)

PRIEST: Your Grace! There are four armed men outside! They say they must see you on behalf of the King. I've barricaded the door but they're breaking it in! They've got hatchets! Quickly! You must go into the back of the church and have the choir gates closed! They're strong enough, they'll hold!

BECKET (*calmly*): It is time for Vespers, William. Does one close the choir gates during Vespers? I never heard of such a thing.

PRIEST (*nonplused*): I know, but. . . .

BECKET: Everything must be the way it should be. The choir gates will remain open. Come, boy, let us go up to the altar. This is no place to be. (*He goes toward the altar, followed by the* YOUNG MONK. *A great crash. The door has given way. The four* BARONS *come in, in their helmets. They fling down their hatchets and draw their swords.* BECKET *turns to face them, grave and calm, at the foot of the altar. They stop a moment, uncertain and disconcerted; four statues, huge and threatening. The tom-tom has stopped. There is nothing now but a heavy silence.* BECKET *says simply*) Here it comes. The supreme folly. This is its hour. (*He holds their eyes. They dare not move. He says coldly*) One does not enter armed into God's house. What do you want?

1ST BARON (*thickly*): Your death. (*A pause.*)

2ND BARON (*thickly*): You bring shame to the King. Flee the country or you're a dead man.

BECKET (*softly*): It is time for the service. (*He turns to the altar and faces the tall crucifix without paying any further attention to them. The throbbing starts again, muffled. The four men close in like automata. The* YOUNG MONK *suddenly leaps forward brandishing the heavy silver cross in order to protect* BECKET, *but one of the* BARONS *swings his sword and fells him to the ground.* BECKET *murmurs, as if in reproach*) Not even one! It would have given him so much pleasure, Lord. (*With a sudden cry*) Oh how difficult You make it all! And how heavy Your honor is to bear! (*He adds, very quietly*) Poor Henry.

(*The four men hurl themselves onto him. He falls at the first blow. They hack at his body, grunting like woodcutters. The* PRIEST *has fled with a long scream, which echoes in the empty cathedral.*

　　Blackout.

　　On the same spot. The* KING, *naked, on bended knees at* BECKET'S *tomb, as in the first scene. Four* MONKS *are whipping him with ropes, almost duplicating the gestures of the* BARONS *as they killed* BECKET.)

KING (*crying out*): Are you satisfied now, Becket? Does this settle our account? Has the honor of God been washed clean? (*The four* MONKS *finish beating him, then kneel down and bow their heads. The* KING *mutters—one feels it is part of the ceremony*) Thank you. Yes, yes, of course, it was agreed, I forgive you. Many thanks. (*The* PAGE *comes forward with a vast cloak, which the* KING *wraps around himself. The* BARONS *surround the* KING *and help him to dress, while the* BISHOPS *and the* CLERGY, *forming a procession, move away solemnly upstage to the strains of the organ. The* KING *dresses hurriedly, with evident bad temper, aided by his* BARONS. *He grimaces ill-humoredly and growls*) The pigs! The Norman Bishops just went through the motions, but those little Saxon monks—my word, they had their money's worth!

(*A* BARON *comes in. A joyful peal of bells is heard.*)

BARON: Sire, the operation has been successful! The Saxon mob is yelling with enthusiasm outside the cathedral, acclaiming your Majesty's name in the same breath as Becket's! If the Saxons are on our side now, Prince Henry's followers look as though they have definitely lost the day.

KING (*with a touch of hypocritical majesty beneath his slightly loutish manner*): The honor of God, gentlemen, is a very good thing, and taken all in all, one gains by having it on one's side. Thomas Becket, who was our friend, used to say so. England will owe her ultimate victory over chaos to him, and it is our wish that, henceforward, he should be honored and prayed to in this Kingdom as a saint. Come, gentlemen. We will determine, tonight, in Council, what posthumous honors to render him and what punishment to deal out to his murderers.

1ST BARON (*imperturbably*): Sire, they are unknown.

KING (*impenetrably*): Our justice will seek them out, Baron, and you will be specially entrusted with this inquiry, so that no one will be in any doubt as to our royal desire to defend the honor of God and the memory of our friend from this day forward.

(*The organ swells triumphantly, mingled with the sound of the bells and the cheering of the crowds as they file out.*)

(*The Curtain Falls.*)

Commentary

Murder in the Cathedral and *Becket* provide more than an occasion for comparing two dramatic studies of an important historical and ecclesiastical figure. Eliot is interested in the spiritual significance of the act of martyrdom, not biography or history. He focuses on what happens within Thomas and what happens because of him. Anouilh concentrates on what happens to him and to his friend and adversary. Anouilh explores the drama of personal relationships that Eliot has described, but not dramatized, as the clash between "the hammer and the anvil." On the other hand, Eliot's central dramatic issue, martyrdom, is not mentioned in *Becket* until Act Four and then only to be contemptuously dismissed by Louis as some kind of neurotic impulse: "You have a taste for martyrdom? You disappoint me. I thought you more healthy-minded" (p. 502).

For Anouilh the powerful excitement of Becket's story lies in the almost endless conflicts it sets vibrating: Becket and Henry, Church and State, England and France, Saxon and Norman, clergy and Henry, clergy and archbishop, king and royal family, court and country, barbarian and civilized courtier, expediency and honor. Anouilh is drawn to Becket because he finds in the archbishop's struggle with his king the clash of ideologies that the playwright has dramatized as a view of life in many of his tragedies and comedies. Wallace Fowlie describes this conflict as a debate between two philosophies:

> one that is determined to exploit human life and profit from it, and another that demands of human life more than it can ever give. On the one side is the character who believes that life has to be tricked and plotted against; and on the other is the character who is determined to ask from life, without subterfuge, without hypocrisy, the ultimate, the absolute.[8]

Anouilh's drama touches upon every phase of man's existence—social, political, economic, religious, moral, philosophical; its 22 scenes enlarge his dramatic arena to include England, France, and Italy—hovel, bedroom, cathedral, palace, dense forest and storm-swept plain. Yet we are never allowed to forget that everything is touched and complicated by the tensions of love and hate informing the friendship of Becket and Henry. Separated by an impossible abyss of nationality, upbringing, character, and way of life, and each incapable ever of understanding the other's feelings or of expressing his own, they are still joined by a bond that even Becket's murder cannot wholly dissolve.

As Becket and Henry begin to relive their memories, after the brief prologue at Becket's grave, Becket, elegant and debonair, is seen dressing his liege. The mood is one of lively good humor and affectionate comradeship, yet underlying it is a subtle crosscurrent hinted at in Anouilh's stage directions: "lightly and inscrutably," "feigning not to understand the question," "putting a touch of contempt in his voice," "a little slyly" (pp. 456-457). The talk is of Becket's Saxon father, "a man of rigid principles," who "contrived" to amass a fortune by collaborating with the Norman conquerors—"a little piece of sleight of hand that men of

---

[8] Wallace Fowlie, *Dionysus in Paris* (New York, 1960), p. 123.

principle are very skillful at in troubled times." Casually and indirectly Anouilh introduces a central condition of his dramatic world, where men of high and responsible position—English monarch and French counterpart, Anglican clergy and Italian Pope—are quite prepared to compromise moral principle for easy expediency and private gain. This world, a far cry from that of *Murder in the Cathedral,* might at first recall *Rosmersholm* except that Anouilh never takes these moral issues with Ibsen's solemnness. Rather, like Shaw, Anouilh laughs at both moral corruption and even those values he affirms.

Because nothing in the world of *Becket* can be taken with the high moral seriousness of *Murder in the Cathedral,* Anouilh replaces Eliot's formal patterns of ritual with a central metaphor of a game in which each character is called upon to play his role to the hilt. In this first scene Becket is playing at being a valet and talks of his father's "sleight of hand." But this topic of conversation itself is a verbal gambit, and Henry would dearly "like to score a point against him occasionally." In the next scene the king thinks he has won a victory when he dramatically appoints Becket chancellor of England and triumphantly declares, "I've managed to surprise you for once" (p. 457). English politics is a chess game for Henry, but one in which he is not always an expert player. Becket, the king believes, will "checkmate" the clergy, and Henry warns them not to rely too much on the chancellor "to play your game" (p. 458). Recurrent metaphors of chess, tennis, hunting, gambling, and magician's tricks define much of the meaning of the action. The games may be as trivial as Henry's use of Becket's forks to bring about a moment of uproarious horseplay at the barons' expense or as serious as Henry's decision to make Becket archbishop of England: ". . . the ball's in our court now" (p. 483). Henry scornfully says to Folliot that he likes playing games, but only with boys his own age (p. 490); yet he is not above playing games with his "great loon" of a son, although his mother reprimands him because "this game is unworthy of you and of us" (p. 508). Louis sees Henry deliberately throwing away political and military advantages against France solely to "score a point" against Becket (p. 502). And Anouilh cannot resist the pleasure of parodying his own metaphor by making an absurd game of the Pope's maneuvering with the cardinal while they discuss Henry's "deep game"; then indeed "the game becomes horribly confusing" (p. 499).

The game well played is at first Becket's highest aim and only love. "Doing what I have to do and doing it well" (p. 476) is his code of personal conduct. Becket throws himself into each role with the zeal of a perfectionist and to the envy of his monarch, who early in the play begrudgingly admits that "drinking and whoring through the town" is "another thing you were better at than me" (p. 455). Becket is the best rider in the kingdom; he is the best host and "the only man in England who knows how to give your friends a royal welcome" (p. 470). Henry has illustration enough to realize that Becket will also, when the time comes, try to be a perfect archbishop ready to declare unflinchingly, "My role is to defend my sheep" (p. 506).

Because Becket sees life as a game in which one must assume many roles, he is very much aware of his clothing and needs a costume symbolic of his role if he is to play the part well. Note how Becket's moral progress can be traced by his changes of costume: an elegant nobleman's short doublet and upturned shoes, the fine coat worn over an even finer doublet, a plain, gray dressing gown, a monk's coarse woolen robe, and at the hour of his death the full vestments of the archbishop of Canterbury. What is the significance of each of these costumes? Becket is also keenly conscious of labels and names which must be assigned these roles. When the king asks if Becket loves him, his friend responds, "I am your servant, my prince" (p. 462). Later he replies to the king's open declaration of love with, "You are our King. We are all your sons and in your hands" (p. 463). When Henry asks the pointed question, "Why do you put labels onto everything to justify your feelings?" Becket answers, "Because, without labels, the world would have no shape, my prince." It is the game, the role, the label that for Becket give form and meaning to a world without order. But the tragedy of living in such a world is that for Becket love is impossible: "How tenderly I would love you, my prince, in an ordered world" (p. 472). At the time of his death he turns wistfully to the young Saxon monk, who wants only a chance to kill one Norman (". . . that will seem fair and right enough to me"), and stroking the boy's hair in a rare gesture of affection, says, "Lucky little Saxon! This black world will have been in order to the end, for you" (p. 512). Despite Becket's earnest prayer the monk dies without striking a blow, and Becket's view of justice is confirmed.

Becket's commitment to the form of things, to the roles in life, raises the central question: Who is Becket? And since Anouilh's drama reflects in its form something of Becket's own capacity for playing games, the playwright gives the question to a stupid baron: "This Becket then, who is he?" Their answers—chancellor of England, a Saxon, a good fighter—do not even satisfy the fourth baron, who waits for Becket to "break cover" (p. 474). But the question is one which Becket's closest friend—and for a time even Becket himself—cannot answer. Note the tones of voice Anouilh gives his hero: "lightly and inscrutably," "smiling," "coldly," "casually," "inscrutably," "stiffly," "icily," "indifferently," "Becket is inaccessible." Only in the brief soliloquies at the ends of the first three acts are we allowed a glimpse under the mask. The old archbishop perhaps best knows the young man who will one day succeed him: "His is a strange, elusive nature. . . . He is as it were detached. As if seeking his real self" (p. 461). Becket is for a long time aware of the limitations and the deficiencies of his attitude toward life. He admits to Gwendolen that he cares for nothing in the whole world and to the king that he is incapable of love. Is he incapable of hatred? Henry perceptively points out that "what looks like morality in you is nothing more than esthetics" (p. 470), and Becket confirms his loyalty only to the form, to the rules of the game, and to the parts he acts. But until his total commitment to the role of archbishop, Becket has not been able to identify himself completely with any role; hence he sees himself as a man without honor: "There is a gap in me where honor ought to be" (p. 471). In a black and disordered world Becket is a man who "tries to save himself from anguish by identifying himself with a role, with a game. Where there is a game, there is a negation of earnestness. But the earnestness is restored in a higher form when there is a total identification with the role."[9]

When Becket early in the play announces that he "adores honor," he means little more than the hedonistic pleasures that Norman luxury provides him, and the scenes of Act One dramatize what Becket calls the improvisation of his honor. But the act closes with the question, "But where is Becket's honor?" The curtain scene of Act Two brings Becket the answer, but even here after he has declared that he cannot serve both God and king, he is self-consciously concerned with the role: "A truly saintly man would never have done the whole thing in one day. . . . I'm setting about it a little clumsily perhaps." In contrast to the agonized soul-searching of Eliot's Becket, he says with gay lightheartedness: "Lord, are You sure You are not tempting me? It all seems far too easy." What position has Becket reached in his ascent by the soliloquy at the close of Act Three: "It has pleased You to make me Archbishop and to set me, like a solitary pawn, face to face with the King, upon the chessboard"?

The death to which Becket inevitably goes is no martyrdom, no earthly fulfilling of God's divine purpose. Becket has been given the responsibility of serving the "honor of God. A frail, incomprehensible honor, vulnerable as a boy-King fleeing from danger" (p. 506). He loves not God but the honor of God, even though he serves God more fully than the self-seeking English clergy or the scheming politician of a Pope, just as earlier he had served the king in battle more courageously than had the barons. The game Becket plays is now for mortal stakes, and his commitment—absurd and courageous—in a world that demands compromise as the price of existence becomes in the hour of supreme folly the honor of man and his destruction: "We must only do—absurdly— what we have been given to do—right to the end" (p. 505). Yet Becket meets his death, not as Eliot's Thomas with a prayer commending his

---

[9] Jacques Guicharnaud (in collaboration with June Beckelman), *Modern French Theatre* (New Haven, 1961), p. 128.

cause and that of the Church to Almighty God, but with the human and personal cry, "Poor Henry."

Becket's dying words echo the king's "O my Thomas," the poignant refrain of a friend who believes himself betrayed. It is easy to point out the faults of Henry as man, king, husband, father, son, and friend. He is, among other things, a coarse sensualist and a conniving ruler who governs by cheap expediency. Yet he has a capacity for friendship greater than any Thomas can experience. When the queen mother acidly scolds her son for allowing Becket to become a threat to the throne, Henry can only cry out, "He is my friend" (p. 486) ; and on another occasion he tells his wife, "I am forced to fight him and crush him, but at least he gave me, with open hands, everything that is at all good in me" (p. 494). Folliot finds it incredible that the king can still love "that mitered hog" even while he plans his destruction (p. 491). There is more than self-pity in Henry's bitter accusation, "Only I loved you and you didn't love me" (p. 488).

When Becket returns the Seal of England, Henry declares with angry determination: "I shall learn to be alone." But without Becket the king's ordered world goes to pieces, for it is Becket who has always shared Henry's pleasure and work and who has taught the king much about the game of statecraft. Without his confidant, adviser, and companion, the king finds himself so bored that he proposes to his barons, "Let us get drunk, like men, all night; until we roll under the table, in vomit and oblivion," and he toasts his "four idiots" and drinks to "comfortable nothingness" (p. 509). Without Becket he is not a man but "a good fat machine." In one of the most theatrically exciting moments of the play, when he learns of Becket's return to England, the king goes berserk, screaming and sobbing hysterically, tearing at the horsehair mattress with his teeth, and eating it until he falls prostrate, "still as death" on the torn mattress, "among the upturned benches, in the deserted hall"— symbols of a disordered world without Becket. As the candle sputters and goes out, as the steady throb of his heartbeat echoes through the dark and lonely palace, we recall the ending of Act One, when Becket shared his bed and comforted his friend, who had been frightened by a nightmare ("My prince . . . my prince . . . sleep in peace. I'm here"), and when the only sound, as the curtain fell, was the contented snoring of the king.

The irreconcilable conflict between the honor of God and the honor of the realm is brought to a stunning climax by the juxtaposition of two formal scenes that dramatize the lonely commitment each man has made. Anouilh resolves his dominant metaphor of life as a game by suggesting that this final game is also a solution and thus more than just another of the games previously played. As Becket prepares to enact his last role at the altar of his cathedral, he straightens and announces gravely, "I'm ready, all adorned for Your festivities, Lord" (p. 512), and a moment later as the barons move toward him with drawn swords, he says softly, "It is time for the service." Following the brief blackout, the ritual is re-enacted on the same spot with four monks flagellating the naked king with gestures that duplicate the barons' hacking at the archbishop's body. The play has come full circle; epilogue is prologue. The king, it would appear, is doing humble penance for his crime, but it is all a masquerade, and Henry admits it is rather absurd. The king is using Becket's death to win the Saxons to his side in the coming struggle with his son. Becket had arrayed himself in the elaborate regalia of an archbishop for his final and finest role; for his masquerade Henry kneels naked—except for his crown—in solitary prayer before the tomb. But what is revealed beneath the cloak is not a man. The mock-ceremony concludes with the king leading a solemn procession of bishops out of the church. "With a touch of hypo-critical majesty beneath his slightly loutish manner," Henry affirms that "the honor of God, gentlemen, is a very good thing, and taken all in all, one gains by having it on one's side." England, he continues, will owe her victory over chaos to Becket, and he talks unctuously of sainthood and posthumous honors and impenetrably of "our justice" that, under the direction of the first baron, will seek out and punish the murderers, so that "no one will be in any doubt as to our royal desire to defend the honor of God and the memory of our friend from this day forward."

At their last meeting on a "vast, arid plain" Becket told his king that he was "waiting for the honor of God and the honor of the King to become one" (p. 505). When the king replied, "You'll wait a long time then!" Becket answered, "Yes. I'm afraid I will." There was a long pause and only the wind was heard "like a shrill dirge." As the final curtain falls, "the organ swells triumphantly, mingled with the sounds of the bells and the cheering of the crowds" to proclaim that the day for which Becket patiently waited has, with devastating irony, come at last.

Questions and Problems

1. Historians have pointed out that Anouilh is in error in making Becket a Saxon when actually he was a Norman whose family came from the vicinity of Rouen. Does this historical inaccuracy damage the play?

2. What is Anouilh's purpose in opening the play with part of the epilogue? What is gained by having the play presented as a flashback?

3. Why does Anouilh provide Becket with the leitmotif of a "gay, ironical Scottish marching song"?

4. Discuss the contribution made by the variety of lighting and sound effects in *Becket*.

5. What does the scene with Gwendolen reveal about Becket and Henry as men? What is the significance of her suicide?

6. On page 474 the fourth baron says that he will wait for Becket "to break cover." Why is the metaphor appropriate? When does Becket break cover?

7. Note how the word *honor* is bandied about by priests and barons, cardinals and kings. What is Anouilh's point in ironically echoing the word throughout the play?

8. Is the scene with the Pope and the cardinal irrelevant? Is it in dubious taste? Can the scene be justified dramatically?

9. What contribution is made by the queen mother and the queen?

10. What does each of these stage properties contribute to the play: the Seal of England, the young Saxon monk's knife, Becket's jeweled crucifix, the archbishop's tall silver cross?

11. What is the function of each of these scenes: a. the visit of Henry and Becket at the Saxon hut; b. the triumphal procession through the French town; c. the last confrontation of Henry and Becket at La Ferté-Bernard?

12. The life and death of the young Saxon monk are an agon in miniature. What is his part in underscoring the central themes, attitudes, and conflicts in *Becket*?

13. Is the total effect of the episodic structure in *Becket* cluttered and confused? What advantages are there in the quick juxtaposition of scenes? What is Anouilh's purpose in presenting so panoramic a view? What devices does he employ to unify his play?

14. Evaluate this opinion of Becket's attitude toward God: "It is clear enough that Thomas doubts the existence of the God whose honor he assumed in that empty cathedral somewhere in France. If he has great faith, it is a faith in himself and in the image he has created of his best self. His prayers and apostrophes to God only reflect the perfectionism of the aesthetic moralist who is playing his role to the fingertips."[10]

15. *Becket* has been called an historical play, a satirical comedy, and a tragedy. Which comes closest to the concerns of the play?

16. The most important and baffling problem of Anouilh's drama is achieving an understanding of the friendship between Henry and Becket. Consider these questions in arriving at some final statement of what the play expresses about the friendship of these men:

Why is each drawn to the other? What characteristics do they share? In what ways are they different? How important is the difference in their nationalities? What is the difference in their views of the meaning of friendship? Why does each think he has been betrayed by the other? To what extent is each correct? Why is total understanding between the two impossible? How close does each come to understanding the other at La Ferté-Bernard? Does either

---

[10] Leonard Cabell Pronko, *The World of Jean Anouilh* (Berkeley and Los Angeles, 1961), pp. 59-60.

want a reconciliation? What does each man most admire in the other after they have become mortal enemies?

Why is Becket unable to love Henry as the king wants him to? What does Becket mean when he tells Gwendolen, "I don't like being loved" (p. 467)? How do you interpret his answer to the king's question: "Tell me, do you believe in love, Thomas?" (p. 469)? What does Becket mean when he declares, "I am no longer like myself" (p. 506)? Compare this statement with Henry's remark that Becket has "made a different man of me, in a way" (p. 470).

Consider each of the following bits of dialogue as it might cast light on a final view of this friendship:

Becket to Henry: "One can permit oneself anything, Sire, but one must never indulge" (p. 480)

Becket to Henry: "If I become Archbishop, I can no longer be your friend" (p. 484)

Henry to Becket: "And you are the only man I trust" (p. 484)

Becket to Louis: "Sire, we loved each other and I think he cannot forgive me for preferring God to him" (p. 502)

Young queen to Henry: "I am tired of having my life encumbered with this man. Becket! Always Becket!" (p. 509).

Since the king frequently asserts that Becket does not love him, how can he say to the queen mother: "I have always been alone, and no one on this earth has ever loved me except Becket!" (p. 495)? How can Henry to the moment of Becket's death declare his love for a man he wants murdered?

Is it possible, finally, to say what *Becket* is dramatizing through this friendship? If life is a game, if public life consists of roles to be chosen and played, must a man ultimately commit himself to one of the roles, even while knowing that it is only a role? Is private life (friendship) the only area of experience in which it is not necessary to assume a role? Must a man sacrifice his private life to the larger demands of his public roles? What is Becket's and Henry's final position on this conflict between public and private interests? Does the play argue that one or the other is right in his commitment, or does it suggest a larger view of life than that held by either the protagonist or the antagonist?

17. Compare the reviews of the two New York productions in the *New York Theatre Critics' Reviews* for 1960 and 1961. Do you agree with their consensus that Henry is a more vivid and successfully created character than Becket? What problems do the critics raise, as members of a first-night audience, that do not trouble the reader?

18. What are some of the dramatic devices Anouilh uses to create humor? To what extent is his comic spirit Shavian?

19. Eddie Carbone in *A View from the Bridge* is another man who dies defending his honor. Contrast the honor of Eddie and Becket. Each play implies that the hero's death is inevitable. Distinguish the reasons for this necessity.

20. Which of Eliot's tempters would Anouilh's Becket be most in danger of yielding to? Which would be no temptation at all? Compare the characters of the two Beckets.

21. Compare Becket's first and last words in *Becket* with those in *Murder in the Cathedral*. What is the difference in the preparations for death made by each? What is the significance of these contrasts? What is the final view of the world in each play?

22. Contrast the differences in the functions of the clergy in *Becket* and the priests in *Murder in the Cathedral*.

23. Which Becket do you prefer—Eliot's or Anouilh's? Why? Which do you think is the better play? Defend your position.

24. Compare *Murder in the Cathedral* and *Becket* with Tennyson's poetic drama *Becket*.

THORNTON WILDER

The Skin of Our Teeth

Biography

THORNTON NIVEN WILDER, three times winner of the Pultizer Prize
and an outstanding figure in contemporary American letters as both
novelist and playwright, was born in Madison, Wisconsin, on April 17,
1897. After living with his family in China for several years, he attended
Oberlin College and in 1917 entered Yale as a junior. Returning to Yale
after serving a year in the Coast Artillery Corps in World War I, Wilder
attracted attention as an able young playwright; several of his one-act
plays written at Yale were later published. After graduating in 1920, he
spent a year abroad studying archaeology at the American Academy in
Rome and then returned to undertake further graduate work at Princeton and to teach at the Lawrenceville School. Later he spent six years
as a member of the English staff at the University of Chicago.

With the publication of his second novel, *The Bridge of San Luis
Rey*, a 1928 Pulitzer Prize winner, Wilder achieved merited recognition
here and abroad. His success as a playwright, however, came much later
with *Our Town*, produced on Broadway in 1938. This experimental
drama, staged without scenery, won him another Pulitzer Prize, as did his
controversial *The Skin of Our Teeth* in 1942. After serving as an officer
in the Air Intelligence Combat Force in North Africa and Italy in World
War II, Wilder resumed his writing. His first play in more than a decade,
The Alcestiad, had its world première in Edinburgh in the summer of
1955. Wilder is now at work on *Plays for Bleecker Street*, a double cycle
of fourteen one-act plays, which is to be his artistic and philosophic
summing up. Two plays from the cycle "The Seven Ages of Man" and
one from the cycle "The Seven Deadly Sins" were produced early in 1962.

All of Wilder's plays are concerned with man in his larger, more
universal aspects. As he writes of *The Alcestiad:* "On one level my play
recounts the life of a woman—of many women—from bewildered bride to
sorely tested wife to overburdened old age. On another level it is a widely
romantic story of gods and men, of death and hell and resurrection, of
great loves, and great trials, of usurpation and revenge. On another level,
however, it is a comedy . . . about the extreme difficulty of any dialogue
between heaven and earth, about the misunderstandings that result from
the 'incommensurability of things human and divine.' " The same univer-
sality is seen in *The Skin of Our Teeth*, a kind of allegorical comedy

tracing the course of human history from Adam and Eve to the present. Despite all tribulations, war, and crises, with faith and knowledge and the will to survive, humanity, says Wilder, will always struggle to rise above chaos and destruction "to build new worlds." The essential dignity of the human being will triumph and endure through the years, although there will always be the struggle between good and evil and man will perennially escape destruction by the skin of his teeth.

Wilder's theme is a traditional one in literature and, when stated in oversimplified, bald prose, may appear trite. It is not what Wilder says but how he says it that is intriguingly new. Like O'Neill a generation ago and Williams today, Wilder is searching for fresh and vital dramatic expression. Not only does he satirize many of the foibles and absurdities of American home life, but he also ridicules his own dramatic medium, the theater, and most of the realistic theatrical conventions set up by Ibsen sixty years earlier. In one sense, Wilder is returning to an earlier mode of drama before the modern realistic theater had created the barrier of a "fourth wall" between audience and actor. Moreover, he keeps his audience fully aware of the fact that they are in a theater, whereas most of his predecessors since Ibsen's time had attempted to create an illusion of reality, a literal copy of life. Wilder's approach to dramaturgy is sometimes called "nonrepresentational" because it does not try to represent on stage life as it is, but rather it creates a view of life while recognizing the distinctly artificial nature of the theater.

Principal Works

NOVELS

The Cabala (1926)
The Bridge of San Luis Rey (1927)
The Woman of Andros (1930)

Heaven's My Destination (1935)
The Ides of March (1948)

COLLECTIONS OF SHORT PLAYS

The Angel That Troubled the Waters (1928)

The Long Christmas Dinner (1931)

PLAYS

The Merchant of Yonkers (1938; rewritten as *The Matchmaker* in 1954)
Our Town (1938)

The Skin of Our Teeth (1942)
The Alcestiad (1955) (first entitled *A Life in the Sun*)
Plays for Bleecker Street (1962-   )

Selected Descriptive Bibliography

Burbank, Rex, *Thornton Wilder,* New York, 1961.
The first full-length book on Wilder. An intelligent critical evaluation of Wilder's artistic achievement and its intellectual tradition.

Cowley, Malcolm, "The Man Who Abolished Time," *Saturday Review* (Oct. 6, 1956), 13-14, 50-52; adapted from his Introduction to *A Thornton Wilder Trio* (New York, 1956).
Cowley reassesses Wilder as "the artist of the anachronism" in an essay on the theme of time in Wilder's novels and plays.

Fergusson, Francis, "The Search for New Standards in the Theatre," *Kenyon Review,* XVII (Autumn, 1955), 581-596.
Studying the American theater between two world wars, Fergusson evaluates Wilder's solutions of the problem of writing for the commercial theater.

_____, "Three Allegorists: Brecht, Wilder and Eliot," *Sewanee Review,* LXIV (Fall, 1956), 544-573; reprinted in his *The Human Image in Dramatic Literature* (New York, 1957), 41-71.
Fergusson criticizes Wilder for his failure to achieve an "imaginative or intellectual unity" of his allegorical meanings and his theatrical devices.

Fuller, Edmund, "Thornton Wilder: the Notation of the Heart," *American Scholar,* XXVIII (Spring, 1959), 210-217.
Fuller finds in Wilder "one of the most searching, balanced and mature visions of ourselves as Man that any American writer offers us."

Hewitt, Barnard, "Thornton Wilder Says 'Yes,' " *Tulane Drama Review,* IV (December, 1959), 110-120.
An analysis of the underlying affirmations in Wilder's three major plays.

Lewis, Flora, "Thornton Wilder at 65 Looks Ahead—and Back," *New York Times,* April 15, 1962, Sec. 6, pp. 28-29, 54-58.
Wilder presents his views of the contemporary scene and discusses his plans for the future.

Wilder, Thornton, "Some Thoughts on Playwriting," in *The Intent of the Artist,* ed. Augusto Centeno (Princeton, 1941), pp. 83-98; reprinted in *Playwrights on Playwriting,* ed. Toby Cole (New York, 1960), pp. 106-115.
Some illuminating observations by the playwright on the nature of his craft.

_____, "The Silent Generation," *Harper's,* CCVI (April, 1953), 34-36.
Wilder sympathetically describes youth in the 1950s and contrasts its problems and aspirations with those a generation ago.

_____, "A Platform and a Passion or Two," *Harper's,* CCXV (October, 1957), 48-51; reprinted as the Preface to *Three Plays* (New York, 1957).
Wilder argues the need for innovation in the modern theater to replace realistic conventions of nineteenth-century drama.

The Skin of Our Teeth THORNTON WILDER

CHARACTERS

ANNOUNCER	DOCTOR	FORTUNE TELLER
SABINA	PROFESSOR	2 CHAIR PUSHERS
MR. FITZPATRICK	JUDGE	6 CONVEENERS
MRS. ANTROBUS	HOMER	BROADCAST OFFICIAL
DINOSAUR	MISS E. MUSE	DEFEATED CANDIDATE
MAMMOTH	MISS T. MUSE	MR. TREMAYNE
TELEGRAPH BOY	MISS M. MUSE	HESTER
GLADYS	2 USHERS	IVY
HENRY	2 DRUM MAJORETTES	FRED BAILEY
MR. ANTROBUS		

ACT ONE: *Home, Excelsior, New Jersey.*
ACT TWO: *Atlantic City Boardwalk.*
ACT THREE: *Home, Excelsior, New Jersey.*

The Skin of Our Teeth was first performed at the Shubert Theater, New Haven, Connecticut, October 15, 1942, and then in New York City at the Plymouth Theater, November 18, 1942.

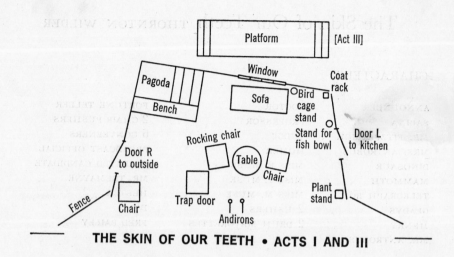

THE SKIN OF OUR TEETH • ACTS I AND III

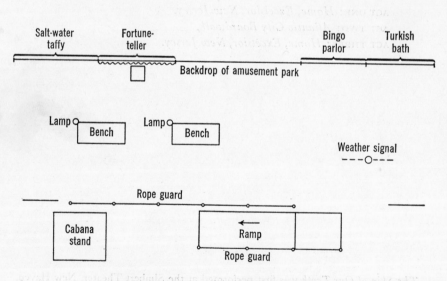

THE SKIN OF OUR TEETH • ACT II

Act One

A projection screen in the middle of the curtain. The first lantern slide: the name of the theatre, and the words: NEWS EVENTS OF THE WORLD. An ANNOUNCER's *voice is heard.*

ANNOUNCER: The management takes pleasure in bringing to you—The News Events of the World. (*Slide of the sun appearing above the horizon*) Freeport, Long Island:

The sun rose this morning at 6:32 a.m. This gratifying event was first reported by Mrs. Dorothy Stetson of Freeport, Long Island, who promptly telephoned the Mayor.

The Society for Affirming the End of the World at once went into a special session and postponed the arrival of that event for TWENTY-FOUR HOURS.

All honor to Mrs. Stetson for her public spirit.

New York City: (*Slide of the front doors of the theatre in which this play is playing; three cleaning* WOMEN *with mops and pails*)

The X Theatre. During the daily cleaning of this theatre a number of lost objects were collected as usual by Mesdames Simpson, Pateslewski, and Moriarty.

Among these objects found today was a wedding ring, inscribed: To Eva from Adam. Genesis II:18.[1]

The ring will be restored to the owner or owners, if their credentials are satisfactory.

Tippehatchee, Vermont: (*Slide representing a glacier*)

The unprecedented cold weather of this summer has produced a condition that has not yet been satisfactorily explained. There is a report that a wall of ice is moving southward across these counties. The disruption of communications by the cold wave now crossing the country has rendered exact information difficult, but little credence is given to the rumor that the ice had pushed the Cathedral of Montreal as far as St. Albans, Vermont.

For further information see your daily papers.

Excelsior,[2] New Jersey: (*Slide of a modest suburban home*)

---

[1] "And the Lord God said, It is not good that the man should be alone; I will make him an help meet for him."

[2] Latin for *higher.*

The home of Mr. George Antrobus,[3] the inventor of the wheel. The discovery of the wheel, following so closely on the discovery of the lever, has centered the attention of the country on Mr. Antrobus of this attractive suburban residence district. This is his home, a commodious seven-room house, conveniently situated near a public school, a Methodist church, and a firehouse; it is right handy to an A. and P. (*Slide of* MR. ANTROBUS *on his front steps, smiling and lifting his straw hat. He holds a wheel*) Mr. Antrobus, himself. He comes of very old stock and has made his way up from next to nothing.

It is reported that he was once a gardener, but left that situation under circumstances that have been variously reported.

Mr. Antrobus is a veteran of foreign wars, and bears a number of scars, front and back. (*Slide of* MRS. ANTROBUS, *holding some roses*) This is Mrs. Antrobus, the charming and gracious president of the Excelsior Mothers' Club.

Mrs. Antrobus is an excellent needlewoman; it is she who invented the apron on which so many interesting changes have been rung since. (*Slide of the* FAMILY *and* SABINA)

Here we see the Antrobuses with their two children, Henry and Gladys, and friend. The friend in the rear is Lily Sabina, the maid. I know we all want to congratulate this typical American family on its enterprise. We all wish Mr. Antrobus a successful future. Now the management takes you to the interior of this home for a brief visit. (*Curtain rises. Living room of a commuter's home.* SABINA—*straw-blonde, over-rouged—is standing by the window back center, a feather duster under her elbow.*)

SABINA: Oh, oh, oh! Six o'clock and the master not home yet.

Pray God nothing serious has happened to him crossing the Hudson River. If anything happened to him, we would certainly be inconsolable and have to move into a less desirable residence district.

The fact is I don't know what'll become of us. Here it is the middle of August and the coldest day of the year. It's simply freezing; the dogs are sticking to the sidewalks; can anybody explain that? No. But I'm not surprised. The whole world's at sixes and sevens, and why the house hasn't fallen down about our ears long ago is a miracle to me. (*A fragment of the right wall leans precariously over the stage.* SABINA *looks at it nervously and it slowly rights itself*)

Every night this same anxiety as to whether the master will get home safely: whether he'll bring home anything to eat. In the midst of life we are in the midst of death, a truer word was never said. (*The fragment of scenery flies up into the lofts.* SABINA *is struck dumb with surprise, shrugs her shoulders and starts dusting* MR. ANTROBUS' *chair, including the under side*)

Of course, Mr. Antrobus is a very fine man, an excellent husband and father, a pillar of the church, and has all the best interests of the community at heart. Of course, every muscle goes tight every time he

---

[3] Antrobus is derived from the Greek *anthrōpos,* meaning *man* or *human being.*

passes a policeman; but what I think is that there are certain charges that ought not to be made, and I think I may add, ought not to be allowed to be made; we're all human; who isn't? (*She dusts* MR. ANTRO-BUS' *rocking chair*)

Mrs. Antrobus is as fine a woman as you could hope to see. She lives only for her children; and if it would be any benefit to her children she'd see the rest of us stretched out dead at her feet without turning a hair,—that's the truth. If you want to know anything more about Mrs. Antrobus, just go and look at a tigress, and look hard.

As to the children—

Well, Henry Antrobus is a real, clean-cut American boy. He'll graduate from High School one of these days, if they make the alphabet any easier.—Henry, when he has a stone in his hand, has a perfect aim, he can hit anything from a bird to an older brother—Oh! I didn't mean to say that!—but it certainly was an unfortunate accident, and it was very hard getting the police out of the house.

Mr. and Mrs. Antrobus' daughter is named Gladys. She'll make some good man a good wife some day, if he'll just come down off the movie screen and ask her.

So here we are!

We've managed to survive for some time now, catch as catch can, the fat and the lean, and if the dinosaurs don't trample us to death, and if the grasshoppers don't eat up our garden, we'll all live to see better days, knock on wood.

Each new child that's born to the Antrobuses seems to them to be sufficient reason for the whole universe's being set in motion; and each new child that dies seems to them to have been spared a whole world of sorrow, and what the end of it will be is still very much an open question.

We've rattled along, hot and cold, for some time now—(*A portion of the wall above the door, right, flies up into the air and disappears*)—and my advice to you is not to inquire into why or whither, but just enjoy your ice cream while it's on your plate,—that's my philosophy.

Don't forget that a few years ago we came through the depression by the skin of our teeth! One more tight squeeze like that and where will we be? (*This is a cue line.* SABINA *looks angrily at the kitchen door and repeats:*)

. . . we came through the depression by the skin of our teeth; one more tight squeeze like that and where will we be? (*Flustered, she looks through the opening in the right wall; then goes to the window and re-opens the Act*)

Oh, oh, oh! Six o'clock and the master not home yet. Pray God nothing has happened to him crossing the Hudson. Here it is the middle of August and the coldest day of the year. It's simply freezing; the dogs are sticking. One more tight squeeze like that and where will we be?

VOICE (*off stage*): Make up something! Invent something!

SABINA: Well . . . uh . . . this certainly is a fine American home . . . and—uh . . . everybody's very happy . . . and—uh . . . (*Suddenly flings pretense to the winds and coming downstage says with indignation:*) I can't invent any words for this play, and I'm glad I can't. I hate this play and every word in it.

As for me, I don't understand a single word of it, anyway,—all about the troubles the human race has gone through, there's a subject for you.

Besides the author hasn't made up his silly mind as to whether we're all living back in caves or in New Jersey today, and that's the way it is all the way through.

Oh—why can't we have plays like we used to have—*Peg o' My Heart,* and *Smilin' Thru,* and *The Bat,* good entertainment with a message you can take home with you?

I took this hateful job because I had to. For two years I've sat up in my room living on a sandwich and a cup of tea a day, waiting for better times in the theatre. And look at me now: I—I who've played *Rain* and *The Barretts of Wimpole Street* and *First Lady*[4]—God in Heaven!

MR. FITZPATRICK (*the* STAGE MANAGER *puts his head out from the hole in the scenery*) : Miss Somerset!! Miss Somerset!

SABINA: Oh! Anyway!—nothing matters! It'll all be the same in a hundred years. (*Loudly*) We came through the depression by the skin of our teeth,—that's true!—one more tight squeeze like that and where will we be?

(*Enter* MRS. ANTROBUS, *a mother.*)

MRS. ANTROBUS: Sabina, you've let the fire go out.

SABINA (*in a lather*) : One-thing-and-another; don't-know-whether-my-wits-are-upside-or-down; might-as-well-be-dead-as-alive-in-a-house-all-sixes-and-sevens. . . .

MRS. ANTROBUS: You've let the fire go out. Here it is the coldest day of the year right in the middle of August, and you've let the fire go out.

SABINA: Mrs. Antrobus, I'd like to give my two weeks' notice, Mrs. Antrobus. A girl like I can get a situation in a home where they're rich enough to have a fire in every room, Mrs. Antrobus, and a girl don't have to carry the responsibility of the whole house on her two shoulders. And a home without children, Mrs. Antrobus, because children are a thing only a parent can stand, and a truer word was never said; and a home, Mrs. Antrobus, where the master of the house don't pinch decent, self-respecting girls when he meets them in a dark corridor. I mention no names and make no charges. So you have my notice, Mrs. Antrobus. I hope that's perfectly clear.

MRS. ANTROBUS: You've let the fire go out!—Have you milked the mammoth?

SABINA: I don't understand a word of this play.—Yes, I've milked the mammoth.

MRS. ANTROBUS: Until Mr. Antrobus comes home we have no food and we have no fire. You'd better go over to the neighbors and borrow some fire.

SABINA: Mrs. Antrobus! I can't! I'd die on the way, you know I would. It's worse than January. The dogs are sticking to the sidewalks. I'd die.

---

[4] Miss Somerset's taste runs to an assortment of conventional popular British and American plays written from 1912 to 1935.

MRS. ANTROBUS: Very well, I'll go.

SABINA (*even more distraught, coming forward and sinking on her knees*):
You'd never come back alive; we'd all perish; if you weren't here, we'd
just perish. How do we know Mr. Antrobus'll be back? We don't know.
If you go out, I'll just kill myself.

MRS. ANTROBUS: Get up, Sabina.

SABINA: Every night it's the same thing. Will he come back safe, or won't
he? Will we starve to death, or freeze to death, or boil to death or will
we be killed by burglars? I don't know why we go on living. I don't know
why we go on living at all. It's easier being dead.

(*She flings her arms on the table and buries her head in them. In each of
the succeeding speeches she flings her head up—and sometimes her hands
—then quickly buries her head again.*)

MRS. ANTROBUS: The same thing! Always throwing up the sponge, Sabina.
Always announcing your own death. But give you a new hat—or a plate
of ice cream—or a ticket to the movies, and you want to live forever.

SABINA: You don't care whether we live or die; all you care about is those
children. If it would be any benefit to them you'd be glad to see us all
stretched out dead.

MRS. ANTROBUS: Well, maybe I would.

SABINA: And what do they care about? Themselves—that's all they care
about. (*Shrilly*) They make fun of you behind your back. Don't tell me:
they're ashamed of you. Half the time, they pretend they're someone else's
children. Little thanks you get from them.

MRS. ANTROBUS: I'm not asking for any thanks.

SABINA: And Mr. Antrobus—you don't understand *him*. All that work he
does—trying to discover the alphabet and the multiplication table. Whenever he tries to learn anything you fight against it.

MRS. ANTROBUS: Oh, Sabina, I know you. When Mr. Antrobus raped you
home from your Sabine hills,[5] he did it to insult me. He did it for your
pretty face, and to insult me. You were the new wife, weren't you? For
a year or two you lay on your bed all day and polished the nails on your
hands and feet. You made puff-balls of the combings of your hair and
you blew them up to the ceiling. And I washed your underclothes and I
made you chicken broths. I bore children and between my very groans
I stirred the cream that you'd put on your face. But I knew you wouldn't
last. You didn't last.

SABINA: But it was I who encouraged Mr. Antrobus to make the alphabet.
I'm sorry to say it, Mrs. Antrobus, but you're not a beautiful woman, and
you can never know what a man could do if he tried. It's girls like I who
inspire the multiplication table. I'm sorry to say it, but you're not a beautiful woman, Mrs. Antrobus, and that's the God's truth.

MRS. ANTROBUS: And you didn't last—you sank to the kitchen. And what
do you do there? *You let the fire go out!* No wonder to you it seems easier
being dead. Reading and writing and counting on your fingers is all very

---

[5] According to legend, the women of the ancient Sabine tribe living in the mountains east of the Tiber were stolen from their families by the Romans in the early
days of Rome.

well in their way,—but I keep the home going.—There's that dinosaur on the front lawn again.—Shoo! Go away. Go away.

(*The baby* DINOSAUR *puts his head in the window.*)

DINOSAUR: It's cold.

MRS. ANTROBUS: You go around to the back of the house where you belong.

DINOSAUR: It's cold.

(*The* DINOSAUR *disappears.* MRS. ANTROBUS *goes calmly out.* SABINA *slowly raises her head and speaks to the audience. The central portion of the center wall rises, pauses, and disappears into the loft.*)

SABINA: Now that you audience are listening to this, too, I understand it a little better. I wish eleven o'clock were here; I don't want to be dragged through this whole play again. (*The* TELEGRAPH BOY *is seen entering along the back wall of the stage from the right. She catches sight of him and calls:*) Mrs. Antrobus! Mrs. Antrobus! Help! There's a strange man coming to the house. He's coming up the walk, help!

(*Enter* MRS. ANTROBUS *in alarm, but efficient.*)

MRS. ANTROBUS: Help me quick! (*They barricade the door by piling the furniture against it*) Who is it? What do you want?

TELEGRAPH BOY: A telegram for Mrs. Antrobus from Mr. Antrobus in the city.

SABINA: Are you sure, are you sure? Maybe it's just a trap!

MRS. ANTROBUS: I know his voice, Sabina. We can open the door. (*Enter the* TELEGRAPH BOY, *12 years old, in uniform. The* DINOSAUR *and* MAMMOTH *slip by him into the room and settle down front right*) I'm sorry we kept you waiting. We have to be careful, you know. (*To the* ANIMALS) Hm! . . . Will you be quiet? (*They nod*) Have you had your supper? (*They nod*) Are you *ready* to come in? (*They nod*) Young man, have you any fire with you? Then light the grate, will you? (*He nods, produces something like a briquet; and kneels by the imagined fireplace, footlights center. Pause*) What are people saying about this cold weather? (*He makes a doubtful shrug with his shoulders*) Sabina, take this stick and go and light the stove.

SABINA: Like I told you, Mrs. Antrobus; two weeks. That's the law. I hope that's perfectly clear. (*Exit.*)

MRS. ANTROBUS: What about this cold weather?

TELEGRAPH BOY (*lowered eyes*): Of course, I don't know anything . . . but they say there's a wall of ice moving down from the North, that's what they say. We can't get Boston by telegraph, and they're burning pianos in Hartford.

. . . It moves everything in front of it, churches and post offices and city halls.

I live in Brooklyn myself.

MRS. ANTROBUS: What are people doing about it?

TELEGRAPH BOY: Well . . . uh . . . Talking, mostly. Or just what you'd do a day in February. There are some that are trying to go South and the roads are crowded; but you can't take old people and children very far in a cold like this.

MRS. ANTROBUS: —What's this telegram you have for me?

TELEGRAPH BOY (*fingertips to his forehead*) : If you wait just a minute; I've got to remember it. (*The* ANIMALS *have left their corner and are nosing him. Presently they take places on either side of him, leaning against his hips, like heraldic beasts*) This telegram was flashed from Murray Hill to University Heights! And then by puffs of smoke from University Heights to Staten Island. And then by lantern from Staten Island to Plainfield, New Jersey. What hath God wrought! (*He clears his throat*)

"To Mrs. Antrobus, Excelsior, New Jersey:

My dear wife, will be an hour late. Busy day at the office. Don't worry the children about the cold just keep them warm burn everything except Shakespeare." (*Pause.*)

MRS. ANTROBUS : Men! —He knows I'd burn ten Shakespeares to prevent a child of mine from having one cold in the head. What does it say next? (*Enter* SABINA.)

TELEGRAPH BOY: "Have made great discoveries today have separated em from en."

SABINA: I know what that is, that's the alphabet, yes it is. Mr. Antrobus is just the cleverest man. Why, when the alphabet's finished, we'll be able to tell the future and everything.

TELEGRAPH BOY: Then listen to this: "Ten tens make a hundred semicolon consequences far-reaching." (*Watches for effect.*)

MRS. ANTROBUS : The earth's turning to ice, and all he can do is to make up new numbers.

TELEGRAPH BOY: Well, Mrs. Antrobus, like the head man at our office said: a few more discoveries like that and we'll be worth freezing.

MRS. ANTROBUS : What does he say next?

TELEGRAPH BOY: I . . . I can't do this last part very well. (*He clears his throat and sings*) "Happy w'dding ann'vers'ry to you, Happy ann'vers'ry to you—"

(*The* ANIMALS *begin to howl soulfully;* SABINA *screams with pleasure.*)

MRS. ANTROBUS : Dolly! Frederick! Be quiet.

TELEGRAPH BOY (*above the din*) : "Happy w'dding ann'vers'ry, dear Eva; happy w'dding ann'vers'ry to you."

MRS. ANTROBUS : Is that in the telegram? Are they singing telegrams now? (*He nods*) The earth's getting so silly no wonder the sun turns cold.

SABINA: Mrs. Antrobus, I want to take back the notice I gave you. Mrs. Antrobus, I don't want to leave a house that gets such interesting telegrams and I'm sorry for anything I said. I really am.

MRS. ANTROBUS : Young man, I'd like to give you something for all this trouble; Mr. Antrobus isn't home yet and I have no money and no food in the house—

TELEGRAPH BOY: Mrs. Antrobus . . . I don't like to . . . appear to . . . ask for anything, but . . .

MRS. ANTROBUS : What is it you'd like?

TELEGRAPH BOY: Do you happen to have an old needle you could spare? My wife just sits home all day thinking about needles.

SABINA (*shrilly*) : We only got two in the house. Mrs. Antrobus, you know we only got two in the house.

MRS. ANTROBUS *(after a look at* SABINA *taking a needle from her collar)* :
Why yes, I can spare this.

TELEGRAPH BOY *(lowered eyes)* : Thank you, Mrs. Antrobus. Mrs. Antrobus,
can I ask you something else? I have two sons of my own; if the cold gets
worse, what should I do?

SABINA: I think we'll all perish, that's what I think. Cold like this in August
is just the end of the whole world.
(Silence.)

MRS. ANTROBUS: I don't know. After all, what does one do about anything?
Just keep as warm as you can. And don't let your wife and children see
that you're worried.

TELEGRAPH BOY: Yes . . . Thank you, Mrs. Antrobus. Well, I'd better be
going.—Oh, I forgot! There's one more sentence in the telegram. "Three
cheers have invented the wheel."

MRS. ANTROBUS: A wheel? What's a wheel?

TELEGRAPH BOY: I don't know. That's what it said. The sign for it is like
this. Well, goodbye.
(The WOMEN *see him to the door, with goodbyes and injunctions to
keep warm.)*

SABINA *(apron to her eyes, wailing)* : Mrs. Antrobus, it looks to me like all
the nice men in the world are already married; I don't know why that is.
(Exit.)

MRS. ANTROBUS *(thoughtful; to the* ANIMALS*)* : Do you ever remember hearing tell of any cold like this in August? *(The* ANIMALS *shake their heads)*
From your grandmothers or anyone? *(They shake their heads)* Have you
any suggestions? *(They shake their heads. She pulls her shawl around,
goes to the front door and opening it an inch calls:)* HENRY. GLADYS.
CHILDREN. Come right in and get warm. No, no, when mama says a
thing she means it. Henry! HENRY. Put down that stone. You know
what happened last time. *(Shriek)* HENRY! Put down that stone!
Gladys! Put down your dress!! Try and be a lady.
(The CHILDREN *bound in and dash to the fire. They take off their winter
things and leave them in heaps on the floor.)*

GLADYS: Mama, I'm hungry. Mama, why is it so cold?

HENRY *(at the same time)* : Mama, why doesn't it snow? Mama, when's
supper ready? Maybe, it'll snow and we can make snowballs.

GLADYS: Mama, it's so cold that in one more minute I just couldn't of
stood it.

MRS. ANTROBUS: Settle down, both of you, I want to talk to you. *(She draws
up a hassock and sits front center over the orchestra pit before the imaginary fire. The* CHILDREN *stretch out on the floor, leaning against her lap.
Tableau by Raphael.*[6] *The* ANIMALS *edge up and complete the triangle)*
It's just a cold spell of some kind. Now listen to what I'm saying: When
your father comes home I want you to be extra quiet. He's had a hard
day at the office and I don't know but what he may have one of his

---

[6] Raffaello Sanzio (1483-1520), the great Italian Renaissance painter, especially
famous for his Madonnas.

moods. I just got a telegram from him very happy and excited, and you know what that means. Your father's temper's uneven; I guess you know that. (*Shriek*) Henry! Henry! Why—why can't you remember to keep your hair down over your forehead? You must keep that scar covered up. Don't you know that when your father sees it he loses all control over himself? He goes crazy. He wants to die. (*After a moment's despair she collects herself decisively, wets the hem of her apron in her mouth and starts polishing his forehead vigorously*) Lift your head up. Stop squirming. Blessed me, sometimes I think that it's going away—and then there it is: just as red as ever.

HENRY: Mama, today at school two teachers forgot and called me by my old name. They forgot, Mama. You'd better write another letter to the principal, so that he'll tell them I've changed my name. Right out in class they called me: Cain.

MRS. ANTROBUS (*putting her hand on his mouth, too late; hoarsely*): Don't say it. (*Polishing feverishly*) If you're good they'll forget it. Henry, you didn't hit anyone . . . today, did you?

HENRY: Oh . . . no-o-o!

MRS. ANTROBUS (*still working, not looking at* GLADYS): And, Gladys, I want you to be especially nice to your father tonight. You know what he calls you when you're good—his little angel, his little star. Keep your dress down like a little lady. And keep your voice nice and low. Gladys Antrobus!! What's that red stuff you have on your face? (*Slaps her*) You're a filthy destestable child! (*Rises in real, though temporary, repudiation and despair*) Get away from me, both of you! I wish I'd never seen sight or sound of you. Let the cold come! I can't stand it. I don't want to go on. (*She walks away.*)

GLADYS (*weeping*): All the girls at school do, Mama.

MRS. ANTROBUS (*shrieking*): I'm through with you, that's all!—Sabina! Sabina!—Don't you know your father'd go crazy if he saw that paint on your face? Don't you know your father thinks you're perfect? Don't you know he couldn't live if he didn't think you were perfect?—Sabina!
(*Enter* SABINA.)

SABINA: Yes, Mrs. Antrobus!

MRS. ANTROBUS: Take this girl out into the kitchen and wash her face with the scrubbing brush.

MR. ANTROBUS (*outside, roaring*): "I've been working on the railroad, all the livelong day . . . etc."
(*The* ANIMALS *start running around in circles, bellowing.* SABINA *rushes to the window.*)

MRS. ANTROBUS: Sabina, what's that noise outside?

SABINA: Oh, it's a drunken tramp. It's a giant, Mrs. Antrobus. We'll all be killed in our beds, I know it!

MRS. ANTROBUS: Help me quick. Quick. Everybody. (*Again they stack all the furniture against the door.* MR. ANTROBUS *pounds and bellows*) Who is it? What do you want?—Sabina, have you any boiling water ready?—Who is it?

MR. ANTROBUS: Broken-down camel of a pig's snout, open this door.

MRS. ANTROBUS: God be praised! It's your father.—Just a minute. George!—Sabina, clear the door, quick. Gladys, come here while I clean your nasty face!

MR. ANTROBUS: She-bitch of a goat's gizzard, I'll break every bone in your body. Let me in or I'll tear the whole house down.

MRS. ANTROBUS: Just a minute, George, something's the matter with the lock.

MR. ANTROBUS: Open the door or I'll tear your livers out. I'll smash your brains on the ceiling, and Devil takes the hindmost.

MRS. ANTROBUS: Now, you can open the door, Sabina. I'm ready.

(*The door is flung open. Silence.* MR. ANTROBUS—*face of a Keystone Comedy Cop[7]—stands there in fur cap and blanket. His arms are full of parcels, including a large stone wheel with a center in it. One hand carries a railroad man's lantern. Suddenly he bursts into joyous roar.*)

MR. ANTROBUS: Well, how's the whole crooked family? (*Relief. Laughter. Tears. Jumping up and down.* ANIMALS *cavorting.* ANTROBUS *throws the parcels on the ground. Hurls his cap and blanket after them. Heroic embraces. Melee of* HUMANS *and* ANIMALS, SABINA *included*) I'll be scalded and tarred if a man can't get a little welcome when he comes home. Well, Maggie, you old gunny-sack, how's the broken down old weather hen?—Sabina, old fishbait, old skunkpot.—And the children,—how've the little smellers been?

GLADYS: Papa, Papa, Papa, Papa, Papa.

MR. ANTROBUS: How've they been, Maggie?

MRS. ANTROBUS: Well, I must say, they've been as good as gold. I haven't had to raise my voice once. I don't know what's the matter with them.

ANTROBUS (*kneeling before* GLADYS): Papa's little weasel, eh?—Sabina, there's some food for you.—Papa's little gopher?

GLADYS (*her arm around his neck*): Papa, you're always teasing me.

ANTROBUS: And Henry? Nothing rash today, I hope. Nothing rash?

HENRY: No, Papa.

ANTROBUS (*roaring*): Well that's good, that's good—I'll bet Sabina let the fire go out.

SABINA: Mr. Antrobus, I've given my notice. I'm leaving two weeks from today. I'm sorry, but I'm leaving.

ANTROBUS (*roar*): Well, if you leave now you'll freeze to death, so go and cook the dinner.

SABINA: Two weeks, that's the law. (*Exit.*)

ANTROBUS: Did you get my telegram?

MRS. ANTROBUS: Yes.—What's a wheel?

(*He indicates the wheel with a glance.* HENRY *is rolling it around the floor. Rapid, hoarse interchange:* MRS. ANTROBUS: *What does this cold weather mean? It's below freezing.* ANTROBUS: *Not before the children!* MRS. ANTROBUS: *Shouldn't we do something about it?—start off, move?* ANTROBUS: *Not before the children!!! He gives* HENRY *a sharp slap.*)

---

[7] In the early days of silent movies Mack Sennett's Keystone Cops were noted for their deadpan acting and wild slapstick escapades.

HENRY: Papa, you hit me!

ANTROBUS: Well, remember it. That's to make you remember today. Today. The day the alphabet's finished; and the day that we *saw* the hundred—the hundred, the hundred, the hundred, the hundred, the hundred—there's no end to 'em. I've had a day at the office! Take a look at that wheel, Maggie—when I've got that to rights: you'll see a sight. There's a reward there for all the walking you've done.

MRS. ANTROBUS: How do you mean?

ANTROBUS (*on the hassock looking into the fire; with awe*): Maggie, we've reached the top of the wave. There's not much more to be done. We're there!

MRS. ANTROBUS (*cutting across his mood sharply*): And the ice?

ANTROBUS: The ice!

HENRY (*playing with the wheel*): Papa, you could put a chair on this.

ANTROBUS (*broodingly*): Ye-e-s, any booby can fool with it now,—but I thought of it first.

MRS. ANTROBUS: Children, go out in the kitchen. I want to talk to your father alone.

(*The* CHILDREN *go out.* ANTROBUS *has moved to his chair up left. He takes the goldfish bowl on his lap; pulls the canary cage down to the level of his face. Both the* ANIMALS *put their paws up on the arm of his chair.* MRS. ANTROBUS *faces him across the room, like a judge.*)

MRS. ANTROBUS: Well?

ANTROBUS (*shortly*): It's cold.—How things been, eh? Keck, keck, keck.—And you, Millicent?

MRS. ANTROBUS: I know it's cold.

ANTROBUS (*to the canary*): No spilling of sunflower seed, eh? No singing after lights-out, y'know what I mean?

MRS. ANTROBUS: You can try and prevent us freezing to death, can't you? You can do something? We can start moving. Or we can go on the animals' backs?

ANTROBUS: The best thing about animals is that they don't talk much.

MAMMOTH: It's cold.

ANTROBUS: Eh, eh, eh! Watch that!—

—By midnight we'd turn to ice. The roads are full of people now who can scarcely lift a foot from the ground. The grass out in front is like iron,—which reminds me, I have another needle for you.—The people up north—where are they? Frozen . . . crushed. . . .

MRS. ANTROBUS: Is that what's going to happen to us?—Will you answer me?

ANTROBUS: I don't know. I don't know anything. Some say that the ice is going slower. Some say that it's stopped. The sun's growing cold. What can I do about that? Nothing we can do but burn everything in the house, and the fenceposts and the barn. Keep the fire going. When we have no more fire, we die.

MRS. ANTROBUS: Well, why didn't you say so in the first place?

(MRS. ANTROBUS *is about to march off when she catches sight of two* REFUGEES, *men, who have appeared against the back wall of the theatre and who are soon joined by others.*)

REFUGEES: Mr. Antrobus! Mr. Antrobus! Mr. An-nn-tro-bus!

MRS. ANTROBUS: Who's that? Who's that calling you?

ANTROBUS (*clearing his throat guiltily*): H'm—let me see.

(*Two* REFUGEES *come up to the window.*)

REFUGEE: Could we warm our hands for a moment, Mr. Antrobus? It's very cold, Mr. Antrobus.

ANOTHER REFUGEE: Mr. Antrobus, I wonder if you have a piece of bread or something that you could spare.

(*Silence. They wait humbly.* MRS. ANTROBUS *stands rooted to the spot. Suddenly a knock at the door, then another hand knocking in short rapid blows.*)

MRS. ANTROBUS: Who are these people? Why, they're all over the front yard. What have they come *here* for?

(*Enter* SABINA.)

SABINA: Mrs. Antrobus! There are some tramps knocking at the back door.

MRS. ANTROBUS: George, tell these people to go away. Tell them to move right along. I'll go and send them away from the back door. Sabina, come with me. (*She goes out energetically.*)

ANTROBUS: Sabina! Stay here! I have something to say to you. (*He goes to the door and opens it a crack and talks through it*) Ladies and gentlemen! I'll have to ask you to wait a few minutes longer. It'll be all right . . . while you're waiting you might each one pull up a stake of the fence. We'll need them all for the fireplace. There'll be coffee and sandwiches in a moment.

(SABINA *looks out door over his shoulder and suddenly extends her arm pointing, with a scream.*)

SABINA: Mr. Antrobus, what's that??—that big white thing? Mr. Antrobus, it's ICE. It's ICE!!

ANTROBUS: Sabina, I want you to go in the kitchen and make a lot of coffee. Make a whole pail full.

SABINA: Pail full!!

ANTROBUS (*with gesture*): And sandwiches . . . piles of them . . . like this.

SABINA: Mr. An . . . !! (*Suddenly she drops the play, and says in her own person as* MISS SOMERSET, *with surprise*) Oh, *I* see what this part of the play means now! This means refugees. (*She starts to cross to the proscenium*) Oh, I don't like it. I don't like it. (*She leans against the proscenium and bursts into tears.*)

ANTROBUS: Miss Somerset!

Voice of the STAGE MANAGER: Miss Somerset!

SABINA (*energetically, to the audience*): Ladies and gentlemen! Don't take this play serious. The world's not coming to an end. You know it's not. People exaggerate! Most people really have enough to eat and a roof over their heads. Nobody actually starves—you can always eat grass or something. That ice-business—why, it was a long, long time ago. Besides they were only savages. Savages don't love their families—not like we do.

ANTROBUS *and* STAGE MANAGER: Miss Somerset!!

(*There is renewed knocking at the door.*)

SABINA: All right. I'll say the lines, but I won't think about the play.

(*Enter* MRS. ANTROBUS.)

SABINA (*parting thrust at the audience*): And I advise *you* not to think about the play, either.

(*Exit* SABINA.)

MRS. ANTROBUS: George, these tramps say that you asked them to come to the house. What does this mean?

(*Knocking at the door.*)

ANTROBUS: Just . . . uh . . . There are a few friends, Maggie, I met on the road. Real nice, real useful people. . . .

MRS. ANTROBUS (*back to the door*): Now, don't you ask them in! George Antrobus, not another soul comes in here over my dead body.

ANTROBUS: Maggie, there's a doctor there. Never hurts to have a good doctor in the house. We've lost a peck of children, one way and another. You can never tell when a child's throat will get stopped up. What you and I have seen—!!! (*He puts his fingers on his throat, and imitates diphtheria.*)

MRS. ANTROBUS: Well, just one person then, the Doctor. The others can go right along the road.

ANTROBUS: Maggie, there's an old man, particular friend of mine—

MRS. ANTROBUS: I won't listen to you—

ANTROBUS: It was he that really started off the A.B.C.'s.

MRS. ANTROBUS: I don't care if he perishes. We can do without reading or writing. We can't do without food.

ANTROBUS: Then let the ice come!! Drink your coffee!! I don't want any coffee if I can't drink it with some good people.

MRS. ANTROBUS: Stop shouting. Who else is there trying to push us off the cliff?

ANTROBUS: Well, there's the man . . . who makes all the laws. Judge Moses!

MRS. ANTROBUS: Judges can't help us now.

ANTROBUS: And if the ice melts? . . . and if we pull through? Have you and I been able to bring up Henry? What have we done?

MRS. ANTROBUS: Who are those old women?

ANTROBUS (*coughs*): Up in town there are nine sisters. There are three or four of them here. They're sort of music teachers . . . and one of them recites and one of them—

MRS. ANTROBUS: That's the end. A singing troupe! Well, take your choice, live or die. Starve your own children before your face.

ANTROBUS (*gently*): These people don't take much. They're used to starving. They'll sleep on the floor. Besides, Maggie, listen: no, listen: Who've we got in the house, but Sabina? Sabina's always afraid the worst will happen. Whose spirits can she keep up? Maggie, these people never give up. They think they'll live and work forever.

MRS. ANTROBUS (*walks slowly to the middle of the room*): All right, let them in. Let them in. You're master here. (*Softly*)—But these animals must go. Enough's enough. They'll soon be big enough to push the walls down, anyway. Take them away.

ANTROBUS (*sadly*): All right. The dinosaur and mammoth—! Come on, baby, come on, Frederick. Come for a walk. That's a good little fellow.

DINOSAUR: It's cold.

ANTROBUS: Yes, nice cold fresh air. Bracing. (*He holds the door open and the* ANIMALS *go out. He beckons to his friends. The* REFUGEES *are typical elderly out-of-works from the streets of New York today.* JUDGE MOSES *wears a skull cap.* HOMER *is a blind beggar with a guitar. The seedy crowd shuffles in and waits humbly and expectantly.* ANTROBUS *introduces them to his wife who bows to each with a stately bend of her head)* Make yourself at home; Maggie, this is the doctor . . . m . . . Coffee'll be here in a minute. . . . Professor, this is my wife. . . . And: . . . Judge . . . Maggie, you know the Judge. (*An old blind man with a guitar*) Maggie, you know . . . you know Homer?—Come right in, Judge.—Miss Muse—are some of your sisters here? Come right in. . . . Miss E. Muse; Miss T. Muse, Miss M. Muse.[8]

MRS. ANTROBUS: Pleased to meet you. Just . . . make yourself comfortable. Supper'll be ready in a minute. (*She goes out, abruptly.*)

ANTROBUS: Make yourself at home, friends. I'll be right back.

(*He goes out. The* REFUGEES *stare about them in awe. Presently several voices start whispering "Homer! Homer!" All take it up.* HOMER *strikes a chord or two on his guitar, then starts to speak:*)[9]

HOMER: Μῆνιν ἄειδε, θεὰ, Πηληϊάδεω ’Αχιλῆος,
ούλομένην, ἥ μυρί’ ’Αχαιοῖς ἄλγε’ ἔθηκε
πολλὰς δ’ ἰφθίμους ψυχὰς—

(HOMER'S *face shows he is lost in thought and memory and the words die away on his lips. The* REFUGEES *likewise nod in dreamy recollection. Soon the whisper "Moses, Moses!" goes around. An aged Jew parts his beard and recites dramatically:*)[10]

MOSES:

בְּרֵאשִׁית בָּרָא אֱלֹהִים אֵת הַשָּׁמַיִם וְאֵת הָאָרֶץ: וְהָאָרֶץ הָיְתָה תֹהוּ

וָבֹהוּ וְחֹשֶׁךְ עַל־פְּנֵי תְהוֹם וְרוּחַ אֱלֹהִים מְרַחֶפֶת עַל־פְּנֵי הַמָּיִם:

(*The same dying away of the words takes place, and on the part of the* REFUGEES *the same retreat into recollection. Some of them murmur, "Yes, yes." The mood is broken by the abrupt entrance of* MR. *and* MRS. ANTRO-BUS *and* SABINA *bearing platters of sandwiches and a pail of coffee.* SABINA *stops and stares at the guests.*)

MR. ANTROBUS: Sabina, pass the sandwiches.

SABINA: I thought I was working in a respectable house that had respectable guests. I'm giving my notice, Mr. Antrobus: two weeks, that's the law.

---

[8] The Muses are the nine goddesses of song, poetry, the arts, and sciences in Greek mythology. Miss E. Muse is either Erato, the muse of lyric and love poetry, or Euterpe, the muse of music. Miss M. Muse is Melpomene, the muse of tragedy. Miss T. Muse is either Terpsichore, the muse of dancing and choral song, or Thalia, the muse of comedy and pastoral poetry.

[9] Homer's lines are from the beginning of the *Iliad:* "The wrath do you sing, O goddess, of Peleus' son, Achilles, that baneful wrath which brought countless woes upon the Achaeans, and sent forth to Hades. . . ."

[10] Moses' lines are from Genesis 1:1-2: "In the beginning God created the heaven and the earth. And the earth was without form, and void; and darkness was upon the face of the deep. And the Spirit of God moved upon the face of the waters."

MR. ANTROBUS: Sabina! Pass the sandwiches.

SABINA: Two weeks, that's the law.

MR. ANTROBUS: There's the law. That's Moses.

SABINA (*stares*): The Ten Commandments—FAUGH!!—(*To Audience*) That's the worst line I've ever had to say on any stage.

ANTROBUS: I think the best thing to do is just not to stand on ceremony, but pass the sandwiches around from left to right.—Judge, help yourself to one of these.

MRS. ANTROBUS: The roads are crowded, I hear?

THE GUESTS (*all talking at once*): Oh, ma'am, you can't imagine. . . . You can hardly put one foot before you . . . people are trampling one another. (*Sudden silence.*)

MRS. ANTROBUS: Well, you know what I think it is,—I think it's sunspots!

THE GUESTS (*discreet hubbub*): Oh, you're right, Mrs. Antrobus . . . that's what it is. . . . That's what I was saying the other day. (*Sudden silence.*)

ANTROBUS: Well, I don't believe the whole world's going to turn to ice. (*All eyes are fixed on him, waiting*) I can't believe it. Judge! Have we worked for nothing? Professor! Have we just failed in the whole thing?

MRS. ANTROBUS: It is certainly very strange—well fortunately on both sides of the family we come of very hearty stock.—Doctor, I want you to meet my children. They're eating their supper now. And of course I want them to meet you.

MISS M. MUSE: How many children have you, Mrs. Antrobus?

MRS. ANTROBUS: I have two,—a boy and a girl.

MOSES (*softly*): I understood you had two sons, Mrs. Antrobus.

(MRS. ANTROBUS *in blind suffering; she walks toward the footlights.*)

MRS. ANTROBUS (*in a low voice*): Abel, Abel, my son, my son, Abel, my son, Abel, Abel, my son.

(*The* REFUGEES *move with few steps toward her as though in comfort murmuring words in Greek, Hebrew, German, et cetera. A piercing shriek from the kitchen,—*SABINA'S *voice. All heads turn.*)

ANTROBUS: What's that?

(SABINA *enters, bursting with indignation, pulling on her gloves.*)

SABINA: Mr. Antrobus—that son of yours, that boy Henry Antrobus—I don't stay in this house another moment!—He's not fit to live among respectable folks and that's a fact.

MRS. ANTROBUS: Don't say another word, Sabina. I'll be right back.

(*Without waiting for an answer she goes past her into the kitchen.*)

SABINA: Mr. Antrobus, Henry has thrown a stone again and if he hasn't killed the boy that lives next door, I'm very much mistaken. He finished his supper and went out to play; and I heard such a fight; and then I saw it. I saw it with my own eyes. And it looked to me like stark murder.

(MRS. ANTROBUS *appears at the kitchen door, shielding* HENRY, *who follows her. When she steps aside, we see on* HENRY'S *forehead a large ochre and scarlet scar in the shape of a C.* MR. ANTROBUS *starts toward him. A pause.* HENRY *is heard saying under his breath:*)

HENRY: He was going to take the wheel away from me. He started to throw a stone at me first.

MRS. ANTROBUS: George, it was just a boyish impulse. Remember how young he is. (*Louder, in an urgent wail*) George, he's only four thousand years old.

SABINA: And everything was going along so nicely!

(*Silence.* ANTROBUS *goes back to the fireplace.*)

ANTROBUS: Put out the fire! Put out all the fires. (*Violently*) No wonder the sun grows cold. (*He starts stamping on the fireplace.*)

MRS. ANTROBUS: Doctor! Judge! Help me!—George, have you lost your mind?

ANTROBUS: There is no mind. We'll not try to live. (*To the* GUESTS) Give it up. Give up trying.

(MRS. ANTROBUS *seizes him.*)

SABINA: Mr. Antrobus! I'm downright ashamed of you.

MRS. ANTROBUS: George, have some more coffee.—Gladys! Where's Gladys gone?

(GLADYS *steps in, frightened.*)

GLADYS: Here I am, mama.

MRS. ANTROBUS: Go upstairs and bring your father's slippers. How could you forget a thing like that, when you know how tired he is? (ANTROBUS *sits in his chair. He covers his face with his hands.* MRS. ANTROBUS *turns to the* REFUGEES) Can't some of you sing? It's your business in life to sing, isn't it? Sabina! (*Several of the women clear their throats tentatively, and with frightened faces gather around* HOMER'S *guitar. He establishes a few chords. Almost inaudibly they start singing, led by* SABINA: *"Jingle Bells."* MRS. ANTROBUS *continues to* ANTROBUS *in a low voice, while taking off his shoes*) George, remember all the other times. When the volcanoes came right up in the front yard. And the time the grasshoppers ate every single leaf and blade of grass, and all the grain and spinach you'd grown with your own hands. And the summer there were earthquakes every night.

ANTROBUS: Henry! Henry! (*Puts his hand on his forehead*) Myself! All of us, we're covered with blood.

MRS. ANTROBUS: Then remember all the times you were pleased with him and when you were proud of yourself.—Henry! Henry! Come here and recite to your father the multiplication table that you do so nicely.

(HENRY *kneels on one knee beside his father and starts whispering the multiplication table.*)

HENRY (*finally*): Two times six is twelve; three times six is eighteen—I don't think I know the sixes.

(*Enter* GLADYS *with the slippers.* MRS. ANTROBUS *makes stern gestures to her: Go in there and do your best. The* GUESTS *are now singing "Tenting Tonight."*)

GLADYS (*putting slippers on his feet*): Papa . . . papa . . . I was very good in school today. Miss Conover said right out in class that if all the girls had as good manners as Gladys Antrobus, that the world would be a very different place to live in.

MRS. ANTROBUS: You recited a piece at assembly, didn't you? Recite it to your father.

GLADYS: Papa, do you want to hear what I recited in class? (*Fierce directorial glance from her mother*) "THE STAR" by Henry Wadsworth LONGFELLOW.

MRS. ANTROBUS: Wait!!! The fire's going out. There isn't enough wood! Henry, go upstairs and bring down the chairs and start breaking up the beds.

(*Exit* HENRY. *The singers return to "Jingle Bells," still very softly.*)

GLADYS: Look, Papa, here's my report card. Lookit. Conduct A! Look, Papa. Papa, do you want to hear "The Star," by Henry Wadsworth Longfellow? Papa, you're not mad at me, are you?—I know it'll get warmer. Soon it'll be just like spring, and we can go to a picnic at the Hibernian Picnic Grounds like you always like to do, don't you remember? Papa, just look at me once.

(*Enter* HENRY *with some chairs.*)

ANTROBUS: You recited in assembly, did you? (*She nods eagerly*) You didn't forget it?

GLADYS: No!!! I was perfect.

(*Pause. Then* ANTROBUS *rises, goes to the front door and opens it. The* REFUGEES *draw back timidly; the song stops; he peers out of the door, then closes it.*)

ANTROBUS (*with decision, suddenly*): Build up the fire. It's cold. Build up the fire. We'll do what we can. Sabina, get some more wood. Come around the fire, everybody. At least the young ones may pull through. Henry, have you eaten something?

HENRY: Yes, papa.

ANTROBUS: Gladys, have you had some supper?

GLADYS: I ate in the kitchen, papa.

ANTROBUS: If you do come through this—what'll you be able to do? What do you know? Henry, did you take a good look at that wheel?

HENRY: Yes, papa.

ANTROBUS (*sitting down in his chair*): Six times two are—

HENRY: —twelve; six times three are eighteen; six times four are—Papa, it's hot and cold. It makes my head all funny. It makes me sleepy.

ANTROBUS (*gives him a cuff*): Wake up. I don't care if your head is sleepy. Six times four are twenty-four. Six times five are—

HENRY: Thirty. Papa!

ANTROBUS: Maggie, put something into Gladys' head on the chance she can use it.

MRS. ANTROBUS: What do you mean, George?

ANTROBUS: Six times six are thirty-six. Teach her the beginning of the Bible.

GLADYS: But, Mama, it's so cold and close.

(HENRY *has all but drowsed off. His father slaps him sharply and the lesson goes on.*)

MRS. ANTROBUS: "In the beginning God created the heavens and the earth; and the earth was waste and void; and the darkness was upon the face of the deep—"

(*The singing starts up again louder.* SABINA *has returned with wood.*)

SABINA (*after placing wood on the fireplace comes down to the footlights and addresses the audience)* : Will you please start handing up your chairs? We'll need everything for this fire. Save the human race.—Ushers, will you pass the chairs up here? Thank you.

HENRY: Six times nine are fifty-four; six times ten are sixty.

(*In the back of the auditorium the sound of chairs being ripped up can be heard.* USHERS *rush down the aisles with chairs and hand them over.*)

GLADYS: "And God called the light Day and the darkness he called Night."

SABINA: Pass up your chairs, everybody. Save the human race.

(*The Curtain Falls.*)

Act Two

Toward the end of the intermission, though with the houselights still up, lantern slide projections begin to appear on the curtain. Timetables for trains leaving Pennsylvania Station for Atlantic City. Advertisements of Atlantic City hotels, drugstores, churches, rug merchants, fortune tellers, Bingo parlors.

When the houselights go down, the voice of an ANNOUNCER *is heard.*

ANNOUNCER: The Management now brings you the News Events of the World. Atlantic City, New Jersey: (*Projection of a chrome postcard of the waterfront, trimmed in mica with the legend: FUN AT THE BEACH*)

This great convention city is playing host this week to the anniversary convocation of that great fraternal order,—the Ancient and Honorable Order of Mammals, Subdivision Humans. This great fraternal, militant and burial society is celebrating on the Boardwalk, ladies and gentlemen, its six hundred thousandth Annual Convention. It has just elected its president for the ensuing term,—(*Projection of* MR. *and* MRS. ANTROBUS *posed as they will be shown a few moments later*)

Mr. George Antrobus of Excelsior, New Jersey. We show you President Antrobus and his gracious and charming wife, every inch a mammal. Mr. Antrobus has had a long and chequered career. Credit has been paid to him for many useful enterprises including the introduction of the lever, of the wheel and the brewing of beer. Credit has been also extended to President Antrobus's gracious and charming wife for many practical suggestions, including the hem, the gore, and the gusset; and the novelty of the year,—frying in oil. Before we show you Mr. Antrobus accepting the nomination, we have an important announcement to make. As many of you know, this great celebration of the Order of the Mammals has received delegations from the other rival Orders,—or shall we say: esteemed concurrent Orders: the WINGS, the FINS, the SHELLS, and so on. These Orders are holding their conventions also, in various parts of the world, and have sent representatives to our own, two of a kind.

Later in the day we will show you President Antrobus broadcasting his words of greeting and congratulation to the collected assemblies of the whole natural world.

Ladies and Gentlemen! We give you President Antrobus!

(*The screen becomes a Transparency.* MR. ANTROBUS *stands beside a pedestal;* MRS. ANTROBUS *is seated wearing a corsage of orchids.* ANTROBUS *wears an untidy Prince Albert; spats; from a red rosette in his buttonhole hangs a fine long purple ribbon of honor. He wears a gay lodge hat,— something between a fez and a legionnaire's cap.*)

ANTROBUS: Fellow-mammals, fellow-vertebrates, fellow-humans, I thank you. Little did my dear parents think,—when they told me to stand on my own two feet,—that I'd arrive at this place.

My friends, we have come a long way.

During this week of happy celebration it is perhaps not fitting that we dwell on some of the difficult times we have been through. The dinosaur is extinct—(*Applause*)—the ice has retreated; and the common cold is being pursued by every means within our power. (MRS. ANTROBUS *sneezes, laughs prettily, and murmurs: "I beg your pardon"*) In our memorial service yesterday we did honor to all our friends and relatives who are no longer with us, by reason of cold, earthquakes, plagues and . . . and . . . (*Coughs*) differences of opinion. As our Bishop so ably said . . . uh . . . so ably said. . . .

MRS. ANTROBUS (*closed lips*): Gone, but not forgotten.

ANTROBUS: "They are gone, but not forgotten." I think I can say, I think I can prophesy with complete . . . uh . . . with complete. . . .

MRS. ANTROBUS: Confidence.

ANTROBUS: Thank you, my dear,—With complete lack of confidence, that a new day of security is about to dawn. The watchword of the closing year was: Work. I give you the watchword for the future: Enjoy Yourselves.

MRS. ANTROBUS: George, sit down!

ANTROBUS: Before I close, however, I wish to answer one of those unjust and malicious accusations that were brought against me during this last electoral campaign.

Ladies and gentlemen, the charge was made that at various points in my career I leaned toward joining some of the rival orders,—that's a lie.

As I told reporters of the *Atlantic City Herald,* I do not deny that a few months before my birth I hesitated between . . . uh . . . between pinfeathers and gill-breathing,—and so did many of us here,—but for the last million years I have been viviparous, hairy and diaphragmatic.

(*Applause. Cries of "Good old Antrobus," "The Prince chap!" "Georgie," etc.*)

ANNOUNCER: Thank you. Thank you very much, Mr. Antrobus. Now I know that our visitors will wish to hear a word from that gracious and charming mammal, Mrs. Antrobus, wife and mother,—Mrs. Antrobus! (MRS. ANTROBUS *rises, lays her program on her chair, bows and says:*)

MRS. ANTROBUS: Dear friends, I don't really think I should say anything. After all, it was my husband who was elected and not I. Perhaps, as president of the Women's Auxiliary Bed and Board Society,—I had some notes here, oh, yes, here they are:—I should give a short report from some of our committees that have been meeting in this beautiful city.

Perhaps it may interest you to know that it has at last been decided that the tomato is edible. Can you all hear me? The tomato *is* edible. A delegate from across the sea reports that the thread woven by the silkworm gives a cloth . . . I have a sample of it here . . . can you see it? smooth, elastic. I should say that it's rather attractive,—though personally I prefer less shiny surfaces. Should the windows of a sleeping apartment be open or shut? I know all mothers will follow our debates on this matter with close interest. I am sorry to say that the most expert authorities have not yet decided. It does seem to me that the night air would be bound to be unhealthy for our children, but there are many distinguished authorities on both sides. Well, I could go on talking forever,—as Shakespeare says: a woman's work is seldom done; but I think I'd better join my husband in saying thank you, and sit down. Thank you. (*She sits down.*)

ANNOUNCER: Oh, Mrs. Antrobus!

MRS. ANTROBUS: Yes?

ANNOUNCER: We understand that you are about to celebrate a wedding anniversary. I know our listeners would like to extend their felicitations and hear a few words from you on that subject.

MRS. ANTROBUS: I have been asked by this kind gentleman . . . yes, my friends, this Spring Mr. Antrobus and I will be celebrating our five thousandth wedding anniversary. I don't know if I speak for my husband, but I can say that, as for me, I regret every moment of it. (*Laughter of confusion*) I beg your pardon. What I *mean* to say is that I do not regret one moment of it. I hope none of you catch my cold. We have two children. We've always had two children, though it hasn't always been the same two. But as I say, we have two fine children, and we're very grateful for that. Yes, Mr. Antrobus and I have been married five thousand years. Each wedding anniversary reminds me of the times when there were no weddings. We had to crusade for marriage. Perhaps there are some women within the sound of my voice who remember that crusade and those struggles; we fought for it, didn't we? We chained ourselves to lampposts and we made disturbances in the Senate,—anyway, at last we women got the ring. A few men helped us, but I must say that most men blocked our way at every step: they said we were unfeminine.

I only bring up these unpleasant memories, because I see some signs of backsliding from that great victory. Oh, my fellow mammals, keep hold of that. My husband says that the watchword for the year is Enjoy Yourselves. I think that's very open to misunderstanding. My watchword for the year is: Save the Family. It's held together for over five thousand years: Save it! Thank you.

ANNOUNCER: Thank you, Mrs. Antrobus. (*The transparency disappears*) We had hoped to show you the Beauty Contest that took place here today. President Antrobus, an experienced judge of pretty girls, gave the title of Miss Atlantic City 1942, to Miss Lily-Sabina[11] Fairweather, charming hostess of our Boardwalk Bingo Parlor. Unfortunately, however, our time is up, and I must take you to some views of the Convention City and conveeners,—enjoying themselves.

(*A burst of music; the curtain rises.*

The Boardwalk. The audience is sitting in the ocean. A handrail of scarlet cord stretches across the front of the stage. A ramp—also with scarlet hand rail—descends to the right corner of the orchestra pit where a great scarlet beach umbrella or a cabana stands. Front and right stage left are benches facing the sea; attached to each bench is a street-lamp.

The only scenery is two cardboard cut-outs six feet high, representing shops at the back of the stage. Reading from left to right they are: SALT WATER TAFFY; FORTUNE TELLER; then the blank space; BINGO PARLOR; TURKISH BATH. They have practical doors, that of the Fortune Teller's being hung with bright gypsy curtains.

By the left proscenium and rising from the orchestra pit is the weather signal; it is like the mast of a ship with cross bars. From time to time black discs are hung on it to indicate the storm and hurricane warnings. Three roller chairs, pushed by melancholy NEGROES, *file by empty. Throughout the act they traverse the stage in both directions.*

From time to time, CONVEENERS, *dressed like* MR. ANTROBUS, *cross the stage. Some walk sedately by; others engage in inane horseplay. The old gypsy* FORTUNE TELLER *is seated at the door of her shop, smoking a corncob pipe.*

From the Bingo Parlor comes the voice of the CALLER.)

BINGO CALLER: A-Nine; A-Nine. C-Twenty-six; C-Twenty-six. A-Four; A-Four. B-Twelve.

CHORUS (*back-stage*): Bingo!!!

(*The front of the Bingo Parlor shudders, rises a few feet in the air and returns to the ground trembling.*)

FORTUNE TELLER (*mechanically, to the unconscious back of a passerby, pointing with her pipe*): Bright's disease![12] Your partner's deceiving you in that Kansas City deal. You'll have six grandchildren. Avoid high places. (*She rises and shouts after another*) Cirrhosis of the liver!

(SABINA *appears at the door of the Bingo Parlor. She hugs about her a blue raincoat that almost conceals her red bathing suit. She tries to catch the* FORTUNE TELLER'S *attention.*)

SABINA: Ssssst! Esmeralda! Ssssst!

FORTUNE TELLER: Keck!

---

[11] In rabbinical literature Lilith is Adam's first wife.
[12] Nephritis, inflammation of the kidneys.

SABINA: Has President Antrobus come along yet?

FORTUNE TELLER: No, no, no. Get back there. Hide yourself.

SABINA: I'm afraid I'll miss him. Oh, Esmeralda, if I fail in this, I'll die; I know I'll die. President Antrobus!!! And I'll be his wife! If it's the last thing I'll do, I'll be Mrs. George Antrobus.—Esmeralda, tell me my future.

FORTUNE TELLER: Keck!

SABINA: All right, I'll tell *you* my future. (*Laughing dreamily and tracing it out with one finger on the palm of her hand*) I've won the Beauty Contest in Atlantic City,—well, I'll win the Beauty Contest of the whole world. I'll take President Antrobus away from that wife of his. Then I'll take every man away from his wife. I'll turn the whole earth upside down.

FORTUNE TELLER: Keck!

SABINA: When all those husbands just think about me they'll get dizzy. They'll faint in the streets. They'll have to lean against lampposts.— Esmeralda, who was Helen of Troy?

FORTUNE TELLER (*furiously*): Shut your foolish mouth. When Mr. Antrobus comes along you can see what you can do. Until then,—go away.

(SABINA *laughs. As she returns to the door of her Bingo Parlor a group of* CONVEENERS *rush over and smother her with attentions:* "Oh, Miss Lily, you know me. You've known me for years.")

SABINA: Go away, boys, go away. I'm after bigger fry than you are.—Why, Mr. Simpson!! How *dare* you!! I expect that even you nobodies must have girls to amuse you; but where you find them and what you do with them, is of absolutely no interest to me.

(*Exit. The* CONVEENERS *squeal with pleasure and stumble in after her. The* FORTUNE TELLER *rises, puts her pipe down on the stool, unfurls her voluminous skirts, gives a sharp wrench to her bodice and strolls towards the audience, swinging her hips like a young woman.*)

FORTUNE TELLER: I tell the future. Keck. Nothing easier. Everybody's future is in their face. Nothing easier. But who can tell your past,—eh? Nobody! Your youth,—where did it go? It slipped away while you weren't looking. While you were asleep. While you were drunk? Puh! You're like our friends, Mr. and Mrs. Antrobus; you lie awake nights trying to know your past. What did it mean? What was it trying to say to you? Think! Think! Split your heads. I can't tell the past and neither can you. If anybody tries to tell you the past, take my word for it, they're charlatans! Charlatans! But I can tell the future. (*She suddenly barks at a passing chair-pusher*) Apoplexy! (*She returns to the audience*) Nobody listens.— Keck! I see a face among you now—I won't embarrass him by pointing him out, but, listen, it may be you: Next year the watchsprings inside you will crumple up. Death by regret,—Type Y. It's in the corners of your mouth. You'll decide that you should have lived for pleasure, but that you missed it. Death by regret,—Type Y. . . . Avoid mirrors. You'll try to be angry,—but no!—no anger. (*Far forward, confidentially*) And now what's the immediate future of our friends, the Antrobuses? Oh, you've seen it as well as I have, keck,—that dizziness of the head; that Great Man dizziness? The inventor of beer and gunpowder. The sudden fits of temper and then the long stretches of inertia? "I'm a sultan; let my slave-girls fan me."

You know as well as I what's coming. Rain. Rain. Rain in floods. The deluge. But first you'll see shameful things—shameful things. Some of you will be saying: "Let him drown. He's not worth saving. Give the whole thing up." I can see it in your faces. But you're wrong. Keep your doubts and despairs to yourselves. Again there'll be the narrow escape. The survival of a handful. From destruction,—total destruction. (*She points sweeping with her hand to the stage*) Even of the animals, a few will be saved: two of a kind, male and female, two of a kind.

(*The heads of* CONVEENERS *appear about the stage and in the orchestra pit, jeering at her.*)

CONVEENERS: Charlatan! Madam Kill-joy! Mrs. Jeremiah![13] Charlatan!

FORTUNE TELLER: And *you!* Mark my words before it's too late. Where'll *you* be?

CONVEENERS: The croaking raven. Old dust and ashes. Rags, bottles, sacks.

FORTUNE TELLER: Yes, stick out your tongues. You can't stick your tongues out far enough to lick the death-sweat from your foreheads. It's too late to work now—bail out the flood with your soup spoons. You've had your chance and you've lost.

CONVEENERS: Enjoy yourselves!!!

(*They disappear. The* FORTUNE TELLER *looks off left and puts her finger on her lip.*)

FORTUNE TELLER: They're coming—the Antrobuses. Keck. Your hope. Your despair. Your selves.

(*Enter from the left,* MR. *and* MRS. ANTROBUS *and* GLADYS.)

MRS. ANTROBUS: Gladys Antrobus, stick your stummick in.

GLADYS: But it's easier this way.

MRS. ANTROBUS: Well, it's too bad the new president has such a clumsy daughter, that's all I can say. Try and be a lady.

FORTUNE TELLER: Aijah! That's been said a hundred billion times.

MRS. ANTROBUS: Goodness! Where's Henry? He was here just a minute ago. Henry!

(*Sudden violent stir. A roller-chair appears from the left. About it are dancing in great excitement* HENRY *and a* NEGRO CHAIR-PUSHER.)

HENRY (*slingshot in hand*): I'll put your eye out. I'll make you yell, like you never yelled before.

NEGRO (*at the same time*): Now, I warns you. I warns you. If you make me mad, you'll get hurt.

ANTROBUS: Henry! What is this? Put down that slingshot.

MRS. ANTROBUS (*at the same time*): Henry! HENRY! Behave yourself.

FORTUNE TELLER: That's right, young man. There are too many people in the world as it is. Everybody's in the way, except one's self.

HENRY: All I wanted to do was—have some fun.

---

[13] An Old Testament prophet who preached that doom and destruction would befall the Hebrew people because of their sins.

NEGRO: Nobody can't touch my chair, nobody, without I allow 'em to. You get clean away from me and you get away fast. (*He pushes his chair off, muttering.*)

ANTROBUS: What were you doing, Henry?

HENRY: Everybody's always getting mad. Everybody's always trying to push you around. I'll make him sorry for this; I'll make him sorry.

ANTROBUS: Give me that slingshot.

HENRY: I won't. I'm sorry I came to this place. I wish I weren't here. I wish I weren't anywhere.

MRS. ANTROBUS: Now, Henry, don't get so excited about nothing. I declare I don't know what we're going to do with you. Put your slingshot in your pocket, and don't try to take hold of things that don't belong to you.

ANTROBUS: After this you can stay home. I wash my hands of you.

MRS. ANTROBUS: Come now, let's forget all about it. Everybody take a good breath of that sea air and calm down. (*A passing* CONVEENER *bows to* ANTROBUS, *who nods to him*) Who was that you spoke to, George?

ANTROBUS: Nobody, Maggie. Just the candidate who ran against me in the election.

MRS. ANTROBUS: The man who ran against you in the election!! (*She turns and waves her umbrella after the disappearing* CONVEENER) My husband didn't speak to you and he never will speak to you.

ANTROBUS: Now, Maggie.

MRS. ANTROBUS: After those lies you told about him in your speeches! Lies, that's what they were.

GLADYS *and* HENRY: Mama, everybody's looking at you. Everybody's laughing at you.

MRS. ANTROBUS: If you must know, my husband's a SAINT, a downright SAINT, and you're not fit to speak to him on the street.

ANTROBUS: Now, Maggie, now, Maggie, that's enough of that.

MRS. ANTROBUS: George Antrobus, you're a perfect worm. If you won't stand up for yourself, I will.

GLADYS: Mama, you just act awful in public.

MRS. ANTROBUS (*laughing*): Well, I must say I enjoyed it. I feel better. Wish his wife had been there to hear it. Children, what do you want to do?

GLADYS: Papa, can we ride in one of those chairs? Mama, I want to ride in one of those chairs.

MRS. ANTROBUS: No, sir. If you're tired you just sit where you are. We have no money to spend on foolishness.

ANTROBUS: I guess we have money enough for a thing like that. It's one of the things you do at Atlantic City.

MRS. ANTROBUS: Oh, we have? I tell you it's a miracle my children have shoes to stand up in. I didn't think I'd ever live to see them pushed around in chairs.

ANTROBUS: We're on a vacation, aren't we? We have a right to some treats, I guess. Maggie, some day you're going to drive me crazy.

MRS. ANTROBUS: All right, go. I'll just sit here and laugh at you. And you can give me my dollar right in my hand. Mark my words, a rainy day is coming. There's a rainy day ahead of us. I feel it in my bones. Go on, throw your money around. I can starve. I've starved before. I know how. (*A* CONVEENER *puts his head through Turkish Bath window, and says with raised eyebrows:*)

CONVEENER: Hello, George. How are ya? I see where you brought the WHOLE family along.

MRS. ANTROBUS: And what do you mean by that?

(CONVEENER *withdraws head and closes window.*)

ANTROBUS: Maggie, I tell you there's a limit to what I can stand. God's Heaven, haven't I worked *enough?* Don't I get *any* vacation? Can't I even give my children so much as a ride in a roller-chair?

MRS. ANTROBUS (*putting out her hand for raindrops*): Anyway, it's going to rain very soon and you have your broadcast to make.

ANTROBUS: Now, Maggie, I warn you. A man can stand a family only just so long. I'm warning you.

(*Enter* SABINA *from the Bingo Parlor. She wears a flounced red silk bathing suit, 1905. Red stockings, shoes, parasol. She bows demurely to* ANTROBUS *and starts down the ramp.* ANTROBUS *and the* CHILDREN *stare at her.* ANTROBUS *bows gallantly.*)

MRS. ANTROBUS: Why, George Antrobus, how can you say such a thing! You have the best family in the world.

ANTROBUS: Good morning, Miss Fairweather.

(SABINA *finally disappears behind the beach umbrella or in a cabana in the orchestra pit.*)

MRS. ANTROBUS: Who on earth was that you spoke to, George?

ANTROBUS (*complacent; mock-modest*): Hm . . . m . . . just a . . . solambaka keray.

MRS. ANTROBUS: What? I can't understand you.

GLADYS: Mama, wasn't she beautiful?

HENRY: Papa, introduce her to me.

MRS. ANTROBUS: Children, will you be quiet while I ask your father a simple question?—Who did you say it was, George?

ANTROBUS: Why-uh . . . a friend of mine. Very nice refined girl.

MRS. ANTROBUS: I'm waiting.

ANTROBUS: Maggie, that's the girl I gave the prize to in the beauty contest,— that's Miss Atlantic City 1942.

MRS. ANTROBUS: Hm! She looked like Sabina to me.

HENRY (*at the railing*): Mama, the life-guard knows her, too. Mama, he knows her well.

ANTROBUS: Henry, come here.—She's a very nice girl in every way and the sole support of her aged mother.

MRS. ANTROBUS: So was Sabina, so was Sabina; and it took a wall of ice to open your eyes about Sabina.—Henry, come over and sit down on this bench.

ANTROBUS: She's a very different matter from Sabina. Miss Fairweather is a college graduate, Phi Beta Kappa.

MRS. ANTROBUS: Henry, you sit here by mama. Gladys—

ANTROBUS (*sitting*): Reduced circumstances have required her taking a position as hostess in a Bingo Parlor; but there isn't a girl with higher principles in the country.

MRS. ANTROBUS: Well, let's not talk about it.—Henry, I haven't seen a whale yet.

ANTROBUS: She speaks seven languages and has more culture in her little finger than you've acquired in a lifetime.

MRS. ANTROBUS (*assumed amiability*) : All right, all right, George. I'm glad to know there are such superior girls in the Bingo Parlors.—Henry, what's that? (*Pointing at the storm signal, which has one black disk.*)

HENRY: What is it, Papa?

ANTROBUS: What? Oh, that's the storm signal. One of those black disks means bad weather; two means storm; three means hurricane; and four means the end of the world.

(*As they watch it, a second black disk rolls into place.*)

MRS. ANTROBUS: Goodness! I'm going this very minute to buy you all some raincoats.

GLADYS (*putting her cheek against her father's shoulder*) : Mama, don't go yet. I like sitting this way. And the ocean coming in and coming in. Papa, don't you like it?

MRS. ANTROBUS: Well, there's only one thing I lack to make me a perfectly happy woman: I'd like to see a whale.

HENRY: Mama, we saw two. Right out there. They're delegates to the convention. I'll find you one.

GLADYS: Papa, ask me something. Ask me a question.

ANTROBUS: Well . . . how big's the ocean?

GLADYS: Papa, you're teasing me. It's—three-hundred and sixty million square-miles — and — it — covers — three-fourths — of — the — earth's — surface — and — its — deepest-place — is — five — and — a — half — miles — deep — and — its — average — depth — is — twelve-thousand — feet. No, Papa, ask me something hard, real hard.

MRS. ANTROBUS (*rising*) : Now I'm going off to buy those raincoats. I think that bad weather's going to get worse and worse. I hope it doesn't come before your broadcast. I should think we have about an hour or so.

HENRY: I hope it comes and zzzzzz everything before it. I hope it—

MRS. ANTROBUS: Henry!—George, I think . . . maybe, it's one of those storms that are just as bad on land as on the sea. When you're just as safe and safer in a good stout boat.

HENRY: There's a boat out at the end of the pier.

MRS. ANTROBUS: Well, keep your eye on it. George, you shut your eyes and get a good rest before the broadcast.

ANTROBUS: Thundering Judas, do I have to be told when to open and shut my eyes? Go and buy your raincoats.

MRS. ANTROBUS: Now, children, you have ten minutes to walk around. Ten minutes. And, Henry: control yourself. Gladys, stick by your brother and don't get lost.

(*They run off.*)

MRS. ANTROBUS: Will you be all right, George?

(CONVEENERS *suddenly stick their heads out of the Bingo Parlor and Salt Water Taffy store, and voices rise from the orchestra pit.*)

CONVEENERS: George, Geo-r-r-rge! George! Leave the old hen-coop at home, George. Do-mes-ticated Georgie!

MRS. ANTROBUS (*shaking her umbrella*): Low common oafs! That's what they are. Guess a man has a right to bring his wife to a convention, if he wants to. (*She starts off*) What's the matter with a family, I'd like to know. What else have they got to offer?

(*Exit.* ANTROBUS *has closed his eyes. The* FORTUNE TELLER *comes out of her shop and goes over to the left proscenium. She leans against it watching* SABINA *quizzically.*)

FORTUNE TELLER: Heh! Here she comes!

SABINA (*loud whisper*): What's he doing?

FORTUNE TELLER: Oh, he's ready for you. Bite your lips, dear, take a long breath and come on up.

SABINA: I'm nervous. My whole future depends on this. I'm nervous.

FORTUNE TELLER: Don't be a fool. What more could you want? He's forty-five. His head's a little dizzy. He's just been elected president. He's never known any other woman than his wife. Whenever he looks at her he realizes that she knows every foolish thing he's ever done.

SABINA (*still whispering*): I don't know why it is, but every time I start one of these I'm nervous.

(*The* FORTUNE TELLER *stands in the center of the stage watching the following.*)

FORTUNE TELLER: You make me tired.

SABINA: First tell me my fortune. (*The* FORTUNE TELLER *laughs drily and makes the gesture of brushing away a nonsensical question.* SABINA *coughs and says*) Oh, Mr. Antrobus,—dare I speak to you for a moment?

ANTROBUS: What?—Oh, certainly, certainly, Miss Fairweather.

SABINA: Mr. Antrobus . . . I've been so unhappy. I've wanted . . . I've wanted to make sure that you don't think that I'm the kind of girl who goes out for beauty contests.

FORTUNE TELLER: That's the way!

ANTROBUS: Oh, I understand. I understand perfectly.

FORTUNE TELLER: Give it a little more. Lean on it.

SABINA: I knew you would. My mother said to me this morning: Lily, she said, that fine Mr. Antrobus gave you the prize because he saw at once that you weren't the kind of girl who'd go in for a thing like that. But, honestly, Mr. Antrobus, in this world, honestly, a good girl doesn't know where to turn.

FORTUNE TELLER: Now you've gone too far.

ANTROBUS: My dear Miss Fairweather!

SABINA: You wouldn't know how hard it is. With that lovely wife and daughter you have. Oh, I think Mrs. Antrobus is the finest woman I ever saw. I wish I were like her.

ANTROBUS: There, there. There's . . . uh . . . room for all kinds of people in the world, Miss Fairweather.

SABINA: How wonderful of you to say that. How generous!—Mr. Antrobus, have you a moment free? . . . I'm afraid I may be a little conspicuous here . . . could you come down, for just a moment, to my beach cabana . . . ?

ANTROBUS: Why-uh . . . yes, certainly . . . for a moment . . . just for a moment.

SABINA: There's a deck chair there. Because: you know you *do* look tired. Just this morning my mother said to me: Lily, she said, I hope Mr. Antrobus is getting a good rest. His fine strong face has deep, deep lines in it. Now isn't it true, Mr. Antrobus: you work too hard?

FORTUNE TELLER: Bingo! (*She goes into her shop.*)

SABINA: Now you will just stretch out. No, I shan't say a word, not a word. I shall just sit there,—privileged. That's what I am.

ANTROBUS (*taking her hand*): Miss Fairweather . . . you'll . . . spoil me.

SABINA: Just a moment. I have something I wish to say to the audience.— Ladies and gentlemen. I'm not going to play this particular scene tonight. It's just a short scene and we're going to skip it. But I'll tell you what takes place and then we can continue the play from there on. Now in this scene—

ANTROBUS (*between his teeth*): But, Miss Somerset!

SABINA: I'm sorry. I'm sorry. But I have to skip it. In this scene, I talk to Mr. Antrobus, and at the end of it he decides to leave his wife, get a divorce at Reno and marry me. That's all.

ANTROBUS: Fitz!—Fitz!

SABINA: So that now I've told you we can jump to the end of it,—where you say—

(*Enter in fury* MR. FITZPATRICK, *the stage manager.*)

MR. FITZPATRICK: Miss Somerset, we insist on your playing this scene.

SABINA: I'm sorry, Mr. Fitzpatrick, but I can't and I won't. I've told the audience all they need to know and now we can go on.

(*Other* ACTORS *begin to appear on the stage, listening.*)

MR. FITZPATRICK: And *why* can't you play it?

SABINA: Because there are some lines in that scene that would hurt some people's feelings and I don't think the theatre is a place where people's feelings ought to be hurt.

MR. FITZPATRICK: Miss Somerset, you can pack up your things and go home. I shall call the understudy and I shall report you to Equity.

SABINA: I sent the understudy up to the corner for a cup of coffee and if Equity tries to penalize me I'll drag the case right up to the Supreme Court. Now listen, everybody, there's no need to get excited.

MR. FITZPATRICK *and* ANTROBUS: Why can't you play it? . . . What's the matter with the scene?

SABINA: Well, if you must know, I have a personal guest in the audience tonight. Her life hasn't been exactly a happy one. I wouldn't have my friend hear some of these lines for the whole world. I don't suppose it occurred to the author that some other women might have gone through the experience of losing their husbands like this. Wild horses wouldn't drag from me the details of my friend's life, but . . . well, they'd been married twenty years, and before he got rich, why, she'd done the washing and everything.

MR. FITZPATRICK: Miss Somerset, your friend will forgive you. We must play this scene.

SABINA: Nothing, nothing will make me say some of those lines . . . about "a man outgrows a wife every seven years" and . . . and that one about "the Mohammedans being the only people who looked the subject square in the face." Nothing.

MR. FITZPATRICK: Miss Somerset! Go to your dressing room. I'll *read* your lines.

SABINA: Now everybody's nerves are on edge.

MR. ANTROBUS: Skip the scene.

(MR. FITZPATRICK *and the other* ACTORS *go off.*)

SABINA: Thank you. I knew you'd understand. We'll do just what I said. So Mr. Antrobus is going to divorce his wife and marry me. Mr. Antrobus, you say: "It won't be easy to lay all this before my wife."

(*The* ACTORS *withdraw.* ANTROBUS *walks about, his hand to his forehead muttering:*)

ANTROBUS: Wait a minute. I can't get back into it as easily as all that. "My wife is a very obstinate woman." Hm . . . then you say . . . hm . . . Miss Fairweather, I mean Lily, it won't be easy to lay all this before my wife. It'll hurt her feelings a little.

SABINA: Listen, George: *other* people haven't got feelings. Not in the same way that we have,—we who are presidents like you and prize-winners like me. Listen, other people haven't got feelings; they just imagine they have. Within two weeks they go back to playing bridge and going to the movies.

Listen, dear: everybody in the world except a few people like you and me are just people of straw. Most people have no insides at all. Now that you're president you'll see that. Listen, darling, there's a kind of secret society at the top of the world,—like you and me,—that know this. The world was made for us. What's life anyway? Except for two things, pleasure and power, what is life? Boredom! Foolishness. You know it is. Except for those two things, life's nau-se-at-ing. So,—come here! (*She moves close. They kiss*) So. Now when your wife comes, it's really very simple; just tell her.

ANTROBUS: Lily, Lily: you're a wonderful woman.

SABINA: Of course I am.

(*They enter the cabana and it hides them from view. Distant roll of thunder. A third black disk appears on the weather signal. Distant thunder is heard.* MRS. ANTROBUS *appears carrying parcels. She looks about, seats herself on the bench left, and fans herself with her handkerchief. Enter* GLADYS *right, followed by two* CONVEENERS. *She is wearing red stockings.*)

MRS. ANTROBUS: Gladys!

GLADYS: Mama, here I am.

MRS. ANTROBUS: Gladys Antrobus!!! Where did you get those dreadful things?

GLADYS: Wha-a-t? Papa liked the color.

MRS. ANTROBUS: You go back to the hotel this minute!

GLADYS: I won't. I won't. Papa liked the color.

MRS. ANTROBUS: All right. All right. You stay here. I've a good mind to let your father see you that way. You stay right here.

GLADYS: I . . . I don't want to stay if . . . if you don't think he'd like it.

MRS. ANTROBUS: Oh . . . it's all one to me. I don't care what happens. I don't care if the biggest storm in the whole world comes. Let it come. (*She folds her hands*) Where's your brother?

GLADYS (*in a small voice*): He'll be here.

MRS. ANTROBUS: Will he? Well, let him get into trouble. I don't care. I don't know where your father is, I'm sure.

(*Laughter from the cabana.*)

GLADYS (*leaning over the rail*): I think he's . . . Mama, he's talking to the lady in the red dress.

MRS. ANTROBUS: Is that so? (*Pause*) We'll wait till he's through. Sit down here beside me and stop fidgeting . . . what are you crying about?

(*Distant thunder. She covers* GLADYS' *stockings with a raincoat.*)

GLADYS: You don't like my stockings.

(*Two* CONVEENERS *rush in with a microphone on a standard and various paraphernalia. The* FORTUNE TELLER *appears at the door of her shop. Other characters gradually gather.*)

BROADCAST OFFICIAL: Mrs. Antrobus! Thank God we've found you at last. Where's Mr. Antrobus? We've been hunting everywhere for him. It's about time for the broadcast to the conventions of the world.

MRS. ANTROBUS (*calm*): I expect he'll be here in a minute.

BROADCAST OFFICIAL: Mrs. Antrobus, if he doesn't show up in time, I hope you will consent to broadcast in his place. It's the most important broadcast of the year.

(SABINA *enters from cabana followed by* ANTROBUS.)

MRS. ANTROBUS: No, I shan't. I haven't one single thing to say.

BROADCAST OFFICIAL: Then won't you help us find him, Mrs. Antrobus? A storm's coming up. A hurricane. A deluge!

SECOND CONVEENER (*who has sighted* ANTROBUS *over the rail*): Joe! Joe! Here he is.

BROADCAST OFFICIAL: In the name of God, Mr. Antrobus, you're on the air in five minutes. Will you kindly please come and test the instrument? That's all we ask. If you just please begin the alphabet slowly.

(ANTROBUS, *with set face, comes ponderously up the ramp. He stops at the point where his waist is level with the stage and speaks authoritatively to the* OFFICIALS.)

ANTROBUS: I'll be ready when the time comes. Until then, move away. Go away. I have something I wish to say to my wife.

BROADCASTING OFFICIAL (*whimpering*): Mr. Antrobus! This is the most important broadcast of the year.

(*The* OFFICIALS *withdraw to the edge of the stage.* SABINA *glides up the ramp behind* ANTROBUS.)

SABINA (*whispering*): Don't let her argue. Remember arguments have nothing to do with it.

ANTROBUS: Maggie, I'm moving out of the hotel. In fact, I'm moving out of everything. For good. I'm going to marry Miss Fairweather. I shall provide generously for you and the children. In a few years you'll be able to see that it's all for the best. That's all I have to say.

BROADCAST OFFICIAL: Mr. Antrobus! I hope you'll be ready. This is the most important broadcast of the year.

BINGO ANNOUNCER: A—nine; A—nine. D—forty-two; D—forty-two. C—thirty; C—thirty. B—seventeen; B—seventeen. C—forty; C—forty.

GLADYS: What did Papa say, Mama? I didn't hear what papa said.

CHORUS: Bingo!!

BROADCAST OFFICIAL: Mr. Antrobus. All we want to do is test your voice with the alphabet.

ANTROBUS: Go away. Clear out.

MRS. ANTROBUS (composedly with lowered eyes): George, I can't talk to you until you wipe those silly red marks off your face.

ANTROBUS: I think there's nothing to talk about. I've said what I have to say.

SABINA: Splendid!!

ANTROBUS: You're a fine woman, Maggie, but . . . but a man has his own life to lead in the world.

MRS. ANTROBUS: Well, after living with you for five thousand years I guess I have a right to a word or two, haven't I?

ANTROBUS (to SABINA): What can I answer to that?

SABINA: Tell her that conversation would only hurt her feelings. It's-kinder-in-the-long-run-to-do-it-short-and-quick.

ANTROBUS: I want to spare your feelings in every way I can, Maggie.

BROADCAST OFFICIAL: Mr. Antrobus, the hurricane signal's gone up. We could begin right now.

MRS. ANTROBUS (calmly, almost dreamily): I didn't marry you because you were perfect. I didn't even marry you because I loved you. I married you because you gave me a promise. (She takes off her ring and looks at it) That promise made up for your faults. And the promise I gave you made up for mine. Two imperfect people got married and it was the promise that made the marriage.

ANTROBUS: Maggie, . . . I was only nineteen.

MRS. ANTROBUS (she puts her ring back on her finger): And when our children were growing up, it wasn't a house that protected them; and it wasn't our love that protected them—it was that promise. And when that promise is broken—this can happen!

(With a sweep of the hand she removes the raincoat from GLADYS' stockings.)

ANTROBUS (stretches out his arm, apoplectic): Gladys!! Have you gone crazy? Has everyone gone crazy? (Turning on SABINA) You did this. You gave them to her.

SABINA: I never said a word to her.

ANTROBUS (to GLADYS): You go back to the hotel and take those horrible things off.

GLADYS (*pert*) : Before I go, I've got something to tell you,—it's about Henry.
MRS. ANTROBUS (*claps her hands peremptorily*) : Stop your noise,—I'm taking her back to the hotel, George. Before I go I have a letter . . . I have a message to throw into the ocean. (*Fumbling in her handbag*) Where is the plagued thing? Here it is. (*She flings something—invisible to us—far over the heads of the audience to the back of the auditorium*) It's a bottle. And in the bottle's a letter. And in the letter is written all the things that a woman knows. It's never been told to any man and it's never been told to any woman, and if it finds its destination, a new time will come. We're not what books and plays say we are. We're not what advertisements say we are. We're not in the movies and we're not on the radio. We're not what you're all told and what you think we are: We're ourselves. And if any man can find one of us he'll learn why the whole universe was set in motion. And if any man harm any one of us, his soul— the only soul he's got—had better be at the bottom of that ocean,—and that's the only way to put it. Gladys, come here. We're going back to the hotel.
(*She drags* GLADYS *firmly off by the hand, but* GLADYS *breaks away and comes down to speak to her father.*)
SABINA: Such goings-on. Don't give it a minute's thought.
GLADYS: Anyway, I think you ought to know that Henry hit a man with a stone. He hit one of those colored men that push the chairs and the man's very sick. Henry ran away and hid and some policemen are look- ing for him very hard. And I don't care a bit if you don't want to have anything to do with mama and me, because I'll never like you again and I hope nobody ever likes you again,—so there!
(*She runs off.* ANTROBUS *starts after her.*)
ANTROBUS: I . . . I have to go and see what I can do about this.
SABINA: You stay right here. Don't you go now while you're excited. Gracious sakes, all these things will be forgotten in a hundred years. Come, now, you're on the air. Just say anything,—it doesn't matter what. Just a lot of birds and fishes and things.
BROADCAST OFFICIAL: Thank you, Miss Fairweather. Thank you very much. Ready, Mr. Antrobus.
ANTROBUS (*touching the microphone*) : What is it, what is it? Who am I talking to?
BROADCAST OFFICIAL: Why, Mr. Antrobus! To our order and to all the other orders.
ANTROBUS (*raising his head*) : What are all those birds doing?
BROADCAST OFFICIAL: Those are just a few of the birds. Those are the dele- gates to our convention,—two of a kind.
ANTROBUS (*pointing into the audience*) : Look at the water. Look at them all. Those fishes jumping. The children should see this!—There's Maggie's whales!! Here are your whales, Maggie!!
BROADCAST OFFICIAL: I hope you're ready, Mr. Antrobus.
ANTROBUS: And look on the beach! You didn't tell me these would be here!
SABINA: Yes, George. Those are the animals.

BROADCAST OFFICIAL (*busy with the apparatus*): Yes, Mr. Antrobus, those are the vertebrates. We hope the lion will have a word to say when you're through. Step right up, Mr. Antrobus, we're ready. We'll just have time before the storm. (*Pause. In a hoarse whisper*) They're wait-ing.
(*It has grown dark. Soon after he speaks a high whistling noise begins. Strange veering lights start whirling about the stage. The other characters disappear from the stage.*)

ANTROBUS: Friends. Cousins. Four score and ten billion years ago our forefather brought forth upon this planet the spark of life,—
(*He is drowned out by thunder. When the thunder stops, the* FORTUNE TELLER *is seen standing beside him.*)

FORTUNE TELLER: Antrobus, there's not a minute to be lost. Don't you see the four disks on the weather signal? Take your family into that boat at the end of the pier.

ANTROBUS: My family? I have no family. Maggie! Maggie! They won't come.

FORTUNE TELLER: They'll come.—Antrobus! Take these animals into that boat with you. All of them,—two of each kind.

SABINA: George, what's the matter with you? This is just a storm like any other storm.

ANTROBUS: Maggie!

SABINA: Stay with me, we'll go. . . . (*Losing conviction*) This is just another thunderstorm,—isn't it? Isn't it?

ANTROBUS: Maggie!!!
(MRS. ANTROBUS *appears beside him with* GLADYS.)

MRS. ANTROBUS (*matter-of-fact*): Here I am and here's Gladys.

ANTROBUS: Where've you been? Where have you been? Quick, we're going into that boat out there.

MRS. ANTROBUS: I know we are. But I haven't found Henry. (*She wanders off into the darkness calling "Henry!"*)

SABINA (*low urgent babbling, only occasionally raising her voice*): I don't believe it. I don't believe it's anything at all. I've seen hundreds of storms like this.

FORTUNE TELLER: There's no time to lose. Go. Push the animals along before you. Start a new world. Begin again.

SABINA: Esmeralda! George! Tell me,—is it really serious?

ANTROBUS (*suddenly very busy*): Elephants first. Gently, gently.—Look where you're going.

GLADYS (*leaning over the ramp and striking an animal on the back*): Stop it or you'll be left behind!

ANTROBUS: Is the kangaroo there? *There* you are! Take those turtles in your pouch, will you? (*To some other animals, pointing to his shoulder*) Here! You jump up here. You'll be trampled on.

GLADYS (*to her father, pointing below*): Papa, look,—the snakes!

MRS. ANTROBUS: I can't find Henry. Hen-ry!

ANTROBUS: Go along. Go along. Climb on their backs.—Wolves! Jackals,— whatever you are,—tend to your own business!

GLADYS (*pointing, tenderly*) : Papa,—look.

SABINA: Mr. Antrobus—take me with you. Don't leave me here. I'll work. I'll help. I'll do anything.

(THREE CONVEENERS *cross the stage, marching with a banner.*)

CONVEENERS: George! What are you scared of?—George! Fellas, it looks like rain.—"Maggie, where's my umbrella?"—George, setting up for Barnum and Bailey?[14]

ANTROBUS (*again catching his wife's hand*) : Come on now, Maggie,—the pier's going to break any minute.

MRS. ANTROBUS: I'm not going a step without Henry. Henry!

GLADYS (*on the ramp*) : Mama! Papa! Hurry. The pier's cracking, Mama. It's going to break.

MRS. ANTROBUS: Henry! Cain! CAIN!

(HENRY *dashes onto the stage and joins his mother.*)

HENRY: Here I am, Mama.

MRS. ANTROBUS: Thank God!—now come quick.

HENRY: I didn't think you wanted me.

MRS. ANTROBUS: Quick! (*She pushes him down before her into the aisle.*)

SABINA (*all the* ANTROBUSES *are now in the theatre aisle.* SABINA *stands at the top of the ramp*) : Mrs. Antrobus, take me. Don't you remember me? I'll work. I'll help. Don't leave me here!

MRS. ANTROBUS (*impatiently, but as though it were of no importance*) : Yes, yes. There's a lot of work to be done. Only hurry.

FORTUNE TELLER (*now dominating the stage. To* SABINA *with a grim smile*) : Yes, go—back to the kitchen with you.

SABINA (*half-down the ramp. To* FORTUNE TELLER) : I don't know why my life's always being interrupted—just when everything's going fine!!

(*She dashes up the aisle. Now the* CONVEENERS *emerge doing a serpentine dance on the stage. They jeer at the* FORTUNE TELLER.)

CONVEENERS: Get a canoe—there's not a minute to be lost! Tell me my future, Mrs. Croaker.

FORTUNE TELLER: Paddle in the water, boys—enjoy yourselves.

VOICE FROM THE BINGO PARLOR: A-nine; A-nine. C-Twenty-four. C-Twenty-four.

CONVEENERS: Rags, bottles, and sacks.

FORTUNE TELLER: Go back and climb on your roofs. Put rags in the cracks under your doors.—Nothing will keep out the flood. You've had your chance. You've had your day. You've failed. You've lost.

VOICE FROM THE BINGO PARLOR: B-fifteen. B-fifteen.

FORTUNE TELLER (*shading her eyes and looking out to sea*) : They're safe. George Antrobus! Think it over! A new world to make,—think it over!

(*The Curtain Falls.*)

---

[14] For many years after its establishment in 1871 Barnum and Bailey's was the most famous circus in the United States.

Act Three

Just before the curtain rises, two sounds are heard from the stage: a cracked bugle call.

The curtain rises on almost total darkness. Almost all the flats composing the walls of MR. ANTROBUS' *house, as of Act One, are up, but they lean helter-skelter against one another, leaving irregular gaps. Among the flats missing are two in the back wall, leaving the frames of the windows and door crazily out of line. Off stage, back right, some red Roman fire is burning. The bugle call is repeated. Enter* SABINA *through the tilted door. She is dressed as a Napoleonic camp follower, "la fille du regiment,"[15] in begrimed reds and blues.*

SABINA: Mrs. Antrobus! Gladys! Where are you? The war's over. The war's over. You can come out. The peace treaty's been signed. Where are they? —Hmpf! Are they dead, too? Mrs. Annnntrobus! Glaaaadus! Mr. Antrobus'll be here this afternoon. I just saw him downtown. Huuuurry and put things in order. He says that now that the war's over we'll have to settle down and be perfect.

(Enter MR. FITZPATRICK, *the stage manager, followed by the whole company, who stand waiting at the edges of the stage.* MR. FITZPATRICK *tries to interrupt* SABINA.*)*

MR. FITZPATRICK: Miss Somerset, we have to stop a moment.

SABINA: They may be hiding out in the back—

MR. FITZPATRICK: Miss Somerset! We have to stop a moment.

SABINA: What's the matter?

MR. FITZPATRICK: There's an explanation we have to make to the audience. —Lights, please. *(To the actor who plays* MR. ANTROBUS*)* Will you explain the matter to the audience?

(The lights go up. We now see that a balcony or elevated runway has been erected at the back of the stage, back of the wall of the Antrobus house. From its extreme right and left ends ladder-like steps descend to the floor of the stage.)

ANTROBUS: Ladies and gentlemen, an unfortunate accident has taken place back stage. Perhaps I should say *another* unfortunate accident.

SABINA: I'm sorry. I'm sorry.

ANTROBUS: The management feels, in fact, we all feel that you are due an apology. And now we have to ask your indulgence for the most serious mishap of all. Seven of our actors have . . . have been taken ill. Apparently, it was something they ate. I'm not exactly clear what happened.

---

[15] Girl of the regiment (French).

(*All the* ACTORS *start to talk at once.* ANTROBUS *raises his hand*) Now, now—not all at once. Fitz, do you know what it was?

MR. FITZPATRICK: Why, it's perfectly clear. These seven actors had dinner together, and they ate something that disagreed with them.

SABINA: Disagreed with them!!! They have ptomaine poisoning. They're in Bellevue Hospital this very minute in agony. They're having their stomachs pumped out this very minute, in perfect agony.

ANTROBUS: Fortunately, we've just heard they'll all recover.

SABINA: It'll be a miracle if they do, a downright miracle. It was the lemon meringue pie.

ACTORS: It was the fish . . . it was the canned tomatoes . . . it was the fish.

SABINA: It was the lemon meringue pie. I saw it with my own eyes; it had blue mould all over the bottom of it.

ANTROBUS: Whatever it was, they're in no condition to take part in this performance. Naturally, we haven't enough understudies to fill all those roles; but we do have a number of splendid volunteers who have kindly consented to help us out. These friends have watched our rehearsals, and they assure me that they know the lines and the business very well. Let me introduce them to you—my dresser, Mr. Tremayne,—himself a distinguished Shakespearean actor for many years; our wardrobe mistress, Hester; Miss Somerset's maid, Ivy; and Fred Bailey, captain of the ushers in this theatre. (*These persons bow modestly.* IVY *and* HESTER *are colored girls*) Now this scene takes place near the end of the act. And I'm sorry to say we'll need a short rehearsal, just a short run-through. And as some of it takes place in the auditorium, we'll have to keep the curtain up. Those of you who wish can go out in the lobby and smoke some more. The rest of you can listen to us, or . . . or just talk quietly among yourselves, as you choose. Thank you. Now will you take it over, Mr. Fitzpatrick?

MR. FITZPATRICK: Thank you.—Now for those of you who are listening perhaps I should explain that at the end of this act, the men have come back from the War and the family's settled down in the house. And the author wants to show the hours of the night passing by over their heads, and the planets crossing the sky . . . uh . . . over their heads. And he says—this is hard to explain—that each of the hours of the night is a philosopher, or a great thinker. Eleven o'clock, for instance, is Aristotle. And nine o'clock is Spinoza.[16] Like that. I don't suppose it means anything. It's just a kind of poetic effect.

SABINA: Not mean anything! Why, it certainly does. Twelve o'clock goes by saying those wonderful things. I think it means that when people are asleep they have all those lovely thoughts, much better than when they're awake.

IVY: Excuse me, I think it means,—excuse me, Mr. Fitzpatrick—

SABINA: What were you going to say, Ivy?

IVY: Mr. Fitzpatrick, you let my father come to a rehearsal; and my father's a Baptist minister, and he said that the author meant that—just like the

---

[16] Benedict Spinoza (1632-1677), a Dutch philosopher, best known for his *Ethics*.

hours and stars go by over our heads at night, in the same way the ideas and thoughts of the great men are in the air around us all the time and they're working on us, even when we don't know it.

MR. FITZPATRICK: Well, well, maybe that's it. Thank you, Ivy. Anyway,— the hours of the night are philosophers. My friends, are you ready? Ivy, can you be eleven o'clock? "This good estate of the mind possessing its object in energy we call divine." Aristotle.

IVY: Yes, sir. I know that and I know twelve o'clock and I know nine o'clock.

MR. FITZPATRICK: Twelve o'clock? Mr. Tremayne, the Bible.

TREMAYNE: Yes.

MR. FITZPATRICK: Ten o'clock? Hester,—Plato? (*She nods eagerly*) Nine o'clock, Spinoza,—Fred?

BAILEY: Yes, *sir*.

(FRED BAILEY *picks up a great gilded cardboard numeral IX and starts up the steps to the platform.* MR. FITZPATRICK *strikes his forehead.*)

MR. FITZPATRICK: The planets!! We forgot all about the planets.

SABINA: O my God! The planets! Are they sick too?

(ACTORS *nod.*)

MR. FITZPATRICK: Ladies and gentlemen, the planets are singers. Of course, we can't replace them, so you'll have to imagine them singing in this scene. Saturn sings from the orchestra pit down here. The Moon is way up there. And Mars with a red lantern in his hand, stands in the aisle over there—Tz-tz-tz. It's too bad; it all makes a very fine effect. However! Ready—nine o'clock: Spinoza.

BAILEY (*walking slowly across the balcony, left to right*): "After experience had taught me that the common occurrences of daily life are vain and futile—"

FITZPATRICK: Louder, Fred. "And I saw that all the objects of my desire and fear—"

BAILEY: "And I saw that all the objects of my desire and fear were in themselves nothing good nor bad save insofar as the mind was affected by them—"

FITZPATRICK: Do you know the rest? All right. Ten o'clock. Hester. Plato.

HESTER: "Then tell me, O Critias, how will a man choose the ruler that shall rule over him? Will he not—"

FITZPATRICK: Thank you. Skip to the end, Hester.

HESTER: ". . . can be multiplied a thousand fold in its effects among the citizens."

FITZPATRICK: Thank you.—Aristotle, Ivy?

IVY: "This good estate of the mind possessing its object in energy we call divine. This we mortals have occasionally and it is this energy which is pleasantest and best. But God has it always. It is wonderful in us; but in Him how much more wonderful."

FITZPATRICK: Midnight. Midnight, Mr. Tremayne. That's right,—you've done it before.—All right, everybody. You know what you have to do.— Lower the curtain. House lights up. Act Three of THE SKIN OF OUR TEETH. (*As the curtain descends, he is heard saying*) You volunteers, just wear what you have on. Don't try to put on the costumes today.

(House lights go down. The Act begins again. The Bugle call. Curtain rises. Enter SABINA.*)*

SABINA: Mrs. Antrobus! Gladys! Where are you? The war's over.—You've heard all this—*(She gabbles the main points)* Where—are—they? Are—they—dead, too, et cetera. I—just—saw—Mr.—Antrobus—downtown, et cetera. *(Slowing up)* He says that now that the war's over we'll all have to settle down and be perfect. They may be hiding out in the back somewhere. Mrs. An-tro-bus.

(She wanders off. It has grown lighter. A trapdoor is cautiously raised and MRS. ANTROBUS *emerges waist-high and listens. She is disheveled and worn; she wears a tattered dress and a shawl half covers her head. She talks down through the trapdoor.)*

MRS. ANTROBUS: It's getting light. There's still something burning over there—Newark, or Jersey City. What? Yes, I could swear I heard someone moving about up here. But I can't see anybody. I say: I can't see anybody.

(She starts to move about the stage. GLADYS' *head appears at the trapdoor. She is holding a* BABY.*)*

GLADYS: Oh, Mama. Be careful.

MRS. ANTROBUS: Now, Gladys, you stay out of sight.

GLADYS: Well, let me stay here just a minute. I want the baby to get some of this fresh air.

MRS. ANTROBUS: All right, but keep your eyes open. I'll see what I can find. I'll have a good hot plate of soup for you before you can say Jack Robinson. Gladys Antrobus! Do you know what I think I see? There's old Mr. Hawkins sweeping the sidewalk in front of his A. and P. store. Sweeping it with a broom. Why, he must have gone crazy, like the others! I see some other people moving about, too.

GLADYS: Mama, come back, come back.

*(*MRS. ANTROBUS *returns to the trapdoor and listens.)*

MRS. ANTROBUS: Gladys, there's something in the air. Everybody's movement's sort of different. I see some women walking right out in the middle of the street.

SABINA'S VOICE: Mrs. An-tro-bus!

MRS. ANTROBUS *and* GLADYS: What's that?!!

SABINA'S VOICE: Glaaaadys! Mrs. An-tro-bus!

(Enter SABINA.*)*

MRS. ANTROBUS: Gladys, that's Sabina's voice as sure as I live.—Sabina! Sabina!—Are you *alive?!!*

SABINA: Of course, I'm alive. How've you girls been?—*Don't* try and kiss me. I never want to kiss another human being as long as I live. Sh-sh, there's nothing to get emotional about. Pull yourself together, the war's over. Take a deep breath,—the war's over.

MRS. ANTROBUS: The war's over!! I don't believe you. I don't believe you. I can't believe you.

GLADYS: Mama!

SABINA: Who's that?

MRS. ANTROBUS: That's Gladys and her baby. I don't believe you. Gladys, Sabina says the war's over. Oh, Sabina.

SABINA (*leaning over the* BABY): Goodness! Are there any babies left in the world! Can it *see?* And can it cry and everything?

GLADYS: Yes, he can. He notices everything very well.

SABINA: Where on earth did you get it? Oh, I won't ask.—Lord, I've lived all these seven years around camp and I've forgotten how to behave.— Now we've got to think about the men coming home.—Mrs. Antrobus, go and wash your face, I'm ashamed of you. Put your best clothes on. Mr. Antrobus'll be here this afternoon. I just saw him downtown.

MRS. ANTROBUS *and* GLADYS: He's alive!! He'll be here!! Sabina, you're not joking?

MRS. ANTROBUS: And Henry?

SABINA (*dryly*): Yes, Henry's alive, too, that's what they say. Now don't stop to talk. Get yourselves fixed up. Gladys, you look terrible. Have you any decent clothes?

(SABINA *has pushed them toward the trapdoor.*)

MRS. ANTROBUS (*half down*): Yes, I've something to wear just for this very day. But, Sabina,—who won the war?

SABINA: Don't stop now,—just wash your face. (*A whistle sounds in the distance*) Oh, my God, what's that silly little noise?

MRS. ANTROBUS: Why, it sounds like . . . it sounds like what used to be the noon whistle at the shoe-polish factory. (*Exit.*)

SABINA: That's what it is. Seems to me like peacetime's coming along pretty fast—shoe polish!

GLADYS (*half down*): Sabina, how soon after peacetime begins does the milkman start coming to the door?

SABINA: As soon as he catches a cow. Give him time to catch a cow, dear. (*Exit* GLADYS. SABINA *walks about a moment, thinking*) Shoe polish! My, I'd forgotten what peacetime was like. (*She shakes her head, then sits down by the trapdoor and starts talking down the hole*) Mrs. Antrobus, guess what I saw Mr. Antrobus doing this morning at dawn. He was tacking up a piece of paper on the door of the Town Hall. You'll die when you hear: it was a recipe for grass soup, for a grass soup that doesn't give you the diarrhea. Mr. Antrobus is still thinking up new things.—He told me to give you his love. He's got all sorts of ideas for peacetime, he says. No more laziness and idiocy, he says. And oh, yes! Where are his books? What? Well, pass them up. The first thing he wants to see are his books. He says if you've burnt those books, or if the rats have eaten them, he says it isn't worthwhile starting over again. Everybody's going to be beautiful, he says, and diligent, and very intelligent. (*A hand reaches up with two volumes*) What language is that? Pu-u-gh,—mold! And he's got such plans for you, Mrs. Antrobus. You're going to study history and algebra—and so are Gladys and I—and philosophy. You should hear him talk. (*Taking two more volumes*) Well, these are in English, anyway.— To hear him talk, seems like he expects you to be a combination, Mrs. Antrobus, of a saint and a college professor, and a dancehall hostess, if you know what I mean. (*Two more volumes*) Ugh. German! (*She is lying on the floor; one elbow bent, her cheek on her hand, meditatively*) Yes, peace will be here before we know it. In a week or two we'll be asking the Perkinses in for a quiet evening of bridge. We'll turn on the radio and hear how to be big successes with a new toothpaste. We'll trot down to the movies and see how girls with wax faces live—all *that* will begin again. Oh, Mrs. Antrobus, God forgive me but I enjoyed the war. Everybody's at their best in wartime. I'm sorry it's over. And, oh, I forgot! Mr. Antrobus sent you another message—can you hear me?—(*Enter* HENRY, *blackened and sullen. He is wearing torn overalls, but has one gaudy admiral's epaulette hanging by a thread from his right shoulder, and there are vestiges of gold and scarlet braid running down his left trouser leg. He stands listening*) Listen! Henry's never to put foot in this house again, he says. He'll kill Henry on sight, if he sees him. You don't know about Henry??? Well, where have you been? What? Well, Henry rose right to the top. Top of *what*? Listen, I'm telling you. Henry rose from corporal to captain, to major, to general.—I don't know how to say it, but the enemy is *Henry*; Henry *is* the enemy. Everybody knows that.

HENRY: He'll kill me, will he?

SABINA: Who are *you*? I'm not afraid of you. The war's over.

HENRY: I'll kill him so fast. I've spent seven years trying to find him; the others I killed were just substitutes.

SABINA: Goodness! It's Henry!—(*He makes an angry gesture*) Oh, I'm not afraid of you. The war's over, Henry Antrobus, and you're not any more important than any other unemployed. You go away and hide yourself, until we calm your father down.

HENRY: The first thing to do is burn up those old books; it's the ideas he gets out of those old books that . . . that makes the whole world so you can't live in it.

(*He reels forward and starts kicking the books about, but suddenly falls down in a sitting position.*)

SABINA: You leave those books alone!! Mr. Antrobus is looking forward to them a-special.—Gracious sakes, Henry, you're so tired you can't stand up. Your mother and sister'll be here in a minute and we'll think what to do about you.

HENRY: What did they ever care about me?

SABINA: There's that old whine again. All you people think you're not loved enough, nobody loves you. Well, you start being lovable and we'll love you.

HENRY (*outraged*): I don't want anybody to love me.

SABINA: Then stop talking about it all the time.

HENRY: I *never* talk about it. The last thing I want is anybody to pay any attention to me.

SABINA: I can hear it behind every word you say.

HENRY: I want everybody to hate me.

SABINA: Yes, you've decided that's second best, but it's still the same thing.—Mrs. Antrobus! Henry's here. He's so tired he can't stand up.

(MRS. ANTROBUS *and* GLADYS, *with her* BABY, *emerge. They are dressed as in Act One.* MRS. ANTROBUS *carries some objects in her apron, and* GLADYS *has a blanket over her shoulder.*)

MRS. ANTROBUS *and* GLADYS: Henry! Henry! Henry!

HENRY (*glaring at them*): Have you anything to eat?

MRS. ANTROBUS: Yes, I have, Henry. I've been saving it for this very day,— two good baked potatoes. No! Henry! One of them's for your father. Henry!! Give me that other potato back this minute.

(SABINA *sidles up behind him and snatches the other potato away.*)

SABINA: He's so dog-tired he doesn't know what he's doing.

MRS. ANTROBUS: Now you just rest there, Henry, until I can get your room ready. Eat that potato good and slow, so you can get all the nourishment out of it.

HENRY: You all might as well know right now that I haven't come back here to live.

MRS. ANTROBUS: Sh. . . . I'll put this coat over you. Your room's hardly damaged at all. Your football trophies are a little tarnished, but Sabina and I will polish them up tomorrow.

HENRY: Did you hear me? I don't live here. I don't belong to anybody.

MRS. ANTROBUS: Why, how can you say a thing like that! You certainly do belong right here. Where else would you want to go? Your forehead's feverish, Henry, seems to me. You'd better give me that gun, Henry. You won't need that any more.

GLADYS (*whispering*): Look, he's fallen asleep already, with his potato half-chewed.

SABINA: Puh! The terror of the world.

MRS. ANTROBUS: Sabina, you mind your own business, and start putting the room to rights.

(HENRY *has turned his face to the back of the sofa.* MRS. ANTROBUS *gingerly puts the revolver in her apron pocket, then helps* SABINA. SABINA *has found a rope hanging from the ceiling. Grunting, she hangs all her weight on it, and as she pulls, the walls begin to move into their right places.* MRS. ANTROBUS *brings the overturned tables, chairs and hassock into the positions of Act One.*)

SABINA: That's all we do—always beginning again! Over and over again. Always beginning again. (*She pulls on the rope and a part of the wall moves into place. She stops. Meditatively*) How do we know that it'll be any better than before? Why do we go on pretending? Some day the whole earth's going to have to turn cold anyway, and until that time all these other things'll be happening again: it will be more wars and more walls of ice and floods and earthquakes.

MRS. ANTROBUS: Sabina!! Stop arguing and go on with your work.

SABINA: All right. I'll go on just out of habit, but I won't believe in it.

MRS. ANTROBUS (*aroused*): Now, Sabina. I've let you talk long enough. I don't want to hear any more of it. Do I have to explain to you what everybody knows,—everybody who keeps a home going? Do I have to say to you what nobody should ever *have* to say, because they can read it in each other's eyes? Now listen to me: (MRS. ANTROBUS *takes hold of the rope*) I could live for seventy years in a cellar and make soup out of grass and bark, without ever doubting that this world has a work to do and will do it. Do you hear me?

SABINA (*frightened*): Yes, Mrs. Antrobus.

MRS. ANTROBUS: Sabina, do you see this house,—216 Cedar Street,—do you see it?

SABINA: Yes, Mrs. Antrobus.

MRS. ANTROBUS: Well, just to have known this house is to have seen the idea of what we can do someday if we keep our wits about us. Too many people have suffered and died for my children for us to start reneging now. So we'll start putting this house to rights. Now, Sabina, go and see what you can do in the kitchen.

SABINA: Kitchen! Why is it that however far I go away, I always find myself back in the kitchen? (*Exit.*)

MRS. ANTROBUS (*still thinking over her last speech, relaxes and says with a reminiscent smile*): Goodness gracious, wouldn't you know that my father was a parson? It was just like I heard his own voice speaking and he's been dead five thousand years. There! I've gone and almost waked Henry up.

HENRY (*talking in his sleep, indistinctly*): Fellows . . . what have they done for us? . . . Blocked our way at every step. Kept everything in their own hands. And you've stood it. When are you going to wake up?

MRS. ANTROBUS: Sh, Henry. Go to sleep. Go to sleep. Go to sleep.—Well, that looks better. Now let's go and help Sabina.

GLADYS: Mama, I'm going out into the backyard and hold the baby right up in the air. And show him that we don't have to be afraid any more. (*Exit* GLADYS *to the kitchen.* MRS. ANTROBUS *glances at* HENRY, *exits into kitchen.* HENRY *thrashes about in his sleep. Enter* ANTROBUS, *his arms full of bundles, chewing the end of a carrot. He has a slight limp. Over the suit of Act One he is wearing an overcoat too long for him, its skirts trailing on the ground. He lets his bundles fall and stands looking about. Presently his attention is fixed on* HENRY, *whose words grow clearer.*)

HENRY: All right! What have you got to lose? What have they done for us? That's right—nothing. Tear everything down. I don't care what you smash. We'll begin again and we'll show 'em. (ANTROBUS *takes out his revolver and holds it pointing downwards. With his back towards the audience he moves toward the footlights.* HENRY'S *voice grows louder and he wakes with a start. They stare at one another. Then* HENRY *sits up quickly. Throughout the following scene* HENRY *is played, not as a misunderstood or misguided young man, but as a representation of strong unreconciled evil*) All right! Do something. (*Pause*) Don't think I'm afraid of you, either. All right, do what you were going to do. Do it. (*Furiously*) Shoot me, I tell you. You don't have to think I'm any relation of yours. I haven't got any father or any mother, or brothers or sisters. And I don't want any. And what's more I haven't got anybody over me; and I never will have. I'm alone, and that's all I want to be: alone. So you can shoot me.

ANTROBUS: You're the last person I wanted to see. The sight of you dries up all my plans and hopes. I wish I were back at war still, because it's easier to fight you than to live with you. War's a pleasure—do you hear me?—War's a pleasure compared to what faces us now: trying to build up a peacetime with you in the middle of it.

(ANTROBUS *walks up to the window.*)

HENRY: I'm not going to be a part of any peacetime of yours. I'm going a long way from here and make my own world that's fit for a man to live in. Where a man can be free, and have a chance, and do what he wants to do in his own way.

ANTROBUS (*his attention arrested; thoughtfully. He throws the gun out of the window and turns with hope*) : . . . Henry, let's try again.

HENRY: Try what? Living *here?*—Speaking polite downtown to all the old men like you? Standing like a sheep at the street corner until the red light turns to green? Being a good boy and a good sheep, like all the stinking ideas you get out of your books? Oh, no. I'll make a world, and I'll show you.

ANTROBUS (*hard*) : How can you make a world for people to live in, unless you've first put order in yourself? Mark my words: I shall continue fighting you until my last breath as long as you mix up your idea of liberty with your idea of hogging everything for yourself. I shall have no pity on you. I shall pursue you to the far corners of the earth. You and I want the same thing; but until you think of it as something that everyone has a right to, you are my deadly enemy and I will destroy you.—I hear your mother's voice in the kitchen. Have you seen her?

HENRY: I have no mother. Get it into your head. I don't belong here. I have nothing to do here. I have no home.

ANTROBUS: Then why did you come here? With the whole world to choose from, why did you come to this one place: 216 Cedar Street, Excelsior, New Jersey. . . . Well?

HENRY: What if I did? What if I wanted to look at it once more, to see if—

ANTROBUS: Oh, you're related, all right—When your mother comes in you must behave yourself. Do you hear me?

HENRY (*wildly*) : What is this?—*must behave* yourself. Don't you say *must* to me.

ANTROBUS: Quiet!

(*Enter* MRS. ANTROBUS *and* SABINA.)

HENRY: Nobody can say *must* to me. All my life everybody's been crossing me,—everybody, everything, all of you. I'm going to be free, even if I have to kill half the world for it. Right now, too. Let me get my hands on his throat. I'll show him.

(*He advances toward* ANTROBUS. *Suddenly,* SABINA *jumps between them and calls out in her own person:*)

SABINA: Stop! Stop! Don't play this scene. You know what happened last night. Stop the play. (*The men fall back, panting.* HENRY *covers his face with his hands*) Last night you almost strangled him. You became a regular savage. Stop it!

HENRY: It's true. I'm sorry. I don't know what comes over me. I have nothing against him personally. I respect him very much . . . I . . . I admire him. But something comes over me. It's like I become fifteen years old again. I . . . I . . . listen: my own father used to whip me and lock me up every Saturday night. I never had enough to eat. He never let me have enough money to buy decent clothes. I was ashamed to go downtown. I never could go to the dances. My father and my uncle put rules in the way of everything I wanted to do. They tried to prevent my living at all.—I'm sorry. I'm sorry.

MRS. ANTROBUS (*quickly*): No, go on. Finish what you were saying. Say it all.

HENRY: In this scene it's as though I were back in High School again. It's like I had some big emptiness inside me,—the emptiness of being hated and blocked at every turn. And the emptiness fills up with the one thought that you have to strike and fight and kill. Listen, it's as though you have to kill somebody else so as not to end up killing yourself.

SABINA: That's not true. I knew your father and your uncle and your mother. You imagined all that. Why, they did everything they could for you. How can you say things like that? They didn't lock you up.

HENRY: They did. They did. They wished I hadn't been born.

SABINA: That's not true.

ANTROBUS (*in his own person, with self-condemnation, but cold and proud*): Wait a minute. I have something to say, too. It's not wholly his fault that he wants to strangle me in this scene. It's my fault, too. He wouldn't feel that way unless there were something in me that reminded him of all that. He talks about an emptiness. Well, there's an emptiness in me, too. Yes,—work, work, work,—that's all I do. I've ceased to *live*. No wonder he feels that anger coming over him.

MRS. ANTROBUS: There! At last you've said it.

SABINA: We're all just as wicked as we can be, and that's the God's truth.

MRS. ANTROBUS (*nods a moment, then comes forward; quietly*): Come. Come and put your head under some cold water.

SABINA (*in a whisper*): I'll go with him. I've known him a long while. You have to go on with the play. Come with me.

(HENRY *starts out with* SABINA, *but turns at the exit and says to* ANTROBUS:)

HENRY: Thanks. Thanks for what you said. I'll be all right tomorrow. I won't lose control in that place. I promise.

(*Exeunt* HENRY *and* SABINA. ANTROBUS *starts toward the front door, fastens it.* MRS. ANTROBUS *goes up stage and places the chair close to table.*)

MRS. ANTROBUS: George, do I see you limping?

ANTROBUS: Yes, a little. My old wound from the other war started smarting again. I can manage.

MRS. ANTROBUS (*looking out of the window*): Some lights are coming on,— the first in seven years. People are walking up and down looking at them. Over in Hawkins' open lot they've built a bonfire to celebrate the peace. They're dancing around it like scarecrows.

ANTROBUS: A bonfire! As though they hadn't seen enough things burning.— Maggie,—the dog died?

MRS. ANTROBUS: Oh, yes. Long ago. There are no dogs left in Excelsior.— You're back again! All these years. I gave up counting on letters. The few that arrived were anywhere from six months to a year late.

ANTROBUS: Yes, the ocean's full of letters, along with the other things.

MRS. ANTROBUS: George, sit down, you're tired.

ANTROBUS: No, you sit down. I'm tired but I'm restless. (*Suddenly, as she comes forward*) Maggie! I've lost it. I've lost it.

MRS. ANTROBUS: What, George? What have you lost?

ANTROBUS: The most important thing of all: The desire to begin again, to start building.

MRS. ANTROBUS (*sitting in the chair right of the table*): Well, it will come back.

ANTROBUS (*at the window*): I've lost it. This minute I feel like all those people dancing around the bonfire—just relief. Just the desire to settle down; to slip into the old grooves and keep the neighbors from walking over my lawn.—Hm. But during the war,—in the middle of all that blood and dirt and hot and cold—every day and night, I'd have moments, Maggie, when I *saw* the things that we could do when it was over. When you're at war you think about a better life; when you're at peace you think about a more comfortable one. I've lost it. I feel sick and tired.

MRS. ANTROBUS: Listen! The baby's crying. I hear Gladys talking. Probably she's quieting Henry again. George, while Gladys and I were living here —like moles, like rats, and when we were at our wits' end to save the baby's life—the only thought we clung to was that you were going to bring something good out of this suffering. In the night, in the dark, we'd whisper about it, starving and sick.—Oh, George, you'll have to get it back again. Think! What else kept us alive all these years? Even now, it's not comfort we want. We can suffer whatever's necessary; only give us back that promise.

(*Enter* SABINA *with a lighted lamp. She is dressed as in Act One.*)

SABINA: Mrs. Antrobus. . . .

MRS. ANTROBUS: Yes, Sabina?

SABINA: Will you need me?

MRS. ANTROBUS: No, Sabina, you can go to bed.

SABINA: Mrs. Antrobus, if it's all right with you, I'd like to go to the bonfire and celebrate seeing the war's over. And, Mrs. Antrobus, they've opened the Gem Movie Theatre and they're giving away a hand-painted soup tureen to every lady, and I thought one of us ought to go.

ANTROBUS: Well, Sabina, I haven't any money. I haven't seen any money for quite a while.

SABINA: Oh, you don't need money. They're taking anything you can give them. And I have some . . . some . . . Mrs. Antrobus, promise you won't tell anyone. It's a little against the law. But I'll give you some, too.

ANTROBUS: What is it?

SABINA: I'll give you some, too. Yesterday I picked up a lot of . . . of beef-cubes!

(MRS. ANTROBUS *turns and says calmly:*)

MRS. ANTROBUS: But, Sabina, you know you ought to give that in to the Center downtown. They know who needs them most.

SABINA (*outburst*): Mrs. Antrobus, I didn't make this war. I didn't ask for it. And, in my opinion, after anybody's gone through what we've gone through, they have a right to grab what they can find. You're a very nice man, Mr. Antrobus, but you'd have got on better in the world if you'd realized that dog-eat-dog was the rule in the beginning and always will be. And most of all now. (*In tears*) Oh, the world's an awful place, and you know it is. I used to think something could be done about it; but I know better now. I hate it. I hate it. (*She comes forward slowly and brings six cubes from the bag*) All right. All right. You can have them.

ANTROBUS: Thank you, Sabina.

SABINA: Can I have . . . can I have one to go to the movies? (ANTROBUS *in silence gives her one*) Thank you.

ANTROBUS: Good night, Sabina.

SABINA: Mr. Antrobus, don't mind what I say. I'm just an ordinary girl, you know what I mean, I'm just an ordinary girl. But you're a bright man, you're a very bright man, and of course you invented the alphabet and the wheel, and, my God, a lot of things . . . and if you've got any other plans, my God, don't let me upset them. Only every now and then I've got to go to the movies. I mean my nerves can't stand it. But if you have any ideas about improving the crazy old world, I'm really with you. I really am. Because it's . . . it's . . . Good night.

(*She goes out.* ANTROBUS *starts laughing softly with exhilaration.*)

ANTROBUS: Now I remember what three things always went together when I was able to see things most clearly: three things. Three things: (*He points to where* SABINA *has gone out*) The voice of the people in their confusion and their need. And the thought of you and the children and this house. . . . And . . . Maggie! I didn't dare ask you: my books! They haven't been lost, have they?

MRS. ANTROBUS: No. There are some of them right here. Kind of tattered.

ANTROBUS: Yes.—Remember, Maggie, we almost lost them once before? And when we finally did collect a few torn copies out of old cellars they ran in everyone's head like a fever. They as good as rebuilt the world. (*Pauses, book in hand, and looks up*)

Oh, I've never forgotten for long at a time that living is struggle. I know that every good and excellent thing in the world stands moment by moment on the razor-edge of danger and must be fought for—whether it's a field, or a home, or a country. All I ask is the chance to build new worlds and God has always given us that. And has given us (*opening the book*) voices to guide us; and the memory of our mistakes to warn us. Maggie, you and I will remember in peacetime all the resolves that were so clear to us in the days of war. We've come a long ways. We've learned. We're learning. And the steps of our journey are marked for us here. (*He stands by the table turning the leaves of a book*)

Sometimes out there in the war,—standing all night on a hill—I'd try and remember some of the words in these books. Parts of them and phrases would come back to me. And after a while I used to give names to the hours of the night. (*He sits, hunting for a passage in the book*) Nine o'clock I used to call Spinoza. Where is it: "After experience had taught me—"

(*The back wall has disappeared, revealing the platform.* FRED BAILEY *carrying his numeral has started from left to right.* MRS. ANTROBUS *sits by the table sewing.*)

BAILEY: "After experience had taught me that the common occurrences of daily life are vain and futile; and I saw that all the objects of my desire and fear were in themselves nothing good nor bad save insofar as the mind was affected by them; I at length determined to search out whether there was something truly good and communicable to man."

(*Almost without break* HESTER, *carrying a large Roman numeral ten, starts crossing the platform.* GLADYS *appears at the kitchen door and moves towards her mother's chair.*)

HESTER: "Then tell me, O Critias, how will a man choose the ruler that shall rule over him? Will he not choose a man who has first established order in himself, knowing that any decision that has its spring from anger or pride or vanity can be multiplied a thousand fold in its effects upon the citizens?"

(HESTER *disappears and* IVY, *as eleven o'clock, starts speaking.*)

IVY: "This good estate of the mind possessing its object in energy we call divine. This we mortals have occasionally and it is this energy which is pleasantest and best. But God has it always. It is wonderful in us; but in Him how much more wonderful."

(*As* MR. TREMAYNE *starts to speak,* HENRY *appears at the edge of the scene, brooding and unreconciled, but present.*)

TREMAYNE: "In the beginning, God created the Heavens and the earth; And the Earth was waste and void; And the darkness was upon the face of the deep. And the Lord said let there be light and there was light."

(*Sudden black-out and silence, except for the last strokes of the midnight bell. Then just as suddenly the lights go up, and* SABINA *is standing at the window, as at the opening of the play.*)

SABINA: Oh, oh, oh. Six o'clock and the master not home yet. Pray God nothing serious has happened to him crossing the Hudson River. But I wouldn't be surprised. The whole world's at sixes and sevens, and why the house hasn't fallen down about our ears long ago is a miracle to me. (*She comes down to the footlights*)

This is where you came in. We have to go on for ages and ages yet. You go home. The end of this play isn't written yet. Mr. and Mrs. Antrobus! Their heads are full of plans and they're as confident as the first day they began,—and they told me to tell you: good night.

Commentary

Of all forms of literary criticism none occupies a more precarious yet responsible position than dramatic criticism. Much of the criticism that the average Broadway play will receive is written only a few hours after the final curtain has fallen on its first-night performance. It is the product, not of any careful, deliberate textual study, but of first impressions by a half-dozen or so critics, highly trained and perceptive observers of a living theatrical performance. It has become almost a sacred Broadway tradition that criticism should be written in a taxicab racing to a newspaper office to meet a deadline for the morning edition. The responsibility of the New York critics is staggering, for upon their judgment of play and performance largely rests the success of the production. A financial investment totaling many thousands of dollars, employment for the actors and crew, and a playwright's reputation often ride on those first notices. As Kenneth Tynan says, "It is no light task to pronounce verdict, in less than an hour of writing time, on an enterprise that has probably been in preparation for a year and may easily, in the course of its casting, financing, rehearsing, and rewriting, have driven several of its participants to the edge of madness or beyond."[17] This is not to suggest that such criticism is arbitrary or capricious; on the contrary, most of it is thoughtful and discriminating, and some of it is brilliant.

The trying circumstances of writing a first-night review produce quite a different brand of commentary than the kind of historical and literary criticism accumulated over the years around Ibsen, Chekhov, and Shaw. As the drama critics left the Plymouth Theater after the first performance of *The Skin of Our Teeth* on November 18, 1942, there were no critical precedents which they could use to substantiate their opinions or behind which they could hide. Therefore the reviews were, as one would expect, highly contradictory and provocative.

Excerpts from these first-night notices have been included here, not to show that there are no absolutes in dramatic criticism nor to imply that all criticism is therefore whimsical and subjective, but to provide a group of considered opinions against which we can measure our own. In one sense, the student is at a disadvantage, for he may not have seen an actual stage performance, which must be the ultimate test of any play; but, on the other hand, he does have a singular advantage over the Broadway critics because with the text at hand and the privilege of re-reading he is able to form a more deliberate judgment of the play as *dramatic literature* without the exigencies of time pressing him. Nor will the student have to aim his criticism at a particular reading public, as newspaper critics to some extent must do.

Without any textual analysis of *The Skin of Our Teeth* as an aid, the student is actually facing the situation that confronts him when he leaves the classroom. The reviews may be of help, but are never a substitute for the critical experience that comes only with reading and studying dramatic literature and attending the theater. From such experience is derived the ability to formulate criteria and to judge independently.

---

[17] Kenneth Tynan, *Curtains* (New York, 1961), p. 367.

Clearly, it is impossible for one to agree with all of the diametrically opposed and outspoken opinions that follow. As qualified readers, we are now in a position to criticize the professional critics, who, although they are acknowledged experts, do not have any claim to final and definitive judgments. If their evaluations, like ours, are to be valid, they must be founded not on whims or prejudices (although sensitivity and taste are not to be overlooked), but upon an honest, intelligent, and judicious understanding of the play. If a survey of the contradictory evaluations of this or any play causes the reader to feel a sense of frustration because there are no "right answers," the solution is to return to the text itself, which contains the only ultimate answers that can ever be given on it.

Before the play began, the première audience at *The Skin of Our Teeth* had nothing to go on but the program notes prepared by an understandably nervous management:

> *The Skin of Our Teeth* is a comedy about George Antrobus, his wife and two children, and their general utility maid, Lily Sabina, all of Excelsior, New Jersey. George Antrobus is John Doe or George Spelvin or you— the average American at grips with a destiny sometimes sour, sometimes sweet. The Antrobuses have survived fire, flood, pestilence, the seven-year locusts, the ice age, the black pox and the double feature, a dozen wars and as many depressions. They have run many a gamut, are as durable as radiators, and look upon the future with a disarming optimism. Ultimately bewitched, befuddled and becalmed, they are the stuff of which heroes are made—heroes and buffoons. They are true offspring of Adam and Eve, victims of all the ills that flesh is heir to. They have survived a thousand calamities by the skin of their teeth, and Mr. Wilder's play is a tribute to their indestructibility.

One Broadway critic, Wilella Waldorf, of the New York *Post,* however, was ready to return the notes to the producer:

> That's what the management says.

> Maybe so. It seems more probable, however, that "The Skin of Our Teeth" is actually less abstruse. Mr. Wilder must simply have decided one night that if Olsen and Johnson can get away with what they've been doing in the theatre all these years, there is no good reason why Thornton Wilder shouldn't turn out something of the kind, with a dash of philosophy tossed in here and there to remind us that he has, after all, a reputation for profound and lofty thinking. . . .

> Mr. Wilder goes to some trouble to indicate that the Antrobuses are actually Adam and Eve, and that their son, an aggressive youth handy with a sling-shot, is named Cain. Moses comes into the first act, and there is a good deal of rebuilding-the-world-after-the-war talk later on, with overtones from the philosophers just out the window. This may set some people a-worrying about allegorical significance and kindred subjects, but "The Skin of Our Teeth" actually is neither a profound nor particularly impressive drama.

It is merely a stunt show with everything tossed into it that the author could dream up. Like all wacky extravaganzas it doesn't always come off, and it is occasionally rather dull, but the evening is saved by some good performances in the leading roles, and especially by the fact that Miss Bankhead is on hand to chatter and flounce her way through the ages, complaining bitterly to the audience every thousand years or so.

Burton Rascoe, of the New York *World-Telegram,* was considerably kinder but for quite contrary reasons:

Mr. Wilder has, indeed, learned enough about the theater to know that it is a medium of entertainment first and of instruction and edification afterwards; and so, in his new play, he kids the life out of his pseudo-philosophic manner and kids life into a play that is genuinely philosophical.

In taking a tip from *Hellzapoppin'*, he has learned that he can slip over on the audience the most serious message that he or anybody else can give in these pessimism-inducing times without having the audience walk out on him and the critics asking rhetorically in their critiques: "What's this hogwash all about?" In various ways Miss Bankhead has asked that same question so many times (and with such hilarious response from the audience each time) during the first act, that by the time the curtain goes down for the intermission you are devoutly hoping that the author won't go serious on you in the next act and pull one of these what-is-its of the drama which is known as a fantasy, and usually is something dreary and unpleasant or so sweet you feel like crying for a shot of insulin. You are hoping, indeed, that you won't ever know what the play is about, being quite content that it should keep on being crazy and funny.

The message of *The Skin of Our Teeth* is a rebuke to our contemporary prophets of doom and an encouraging reminder that since the first man and his wife appeared on earth he and their descendants have, as the program note seriously understates, "survived fire, flood, pestilence, the seven-year locusts, the ice age, the black pox and the double feature, and as many depressions" and the odds are heavily in favor of their surviving the present world catastrophe. Incidentally, there is the profound observation that, curiously enough, people are the noblest of their lives in time of war—sacrificing, aspiring, working in harmony and unselfishly, dreaming and hoping for a better world, full of heroic high resolve—and, then, when they have peace, security, leisure, they slip back into the old habits of human beings. And yet, says Mr. Wilder, the torch of progress and high aspiration is passed on after each catastrophe through books and the thoughts embodied in them by the philosophers, scientists, poets and artists. . . .

In my opinion this is the best play the war is likely to produce. Certainly it is bound to be the most comforting.

If Mr. Rascoe liked the play because it stayed thoroughly amusing as entertainment, John Anderson, of the New York *Journal American,* thought the fun obscured a seriously challenging theme; he would have preferred Wilder somberly to develop the exalting "tragic core" of his drama:

Yet it seems to me that the fun is too often superficial, that it touches no serious depths of emotion, so that the play fails to reach the wrenching intensity for which its laughter should be a profound release. Mr. Wilder takes a challenging theme and uses it for momentary effects with gadgets that are more theatrical than imaginative. It has a funny-paper inventiveness which finally gets in the way of what Mr. Wilder is trying to say. . . .

The terms Mr. Wilder has chosen to express this heroic optimism are clever, immediately challenging, and pictorially effective. Where he transcended space in "Our Town" and made his New England village a simple pattern of the whole world he has here kaleidoscoped time, and in Mr. and Mrs. Antrobus, of Excelsior, New Jersey, he has snapshotted the human family of all ages. He has outdone the classical unities by boiling them in Einstein. . . .

The Antrobus son is firmly called Henry to disguise the fact that he is really Cain, yet even in their moment of deepest dejection and grief they protect Cain, knowing the sorrow he will cause again and again in bathing the earth in blood.

It is in handling this, the tragic core of the play (since it is the fate humanity must triumph over), that Mr. Wilder seems to me to be too glib to be either searching or truly effective. Though his world is again in smoking ruins, and though Cain is back in the protective shelter of his own house (safe in the heart of the human race) Mr. Antrobus struggles up, clinging to a few printed pages of wisdom—trying to build his dream all over again on the ashes of his perpetual disillusion.

It is a valiant gesture, almost foolhardy in its unflinching purpose, and yet it doesn't hold much stature against the rest of the play, against the careful fantasy and occasional cuteness which Mr. Wilder indulges in for the general tone. It lacks scale, and so misses the exaltation which, however temporary, an audience of Antrobuses has a right to feel for a brief moment, even in their own tear-strewn merriment. We are asked to laugh at the cosmic kick in the pants, without feeling the pain.

Louis Kronenberger, writing for *PM,* considered the first act much the best and believed that by the third the drama had come to a standstill:

Dramatically Mr. Wilder cannot sustain what he sets out to do. Only his first act has a real freshness and lift, partly because everything is still new and sudden and amusingly incongruous, but partly because it is full of impudent monkeyshines that, besides being hilarious in themselves, act as a kind of fourth-dimensional commentary on the illogic of man's experiences. The play, after that, starts bumping up and down. There are still hilarious moments, but the humor on the whole is less frequent and more forced. Since there is no narrative worth mentioning, it is only by fresh spurts of the imagination that the play can sail ahead, and the spurts are not many. By the third act, the play bogs down in talk, and Mr. Wilder even succumbs to the temptation of orchestrating his theme with some pretty set speeches. . . .

For Howard Barnes, of the New York *Herald Tribune,* conversely, the third act was worth the whole play:

> To some it may seem that Wilder is having fun at an audience's expense in his cockeyed panorama of human existence. There are several supposedly antic touches in the exposition which are definitely hard to take. When the play flames up in moments of great eloquence and imagery, though, it needs neither glossary nor an approach of detached amusement. "The Skin of Our Teeth" is wonderfully wise as well as wacky. It uses the language of the theater triumphantly to make its points.
>
> Like all daring and exciting works of art, it is rewarding in just such measure as one wishes to find it so. Viewed merely as a prank, it is frequently amusing, but often wearisome. Contemplated as a sometimes stuttering but splendidly sincere attempt to make some sense out of this poor old world, it is a challenging and unforgettable communication between a group of artists and spectators. The final act, with its trenchant observations on the current scene, would have sufficed by itself to have made "The Skin of Our Teeth" a glowing play. With the satirical matter that is woven into earlier scenes, the show has real dimensions. . . .

But George Jean Nathan would have very little of it at any time in any mood.

> This play once again reinforces the conviction that Thornton Wilder remains merely a talented dilettante. Apparently determined at all costs to be different, his stage writing, while it accomplishes that end, does not succeed in investing the difference with enough weight to give it an even relative importance. He is at times agreeably humorous; he is at moments remotely inventive; he is at times even moderately moving. But it is all on the surface; there is little or no plumbing of the depths; and the final impression, after the pleasant little moments have been forgotten, is of one of those imitation gold bracelets hung with newfangled charms that one sees in the so-called novelty shops. It is pretty and it is cute, but it isn't the real article, and its novelty very quickly wears off. . . .[18]

The years have shown Mr. Nathan's last remark to be rather too sweeping, for 1955 and 1961 brought full-scale revivals of the play here and abroad. We today, however, have one advantage denied the critics of 1942—perspective. The shock and surprise at the novelty have worn off for those now thoroughly familiar with it, although perhaps not for one viewing the play for the first time. But the last two decades have shown that the play has more than the surface appeal of entertainment; it has a theme that is significant not only in the dark days of a world at war

---

18 George Jean Nathan, *The Theatre Book of the Year, 1942-1943* (New York, 1943), pp. 132-133.

but also at a time when the world hovers near the brink of nuclear disaster. Wilder has noted that his play

> mostly comes alive under conditions of crisis. It has been often charged with being a bookish fantasia about history, full of rather bloodless schoolmasterish jokes. But to have seen it in Germany soon after the war, in the shattered churches and beer halls that were serving as theatres, with audiences whose price of admission meant the loss of a meal and for whom it was of absorbing interest that there was a "recipe for grass soup that did not cause the diarrhea," was an experience that was not so cool.[19]

Today we can see more clearly that whatever judgments ultimately are made about *The Skin of Our Teeth* must not attempt to separate the external theatrical form from its thematic content. The artistic unity of the drama defies any such easy dichotomy. Brooks Atkinson, in the *New York Times* of August 7, 1955, could thus add a new dimension to the criticism of Wilder's play because thirteen years gave him the advantage of an aesthetic distance. It is significant that Mr. Atkinson's verdict should be more favorable than any rendered in 1942, for every play needs to be reassessed at every reading and every performance.

> The breezy form gives the impression that mankind carries forward its ancient and honorable traditions unconsciously in the midst of squalor, vulgarity and muddle—never aware of its spiritual valor. In this way the slapstick form provides perspective.
>
> In 1942, after the anxious years of the depression and in the depths of World War II, "The Skin of Our Teeth" was a tonic. . . . Thirteen years later, the play is still a vital piece of dramatic literature. Even when detached from the emergencies of its own period, it has intellectual stature. It is an expression of faith by a man of knowledge and principle. It reflects some of the light referred to in the quotation from Genesis that brings the story to a close—"And the Lord said, let there be light and there was light." When he was writing his play Mr. Wilder caught some of the light.

Questions and Problems

1. What are the various theatrical devices that Wilder uses in Act One to baffle an unsuspecting audience?

2. What is the playwright alluding to on page 532 when he says that Mrs. Antrobus "invented the apron on which so many interesting changes have been rung since"? What other similar allusions are there in Act One?

---

[19] Thornton Wilder, "A Platform and a Passion or Two," *Harper's*, CCXV (October, 1957), 51.

3. What are the pertinent facts of exposition derived from the announcer and Sabina? Why all the apparent irrelevancies, such as the location of the Antrobus home near an A & P, or Mr. Antrobus' scars?

4. What is the function of Sabina's interrupting the dialogue to address the audience?

5. List all the anachronisms and incongruities in the play up to the time of Mr. Antrobus' arrival. What is the author's purpose in introducing them?

6. How would you direct the scene in Act One in which the Refugees appear? With a stage full of people, how can you keep these minor characters from appearing wooden and lifeless?

7. Since Moses, Homer, and the Muses have no direct relationship to the Antrobuses' present dilemma, why are they included in the play?

8. Discuss the theatrical effectiveness of the curtain scene in Act One. How does it help Wilder's theme to emerge more clearly?

9. How does the prophecy of the Fortune Teller establish the variations on the theme developed in Act Two?

10. In Act Two what is the symbolic meaning of (a) the set; (b) the conveeners; (c) the Fortune Teller; (d) the convention speeches of Mr. and Mrs. Antrobus?

11. What new light is shed on the character of each of the Antrobuses during Act Two?

12. What functions are served by the minor characters in each act?

13. Evaluate the analysis of the function of the hours that is spoken by Ivy on pages 566-567.

14. What reasons could there be for Wilder's going through the elaborate stage business of the interruption and rehearsal in Act Three?

15. Act Three takes place immediately after World War II, or after any and all of the wars of mankind. What traditional attitudes toward peace are dramatized here?

16. What is the dramatist's purpose in revealing the character of the boy playing the part of Henry in the quarrel on pages 573-574?

17. Discuss the range of the historical and mythical allusions in the play as a whole. Does the dramatist's theme gain or lose impact because of such a multiplicity of references?

18. The Broadway critics are sharply divided on the structural unity of *The Skin of Our Teeth*. What reasons might Wilder have had for combining a serious theme with a novel and amusing dramatic style?

19. In the absence of a conventional plot, on what unifying principle are the three acts organized?

20. What happens to the character of Henry during the play? How is he made a significant part of Wilder's meaning?

21. Discuss the various people and symbols represented in each of the Antrobuses and in Sabina. All these characters also represent traits of character that Wilder considers universal. Illustrate.

22. What is Wilder satirizing in Sabina's opening scene? What other elements of satire are there in *The Skin of Our Teeth*?

23. Defend, qualify, or refute each of these judgments of *The Skin of Our Teeth*:

a. "Where the inclusiveness of a fully developed conflict is absent, Wilder achieves his moral and religious affirmations too easily. Antrobus in *The Skin of Our Teeth* survives the disasters that beset mankind, but most of mankind is destroyed by them; and we see no real suffering during his times of crisis. Granting that moral courage can help minimize the tyranny of circumstance, we do not see Antrobus' courage tested in serious conflict on the stage."[20]

b. "Man, says Mr. Wilder, from time to time gets puffed up with pride and prosperity, he grows envious, covetous, lecherous, forgets his conjugal duties, goes whoring after women; portents of disaster appear, but he is too blind to see them; in the end, with the help of the little woman, who has never taken any stock in either pleasure or wisdom, he escapes by the skin of his teeth. *Sicut erat in principio*. . . .

"It is a curious view of life. It displays elements of Christian morality. Christ, however, was never so simple. . . ."[21]

c. "In the third act, which deals with contemporary disaster, the theatricalism is not only inappropriate because it is played in the wrong key and is perhaps insufficiently climactic for a dramatic masterpiece, but it is evasive as well. The author has apparently nothing to say that he hasn't already told us twice. So he repeats himself again, quotes the right authors, who give us the right schoolbook assurances in a pageant-like procession of the show's backstage personnel; and he reminds us for a third time that *The Skin of Our Teeth* is just a show. Ibsen and Shaw would have scorned to beg off so lightly."[22]

24. Compare Shaw and Wilder as dramatic satirists. How does each parody what he considers old-fashioned playwriting? Which seems to be the more successful dramatist? Why?

25. Contrast the roles of Sabina and Mrs. Helseth in *Rosmersholm* as maids.

26. On page 576 Antrobus declares, "All I ask is the chance to build new worlds." At some point in their lives the same thought may have occurred to characters in *Rosmersholm, Desire under the Elms*, and *A View from the Bridge*. For each character define the vision of the "new world." In each case why is the vision never to be fulfilled? In the last act of *The Cherry Orchard*, on the other hand, Anya exultantly asserts, "A new life is beginning, mamma." What are her chances of fulfilling the dream? Is Trofimov Chekhov's Antrobus? Would you support the critic who argues, "At the end of *The Cherry Orchard*, the main characters are set free from the past. Each goes off in isolation. They have all learned how to live better, abandoning a nonproductive, dead society which glories in its past. They go away to do and to produce"?[23]

---

[20] Rex Burbank, *Thornton Wilder* (New York, 1961), p. 133.

[21] Mary McCarthy, *Sights and Spectacles* (New York, 1956), pp. 54-55.

[22] John Gassner, *Form and Idea in Modern Theatre* (New York, 1956), p. 143.

[23] Norman Silverstein, "Chekhov's Comic Spirit and *The Cherry Orchard*," *Modern Drama*, I (September, 1958), 99.

27. What comments are made in *The Devil's Disciple, The Glass Menagerie, Becket,* and *The Skin of Our Teeth* about the impact of war on the individual?

28. *Rosmersholm, Desire under the Elms, The Glass Menagerie, A View from the Bridge, The Cherry Orchard,* and *The Skin of Our Teeth* are all in some way plays about home. What similarities and differences are noteworthy in the sets which reveal both the physical dimensions of these homes and their larger thematic or symbolic implications? Why does each playwright center the dramatic action upon the home? In each case, with the exception of *Rosmersholm,* consider the significance of the parent-child relationship to the play as a whole. How do these relationships underscore the view of life which each play dramatizes? In every play except *The Skin of Our Teeth* the home is badly shaken or destroyed by the dramatic events. Describe the nature of these destructive forces. Are they usually internal or external? Are they inevitable? Are members of the families innocent victims or responsible agents in the breakup of these homes and families? Could the family have survived them? What view of these questions is taken by *The Skin of Our Teeth?*

EDWARD ALBEE

The Sandbox

*A brief play, in memory of
my grandmother (1876–1959)*

Biography

BORN ON March 12, 1928, in Washington, D. C., Edward Albee was adopted two weeks later by Reed and Frances Albee and grew up in and around New York City. He attended preparatory schools at Lawrenceville, Valley Forge Military Academy, and Choate and left Trinity College in Hartford, Connecticut, during his sophomore year. After college he worked in New York City at various odd jobs, among them that of Western Union messenger. During these years he wrote poetry and attempted a novel before deciding to write plays.

Albee's first play, *The Zoo Story*, had its première in a German translation in Berlin on September 28, 1959, and its first American production, Off Broadway, in January, 1960, on a double bill with Samuel Beckett's *Krapp's Last Tape*. In the introduction to a collection of his first three plays in 1960 Albee writes:

> *The Sandbox*, which is fourteen minutes long, was written to satisfy a commission from the Festival of Two Worlds for a short dramatic piece for the Festival's summer program in Spoleto, Italy—where it was not performed. I was, at the time of the commission, at work on a rather longer play, *The American Dream*, which I subsequently put aside and have, at this writing, just taken up again. For *The Sandbox*, I extracted several of the characters from *The American Dream* and placed them in a situation different than, but related to, their predicament in the longer play. They seem happy out of doors, in *The Sandbox*, and I hope they will not be distressed back in a stuffy apartment, in *The American Dream*.[1]

The American Dream parodies American family life, togetherness, and physical fitness as sentimental middle-class ideals. In his first full-length drama, *Who's Afraid of Virginia Woolf?*, which is set in the living room of a faculty couple of a New England college, Albee again attacks people living with false values. As one of the most promising of the "new wave" playwrights writing for Off-Broadway productions, Albee has already won the respect of Tennessee Williams, who says of him, "Edward Albee is a man who's never compromised and I doubt he ever will."[2]

---

[1] Edward Albee, *Three Plays* (New York, 1960), p. 5.
[2] Seymour Peck, "Williams and 'The Iguana,'" *New York Times,* December 24, 1961, Sec. 2, p. 5.

Plays

The Zoo Story (1958)
The Death of Bessie Smith (1959)
The Sandbox (1959)

The American Dream (1960)
Who's Afraid of Virginia Woolf?
(1961)

Selected Descriptive Bibliography

Albee, Edward, "Which Theatre Is the Absurd One?" *New York Times,* February 25, 1962, sec. 6, pp. 30-31, 64-66.
In a lively attack on the failures of Broadway, Albee discusses the nature and aims of the Off-Broadway theater today.

Esslin, Martin, *The Theatre of the Absurd,* New York, 1961.
An intelligent and searching analysis of the history, tradition, and significance of the experimental "Theatre of the Absurd," with which Albee has become identified.

The Sandbox EDWARD ALBEE

CHARACTERS

THE YOUNG MAN, *25, a good-looking, well-built boy in a bathing suit*

MOMMY, *55, a well-dressed, imposing woman*

DADDY, *60, a small man; gray, thin*

GRANDMA, *86, a tiny, wizened woman with bright eyes*

THE MUSICIAN, *no particular age, but young; would be nice*

NOTE: *When, in the course of the play, MOMMY and DADDY call each other by these names, there should be no suggestion of regionalism. These names are of empty affection and point up the presenility and vacuity of their characters.*

THE SCENE: *A bare stage, with only the following: Near the footlights, far stage-right, two simple chairs set side by side, facing the audience; near the footlights, far stage-left, a chair facing stage-right with a music stand before it; farther back, and stage-center, slightly elevated and raked, a large child's sandbox with a toy pail and shovel; the background is the sky, which alters from brightest day to deepest night.*

At the beginning, it is brightest day; the YOUNG MAN is alone on stage, to the rear of the sandbox, and to one side. He is doing calisthenics; he does calisthenics until quite at the very end of the play. These calisthenics, employing the arms only, should suggest the beating and fluttering of wings. The YOUNG MAN is, after all, the Angel of Death.

The Sandbox was first performed at the Jazz Gallery in New York City on April 15, 1960.

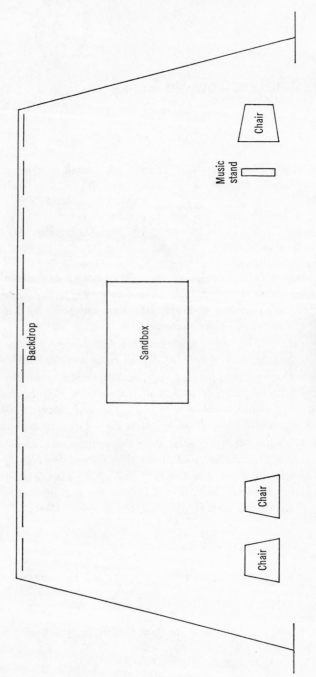

THE SANDBOX

The Sandbox

MOMMY *and* DADDY *enter from stage-left,* MOMMY *first.*

MOMMY (*motioning to* DADDY) : Well, here we are; this is the beach.

DADDY (*whining*) : I'm cold.

MOMMY (*dismissing him with a little laugh*) : Don't be silly; it's as warm as toast. Look at that nice young man over there: *he* doesn't think it's cold. (*Waves to the* YOUNG MAN) Hello.

YOUNG MAN (*with an endearing smile*) : Hi!

MOMMY (*looking about*) : This will do perfectly . . . don't you think so, Daddy? There's sand there . . . and the water beyond. What do you think, Daddy?

DADDY (*vaguely*) : Whatever you say, Mommy.

MOMMY (*with the same little laugh*) : Well, of course . . . whatever I say. Then, it's settled, is it?

DADDY (*shrugs*) : She's *your* mother, not mine.

MOMMY: *I* know she's my mother. What do you take me for? (*A pause*) All right, now; let's get on with it. (*She shouts into the wings, stage-left*) You! Out there! You can come in now.

(*The* MUSICIAN *enters, seats himself in the chair, stage-left, places music on the music stand, is ready to play.* MOMMY *nods approvingly.*)

MOMMY: Very nice; very nice. Are you ready, Daddy? Let's go get Grandma.

DADDY: Whatever you say, Mommy.

MOMMY (*leading the way out, stage-left*) : Of course, whatever I say. (*To the* MUSICIAN) You can begin now.

(*The* MUSICIAN *begins playing;* MOMMY *and* DADDY *exit; the* MUSICIAN, *all the while playing, nods to the* YOUNG MAN.)

YOUNG MAN (*with the same endearing smile*) : Hi!

(*After a moment,* MOMMY *and* DADDY *re-enter, carrying* GRANDMA. *She is borne in by their hands under her armpits; she is quite rigid; her legs are drawn up; her feet do not touch the ground; the expression on her ancient face is that of puzzlement and fear.*)

DADDY: Where do we put her?

MOMMY (*the same little laugh*) : Wherever I say, of course. Let me see . . . well . . . all right, over there . . . in the sandbox. (*Pause*) Well, what are you waiting for, Daddy? . . . The sandbox!

(*Together they carry* GRANDMA *over to the sandbox and more or less dump her in.*)

GRANDMA (*righting herself to a sitting position; her voice a cross between a baby's laugh and cry*): Ahhhhhh! Graaaaa!

DADDY (*dusting himself*): What do we do now?

MOMMY (*to the* MUSICIAN): You can stop now. (*The* MUSICIAN *stops. Back to* DADDY) What do you mean, what do we do now? We go over there and sit down, of course. (*To the* YOUNG MAN) Hello there.

YOUNG MAN (*again smiling*): Hi!

(MOMMY *and* DADDY *move to the chairs, stage-right, and sit down. A pause.*)

GRANDMA (*same as before*): Ahhhhhh! Ah-haaaaaa! Graaaaaa! *~ older she gets, more childish she gets treated as a child Mommy*

DADDY: Do you think . . . do you think she's . . . comfortable?

MOMMY (*impatiently*): How would I know?

DADDY (*pause*): What do we do now?

MOMMY (*as if remembering*): We . . . wait. We . . . sit here . . . and we wait . . . that's what we do.

DADDY (*after a pause*): Shall we talk to each other?

MOMMY (*with that little laugh; picking something off her dress*): Well, *you* can talk, if you want to . . . if you can think of anything to *say* . . . if you can think of anything *new*.

DADDY (*thinks*): No . . . I suppose not.

MOMMY (*with a triumphant laugh*): Of course not!

GRANDMA (*banging the toy shovel against the pail*): Haaaaaa! Ah-haaaaaa!

MOMMY (*out over the audience*): Be quiet, Grandma . . . just be quiet, and wait.

(GRANDMA *throws a shovelful of sand at* MOMMY.)

MOMMY (*still out over the audience*): She's throwing sand at me! You stop that, Grandma; you stop throwing sand at Mommy! (*To* DADDY) She's throwing sand at me.

(DADDY *looks around at* GRANDMA, *who screams at him.*)

GRANDMA: GRAAAAA!

MOMMY: Don't look at her. Just . . . sit here . . . be very still . . . and wait. (*To the* MUSICIAN) You . . . uh . . . you go ahead and do whatever it is you do.

(*The* MUSICIAN *plays.* MOMMY *and* DADDY *are fixed, staring out beyond the audience.* GRANDMA *looks at them, looks at the* MUSICIAN, *looks at the sandbox, throws down the shovel.*)

GRANDMA: Ah-haaaaaa! Graaaaaa! (*Looks for reaction; gets none. Now . . . directly to the audience*) Honestly! What a way to treat an old woman! Drag her out of the house . . . stick her in a car . . . bring her out here from the city . . . dump her in a pile of sand . . . and leave her here to set. I'm eighty-six years old! I was married when I was seventeen. To a farmer. He died when I was thirty. (*To the* MUSICIAN) Will you stop that, please? (*The* MUSICIAN *stops playing*) I'm a feeble old woman . . . how do you expect anybody to hear me over that peep! peep! peep! (*To herself*) There's no respect around here. (*To the* YOUNG MAN) There's no respect around here!

YOUNG MAN (*same smile*): Hi!

GRANDMA (*after a pause, a mild double-take, continues, to the audience*):

My husband died when I was thirty (*indicates* MOMMY), and I had to raise that big cow over there all by my lonesome. You can imagine what *that* was like. Lordy! (*To the* YOUNG MAN) Where'd they get *you?*

YOUNG MAN: Oh . . . I've been around for a while.

GRANDMA: I'll bet you have! Heh, heh, heh. Will you look at you!

YOUNG MAN (*flexing his muscles*): Isn't that something? (*Continues his calisthenics.*)

GRANDMA: Boy, oh boy; I'll say. Pretty good.

YOUNG MAN (*sweetly*): I'll say.

GRANDMA: Where ya from?

YOUNG MAN: Southern California.

GRANDMA (*nodding*): Figgers; figgers. What's your name, honey?

YOUNG MAN: I don't know. . . .

GRANDMA (*to the audience*): Bright, too!

YOUNG MAN: I mean . . . I mean, they haven't given me one yet . . . the studio . . .

GRANDMA (*giving him the once-over*): You don't say . . . you don't say. Well . . . uh, I've got to talk some more . . . don't you go 'way.

YOUNG MAN: Oh, no.

GRANDMA (*turning her attention back to the audience*): Fine; fine. (*Then, once more, back to the* YOUNG MAN) You're . . . you're an actor, hunh?

YOUNG MAN (*beaming*): Yes. I am.

GRANDMA (*to the audience again; shrugs*): I'm smart that way. *Anyhow,* I had to raise . . . *that* over there all by my lonesome; and what's next to her there . . . that's what she married. Rich? I tell you . . . money, money, money. They took me off the *farm* . . . which was real decent of them . . . and they moved me into the big town house with *them* . . . fixed a nice place for me under the stove . . . gave me an army blanket . . . and my own dish . . . my very own dish! So, what have I got to complain about? Nothing, of course. I'm not complaining. (*She looks up at the sky, shouts to someone off stage*) Shouldn't it be getting dark now, dear?

(*The lights dim; night comes on. The* MUSICIAN *begins to play; it becomes deepest night. There are spots on all the players, including the* YOUNG *man, who is, of course, continuing his calisthenics.*)

DADDY (*stirring*): It's nighttime.

MOMMY: Shhhh. Be still . . . wait.

DADDY (*whining*): It's so hot.

MOMMY: Shhhhhh. Be still . . . wait.

GRANDMA (*to herself*): That's better. Night. (*To the* MUSICIAN) Honey, do you play all through this part? (*The* MUSICIAN *nods*) Well, keep it nice and soft; that's a good boy. (*The* MUSICIAN *nods again; plays softly*) That's nice.

(*There is an off-stage rumble.*)

DADDY (*starting*): What was that?

MOMMY (*beginning to weep*): It was nothing.

DADDY: It was . . . it was . . . thunder . . . or a wave breaking . . . or something.

MOMMY (*whispering, through her tears*): It was an off-stage rumble . . . and you know what *that* means. . . .

DADDY: I forget. . . .

MOMMY (*barely able to talk*): It means the time has come for poor Grandma . . . and I can't bear it!

DADDY (*vacantly*): I . . . I suppose you've got to be brave.

GRANDMA (*mocking*): That's right, kid; be brave. You'll bear up; you'll get over it.

(*Another off-stage rumble . . . louder.*)

MOMMY: Ohhhhhhhhhh . . . poor Grandma . . . poor Grandma. . . .

GRANDMA (*to* MOMMY): I'm fine! I'm all right! It hasn't happened yet!

(*A violent off-stage rumble. All the lights go out, save the spot on the* YOUNG MAN; *the* MUSICIAN *stops playing.*)

MOMMY: Ohhhhhhhhhh. . . . Ohhhhhhhhhh. . . .

(*Silence.*)

GRANDMA: Don't put the lights up yet . . . I'm not ready; I'm not quite ready. (*Silence*) All right, dear . . . I'm about done.

(*The lights come up again, to brightest day; the* MUSICIAN *begins to play.* GRANDMA *is discovered, still in the sandbox, lying on her side, propped up on an elbow, half covered, busily shoveling sand over herself.*)

GRANDMA (*muttering*): I don't know how I'm supposed to do anything with this goddam toy shovel. . . .

DADDY: Mommy! It's daylight!

MOMMY (*brightly*): So it is! Well! Our long night is over. We must put away our tears, take off our mourning . . . and face the future. It's our duty.

GRANDMA (*still shoveling; mimicking*): . . . take off our mourning . . . face the future. . . . Lordy!

(MOMMY *and* DADDY *rise, stretch.* MOMMY *waves to the* YOUNG MAN.)

YOUNG MAN (*with that smile*): Hi!

(GRANDMA *plays dead.* (!) MOMMY *and* DADDY *go over to look at her; she is a little more than half buried in the sand; the toy shovel is in her hands, which are crossed on her breast.*)

MOMMY (*before the sandbox; shaking her head*): Lovely! It's . . . it's hard to be sad . . . she looks . . . so happy. (*With pride and conviction*) It pays to do things well. (*To the* MUSICIAN) All right, you can stop now, if you want to. I mean, stay around for a swim, or something; it's all right with us. (*She sighs heavily*) Well, Daddy . . . off we go.

DADDY: Brave Mommy!

MOMMY: Brave Daddy! (*They exit, stage-left.*)

GRANDMA (*after they leave; lying quite still*): It pays to do things well. . . . Boy, oh boy! (*She tries to sit up*) . . . well, kids . . . (*but she finds she can't*) . . . I . . . I can't get up. I . . . I can't move. . . .

(*The* YOUNG MAN *stops his calisthenics, nods to the* MUSICIAN, *walks over to* GRANDMA, *kneels down by the sandbox.*)

GRANDMA: I . . . can't move. . . .

YOUNG MAN: Shhhhh . . . be very still. . . .

GRANDMA: I . . . I can't move. . . .

YOUNG MAN: Uh . . . ma'am; I . . . I have a line here.

GRANDMA: Oh, I'm sorry, sweetie! you go right ahead.

YOUNG MAN: I am . . . uh . . .

GRANDMA: Take your time, dear.

YOUNG MAN (*prepares; delivers the line like a real amateur*): I am the Angel of Death. I am . . . uh . . . I am come for you.

GRANDMA: What . . . wha . . . (*Then, with resignation*) . . . ohhhh . . . ohhhh, I see.

(*The* YOUNG MAN *bends over, kisses* GRANDMA *gently on the forehead.*)

GRANDMA (*her eyes closed, her hands folded on her breast again, the shovel between her hands, a sweet smile on her face*): Well . . . that was very nice, dear. . . .

YOUNG MAN (*still kneeling*): Shhhhhh . . . be still. . . .

GRANDMA: What I meant was . . . you did that very well, dear. . . .

YOUNG MAN (*blushing*): . . . oh . . .

GRANDMA: No; I mean it. You've got that . . . you've got a quality.

YOUNG MAN (*with his endearing smile*): Oh . . . thank you; thank you very much . . . ma'am.

GRANDMA (*slowly; softly—as the* YOUNG MAN *puts his hands on top of* GRANDMA'S): You're . . . you're welcome . . . dear.

(*Tableau. The* MUSICIAN *continues to play as the curtain slowly comes down.*)

A Note on the Musical Score

"In approaching the curious and arresting problem of composing music for this short play, I found that, even within the limitation imposed by the use of one instrument, the score would of necessity function on two levels. It must, in a sense, 'speak' lines (the musician is, after all, a character in the play); at the same time, it must underline the moods involved and characterize the people on the stage. My first impulse was to make it all 'funny,' so as to run counter to the obvious seriousness of the literary theme. But such a solution, it seemed to me, would render the whole business a stunt, a mere gimmick.

"As the score stands, the musician plays two kinds of music under two different circumstances—when he is *asked* specifically to do so by MOMMY, and when he does so of his own volition. Since he has probably been hired for the occasion (like an organist at a funeral, 'It pays to do things well,' MOMMY says at one point), the differentiation seems inherent in the dramatic structure.

"Therefore: for those situations involving the clearly indicated hypocrisy of MOMMY and DADDY in disposing of GRANDMA, I have composed a twelve-tone row and a simple set of variations on its structure. . . .

"Elsewhere, the music is diatonic and directly, simply lyrical. . . . As the tender situation with the YOUNG MAN approaches, the music makes its transition from the angularity of the twelve-tone commentary to a simple, lyrical piece, which, correspondent to the closing mood of the situation itself, ends the play."[3]

Commentary

In *The Devil's Disciple* Shaw finds amusement in presenting his sophisticated, modern ideas in the old-fashioned forms of nineteenth-century comedy, which he ridicules even as he turns them to his advantage, and in creating characters who play traditional roles until their "hour of trial," when their inner nature is at last revealed. Shaw's hero Dick Dudgeon is prepared to sacrifice his life to save another, not out of love or duty, but because of an instinctive moral compulsion which asserts his dignity as a man and demonstrates his capacity for an heroic act. In *The Skin of Our Teeth* Wilder reverses the process of Shavian humor by dramatizing traditional ideas by means of unconventional and bizarre theatrical effects, but like Shaw, Wilder pokes fun at American home life as well as at the dramatic medium through which he presents it. In each play comedy prepares the way for the playwright's affirmations. For Wilder there is a commitment to the Judaic-Christian religious and the Greek cultural heritages of our civilization. Wilder's play declares the worth of the individual, his family, and his society. Wilder's hero has, despite all of his ridiculousness and his lapses, the indomitable will to start erecting the foundations of a new world. He has faith in himself, in those he loves, and in his future. He recognizes that his way of life is precariously achieved at best, but he is prepared to make a total commitment to preserving it.

Anouilh's Becket provides a bridge between Shaw's Dudgeon and Wilder's Antrobus on the one side and Albee's nameless characters on the

---

[3] William Flanagan, "Notes on the Performance of the Musical Score for *The Sandbox*," *The Best Short Plays 1959-1960*, ed. Margaret Mayorga (Boston, 1960), p. 69. Miss Mayorga includes the score of the music composed by William Flanagan for *The Sandbox*.

other, because Becket too in his "hour of trial" is ready to die for a cause, although he recognizes the absurdity of such an heroic stance: "We must only do—absurdly—what we have been given to do—right to the end" (p. 505), and he calls the moment of his death "the supreme folly" (p. 512). No such commitment is made in the world of *The Sandbox,* and one wonders whether it could be. Does Albee parody theatrical conventions and unsettle an audience's stereotyped attitudes about the dramatic experience so that he can deny the validity of the premises for a meaningful act? Or does his play challenge only the *possibility* of a fruitful realization of man's heroic qualities in our time? Or is Albee, like Shaw, satirizing his characters and their absurd actions in order to make us scrutinize ourselves with amused detachment?

A play in which an aged mother is abandoned to die alone and forgotten on the seashore might well be a tragedy concerned with an act of monstrous cruelty which would arouse pity and terror in an audience. Substitute "in a sandbox" for "on the seashore" as the dramatic arena, and the action turns into a grotesque and distorted nightmare. But note that the final tableau of the play consists of a bare-chested young man kneeling beside a sandbox and holding hands with an eighty-six-year-old lady lying half-buried in the sand, and one senses the complex interplay of satiric tones in *The Sandbox.* On the surface the action is absurd. But the generic meaning of *absurd* is not simply *ridiculous* but *out of harmony* in a musical sense. Albee's drama is an attempt to explore the deeper implications of a world in which man is out of harmony with himself, his fellowman, and his environment. His is a rootless world in which belief in Wilder's affirmations—or Shaw's or Anouilh's—may no longer be possible. At such a time, as Martin Esslin says, "The dignity of man lies in his ability to face reality in all its senselessness; to accept it freely, without fear, without illusions—and to laugh at it."[4]

Albee's effort to find a new dramatic mode to contain his view of the world is itself a necessary but quite conventional impulse, and each of the playwrights in this volume has to some extent been an innovator and an experimenter. Rebellion against established dramatic forms is an essential condition for a healthy theater. It has been argued that Albee, like other young playwrights today, is in revolt against the theater of external reality of Ibsen and Miller, but actually *The Sandbox* is only a natural transition from a play like *A View from the Bridge.* Miller himself has pointed the way Albee has taken when he writes of his own craft:

> The moment realistic behavior and psychology disappear from the play all the other appurtenances of Realism vanish too. The stage is stripped of knickknacks; instead it reveals symbolic *designs* which function as overt pointers toward the moral to be drawn from the action. We are no

---

[4] Martin Esslin, *The Theatre of the Absurd* (New York, 1961), p. 316.

longer under quite the illusion of watching through a transparent fourth wall. Instead we are constantly reminded, in effect, that we are watching a theater piece. In short, we are not bidden to lose our consciousness of time and place, the consciousness of ourselves, but are appealed to through our intelligence, our faculties of knowing rather than of feeling.[5]

Although one could argue that the symbolic design in *The Sandbox* does not lead with any certainty to a moral implication, a more real difference between the two playwrights is that Miller is concerned primarily with the social and psychological implications of a human situation, whereas Albee is attempting symbolically to expose the essence of the human condition itself.

In *The Sandbox* Albee has abandoned the formal dramatic structure and lucid design of Ibsen's *Rosmersholm* and O'Neill's *Desire under the Elms*. He has even disposed of a conventional plot and setting, and his characters do not give the illusion that they are people. The Young Man says that he is the Angel of Death, and Grandma reports that in her new home she was fixed up with a nice place under the stove and was given an army blanket and her own dish. Drama is the management of an illusion, but Albee's characters, like Wilder's, keep reminding us that we are watching a play in which they are acting parts. Grandma much prefers talking to the audience, Mommy orders the Musician around like a stage manager, and the Young Man has to remind Grandma that it is his turn to deliver a line.

Nonetheless, although Albee has got rid of traditional dramatic modes, the play still has an inner symbolic design which is the playwright's way of expressing his themes. Without this structure *The Sandbox* would be only a brief and pleasantly diverting showpiece. The clue to this design of the play lies in the recognition that although the characters are very much aware that they are in Albee's play and are acting before an audience, they are also conscious of their roles in an inner play which is like a ceremony or a ritual. Mommy is quite clearly creating her own play; she selects the setting ("This will do perfectly."), and she directs the players (". . . let's get on with it. . . . You can come in now." "Are you ready, Daddy?" "You can begin now."). Daddy seems less familiar with the ceremony: "What do we do now?" Mommy responds as one who has played the part many times before: "We go over there and sit down, of course." When Daddy repeats the question, Mommy answers "as if remembering." Grandma, however, is uncoöperative and, as children sometimes behave on formal occasions, she tries to stir up some excitement by throwing sand at Mommy. Mommy's outrage seems to be caused as much by Grandma's breaking of the ritual pattern as by her

---

[5] Arthur Miller, "The Family in Modern Drama," *Atlantic*, CXCVII (April, 1956), 37.

throwing sand. As is customary at important ceremonies, Mommy has arranged for a musician. What other examples of an observance of a ritual are there?

The dimming of the lights and the off-stage rumble make it clear that the characters in *The Sandbox* are enacting an absurd parody of a wake and a funeral service for someone who is—ironically—the liveliest person on stage. Ritual is symbolic re-enactment in which the communicants join in what is usually a service of devotion and spiritual renewal. But in the world of *The Sandbox* religious symbols have been stripped of their meaning. Here there is not the kind of divine thunder reverberating in Sophocles' *Oedipus at Colonus* as God calls to Oedipus, "It is time; you stay too long"; Mommy corrects Daddy's notion that the rumble is thunder. It is literally only a noise made by a stagehand off stage. If, as Mommy says, "It means the time has come for poor Grandma," it is only because Mommy has grown tired of putting up with Grandma around the house. A religious ritual, such as the Order for the Burial of the Dead in the *Book of Common Prayer* or the liturgy of the Catholic Mass for the Dead—echoes of which are parodied in the play—evokes traditional and ceremonious responses from the communicants. But in *The Sandbox* there are only the stereotyped verbal gestures and expected *social* formulas: "Well! Our long night is over. We must put away our tears, take off our mourning . . . ," says Mommy as though she were undecorating the Christmas tree and storing the ornaments for another year. Then after she bids farewell to her mother with pious platitude, self-congratulation, and praise for the undertaker's dexterity—"Lovely! It's . . . it's hard to be sad . . . she looks . . . so happy. . . . It pays to do things well"— she and Daddy bravely march off to face the future. That Grandma is still very much alive does not matter; the ceremony has been perfectly executed, although the worship service in Mommy's competent hands has become in the euphemism of the obituary column only "funeral arrangements." Thus, by ironic contrast, the amusing final tableau, although formal and posed, comes closer to the spiritual significance of the burial service than Mommy's empty mockery, for at least here there is a kiss and a handclasp—the only gestures of unselfish love in the play— and a quiet acceptance of the inevitable.

Besides this structural device of celebrating a meaningless ritual, another of Albee's chief means for creating a world devoid of spirit and humanity is the language he uses to demonstrate the impossibility of communication, even if people like Daddy had anything to say. The dialogue of *The Sandbox* is an expertly poised sequence of clichés, meaningless expressions, and euphemistic double talk, interspersed with vacant pauses. Even ritual response has lost its spiritual significance. Because Mommy uses words either to intimidate or to conceal, rather than to reveal her thoughts and emotions, the play can expose her as a selfish fraud simply by having Grandma mimic her daughter's words: ". . . take off our mourning . . . face the future. . . . Lordy!" On the other hand Daddy's brief lines consist of empty-headed questions, whines of "I'm cold" or "It's so hot," and observations like "It's nighttime" and "Mommy! It's daylight!" The Young Man substitutes his "endearing smile" for conversation, and he has not so mastered the finer points of articulation as to be ready to undertake, say, the role of Shaw's Dick Dudgeon. The only character who is capable of perceptive, witty conversation and whose colloquial idiom reveals a lively interest in all about her is Grandma, whose burial service is celebrated by her spiritually and emotionally dead family.

Questions and Problems

1. Why are the members of Albee's family called Mommy, Daddy, and Grandma?

2. What is your interpretation of the set of *The Sandbox*? Why the sandbox? Why the seashore? Is this another "view from a bridge"?

3. Is Grandma the heroine of *The Sandbox*? What, if anything, is heroic about her life? her dying?

4. What is Albee's point in making his Angel of Death a California beach boy? How are we to interpret his "endearing smile" and cheery "Hi"? Why should the playwright make him an aspiring movie actor?

5. To what extent is this a play about the meaning of death? What attitudes toward dying are held by Mommy, Daddy, Grandma, and the Young Man?

6. One of Albee's problems is the question of how a playwright can dramatize a failure to communicate. If dead people are using a dead language, how is drama possible? Study the ways in which Albee employs words. Illustrate how the dialogue of *The Sandbox* frequently contains hackneyed expressions. Point out banalities which are not really communication but only conventional noises which say nothing and mean nothing. Find moments in which a character wants to communicate and tries to be articulate but fails because the right words cannot be found.

7. Albee establishes his meaning in part by making the action in *The Sandbox* unrealistic. How are we to interpret a. the one character who is on stage the entire time, yet does nothing but the same arm exercise until the last minute of the play; b. Grandma's entrance; c. Mommy and Daddy "fixed, staring out beyond the audience"; d. Grandma and her toy shovel; e. the presence of the Musician; f. the final tableau?

8. What attitudes and values are satirized in *The Sandbox*? In general, what is wrong with the characters? Does the play hold out hope for reform? Are any affirmations implied? If so, of what sort?

9. Does *The Sandbox* suggest that if man is not tragic, he is absurd?

10. When *The Sandbox* first appeared Off Broadway, at least one critic dismissed it as the disappointing work of a talented writer. Do you agree with the judgment? Defend your position.

11. *The Sandbox, The Glass Menagerie,* and *The Cherry Orchard* have titles which call attention to the central symbol of each play. What dramatic advantages are gained by these organizing symbols? Do they have any meanings in common? What is unique about each?

12. Compare Albee's use of music with Williams' in *The Glass Menagerie,* Eliot's in *Murder in the Cathedral,* and Anouilh's in *Becket.*

13. Compare the purposes achieved by the off-stage rumble in *The Sandbox* with the storms in *The Glass Menagerie* and *The Skin of Our Teeth.*

14. Compare Sabina in *The Skin of Our Teeth* and Grandma as commentators who take the audience into their confidence.

15. Like Eliot's chorus in *Murder in the Cathedral,* Mommy and Daddy sit and wait, mourn and rejoice. Contrast the implications of these acts and emotions for their plays.

16. Contrast Eliot's use of ritual in *Murder in the Cathedral* with Albee's in *The Sandbox.*

17. Mommy announces that it is her duty to "face the future," and together she and Daddy exit from the play. What is Albee implying by their departure? Compare the endings of *The Cherry Orchard* and *The Skin of Our Teeth,* which conclude on a similar note. What is the attitude of the characters toward their future? What will the future apparently be like in each case?

18. *The Sandbox* and *The Cherry Orchard* end with the abandoning of an elderly person on stage. Compare the significance of these curtain scenes.

19. How does Albee's view of the American family differ from that found in *Desire under the Elms, The Glass Menagerie, A View from the Bridge,* and *The Skin of Our Teeth?*

20. Shaw's and Albee's dialogue frequently provokes laughter from an audience. What are the differences between the dialogue of the two playwrights?

21. In *The Cherry Orchard* characters often hold conversations which are essentially monologues. How does Chekhov handle this breakdown in communication? How does his treatment differ from Albee's? In what other plays in this text is the inability to communicate a problem? Is it language itself which is the cause or the characters and attitudes of the speakers which create the difficulty?

22. The characters in *The Sandbox* act like children. Daddy is constantly whining, the Young Man's only interest is his calisthenics, and even Grandma plays with a toy shovel in a sandbox, throws sand at Mommy, and cries like a baby. What is Albee suggesting? In *A View from the Bridge* Eddie treats Catherine as though she were a little girl. Many of the characters in *The Cherry Orchard* behave like children. At the opening of Act Three of *Becket* Henry is in a corner playing at cup-and-ball. Compare the various reasons why Albee, Miller, Chekhov, and Anouilh have treated adults as though they were children.

23. The heroes of Shaw's, Eliot's, Anouilh's, and Wilder's plays all have or attain a high degree of self-knowledge. The characters of *The Sandbox* are only concerned with themselves. Why are they incapable of attaining self-awareness?

24. One critic of Tennessee Williams writes: "The underlying belief in *The Glass Menagerie* is that there is very little, if any, reason for living. Man is by nature incomplete because his universe is fragmented. There is nothing to be done about this condition because nothing *can* be done about it. Human guilt becomes a corollary of universal guilt and man's life is an atonement for the human condition."[6] How accurate an assessment is this of the plight of the Wingfields? To what extent would *Rosmersholm, Desire under the Elms, A View from the Bridge, Murder in the Cathedral, Becket,* and *The Sandbox* substantiate this view of man's guilt and responsibility in a fragmented universe?

---

[6] Benjamin Nelson, *Tennessee Williams: The Man and His Work* (New York, 1961), p. 112.

General Descriptive Bibliography and Glossary

General Descriptive Bibliography

Bentley, Eric, *The Dramatic Event,* New York, 1954.

————, *In Search of Theatre,* New York, 1953.

————, *The Playwright as Thinker,* New York, 1946.
Collected essays and reviews by one of the best critics and teachers of the drama.

Clark, Barrett H., *European Theories of the Drama,* New York, 1947.
A collection of dramatic criticism since Aristotle.

————, and George Freedley, *A History of Modern Drama,* New York, 1947.
A detailed factual account of the origin and development of modern drama from 1850 through World War II.

Cole, Toby, ed. *Playwrights on Playwriting,* New York, 1960.
An anthology of comments that playwrights from Ibsen to Ionesco have made about their plays.

Downer, Alan, *Fifty Years of American Drama: 1900-1950,* Chicago, 1951.
A brief analysis of recent American drama in terms of dramatic form and subject matter.

Drew, Elizabeth, *Discovering Drama,* New York, 1937.
A highly readable and enjoyable introduction to drama. Miss Drew's comments on themes and techniques of modern drama are placed in the context of Greek and Elizabethan drama.

Dusenbury, Winifred L., *The Theme of Loneliness in Modern American Drama,* Gainesville, Florida, 1960.
A study of a recurrent theme in the works of many American dramatists such as O'Neill, Williams, and Miller.

Fergusson, Francis, *The Idea of a Theater,* New York, 1953.
A brilliant analysis of the underlying structure of incident and character in drama. Fergusson's discussion of Ibsen, Shaw, Chekhov, and Eliot places them in a more complex relation to their predecessors than simply one of historical development.

Flexner, Eleanor, *American Playwrights, 1918-1938,* New York, 1938.
A good example of the social criticism of drama current in the 1930s.

Gagey, Edmond M., *Revolution in American Drama,* New York, 1947.
A survey of the popular American theater prior to World War II. In its brief comments on hundreds of plays, the book unintentionally reveals the appalling amount of trash that has appeared on Broadway since 1920.

Gassner, John, *Form and Idea in Modern Theatre*, New York, 1956.
All of Gassner's books are indispensable for an introduction to a study of modern drama. This one discusses such dramatic types as realism, expressionism, symbolism, and formalism.

———, *Masters of the Drama*, 3rd ed., New York, 1954.
The most complete and satisfactory survey of world drama from Aeschylus to Miller. Bibliography.

———, *Theatre at the Crossroads*, New York, 1960.
In a review of plays and productions since World War II, Gassner assesses the American theater at midcentury.

———, *The Theatre in Our Times*, New York, 1954.
The most thoroughly detailed account of twentieth-century drama. Chapters on history, dramatic criticism, and dramatic theory. A most useful reference.

Krutch, Joseph Wood, *The American Drama Since 1918*, rev. ed., New York, 1957.
A competent survey of modern American drama with a good chapter on O'Neill. The book is weakest in its discussion of drama since World War II.

Lamm, Martin, *Modern Drama*, trans. Karin Elliott, Oxford, 1952.
A good introductory study to the major modern dramatists whose careers have ended. Chapters on Ibsen, Chekhov, Shaw, and O'Neill.

Lumley, Frederick, *Trends in 20th-Century Drama*, Fair Lawn, N. J., 1956.
A descriptive, often superficial, survey of modern plays and playwrights. Lumley's judgments are not always reliable.

McCarthy, Mary, *Sights and Spectacles*, New York, 1956.
A collection of the judgments, usually harsh, of one of the most colorful and controversial of drama critics.

McCollom, William G., *Tragedy*, New York, 1957.
A helpful study of the major problems of tragedy: the hero and his fate, tragic theme and structure, tragedy and society.

Modern Drama, 1958 to date.
A first-rate critical quarterly of modern drama. Especially noteworthy are the special issues devoted to a single playwright. Annual Bibliography.

Muller, Herbert J., *The Spirit of Tragedy*, New York, 1956.
In one of the best studies of tragedy, Muller evaluates both its historical development and its philosophical issues.

Myers, Henry Alonzo, *Tragedy: a View of Life*, Ithaca, New York, 1956.
Although Myers does not explore the problem of modern tragedy, his discussion of tragedy as form and value raises the central issues for such a study.

New York Theatre Critics' Reviews, New York, 1940 to date.
A weekly report of opening-night reviews of each Broadway play by New York newspaper critics. Few reviews of Off-Broadway plays are included.

O'Hara, Frank H., and Margueritte H. Bro, *Invitation to the Theatre,* New York, 1951.
A helpful handbook that discusses briefly dramatic types and terms.

Olson, Elder, *Tragedy and the Theory of Drama,* Detroit, 1961.
An inquiry into the nature of dramatic principles seen from the point of view of the dramatist.

Peacock, Ronald, *The Art of Drama,* London, 1957.
A stimulating search for a modern theory of drama.

_____, *The Poet in the Theatre,* London, 1946.
A monograph on the nature of poetic drama in England and on the Continent since Ibsen.

Rowe, Kenneth Thorpe, *A Theater in Your Head,* New York, 1960.
A good introduction to the problems of the theater and of theatrical productions.

Styan, J. L., *The Elements of Drama,* Cambridge, 1960.
An excellent study of the question of how to read a play. Styan makes his critical points by the close textual analysis of dramatic fragments.

Thompson, Alan R., *The Anatomy of Drama,* Berkeley and Los Angeles, 1942.
An inquiry into the philosophy of drama from the Greek tragedians to O'Neill, seen in terms of the civilizations that produced them.

Tulane Drama Review, 1957 to date.
TDR, published quarterly, contains some of the best critical studies in modern drama.

Tynan, Kenneth, *Curtains,* New York, 1961.
A collection of bright and witty theater reviews and articles by one of the sharpest young critics in the business.

Williams, Raymond, *Drama from Ibsen to Eliot,* London, 1952.
A vigorous revaluation of the leading playwrights from 1850 to 1950, but with little emphasis on American drama.

Glossary

antagonist. The character who most directly and forcefully opposes the protagonist, or main character.

attitude. The emotions, feelings, or state of mind of a character, the dramatist, or the audience.

backdrop. The rear curtain of a stage setting.

climax. The most intense point of conflict in a play; the turning point in the action.

comedy of manners. A comedy which wittily satirizes the foibles and artificialities of sophisticated characters in fashionable society.

curtain scene. The last moments of action before the curtain falls on a scene.

cyclorama. The curving drop curtain for an exterior stage setting, used to represent sky or open space or to conceal the rear or the sides of the stage.

denouement. The resolution or final working out of the complications of the plot.

dialogue. The conversation between or among characters.

diction. The words the dramatist chooses, considered in regard to their connotations (i.e., their suggestive or associative value).

downstage. At or toward the front of the stage.

dramatic irony. Irony which exists when the audience is aware of facts or a situation of which the characters on stage are ignorant.

exposition. The process of providing an audience the information necessary for understanding the background of the story.

expressionism. The dramatic representation of a subjective emotion or psychological state of mind by means of an objective stage technique, such as use of lighting, scenery, or properties.

farce. Broadly humorous drama based on the outrageous absurdity of the situations and unsubtle in characterization and ideas.

flies. The space above the stage behind the proscenium and out of view of the audience. It is used temporarily during a performance for storage of hanging scenery or lighting equipment.

foil. A minor character used to set off a major one more distinctly by sharp contrast.

foreshadowing.   The indication of an action which is to occur later in the play.

function.   The contribution made by character, scene, symbol, dialogue, stage property, and so on, to the achievement of the dramatist's total effect. In dramatic art everything should exist for a purpose, not for its own sake or merely for decoration; it should be integrally related to the total unity of the play.

imagery.   Comparisons used for their associative, connotative, and emotional significance. Expressed comparisons are similes; implied comparisons are metaphors.

melodrama.   A play which places emphasis on complicated involvements of plot, heightened suspense, and elaborate theatrical effects.

motivation.   The playwright's providing the actions of his characters with adequate and proper cause, reason, or justification.

naturalism.   An attempt to intensify realism by portraying events and characters as close to objective reality as possible. Naturalistic plays are based on the principle that cause and effect govern human conduct. The naturalist avoids all moral and ethical pronouncements.

pace.   The speed at which the action of a play moves.

parody.   A drama that imitates the language or style of an author for comic effect or in ridicule.

pathos.   The emotional quality in a situation which evokes sympathy and compassion from an audience.

plot, subplot.   The ordered arrangement of actions and characters which develops the story of the play. The subplot is a secondary story often involving a group of minor characters but related to the action of the main plot.

prop, properties.   Movable objects or furniture used in the action. Large pieces of furniture are considered part of the set.

proscenium.   The opening through which the audience sees the acting area of a stage. The proscenium arch is the frame for this opening.

protagonist.   The leading character in a play.

realism.   An attempt to represent on stage the generally observed facts of experience. Realism tends to be less deterministic than naturalism in working out characterization. A realistic dramatist often criticizes the pattern of life he is arranging, whereas a naturalistic dramatist tries to refrain from any personal interpretations.

sentimentality.   An emotional response in a character greater than the circumstance calls for; in a play, the attempt to obtain an emotion, frequently a stock response, that is not adequately prepared for or justified by the character and situation.

soliloquy.   A monologue delivered as though the speaker were talking to himself but overheard by the audience.

stage left and *stage right.*   Stage left is the actor's left and the audience's right; stage right is the actor's right, the audience's left. Unless specifically indicated, a dramatist means "stage left" when he indicates simply "left."

structure.   The artistic arrangement or pattern of the episodes and details of action. Structure is not simply a matter of division into acts and scenes, but is the dramatic organization of the conflicts, contrasts, and interrelations of plot and subplot which compose the organic unity of the play.

symbol.   An image in which a material object stands for an abstract or generalized idea.

tag.   The last line in a play.

tempo.   The timing or rate of speed of the action.

theatrical technique.   Any device available to a dramatist to achieve the effect he desires on stage.

theme.   The central idea developed by a play.

tone.   The emotional qualities of the play as a whole or of any part of it. It consists of atmosphere or mood as well as the attitudes of the characters.

upstage.   The back of the stage.